DISPARITIES IN INDIA

A Development Perspective

DISPARITIES IN INDIA

A Development Perspective

- Disparity in Growth and Development
- Disparity in Agriculture and Allied Activities
- Disparity in Social Sector
- Disparity in Infrastructure and Development
- Disparity in Employment
- Disparity in Financial System and Policy Formulation

Edited by

DR. ANIL KUMAR THAKUR

and

DR. DALIP KUMAR

Published on behalf of
THE INDIAN ECONOMIC ASSOCIATION

DEEP & DEEP PUBLICATIONS PVT. LTD.
F-159, Rajouri Garden, New Delhi-110027

DISPARITIES IN INDIA
A Development Perspective

ISBN 978-81-8450-316-6

Typeset by S.S. COMPOSERS
3190, Mohindra Park, Shakur Basti, Delhi-110034.

Printed in India at NEW ELEGANT PRINTERS,
A-49/1, Maya Puri, Phase-I, New Delhi-110064.

Published by DEEP & DEEP PUBLICATIONS PVT. LTD.
F-159, Rajouri Garden, New Delhi-110027.
Phones: 25435369, 25440916
E-mail: ddpbooks@yahoo.co.in • ddpubs@gmail.com
Showroom:
2/13, Ansari Road, Daryaganj, New Delhi-110002 • Telefax: 23245122

Contents

PART B

DISPARITY IN AGRICULTURE AND ALLIED ACTIVITIES

Part C

DISPARITY IN SOCIAL SECTOR

Part D

DISPARITY IN INFRASTRUCTURE AND DEVELOPMENT

Part E

DISPARITY IN EMPLOYMENT

PART F

DISPARITY IN FINANCIAL SYSTEM AND POLICY FORMULATION

Foreword

It is a pleasure for me to write a foreword to "Disparities in India" edited by Dr. Anil Kumar Thakur, Professor, and Secretary of the Indian Economic Association, and Dr. Dalip Kumar, National Council for Applied Economics Research. The book consists of a collection of selected papers presented at the Annual Conference of the Indian Economic Association in 2008. The papers in this volume cover a variety of themes and approaches. A number of papers focus on inter-state income disparities, while some others dwell on intra-state income disparities. Going beyond income, a group of papers in the volume focus on disparities in the agricultural sector. A third section in the book brings together papers on disparities in the social sector development. These papers deal with synthetic indicators of the levels of living, human development, health, education, and social groups. A whole section in this book deals with employment disparities. Another section comprises of papers on infrastructure and industrial development. A final section covers papers on fiscal flows and the financial sector. Taken together, the papers in this volume offer a rich analysis of the empirical trends in regional disparity in India, the proximate determinants and relevant policy issues.

Development theory makes a strong case for uneven spatial development. But disparities are expected to follow and inverted U curve and therefore to decline after increasing in the first phase of industrial development. Paul Krugman and the other prominent exponents of "New Economic Geography" have now offered analytical models explaining the existence of strong centripetal forces leading to the agglomeration of economic activities in certain locations. But after a period of growth, centrifugal tendencies are expected to become stronger leading to the development of new growth centres. The resultant growth is expected to continue to be spatially uneven but less unequal. If growth is inherently unbalanced, intervening strongly to reduce disparities could amount to dampening the growth stimulus and to throwing out the baby with the bath water. This is essentially what the World Bank World Development Report 2009 (Reshaping Economic Geography) argues.

However, there are at least two strong reasons why we remain concerned with regional disparities.

First and foremost, because spatial inequalities determine the quality of life of people living in different locations, most of whom lack opportunities to access better alternatives elsewhere. In India, spatial inequalities are reinforced by intolerably low levels of living and high deprivations in less developed areas.

Second, the disparities which exist are not only the result of market forces but are nurtured and promoted by national and international policies and institutions. A realignment of these policies has large and dramatic impact on spatial disparities. A result of the specific type of globalization policies followed internationally in the last two decades or so has been a sharp increase in inter-group and regional inequalities within both developed and developing countries. The Indian case is brought out by the papers in this volume, most of which attest to growing inequalities in the post-reform period. It is therefore an oversimplification to suggest that the relationship between growth and inequality has a pre-specified form and is independent of policy regimes.

Presently, the pattern of development has led to sharp political cleavages and the reemergence of strong movements in many less developed regions. After more than a decade of neglect in the post-reform period, regional policy has resurfaced as part of a broader policy agenda of inclusive development.

The papers in this volume therefore offer timely

analysis of a range of issues concerned with regional disparities and I commend this volume to interested readers.

PROF. RAVI S. SRIVASTAVA
Chairperson,
Centre for the Study of
Regional Development,
New Delhi
and
Former Member
National Commission for Enterprises
in the Unorganised Sector,
Government of India

Acknowledgements

The book 'Disparities in India' is divided in 6 parts along with 53 papers contributed by authors. This book is an outcome of the 91st Annual Conference of Indian Economic Association, which was organised by the Department of Economics, Mohan Lal Sukhadia University, Udaipur, Rajasthan during December 27-29, 2008. We are thankful to Professor G.K. Chadha, the Conference President of the Indian Economic Association for his valuable guidance and immense cooperation.

The success of the conference was reflected in the lively debate among all the paper writers and discussants. The session attracted more than 100 papers, including the concern of economists for a sensitive topic, which is likely to have a major impact on the state as well as Indian economy. Thanks to the Chairman of the technical session Prof. T.S. Papola, who spent enormous time and energy for conducting the technical session and valuable comments. We are also grateful to all the paper writers who, despite their busy schedules, for incorporated the desired comments in revising their papers.

We extend our heartfelt thanks to Prof. Anju Kohali and Arun Prabha Choudhary from Department of Economics, organizers of the conference and her Colleagues, and all the teaching and administrative staff of the Sukhadia University for their active support in organising and making this conference a success.

Our special appreciation is due to Dr. Anjani Kumar Jha, the Chairman, Development of Indian Society and Culture (DISC), Dr. Rajesh Jaiswal, Associate Fellow, National Council of Applied Economic Research, New Delhi for a helping hand in bringing out this publication. We are indebted to many friends, colleagues, and teachers for their careful guidance and constant support.

The views expressed in the book are of the respective authors and do not reflect the opinion of the book editors or the publisher. They shall not be held accountable for the views expressed.

Finally, we would be thankful to Mr. Bhatia and his staff of M/s Deep and Deep Publications Pvt. Ltd., Delhi who deserve thanks for all the designing, typesetting and printing work to bring out this volume.

ANIL KUMAR THAKUR
DALIP KUMAR

List of Contributors

A.S. Mohammad, Mohammadpur, Mahnar, Vaishali.

Abhas Saurabh, Research Scholar, Institute for Rural Development, Hajipur, Bihar.

Abhishek Kumar Pandey, Research Scholar, Department of Economics, University of Allahabad, Allahabad.

Achal Kumar Gaur, Reader, Department of Economics, Faculty of Social Science, B.H.U., Varanasi.

Alpana Kateja, Reader, Department of Economics, Banaras Hindu University, Varanasi.

Amrita Nandi, Building No. 3B, Flat No. 102, Shanti Dham C.H.S, New Mhada Colony, Mahakali Caves Road, Andheri (East), Mumbai.

Anil Kumar, Reader, Haryana School of Business, Guru Jambheshwar University of Science and Technology, Hisar (Haryana).

Archana Rani Srivastava, Research Scholar, Department of Economics, University of Allahabad, Allahabad.

Ashok B. Trivedi, Lecturer, Shree B.K. Patel Arts and Smt. L.M. Patel Commerce College, Savli Dist., Vadodara (Gujarat).

B. Karthikeyan, Post-Graduate Student, Department of Economics, Bharathiar University, Coimbatore, TN.

B. Sudhakar Reddy, Assistant Professor, Department of Economics, Osmania University, Hyderabad, AP.

B.G. Lobo, Lecturer of Economics, Sinhgad Institute, N.B. Navale College of Commerce, Lonavala.

Bhavesh N. Desai, Lecturer, S.C.A. Patel Arts College, Sadhali Dist., Vadodara (Gujarat).

Binoy N. Verma, Ex University Professor and Chairman, Department of Agricultural Economics, Rajendra Agricultural University, Pusa, Samastipur, Bihar.

Bipul Malakar, Professor, Department of Economics, Jadavpur University, Kolkata.

Brajesh Srivastava, Research Scholar (Economics), University of Allahabad, Allahabad.

D. Kailasa Rao, Reader, Department of Economics, Sarada College, Vijayawada, Andhra Pradesh.

D.C. Pathak, Doctoral Fellow, G.B. Pant Social Science Institute, Allahabad.

Dalip Kumar, Project Officer, National Council of Applied Economic Research, New Delhi.

Dastgir Alam, Department of Economics, A.M.U., Aligarh, UP.

Dhiraj Kumar Bandyopadhyay, Associate Professor in Economics, Centre for Urban Economic Studies, Department of Economics, Calcutta University, Kolkata.

Dipak R. Chaudhari, Lecturer, Shree B.K. Patel Arts and Smt. L.M. Patel Commerce College, Savli Dist., Vadodara (Gujarat).

Firdaus Fatima Rizvi, Associate Fellow, Council for Social Development, New Delhi.

G. Vanithamani, M.Phil. Research Scholar, Department of Economics, Bharathiar University, Coimbatore.

Girish Chandra Tripathi, Professor, Department of Economics, University of Allahabad, Allahabad.

H.C.L. Das, P.G. Department of Economics, M.S. College, Motihari, Bihar.

Hira Lal Ram, Reader in Economics, S.P. Mahila College, Dumka, S.K.M. University, Dumka.

Inderjeet Singh, Professor, Department of Economics, Punjabi University, Patiala (Punjab).

J.R. Gupta, (Retd.) Professor, Department of Economics, Punjabi University, Patiala.

Jagannath Lenka, Prof. and Head, Department of Economics, North Orissa University.

Jagdish Narayan, Professor, Department of Economics, University of Allahabad, Allahabad.

Jyoti Obia, Research Scholar, Department of Economics, Aligarh Muslim University, Aligarh.

K. Madhu Babu, Assistant Professor, Department of Economics, Acharya Nagarjuna University, Nagarjuna Nagar, Guntur, Andhra Pradesh.

K. Pazhani, Reader and Head, Department of Economics, T.D.M.N.S. College, T. Kallikulam, Tamil Nadu.

K. Raja Babu, Professor, Department of Economics and Applied Economics, Acharya Nagarjuna University, Nagarjunanagar, AP.

Kaveri Sarkar, Reader in Ẹconomics, G.H. College, Kolkata.

Kavita S. Sharma, HOD in Economics, Dr. Ambedkar College, Wadala, Mumbai.

Kuldip Kaur, Reader, Punjab School of Economics, GNDU, Amritsar.

Kulwant Singh Phull, Lecturer (Selection Grade) and Head, Department of Economics, Guru Nanak College, Sukhchainana Sahib, Phagwara.

Kumud Bhagawati, Department oF Economics, D.K. College, Mirza.

M. Sridevi, Research Scholars, Department of Economics and Applied Economics, Acharya Nagarjuna University, Nagarjunanagar, AP.

M.V. Narasimha Sarma, Professor, Department of Economics and Applied Economics, Acharya Nagarjuna University, Nagarjuna Nagar, Guntur, Andhra Pradesh.

Mahalaya Chatterjee, Reformatory Street, Calcutta University Alipur Campus, Kolkata.

Mandakini R. Mahore, Reader, Jawaharlal Nehru College, Wadi Nagpur (Maharashtra).

Manju Yadav, Lecturer, Department of Economics, Government College, Kishangarh, Ajmer, Rajasthan.

Manjushri Gupta, Lecturer, Department of Economics, Government Girls College, Ajmer, Rajasthan.

Minati Mallick, Lecturer in Economics, Department of Economics, North Orissa University.

Mohammad Asif, Senior Lecturer, Department of Economics, Aligarh Muslim University, Aligarh.

Mona Khare, Professor of Economics, Department of Regional Planning and Economic Growth, Barkatullah University, Bhopal (MP).

Montu Bose, Department of Economics, Rabindra Bharati University, Kolkata.

N.K. Thakur, Sr. Marketing Manager, GNFC Ltd. Lucknow (UP).

Nazia Iqbal Hashmi, Research Scholar, Department of Economics, Aligarh Muslim University, Aligarh.

Nidhi Sharma, Reader in Economics, MMV, Banaras Hindu University, Varanasi, UP.

Nighat Ahmad, A-13, Medical Colony, AMU, Aligarh.

Nisar Ahmad Khan, Reader, Department of Economics, Aligarh Muslim University, Aligarh, UP.

Nisha, Post-Doctoral Fellow, UNCTAD India Programme, Department of Economics, University of Allahabad, Allahabad.

Paramjeet Kaur Dhindsa, Professor, Punjab School of Economics, GNDU, Amritsar.

Pooja Sikka, S.R.F. (Senior Research Fellow), Department of Economics, Punjabi University, Patiala.

Pradeep Punjabi, Head, Department of Economics, Associate Professor, MVS College, JRN Rajasthan Vidhyapeeth University, Udaipur.

Prahlad Kumar, Professor and Co-ordinator, UGC SAP III Programme, Department of Economics, University of Allahabad, Allahabad.

Prashant Bhardwaj, Assistant Professor, Department of Economics, JRN Rajasthan Vidhyapeeth University, Udaipur.

R. Rohini, Research Scholar, Department of Economics and Applied Economics, Acharya Nagarjuna University Nagarjunanagar, AP.

R.K. Bansal, Professor, Department of Economics, Punjabi University, Patiala.

R.K. Panda, Professor of Economics, Utkal University, Orissa.

Rajesh Kumar Singh, Lecturer in Commerce, DAV PG College (Banaras Hindu University), Varanasi (UP).

Rama J. Shah, Arts and Commerce College, Dhansura.

Rita N. Patel, Professor, Arts and Science College, Kalol.

Roopali Shevalkar,

S. Jesi Isabella, Reader in Commerce, Holy Cross College, Nagercoil, Tamil Nadu.

S.K. Dhage, Reader and H.O.D. of Business Economics, Baburaoji Gholap College, Sangvi, Pune.

S.K. Pant, Reader, G.B. Pant Social Science Institute, Allahabad.

S.N. Kukale, Principal, Baburaoji Gholap College, Sangvi, Pune.

S.P. Singh, Professor of Economics, Department of Humanities and Social Sciences, Indian Institute of Technology, Roorkee.

Samik Shome, Assistant Professor, Alliance Business School, Bangalore.

Seozy Bhatia, Junior Research Fellow, Punjab School of Economics, GNDU, Amritsar.

Shakshi Chaudhary, Lecturer in Commerce, DAV PG College, Banaras Hindu University, Varanasi.

Shilpi Tiwari, Research Scholar, Department of Economics, University of Allahabad, Allahabad.

Shiny Thankachan, M.Phil. Research Scholar, Department of Economics, Bharathiar University, Coimbatore.

Uma Shankar Bharti, Research Scholar, University Department of Economics, T.M. Bhagalpur University, Bhagalpur.

Upendra Sah, Reader in Economics, University Department of Economics, T.M. Bhagalpur University, Bhagalpur .

V.L. Lavanya, Research Scholar, Department of Economics, Bharathiar University, Coimbatore, TN.

Venkata Narayana, Research Scholar, Department of Economics and Applied Economics, Acharya Nagarjuna University, Nagarjunanagar, AP.

Vinay Nath Dubey,

Vinayak Kant Mishra, Research Scholar, Department of Economics, University of Allahabad, Allahabad.

Abbreviations

ADF	:	Additional Director of Fisheries
AICTE	:	All-India Council of Technical Education
AIDS	:	Acquired Immune Deficiency Syndrome
ANC	:	Anti Netal Care
APC	:	Agriculture Price Commission
AYF	:	Average Yield of Foodgrain
BIMARU	:	Bihar , MP, Assam, Rajasthan, Orissa and UP
BKR	:	Backward Region
BR	:	Birth Rates
BSNL	:	Bharat Sanchar Nigam Limited
CABE	:	Central Advisory Board on Education
CAGR	:	Compound Annual Growth Rates
CAZRI	:	Carbon Arid Zone Research Institute
CBFM	:	Community-based Fisheries Management
CBR	:	Crude Birth Rates
CDR	:	Crude Death Rates
CHC	:	Community Health Centre
CID	:	Composite Index of Development
CIED	:	Composite Index of Economic Development
CIH	:	Composite Index of Health
CMIE	:	Centre for Monitorting Indian Economy
CR	:	Central Region
CRI	:	Cropping Intensity
CSO	:	Central Statistical Organisation
CSRE	:	Centre of Study in Resources Enginnering
CVs	:	Co-efficients of Variations
DEA	:	Data Envelopment Analysis
DOT	:	Department of Telecommunication
DOT	:	Department of Telematrics
EEZ	:	Exclusive Economic Zones

ER	:	Eastern Region
FCI	:	Food Corporation of India
FDI	:	Final Development Index
GCA	:	Gross Cropped Areas
GDP	:	Gross Domestic Product
GEM	:	Gender Related Development Index
GIA	:	Gross Irrigated Areas
GR	:	Green Revolution
GSDP	:	Gross State Domestic Product
HER	:	Human Expenditure Ratio
HDI	:	Human Development Index
HCR	:	Head Count Ratio
HYV	:	High Yield Verieties
IAR	:	Institute of Audio Research
IAY	:	Indira Awaas Yojana
ICAR	:	Indian Council of Agricultural Research
ICT	:	Information and Comunication Technology
IISc	:	Indian Institute of Sciences
IMR	:	Infant Mortality Rate
ITDP	:	Institute for Technology Development Programs
ITES	:	Information Technology Enabaled Services
ITI	:	Industrial Training Institute
KTMFA	:	Kalinga Traditional Marin Fisherman Association
LDCs	:	Less Developed Countries
LE	:	Life Expectancy
LOU	:	Lavel of Urbanisation
LPG	:	Liberalisation, Privatisation and Globalisation
MFALDA	:	Marin Fisherman Association Local Area Development
MHRD	:	Ministry of Humand Resource Development
MIT	:	Ministry of Information Technology
MLAs	:	Members of Legislative Assembly
MMR	:	Matternal Mortality Ratio
MNC	:	Multi National Corporation
MOU	:	Minutes of Usages.
MPCE	:	Monthly Per-capita Expenditure
MPLAD	:	Member of Parliament Local Area Development Scheme
MPs	:	Members of Parliament
MRD	:	Mixed Recall Period

MSY : Maximum Sustainable Yield
NABARD : National Bank of Agriculture and Rural Develpment
NASSCOM: National Association of Software and Services Companies
NCAER : National Council of Applied Economic Research
NCERT : National Council of Education Research and Training
NF/L : Number of Factory Per·Lakh Population
NFFW : National Food for Work Programme
NFHS : National Family Health Survey
NGO : Non Government Organisation
NHP : National Health Policy 2002
NIEPA : National Institute of Education and Planning Administration
NMR : Nuclear Magnetic Resonance
NREP : National Rural Employment Programme
NSDP : Net State Domestic Product
NSSO : National Sample Survey Organisation
OBCs : Other than Backward Castes
OECD : Organisation for Economic CO-operation and Development
OMFRA : Orissa Marine Fisheries Regulation Act
PBC : Per-capita Bank Credit
PCDDP : Per-capita District Domestic Product
PCNSDP : Per-capita Net State Domestic Product
PDS : Public Distribution System
PEC : Per-capita Consumption of Electricity
PER : Public Expenditure Ratio
PGI : Poverty Gap Index
PHCs : Primary Health Centres
PMGSY : Pradhan Mantri Gram Sadak Yojana
PMP : Per-capita Milk Production
PQLI : Physical Quality of Life Index
PS : Principal Status
PVM : Per-capita Net Value Added in Manufacturing Sector.
QLI : Quality of Life Index.
QLWI : Quality of Life and Work Index
RCP : Rural Community Phone

RLEGP : Rural Landless Employment Gurantee Programme
RSVY : Rastriya Sum Vikas Yojana
SAR : Social Allocation Ratio
SC&ST : Sechdueld Caste and Secheduled Tribes
SCB : Sechedued Commercial Banks
SEZ : Special Economic Zones
SFDA : State Food and Drug Administration
SJSRY : Sawarn Jayanti Sahari Rojgar Yojana
SGSY : Swarnjayanti Gramin Swarojgar Yojana
SNA : System of National Accounts
SP : State Plan
SPSS : Statistical Pakage of Social Sciences.
SS : Subsidiary Status.
SUCCESS : Scheme for Universal Access and Quality at the Secondary Stage
TAI : Technology Achievement Index
TED : Turle Excluder Device
TEMPO : Technology Mission on Pulses and Oilseeds
TMC : Thousand Cubic Million Feet
TRAI : Telecom Regulatory Authority of India
TRYSEM : Training of Rural Youth for Self-Employment
UNDP : United Nations Development Programme
UNFPA : United Nations Population Fund
UNICEF : United Nations Children Funds
UPA : United Progressive Alliance
URGD : Urban Rural Growth Differentials
URP : Uniform Recall Period
VPTs : Village Public Telephones
WHO : World Health Organisation
WPR : Worker Participation Rates
WPR : Worker Participation Ratio
WR : Western Region

Introduction

Disparities in India are inter-related and each of the individual concepts like globalization, income inequality, and regional disparity has contributed to the rise in poverty in India in spite of the immense growth of the Indian economy. Disparities are most easily identified when there is a clear reference point for what is appropriate and reasonable to expect. While there may be uncertainty regarding many aspects of clinical care, the quality measures presented here have been developed around health care interventions for which there is sound scientific evidence of effectiveness and for which there is a professional consensus and expectation that these services would be provided to all patients. Even after consideration of variation in patients' medical conditions and severity of illness, there should be little deviation from specific quality measures associated with population.

To understand the disparities, it is pertinent to peep through the ideas of various theorists who tried to focus attention on economic development, regional economic thoughts and their theoretical and empirical investigations. Elements of development economics can be traced back to the classical works of David Ricardo, Karl Marx and Schumpeter. Regional economics can be said to have originated in the writings of German Economists like Von Thunen's spatial contours of agriculture production and Alfred Weber's theory of industrial location. According to neo-classical economists like Robert Solow (1956), regional disparities are self-limiting in character. But Gunner Myrdal (1957) differed from Solow's views. To him, the factor movements themselves were likely to have disequilibrating rather than equilibrating on account of the backwash effect. Labour migration was considered to be widening the disparity. The approach taken by Hirschman (1958) closely resembles with that of Myrdal.

Repatriation of income by migrants and rise in demand of goods in the backward regions are supposed to bring about a reversal in the trend of widening regional economic disparities. It was further explained by Jeffery Williamson (1965) who examined the relationship between magnitude of regional per-capita disparities in 24 nations and the level of development of those nations.

However, the Latin American Schools of thoughts were skeptical about second phase of inverted U-shaped curve of disparities emerging on the global level within the framework of production based on capitals. According to Andre Gunder Frank (1967) the greater integration between metropolis and their satellites fuelled only the growth in the metropolis. This widened the disparities instead of bringing about a trickle down effect of prosperity from more developed metropolis to the backward nations and regions. Economic history suggests that trickle down effects on the economy and region takes place only within the framework of sustained high economic growth over a period of time complemented by sound macro-economic policies and selective states intervention. It is not purely the market forces which help attain the goal of high economic growth and its dispersal over the regions and various segments of the population. The experience of East and Southeast Asia and China bears witness to this fact. Similar views can be found in the Paul Baran's theory (1957) of surplus or Emmanuel's (1972) thesis of unequal exchange.

Paul Bairoch's work (1981) is perhaps the only study which made herculean attempt to delineate the behaviour of international disparities in the per-capita income since the period even before the advent of the industrial revolution in the mid-18th century. He found that at the time of industrial revolution, the maximum inter-country deviation in per-capita income never exceeded. Considering the present day less developed countries (LDCs) as one group and the Developed countries as another group, he finds that the gap between these two groups continued to widen reaching a ratio of nearly seven by the year 1977. However, within the developed counties group, the inter-country disparities had reduced.. Sen and Himanshu (2004) have argued, inter-state as well as intra-state inequality increased between 1993-94 and 2001-02.

The articles in this book are presented in six parts. Part (A) Disparity in growth and development issues, (B) Disparity in agriculture and allied activities, (C) Disparity in social sector, (D) Disparity in infrastructure and development, (E) Disparity in employment, and (F) Disparity in financial system and policy formulation.

(A) Disparity in Growth and Development Issues

The idea of regional development originated with Stalin who wanted to develop each region in the former Soviet Russia in such a way that in the event of an invasion, the occupation of any region by the capitalist powers might not cripple the economic power of the country. Regional development began to receive attention in the Western countries in the 1930, on welfare considerations. Specially, the need was to relieve from (i) mass unemployment and distress in the depressed regions, such as the northern and western industrial regions of the UK, which had suffered severely during the depression, and (ii) poverty and backwardness in regions such as Appalachia in the US and Italian South, which had been by-passed in the course of the economic development of these countries (Nath, 1970). The pressure for development of backward regions is stronger and the most persistent among regional development pressures and, it can be harnessed in support of the political objective of creation of separate States. (Nath, 1971).

The paper on "Rural-Urban Development Disparities in India" written by Kaveri Sarkar tries to analyze the disparities in development with respect to the rural and urban sectors of twenty major states of India. Author has used secondary data which covered disparities in growth of NSDP, Population, and Poverty along with HDI and consumption pattern of the people. Author has also taken some indicators related to employment, education and health infrastructure. The author tenders several suggestions to reduce rural-urban disparities. Some states are in good position to exploit some new opportunities that arise.

Balanced regional development should not be achieved by leveling down some state by preventing them from reaching their full growth potential in order to bring equality. Poorer states may learn lessons from better states. Kuznets (1955) examined the extent of economic inequality and its major determinants in an inter-temporal context. He observed and explained that the inverted-U-relation between income inequality and per-capita income runs in term of change in (i) rural-urban disparities in per-capita income; (ii) rural-urban intra-sectoral inequalities in income distribution; and (iii) sectoral allocation of workforce and origin of income.

The paper "Regional Disparity in India: Issues Related to Inter-State Variations" prepared by Dhiraj Kumar Bandyopadhyay tries to explain the picture of wide regional variations in the socio-economic indicators like per-capita income, poverty line, literacy rate, infant mortality rate, life expectancy at birth and social and physical infrastructures. Author also tries to examine regional variation at the inter-state and intra-state level in term of urbanization, industrialization and some socio-economic indicators. Author has classified Indian States into two major groups: forward states and backward states. Among the forward states author includes Karnataka, Tamil Nadu, Kerala, Andhra Pradesh, West Bengal, Maharashtra, Punjab and Gujarat. On the other hand, the backward states are Assam, Bihar, Uttar Pradesh, Rajasthan, Orissa and Madhya Pradesh. Author has also used huge data and some statistical tools to find out the objective. Lastly author reached the conclusion that the poverty levels in developed and more urbanized states have surprisingly been high and highest incidence of poverty in urban areas of India was mostly in the small towns.

Dalip Kumar's paper "Regional Pattern of Disparities and Levels of Living in India" tries to explain the disparities in levels of living in India by using the secondary sources of data. The measurement of levels of living depends on so many components like health, food consumption and nutrition, level of education, level of employment and condition of work, housing status, social security, quality of clothing, types of recreation and entertainment, Communication, quality of transportation, levels of aged population and its economic freedom, etc. The data concerning social indicators, especifically standards of living, are included as population, economy, education, working conditions, financial resources, consumer durable, housing, home environment, transportation, leisure, social environment, health, social mobility, minorities, levels of and class differences in material standard of living, and equality between the sexes. This paper discusses Educational disparities, health disparities and Housing infrastructure disparities among the major States of India. Educational disparities can be seen by the literacy rates, Gross enrolment ratio, etc. health-related disparities can be seen by the indicators like CBR, CDR, IMR, Life Expectancy, and housing infrastructure disparities, housing status, drinking water and toilet facility, uses of cooking gas, levels of aged population, etc. Analysis is on the basis of Socio-economic indicators among 16 major states of India which have been categorized into three categories. The ranking is done with the help of various health indicators and social and economic indicators like Literacy rates, per-capita expenditure on health, per-capita GSDP, etc. As per these indicators better level of living states are Kerala, HP, Punjab, Haryana, Maharashtra and Tamil Nadu. On the other hand, states like Rajasthan, Assam, Bihar, Orissa, UP find place only in low level of living states.

The paper "Regional Disparities in Levels of Living in India" is written by H.C.L. Das. Mr. Das has been attempting to identify the degree of inter-state disparities in respects of levels of living mainly in the context of quality of life and work in major 15 Indian states. This paper is purely based on secondary data. Author has used statistical tools to find the proposed objective. The correlation coefficients among the three indices namely, final development index, human development index and quality of life and work index have been computed. The correlation coefficients among these indices have been found highly significant.

Paper "Inter-State Disparities in India under Liberalised Regime: Extent, Trends and Sources" written by Kulwant Singh Phull to analyse the extent and trends of inter-sate disparities in economic development of India, particularly under the liberalized policy implication with the view to explore effective corrective measures. Author has suggested that there is a need to encourage the investment in manufacturing sector along with diversification of agriculture in the backward states, to reduce the inter-state disparities in the country. For this purpose, private investment, both domestic as well as foreign should be encouraged, especially in the backward states together by the central and state governments. More financial powers should be given to state to encourage the state planning to minimize the inter-state disparities.

S.K. Pant, Firdaus Fatima and D.C. Pathak have jointly contributed paper on "Inter-Regional Disparities: Threats and Challenges". In this paper authors try to explain and explore the nature, magnitude and trend of inter-regional imbalances. Authors used some economic indicators like as gender disparity, State Domestic product and poverty and social indicators as education and health. Authors have reached on conclusion, that SC, ST and OBC households start declining both in rural as well as urban setting, thereby upholding the fact that poverty alleviation and other social welfare programmes of the government have, so far, failed to mitigate the incidence of poverty and accordingly increasing the gap of disparities.

Paper on "Inter-Regional Disparities with Multi-dimensional Aspects in India" is prepared by V.L. Lavanya and B. Karthikeyan. Authors have explained the disparities with multi-dimensional aspects in India. Some of its major dimensions include: the level of economic growth, level of education, level of health services, degree of modernization, status of women, level of nutrition, quality of housing, distribution of goods and services.

Paper on "Inter-Regional Disparities in India" is jointly written by Pradeep Punjabi and Prashant Bhardwaj. Authors have referred to some historical trends and try to prove the glorious past of this country. Authors used the data related to bank branches, deposit in and credit by the bank. As per this data they want to show the disparities status among 15 major states in the country.

Mandakini R. Mahore and A.S. Mohammad have contributed the paper entitled "Inter-Regional Disparities in

India's Development". They focused in the paper related to disparities in national income and poverty among major fifteen states. Authors have also mentioned some cases where intra-state regional disparities have been reduced through public policies particular in Kerala, Tamil Nadu and Haryana states. The development of the drought prone districts of Haryana through irrigation is a remarkable example of reduction in economic disparities across the regions within a state.

The paper "Inter-Regional Disparities in India's Development" is written by Rama J. Shah and Rita N. Patel. Authors try to describe the importance of balanced regional development (BRD). BRD is one of the important objectives for reducing regional disparities in the development of Indian economy. The result on the basis of available data indicates that inter-regional disparities in per-capita income are on the increase in the period 1990-91 to 2001-02.

The paper of Rajesh Kumar Singh and Vijay Nath Dubey on "Industrial Disparity in India: An Analysis of UP *vis-à-vis* Maharashtra and Gujarat". The objective of the paper is to enquire into the industrial disparity across states in India. Authors of this paper analyse the number of factories, invested capital, employment and output of factories across the India. This is the result, that the number of factories in UP is very much lower than that in Maharashtra and Gujarat. Another is the input-output ratio of factories in UP which is similar to that of India, Maharashtra and Gujarat. Authors have suggested that the number of factories/industries and amount of invested capital should be accelerated in the backward states.

The paper "Regional Disparity in Indian Development" is written by Bhavesh N. Desai, Ashok B. Trivedi and Dipak R. Chaudhari. Authors have explained the various variables of disparities like poverty, employment GSDP, per-capita income, and human development index. This paper is based on secondary data. Data show that the average growth rate of GSDP was found high before reforms in Maharashtra, Andhra Pradesh and Haryana than average of India. While average growth rate of GSDP was found lower in Gujarat, Karnataka and Bengal. There was not found the inverse relationship between growth rate of GSDP and poverty ratio in Punjab. The growth rate of GSDP and poverty ratio both were lower in Punjab.

Pooja Sikka's paper on "Regional Disparities Across Indian States: A Sector-wise Analysis" tries to examine the sectoral composition of growth performance of major 14 states in the post-reform period. Secondly, author has also worked out the sect oral growth rates of SDP in various sectors.

The paper on "Reforms and Regional Disparities in India" is written by Upendra Sah, Hira Lal Ram and Uma Shankar Bharti. In this paper authors try to focus on the analysis of growth and disparity among major states of India in the pre-reform and post-reform era as per some socio-economic parameters. The authors tender several suggestions to reduce regional inequality across the Indian States. Main suggestion to speed up socio-economic development of the state is quality of governance. A better administered state is more efficient in raising resources and putting them to better uses. Hence governance needs to be given more attention in the backward states.

S.K. Dhage, B.G. Lobo and S.N. Nukale's paper on "Inter-Regional Disparities in India" tries to initiate a debate on the various issues involved with a view explore effective corrective measures without any further delay. This paper gives an idea and tries to give some extent of theoretical analysis of the problem. The authors have several suggestions to reduce regional inequality across the Indian States. They suggest the need for higher level of investment in the social services and infrastructure in backward states as compared to forward states. The backward states are unable to attract private investments because of unfavorable investment climate including poor infrastructure.

"Disparities within India's Different Regions: Why Does the Same Countries Government Work Differently in Different States?" written by G. Vanithamani and Shiny Thankachan. Authors explain the disparities on the basis of some important indicators like per-capita income, population below the poverty line, population engaged in agriculture and manufacturing sectors. Authors have suggested that it is necessary to replace financial attitude with planning attitude. It will be appropriate to take proper account of resources available in backward states so that appropriate special plan can be prepared in favour of individual states.

Achal Kumar Gaur's paper is on "Estimating Regional Disparities in Economic Growth: A Case Study of Indian States". Author tries to examine the inter-state disparity in SDP with the help of several inequality indices that are based on properties of Lorenz Curve, Atkinson's Social Welfare Function, Herfindahl's indices followed by traditional measures like CV and Log Normal Distribution. In addition author has used so many statistical tools for testing the inter-state disparities in major twenty states.

The paper on "Inter-State Disparities in India: A Similarity Matrix Approach" written by Mahalaya Chatterjee. Author tries to explain inter-state disparities in India by the Matrix Approach. He used various factors such as the level of literacy, infant mortality; political commitments and their corresponding interactions contributing to this striking variation among states. The methodology for similarity matrix is briefly discussed in this paper. Author gives more emphasis on spread of primary education through incentives as mid-day meals and free books should be given in poor performing and backward states. Public investment should be stepped up in the health and education infrastructure particularly in poor and less developed states.

The paper on "Regional Development and Locational Dynamics in Andhra Pradesh" written by K. Madhu Babu, is an attempt to examine the regional disparities in concentration of medium and small scale industries of Andhra Pradesh. This paper is mainly intended to explain locational dynamics of the medium and small scale industries in the state of Andhra Pradesh. Two time periods have been selected to make comparative analysis, i.e. 1995 and 2005. Author used simple statistical techniques like annual compound growth rate for above periods.

Kumud Bhagawati's paper on "Regional Socio-economic Disparities in India: With Special Reference to Assam Economy" tries to investigate into the depth of regional disparities in India with special reference to Assam economy and to find out the reasons for it and provides some suggestions to reduce this crucial disparities. The author has several suggestions to reduce region disparities. By making proper identification of the backward regions the integrated programms should be taken up for the development of small scale and cottage industries which are cost effective and labour intensive. Decentralization of economic plans would help in reducing the gap between the developed and developing regions. For this purpose Panchayati Raj Institution should be empowered.

The paper on "Economic Development and Disparities in Maharashtra", written by Kavita S. Sharma tries to explain the district-wise rural-urban disparities in Maharashtra. Author analysed the data related to Human Development Index and per-capita district domestic product. Health and Education-related indicators are used in the analysis. There is a wide gap in the health care infrastructure available in Maharashtra. In the health sector around fifty per cent of doctors in Maharashtra worked in Mumbai.

S.P. Singh's paper on "Economic Growth and Regional Disparity in Uttar Pradesh" examines economic growth and regional disparity in UP. Sector-wise growth rates in the NSDP are estimated for the period 1993-94 to 2004-05. Author used some statistical tools for finding the useful result. The paper has suggested the region specific and sector specific policy interventions required to achieve balanced and inclusive development of all the regions.

The paper on "Inter-Regional Disparities: A Study of Uttar Pradesh" written by Nidhi Sharma highlights the issue related to disparities in wealth concentration across the households, individuals, regions and groups. Author has suggested that there is an urgent need of industrialization in the poor performing regions. Service sector's growth rate is to be accelerated through urbanization process. Agricultural sector needs serious attentions through several institutional and non-institutional reforms such as land reforms, diversification and commercialization of agriculture.

The paper on "Inter-State Disparities in Marine Fisheries Development" written by K. Pazhani and S. Jesi Isabella tries to explain the disparities in marine fisheries development in coastal areas in India. Authors have explained the existing disparities in factor and resources endowments and also the available infrastructures—basic financial and marketing. Authors suggest that the Central as well as State governments should frame policies with the participation of representative of fishermen communities for the equitable and sustainable use of marine resources with better infrastructure.

(B) Disparity in Agriculture and Allied Activities

Agriculture sector plays important role in development of the economy. Agriculture occupies a key position in the Indian economy because of its contribution to over-all economic growth through supplies of food, raw materials and exports. It is a source of livelihood for a majority of the population and provides a large market for non-agricultural goods and services. Disparity is a reason behind inequality in India. The unskilled labour in India is mainly engaged in the manufacturing and the agricultural sector. The aspect of disparity in Indian agriculture concerns crop-wise disparities in growth, between food grains and non-food grains on the one hand, and among different food grains themselves on the other. Part of this inter-crop imbalance derives from regional disparities. Agricultural growth through infrastructure development, e.g., irrigation, drainage, roads, markets and credit institutions in the less developed regions, extension of new technology, particularly breakthrough in dry land farming, afforestration and appropriate price and procurement policies for crops are essential for accelerating the growth of agricultural output, reducing annual fluctuations in output and for correcting inter-regional, inter-crop and inter-class disparities. Agricultural inequality across states as observed in better performing states are mostly in western and southern regions of the country whereas non-performing states are in the northern and eastern region. Some of the important reasons for disparities in agriculture output are studied in detail. These determinants are mainly size of operational holdings, irrigation facilities, cropping intensity, application of new farm technology, HYV seed, fertilizers, pesticides, extension services, rural infrastructure, quality of land and rainfall, etc

The paper on "Inter-State and Inter-Regional Disparities in Production and Productivity in Food Grains in India (1970-71 to 2006-07)" written by Amrita Nandi explains the variation across the Indian States in terms of foodgrain production. The food grain production in this country is enormous and it has raised some policy questions within the country. Reduction of regional disparities is one of the key challenges in agricultural growth in India.

The paper on "Inter-Regional Disparities in India: A Comparative Study in Agricultural Development in Each Zonal State", is written by N.K. Thakur. He considers regional disparities as an issue of deep concern. This paper tries to explain the explicit imbalances in several parameters of agricultural growth in various agro-climatic zones and emphasizes to reduce the imbalance as agriculture provides social justice, peace, prosperity and social harmony.

The paper "Regional Disparity in Agri-Infrastructure with Particular Reference to Irrigation Development in Post-Reform Period" is prepared by R.K. Panda. The author finds wide inequality prevailing in the irrigational development across states. It results into lope-side development in agriculture. This is the result of declining public investment and more emphasis on private investment in agriculture. There is earnest need of providing direct credit facilities to farmers by institutional agencies.

"Growing Inter-State Disparities in Indian Agriculture" written by Nazia Iqbal Hashmi is an explanation based on several tables containing relevant data. India has witnessed green, white, yellow and blue revolution resulting into the economic growth and increase in the per-capita availability of food grain. But that has not been even growth. The author tenders several suggestions to reduce regional inequality in agriculture across Indian States.

B. Sudhakar Reddy has contributed the chapter on "Regional Disparities in Agricultural Development of Andhra Pradesh—A Factor Analysis". Regional disparities are universal phenomenon. He tries to study the inter-regional and intra-regional disparities in the agricultural development of Andhra Pradesh and to identify the factors resulting into the regional disparities in the state. It provides some suggestions and remedial measures with special emphasis on irrigation and priorities to backward and areas with scanty rainfall.

"Removing Regional Differences through Improved Irrigation Facilities in Andhra Pradesh (Jalayagram) is jointly written by K. Raja Babu, M. Sridevi, R. Rohini and Venkata Narayana. The paper analyses existing regional disparities and examines the Jalayagram project in eradicating regional disparities as well as the changes in the structure of land holdings after execution of the project. With the help of tables and maps it has been shown that how much irrigation will have its impacts in the lives of the people in Andhra Pradesh. The authors do not see any politics in the proposed project as the irrigation improvement in evenly spread over all regions.

Anil Kumar and Inderjeet Singh have jointly contributed paper on "Inter-district Variations in the Average Yield of Selected Crops in State of Haryana". Agricultural development is a catalyst for economic growth and development of the country. This paper attempts to analyse the inter-district variations in terms of average yield of main crops. In Haryana in comparison with those at All-India level. The aim of the paper is to examine factors responsible for the increase in average yield in the state of Haryana.

The paper on "An Analysis of Inter-district Variations in the Level of Food Grains Productivity in Rajasthan" is written jointly by Manjushree Gupta and Manju Yadav. This paper explains regional disparities in food grain productivity after 1990-91 and finds out main reasons for it. It also provides some suggestions to reduce inter-state disparities.

(C) Disparity in Social Sector

Increasing regional and sectoral disparities and its possible consequences for social and economic instability are of growing concern in India. Today is one of huge disparities among the social groups and social sector. There are many factors that contribute to the disparity in education. Education disparity was aggravate by economic disparity, gender disparity and rigid social stratifications. In India, educational disparities persist in the Literacy rates, enrolment ratio between boys and girls at all levels, expenditure on education, drop-out rate, etc. The average literacy rate of this country was 65.20 per cent in 2001. The literacy rate among male and female was 76 and 54 per cent respectively. But there are many disparities among the states. On the one side the Kerala has the highest literacy rate of 90.92 per cent followed by Maharashtra (77.27%), Himachal Pradesh (75.91%), Tamil Nadu (73.47%), Punjab (69.75%), West Bengal (69.22%), Karnataka (67.04%), and Gujarat was (66.43%). Rest of the states has literacy levels below the national average. The lowest literacy level is in Bihar (47.53%) followed by Uttar Pradesh (57.36%), Rajasthan (61.03%), Andhra Pradesh (61.11%), MP (64.08%) and Assam (64.28%). High spending in the social sector is one of the major reason for the high revenue deficit and fiscal imbalance in the state.

Literacy Disparities among Religious Groups

In the distribution of persons aged 7 years and above by each sector and religions it is noticed that the literacy rate was lower in rural India for 'Islam' compared to other religions. Literacy rate for all the religious groups, as revealed again for the first time in 2001 Census, were very encouraging, shattering many myths earlier when such a data set was not available for the country as a whole. The literacy rate among Hindus (65.1%) was slightly better than the national average (64.8%) for all religious groups combined. Among Muslims the literacy rate is 59.1%, below the national average. The highest literacy rate is recorded among the Jains (94.1%), followed by Christians (80.3%), Buddhists (72.7%) and Sikhs (69.4%). Against the existing popular perceptions, the female literacy rate among different religious groups does not show wide variations. Among the Muslims, for instance, the literacy rate among the females was stagnant at 50.1 per cent, below the national average of 53.7 per cent. Slightly better is the female literacy rate among the Hindus (53.2%), again below the national average. The highest literacy rate among the females was recorded among the Jains (90.6%), like their male counterparts. Female literacy rate among Christians was 76.2 per cent, followed by Sikhs (63.1%) and Buddhists (61.7%) (Census, 2001).

The paper on "Problem of Regional Imbalances—An

Analysis of Social Sector" is written by Dastgir Alam. The author's opinions that main cause of regional disparities in terms of economic development is the variations in the distribution of production assets. The gap between the two regions' is ever increasing due to free play of market force. The long-term existence of regional inequality is dangerous for national solidarity and peace. He analyses various aspects of economic and social disparities and concluded that each and every state has improved in general but the differences among states remain unchanged because the rate of development in poor states have been lower than that of the rich states. Hence there is need of some special care for backward states.

The paper on "Public Health Expenditure and Health Status in India: An Inter-State Analysis" is jointly written by Kuldip Kaur, Seozy Bhatia and Paramjeet Kaur Dhindsa. The paper elabourates on government health policies in different phase after independence and gives some findings and points towards the areas of concerns. It is a matter of great concern that in India more than 1.72 million children die before celebrating their first birth day. The paper suggests for concerted efforts to develop health infrastructure, empowering the Panchayati Raj Institutions (PRIs) to manage the health services at community levels and increase the budget allocation on health sector. Only then India can realize the dream of becoming "World Class" in health care system. In Kerala social sector spending as a percentage of gross domestic product (GDP) remained much higher than all state spending. The large expenditure on health and education remained the main focus of fiscal policy during the early 1970s and during the 1990s, Kerala has been able to reduce it in recent years.

The paper contributed by Nighat Ahmad is "Rural/ Urban Health Disparity in India". The author concludes that though there has been some improvement in health outcomes but rural-urban disparities is still significant. Disparities breed discontent and dissatisfaction. In the effort to reduce the disparities in health sectors, the National Rural Health mission is a significant step which proposes to raise public expenditure on health from one per cent to three per cent of

GDP. The mission should be launched with all seriousness so that it does not remain only a political gimmick. For this there is need of good governance.

The paper "Inter-State Variations in Health Status in India: Significance of Nutritional Status and Health Awareness" is written by Bipul Malakar and Montu Bose. The health condition of a country depends on the level of nutrition, per head per day calories intake, vaccination and Immunization, educational level and awareness. With the help of some relevant data authors give some suggestions to ameliorate the imbalances in health status in the country.

"Regional Imbalances in Health Facilities in Coastal Andhra Pradesh" is jointly prepared by M.V. Narasimha Sarma and D. Kailasa Rao. The paper throws light on perception of state responsibilities for providing health facilities and conclude that priorities in health are not given equal opportunities in the three regions of Andhra Pradesh. The priority has shifted from health to other sectors. It also gives a few suggestions to improve the health status.

The paper on "Determinants of Health Disparities in Madhya Pradesh: Need for Region Specific Approach" is written by Mona Khare. Madhya Pradesh is passing through the phase of transition. There is a big gap between per-capita income of MP and other developed states. The paper tries to measure the level of health status of major 45 districts of MP and to identify the determinants of intra-district variations therein. The author conclude with a few suggestions like public private partnership, governmental responsibility for providing good quality health facilities at subsidized rate and differential charges from individuals according to their paying capacities.

The elimination of disparities in health is a goal of Healthy People. Disparities in health care can only be interpreted within the context of disparities in health. Disparities in health sector contribute to overall disparities in health. Eliminating disparities in health care is a logical method for eliminating associated disparities in health. Disparities may be differing perspectives regarding the appropriate division of responsibility between the public sector, and the private sector. The health status is generally measured in terms of life expectancy at birth, Infant mortality rate, fertility rate, crude birth rate and crude death rate. Investment and reforms in health sector not only leads to the improvement in quality of life but also to human resource development which in turn affects various sectors of national economy. Health covers a wide range of activities like population control, family planning, prevention of food adulteration, drug control, immunization and eradication of major communicable and non-communicable diseases. According to WHO, health is a state of complete physical, mental and social well-being and not merely the absence of disease or infirmity. The indicators of health status, the birth and death rates are more reflective of the demographic changes taking place in the country. The life expectancy and the infant mortality rate are better indicators of the health status of the population. A look at the relationship among these four indicators is sufficient enough to confirm that these indicators are inter-dependent over the time

The paper on "Regional Disparities in Education with Special Reference to Secondary Level: Issues and Challenges" is prepared jointly by Vinayak Kant Mishra and Prahlad Kumar. It tries to make a comparative analysis of the emerging trends in 15 Major States in respect of a few key parameters which have intrinsic bearing upon the socio-economic development. With the help of secondary data, authors conclude that there is earnest need of holistic convergent framework for implementation of various schemes in secondary education, so that it may be available, accessible and affordable to all students by 2015.

The paper on "Inter-State Disparities in Technical Education in India: Challenges for 2030" is prepared by Nisha and Prahlad Kumar. It throws some light on the growth of technical education during Eleventh Five Year Plan Periods and concludes with some fruitful suggestions like more equitable development of engineering institutions in various regions and efforts to make engineering education more Qualitative and industry-based.

The paper on "Human Development in India: An Inter-State Analysis" is written by Minati Mallick and Jagannath Lenka. It finds that the rank correlation co-efficient between income and human development indexes stands in the order of 0.94 and 0.91 in the year 2001 and 2005 respectively. It indicates the fact that economic growth is the major determinants of human development. Hence there is need to rethink and reformulate our policy approaches up to break vicious cycle of widespread underdevelopment in low-income category states. There is need of development of both the physical and social infrastructure.

(D) Disparity in Infrastructure Development

Disparity in regional infrastructural has been a major reason behind development in India. Infrastructure development has played an important role for development of economy. The increase in regional disparity in infrastructure reflects the enlarging gap between the super rich regions and the rest of the economy within each of the States.

The paper on "A Review of Inter-State Disparities in Telecom Sector in India" is joint contribution of Archana Rani Srivastava and Jagdish Narayan. It is an attempt to identify disparity among states on the basis of Net State Domestic Product (NSDP), contribution of telecom sector and the disparity on the basis of tele-density. India's phone network is fifth largest in the world. Authors try to explain the growth of telecom sector in its historical perspective, the present scenario and the opportunities ahead. Private operators had 53.76 million subscribers in the end of July 2005, while the two PSUs had 53.24 millions. The subscriber base of private telecom operators is now more than that of public sector companies—BSNL and MTNL. Private operator owned 50.24 per cent of the total 107 million subscribers' market, comprising both landlines and mobile segments. The private operators are largely due to the growth in mobile usage. With the help of several tables they conclude that Indian Telecom Sector is witnessing a resurgent growth and has emerged as the fastest growing telecom market in the world with the addition of more than 7 million subscribers per year. The chapter highlights the strong competition between mobile communication channels and the basic telephone lines. Hence, there is need for governmental steps to stop the cut-throat competition by making it more eco-friendly and based on private-public partnership (PPP).

The paper "Infrastructure Disparity and Role of MPLAD Scheme: A Case Study of Allahabad (UP)" is contribution by authors Girish Chandra Tripathi, Abhishek Kumar Pandey and Shilpi Tiwari. From very beginning regional balance has attracted the attention of the planners as per the directive principles enshrined in the consultation. Authors have identified disparity in telecom sector in different constituencies in the district of Allahabad in UP. On the basis of certain findings of the case study, authors render some relevant suggestions to achieve the optimum benefits from the growth process.

The paper written by Alpana Kateja, "Inter-State Pattern of Technology Achievement in India" is an attempt to identify the elements of disparities in terms of Infrastructure, human skill, and Information technology achievement. It has been found that economic well-being of a state is directly related to ICT growth. There is a direct correlation between technology and e-readiness Index. There is a need to reduce the growing disparity in the interest of regional balance.

The paper on "Inter-State Disparities on Banking Operations in India: A Study of UP and Uttarakhand" are jointly contributed by Nisar Ahamad Khan. The chapter is based on the basic of survey on Inter-State disparities, banking development in UP and Uttrakhand, role of banks in providing credit, Inter-State variations in banking operations and SHGs credit linkage by Reserve Bank of India.

In the paper "Regional Imbalances in India—An Analysis of Industrial Disparity in UP, MP, Rajasthan and Maharashtra", the author Shakshi Chaudhary tries to analyse the growth pattern of number of factories, capital investment, employment opportunities and the output of some factories in the states of UP, MP, Rajasthan and Maharashtra. In context of macro-economic stabilization policies initiated in 1991, the government has not been able to make public investment by borrowings. More private investments were made only in developed regions which have better economic and social infrastructure as well as more efficient and investor-friendly state governments.

(E) Disparity in Employment

The National Commission for Enterprises in the Unorganized Sector (NCEUS), report titled "The Challenge of Employment in India: An Informal Perspective" starts by talking of issues that have already discussed in numerous economic circles. The fact that the Indian economy's high growth rate hasn't translated into employment growth leading to a greater disparity between the rich and the poor has been talked about for a long time. According to the World Economic and Social Survey 2008: Overcoming Economic Insecurity, numerous developing economies in South East Asia, Africa, Latin America and the Caribbean have to deal with the issue of a declining employment growth while sustaining their high growth rate. China, for example, is the fastest growing economy in the world; however in the period 2000-06 its employment growth rate was a mearely 1 per cent. (Das, 2009)

National Sample Survey Organization's Report on Employment-Unemployment Situation in India, 2001-02 has observed that at an all-India level, "the employment scenario has remained generally stable over the years 1983 to 2002". What it did not mention was that this was true only for males in rural India; that females are having a much tougher time in the urban work-place with evidence of higher unemployment and withdrawal from the labour force. The employment scenario for women has been far from stable as their urban worker population ratios (number of persons usually employed per 1,000 persons) have drifted lower. If we take the usual status classification in which a person is counted as employed if he or she was engaged in a principal or a subsidiary occupation for the major part of the year—this ratio rose to a peak of 155 in 1993-94 and declined to 139 in 2002.

The decline in the number of women working is partly on account of their spending more years in higher education. In the age group 15-29, for instance, the number of females usually employed per 1,000 persons in urban India has been steadily falling from 149 in 1999-2000 to 136 in 2002. This broad downward drift in age-specific work participation rates has been observed even between 1983-99/2000. These changes are not necessarily regressive as they are in line with development. (*Financial Express*, December 22, 2003)

Employment in organized sector has gone up from 264.58 lakh in March 2005 to 269.93 lakh in March 2006 recording an increase of 2.02 per cent. Public and private sector's employment showed an increase of 1.01 and 4.18 per cent respectively during 2005-06. Employment in private sector has risen significantly as compared to public sector. Region-wise disparities in employment during 2005-06 are also noticed. South Region and Central Region recorded a negative growth (0.9% and 0.2%) in employment. There was an increasing trend of employment in North-Eastern Region (7.3%) followed by Eastern Region (4.2%), Western Region (2.7%) and Northern Region (2.0%). (DGET, 2008)

The chapter on "Regional Disparities in Growth and Employment in India" is written by Samik Shome. On the basis of some relevant secondary data, the author has analysed demographic and social characteristics, Inter-State growth comparison, disparity in per-capita SDP growth and disparity in employment growth. There is a variation in compound annual growth rate of employment not only among state but also within the rural and urban areas within the states. In terms of employment western states have better record due to huge flow of Foreign Direct Investment. The author feels it prudent to arrest the present trends in the differential rate of development. Hence, there is urgent need of growth of non-farm employment, more investment in social infrastructure and focus on public-private partnership.

The paper "Regional Disparities and Level of Employment in India" is contributed by Mohamad Asif and Jyoti Obia. Prevailing wide disparities are main causes of socio-economic and political unrest. The authors explain growth and its trend in employment in organized sector, regional disparities and incidence of employment, employment prospects and governmental efforts for employment generation. This paper also prescribes certain recommendations and concludes that reform process should be such that promotes growth with equity.

The paper "Regional Development and Occupational Shift in MP: An Inter-Temporal Analysis" is authored by

Roopali Shevalkar. It analysis the shift in occupational pattern in the period 1981-2001, makes comparative analysis of regional disparities and development and tries to identify the relationship between index of regional development and occupational pattern.

(F) Disparity in Financial System and Policy Formulation

The financial system in India is the most extensive. The total asset value of the entire banking sector in India is nearly US$ 270 billion. The total deposits are nearly US$ 220 billion. Banking sector in India has been transformed completely. Presently the latest inclusions Internet banking and Core banking have made banking operations more user-friendly and easy. The major step towards opening up of the financial market further was the nullification of the regulations restricting the growth in the financial sector. To maintain such a growth for a long-term the inflation has to come down further. The analysis of Indian financial sector shows the growth of the sector was the result of the individual development of the divisions under the sector. The question of disparity between different regions within states has become politically important with the contradictions in centre-state relations exacerbated by neoliberalism even as the finance commission strictures-based on fiscal discipline being institutionalized.

The paper "Need of an Integrated Price Policy in an Inter-Regional and Inter-Sectoral Frame of Indian Economy" is contributed jointly by Binoy N. Verma and Abhas Saurabh. The authors suggests for liberal credit policy for small and marginal farmers and a coordinated approach in formulating the agricultural price policy in order to achieve the goal of social justice.

"Inter-Regional Disparity of Foreign Direct Investment in India after Economic Reforms" is authored by Brajesh Srivastava. The author suggests for improvement in basic infrastructure, quacking and transparency in official dealings and bringing more FDI and its investment in new destinations also.

In the paper "Inter-State Income Disparity and the Transfer of Resources from the Union to the States" the authors duo R.K. Bansal and J.R. Gupta make use of several tables to conclude that self-dependence of the better-off states is more responsible for keeping them ahead of others than the distribution of sources from the centre.

Kerala ranked first among the major Indian States on the basis of its human development index in 1981, 1991 and 2001 despite its per-capita income being much below the national average. Regional inequality in states needs to be seen in the context of its development challenges, which are different from those of the rest of India. For the low performing region, the development strategy would need drastic modifications. The major thrust of strategy has to be fast human capital development (i.e. education, health and nutrition), agricultural modernization and rural industrialization. In order to introduce and expend growth centers in rural areas, infrastructure on transport and communication should occupy the highest priority. For agriculture modernization, there is a need to enhance both public and private sector investment, particularly in various areas of irrigation development. Available statistic reveal that those states which have continuously increased investment in irrigation, agricultural productivity has increased. As a result, the level of employment has gone up and incidence of poverty has declined. The reverse is the case with the low performing regions which has reduced the level of investment in agriculture sector. Second major constraint to the low performing region has been the weak organization of economic institutions. One of the major task for the state would be a bring significant improvement and strengthening in the organization of such institutions at various level. It should be done most urgently in order to encourage the initiative and participation of private sector.

If curse of India's disparity is to be removed, all attempts have to be made to adopt sound macro as well as micro-economic policies, pragmatic development strategy specific to each State, revamping of institutions and delivery mechanism, and involvement of people as practitionor of development at the grass-root level. It is also for the national leaders, planners and policy-makers to realize that if the curse of India's disparity is not removed, India would never be able to realize the dream of becoming a World's Economic Power.

References

Das, Debabrata (2009), Growth, Employment and Economic Disparity, *Business Line*, August 4, 2009.

DGET (2009), *Employment Review*, 2005-06, Government of India, Ministry of Labour and Employment, Director General of Employment and Training, New Delhi.

Financial Express, (2003), Gender Disparity in Urban India, *Financial Express*, December 22, 2003.

Kuznets, Simon (1955), Economic Growth and Income Inequality, *The American Economic Review*, Vol. 45, No. 1, pp. 1-28.

Nath, V. (1970), Regional Development in Indian Planning, *Economic and Political Weekly*, Volume V, Issues 3-5, Special Article, p. 247.

Nath, V. (1971), Regional Development Policies, *Economic and Political Weekly*, Volume VI, Issues 30-32, pp. 1601-03.

Planning Commission (2004), West Bengal Human Development Report, Government of India.

Sen, A. and Himanshu (2004), Poverty and Inequality in India—I and II, *Economic and Political Weekly*, 18 and 25, September.

1

Rural-Urban Development Disparities in India

KAVERI SARKAR

Economic development is the result of a combination of economic growth, social progress and political stability of a country. A rapid rate of growth may be achieved by integrating with the world economy, or by liberalisation and privatisation policies, but such a strategy does not necessarily aim at a commensurate human development and poverty alleviation.

The fruits of development need to cover equally all sections of the population and every segment of the country. Economic growth is a function of increase in investment and productivity, but economic equality necessitates investment in the areas where most of the poor, unemployed or underemployed people are living or working. Use of labour-intensive techniques is necessary to provide gainful employment otherwise economic growth implies jobless growth. Economic reforms in the true sense of the term requires reformative measures which would not only accelerate growth but also ensure equality in all sections of the population and allover the country. Economic reforms in

India since 1991 though has achieved a higher rate of growth in the recent years but India still possesses the characteristics of an under developed country. India's per-capita income is rising despite a rapid growth of population, but it is still well within the range of low income countries as classified by world development report (2005). Dependence on agriculture is still very high and almost 70 per cent population depends on agriculture which produces only 24 per cent of national income. Unemployment is very high and almost 24 per cent people live below poverty line. The social objective of Indian economic development has been growth with equitable distribution of income, but the problem lies in reconciling growth with equality.

This paper aims at analyzing the disparities in development with respect to the rural and urban sectors of roughly twenty major states of the country. The study has been divided in four sections. The first one will cover the disparities in growth of NSDP, population, poverty alleviation, along with changes in HDI and consumption patterns of the people.

The second one will discuss the employment and literacy situations, and the third one will analyze the health indicators. The fourth one will show the infrastructural developments.

The data obtained are in most cases for twenty major states of the country. The data are everywhere not for the same periods also. The study has been conducted with data which were easily accessible to the author so comparative analysis from all aspects has been restricted.

SECTION I

The per-capita NSDP growth was 31 per cent from 1991 to 1997 in India with a rise in disparity from 34.3 per cent to 39.7 per cent. Gujarat was the leading state with a growth of 41 per cent, followed by Maharashtra and Tamil Nadu. The number of states having higher per-capita NSDP than the national level declined from 1991 to 1997. Bihar was the state with the lowest growth in per-capita NSDP followed by Uttar Pradesh, Meghalaya, Manipur, Assam (See Table 1 in Appendix).

Economic development is a three stage process. The dominance of the service sector in the growth process is associated with the third stage of growth. In developed economies service sector contributes a major share in GDP. During the process of growth the Indian economy too experienced a rise in the share of industry and service sector in GDP. The contribution of the service sector has rapidly been increasing in the recent years by growth in trade, hotel services, storage, communication, financing, insurance, real estate and business services, all of which are experiencing high trend growth rates.

The contribution of different sectors in SDP shows the maximum disparity among the states in case of the industrial sector where the disparity was 28 per cent in 1993, though it declined to 24 per cent in 2001. In case of agriculture the disparity was 25 per cent in 2001 and for services all the states had an equitable rise with disparity of only 14 per cent among the states. There was a commendable rise in India in the service sector contribution, in almost all the states. The share of agriculture in GDP declined from 30 per cent to 24 per cent, but there was a flat growth of the industrial sector, which had a contribution of only 26 per cent in both 1993 and 2001. The service sector had a marked increase in contribution to GDP from 42 per cent in 1993 to 48 per cent in 2001. Apart from Punjab, Bihar had a good contribution of the agriculture sector, as well as the services sector, but very low contribution of the industrial sector. Service sector contribution was high in Kerala, Maharashtra, West Bengal, Tamil Nadu, Jannu & Kashmir, etc. The industrial sector contribution was good in Gujarat, Himachal Pradesh, Madhya Pradesh and Tamil Nadu (See Table 2 in Appendix).

The rate of urbanization was 27.78 per cent in India, with an increase of 1.95 per cent in 2001 over 1991. Gujarat had the highest rate in urbanization followed by Haryana. On the other hand, West Bengal and Bihar showed a marked decline in urbanization as also Kerala and Manipur. The degree of disparity in urbanization showed a rise from 35 per cent in 1991 to 39 per cent in 2001. The number of states showing above average rate of urbanization than all-India declined in 2001 from 1991. The population growth rate was

1.95 in India in the period 1991-2001. Jammu & Kashmir showed the highest rate of growth followed by Meghalaya, Manipur, Rajasthan, Bihar and Haryana. The degree of disparity among the states was as high as 29 per cent in population growth (See Table 3 in Appendix).

Poverty at the national level is estimated as the weighted average of state-wise poverty levels. The state-wise poverty index is measured by state specific poverty lines and distribution of persons by expenditure growths obtained from the NSS data on consumption expenditure. The state specific poverty ratios have witnessed a secular downward trend since the seventies. Poverty has declined at the macro-level, but rural-urban and inter-state disparities are very much there.

The percentage of people below poverty line declined from 32 per cent in 1993-94 in urban India to 23 per cent in 1991-2000 whereas in the rural areas it fell from 37 per cent to 27 per cent. Though the population below poverty line decreased still the inequality index has increased. The degree of disparity among the states was 56 per cent in 1993-94 in the urban areas which rose to 63 per cent in 1999-2000. The same also rose for the rural areas and this was much higher than the urban areas, i.e., from 33 per cent to 60 per cent (See Table 4 in Appendix). The following are the states with higher percentage of population below poverty line than all-India average:

Urban		*Rural*	
1993	*1999*	*1993*	*1999*
Orissa	Uttar Pradesh	Assam	Assam
Madhya Pradesh	Orissa	Bihar	Bihar
Bihar	Tamil Nadu	West Bengal	West Bengal
Uttar Pradesh	Madhya Pradesh	Tripura	Tripura
Maharashtra	Maharashtra	Uttar Pradesh	Uttar Pradesh
Andhra Pradesh	Karnataka	Madhya Pradesh	Madhya Pradesh
Karnataka	Andhra Pradesh	Maharashtra	Maharashtra
	Bihar	Manipur	Manipur
		Meghalaya	Meghalaya
		Orissa	Orissa

The states of Punjab and Haryana have advanced through massive agricultural development, Kerala has progressed through human resource developments, West Bengal through massive land reforms efforts and panchayat system, and Andhra Pradesh through direct public intervention in the form of public distribution of food grains.

The HDI has improved significantly over 1980 to 2001. In India HDI has increased by 26 per cent in the eighties and by another 24 per cent during the nineties. India's rank is 127 among 177 nations in HDI. India's HDI was 0.595 at 2002 and India is now a medium human development country of the world. There have been improvements in both rural and urban areas, though the rural-urban gap in human developments continues to be significant but declining. The disparity among states in HDI is less than that of per-capita NSDP. There has been a one to one correspondence between the low income states having lower HDI. But the states having higher income level are not showing higher HDI. As for example, Kerala shows higher HDI with middle income, on the other hand, West Bengal, Andhra Pradesh have higher incomes but not high HDI. Hence higher income is not enough for human development, social mobilization is needed for better and improved quality of life to all and everyone of the country.

When we look at the HDI we find that in general India recorded an increase over the years 1981, 1991, 2001 with HDI 0.302, 0.381 and 0.472 respectively. The disparity among the states also declined with respect to human development. The states which show a lower level of development are Bihar, Madhya Pradesh, Uttar Pradesh, Assam, Rajasthan, Orissa and Andhra Pradesh in 2001. The number of states showing lower than average HDI were more in 1991. Kerala, Punjab, Manipur were among the high ranked states both in 1991 and 2001 (See Table 5 in Appendix).

There was not much inequality in case of expenditure on consumption of the population in different states of India, both in rural and urban sectors, though the degree of disparity was more in the rural sector than the urban. There has been a steady decline in consumption expenditure on food items and rise in non-food items both in the rural and urban sectors. The fall in consumption expenditure on food items was from 63 per cent to 59 per cent in the rural sector over 1993 to 2000, and from 55 per cent to 48 per cent in the urban sector. On the other hand, rise in consumption expenditure on non-food items was from 37 per cent to 41 per cent in the rural sector, whereas it was from 45 per cent to 52 per cent in the urban sector (See Table 6 in Appendix). The Gini ratio in consumption expenditure is very high for the urban sector in most of the states and it remained almost same in both 1993 and 2000, but for the rural sector there has been a decline. Karnataka Maharashtra, Tamil Nadu and West Bengal showed very high Gini ratio in the urban sector in 2000 and Maharashtra, Madhya Pradesh, Himachal Pradesh, Uttar Pradesh, Tamil Nadu in the rural (See Table 7 in Appendix).

Section II

There have been significant improvements in the literacy condition of the states. In general in India, there has been a steady increase from 45 per cent to 59 per cent in the rural areas from 1991 to 2001, which was from around 75 per cent to 81 per cent in the urban areas. The degree of disparity among the states also fell from 27 per cent to 16 per cent in the rural areas and from 10 per cent to 7 per cent in the urban areas. Kerala, Himachal Pradesh, Tripura, Maharashtra were the states having good literacy rates in 2001 in the rural areas and Kerala, Himachal Pradesh, Tripura, Maharashtra, Assam, Meghalaya in the urban areas (See Table 8 in Appendix).

There have been numerous employment guarantee programmes in various states. But there have been high proportions on non-poor, non-eligible persons among the beneficiaries. Leakages due to inappropriate works, inefficient implementation and corruption are high. The employment growth rate was only 1.3 per cent in the rural areas and 2.4 per cent in the urban areas over 1993-99. The degree of disparity among the states was as high as 60 per cent which rose from 39 per cent in 1983-93 in the urban areas and in the rural areas the same was from 45 per cent to 52 per cent.

This indicates the phenomenon of jobless growth. The states with high rural employment growth rate were Punjab, Bihar, Assam in 1993-99 and Assam, Kerala, Madhya Pradesh, Uttar Pradesh, Manipur, Orissa with high urban employment growth rate (See Table 9 in Appendix). The degree of disparity among the states in incidence of unemployment in rural India was very high in both 1993 and 2000. Incidence of unemployment increased in case of both rural and urban India from 1993 to 2000. Assam, Kerala and West Bengal recorded very high incidence in the rural areas and Assam, Bihar, Himachal Pradesh, Manipur, Kerala, Orissa and West Bengal showed very high incidence in the urban areas (See Table 10 in Appendix).

The per worker value of output showed high degree of disparity among the states in 2001-02 and it even increased from 1996-97. Gujarat, Haryana, Madhya Pradesh, Himachal Pradesh, Maharashtra showed higher per worker value of output in 2001-02. The input-output ratio increased from 0.75 to 0.8 during this period in India, almost all the states had it around 0.8, showing a very low degree of disparity, only Tripura had it as low as 0.6 (See Table 11 in Appendix).

SECTION III

In this section we will show the rural urban disparities with respect to health indicators. There has been not much disparity in expectation of life in the urban areas in 1992-96, which was 4.57 per cent and on the other hand it was 8 per cent in the rural areas. In rural India expectation of life was 59 years and in urban areas it was 66 years during the same period. The states with lower life expectancy in both rural and urban areas were, Uttar Pradesh, Madhya Pradesh, Assam, Orissa and Rajasthan (See Table 12 in Appendix).

In rural India 36 per cent child birth were without any kind of medical attendance in 1995-96, whereas 16 per cent were without any kind of medical attendance in the urban areas. The degree of disparity among the states was as high as 68 per cent in the urban areas and 54 per cent in the rural areas. Punjab, Kerala,

Andhra Pradesh, Tamil Nadu were the better states

with lower percentage in this regard in the rural areas. On the other hand, Punjab, Kerala, Haryana, Tamil Nadu, West Bengal were the better states with lower percentage in this regard in the urban areas. The states with high percentage of child birth without any medical attendance in both rural and urban areas were Bihar, Uttar Pradesh, Madhya Pradesh, Rajasthan, Orissa whereas Assam and Jammu & Kashmir had very high percentage of child birth without any medical attendance in the rural areas (See Table 13 in Appendix).

The percentage of children fully vaccinated increased from 31 per cent to 37 per cent in the rural areas over the years 1992-93 to 1998-99 in India as also from 51 per cent to 61 per cent in the urban areas. But the degree of disparity among the states increased to a very high extent in the rural areas from 45 per cent to 53 per cent over this period, and for the urban areas also there was a rise from 31 per cent to 34 per cent. In the rural areas the states of Assam, Uttar Pradesh, Madhya Pradesh, Rajasthan, Bihar had a very less percentage of children fully vaccinated, whereas these states also faired badly in the urban counterpart along with the states of West Bengal, Gujarat, Orissa and Karnataka (See Table 14 in Appendix).

India has a very high rate of anaemic people and it is widespread among women. During 1998-99 the percentage of anaemic women in India in the rural areas was 54 per cent as against 46 per cent in the urban areas. There was a moderate disparity of 21 per cent among the states in the rural areas and 23 per cent in the urban areas. The states of Assam, Bihar, Orissa, West Bengal had very high percentage of anaemic women in both the rural and urban areas (See Table 15 in Appendix).

The death rate also decreased in both rural and urban areas from 1991 to 1997, and the degree of disparity among the states was moderate and it also declined over the same period. Uttar Pradesh, Orissa and Madhya Pradesh were the states with higher death rates in both the rural and urban areas in 1997 (See Table 16 in Appendix).

The number of females per thousand males increased from 939 to 946 over 1991 to 2001 in the rural areas and from 894 to 901 in the urban areas. Interestingly enough the ratio was less in the urban areas. The degree of disparity was not much among the states. Haryana, Punjab, Jammu & Kashmir were the states with lesser number of females (See Table 17 in Appendix).

Section IV

High growth of income on its own is not enough to improve the quality of life of the poor unless the poor have certain basic minimum services. These include universal primary education, employment, primary health care, safe drinking water, shelter for the poor, road connectivity for all villages and habitations and nutritional security.

In this section the relative developments in the basic minimum infrastructural facilities can be studied. If we look at the figures of road connectivity at village level we will see that from 1992-93 to 1996-97 there has been a decline in road connectivity from 90 per cent to 78 per cent villages with a population of over 1500. There have been moderate levels of disparity in both the years but the degree of disparity increased from 1992-93 to 1996-97. There was worse road connectivity in the states of Uttar Pradesh, Madhya Pradesh, Himachal Pradesh, West Bengal, Bihar, Meghalaya in 1996-97. There were drastic fall in connectivity in the states of Uttar Pradesh, Madhya Pradesh, Meghalaya from 1992-93 to 1996-97 and moderate fall in Andhra Pradesh, Orissa and Jammu & Kashmir (See Table 18 in Appendix).

Regarding electricity connection in the rural areas there was an increase from 14.7 per cent to 30.5 per cent in 1991 from 1981. The degree of disparity also decreased from 76 per cent to 59 per cent. On the other hand in the urban areas the increase was from 62.5 per cent to 75.8 per cent with a decline in degree of disparity from 26 per cent to 14 per cent. Uttar Pradesh, West Bengal, Orissa, Assam, Bihar had the worse conditions in the rural areas and Assam, Bihar and Orissa were the worse states in relation to the conditions in the urban areas (See Table 19 in Appendix).

Safe drinking water availability increased from 26.5 per cent to 55.5 per cent households in 1991 from 1981 in the rural areas. The degree of disparity declined from 72 per cent to 38 per cent among the states. The availability increased from 75 per cent to 81 per cent households in the urban areas during the same period. The degree of disparity among the states fell to 19 per cent from 24 per cent in 1981. The north-eastern states had less availability of safe drinking water, viz. Meghalaya, Assam, Manipur, Tripura especially in the rural areas. Other states like, Madhya Pradesh, Orissa, Andhra Pradesh also lagged behind in this regard. Kerala has been in the worst position with only 12 per cent availability. On the contrary, Haryana, Punjab had the best record in this regard (See Table 19 in Appendix).

The percentage of pucca houses increased in the rural areas from 22 per cent in 1981 to 29 per cent households in 1993-94. It should be noted that the degree of disparity among the states increased from 61 per cent to 66 per cent in these years. In the urban areas the percentage of pucca houses increased from 65 per cent in 1981 to 71 per cent households in 1993-94. The degree of disparity among the states was almost the same at 33 per cent in the two time periods. The north-eastern states along with Bihar, Orissa, Madhya Pradesh and West Bengal were in worse positions in this regard (See Table 20 in Appendix).

Access to sanitation facilities is one of the basic minimum needs of the poor. Only 9 per cent households got access to toilet facilities in the rural areas in 1991 as compared to 64 per cent in the urban areas. The degree of disparity among the states was as high as 104 per cent in the rural areas as compared to a moderate 19 per cent in the urban areas in 1991. Bihar, Madhya Pradesh, Orissa were in the worst positions with Uttar Pradesh, Karnataka, Andhra Pradesh, Himachal Pradesh, Haryana, Maharashtra, Rajasthan, Tamil Nadu coming next in the rural areas. In the rural urban combined figure we find that in 1991, 24 per cent households got access to toilet facilities, which was 49 per cent in 1997.

The degree of disparity among the states increased from 15 per cent in 1991 to 25 per cent in 1997. The conditions of Assam, Jammu & Kashmir, Orissa, Madhya Pradesh were worse in 1997 among the states (See Table 21 in Appendix).

CONCLUSION

The mere fact that different states grow at different rates is not a failure of policy. India is a very large and vastly diversified country. Some states are at times in a good position to exploit some new opportunities that arise. Some states are better managed and are able to create better environment which generates higher rate of growth. Balanced regional development should not be achieved by leveling down some states by preventing them from reaching their full growth potential in order to bring equality. The inter-state differences can have a healthy demonstration effect, i.e., the poorer states may learn lessons from their superior counterparts.

References

Economic Survey, Various issues, Ministry of Finance, Government of India.

Gupta, K.R. (ed.), Liberalisation and Globalisation of Indian Economy.

Kapila, Uma, Understanding the Problems of Indian Economy.

Planning Commission, Human Development Report, 2001.

Planning Commission, (2005), Mid-term Appraisal of the Tenth Five Year Plan.

Saksena, K.D., Economic Reforms: The Indian Experience.

Statistical Hand Book, Various issues, Reserve Bank of India.

TABLE I

Per-capita NSDP

Sl. No.	*States*	*1990-91*	*1997-98*	*% Change*	*Rank*	*States above Average*	
						1991	*1997*
1.	Andhra Pradesh	2099	2550	21.49	8	West Bengal	West Bengal
2.	Assam	1579	1675	6.08	16	Tamil Nadu	Tamil Nadu
3.	Bihar	1120	1126	0.54	20	Punjab	Punjab
4.	Gujarat	2738	3918	43.10	1	Maharashtra	Maharashtra
5.	Haryana	3521	4025	14.31	11	Karnataka	Gujarat
6.	Himachal Pradesh	2268	2556	12.70	12	Gujarat	Haryana
7.	Jammu & Kashmir	1815	1932	6.45	15	Haryana	
8.	Karnataka	2215	2866	29.39	6	Himachal Pradesh	
9.	Kerala	1876	2490	32.73	4		
10.	Madhya Pradesh	1636	1922	17.48	9		
11.	Maharashtra	3615	5032	39.20	2		
12.	Manipur	1847	1948	5.47	17		
13.	Meghalaya	1734	1804	4.04	19		
14.	Orissa	1480	1666	12.57	13		
15.	Punjab	3873	4389	13.32	14		
16.	Rajasthan	1916	2226	16.18	10		
17.	Tamil Nadu	2303	3141	36.39	3		
18.	Tripura	1671	2117	26.69	7		
19.	Uttar Pradesh	1648	1725	4.67	18		

20. West Bengal	2257	2977	31.90	5
All-India	2213	2890	30.59	
Degree of Disparity	34.38	39.8		

Source: Planning Commission, Human Development Report, 2001

TABLE 2

Change in Structure of SDP

Sl. No	States	% Share of Agriculture			% Share of Industry			% Share of Services		
		1993-94	2001-02	% change	1993-94	2001-02	% change	1993-94	2001-02	% change
1.	Andhra Pradesh	33.3	27.6	-17	24.4	25.3	4	42.4	47.1	11.1
2.	Assam	39.4	32.8	-17	22.4	22.7	1	38.2	44.5	16.5
3.	Bihar	48.6	38.5	-21	10.1	12.3	22	41.3	49.2	19.1
4.	Gujarat	22.4	17.3	-23	38.8	41.2	6			
5.	Haryana	42.2	31.1	-26	26.5	28.6	8	31.3	40.3	28.8
6.	Himachal Pradesh	32.2	22	-32	28.1	35.8	27	39.8	42.2	6
7.	Jammu & Kashmir	32.9	32.1	-2	21.8	16.9	-22	45.4	51	12.3
8.	Karnataka	35.6	26.2	-27	26.2	27.7	6	38.3	46.2	20.6
9.	Kerala	30.3	23.2	-23	20.9	20.4	2	48.1	56.4	15.6
10.	Madhya Pradesh	39.8	28.9	-27	24.6	33.1	35	35.7	38	6.4
11.	Maharashtra	19.5	15.1	-23	33.4	29.8	-11	47.8	55.1	17
12.	Manipur	35.5	27.5	-23	18.7	24.1	29	45.9	48.4	5.4
13.	Meghalaya	25.3	23.6	-7	20.6	23.6	15	54.1	52.8	-2.4
14.	Orissa	29.8	30.5	-15	21.8	24.6	13	32.1	36.2	12.8
15.	Punjab	46.1	39.3	-15	21.8	24.6	13	32.1	36.2	12.8
16.	Rajasthan	34	29.5	-13	27.3	30.4	11	38.8	40.1	3.3
17.	Tamil Nadu	24.1	16.4	-32	34.4	32.9	-4	41.5	50.6	21.9
18.	Tripura	35.3	21.7	-38	11	30	173	53.7	48.3	-10

19.	Uttar Pradesh	39	35.1	-10	22.2	25.8	16	38.8	39.1	0.8
20.	West Bengal	32.4	26.2	-19	24.5	22.9	-6	43.1	51	18.3
	All-India	30.97	24.31	-21	26.66	26.72	0.2	42.77	48.97	14.5
	Degree of Disparity	22.23	24.93		28.49	24.55		15.57	13.62	

Source: *Economic Times*, Trends, 26 January 2004, p. 12

States with Higher than Average Share of Service Sector		*States with Higher than Average Share of Industrial Sector*	
2001	*1993*	*2001*	*1993*
Maharashtra	Tripura	Himachal Pradesh	Tamil Nadu
Meghalaya	Kerala	Madhya Pradesh	Maharashtra
West Bengal	Maharashtra	Tamil Nadu	Himachal Pradesh
Jammu & Kashmir	Manipur	Rajasthan	Rajasthan
Tamil	Jammu & Kashmir	Tripura	
	West Bengal	Maharashtra	
		Haryana	
		Karnataka	

TABLE 3

Urbanisation and Population Growth (% per annum)

Sl. No	States	Urbanisation Rate (%)			Annual Average Growth		States with above Average Urbanisation	
		1991	2001	% change	1991-2001	Rank	1991	2001
1.	Andhra Pradesh	26.89	27.08	0.71	1.31	18	West Bengal	Tamil Nadu
2.	Assam	11.10	12.72	14.59	1.74	12	Tamil Nadu	Punjab
3.	Bihar	13.14	10.47	-20.32	2.43	6	Punjab	Maharashtra
4.	Gujarat	34.49	37.35	8.29	2.05	9	Manipur	Karnataka
5.	Haryana	24.83	29.00	16.79	2.50	5	Maharashtra	Gujarat
6.	Himachal Pradesh	8.69	9.79	12.66	1.63	14	Karnataka	Haryana
7.	Jammu & Kashmir	23.83	24.88	4.41	2.69	1	Kerala	
8.	K.arnataka	30.92	33.98	9.90	1.60	15	Gujarat	
9.	Kerala	26.39	25.97	-1.59	0.90	20		
10.	Madhya Pradesh	23.18	26.67	15.06	2.06	7		
11.	Maharashtra	38.69	42.40	9.59	2.06	7		
12.	Manipur	27.52	23.88	-13.23	2.66	2		
13.	Meghalaya	18.60	19.63	5.54	2.65	3		
14.	Orissa	13.38	14.97	11.88	1.49	16		
15.	Punjab	29.55	33.95	14.89	1.82	10		
16.	Rajasthan	22.00	23.38	6.27	2.53	4		
17.	Tamil Nadu	34.15	43.86	28.43	1.07	19		
18.	Tripura	15.29	17.02	11.31	1.47	17		

19.	Uttar Pradesh	19.84	20.78	4.74	1.79	11
20.	West Bengal	27.84	20.03	-28.05	1.65	13
	All-India	25.71	27.78	8.05	1.95	
	Degree of Disparity	35.22	39.41		28.33	

Source: Planning Commission, Human Development Report, 2001.

TABLE 4

Per cent of Population below Poverty Line

Sl. No.	States	Urban					Rural				
		1993-94		1999-2000		1999-2000 over 1993-94	1993-94		1999-2000		1999-2000 over 1993-94
		% of Persons	Poverty Line (Rs.)	% of Persons	Poverty Line (Rs.)	% of Persons	% of Persons	Poverty Line (Rs.)	% of Persons	Poverty Line (Rs.)	% change in % of persons
1.	Andhra Pradesh	38.33	278.14	26.63	457.4	-30.52	15.9	163	11.05	262	-30.6
2.	Assam	7.73	212.42	7.47	343.99	-3.36	45.1	232	40.04	365	-11.04
3.	Bihar	34.5	238.49	32.91	379.78	-4.61	58.2	212	44.3	333	-23.9
4.	Gujarat	27.89	297.22	15.59	474.41	-44.10	22.2	202	13.1	318	-40.6
5.	Haryana	16.38	258.33	9.99	420.2	-39.01	28.02	233	8.2	362	-70.5
6.	Himachal Pradesh	9.18	253.61	9.63	420.2	4.90	30.3	233	7.9	367	-73.8
7.	Jammu & Kashmir	9.18	253.61	1.98	420.2	-78.43	30.3	233	3.9	367	-86.9
8.	Karnataka	40.14	302.89	25.25	511.44	-37.10	29.9	186	17.4	309	-41.8
9.	Kerala	25.55	280.54	20.27	477.06	-20.67	25.7	243	9.4	374	-63.6
10.	Madhya Pradesh	48.38	317.16	38.44	481.65	-20.55	40.6	193	37.1	311	-8.8
11.	Maharashtra	35.15	328.56	26.81	539.71	-23.73	37.9	194	23.7	318	-37.5
12.	Manipur	7.73	212.42	7.47	343.99	-3.36	45.01	232	40.04	365	-11.04
13.	Meghalaya	7.73	212.42	7.47	343.99	-3.36	45.01	232	40.04	365	-11.04

14.	Orissa	41.64	298.22	42.83	473.12	2.86	49.7	194	48.01	323	-3.4
15.	Punjab	11.35	253.61	5.75	385.15	-49.34	11.9	233	6.35	362	-46.9
16.	Rajasthan	30.49	280.85	19.85	465.92	-34.90	26.4	215	13.7	344	-48.1
17.	Tamil Nadu	39.77	296.63	22.11	475.6	-44.41	32.5	196	20.6	307	-36.7
18.	Tripura	7.73	212.42	7.47	343.99	-3.36	45.01	232	40.04	365	-11.04
19.	Uttar Pradesh	35.39	258.65	30.89	416.29	-12.72	42.3	213	31.2	336	-26.2
20.	West Bengal	22.41	247.53	14.86	409.22	-33.69	40.8	220	31.9	350	-21.9
	All-India	32.46	291.35	23.62	454.11	-27.23	37.3	205	27.1	327	-27.3
	Degree of Disparity	56.57	13.58	63.13	13.79		33.49	9.98	60.83	8.66	

Source: Planning Commission, Human Development Report, 2001.

TABLE 5

Human Development Index

Sl. No.	States	1981		1991		2001		States Below National Average	
		Value	Rank	Value	Rank	Value	Rank	1991	2001
1.	Andhra Pradesh	0.30	23	0.38	23	0.42	10	Bihar	Bihar
2.	Assam	0.27	26	0.35	26	0.39	14	Uttar Pradesh	Assam
3.	Bihar	0.24	32	0.31	32	0.37	15	Madhya Pradesh	Uttar Pradesh
4.	Gujarat	0.36	14	0.43	17	0.48	6	Orissa	Madhya Pradesh
5.	Haryana	0.36	15	0.44	16	0.51	5	Rajasthan	Orissa
6.	Himachal Pradesh	0.40	10	0.47	13	--		Assam	Andhra Pradesh
7.	Jammu & Kashmir	0.34	19	0.40	21	--		Meghalaya	Rajasthan
8.	Karnataka	0.35	16	0.41	19	0.48	7	Andhra Pradesh	
9.	Kerala	0.50	2	0.59	3	0.64	1		
10.	Madhya Pradesh	0.25	30	0.33	30	0.39	12		
11.	Maharashtra	0.36	13	0.45	15	0.52	4		
12.	Manipur	0.46	4	0.54	9	--			
13.	Meghalaya	0.37	21	0.37	24	--			
14.	Orissa	0.27	27	0.35	28	0.40	11		
15.	Punjab	0.41	9	0.48	12	0.54	2		
16.	Rajasthan	0.26	28	0.35	27	0.42	9		
17.	Tamil Nadu	0.34	17	0.47	14	0.53	3		
18.	Tripura	0.29	24	0.39	22	--			
19.	Uttar Pradesh	0.26	29	0.31	31	0.39	13		

20.	West Bengal	0.31	22	0.40	20	0.47	8
	All-India	0.30		0.38		0.47	
	Degree of Disparity	21.74		18.11		16.30	

Source: Planning Commission, Human Development Report, 2001.

TABLE 6

Composition of Per-capita Expenditure (%)

Sl. No.	States	Rural						Urban					
		Food			Non-Food			Food			Non-Food		
		1993-94	1999-2000	% change	1993-94	1999-2000	% change	1993-94	1999-2000	% change	1993-94	1999-2000	% change
1.	Andhra Pradesh	59.58	60.50	1.54	40.42	39.50	-2.28	53.84	47.44	-11.89	46.16	52.56	12.18
2.	Assam	72.26	67.63	-6.41	27.74	32.27	16.33	59.68	55.38	-7.21	40.32	44.62	9.64
3.	Bihar	71.00	66.54	-6.28	29.00	33.46	15.38	62.92	57.24	-9.03	37.08	42.76	13.28
4.	Gujarat	67.10	59.82	-10.85	32.90	40.18	22.13	58.41	49.58	-15.12	41.54	50.42	17.61
5.	Haryana	60.05	55.51	-7.56	39.95	44.49	11.36	53.87	45.87	-14.85	46.13	54.13	14.78
6.	Himachal Pradesh	60.02	56.00	-6.70	39.98	44.00	10.06	42.45	45.34	6.81	57.55	54.66	-5.29
7.	Jammu and Kashmir	61.78	62.60	1.33	38.22	37.40	-2.15	56.71	55.51	-2.12	43.59	44.49	2.02
8.	Karnataka	61.95	59.08	-4.63	38.05	40.92	7.54	55.71	46.32	-16.86	44.29	53.68	17.49
9.	Kerala	60.45	53.70	-11.17	39.55	46.30	17.07	53.93	49.04	-9.07	46.07	50.96	9.60
10.	Madhya Pradesh	61.19	58.09	-5.07	38.81	41.91	7.99	52.85	47.60	-9.93	47.15	52.40	10.02
11.	Maharashtra	59.48	54.71	-8.02	40.52	45.29	11.77	53.02	45.31	-14.54	46.98	54.69	14.10
12.	Manipur	67.48	63.12	-6.46	32.52	36.88	13.41	63.82	56.40	-11.63	36.18	43.60	17.02
13.	Meghalaya	60.83	60.44	-0.64	39.17	39.36	0.49	56.38	47.02	-16.60	43.62	52.98	17.67

14.	Orissa	68.06	64.11	-5.80	31.94	35.89	12.37	57.79	56.95	-1.45	42.21	43.05	1.95
15.	Punjab	57.92	52.29	-9.72	42.08	47.71	13.38	53.03	47.12	-11.14	46.97	52.88	11.18
16.	Rajasthan	62.28	59.50	-4.46	37.72	40.50	7.37	56.65	50.85	-10.24	43.35	49.15	11.80
17.	Tamil Nadu	62.84	58.74	-6.52	37.16	41.26	11.03	54.60	45.61	-16.47	45.40	54.39	16.53
18.	Tripura	64.85	65.20	0.54	35.15	34.80	-1.00	56.96	56.18	-1.37	43.04	43.82	1.78
19.	Uttar Pradesh	61.47	57.42	-6.59	38.53	42.58	10.51	55.99	50.49	-9.82	44.01	49.51	11.11
20.	West Bengal	66.82	65.90	-1.38	33.18	34.10	2.77	55.93	52.28	-6.53	44.07	47.72	7.65
	All-India	63.18	59.41	-5.97	36.82	40.59	10.24	54.65	48.06	-12.06	45.35	51.94	12.69
	Degree of Disparity	6.42	7.38		11.11	11.11		7.80	8.72		9.81	8.85	

Source: Planning Commission, Human Development Report, 2001

TABLE 7

Gini Ratio for Per-capita Consumption Expenditure

Sl. No.	States	Rural		Urban	
		1993-94	1999-2000	1993-94	1999-2000
1.	Andhra Pradesh	0.26	0.24	0.32	0.31
2.	Assam	0.18	0.20	0.29	0.31
3.	Bihar	0.22	0.21	0.31	0.32
4.	Gujarat	0.24	0.23	0.29	0.29
5.	Haryana	0.30	0.24	0.28	0.29
6.	Himachal Pradesh	0.28	0.24	0.44	0.30
7.	Jammu & Kashmir	0.23	0.18	0.28	0.22
8.	Karnataka	0.27	0.24	0.32	0.32
9.	Kerala	0.29	0.27	0.34	0.32
10.	Madhya Pradesh	0.28	0.24	0.33	0.31
11.	Maharashtra	0.30	0.26	0.35	0.35
12.	Manipur	0.15	0.19	0.15	0.22
13.	Meghalaya	0.27	0.15	0.24	0.21
14.	Orissa	0.24	0.24	0.30	0.29
15.	Punjab	0.26	0.24	0.28	0.29
16.	Rajasthan	0.26	0.21	0.29	0.28
17.	Tamil Nadu	0.31	0.28	0.34	0.40
18.	Tripura	0.24	0.19	0.28	0.29
19.	Uttar Pradesh	0.28	0.25	0.32	0.33
20.	West Bengal	0.25	0.22	0.34	0.33
	All-India	0.28	0.26	0.34	0.34
	Degree of Disparity	15.64	13.98	17.70	14.91

Source: Planning Commission, Human Development Report, 2001.

TABLE 8

Rate of Literacy

(% of population)

Sl. No.	States	Rural Areas 1991	Rural Areas 2001	Rural Areas % change	Urban Areas 1991	Urban Areas 2001	Urban Areas % change
1.	Andhra Pradesh	35.74	55.33	54.81	66.35	76.39	15.13
2.	Assam	49.32	60.92	23.52	79.39	85.76	8.02
3.	Bihar	33.83	44.42	31.30	67.89	72.71	7.10
4.	Gujarat	53.09	58.53	10.25	76.54	79.24	3.53
5.	Haryana	49.85	68.82	38.05	73.66	79.89	8.46
6.	Himachal Pradesh	61.86	74.38	20.24	84.17	89.59	6.44
7.	Jammu and Kashmir	-	48.22	-	-	72.17	-
8.	Karnataka	47.69	59.68	25.14	74.2	81.05	9.23
9.	Kerala	88.92	90.95	2.28	92.25	93.38	1.22
10.	Madhya Pradesh	35.87	58.1	61.97	70.81	79.67	12.51
11.	Maharashtra	55.52	70.84	27.59	79.2	85.76	8.28
12.	Manipur	55.79	65.33	17.10	70.53	80.04	13.48
13.	Meghalaya	41.05	57	38.86	81.74	87.12	6.58
14.	Orissa	45.46	60.44	32.95	71.99	80.95	12.45
15.	Punjab	52.77	65.16	23.48	72.08	79.13	9.78
16.	Rajasthan	30.37	55.92	84.13	65.33	76.89	17.69
17.	Tamil Nadu	54.59	66.66	22.11	77.99	82.07	5.23
18.	Tripura	56.08	70.23	25.23	83.09	89.51	7.73
19.	Uttar Pradesh	36.66	53.68	46.43	61	70.61	15.75
20.	West Bengal	50.5	64.06	26.85	75.27	81.63	8.45
	All-India	44.69	59.21	32.49	-	80.06	-
	Degree of Disparity	26.74	16.17		10.01	7.40	

Source: Planning Commission, Human Development Report, 2001.

Table 9

Growth of Employment

(% per annum)

Sl. No.	States	Rural 1983-93	Rural 1993-99	Rural % change	Urban 1983-93	Urban 1993-99	Urban % change
1.	Andhra Pradesh	2.00	0.80	-60.00	3.70	2.20	-40.54
2.	Assam	1.70	2.40	41.18	1.00	2.70	170.00
3.	Bihar	0.90	2.30	155.56	0.90	3.60	300.00
4.	Gujarat	1.70	2.00	17.65	3.30	2.30	-30.30
5.	Haryana	2.80	0.50	-82.14	3.80	0.80	-78.95
6.	Himachal Pradesh	2.90	1.50	-48.28	2.60	0.80	-69.23
7.	Jammu and Kashmir	2.90	1.30	-55.17	3.10	0.30	-90.32
8.	Karnataka	2.30	1.20	-47.83	2.20	2.80	27.27
9.	Kerala	-0.10	0.90	-1000.00	4.40	3.20	-27.27
10.	Madhya Pradesh	1.90	1.40	-26.32	3.30	3.30	0.00
11.	Maharashtra	1.90	0.60	-68.42	2.90	1.90	-34.48
12.	Manipur	3.10	0.60	-80.65	3.90	5.40	38.46
13.	Meghalaya	3.40	3.00	-11.76	4.00	-0.10	-102.50
14.	Orissa	2.00	1.00	-50.00	3.30	3.40	3.03
15.	Punjab	0.60	2.50	316.67	2.10	2.60	23.81
16.	Rajasthan	2.50	1.40	-44.00	2.80	2.40	-14.29
17.	Tamil Nadu	1.60	0.40	-75.00	2.40	1.60	-33.33
18.	Tripura	3.90	1.40	-64.10	6.30	1.30	-79.37
19.	Uttar Pradesh	1.80	1.40	-22.22	2.90	3.30	13.79
20.	West Bengal	2.50	1.20	-52.00	2.00	0.80	-60.00
	All-India	1.80	1.30		2.90	2.40	
	Degree of Disparity	45.18	51.93		39.49	59.90	

Source: Planning Commission, Human Development Report, 2001.

TABLE 10

Incidence of Unemployment

(% per annum)

Sl. No.	States	Rural			Urban			Higher than Average Incidence	
		1993-94	1999-2000	% change	1993-94	1999-2000	% change	Rural 1999-2000	Urban 1999-2000
1	2	3	4	5	6	7	8	9	10
1.	Andhra Pradesh	0.50	0.70	40.00	3.20	4.00	25.00	West Bengal	West Bengal
2.	Assam	5.30	4.00	-24.53	8.70	9.80	12.64	Tamil Nadu	Tripura
3.	Bihar	1.70	1.80	5.88	7.30	7.40	1.37	Orissa	Orissa
4.	Gujarat	0.90	0.30	-66.67	3.30	2.00	-39.39	Punjab	Maharashtra
5.	Haryana	1.20	0.80	-33.33	2.70	2.70	0.00	Manipur	Manipur
6.	Himachal Pradesh	0.60	1.30	116.67	2.70	6.80	151.85	Kerala	Kerala
7.	Jammu & Kashmir	0.80	1.10	37.50	8.40	4.90	-41.67	Assam	Himachal Pradesh
8.	Karnataka	0.70	0.70	0.00	3.70	3.40	-8.11	Bihar	Jammu & Kashmir
9.	Kerala	6.80	8.10	19.12	10.20	10.00	-1.96		Assam
10.	Madhya Pradesh	0.50	0.50	0.00	5.00	3.60	-28.00		Bihar
11.	Maharashtra	0.80	1.40	75.00	4.30	5.70	32.56		
12.	Manipur	0.90	2.00	122.22	4.20	6.70	59.52		
13.	Meghalaya	0.20	0.40	100.00	1.70	4.50	164.71		

(Contd.)

TABLE 10 (*Contd.*)

1	2	3	4	5	6	7	8	9	10
14.	Orissa	1.50	2.00	33.33	6.60	6.70	1.52		
15.	Punjab	1.30	1.80	38.46	8.40	2.80	-66.67		
16.	Rajasthan	0.30	0.40	33.33	1.50	2.50	66.67		
17.	Tamil Nadu	1.30	2.00	53.85	4.90	3.80	-22.45		
18.	Tripura	2.40	1.20	-50.00	8.40	5.80	-30.95		
19.	Uttar Pradesh	0.70	0.80	14.29	2.90	4.10	41.38		
20.	West Bengal	1.80	2.70	50.00	7.90	7.60	-3.80		
	All-India	1.20	1.50		4.60	4.80			
	Degree of Disparity	110.15	103.48		50.66	44.43			

Source: Planning Commission, Human Development Report, 2001.

TABLE 11

Growth of Labour Productivity

Sl. No.	States	Per worker value of output (Rs. Lakhs)			Input-output ratio			States with Above Average No. Value of Output per Worker	
		1996-97	2001-02	% change	1996-97	2001-02	% change	2001	1996
1	2	3	4	5	6	7	8	9	10
1.	Andhra Pradesh	4.80	6.90	43.20	0.75	0.78	4	Madhya Pradesh	Bihar
2.	Assam	4.70	7.10	50.60	0.76	0.81	7	Maharashtra	Gujarat
3.	Bihar	8.10	10.50	28.80	0.73	0.87	19	Gujarat	Haryana
4.	Gujarat	10.70	20.40	91.30	0.73	0.83	14	Haryana	Madhya Pradesh
5.	Haryana	9.20	15.70	70.30	0.81	0.82	1	Himachal Pradesh	Maharashtra
6.	Himachal Pradesh	6.20	14.40	132.90	0.64	0.76	19	Meghalaya	Rajasthan
7.	Jammu & Kashmir	4.50	6.20	38.00	0.78	0.85	9	Rajasthan	Uttar Pradesh
8.	Karnataka	6.80	11.00	62.30	0.74	0.82	11	Uttar Pradesh	
9.	Kerala	5.50	7.30	31.80	0.79	0.82	4		
10.	Madhya Pradesh	9.40	16.40	74.10	0.72	0.81	12		
11.	Maharashtra	10.90	14.50	32.50	0.74	0.78	5		
12.	Manipur	1.90	1.50	-18.30	0.41	0.80	17		
13.	Meghalaya	2.10	13.00	523.00	0.43	0.84	95		

(Contd.)

TABLE 11 (*Contd.*)

1	2	3	4	5	6	7	8	9	10
14.	Orissa	7.60	11.20	48.30	0.70	0.82	17		
15.	Punjab	6.30	9.30	47.90	0.74	0.82	11		
16.	Rajasthan	8.60	13.70	59.60	0.74	0.82	11		
17.	Tamil Nadu	6.40	8.60	34.20	0.77	0.80	4		
18.	Tripura	1.90	2.80	47.90	0.65	0.60	-8		
19.	Uttar Pradesh	8.10	12.80	58.30	0.76	0.79	4		
20.	West Bengal	4.70	7.50	39.50	0.74	0.81	9		
	All-India	7.80	11.90	52.70	0.75	0.80	7		
	Degree of Disparity	42.22	44.67		15.01	6.70			

Source: *Economic Times*, Trends, 1 Sept. 2003, p. 10.

TABLE 12

Expectation of Life at Birth (years)

Sl. No.	*States*	*1992-96 Rural*	*1992-96 Urban*	*States with % below Average Rural*	*States with % below Average Urban*
1.	Andhra Pradesh	61	66	Uttar Pradesh	Uttar Pradesh
2.	Assam	56	65	Rajasthan	Rajasthan
3.	Bihar	59	66	Orissa	Orissa
4.	Gujarat	60	64	Madhya Pradesh	Madhya Pradesh
5.	Haryana	63	68	Assam	Assam
6.					Gujarat
7.					
8.	Karnataka	61	67		
9.	Kerala	73	74		
10.	Madhya Pradesh	54	63		
11.	Maharashtra	63	69		
12.					
13.					
14.	Orissa	56	65		
15.	Punjab	67	70		
16.	Rajasthan	57	64		
17.	Tamil Nadu	62	67		
18.					
19.	Uttar Pradesh	56	62		
20.	West Bengal	61	68		
	All-India	59	66		
	Degree of Disparity	8.03	4.57		

Source: Planning Commission, Human Development Report, 2001.

TABLE 13

No Medical Attendance at Child Birth (%)

Sl. No.	States	1995-96		States with % above Average	
		Rural	Urban	Rural	Urban
1.	Andhra Pradesh	13	8	Assam	Himachal Pradesh
2.	Assam	40	11	Bihar	Bihar
3.	Bihar	47	40	J & K	Madhya Pradesh
4.	Gujarat	20	9	Madhya Pradesh	Manipur
5.	Haryana	19	7	Orissa	Orissa
6.	Himachal Pradesh	25	23	Rajasthan	Rajasthan
7.	Jammu & Kashmir	47	15	Uttar Pradesh	Uttar Pradesh
8.	Karnataka	30	12		
9.	Kerala	4	3		
10.	Madhya Pradesh	39	22		
11.	Maharashtra	24	11		
12.	Manipur	19	25		
13.	Meghalaya	32	10		
14.	Orissa	45	29		
15.	Punjab	2	1		
16.	Rajasthan	51	27		
17.	Tamil Nadu	12	5		
18.	Tripura	32	15		
19.	Uttar Pradesh	50	30		
20.	West Bengal	14	7		
	All-India	36	16		
	Degree of Disparity	54.50	68.10		

Source: Planning Commission, Human Development Report, 2001.

TABLE 14

Per cent of Children Vaccinated Fully (12-23 months)

Sl. No.	States	Rural			Urban			States with % below average (1998-99)	
		1992-93	1998-99	% change	1992-93	1998-99	% change	Rural	Urban
1	2	3	4	5	6	7	8	9	10
1.	Andhra Pradesh	40	49	22.5	58	61	5.17	Assam	Uttar Pradesh
2.	Assam	17	15	-11.76	40	50	25.00	Bihar	West Bengal
3.	Bihar	9	9	0	22	22	0.00	Madhya Pradesh	Rajasthan
4.	Gujarat	46	45	-2.174	57	54	-5.26	Rajasthan	Orissa
5.	Haryana	52	58	11.54	58	77	32.76	Uttar Pradesh	Madhya Pradesh
6.	Himachal Pradesh	61	84	37.70	82	80	-2.44		Karnataka
7.	Jammu & Kashmir	63	53	-15.88	85	73	-14.12		Assam
8.	Karnataka	50	60	20	58	59	1.72		Bihar
9.	Kerala	54	78	44.44	56	85	51.79		Gujarat
10.	Madhya Pradesh	26	17	-34.61	43	41	-4.65		
11.	Maharashtra	66	77	16.67	62	80	29.03		
12.	Manipur	-	-	-	-	-	-		
13.	Meghalaya	-	-	-	-	-	-		
14.	Orissa	35	42	20	44	56	27.27		
15.	Punjab	58	66	13.79	76	86	13.16		
16.	Rajasthan	16	13	-18.75	46	26	-43.48		

(Contd.)

TABLE 14 (Contd.)

1	2	3	4	5	6	7	8	9	10
17.	Tamil Nadu	60	77	28.33	73	81	10.96		
18.	Tripura	-	-	-	-	-	-		
19.	Uttar Pradesh	17	19	11.76	33	32	-3.03		
20.	West Bengal	31	41	32.26	44	56	27.27		
	All-India	31	37		51	61			
	Degree of Disparity	45.84	53.43		31.23	34.68			

Source: Planning Commission, Human Development Report, 2001.

TABLE 15

Anaemia among Women

(%)

Sl. No.	States	1998-99 Rural	1998-99 Urban	States with % above Indian Average Rural	States with % above Indian Average Urban
1.	Andhra Pradesh	51	47	Assam	Andhra Pradesh
2.	Assam	69	67	Bihar	Assam
3.	Bihar	64	60	Jammu & Kashmir	Bihar
4.	Gujarat	51	40	Madhya Pradesh	Jammu & Kashmir
5.	Haryana	48	46	Orissa	Orissa
6.	Himachal Pradesh	41	38	Tamil Nadu	Rajasthan
7.	Jammu & Kashmir	60	54	West Bengal	Tamil Nadu
8.	Karnataka	46	36		West Bengal
9.	Kerala	23	20		
10.	Madhya Pradesh	57	46		
11.	Maharashtra	51	45		
12.	Manipur	-	-		
13.	Meghalaya	-	-		
14.	Orissa	64	55		
15.	Punjab	43	39		
16.	Rajasthan	49	47		
17.	Tamil Nadu	59	52		
18.	Tripura	-	-		
19.	Uttar Pradesh	49	46		
20.	West Bengal	64	58		
	All-India	54	46		
	Degree of Disparity	21.24	23.14		

Source: Planning Commission, Human Development Report, 2001.

TABLE 16

Death Rate

Sl. No.	States	1991		1997		% change		States having above Average Rate	
		Rural	Urban	Rural	Urban	Rural	Urban	1997 Rural	1997 Urban
1.	Andhra Pradesh	10	7	9	6	-10.00	-14.29	Uttar Pradesh	Uttar Pradesh
2.	Assam	12	7	10	6	-16.67	-14.29	Orissa	Orissa
3.	Bihar	10	6	10	7	0.00	16.67	Madhya Pradesh	Madhya Pradesh
4.	Gujarat	9	8	8	6	-11.11	-25.00		
5.	Haryana	9	7	8	7	-11.11	0.00		
6.	Himachal Pradesh	9	5	8	6	-11.11	20.00		
7.	Jammu & Kashmir								
8.	Karnataka	10	7	9	5	-10.00	-28.57		
9.	Kerala	6	5	6	6	0.00	20.00		
10.	Madhya Pradesh	15	9	12	8	-20.00	-11.11		
11.	Maharashtra	9	6	9	5	0.00	-16.67		
12.	Manipur	5	6	6	6	20.00	0.00		
13.	Meghalaya	10	4	10	4	0.00	0.00		
14.	Orissa	13	7	11	8	-15.38	14.29		
15.	Punjab	9	6	8	6	-11.11	0.00		
16.	Rajasthan	11	8	9	7	-18.18	-12.50		
17.	Tamil Nadu	10	8	9	7	-10.00	-12.50		
18.	Tripura	8	6	7	6	-12.50	0.00		

19.	Uttar Pradesh	12	8	11	8	-8.33	0.00
20.	West Bengal	9	7	8	7	-11.11	0.00
	All-India	11	7	10	7		
	Degree of Disparity	23.24	18.69	18.18	16.72		

Source: Planning Commission, Human Development Report, 2001.

TABLE 17

Change in Sex Ratio (Female per 1000 Males)

Sl. No.	States	Rural			Urban			Ratio above Indian Average (2001)	
		1991-92	2001-02	% change	1991-92	2001-02	% change	Urban	Rural
1.	Andhra Pradesh	977	983	0.614	959	965	0.63	Assam	Assam
2.	Assam	921	940	2.063	838	878	4.77	Bihar	Bihar
3.	Bihar	934	927	-0.749	844	869	2.96	Gujarat	Haryana
4.	Gujarat	949	946	-0.316	907	880	-2.98	Haryana	Jammu & Kashmir
5.	Haryana	864	867	0.347	868	847	-2.42	Himachal Pradesh	Madhya Pradesh
6.	Himachal Pradesh	990	991	0.101	831	797	-4.09	Jammu & Kashmir	Punjab
7.	Jammu & Kashmir	-	927	-	-	822	-	Madhya Pradesh	Rajasthan
8.	Karnataka	973	976	0.308	930	940	1.08	Maharashtra	Uttar Pradesh
9.	Kerala	1037	1059	2.122	1034	1058	2.32	Orissa	
10.	Madhya Pradesh	943	927	-1.697	893	899	0.67	Punjab	
11.	Maharashtra	972	959	-1.337	875	874	-0.11	Rajasthan	
12.	Manipur	951	969	1.893	975	1009	3.49	Uttar Pradesh	
13.	Meghalaya	966	972	0.621	910	985	8.24	West Bengal	
14.	Orissa	988	986	-0.202	866	895	3.35		
15.	Punjab	988	887	-10.223	868	848	-2.30		
16.	Rajasthan	919	932	1.415	879	890	1.25		
17.	Tamil Nadu	981	992	1.121	960	980	2.08		
18.	Tripura	942	948	0.637	958	962	0.42		

19.	Uttar Pradesh	884	904	2.262	860	879	2.21
20.	West Bengal	940	950	1.064	858	893	4.08
	All-India	939	946		894	901	
	Degree of Disparity	6.41	6.81		9.27	7.32	

Source: Planning Commission, Human Development Report, 2001.

TABLE 18

Growth of Road Connectivity at Village Level

(% of villages connected by roads)

Sl. No.	States	Population above 1500			States having Lower than Average Connectivity	
		1991-92	1996-97	% change	1991-92	1996-97
1.	Andhra Pradesh	95	86	-9.474	Bihar	Bihar
2.	Assam	100	100	0	HP	HP
3.	Bihar	65	72	10.77	Karnataka	MP
4.	Gujarat	99	99	0	West Bengal	Meghalaya
5.	Haryana	100	100	0		UP
6.	Himachal Pradesh	40	65	62.5		West Bengal
7.	Jammu & Kashmir	92	83	-9.78		
8.	Karnataka	83	100	20.48		
9.	Kerala	100	99	-1		
10.	Madhya Pradesh	92	58	-36.96		
11.	Maharashtra	99	98	-1.01		
12.	Manipur	99	90	-9.09		
13.	Meghalaya	100	64	-36		
14.	Orissa	99	83	-16.16		
15.	Punjab	100	100	0		
16.	Rajasthan	94	94	0		
17.	Tamil Nadu	99	100	1.01		
18.	Tripura	100	100	0		
19.	Uttar Pradesh	96	49	-48.96		
20.	West Bengal	61	64	4.92		
	All-India	90	78			
	Degree of Disparity	18.07	19.97			

Source: Planning Commission, Human Development Report, 2001.

TABLE 19

Drinking Water and Electricity Connection

Sl. No.	States	Safe Drinking Water						Electricity Connection					
		Rural Areas (%)			Urban Areas (%)			Rural Areas (%)			Urban Areas (%)		
		1981	1991	% change	1981	1991	% change	1981	1991	% change	1981	1991	% change
1	2	3	4	5	6	7	8	9	10	11	12	13	14
1.	Andhra Pradesh	15.12	48.98	223.94	63.27	73.82	16.67	12.53	37.50	199.28	32.22	73.31	127.53
2.	Assam	-	43.28	-	-	64.07	-	-	12.44	-	-	63.21	-
3.	Bihar	33.77	56.55	67.46	65.36	73.39	12.29	3.48	5.57	60.06	50.09	58.77	17.33
4.	Gujarat	36.16	60.04	66.04	86.78	87.23	0.52	30.83	58.43	89.52	74.40	82.96	11.51
5.	Haryana	42.94	67.14	56.36	90.72	93.18	2.71	41.04	63.20	54.00	82.22	89.13	8.40
6.	Himachal Pradesh	39.56	75.51	90.87	39.56	91.93	132.38	51.08	85.86	68.09	89.36	96.24	7.70
7.	Jammu and Kashmir	27.95	-	-	86.67	-	-	52.54	-	-	92.18	-	-
8.	Karnataka	17.63	67.31	281.79	74.40	81.38	9.38	21.35	43.75	104.92	61.98	76.27	23.06
9.	Kerala	6.26	12.22	95.21	39.72	38.68	-2.62	23.21	41.95	80.74	54.57	67.65	23.97
10.	Madhya Pradesh	8.09	45.56	463.16	66.65	79.45	19.20	6.89	34.49	400.58	56.42	72.52	28.54
11.	Maharashtra	18.34	54.02	194.55	85.56	90.50	5.77	24.12	53.45	121.60	70.53	86.07	22.03

(Contd.)

TABLE 19 (Contd.)

1	2	3	4	5	6	7	8	9	10	11	12	13	14
12.	Manipur	12.91	33.72	161.19	38.71	52.10	34.59	10.28	41.73	305.93	48.32	75.45	56.15
13.	Meghalaya	14.26	26.82	88.08	74.40	75.42	1.37	7.44	16.34	119.62	59.59	83.04	39.35
14.	Orissa	9.47	35.32	272.97	51.33	62.83	22.40	13.03	17.45	33.92	51.74	62.11	20.04
15.	Punjab	81.80	92.09	12.58	91.13	94.24	3.41	50.61	76.98	52.10	85.44	94.60	10.72
16.	Rajasthan	13.00	50.62	289.38	78.65	86.51	9.99	8.70	32.44	272.87	63.67	76.67	20.42
17.	Tamil Nadu	30.97	64.28	107.56	69.44	74.17	6.81	26.03	44.49	70.92	61.59	76.80	24.70
18.	Tripura	22.47	30.60	36.18	67.92	71.12	4.71	16.52	28.50	72.52	92.10	80.43	-12.67
19.	Uttar Pradesh	25.31	56.62	123.71	73.23	85.78	17.14	3.97	10.96	176.07	54.61	67.76	24.08
20.	West Bengal	65.78	80.26	22.01	71.28	86.23	20.97	7.02	17.75	152.85	57.86	70.19	21.31
	All-India	26.50	55.54	109.58	75.06	81.38	8.42	14.69	30.54	107.90	62.51	75.78	21.23
	Degree of Disparity	72.01	37.67		24.19	19.06		76.37	58.99		25.67	13.74	

Source: Planning Commission, Human Development Report, 2001.

TABLE 20

Growth (%) in Number of Households with Pucca Houses

Sl. No.	*States*	*Rural Area*			*Urban Area*		
		1981	*1993-94*	*% change*	*1981*	*1993-94*	*% change*
1.	Andhra Pradesh	18.62	32.60	75.08	52.39	66.50	26.93
2.	Assam	-	5.40	-	-	45.90	-
3.	Bihar	17.77	17.50	-1.52	65.66	64.30	-2.07
4.	Gujarat	36.42	36.70	0.77	75.49	80.00	5.97
5.	Haryana	31.09	72.50	133.19	65.39	90.00	37.64
6.	Himachal Pradesh	41.02	43.90	7.02	70.59	86.70	22.82
7.	Jammu & Kashmir	16.58	30.30	82.75	62.41	86.40	38.44
8.	Karnataka	19.19	28.70	49.56	54.64	67.20	22.99
9.	Kerala	35.07	51.50	46.85	56.08	67.70	20.72
10.	Madhya Pradesh	16.97	13.30	-21.63	56.02	38.20	-31.81
11.	Maharashtra	25.78	34.10	32.27	64.63	74. 7	-
12.	Manipur	1.20	3.20	166.67	9.83	12.20	24.11
13.	Meghalaya	7.03	24.00	241.39	30.67	72.90	137.69
14.	Orissa	8.32	10.20	22.60	46.70	59.00	26.34
15.	Punjab	49.59	67.80	36.72	78.43	89.10	13.60
16.	Rajasthan	40.36	46.30	14.72	80.82	85.70	6.04
17.	Tamil Nadu	25.57	36.40	42.35	60.74	64.10	5.53
18.	Tripura	1.43	1.80	25.87	20.70	24.30	17.39
19.	Uttar Pradesh	21.56	32.20	49.35	65.40	73.10	11.77
20.	West Bengal	11.96	15.60	30.43	71.37	68.10	-4.58
	All-India	22.53	29.20	29.60	64.70	70.70	9.27
	Degree of Disparity	61.41	65.62		33.05	33.26	

Source: Planning Commission, Human Development Report, 2001.

TABLE 21

Access to Toilet Facilities (per cent of Households)

Sl. No.	States	Rural 1991	Urban 1991	Rural-Urban Combined 1991	1997	% change
1.	Andhra Pradesh	6.62	54.6	18.4	35.06	90.54
2.	Assam	30.52	86.06	37.4	6.44	-82.78
3.	Bihar	4.96	56.54	11.75	58.14	394.81
4.	Gujarat	11.16	55.71	30.69	66.74	117.46
5.	Haryana	6.53	64.25	22.45	60	167.26
6.	Himachal Pradesh	6.42	59.98	12.39	43.22	248.83
7.	Jammu & Kashmir	-	-	-	9.61	-
8.	Karnataka	6.85	62.52	24.13	90.14	273.56
9.	Kerala	44.07	72.66	51.28	73.05	42.45
10.	Madhya Pradesh	3.64	53	15.07	7.87	-47.78
11.	Maharashtra	6.64	64.45	29.56	64.13	116.95
12.	Manipur	33.2	70.16	43.13	12.41	-71.23
13.	Meghalaya	18.13	85.69	31.11	26.61	-14.46
14.	Orissa	3.58	49.27	9.81	9.46	-3.57
15.	Punjab	15.79	73.23	33.18	66.68	100.96
16.	Rajasthan	6.65	62.27	19.57	65.4	234.18
17.	Tamil Nadu	7.17	57.47	23.13	37.13	60.53
18.	Tripura	62.43	96.32	67.93	46.72	-31.22
19.	Uttar Pradesh	6.44	66.54	18.02	33.15	83.96
20.	West Bengal	12.31	78.75	31.51	50.19	59.28
	All-India	9.48	63.85	23.7	49.32	108.10
	Degree of Disparity	103.76	18.96	52.38	58.27	

Source: Planning Commission, Human Development Report, 2001

2

Regional Disparity in India: Issues Related to Inter-State Variations

DHIRAJ KUMAR BANDYOPADHYAY

I. INTRODUCTION

Balanced regional growth is a crucial issue for the harmonious development of federal state. India, however, presents a economic picture of wide regional variations, in terms of such socio-economic indicators of economic growth as per-capita income, the proportion of population living below the poverty line, working population in agriculture and industry, the literacy rate, the infant mortality rate, life expectancy at birth, physical and social infrastructure (in terms of availability and accessibility of education and health care), the percentage of urban population to total population. It is important to note that some states and districts are economically advanced while others are relatively backward. Even within each state and each district, some regions are more developed while others are almost backward. We know that the regional imbalances may be natural due to unequal natural endowment and in the sense of neglect of some regions and preference of others for investment and development efforts.

We argue that economic backwardness of a region is indicated by indicators of high population growth, excessive dependence of agriculture leading to high incidence of poverty, unemployment, absence of large scale of urbanization, low productivity in agriculture and small scale industries. Our study of regional variations covers the fifteen major states (as well as districts when it would necessary to deal with) of India have been classified into two major groups: forward states and backward states. Among the forward states we include Karnataka, Tamil Nadu, Kerala, Andhra Pradesh, West Bengal, Maharashtra, Punjab and Gujarat. On the other hands the backward states are Assam, Bihar, Uttar Pradesh, Rajasthan, Orissa and Madhya Pradesh. These major fifteen states taking together accounted for 90 per cent of total population in 2001.

We know that in spite of planning, however, regional disparity remained a serious problem in India. A new controversy in this respect is whether growth rates and standards of living in different regions would eventually converge or not.

The main objective of this study is to examine regional variation at the inter-sate and intra-state level in terms of level of urbanization, industrialization and some socio-economic indicators. Section-II has been presented an overview of some recent literatures related to the issue of regional variation. The methodology of this study and issues related to regional variation, level of urbanization, industrialization and socio-economic development have been discussed in Section-III. Then we have been examined in Section-IV the regional variation of state domestic product (SDP) as well as relationship between SDP and population growth with a view to observe the empirical evidence of 'convergence theorem' in India. Section-V examine regional variation and relationship between urbanization and socio-economic indicators at states level. Intra-state and inter-dependencies between urbanization development indicators in elect states are examined in Section-VI. Conclusions are drawn in Section-VII.

II. REVIEW OF LITERATURE

The convergence theorem (Barro, 1991) postulates that when the growth rate of an economy accelerates, initially some regions with better resources would grow faster than others. But after sometime, when the law of diminishing marginal returns set in, first growth rates would converge, due to differential marginal productivity of capital (higher in poorer regions and lower in richer regions), and this in turn would bridge the gaps in the levels of income across regions. The related empirical evidence is however very controversial. On the other hand, the widespread acceptance of Myrdal's (1963) concept of 'Cumulative Causation' has led to the belief that developed regions would always continue to grow at the expense of the poor regions. We know that the theory of geographical dualism is virtually based on the hypothesis of cumulative causation as explained by Myrdal. This type of dualism, in fact, refer to the persistence of spatial differences in a wide variety of development indices including per-capita income, rates of growth of industrialization, trade and levels of unemployment. The regions more urbanized used to be claimed as 'advantage' over others which are less-urbanized. It has also been observed that when an economy is liberated, especially after controls on investment are lifted, regions with better infrastructure attract more investment, especially foreign capital through market mechanisms, and this in turn leads to regional inequity, at least in the early phase of reforms. The regional disparity in China after economic reform is a classic example of this. In the recent period, a number of studies (for instance, Ahluwalia, 2000 and 2002; B.B. Bhattacharya and S. Sakthivel, 2004; Nagaraj, Varoudakis and Veganzous, 1998; Rao, Shand and Kalirajan, 1999; Shand and Bhide, 2000) have observed that the regional disparity in India has widened, especially during the 1990s.

In our study we like to examine regional disparity or variation in the context of urbanization, industrialization and some important socio-economic indicators. Besides, we like examine the regional variation at the intra-state level with a view to conceptualize that the district which is characterized as 'developed' at national but has some serious problem at the district level and beyond that.

III. METHODOLOGY USED AND ISSUES RELATED TO REGIONAL VARIATION, LEVEL OF URBANIZATION AND SOCIO-ECONOMIC DEVELOPMENT

This study uses census data of 1981, 1991 and 2001 on socio-demographic indicators and employment data has been taken from NSS, on various rounds. Per-capita income data has been taken from *Economic Survey,* and data on infrastructure has been taken from both census and India Infrastructural Report and also from Hand Book of Urbanization written by K. Sivaramakrishnan, A.K. Kundu and B.N. Singh. The degree of interdependency between the level as well as growth of urbanization with selected indicators has been examined by using Pearson's co-efficients or correlations, computed for the three years 1981, 1991 and 2001. We have avoided large data base for space constraints and only presented some calculated correlation matrix tables and only two calculated database tables for useful discussion.

A positive correlation of urbanization with any indicator signifies that the states for which the indicator obtains higher values, urbanization also shows higher values Then treated as developed states and converse is also true. In case of district level analysis same criteria has also been followed. We also assumed that Indian urbanization has been characterized by economic activities of industry and services.

The indicators in the process of socio-economic development of a state can broadly be placed into four categories. These are: (a) economic, (b) employment and poverty, (c) infrastructure development, and (d) socio-demographic development. The economic indicators can further be classified into macro-indicators such as per-capita income, per-capita foreign direct investment (FDI), agricultural development, such as productivity per hectare, size of landholding, and industrial indicators such as percentage share of industrial production, worker enterprise ratio, etc. Employment and poverty dimension comprise Work Participation Rate (WPR), unemployment rates, and poverty ratios taken separately for rural and urban areas. The infrastructural development indicators relating to the facilities that promote the development and growth of other sectors, such as roads per 100 sq. km., railways per 100 sq. km, telephone lines per 100 persons, percentage of villages electrified. The socio-demographic indicators constitute the demographic dimension relating to urban-rural growth differentials and indicators of social development like literacy in rural and urban areas, schooling facility (middle and higher secondary) per thousand persons, hospitals and dispensaries per thousand persons, and basic amenities for urban areas such as percentage of urban households, access to safe drinking water, sanitation facilities, and electricity use.

IV. VARIATION ON ECONOMIC AND SOCIAL INDICATORS AMONG DIFFERENT STATES IN INDIA

In India, the growth rate of gross domestic product (GDP) has accelerated since 1980s. the average annual GDP growth rate in the first three decades (1950s to 1980s) was only 3.6 per cent. During the 1980s, the GDP growth rate accelerated to 5.6 per cent, and after economic reforms in the 1990s, it has further accelerated to 6 per cent. The reforms led to a lot of structural changes in the Indian economy, such as, deregulation of investment—both domestic and foreign—and liberalization of trade, exchange rate, interest rate, capital flows and prices. The post-reform period also witnessed a sharp deceleration in public investment due to fiscal constraints. At the aggregate level, the average share of public investment in total investment has declined from 45 per cent in the early 1980s to about one-third in early 2000s. Although, there is little information on investment at the regional level, the available indicators suggest that more and more investments are now being made in richer states. The RBI data on capital flows show that four to five developed states have covered the major chunk of foreign direct investment in India. The poorer states with inadequate infrastructure are not able to attract foreign investment. The poorer states are also investing less because historically they mobilized resources for public investment mainly through grants and assistance from the centre, which are now declining due to fiscal constraints.

Our Table 1 on state domestic products of various states indicates that regional disparity has widened since 1990. The coefficient of variation of SDP growth rates among

TABLE I

State-wise Net Domestic Product at Constant Prices (1993-94)

	Rs. Crores		Annual Average growth Rate 1990-91 to 2002-03	Growth rate of SDP (2002-07)	Average annual per-capita rate of growth (1990-91 to 2002-03)
Forward States	**1990-91**	**2002-03**			
1. Punjab	23,693	37,582	3.9	4.5	2.2
2. Maharashtra	79,869	153,429	5.6	7.9	3.6
3. Haryana	18,215	31,952	4.8	7.6	2.3
4. Gujarat	36,207	75,447	6.3	10.6	4.3
5. West Bengal	40,633	89,792	6.8	6.1	5.2
6. Karnataka	29,845	63,978	6.6	7.0	4.9
7. Kerala	19,774	37,037	5.4	7.2	4.3
8. Tamil Nadu	43,937	81,019	5.2	8.0	4.2
9. Andhra Pradesh	45,131	82,046	5.1	6.7	3.7
Sub-total	337,304	652,282	5.6		
Backward States					
10. Madhya Prdesh	41,833	43,770	0.4	4.3	0.8
11. Assam	12,299	16,788	2.6		0.9
12. Uttar Pradesh	74,791	96,011	2.1	4.6	0.4
13. Rajasthan	29,713	44,769	3.5	5.0	1.0
14. Orissa	13,450	21,862	4.1	9.1	2.6
15. Bihar	37,607	34,553	-0.7	4.7	-0.8
Sub-total	209,693	257,753	1.7		
All-India	623,407	1,169,793	5.4		

Sources: Ministry of Finance, Indian Public Finance Statistics (2004-05); 11th Five Year Plan (2007-12), Vol. I.

states has jumped from 0.14 in the 1980s to 0.29 in the 1990s and to 0.32 in 2002-07. In terms of per-capita SDP, the coefficient of variation have become even worse in the 1990s and in 2002-07: from 0.22 in the 1980s to 0.43 in the 1990s and to 0.45 in 2007. And this has happened despite a very modest rise in average GDP growth rate at the all-India level, from 5.6 per cent in the 1980s to 6.0 in the 1990s and to 6.8 per cent in 2002-07. This reflects an uneven regional development in the post-reform years and is corroborated by other studies as well.

However, a rise in the coefficient of variation does not necessarily imply a lack of convergence. We know that proper test of convergence would require estimating the marginal impact of initial levels of income (imply for convergence a negative value is required) on subsequent periods of growth after considering the impact of growth of different factors such as capital, labour, technology, etc. It is important to note that at the state, intra-state (i.e. district level) and intra-districts level, there are paucity of data on capital and other relevant variables of estimating a growth function. Even keeping it aside, an inference can be derived from the coefficient of correlation between average growth rates of SDP in the 1980s, 1990s and 2001-06. The estimated coefficient turns out to be 0.50, which is positive and statistically significant at 5 per cent level. This means that states which had higher rates of SDP growth in the 1980s had continued to experience higher growth rates in the 1990s as well as during 2002-07 or in other words there is no evidence of convergence.

We have noted that regional disparity has widened since 1990, and that there is no evidence of convergence between states. In general, the poorer states—notably, Bihar and UP—with higher population growth have performed badly in terms of SDP growth in the 1990s. It may be therefore worth investigating the relationship between SDP growth and population growth at the state level. We have calculated the compound growth rate of population in the 1980s and 1990s based on decennial Censuses 1981, 1991 and 2001. The simple correlation between population growth and SDP growth at constant prices in the 1980s turn out to be positive (0.25) but not significant, which means that SDP growth in the 1980s was neutral with respect to population growth. However, in the 1990s, the relationship between population growth and SDP growth becomes negative (-.22). Population growth in Orissa, a backward state, was unusually low at 1.5 per cent per annum in the 1990s due to a high mortality rate. Assam on the other hand, recorded very poor SDP growth (2.47% per annum) due to terrorism in the 1990s. If a dummy variable is used for abnormal behaviour in these two states, then the correlation coefficient between SDP growth and population growth in the 1990s rises to -0.69 and becomes statistically significant at 1 per cent level.

The inverse relationship becomes even stronger in terms of per-capita SDP growth. The correlation coefficient between population growth rate and per-capita SDP growth, which was -0.22 in the 1980s, shoots up to -0.39 (significant at 10 per cent level) in the 1990s. If a dummy variable is used for abnormal behaviour in Assam and Orissa, then the correlation coefficient of -0.76 turns out to be highly significant at 1 per cent level. The direction of causality however cannot be attributed from this result. It may imply either that higher income growth has begun to slow down population growth, or that population growth is constraining development. If the former is true then it is a positive sign because development is expected to be the best deterrent to population growth. However, if the latter is true, then it can create a serious anomaly: higher population and its attendant workforce growth along with lower SDP and job creation growth means higher unemployment. In the pre-reform era, public investment was made mainly in backward states. Even private investment was directed towards backward regions by practices such as licensing, etc. These policy measures therefore restrained the inverse relationship between population growth and SDP growth. In the post-reform era, private investment is deregulated and public investment has shrunk and consequently, the inverse relationship between income and population growth has become a serious problem. It is important to note that there has a remarkable structural change in composition of SDP in developed states, i.e. from primary sector to industry and more in favour of services sector.

V. VARIATION AND RELATIONSHIP BETWEEN URBANIZATION AND SOCIO-ECONOMIC INDICATORS AT STATE LEVEL

The all-India average of per-capita net state domestic product or per-capita income in 1981 was Rs. 1630. The states showing much higher per-capita income were Delhi, Maharashtra, Gujarat, Punjab, and Haryana. On the other hand, Bihar, Orissa, Uttar Pradesh, and Rajasthan reported per-capita income of less than Rs. 1400. West Bengal, Tamil Nadu, and Karnataka constitute the moderately developed states in terms of per-capita income but their level of urbanization is high. The only major exception is Himachal Pradesh wherein the per-capita income was higher than the average per-capita income of the country but the percentage of urban population was only 7.6 per cent—much below the national average of 23.73 per cent.

It is important to note that the coefficient of variation in the level of urbanization across the states has been estimated to be 73 per cent, which is very high. Besides this, the correlation of the level of urbanization with per-capita income is also very high viz. 0.85 which is significant at one per cent level. So, this attribute confirms the fact that the economically better-off states tend to have higher percentage of urban population in the country.

Again, for the period 2001, the pattern has altered but the correlations are high and positive as before. But still, the developed states have been maintaining their urban status. However, Kerala improved its position in terms of per-capita income, crossing the all-India average of Rs. 9660. But in terms of urbanization it shows a mixed trend. The percentage of urban population in Kerala state had gone up from 18.7 per cent in 1981 to 26.4 per cent in 1991 but has subsequently reduced to 25.9 per cent in 2001. Now, by examining at the interdependence between per-capita income and level of urbanization for 2001, the correlation coefficient has also exhibited a highly significant positive value of 0.84 which confirms the phenomenon that the developed states constitute a higher percentage of urban population than the poorer ones. The correlation coefficient between per-capita income and growth of urban population is 0.43. This is statistically significant at one per cent level. We can observe that several of the developed states have reported growth of urban population, which is at par with the national average of 2.7 or slightly higher than that. The growth rates of urban population in the backward states have gone down; these are often similar to the national urban growth rate or less than that. We argue that this can possibly be attributed to the process of liberalization which has resulted in the shift of population to urban centers in developed states which have received a large part of the industrial and infrastructural investment.

Now, by analyzing the data for Foreign Direct Investment (FDI) from 1990-1 to 2000-1, We have observed that the inflow varies widely across the states. Gujarat, Maharashtra, Delhi, Tamil Nadu, and Karnataka are the states that benefited the most whereas Assam, Bihar, Orissa, Rajasthan, and Uttar Pradesh lagged far behind the national average. The correlation coefficient is as high as 0.92. So, the states exhibiting a high percentage of urban population in the base year received higher FDIs, compared to other states. Again, another important dimension is that the correlation between per-capita flow of FDI and infrastructure indicators like road, railways, and telecom are positive and very strong, suggesting that these investments directly or indirectly became instrumental in infrastructural development. It also shows that the states providing better basic infrastructure facilities have been able to receive higher FDI.

It is important to note that flow of FDI is strongly correlated with Urban Rural growth differentials (URGD), which means wider the gap between urban to rural, greater the flow of FDIs. Eventually, this will accentuate the disparity and make the rich states richer relative to the poorer states. The relationship of flow of FDI is also positively related with the growth of urban population, although the value of correlation co-efficient (0.44) in 2001 is not statistically significant at one per cent level. Thus, while urban infrastructural development in country during the 1990s has facilitated FDI, it has also led to a widening of regional inequality.

Now, we have observed that the correlation between agricultural productivity and level of urbanization is not statistically significant, reflecting a pattern during the two decades ending 1981 as well as 1991. The coefficient of correlation between per-capita income and agricultural productivity is also statistically insignificant, indicating that the relative performance of other sectors has influenced urbanization much more. However, the state of Punjab has shown some direct correlation between urbanization and agricultural productivity. In the developed states of Maharashtra, Tamil Nadu, Gujarat, West Bengal and others such as Andhra Pradesh, Uttar Pradesh, and Orissa, the increase in agricultural productivity has been accompanied by increased urbanization.

Again, industrial production as percentage of aggregate state domestic product shows positive correlation with the level of urbanization in all the three periods (1981, 1991 and 2001). The worker enterprise ratio in rural and urban areas has been correlated with the level and growth of urbanization separately. The correlation coefficients, however, work out as negative when we relate industrialization with the growth of urban population during the 1970s and 1980s. We argue that urban growth is characterized by dualism and both developed and backward states had experienced high growth of population in urban areas. The pattern, however, has changed during the 1990s. The correlation coefficient is no longer negative as the capacity of industrially backward states to attract migrants has gone down over the years. Worker enterprise ratio in urban areas correlates positively and with highly statistically significant, with both the level as well as growth of urban population in 2001. So, it again confirms the proposition that industrialization continues to be a significant though not uniform factor in explaining the level and growth of urbanization across the states in the 1990s.

But, what is more is that the WPR for the fifteen-plus age group shows no significant correlation (rural as well as urban) with the level as well as growth of urban population in 1991 and 2001. Similarly, unemployment rate adjusted for usual status does not reveal any significant relationship with the level of urbanization, though the correlations are negative in both rural and urban and in 1991 as well as 2001. The correlation coefficient observed is -0.54 which is significant at 5 per cent level. It implies that urban unemployment rate has diminished in the states as a result of rapid urban growth. Unfortunately, rural unemployment rate has not exhibited a similar correlation. It is, therefore, difficult to argue that urbanization per se would lead to growth in employment rate or bring down the unemployment rate. In fact, there is a complex interaction among various forces that are linked with urban growth, affecting employment scenario in more than one way. So, there emerges no clear relationship between the two. Interestingly, the correlation of rural WPR with infrastructural indicators like roads and railways works out as significantly negative in 2001. This implies that the states where roads and railways are not developed, rural workforce participation tends to be high. This implies that high WPR could be due to excessive dependence on agriculture and cannot be taken as a development indicator.

Therefore, it may be the fact that urbanization results in growth of regular jobs. The states with high levels of urbanization or experiencing high urban growth have indeed provided job opportunities which are somewhat stable and of long-term nature. Both the level of urbanization and growth of urban population correlates positively with the percentage of regular workers in urban areas at both the time points, 1991 and 2001. Importantly, the correlation has improved over time. One would infer that the regular (urban) jobs have come up more in the urbanized states in the 1990s. Furthermore, the impact is not restricted to the rural areas only. In case of rural areas, the correlation coefficients are much higher than urban areas.

Now, in the context of poverty, we have observed that apart from Bihar, Madhya Pradesh, Rajasthan, and Uttar Pradesh, the incidence of poverty is high in Orissa and Assam as well. We have already been mentioned that the level of urbanization correlates positively with economic development at all the time points under consideration. One would, therefore, expect a negative correlation between urbanization and rural poverty. This is indeed the case. The value was -0.44 in 1981 and became -0.6 in 2001. The correlations work out as negative even with urban poverty but the values are somewhat lower. For qualifying more another indicator, linked to poverty, is average monthly per-capita expenditure. In rural areas, it exhibits highly positive correlation with the level of urbanization during the entire period, as expected. The correlation, however, is not so high in case of urban areas and this has gone down further in 2001. This may be attributed to the growing slum-population in urban areas.

As per Planning Commission 1993 methodology, at the macro level, the percentage of people below the poverty line has gone down to 25.35 in 2000-01. The head count ratio (HCR) of the poor in urban areas has been significantly below (5 percentage points) that in rural areas during the 1970s and 1980s based on the NSS data. We have examined that the gap between the two poverty levels narrowed down so much that in 1987-8, urban poverty works out higher than rural poverty. The poverty figure for rural areas was again higher than that of urban areas but rural-urban poverty differential in the late 1990s was noted as less than that of the 1970s. Again sample data from NSS, tends to say that the poverty scenario has changed significantly since the mid-1990s. The poverty levels in developed states like Maharashtra, Tamil Nadu and Gujarat have surprisingly been high. Industrial growth in recent years did not lead to any significant decline in poverty in these states. Based on NSS data, the poverty scenario has changed significantly in the mid-1990s. The percentage of people below poverty line in rural areas has increased by one percentage point in 1994-95 compared to that of the previous year. It remained at the level until 1997. The proportion of people living below the poverty line in many states is now higher in urban areas than in rural areas. Developed states, such as Punjab and Karnataka, and the less developed states like Andhra Pradesh, Kerala, Madhya Pradesh, Uttar Pradesh, and Rajasthan, have reported higher levels of urban poverty than rural poverty for a number of years.

The data on infrastructure facilities have been taken from the CMIE Report (2000) for the three periods. The physical infrastructure, viz. roads, railway lines, telephones connections, village electrification exhibit highly significant correlations with urbanization level at all the three points of time under consideration. Except in village electrification, all are also showing very high correlation values with per-capita income and expenditure. Moreover, correlations have remained almost the same, suggesting that no substantial changes have occurred in the ranking of the states. In other words, the poorer states have not been able to improve their position relative to richer states. The relationship of infrastructural facilities with growth of urban population is also positive and generally significant at the three points. This implies that the process of urbanization is directly related to improvement in infrastructural facilities across the states.

The levels of urban basic amenities like access to safe drinking water, sanitation facilities, and electricity are positively correlated with urbanization although the values are statistically insignificant. It is thus not possible to argue that the more urbanized states provide basic amenities to a larger percentage of their urban population. On the other hand, the correlation of these indicators with urban growth has become negative over the years. Here it appears that the growth of urban population over the decades has led to increased pressure on basic amenities and resulted in deterioration in standards of living. Again correlation of percentage of urban population with hospitals per thousand persons is highly positive. But its value has decreased continuously from 0.61 in 1981 to 0 55 in 1991 and then to 0.49 in 2001. Furthermore, its correlation with middle higher secondary schools has been negative and has been maintained as such in 2001 as well. Therefore, this apparently reflects the pressure of the growing urban population on the limited infrastructure. We have argued before that urbanization in the later years has been backed up by industrialization. Unfortunately, a similar relationship does not exist between indicators of urbanization, social development, and access to basic services.

It is important to note at this juncture the existence and rapid growth of slum-settlements has been noted as a general urban phenomenon in recent years. The previous Indian censuses had not gathered any information regarding this aspect of urbanization. For the first time, the Census 2001 has collected demographic data regarding the slum-settlements in all urban centers with a population of 50,000 or more throughout the country. In India the total slum-population in the country works out as above 40 million, which is 14.12 per cent of the total urban population. We have observed that the states with high share of slum-population in total urban population are Maharashtra, Andhra Pradesh, and Haryana, constituting 25.9 per cent, 25.1 per cent, and 23 per cent of the urban population respectively. West Bengal and Delhi too have exhibited moderately higher shares of slum-population than the national average. So it is more important to note that these states are relatively well off economically and have higher levels of urbanization than other states. Evidently, the correlations between the indicators of urbanization (Both the level and growth) and slum-population are positive and which confirms the fact that slum-settlements have generally increased in highly urbanized states.

Interestingly, some of the developed state which are also highly urbanized, like Gujarat, Karnataka, Punjab, and Tamil Nadu have reported shares of slum-population, which as much below the national average. We would, therefore, like to examine into the structural conditions of the states which influence rural-urban migration, thereby increasing slum-population. So, by analyzing the interdependence between the indicators of socio-economic development and share of slum-population, it has been found that indicators on per-capita income and industrialization have exhibited highly positive correlation with regular workers in urban area. On the other hand, it has shown negatively high correlation with urban unemployment rate. This shows that increase in job opportunities is conducive for growing slum-population. On the contrary, existence of high unemployment rate in the state discourages rural-urban migration, and thereby, does not provide a conducive atmosphere for increase in slum-population in the state. These facts confirm the generally perceived conclusion that increasing slum-population has been prompted by rapid industrialization and growing job opportunities in selected pockets of the country.

VI. INTRA-STATE VARIATION AND INTER-DEPENDENCIES BETWEEN URBANIZATION AND DEVELOPMENTAL INDICATORS IN SELECT STATES (WEST BENGAL, MAHARASHTRA, PUNJAB, BIHAR, RAJASTHAN)

In this section a number of indicators have been considered at the district-level analysis as has been done for analyzing the pattern of interdependence at the state level. These include—(1) the level of urbanization (LoU); (2) growth of urban population GR (U). The indicators of socio-economic development that are included in the analysis can be broadly classified as economic development indicators, viz.; (3) Size of industrial enterprise; (4) Value of agricultural output per hectare; (b) Infrastructural Development Indicators; (5) Road length per 100 sq. km; (6) Railway lines per 100 sq. km; (7) Telephone connections per 100 persons; (8) Per-capita bank deposits; (9) Per-capita industrial credit. (c) Socio-demographic Development Indicators; (10) Females per thousand males in urban areas; (11) Literacy in rural areas; (12) Literacy in urban areas; (13) Middle and higher secondary schools per thousand persons; and (14) Hospitals and dispensaries per thousand persons. Here some of the indicators have not shown in correlation tables of different states due space constraint.

West Bengal

In case of West Bengal, levels of urbanization across districts have been exhibited strong correlation with the developmental indicators at all three years 1981, 1991, 2001. The same is true for the growth of urban population. This relates very strongly and positively to the share of manufacturing output in 2001, much more than the urbanization due to increasing industrial activity in the post-liberalization phase. The correlation coefficient of the indicators of urbanization with agricultural productivity has been exhibited positive relationship in 1980s and 1990s (*Economic Survey*, Government of West Bengal). Availability of physical infrastructure has played an important role in the process of urbanization across the districts in West Bengal.

The districts have better social infrastructure as well as social indictors (like hospitals, availability of beds, total number of schools, literacy rate, etc.) are likely to have a higher share of level of urbanization than those with poor infrastructure and social indicators.

Maharashtra

We have observed that levels of urbanization across districts in the state of Maharashtra exhibit strong correlation with the developmental indicators at all the three point of time 1981, 1991, 2001. The same is generally true for the growth of urban population as well. This relates very strongly and positively to the size of factories in 2001, much more than the urbanization due to the increasing industrial activity in the post-liberalization phase. Again, the correlation of the indicators of urbanization (level and growth) with agricultural productivity does not show any significant relationship in the early 1980s or early 1990s. However, there was a positive relationship between the two during the early 1980s, which subsequently became negative over a decade in the early 1990s. Hence, positive and strong interdependence of level of urbanization with factory size on the one hand (as shown below) and its inverse relationship with agricultural productivity, on the other, reflects the shifting of occupational structure over time, along with increasing level of urbanization in the state of Maharashtra. In other words, increasing level of urbanization can be attributed to the development of industrial activity in the state.

Moreover, availability of physical infrastructure has played an important role in the process of urbanization in the state of Maharashtra. This may be inferred from the strong interdependencies between level of urbanization and the infrastructural indicators at all three years 1981, 1991, 2001. What is more, the correlations of the former with railways per 100 sq. km. and telephone connections per 100 persons are very high at all the three points of time. The relationship of road network with level of urbanization is negative, that is -0.38 in 1981 and -0.18 in 1991, but the correlation has improved 0.33 in 2001, suggesting increasing importance of road as a factor in the urbanization process. Consequently,

TABLE 2

Correlations of Level of Urbanization and Development Indicators—West Bengal

		Level of Urbanization	Literacy rate	Enrolment primary education	Enrolment secondary education	Enrolment higher secondary education	Availability of beds per 10,000 population	NDDP at constant prices (1993-94) in Rs. Lakh	District per capita income at current prices	Share of manufacturing in DDP at constant prices 1993-94	Share of workers in total population	Share of urban workforce	Sex ratio (female per 1000 males) overall
Level of Urbanization	Pearson Correlation	1.000	.703	.264	.561	-.109	.697	.128	.836	.335	-.383	.997	-920
	Sig. (2-tailed)	.	.001	.274	.013	.656	.001	.603	.000	.161	.106	.000	.000
	N	19	19	19	19	19	19	19	19	19	19	17	18
Literacy rate	Pearson Correlation	.703	1.000	.030	.451	.288	.405	.166	.561	.491	-.438	.683	-509
	Sig. (2-tailed)	.001	.	.902	.053	.231	.085	.497	.012	.033	.060	.003	.031
	N	19	19	19	19	19	19	19	19	19	19	17	18
Enrolment primary education	Pearson Correlation	.264	.030	1.000	.288	-.151	.713	-.078	.613	-.580	.228	.283	.434
	Sig. (2-tailed)	.274	.902	.	.231	.538	.001	.751	.005	.009	.347	.272	.072
	N	19	19	19	19	19	19	19	19	19	19	17	18
Enrolment secondary education	Pearson Correlation	.561	.451	.288	1.000	-.165	.587	.119	.712	-.001	.091	.556	.580
	Sig. (2-tailed)	.013	.053	.231	.	.501	.008	.628	.001	.996	.711	.020	.012

	N	19	19	19	19	19	19	19	19	19	19	17	18
Enrolment higher secondary education	Pearson Correlation	-.109	.288	-.151	-.165	1.000	-.103	.039	-.175	.244	-.176	-.107	.364
	Sig. (2-tailed)	.656	.231	.538	.501	.	.674	.873	.472	.315	.471	.683	.138
	N	19	19	19	19	19	19	19	19	19	19	17	18
Availability of beds per 10,000 population	Pearson Correlation	.697	.405	.713	.587	-.103	1.000	.014	.909	-.291	.019	.700	.757
	Sig. (2-tailed)	.001	.085	.001	.008	.674	.	.954	.000	.227	.940	.002	.000
	N	19	19	19	19	19	19	19	19	19	19	17	18
NDDP at constant prices (1993-94) in Rs. Lakh	Pearson Correlation	.128	.166	-.078	.119	.039	.014	1.000	.086	.160	-.126	.575	.497
	Sig. (2-tailed)	.603	.497	.751	.628	.873	.954	.	.725	.513	.607	.016	.036
	N	19	19	19	19	19	19	19	19	19	19	17	18
District per-capita income at current prices	Pearson Correlation	.836	.561	.613	.712	-.175	.909	.086	1.000	-.094	-.063	.822	.868
	Sig. (2-tailed)	.000	.012	.005	.001	.472	.000	.725	.	.703	.799	.000	.000
	N	19	19	19	19	19	19	19	19	19	19	17	18
Share of manufacturing in DDP at constant prices 1993-94	Pearson Correlation	.335	.491	-.580	-.001	.244	-.291	.160	-.094	1.000	-.675	.347	.112
	Sig. (2-tailed)	.161	.033	.009	.996	.315	.227	.513	.703	.	.002	.173	.658
	N	19	19	19	19	19	19	19	19	19	19	17	18
Share of workers in total population	Pearson Correlation	-.383	-.438	.228	.091	-.176	.019	-.126	-.063	-.675	1.000	-.374	.233
	Sig. (2-tailed)	.106	.060	.347	.711	.471	.940	.607	.799	.002	.	.139	.351
	N	19	19	19	19	19	19	19	19	19	19	17	18
Share of urban workforce	Pearson Correlation	.997	.683	.283	.556	-.107	.700	.575	.822	.347	-.374	1.000	.922
	Sig. (2-tailed)	.000	.003	.272	.020	.683	.002	.016	.000	.173	.139	.	.000
	N	17	17	17	17	17	17	17	17	17	17	17	17
Sex ratio (female per 1,000 males) Overall	Pearson Correlation	-.920	-.509	-.434	-.580	.364	-.757	-.497	-.868	-.112	.233	-.922	1000
	Sig. (2-tailed)	.000	.031	.072	.012	.138	.000	.036	.000	.658	.351	.000	.
	N	18	18	18	18	18	18	18	18	18	18	17	18

** Correlation is significant at the 0.01 level (2-tailed).

* Correlation is significant at the 0.05 level (2-tailed

TABLE 3

Maharashtra—Indicators of Urbanization and Economic Development

	LoU	*GR (U)*	*Ind. enterprise*	*Agri. Output*	*Road*	*Railway*	*Telephone*	*Bank deposits*	*Ind. credit*	*Literacy (U)*	*Sex ratio (U)*	*Hospital*	*School*
LoU	1.00	.380(*)	0.16	0.19	0.33	0.742(**)	.712(**)	.702(**)	0.04	-0.02	-0.743	.559(**)	-0.543(**)
GR (U)	.380(*)	1.00	.347(*)	0.21	0.14	0.06	0.03	0.01	-0.04	-0.18	-0.563	0.08	-0.015
Ind. enterprise	0.16	.347(*)	1.00	0.03	0.06	0.15	0.17	0.17	0.07	0.02	-0.437	0.03	-0.101(**)
Road	0.19	0.21	0.03	1.00	0.25	0.09	0.04	0.04	0.25	0.09	-0.19	0.28	-0.159
Railway	0.33	0.14	0.06	0.25	1.00	0.09	0.05	0.04	0.28	0.21	-0.14	0.31	-0.201
Telephone	.742(**)	0.06	0.15	0.09	0.09	1.00	.989(**)	.987(**)	-0.02	0.14	-0.639(**)	.617(**)	-0.362(*)
Bank deposits	.712(**)	0.03	0.17	0.04	0.05	.989(**)	1.00	.998(**)	0.01	0.17	-0.598(**)	.607(**)	-0.309
Ind. credit	.702(**)	0.01	0.17	0.04	0.04	.987(**)	.998(**)	1.00	0.00	0.15	-0.592(**)	.594(**)	-0.327
Literacy (R)	0.04	-0.04	0.07	0.25	0.28	-0.02	0.01	0.00	1.00	.435(*)	0.18	0.27	0.07
Literacy (U)	0.02	-0.18	0.02	0.09	0.21	0.14	0.17	0.15	.435(*)	1.00	0.10	.367(*)	0.044
Sex ratio (U)	-.743(**)	-.563(**)	-.437(**)	-0.19	-0.14	-.639(**)	-0.60	-592(**)	0.18	0.01	1.00	-0.30	.382(*)
Hospital	0.559	0.08	0.03	0.28	0.31	.617(**)	.607(**)	.594(**)	0.27	0.367	-0.30	1.00	-0.321
School	-.543(**)	-0.10	-0.10	-0.16	-0.20	-0.36	-0.31	-0.33	0.07	0.04	.382(*)	-0.32	1

Notes: *Correlation is significant at the 0.05 level (2-tailed). ** Correlation is significant at the 0.01 level (2-tailed).

the districts having better infrastructural facilities are likely to have a higher share of urban population than those with poor infrastructure.

In the way, all the indicators of financial infrastructure have reflected a positive and significant correlation with urbanization level. We can note this interdependency to exist generally between economic indicators and urbanization levels. The infrastructural facilities also seem to have accelerated the tempo of urbanization. One odd observation is that the number of middle and higher schools (per thousand persons) has not increased with the level of urbanization. This is reflected in the negative correlation between the indicators during the

1980s as well as the 1990s. However, health facilities tend to go up with urbanization. The number of hospital per thousand population exhibits a positive correlation with the level of urbanization.

The socio-demographic indicator, literacy in urban area has a positive correlation with the level of urbanization, both in 1981 and 1991. The correlation coefficients, however, are not very high ranging between 0.17 and 0.34. Urban literacy tends to go down for higher levels of urbanization, at all the three points of time. This can be attributed to inflow of illiterate migrants to the cities and town in the urbanized districts in search of livelihood.

Punjab

In case of Punjab the correlation matrix has not been shown in table format due to space constraint. Our study shows that Punjab exhibits somewhat similar pattern of interdependence between urbanization and the developmental indicators excepting the indicators on agricultural productivity. Unlike Maharashtra, the correlation between level of urbanization and value of agricultural output is positive and significant in the early 1980s. Even the growth of urbanization has shown a stronger positive relationship with agricultural productivity in the latter period. In fact, the pattern of urbanization in Punjab is different from that of other states, as urbanization here is not restricted to a few industrialized towns. With the advent of the Green

Revolution, agriculture network led to the growth of agro-allied industries in the vicinity. Consequently, regions with high productivity in agriculture encouraged urban centers in a more decentralized way. This has produced a positive correlation of urbanization with agricultural productivity.

The relationships of roads (for which information was available only for the last decade of 1991-2001) with the level of urbanization is positive though not statistically significant. Per-capita credit to industry exhibits the strongest and the most significant relationship with the percentage of urban population in all the three years (1981, 1991, 2001) which underlines the impotence of this factor. Correlation is also positive in case of per-capita availability of bank credit, though the values are not significant. The values, however, have improved over the time. Interestingly, a pattern similar to Maharashtra is noticed with regard to urban sex ratio and middle and high school education. The correlation between growth of population and sex ratio in urban areas is -0.59 which is significant at 5 per cent level in 1981. it goes down to -0.44 and -0.13 in 1991 and 2001 respectively but still the correlation remains negative, suggesting male dominance in rapidly urbanizing districts. The negative relationship of urbanization with the indicators of middle and higher schools indicates that the facilities have not kept pace with the level and growth of urbanization in the state. The other infrastructural indicator, hospitals per thousand populations, relates positively and significantly with the level of urbanization in 1991 as well as 2001. the correlations are as high as 0.70 and 0.51 respectively. However, the decline in their values suggests that the medical facilities, too, have failed to increase corresponding to the increase in urban population during the 1990s, as noted in case of schooling.

Socio-economic indicators like urban literacy exhibit positive but insignificant relationship with the level as well as growth of urban population across the districts. The difference between rural and urban literacy in Punjab is much less than the national average in 1981, 1991, and 2001. This, possibly, is due to lesser number of illiterate migrants in the urban areas. Reduction in the 0-6 age group of population would also enhance the crude literacy rate. Punjab, as a matter of fact, has reported a larked decrease in its 0-6 age group of population due to decline in birth rate between 1991-2001—much more than the national average.

Bihar

It is to be noted that the number of indicators available in case of Bihar is less as compared to the other two states discussed already. Temporal comparability of the interdependency between urbanization and other socio-economic indicators at the district level would, therefore, have certain additional limitations here. The agricultural productivity data for some of the districts of Bihar are not available and they are substituted by the mean value to keep the correlations unbiased. The correlations between the indicators of urbanization and agricultural productivity were insignificant in both the temporal periods under consideration. However, the correlation between level of urbanization and agricultural output was positive during the early 1980s as well as early 1990s. Importantly, the growth of urbanization has exhibited a negative relationship with agricultural productivity and it has become stronger over time. This is evident from the fact that districts which exhibited increase in urbanization have witnessed a declining trend in terms of agricultural productivity.

Again, the indicator on roads per sq. km. does not show any positive relationship with the level or growth of urban population in 1981. Correlations of level of urbanization with per-capita bank credit and credit to industry per-capita, however, are positive and highly significant in 1981. The correlations, however, have weakened over the subsequent decades. What is more, interrelation of these indicators with the growth of urban population is neither significant nor gives a consistent correlation over the years.

Besides, urban and rural literacy relate positively with the level of urbanization across the districts. A marked gap can be noticed between urban and rural literacy rates. The strong positive correlation between level of urbanization and urban literacy suggests that there is a concentration of educated persons in a few large cities and urbanized districts of the state. It is evident from our analysis that unlike Maharashtra and Punjab, Bihar has not been able to enjoy the benefits of urbanization. The numbers and percentage of urban population in the state have of course gone up due to natural growth and poverty-induced migration. Interestingly, the level as well as growth in urban population has exhibited an inverse relation with the urban sex ratio in all the three decades. Poverty and lack of job opportunities in rural Bihar seem to be the main factors behind the rural-urban migration which has been highly male selective. This has lowered the female-male ratio in the relative urbanized districts of the state.

TABLE 4

Interdependence Indicators—Urbanization and Socio-economic Development

	LoU	*GR (U)*	*Literacy (R)*	*Literacy (U)*	*Sex ratio (U)*
LoU	1.00	-0.16	.473(**)	.400(**)	-0.191
GR (U)	-0.16	1.00	-284	0.061	-0.045
Literacy (R)	.473(**)	-0.284(*)	1.00	.445(**)	0.204
Literacy (U)	.400(**)	0.061	.445(**)	1.00	0.053
Sex ratio (U)	-0.191	0.0045	0.204	0.053	1.00

Rajasthan

The state of Rajasthan is also constrained by the non-availability of data on the selected indicators, as in the case of Bihar. However, we have tried to evaluate the nature of relationship of the level and growth of urbanization with the available developmental indicators. Urbanization in the state of Rajasthan has witnessed inverse relationship with agricultural productivity. This phenomenon was evident from the negative correlations in level as well as growth of urbanization in the early 1980s and in later years. This seems to be obvious, since agriculture is a component of village-oriented economy. Interestingly, its correlation with the growth of urbanization has become positive and significant in the early 1990s. This implies that much of the urban growth is occurring in the agriculturally developed areas.

Again, the correlation matrix for 1981 shows positive and significant relationship of per-capita bank credit and per-capita credit available to industries with level of urbanization. This has been noticed throughout the 1980s and the 1990s.

TABLE 5

Interdependence among Indicators of Urbanization and Socio-economic Development in Rajasthan

	LoU	*GR (U)*	*Bank deposits*	*Ind. credit*	*Literacy (R)*	*Literacy (U)*	*Sex ratio (U)*	*Hospital*	*School*
LoU	1.00	0.259	.727(**)	.418(*)	0.316	0.155	-0.049	-0.361(*)	0.004
GR (U)	0.259	1.00	0.23	0.303	0.086	-0.26	-0.259	-0.009	0.138
Bank deposits	.727(**)	0.23	1.00	.605(**)	0.125	.408(*)	-0.074	-0.305	-0.041
Ind. credit	.418(*)	0.303	.605(**)	1.00	-0.02	.354(*)	-0.157	-0.284	0.01
Literacy (R)	0.316	0.086	0.125	-0.02	1.00	-0.117	-0.01	-0.234	0.151
Literacy (U)	0.155	-0.26	.408(*)	.354(*)	-0.117	1.00	0.046	-0.26	0.101
Sex ratio (U)	-0.049	-0.259	-0.074	-0.157	-0.01	0.046	1.00	-0.413(*)	-0.289
Hospital	-0.361(*)	-0.009	-0.305	-0.284	-0.234	-0.26	-0.413(*)	1.00	-0.16
School	0.004	0.138	-0.041	0.01	0.151	0.101	-0.289	-0.16	1.00

Notes: *Correlation is significant at the 0.05 level (2-tailed). ** Correlation is significant at the 0.01 level (2-tailed).

But, per-capita bank credit does not show such high correlation with the growth of urban population. Of course, the correlation has improved over time but still remains statistically insignificant even in 2001. Similarly, credit to industry shows positive correlation with the growth of urban population since 1981 and the value has increased over the time. And, yet, it is not significant even at the 5 per cent level.

Besides, this the level of urbanization exhibits positive relation with urban literacy, though the values are insignificant at all the three points of time. In case of the growth rate, however, there exists no consistent pattern in the relationship. High growth of urban population seems to be having a negative impact on urban literacy at the district level in Rajasthan, as is the case in many other states. The reason lies in the fact that most of the rural migrants to urban areas, who come to cities and town in search of jobs, are illiterate. Corroborating evidence is also the fact there exists a marked differential in urban and rural literacy in the state. Interestingly, level of urbanization exhibits insignificant positive relation with urban sex ratio both in 1981 and 1991 whereas in 2001 the value is still less. In case of growth of urban population, however, the correlation with the sex ratio is negative and significant. As elsewhere high urban growth is associated with male selective migration leading to low female-male ratio.

Among the other infrastructure indicators like hospitals and middle and higher schools per thousand populations, the data are available only for medical facilities. We have observed that the indicator pertaining to middle and higher schools however shows a negligible positive correlation with both the level and growth of urban population. We argue that with the increased in the levels and growth in urban population, infrastructure facilities come under stress, reflected in low per-capita values in the urbanized districts.

VII. SUMMARY AND CONCLUDING REMARKS

From our foregoing analysis we have been observed that foreign direct investment has facilitated the development of more urbanized states where infrastructure facilities are better compare to other states but it has led to a widening of regional inequality. Again, it is difficult to argue that urbanization per se would lead to growth in employment rate or bring down the unemployment rate. What is more, the poverty levels in developed and more urbanized states have surprisingly been high and highest incidence of poverty in urban areas of India was mostly in the small towns. An analysis of the growth performance and structural changes in the SDP in Indian states since 1981 reveals that the development process has been uneven across states and intra-state level. Besides this, advanced industrial states have tended to leap forward since 1990, while other states have lagged behind. This pattern is also same in case of advanced districts which have been benefited from economic reform and poorer districts even in advanced state lagged behind as well as suffered most.

We know that the record of economic and social

development in India since independence, though highly uneven and far from exemplary, includes substantial overall progress in many fields. India's recent success story of raising its GDP growth rate is explained primarily by the performance of the services sector.

REFERENCES

Census of India 1981, 1991 and 2001, Government of India.

Economic Census 1990, 1998 and 2006, Government of India.

NSS Organization, Employment and Unemployment in India, 1993-4, 50th Round and 1999-2000, 55th Round

Economic Survey, Government of India, Various issues.

Eleventh Five Year Plan (2007), Government of India.

CMIE (2000), Economic Intelligence Service—Profiles of Districts.

Expert Group of Commercialization of Infrastructure (1996), The Indian Infrastructure Report: Policy Imperatives for Growth and Welfare, Ministry of Finance, Government of India, New Delhi.

Jean Dreze and A.K. Sen (2002), India: Development and Participation, Oxford, 2002.

K.C. Sivaramkrishnan, A.K. Kundu and B.N. Singh (2005), Handbook Urbanization in India, Oxford.

Solow, R.M. (1974), 'The Economies of Resources or the Resources of Economics', *American Economic Review,* Papers and Proceedings, Richard T. Elly Lecture.

——— (1997), 'Georgescu-Roegen *versus* Solow and Stiglitz', Replky, Ecological Economics, 22, 267-68.

Smith, Adam (1776), Inquiry into the Nature and Causes of the Wealth of Nations.

Bhattacharya, B.B., Sakthvel, S. (2004), Regional Growth and Disparity in India, Comparison of Pre- and Post-Reform Decades, *EPW,* March 6.

Shand, Ric, Bhide, S. (2000), Sources of Economic Growth—Regional Dimensions of Reforms, *EPW,* October 14.

APPENDIX TABLE I

Level and Growth of Urbanization and Socio-economic Indicators among Different States of India, 2001

States	*LoU*	*Growth rate (U)*	*Per capita income (Rs. Crore)**	*Per capita FDI Rs.*	*Average size of land holding (ha.)*	*Industrial production as % of NSDP*	*WE ratio (rural)*	*WE ratio (urban)*	*WPM (P+S) in 15+ age by usual status (%) (rural)*	*WPM (P+S) in 15+ age by usual status (%) (urban)*	*% of Reg. workers to total workers (rural)*
1	*2*	*3*	*4*	*5*	*6*	*7*	*8*	*9*	*10*	*11*	*12*
Andhra Pradesh	27.08	1.40	9118	1597.98	1.56	20.91	3.43	3.96	76.70	50.10	5.90
Assam	12.72	3.10	5942	0.56	1.31	3.10	9.46	4.17	53.90	45.40	16.60
Bihar	13.00	2.60	4397	85.41	0.93	12.30	2.55	4.16	57.20	42.40	3.50
Delhi	93.01	4.10	19,091	23,387.20	1.17	5.49	5.31	11.59	47.20	46.80	45.40
Gujarat	37.35	2.80	13,709	2209.50	2.93	30.90	4.59	6.89	73.90	48.30	6.30
Haryana	29.00	4.10	13,084	1418.89	2.43	9.19	4.94	7.04	55.40	46.90	12.40
Himachal Pradesh	9.79	2.80	8864	595.10	1.20	2.39	2.41	6.26	73.70	45.20	10.10
Karnataka	33.98	2.50	11,153	3777.71	2.13	23.18	3.15	3.91	71.60	50.30	5.30
Kerala	25.97	0.70	9807	405.88	0.33	9.76	3.61	3.78	52.50	49.40	13.70
Madhya Pradesh	25.00	2.80	7350	1513.63	2.63	19.48	2.38	3.89	74.30	48.60	3.50

Maharashtra	42.40	2.90	15805	4315.16	2.21	67.25	3.69	6.58	72.90	49.10	7.30
Orissa	14.97	2.60	5648	2175.83	1.34	4.44	2.13	5.49	63.20	46.60	4.20
Punjab	33.95	3.20	14,457	803.61	3.61	11.38	4.41	6.07	61.40	49.90	13.00
Rajasthan	23.38	2.70	7694	458.82	3.95	12.45	2.59	3.91	72.10	49.00	4.90
Tamil Nadu	43.86	3.60	12,287	3049	0.93	28.93	3.94	4.28	69.90	53.40	11.80
Uttar Pradesh	21.00	2.80	5890	241.86	0.89	29.25	3.59	4.11	58.60	47.70	5.60
West Bengal	28.03	1.80	8622	1045.73	0.90	21.36	2.94	6.22	54.30	46.40	7.00
All-India	27.78	2.70	9660	2402.13	1.57	85.60	3.29	5.39	64.70	48.60	6.80
CV	62.92	31.34	40.05	197.30	57.74		45.12	36.81	14.94	5.22	95.05

(Contd.)

APPENDIX TABLE I (*Contd.*)

1	13	14	15	16	17	18	19	20	21	22	23
States	*per cent of Reg. workers to total workers (urban)*	*Usual status (adj.) Unemp. Rate (%) in 15+ age (R)*	*Usual status (adj.) Unemp. Rate (%) in 15+ age (U)*	*Rural poverty (%)*	*Urban poverty (%)*	*Average age MPCE (R)*	*Average Average Average (U)*	*Road (per 100 sq. km.)*	*Railways (per 100 popn)*	*Tele-phone (per 100 popn.)*	*Village electri-fied (%)*
Andhra Pradesh	38.70	6.80	6.90	11.05	26.63	453.61	773.52	58.27	1.84	1.99	99.92
Assam	42.90	15.20	14.10	40.04	7.47	426.12	814.12	87.22	3.10	0.86	76.97
Bihar	30.20	6.50	13.20	44.30	32.91	384.72	601.88	50.81	3.02	0.49	70.85
Delhi	54.80	6.50	4.60	0.40	9.42	917.21		1796.08	11.55	12.50	100.00
Gujarat	34.10	1.10	2.80	13.17	15.59	551.33	891.68	46.37	2.72	3.21	99.44
Haryana	42.80	1.10	3.90	8.27	9.99	714.37	912.07	63.71	3.42	2.63	96.72
Himachal Pradesh	51.60	3.70	9.60	7.94	4.63	684.50	1242.93	54.24	0.48	3.74	97.87
Karnataka	39.60	4.50	5.50	17.38	25.25	499.78	910.99	75.09	1.59	2.79	98.51
Kerala	29.10	19.80	17.50	9.38	20.27	765.70	932.61	374.95	2.70	4.18	100.00
Madhya Pradesh	33.00	3.90	5.50	37.06	38.44	401.50	693.56	45.13	1.33	1.18	94.37
Maharashtra	51.50	6.10	6.90	23.72	26.81	496.77	973.32	117.61	1.80	4.10	100.00
Orissa	35.80	15.70	15.30	48.01	42.83	373.17	614.48	168.71	1.41	0.91	69.86

Punjab	40.90	4.90	4.40	6.35	5.75	742.43	898.82	127.78	4.25	4.59	100.00
Rajasthan	36.50	2.00	3.50	13.74	19.85	548.88	795.81	37.89	1.72	1.72	88.56
Tamil Nadu	44.10	10.60	6.60	20.55	22.11	513.97	971.61	158.78	3.07	3.43	100.00
Uttar Pradesh	32.30	2.80	7.30	31.22	30.89	466.68	690.67	86.77	3.02	1.01	77.20
West Bengal	40.00	11.10	11.20	31.85	14.86	454.50	866.59	19.63	4.25	1.56	77.21
All-India	40.00	6.70	7.40	27.096	23.62	486.07	854.96	75.01	1.91	2.15	85.95
CV	18.90	76.19	55.30	68.52	55.22	28.30	18.70	211.93	80.65	92.84	12.70

(Contd.)

APPENDIX TABLE I (Contd.)

1	24	25	26	27	28	29	30	31	32
States	*URGD (1981-91)*	*Slum pop. as % of urban popn.*	*Literacy (rural)*	*Literacy (urban)*	*Hospital (per '000 popn.)*	*School (per '000 popn.)*	*Access to safe drink water (% U HH) (1991)*	*Sanitation facilities (% U HH) (1991)*	*Electricity use (% U HH) (1991)*
Andhra Pradesh	0.12	25.11	48.01	67.55	0.436	0.105	73.82	54.60	73.31
Assam	1.60	2.50	50.48	76.44	0.523	0.304	64.07	86.06	63.21
Bihar	0.17	5.85	35.93	64.53	1.070	0.134	73.39	56.54	58.77
Delhi	4.08	15.80	65.86	70.74	1.764	0.047	96.24	66.64	81.38
Gujarat	1.31	7.13	49.96	69.92	1.971	0.424	87.23	65.71	82.96
Haryana	2.21	23.25	53.46	69.06	0.623	0.088	93.18	64.25	89.13
Himachal Pradesh	1.32		64.77	80.37	1.657	0.183	91.93	59.98	96.24
Karnataka	1.43	7.07	51.60	71.49	1.128	0.373	81.38	62.52	76.27
Kerala	-0.25	0.55	79.53	83.20	1.343	0.096	38.62	72.66	67.65
Madhya Pradesh	0.99	14.83	48.04	68.68	0.440	0.263	79.45	53.00	72.52
Maharashtra	1.56	25.95	60.51	75.19	2.312	0.248	90.50	64.45	86.07
Orissa	1.29	11.56	51.63	71.68	0.489	0.342	62.83	49.27	62.11
Punjab	1.99	13.97	56.64	69.94	1.097	0.112	94.24	73.23	94.60
Rajasthan	0.29	9.13	45.00	65.24	0.755	0.291	86.51	62.27	76.67
Tamil Nadu	4.14	9.29	58.99	73.62	1.175	0.090	74.17	57.47	76.80

Uttar Pradesh	0.71	12.04	43.96	60.90	0.501	0.128	85.78	66.54	67.76
West Bengal	0.32	17.00	54.14	73.67	0.902	0.033	86.23	78.75	70.19
All-India	1.05	14.12	49.44	70.10	0.945	0.197	81.38	63.90	75.78
CV	90.58	62.85	18.52	7.82	0.541	0.636	18.33	14.67	14.49

Sources: Census of India, 2001: *Economic Survey*, Government of India, NSS, Economic Census, Various Issues.

3

Regional Pattern of Disparities and Levels of Living in India

DALIP KUMAR

A. INTRODUCTION

To understand the pattern of regional disparities, it is pertinent to peep through the ideas of various theorists who tried to focus attention on economic development, regional economic thoughts and their theoretical and empirical investigations. Elements of development economics can be traced back to the classical works of David Recardo, Karl Marx and Schumpeter. Regional economics can be said to have originated in the writings of German Economists like Von Thunen's spatial contours of agriculture production and Alfred Weber's theory of industrial location. According to neo-classical economists like Robert Solow (1956), regional disparities are self-limiting in character. But Gunner Myrdal (1957) differed from Solow's views. To him, the factor movements themselves were likely to have disequilibrating rather than equilibrating on account of the backwash effect. Labour migration was considered to be widening the disparity. The approach taken by Hirschman (1958) closely resembles with that of Myrdal.

Repatriation of income by migrants and rise in demand of goods in the backward regions are supposed to bring about a reversal in the trend of widening regional economic disparities. It was further explained by Jeffery Williamson (1965) who examined the relationship between magnitude of regional per-capital disparities in 24 nations and the level of development of those nations.

However, the Latin American Schools of thoughts were skeptical about second phase of inverted U-shaped curve of disparities emerging on the global level within the framework of production based on capitals. According to Andre Gunder Frank (1967) the greater integration between metropolis and their satellites fuelled only the growth in the metropolis. This widened the disparities instead of bringing about a trickle down of prosperity from more developed metropolis to the backward nations and regions. Similar views can be found in the Paul Baran's theory (1957) of surplus or Emmanuel's (1972) thesis of unequal exchange.

Paul Bairoch's work (1981) is perhaps the only study which made herculian attempt to delineate the behaviour of international disparities in the per-capita income since the period even before the advent of the industrial revolution in the mid-18th century. He found that at the time of industrial revolution, the maximum inter-country deviation in per-capita income never exceeded, i.e. or su. Considering the present day less developed countries (LDCs) as one group and the Developed countries as another group, he finds that the gap between these two groups continued to widen reaching a ratio of nearly seven by the year 1977. However, within the developed counties group, the inter-country disparities had reduced.

Level of living depends on personal income and consumption expenditure of a household. A level of income or expenditure higher than this means better conditions of living. The proportion of personal consumption expenditure is distributed among the various items of consumption. While comparing the levels of living of the people in terms of the level of expenditure as a whole and on individual items of expenditure, we are beset with the problem of price. We can also bypass the problem of prices, as also the problems connected with the supply of goods and services by the state, which is known to have an impact on the level of living. One important aspect of the indicator of the levels of living is their utility from the point of view of measurement of the degree of inequality in the levels of living in states.

The measurement of levels of living depends on so many components like health, food consumption and nutrition, level of education, level of employment and condition of work, housing status, social security, quality of clothing, types of recreation and entertainment, Communication, quality of transportation, levels of aged population and its economic freedom, etc. These data concerning social indicators, specifically standards of living, are included as population, economy, education, working conditions, financial resources, consumer durable, housing, home environment, transportation, leisure, social environment, health, social mobility, minorities, levels of and class differences in material standard of living, and equality between the sexes. This paper discusses Educational disparities, health disparities and Housing infrastructure disparities among the major States of India. Educational disparities can be seen by the literacy rates, Gross enrolment ratio, etc., health-related disparities can be seen by the indicators like CBR, CDR, IMR, Life Expectancy, and housing infrastructure disparities housing status, drinking water and toilet facility, uses of cooking gas, levels of aged population, etc.

Disparities in Distribution of HHs by Monthly Per-capita Expenditure (MPCE)

'Levels of living' is highly related with the good health of the household members as well as to the extent of medical care received by them. The distribution of Households and population by income level is useful information for health sector. NSSO collected data on consumption expenditure in its survey. Since Monthly per-capita expenditure (MPCE) provides the basis for ranking of the households according to level of living, the distributions of households by MPCE class for rural and urban India are presented in the Table 1.

TABLE I

Per 1000 Distribution of Households by MPCE Class during January-June 2004

Rural		*Urban*	
MPCE class (Rs.)	*Households*	*MPCE class (Rs.)*	*Households*
Less than 225	46	Less than 300	27
225-255	38	300-350	19
255-300	88	350-425	51
300-340	78	425-500	99
340-380	93	500-575	45
380-420	99	575-665	81
420-470	102	665-775	110
470-525	110	775-915	101
525-615	109	915-1120	149
615-775	113	1120-1500	158
775-950	58	1500-1925	48
950 or more	66	1925 or more	110
All	1000	All	1000

Source: NSSO 60th Round, Report No. 507, January-June 2004.

The above table shows data related to Monthly Per-capita Expenditure (MPCE) by HHs categorised for the convenience of comparative studies both in rural as well as urban areas. It may be recalled here that the poverty lines are fixed art Rs. 328 and Rs. 454 for rural and urban respectively. Out of 1000 HHs 250 HHs spend less than Rs. 340 in rural areas and 196 HHs MPCE in urban areas is less than Rs. 500 MPCE of 66 out of 1000 HHs in rural areas is more than Rs. 950, whereas 110 HHs in urban areas spend more than Rs. 1925. Maximum number of HHs (110) in rural areas spend only Rs. 470-525 whereas in the urban areas a maximum of 158 out of 1000 HHs are capable enough to spend Rs. 1120-1500 per person per month on health. Brief summaries of analysis of MPCE figure reflect very gloomy pictures especially for rural HHs. Its commutative impacts can be seen on education and health indicators like literacy rate, crude death rate, infant mortality rate, life expectancy. It affects directly working population and its levels of living in the country.

B. EDUCATIONAL DISPARITIES

(i) Trends and Disparities of Literacy in India

All-India average of percentage of literacy in the country was 5.36 in 1901. The literacy ratio of male was 9.80 per cent and female less than one (0.60). In 1931 the average literacy rate was 9.51. During 30 years period there was no more change in this rate. The drastic change started only after 1941.

TABLE 2

Literacy in India (1901-2001)

Year	*Age Group*	*(In Million)*			*(Percentage)*		
	All	*Population*	*Illiterate*	*Literate*	*Person*	*Male*	*Female*
1901	All	235.10	225.50	12.60	5.36	9.80	0.60
1911	All	248.20	233.50	14.70	5.92	10.60	1.00
1921	All	246.70	229.00	17.70	7.17	12.20	1.80
1931	All	273.40	247.40	26.00	9.51	15.60	2.90
1941	All	312.00	261.80	50.20	16.09	25.00	7.30
1951	5 and above	316.10	300.00	60.19	19.04	27.20	8.90
1961	5 and above	372.84	267.30	105.52	28.30	40.40	15.30
1971	5 and above	468.60	307.10	161.41	34.45	45.95	22.00
1981	7 and above	581.78	340.70	241.03	41.43	56.50	29.80
1991	7 and above	688.16	328.80	359.28	52.21	64.10	39.30
2001	7 and above	869.15	302.44	566.71	65.20	75.80	54.20

Sources: Census of India, Various Issue, Government of India

CHART I

Literacy Rate in India (1901-2001)

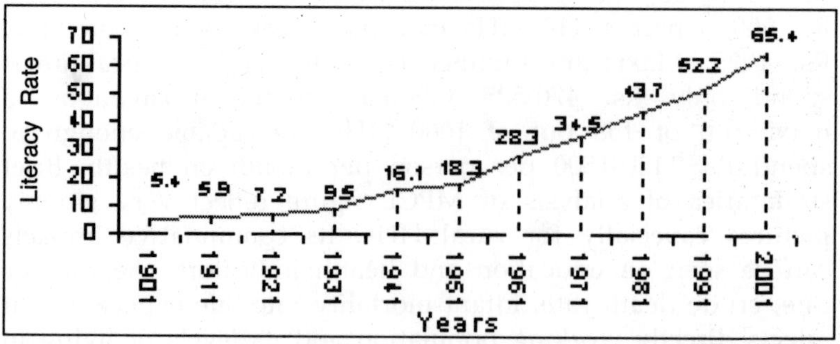

CHART 2

Disparities in Literacy Rate of Male and Female in India (1901-2001)

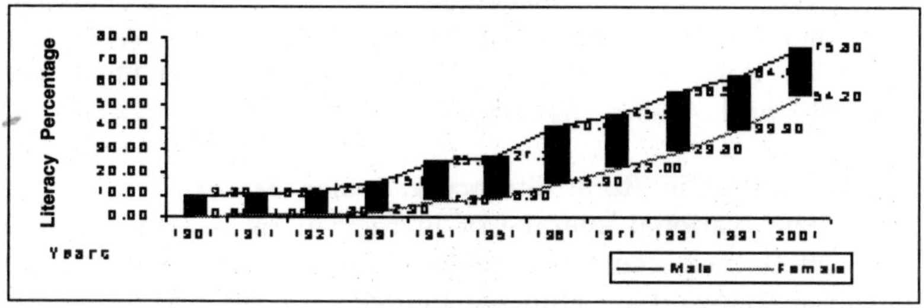

In the period from 1901 to 1931, the spread of literacy in India was almost stagnant. In 30 years, it increased from 5.36 per cent to only 9.5 per cent. After 1931, there was steady growth in the literacy percentage. In the period between 1931 and 2001, the literacy expansion was almost seven times, i.e. from 9.51 per cent to 65.20 per cent. This positive trend can be seen both in case of male as well as female literacy as given in the Table 2 and Charts 1 and 2.

(ii) Regional Disparities in Literacy

The average literacy rate of this country was 65.20 per cent in 2001. The literacy rate among male and female was 76 and 54 per cent respectively. But in the above table there are much disparities among the states. On the one side Kerala has the highest literacy rate of 90.92 per cent followed by

CHART 3

Male and Female Literacy as per Census-2001

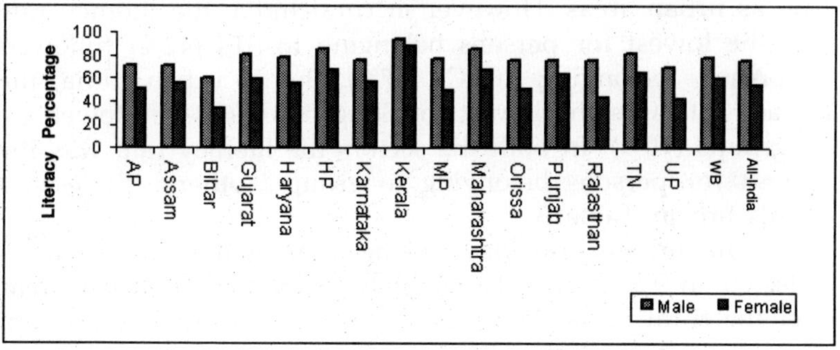

Maharashtra (77.27%), Himachal Pradesh (75.91%), Tamil Nadu (73.47%), Punjab (69.75%), West Bengal (69.22%), Karnataka (67.04%), and Gujarat (66.43%) but rest of the states have literacy levels below than the national average. The lowest literacy level is in Bihar (47.53%) followed by UP (57.36%), Rajasthan (61.03%), Andhra Pradesh (61.11%), MP (64.08%) and Assam (64.28%).

(iii) Disparities in Rural Literacy in Indian States

The National average of literacy in rural areas in 2001 was 59.21 per cent, the highest literacy being in Kerala (90.05%) followed by Himchal Pradesh (74.38%), Maharashtra (70.84%), Haryana (68.82%), TN (66.66%), Punjab (65.16%), WB (64.06%), Assam (60.92%) and Orissa (60.44%). The lowest literacy rates in rural India were in Bihar (44.42%), UP (53.68%), AP (55.33%) Rajasthan (55.92%), MP (58.10%) and Gujarat (58.53%).

(iv) Disparities in Urban Literacy in Indian States

The national average of Literacy in urban areas was 80.06 per cent in 2001, the highest rate being in Kerala (93.38%) followed by HP (89.59%), Assam (85.76%), Maharashtra (85.76%), TN (82.07%), Karnataka (81.05%), WB (81.63%) and Orissa (80.95%). Remaining other states had literacy rates below the national average.

(v) Literacy Disparities among Social Groups

This table presents distributions of persons aged 7 years and above by major social groups. The pattern of variation in the literacy rate was almost the same in rural as well as urban areas. However in rural India, the literacy rate was the lowest for persons belonging to STs (42%) followed by persons belonging to SCs (47%). But in urban India, the literacy rate was the lowest for SC groups (66%) followed by ST groups (70%). In both the sectors the literacy rate was the highest for persons belonging to group ' others'. State-wise details are in Table 3.

The urban-rural bias can be seen in the literacy as is reflected in Table 3. Urban literacy exceeded in urban areas over the rural India. The urban literacy stood at 79.8 per cent

TABLE 3

Percentage of Literate Persons Aged 7 Years and Above in Rural and Urban Areas by Social Groups Based on 55th Rounds

State	*ST*		*SC*		*OBC*		*Others*		*All*	
	Rural	*Urban*	*Rural*	*Urban*	*Rural*	*Urban*	*Rural*	*Urban*	*Rural*	*Urban*
Andhra Pradesh	26.1	57.5	39.4	67.3	42.5	68.8	62.3	82.2	45.8	74.5
Assam	71.6	85.3	69.7	69.2	72.9	80.1	66.7	89.7	69.0	86.1
Bihar	34.4	69.7	25.7	47.5	42.4	63.6	59.2	84.0	41.8	69.6
Gujarat	50.3	66.8	55.5	71.2	55.8	76.7	75.0	91.2	62.0	84.1
Haryana	48.3	93.7	50.7	53.4	58.1	75.5	67.7	84.6	61.2	76.6
HP	73.1	85.4	67.7	81.2	81.1	78.9	74.2	93.3	73.4	90.2
Karnataka	41.3	53.9	44.3	65.6	56.6	79.6	65.2	88.9	55.9	82.1
Kerala	80.2	97.5	79.1	87.9	88.3	92.3	94.1	96.4	89.4	93.7
MP	32.4	59.8	46.0	64.0	55.6	73.5	67.8	87.9	49.8	77.5
Maharashta	49.9	79.4	63.5	80.1	69.0	83.0	72.2	88.3	66.5	86.0
Orissa	33.1	55.2	47.8	53.2	61.6	79.4	73.9	85.8	53.8	75.5
Punjab	69.2	75.5	51.9	60.1	63.5	80.3	70.4	87.2	62.5	78.9
Rajasthan	38.4	69.1	36.7	56.0	46.3	70.0	57.8	84.4	46.5	75.1
Tamil Nadu	50.8	95.7	55.9	74.1	66.3	84.0	81.7	92.9	63.8	84.5
UP	47.7	78.5	40.7	58.1	47.6	59.3	64.9	79.7	51.1	70.1
West Bengal	41.6	63.2	57.1	67.4	74.6	81.2	64.7	86.2	61.7	82.2
All-India	42.2	70.0	46.6	66.2	54.8	75.3	67.7	86.5	56.0	79.8

Source: NSSO Report No. 473: Literacy and Levels of Education in India, 1999-2000, Tables 3R and 3U.

whereas it was just 56 per cent in rural area. The gap is explicit more in states like Rajasthan where in urban literacy stood at 75.1, which is far more than just 46.5 per cent in rural Rajasthan.

CHART 4

Literacy By Social Groups

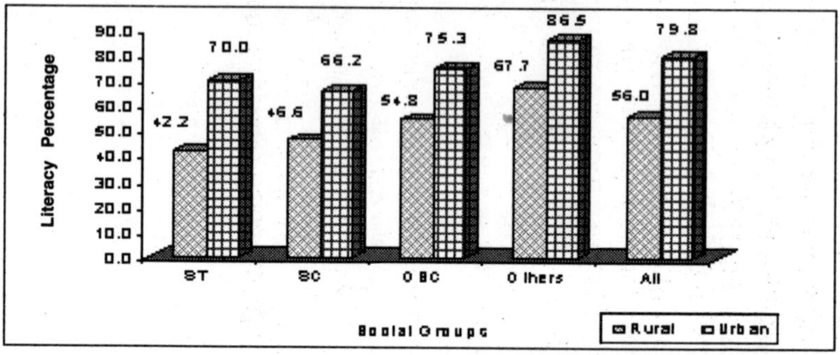

(vi) Disparities of Literacy among Religious Groups

This Table 4 shows the distribution of persons aged 7 years and above by each sector and religions. It is noticed that the literacy rate was lower in rural India for 'Muslims' compared to other religious groups. Literacy rate for all the religious groups, as revealed for the first time in 2001 Census, were very encouraging, shattering many myths earlier when such a data set was not available for the country as a whole. The literacy rate among Hindus (65.1%) was slightly better than the national average (64.8%) for all religious groups combined. Among Muslims the literacy rate is 59.1%, below the national average. The highest literacy rate is recorded among the Jains (94.1%), followed by Christians (80.3%), Buddhists (72.7%) and Sikhs (69.4%). Against the existing popular perceptions, the female literacy rate among different religious groups does not show wide variations. Among the Muslims, for instance, the literacy rate among the females was stagnant at 50.1 per cent, below the national average of 53.7 per cent. Slightly better is the female literacy rate among the Hindus (53.2%), again below the national average. The highest literacy rate among the females was recorded among

TABLE 4

Percentage of Literate Persons Aged 7 Years and above in Religious Groups Based on 55th Rounds

State	*Hinduism*		*Islam*		*Christianity*		*Others*		*All*	
	Rural	*Urban*	*Rural*	*Urban*	*Rural*	*Urban*	*Rural*	*Urban*	*Rural*	*Urban*
AP	45.4	75.0	51.0	70.7	51.5	78.9	55.5	96.1	45.8	74.5
Assam	74.5	87.0	59.4	79.7	53.5	80.5	85.7	-	69.0	86.1
Bihar	42.6	70.7	36.1	61.1	44.7	83.5	41.3	96.0	41.8	69.6
Gujarat	61.8	83.7	69.1	82.7	62.5	94.2	-	-	62.0	84.1
Haryana	61.7	76.9	31.0	54.5	-	-	-	-	61.2	76.6
HP	73.7	90.2	56.9	73.6	-	-	83.2	-	73.4	90.2
Karnataka	55.3	82.9	63.2	77.1	68.0	95.5	52.0	73.4	55.9	82.1
Kerala	88.4	94.2	87.2	91.0	95.1	95.8	-	-	89.4	93.7
MP	49.1	77.5	60.3	73.6	66.5	89.1	-	61.3	49.8	77.5
Maharashta	66.2	87.3	67.1	79.9	61.4	95.3	76.4	86.6	66.5	86.0
Orissa	53.7	76.6	67.1	56.7	48.5	63.7	62.6	-	53.8	75.5
Punjab	68.4	79.2	62.9	65.4	44.2	77.7	84.7	-	62.5	78.9
Rajasthan	46.7	76.0	38.4	64.9	-	100.00	47.8	92.6	46.5	75.1
Tamil Nadu	61.7	84.3	84.1	81.6	83.6	91.2	-	90.6	63.8	84.5
UP	52.9	76.8	38.9	52.6	66.4	100.00	37.6	59.7	51.1	70.1
WB	65.5	84.3	53.7	66.6	79.6	91.8	57.7	87.3	61.7	82.2
All-India	55.7	81.1	52.1	69.8	73.7	91.1	54.2	87.1	56.0	79.8

Source: NSSO Report No. 473: Literacy and Levels of Education in India, 1999-2000, Tables 3R and 3U.

the Jains (90.6%), like their male counterparts. Female literacy rate among Christians was 76.2 per cent, followed by Sikhs (63.1%) and Buddhists (61.7%) (Census, 2001).

CHART 5

Literacy Rate among Religious Based on 55th Rounds NSSO

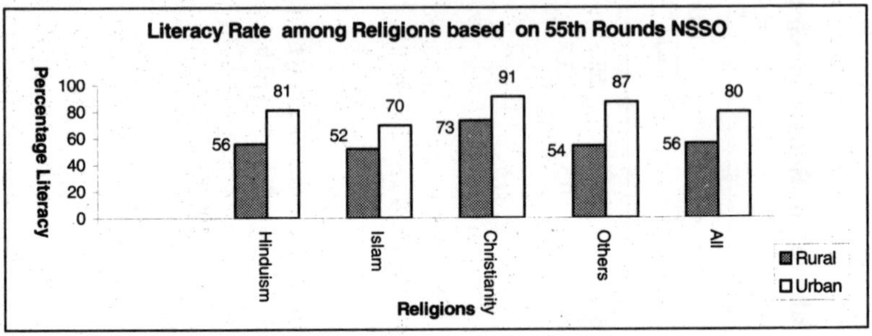

The 55th Round NSSO Report reveals the difference in literacy indifferent religious communities. The literacy rate in Christians is the highest both in rural as well as urban areas. Hindus stand at the second place whereas Muslims occupy the third place with 52 and 70 per cent literacy respectively in rural as well as urban areas.

CHART 6

Literacy Rate among Urban Hindus and Muslims

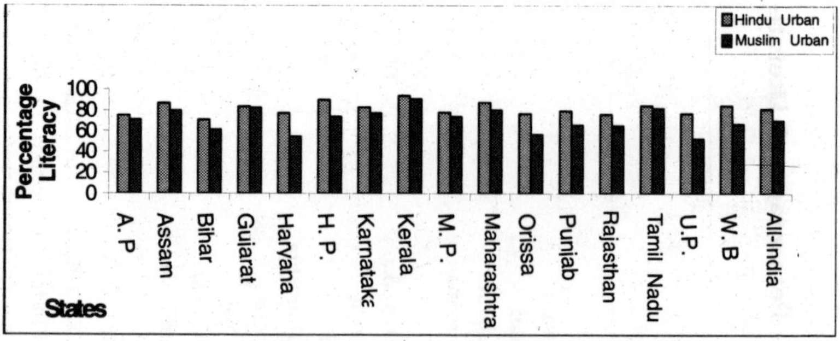

(vii) Disparities in Student-Teacher Ratio

Only 5 out of 29 States and UTs have above 40:1 Pupil-Teacher Ratio in Primary schools. The heaviest student-teacher ratio in primary schools is observed in Bihar (76:1), followed by UP (74:1), Jharkhand (54:1) and WB (50:1). Bihar too has a high ratio both in case of Government (76) and Private managed (78) schools. In addition, many schools are single-teacher and single classroom schools. Student-classroom ratio is analyzed as heavy as 91 in case of Bihar and 65 in UP. On an average, the student-classroom ratio in a primary school is 45:1, which, in other school types, is lower than that in Primary schools. In Bihar it is not only student-classroom ratio in Primary schools that is high but pupil-teacher ratio is also very high in the case of independent Elementary schools (85:1), Upper Primary schools (68) and Higher Secondary schools (62:1).

CHART 7

Literacy Rate among Rural Hindus and Muslims

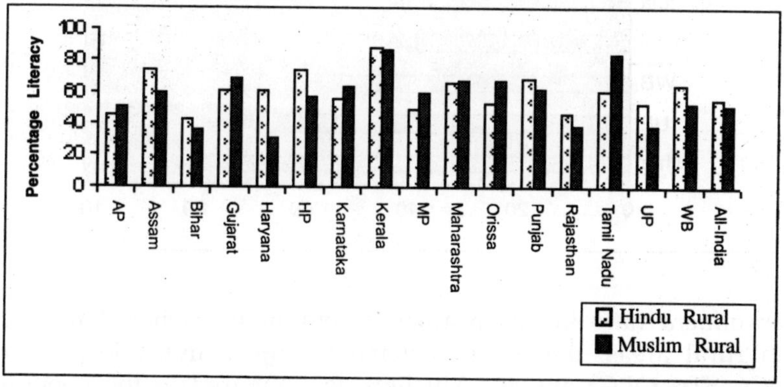

(viii) Regional Disparities in Gross Enrolment Ratio in Higher Education (All Categories, 18-24 Years) in year 2004-05

Gross enrolment ratio (GER), as defined by UNESCO, designates a nation's total enrolment "in a specific level of education, regardless of age, expressed as a percentage of the population in the official age group corresponding to the level of education." In the country as a whole, gross

CHART 8

Disparities between Teacher-Pupil Ratio in Year 2005

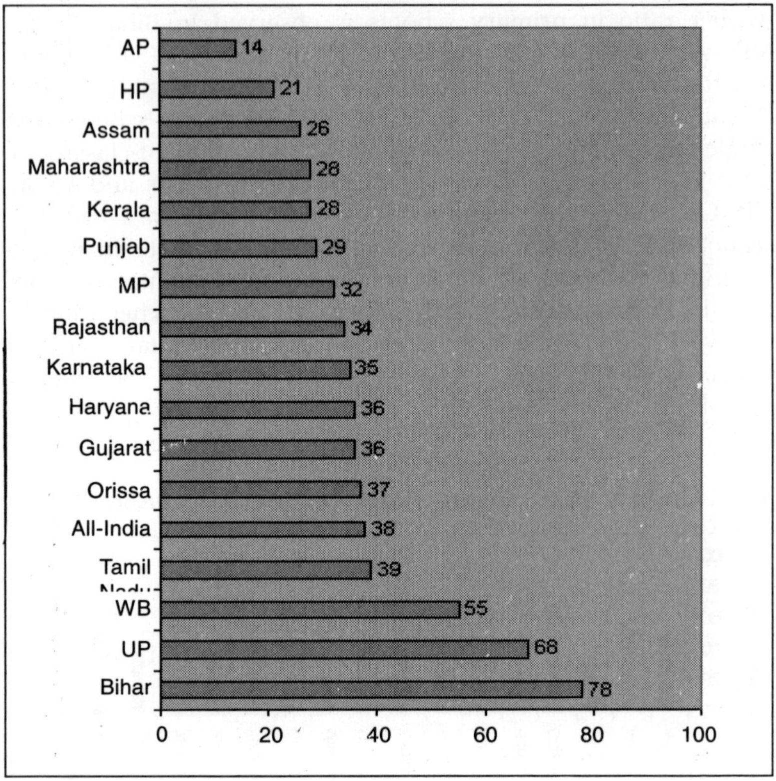

enrolment ratio in urban areas is four times higher than that in rural areas; the gross enrolment ratio is much lower for SCs, STs, OBCs and for Muslims as compared to the general population; the ratio is 11 per cent for females as compared to over 15 per cent for males; the poor also have a low gross enrolment ratio, that is one fifth of that of the non-poor. Enrolment rates have increased from 0.2 per cent in 1947-48, to 2.0 per cent in year 1970-71, 4.4 per cent in year 1990-91 to 10 per cent in 2005-06. According to the NSS survey and Population Census, if diploma and certificate courses are also included, then the ratio has increased to about 13-14 per cent.

TABLE 5

Pupil-Teacher Ratio by School Category in Indian States in 2005

States	*Primary Only*	*Upper Primary with Sec./H/Sec.*	*All Schools*
AP	28	19	14
Assam	34	21	26
Bihar	76	40	78
Gujarat	31	33	36
Haryana	44	25	36
HP	21	24	21
Karnataka	25	31	35
Kerala	26	36	28
MP	36	29	32
Maharashtra	30	23	28
Orissa	36	37	37
Punjab	37	24	29
Rajasthan	37	26	34
Tamil Nadu	34	50	39
UP	74	60	68
WB	50	68	55
All-India	42	31	38

Source: NIEPA-2006.

With an aim to increase the Gross Enrolment Ratio in higher education institutions from the current 10 per cent to 15 per cent by the end of 11 th Five Year Plan (2011-12) and to bring more equity in the education system, the University Grant Commission will increase the number of universities and colleges across the country to add to the present intake capacity.

Chinese higher education has expanded rapidly over the past decade-with gross enrolment rates increasing from 3.4 per cent in 1990 to 7.2 per cent in 1995, and to 11 per cent in 2000. Quantitative growth continued till date and reached 22 per cent in year 2006. China started to control excessive enrolment in 2006, and to invest its effort on

TABLE 6

Gross Enrolment Ratio in Higher Education (18-24 years)

	Boys	*Girls*	*Total*
Andhra Pradesh	14.57	8.55	11.52
Arunachal Pradesh	7.12	4.50	5.85
Assam	8.17	5.70	6.94
Bihar	8.44	3.19	6.02
Chhattisgarh	9.43	5.54	7.51
Gujarat	11.88	9.29	10.67
Haryana	11.07	10.06	10.63
Himachal Pradesh	14.59	13.58	14.10
Jammu & Kashmir	6.76	6.29	6.54
Jharkhand	8.66	5.32	7.05
Karnataka	12.72	10.36	11.58
Kerala	8.15	9.96	9.08
Madhya Pradesh	14.15	7.40	11.02
Maharashtra	15.17	10.92	13.24
Orissa	13.62	3.48	8.59
Punjab	9.40	11.23	10.24
Rajasthan	7.55	4.31	6.04
Tamil Nadu	13.03	9.95	11.47
Uttar Pradesh	9.21	6.84	8.13
Uttaranchal	13.22	12.70	12.97
West Bengal	10.00	6.09	8.09
Chandigarh	30.93	46.12	37.01
Delhi	33.15	42.94	37.25
All-India	11.58	8.17	9.97

improving the quality of higher education. In 2006, 7.24 million Chinese entered colleges. By the end of 2006, there were 25 million college students in China, The number of post-graduate students reached 1,100,000 for the first time in 2006, a 12.88 per cent growth from 2005. The trends of GER in China can be seen in Figure 5.

In developed countries population growth is very low and the growth in infrastructures is higher than that in developing countries. So the gross enrolment of developed countries are much higher than in developing countries. GER

CHART 9

State-wise Gross Enrolment in Higher Education, 2005

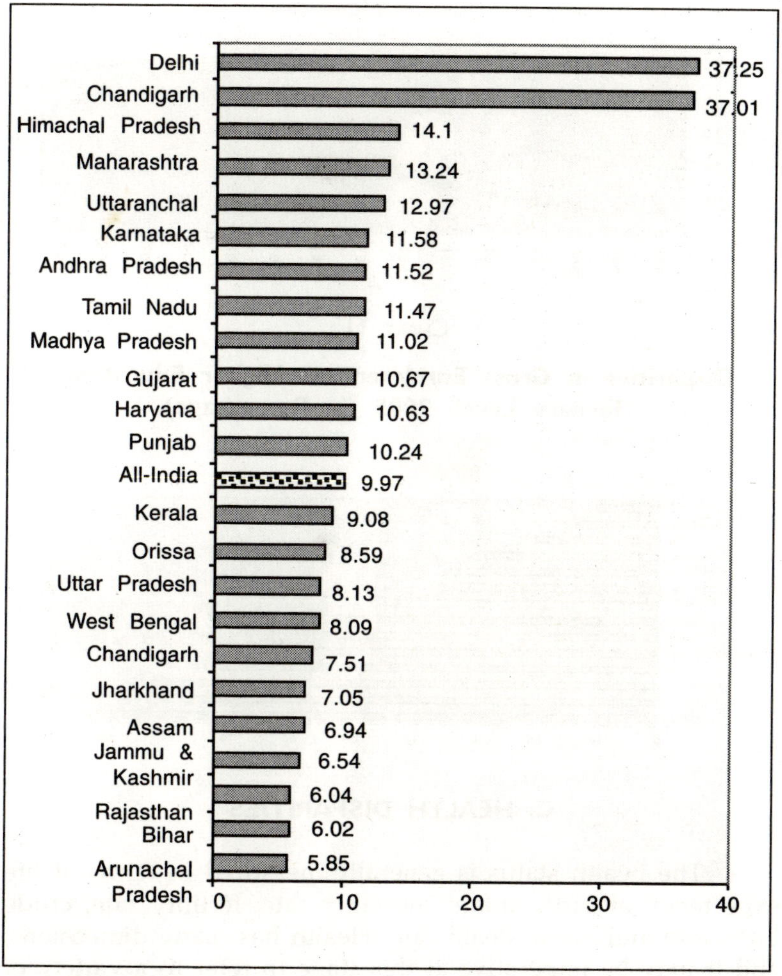

at Tertiary level of Developed countries like Korea, United States, Australia are more than seven-eight times than those in the developing country like India. Gross enrolment ratio at higher education of some developed and developing countries can be seen in Chart 11.

CHART 10

Trends of GER in China's Higher Education

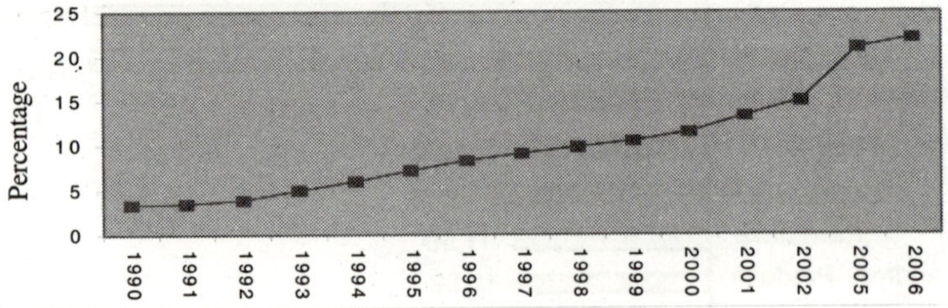

CHART 11

Disparities in Gross Enrolment at Higher Education/ Tertiary Level, 2005 (in Percentage)

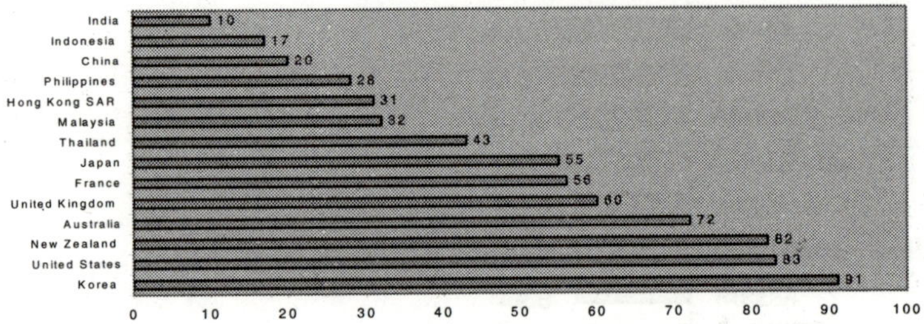

C. HEALTH DISPARITIES

The health status is generally measured in terms of life expectancy at birth, Infant mortality rate, fertility rate, crude birth rate and crude death rate. Health has many dimensions, and it may be imperative at this stage to refer to a variety of indicators of health status rather than select one as preferred. The most commonly cited health indicator is life expectancy. It has the appeal of an intrinsic capability on which personal welfare depends (Sen, 1998) According to WHO, health is a state of complete physical, mental and social well-being and not merely the absence of disease or infirmity. The indicators

TABLE 7

States	*Population 2001*	*Per Capita GSDP (Rs.) current prices*	*Literacy 2001*	*Birth Rate/ 1000 (2000)*	*Death Rate/ 1000 (2000)*	*IMR/ 1000 (2000)*	*Per capita Public health expenditure in 2001-02*	*Life expectancy at Birth (1998-2002)*
AP	76,210,007	19877	60.47	21.30	8.20	65.00	179,45	63.5
Assam	26,655,528	12886	63.25	26.90	9.60	75.00	135.14	57.9
Bihar	82,998,509	5677	47.00	31.90	8.80	62.00	66.13	60.8
Gujarat	50,671,017	23887	69.14	25.20	7.50	62.00	143.82	63.4
Haryana	21,144,564	28642	67.91	26.90	7.50	67.00	152.25	65.2
HP	6,077,900	24628	76.48	22.10	7.20	60.00	130.50	65.1
Karnataka	52,850,562	20627	66.64	22.00	7.80	57.00	205.45	64.5
Kerala	31,841,374	22738	90.86	17.90	6.40	14.00	237.45	73.5
MP	60,348,023	13950	76.88	31.40	10.30	87.00	84.77	56.9
Maharashta	96,878,627	27550	63.74	21.00	7.50	48.00	189.39	66.2
Orissa	36,804,660	11438.	63.08	24.30	10.50	95.00	122.15	58.5
Punjab	24,358,999	29113.	69.65	21.60	7.40	52.00	253.83	68.5
Rajasthan	56,507,188	15587	60.41	31.40	8.50	79.00	176.45	61.1
Tamil Nadu	62,405,679	23004	73.45	19.30	7.90	51.00	195.44	65.2
UP	166,197,921	10909	56.27	32.80	10.30	83.00	78.80	59.1
WB	80,176,197	19191	68.64	20.70	7.00	51.00	176.26	63.9
All-India	1028610000	17947	65.49	25.80	8.50	68.00	184.97	62.5

Source: Computed from SRS Bulletin, Various years and National Health Account India 2001-02, MOH and FW, GOI (2005).

of health status, the birth and death rates are more reflective of the demographic changes taking place in the country. The life expectancy and the infant mortality rate are better indicators of the health status of the population. A look at the relationship among these four indicators is sufficient enough to confirm that these indicators are inter-dependent over the time.

The National Health Policy (NHP), 2002 has set out the basic objective of achieving good health and providing best level of living to all population of the country . Accordingly, the targets are to reduce the Maternal Mortality Rate (MMR)

CHART 12

Disparities of Birth Rates/1000 in Year 2001-02

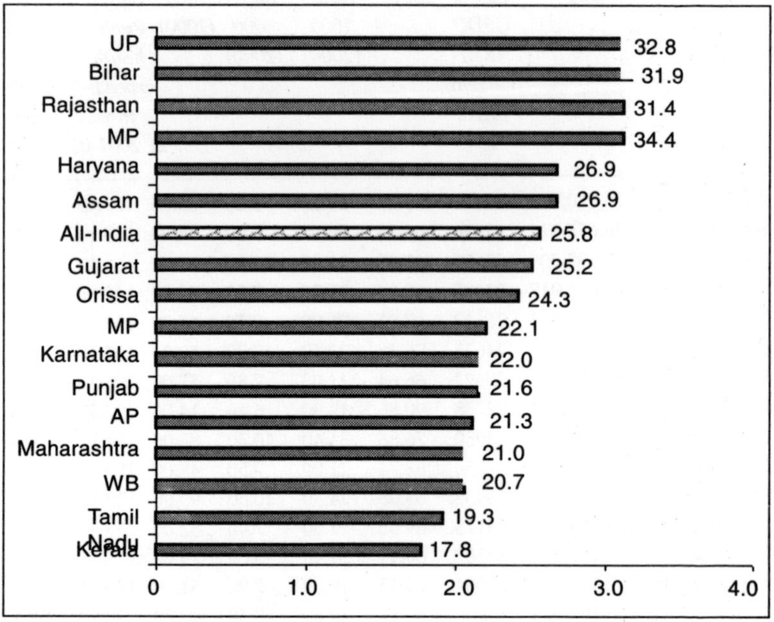

to 100 per 100,000 live births by 2012; the Total Fertility Rate (TFR) to be reduced to 2.1 by 2012; and the Infant Mortality Rate (IMR) to be reduced to 30 per 1000 live births by 2012. The data of National Family Health Survey (NFHS-3) shows malnutrition status of Indian kids and say that as many as 45.9 per cent of children are under weight, 38.4 per cent stunted and 19.1 per cent are wasted. The figure for Anemia are even more alarming. 79 per cent of kids aged between six and 35 months are anemic whereas 56 per cent of women aged between 15-49 are anemic.

(i) Crude Birth Rate

The Crude Birth Rate (CBR) is defined as the number of live births in a year per 1000 of the mid-year population. The Crude Birth Rate is called "crude" because it does not take into account age or sex differences among the population.

CHART 13

Disparities of Death Rates/1000 in Year 2001-02

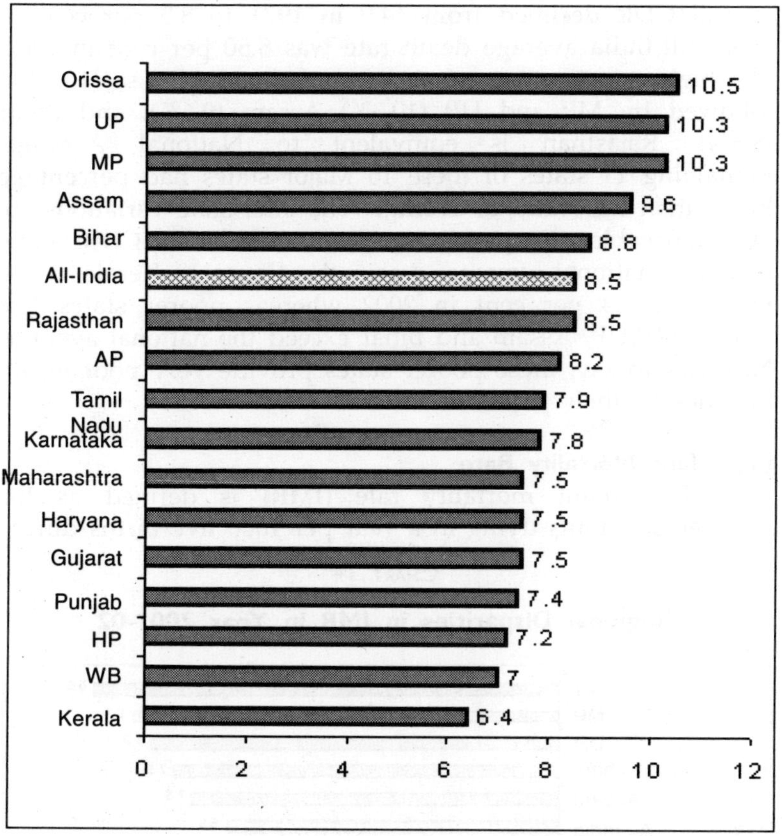

All-India average birth rate was 25.80 per cent in 2002. The highest percentage of such rate being in UP (32.8%) followed by Bihar (31.9%), MP and Rajasthan (31.4%), Assam and Haryana (26.9%),. Gujarat is near to National Average. Remaining 10 states of these 16 Major states had percentage lower than the National average. The inter-state variations are also noticeable. Comparatively richer states have CBR below than the national average. Again the figure in Kerala is the lowest at 17.9 per cent in 2002 whereas poorer states like, MP, UP, Assam, Rajasthan and Bihar exceed the national average.

(ii) Crude Death Rate

The Crude Death Rate (CDR) is defined as the number of deaths in a year per 1000 of the mid year population. The overall CDR declined from 14.9 in 1971 to 8.5 per cent in 2002. All-India average death rate was 8.50 per cent in 2002. The highest percentage of such rate being in Orissa (10.50%) followed by MP and UP (10.3%) Assam (9.6%), and Bihar (8.8%). Rajasthan is equivalent to National Average. Remaining 11 states of these 16 Major states had percentage lower than the National average. The inter-state variations are also noticeable. Comparatively richer states have CDR below than the national average. Again the figure in Kerala is the lowest at 6.4 per cent in 2002 whereas poorer states like Orissa, MP,UP, Assam and Bihar exceed the national average. Needless to say, these poorer states provide very poor health facilities to their population.

(iii) Infant Mortality Rate

The infant mortality rate (IMR) is defined as the number of infants dying in a year per 1000 live births during

CHART 14

Regional Disparities in IMR in Year 2001-02

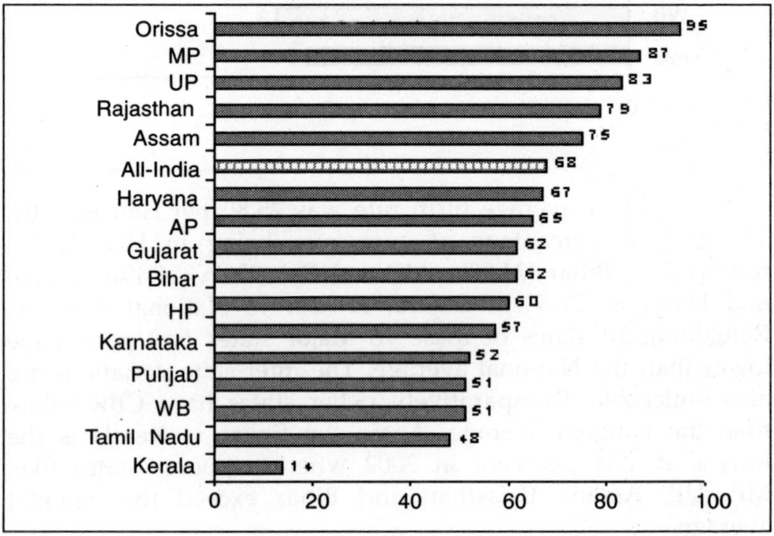

the year. IMR was reported to be 79 per 1000 live births in 1991-92 and now it has reduced to 58 per 1000 live births in 2004. The main causes of death are diseases of circulatory system, infections and parasitic diseases, injury, poisoning, pre-natal conditions, and diseases of respiratory system. The main constraints are low literacy and income levels, socio-cultural beliefs and practices, and sub optimal utilization of health facilities. The infant mortality rate is also called the infant death rate.

There is a wide inter-state disparity in infant mortality rates. All-India average Infant mortality Rate (IMR) was 6.8 per cent in 2002. The highest percentage of such rate being in Orissa (9.5%) followed by MP (8.7%), UP (8.3%) Assam (9.6%), Rajasthan (7.9%). Haryana is equivalent to National Average. Remaining 11 states of these 16 Major states had percentage lower than the National average. The inter-state variations are also noticeable. Comparatively richer states have IMR below than the national average. Again the figure in Kerala is the lowest at 1.4 per cent in 2002 whereas poorer states like Orissa, MP, UP, Assam exceed the national average. Needless to say, these poorer states provide very poor health facilities to their population

The infant mortality rate in India is steadily decreasing; IMR is currently estimated at 57 deaths before the age of one year per 1000 live births, down from NFHS-II estimate of 68 and NFHS-I estimate of 79. IMR in rural areas is 50 per cent higher than that in urban areas. Children whose mothers have no education are more than twice as likely to die before their first birth days as children whose mothers have completed at least 10 years of schooling. (GOI, 2007).

61.3 per cent of infant deaths in rural areas is directly or indirectly related to maternal/child malnutrition, viz., Prematurity (30%), Pneumonia (14.5%), Respiratory Infection (11%), Anemia (2.9%), Diarrhoea (2.9%). (Rao, 2008).

(iv) Life Expectancy

India has made substantial progress in terms of health indicators over the past few decades. Life expectancy increased from 54 year in 1980 to 64.7 years in 2006. This increase in life expectancy is the result of an overall decline

CHART 15

Disparities in Life Expectency (LE) in Year 1998-02

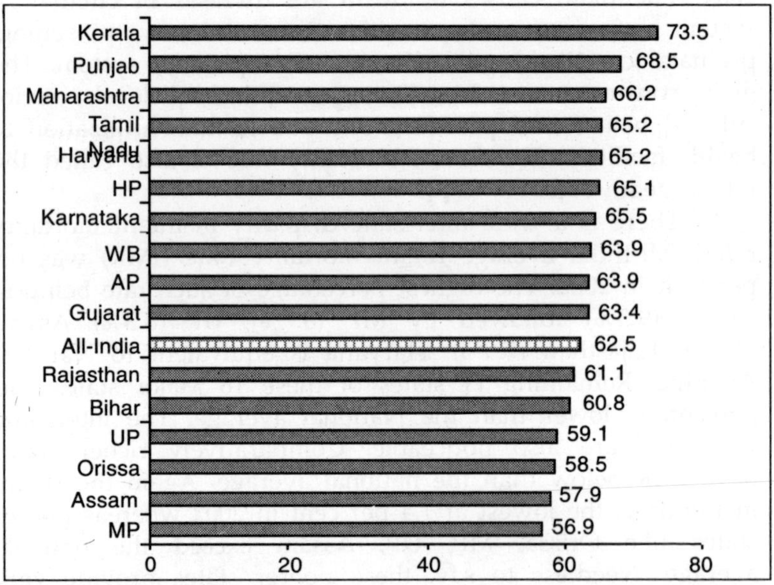

in mortality. Japan has the highest life expectancy in the world and on an average a Japanese is expected to live 19 more years than a South Asian (Haq, 2004). Knowles and Owen (1997) and Jamison and Wang (1998) find that life expectancy contributes to economic growth more than education. This is obvious as higher life expectancy means sound health, better physical strength and lesser mandays' loss due to illness.

Life expectancy at birth has increased for male and female in India. It is 64.1 years for males and 65.8 years for females (2005). This has revealed the decrease in death rate and the better improvement of quantity and quality health services in India. In Kerala, a person at birth is expected to live for 73 years while in states like Bihar, Assam, Madhya Pradesh, Uttar Pradesh, etc. the expectancy is in the range of 55-60 years.

All-India average Life expectancy (LE) was 62.5 year in 1998-02.. The highest percentage of such rate being in Kerala

TABLE 8

Public and Private Expenditure on Health in Indian States, 2001-02

States	*Per-capita Expenditure in Rs.*			*Pub. Exp. as % of Total Exp.*	*Private Exp. as % of Total Exp.*
	Public	*Private*	*Total*		
AP	182	857	1039	17.5	82.5
Assam	176	393	569	30.9	69.1
Bihar	92	687	779	11.8	88.2
Gujarat	147	670	816	18.0	82.0
Haryana	163	1408	1570	10.4	89.6
HP	493	812	1305	37.8	62.2
Karnataka	206	506	712	28.9	71.1
Kerala	240	1618	1858	12.9	87.1
MP	132	733	864	15.3	84.7
Maharashta	196	815	1011	19.4	80.6
Orissa	134	449	582	23.0	77.0
Punjab	258	1273	1530	16.9	83.1
Rajasthan	182	415	597	30.5	69.5
Tamil Nadu	202	644	846	23.9	76.1
UP	84	1040	1124	7.5	92.5
WB	181	593	775	23.4	76.6
All-India	207	790	997	20.8	79.2

Source; National Health Account India, 2001-02.

(73.5 years) followed by Punjab 68.5 year, Maharashtra (66.2 years), TN (65.2 years), Haryana and HP (65.2 years). Rajasthan is near to National Average. Remaining 6 states of these 16 Major states average life expectancy had lower than the National average. The inter-state variations are also noticeable. Comparatively richer states have LE above than the national average. Again the figure in Kerala is the highest at 73.5 years in 1998-02. whereas poorer states like Orissa, MP, UP, Assam below the national average. However, there are inter-state, inter-district and rural-urban differences in life expectancy at birth due to low literacy, differential income levels and socuo-economic conditions and beliefs.

CHART 16

Public and Private Expenditure on Health, 2001-02

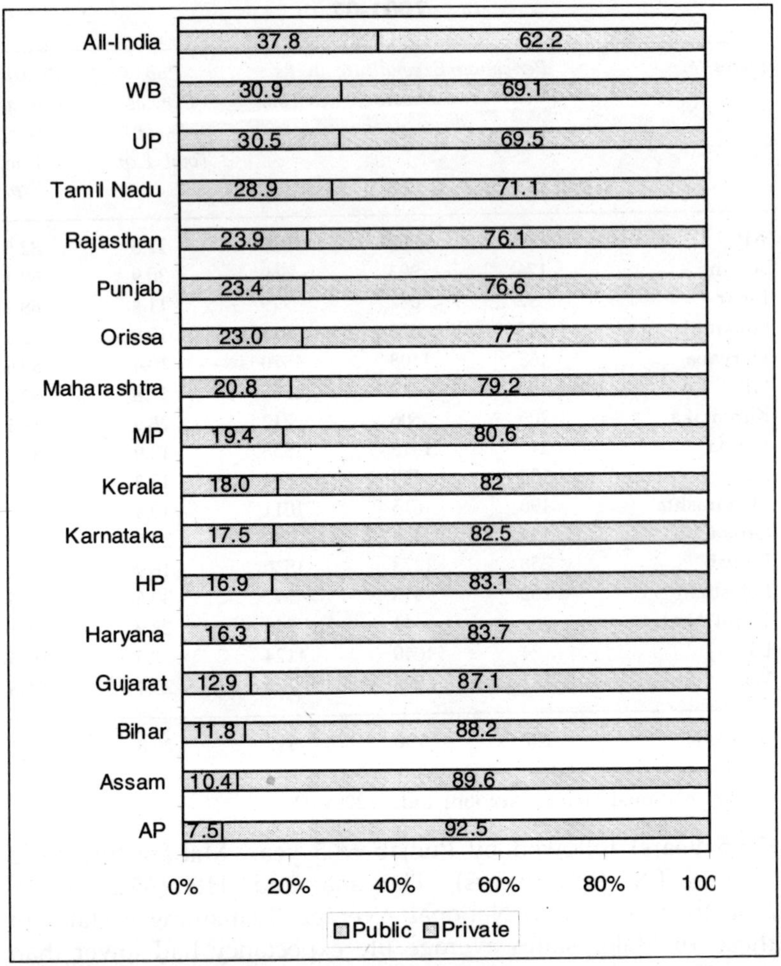

(v) Disparities of Expenditure on Health

The private and public expenditure in states has been presented in table 08 and Chart 16. Per-capita health expenditure in India during 2001-02 was Rs. 997 (Chart 17) of which public expenditure amounted to Rs. 207 and private expenditure to Rs. 790. The per-capita health expenditure of major states for the year 2001-02 indicated that the level of

TABLE 9

Disparities on Health Expenditure in Various Countries, 2001

Countries	*Total expenditure on health as % of GDP*	*Government expenditure on health as % of total expenditure on health*	*Private expenditure on health expenditure on health as % of total*
UK	7.7	83.4	16.6
Germany	10.9	78.5	21.5
France	9.7	76	24
Canada	9.6	69.9	30.1
Malaysia	3.8	53.8	46.2
Sri Lanka	3.7	48.9	51.1
Thailand	4.4	46.7	53.3
Brazil	7.9	45.9	54.1
USA	14.6	44.9	55.1
Bangaladesh	3.1	44.2	55.8
Indonesia	3.2	36	64
China	5.8	33.7	66.3
Nepal	5.2	29.7	70.3
Pakistan	3.2	24.4	75.6
India	5.1	17.9	82.1

Source: WHO, 2003, World Health Report, 2005.

CHART 17

Public-Private Expenditure on Health, 2001-02

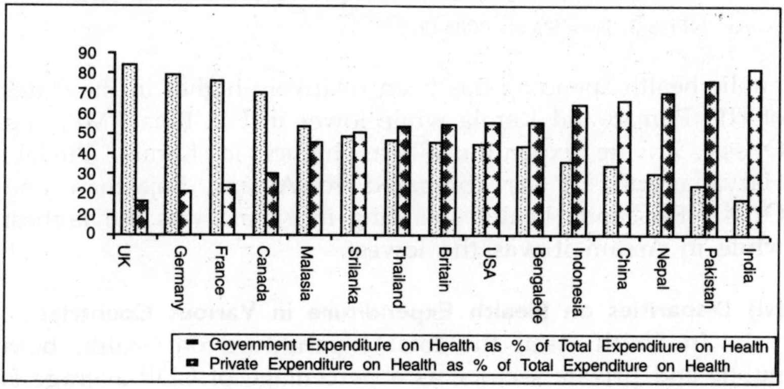

TABLE 10

Stunting/Wasting/Underweight among Children Under 3 in Major States

Sr. No.	*Major States*	*Key Indicators (NFHS-3)*		
		Children under-3 who are	*Children under-3 stunted (%)*	*Children under-3 who are under-weight (%)*
1.	Assam	34.8	13.1	40.4
2.	Bihar	42.3	27.7	58.4
3.	Chhattisgarh	45.4	17.9	52.1
4.	Gujarat	42.4	17.0	47.4
5.	HP	26.6	18.8	36.2
6.	J&K	27.6	15.4	29.4
7.	Jharkhand	41.0	31.1	59.2
8.	Karnataka	38.0	17.9	41.1
9.	Kerala	21.1	16.1	28.8
10.	MP	39.9	33.3	60.3
11.	Maharashtra	37.9	14.6	39.7
12.	Orissa	38.3	18.5	44.0
13.	Punjab	27.9	9.0	27.0
14.	Rajasthan	33.7	19.7	44.0
15.	TN	25.1	21.5	33.2
16.	UP	46.0	13.5	47.3
	All-India	38.4	19.1	45.9

Source: NFHS-3, Fact Sheet (2005-06).

public health spending has been relatively higher in the states of HP, Punjab and Kerala while lower in UP, Bihar, MP, and Orissa. Private expenditure was higher in Kerala, Punjab, Haryana and UP as compared to Assam, Rajasthan and Orissa. Per-capita health spending in Kerala was the highest while in Assam it was the lowest.

(vi) Disparities on Health Expenditure in Various Countries

In South Asia, the total expenditure on health, both public and private sectors, as a percentage of GDP average is

4.8 per cent. Private sector is the major provider of health services, accounting to the 78 per cent of total expenditure. Per-capita expenditure is also the lowest in the world. High-income country's spending on health is more than 10 per cent of GDP. Maldives is the only country in South Asia, which is spending more than six per cent on health as a percentage of GDP. Lack of access is one of the major failures of the health system in South Asia. Access to safe drinking water, Sanitation, health facilities, doctors and transport facilities are limited.

(vii) Disparities in Nutritional Status of Children

Stunting (deficit in height for age), Wasting (deficit in weight for height) and Under Weight (deficit in weight for age) are three critical indicators for determining the nutritional status of children. NFHS-3 provides a picture of nutritional status of children in major states. This can see in Table 10.

The NFHS-3 data reveal that 46 per cent of children below 3 years of age are underweight, 38 per cent are stunted and 19 per cent are wasted. It is a matter of grave concern for the optimal development of our human resources that are the greatest asset for any country. It is logical to forecast that this group of children will never achieve their complete physical and cognitive potential, will have poor health, and remain within the poverty trap as adults. In addition to the causes stated in connection with low birth weight and mortality rates, lack of exclusive breast feeding for the first six months, poor quality of breast milk on account of maternal malnutrition, delayed complementary feeding, inadequate calorie protein intake, poor caring practices, ignorance regarding proper dietary intake even within the purchasing power of the family, infections and disease, are predominant causes for the high percentage of underweight, stunted and wasted children.

According to the recent global report on the status of children, India has higher rate of undernutrition among children below five years of age (48% of children have stunting and 43% of them have under weight) than whole of sub-Saharan Africa (38% and 28% stunting and underweight respectively) despite having higher per-capita income as well as Dross Domestic Product than any individual country of that region (UNICEF, 2008)

It is equally a cause of concern that improvements in the indicators of stunted and underweight children in the last decade have been marginal nationally and in certain States they have been negative Karnataka (stunting), Bihar, Gujarat, Himachal Pradesh, Jammu & Kashmir, Kerala, Madhya Pradesh, Punjab, Rajasthan, Tamil Nadu and Uttar Pradesh (wasting), Assam, Bihar, Gujarat, Jharkhand, Kerala, Madhya Pradesh, (underweight). Though some States such as Assam, Bihar, Chhattisgarh, Himachal Pradesh, Jammu & Kashmir, Madhya Pradesh, Punjab and Rajasthan have shown improvement of more than 10 per cent in reduction of stunting of children Under 3 and Underweight Children .

(viii) Disparities in Anemia among Children

High prevalence of anemia also indicates that it is not limited to below poverty line population only. Its causes are heterogeneous, both for the poor as well as those with low purchasing power. NFHS-3 data indicates that there has been an alarming increase in the prevalence of anemia in the national average and in all States except Chhattisgarh, Jammu & Kashmir, Jharkhand, Maharashtra, Rajasthan. (Chart 18).

CHART 18

Anemia among Children (06-35 Months) in Major States, 2005-06

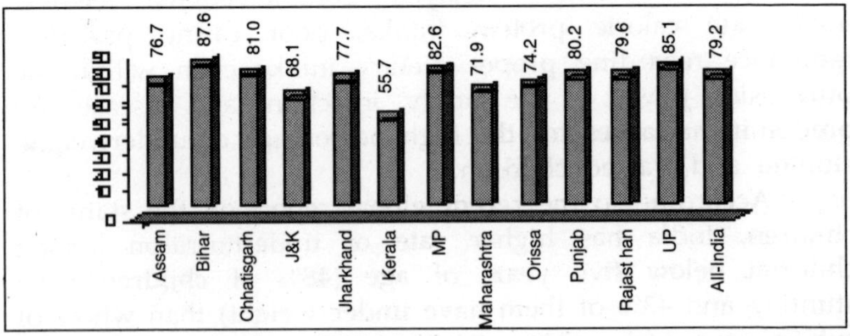

Source: NFHS-3 Fact Sheet (2005-06)

The major reasons for incidence of anemia may be attributed to late complementary feeding, lack of awareness and information regarding the importance of iron rich foods for children, worm infestation, unsafe drinking water and poor sanitary conditions, prolonged infection and diarrhoea, lack of fortification and supplementation in the diets of the poor, and unhealthy eating habits among families with purchasing power.

D. HOUSING DISPARITIES

(i) Disparities in Type of Structure of Housing

The National Sample Survey Organisation collects data on housing conditions and also gives us a statewise break ups. Structure of the housing not only reflects the levels of living condition of the HH and its members but also has a bearing upon the health conditions of the members of HH. The distribution of HHs by type of structure of their housing units by each HH for the rural and urban areas statewise can be seen in the Table 11.

Roti, Kapara and Makan are the three most basic needs of mankind. In terms of housing, the picture in Indian states is not good and that is evident by the data collected by NSSO 60th Round in the first half of the year 2004. On an average 48 per cent HHs in India live in Pucca houses, 33 per cent in semi-pucca and 19 per cent HHs live in kuccha houses in rural areas. The scene in urban areas is obviously better, where in 84.2 per cent HHs live in Pucca, 11.5 per cent in semi-pucca and around 4 per cent HHs dwell in kuccha houses.

There are some states like Haryana and Punjab where in 94 per cent and 84 per cent rural HHs respectively afford to take selteer in pucca houses. The figure for urban areas in thse two ststes are 97.5 per cent and 91.3 per cent HHs. But all is not well in many poor states. In state like Orissa, Assam and Bihar 50 per cent, 40 per cent and 31 per cent rural HHs are destined to dwell in Kuccha houses. Other state such as WB, UP, TN, Rajasthan, Jharkhand and J and K the kuccha houses are available to more HHs than the all-India figure of 18.8 per cent of kuccha houses. In the urban areas some states like Uttaranchal, Haryana, Chhattisgarh and

TABLE 11

Per 1000 Distribution of HHs by Structure of Dwelling for Major States

Sr. No.	States	Rural				Urban			
		Pucca	Semi-Pucca	Kuccha	Total	Pucca	Semi-Pucca	Kuccha	Total
1.	AP	616	181	203	1000	864	70	66	1000
2.	Assam	165	433	402	1000	622	311	64	1000
3.	Bihar	431	255	313	1000	825	60	114	1000
4.	Chhattisgarh	91	894	15	1000	706	281	8	1000
5.	Gujarat	594	349	57	1000	926	57	16	1000
6.	Haryana	940	34	26	1000	975	18	7	1000
7.	HP	723	251	26	1000	843	89	68	1000
8.	J & K	352	444	204	1000	714	227	59	1000
9.	Jharkhand	220	564	214	1000	809	170	21	1000
10.	Karnataka	466	473	60	1000	746	224	29	1000
11.	Kerala	730	198	72	1000	847	129	24	1000
12.	Madhya Pradesh	313	588	99	1000	788	196	15	1000
13.	Maharashtra	532	418	50	1000	864	117	19	1000
14.	Orissa	209	289	502	1000	651	153	189	1000
15.	Punjab	840	135	26	1000	913	63	24	1000
16.	Rajasthan	596	214	189	1000	961	29	9	1000
17.	TN	535	217	248	1000	779	119	102	1000
18.	UP	561	244	195	1000	868	88	44	1000
19.	Uttaranchal	837	14	149	1000	968	29	3	1000
20.	WB	262	469	269	1000	789	166	45	1000
	All-India	480	332	188	1000	842	115	43	1000

Source: NSSO 60th Round, Report No. 507, January-June 2004,

Rajasthan correspounding figures for HHs living in kuccha houses are 3 per cent, 7 per cent, 8 per cent and 9 per cent respectively. But in states like Orissa, Bihar and Tamil Nadu 18.9 per cent, 11.4 per cent and 10.2 per cent HHs are destined to live in kuccha houses. The type of houses where in the rural and urban HHs live reflect not only the economic status but also showing the level of living of peoples.

TABLE 12

Distribution of Households by Major Source of Drinking Water: 2004

Sr. No.	States	*Per 1000 distribution of HHs by Major Sources of Drinking Water (Rural India)*				*Per 1000 distribution of HHs by Major Sources of Drinking Water (Urban India)*			
		Tap	*Tube well/ Hand Pump*	*Pucca well*	*Others**	*Tap*	*Tube well/ Hand Pump*	*Pucca well*	*Others**
1.	AP	572	279	99	50	783	127	25	65
2.	Assam	63	609	201	127	321	494	164	21
3.	Bihar	23	925	46	6	310	680	9	1
4.	Chhattisgarh	48	763	164	25	688	230	68	14
5.	Gujarat	470	386	88	56	859	91	2	48
6.	Haryana	445	446	94	15	752	229	11	8
7.	HP	758	56	25	161	819	53	4	124
8.	J&K	493	157	12	338	859	48	0	93
9.	Jharkhand	19	473	458	50	435	331	185	49
10.	Karnataka	563	307	104	26	815	117	20	48
11.	Kerala	107	62	766	65	347	49	591	13
12.	MP	116	625	237	22	648	278	48	26
13.	Maharashtra	415	259	213	113	879	55	27	39
14.	Orissa	64	718	183	35	492	278	221	9
15.	Punjab	302	687	4	7	682	239	0	79
16.	Rajasthan	236	493	133	138	828	99	23	50
17.	TN	815	100	48	37	691	58	13	238
18.	Uttaranchal	614	269	1	116	894	41	0	65
19.	UP	39	883	75	3	407	585	6	2
20.	WB	67	854	65	14	575	398	12	15
	India	248	564	139	49	676	224	44	56

*Others included bottle water, tanker, tank, pond, river, cannal, etc.
Source: NSSO, Report No. 507, January-June 2004, pp. 38-39.

(ii) State-wise Disparities in Source of Drinking Water

Sources of drinking water are the clear indicators of levels of living. Water-related diseases include those due to micro-organisms and chemicals in water people drink, diseases like malaria, Diarrhoea, Hepatitis, Cholera, Fluorosis, Dengue, etc. They highly affect the levels of living in society. Quality of Drinking water is also an important determinant of level of living to the HHs.

As per NSS report, highest proportion of rural HHs having hand pump/tube well as a source of drinking water, it is (56.4%), tap (24.8%), Pucca well(14%) and (5%) 'others' type of drinking water in the country. In the urban areas, HHs are using tap (67.6%), hand pump/tube well (22.4%), Well (4%) and other (5.6%) sources of drinking water at national Level. One side in rural areas TN is using Tape water (81.5%) of HHs, Tube well and Hand pump (10%), 4 per cent pucca well and around 4 per from the other sources like as bottle water, tanker, tank pond and river, etc. Other side in developed state like Kerala only 10 per cent of HHs using tap water, 6 per cent of tube well/hand pump and more than 76 per cent of HHs using pucca well as sources of drinking water. Kerala is only state where more than 76 per cent rural HHs and 60 per cent of urban HHs are using pucca well as a source of drinking water. In Bihar more than 92.5 per cent of rural HHs and 68 per cent of urban HHs are using hand pump and tube well pump as a source of drinking water. Details are available in Table 12

(iii) Disparities in Toilet Facilities

Toilet facility is a critical link between good and bad levels of living. Open defeacation and unavailability of toilet facilities are the symbols of lower levels of living. These indicate the lower levels of education, cultural value, awareness to health and hygiene. Around 1.2 billion people worldwide have no access to toilets and India tops the list of countries with the most number of people defecating in the open, at 665 million—about half its population, the World Health Organisation (WHO) said. According to a report jointly conducted by WHO and UNICEF (United Nations Children's Fund), the next three most offending countries are Indonesia, Ethiopia and Pakistan. While 66 million people in Indonesia have no access to toilets, in Ethiopia it is 52 million and 50 million in Pakistan. In China, a whopping 32 million people don't have access to toilets. In Nigeria, 29 million

TABLE 13

Distribution of HHs by Availability of Toilet within the House 2001

Sr. No.	States	*Availability of Toilet*			*Not Availability of Toilet*		
		Total	*Rural*	*Urban*	*Total*	*Rural*	*Urban*
1.	AP	32.99	18.15	78.07	67.01	81.85	21.93
2.	Assam	64.64	59.57	94.6	35.36	40.43	5.4
3.	Bihar	19.19	13.91	69.69	80.81	86.09	30.31
4.	Chhattisgarh	14.20	5.18	52.59	85.8	94.82	47.41
5.	Gujarat	44.60	21.65	80.55	55.4	78.35	19.45
6.	Haryana	44.50	28.66	80.66	55.5	71.34	19.34
7.	HP	33.43	27.72	77.22	66.57	72.28	22.78
8.	J&K	53.14	41.8	86.87	46.86	58.2	13.13
9.	Jharkhand	19.67	6.57	66.68	80.33	93.43	33.32
10.	Karnataka	37.50	17.4	75.23	62.5	82.6	24.77
11.	Kerala	84.01	81.33	92.02	15.99	18.67	7.98
12.	MP	23.99	8.94	67.74	76.01	91.06	32.26
13.	Maharashtra	35.09	18.21	58.08	64.91	81.79	41.92
14.	Orissa	14.89	7.71	59.69	85.11	92.29	40.31
15.	Punjab	56.84	40.91	86.52	43.16	59.09	13.48
16.	Rajasthan	29.00	14.61	76.11	71	85.39	23.89
17.	TN	35.16	14.36	64.33	64.84	85.64	35.67
18.	Uttaranchal	45.20	31.6	86.88	54.8	68.4	13.12
19.	UP	31.43	19.23	80.01	68.57	80.77	19.99
20.	WB	43.71	26.93	84.85	56.29	73.07	15.15
	All-India	36.4	21.92	73.72	63.6	78.08	26.28

Source: Census of India, Housing Atlas of India-2001, Office of Registrar General, Government of India, New Delhi.

people use the open spaces while 18 million each in Brazil and Bangladesh do so. Most of the 1.2 billion defecting in the open—83 per cent—are from 13 countries, especially Asia and Africa. Both global health watch dogs have said that it's the "riskiest sanitary practice of all" in its report released on the International Year for Sanitation (2008). (IBN LIVE, 18 July, 2008)

As per Census 2001, the percentage data have been categorized into three types of latrines, i.e. Pit latrine, Water

SUMMARY INDICATORS: AS PER RANKING

Ranking of Major States

Sr. No.	Life Expectancy at Birth Year-1998-2002)	CBR/000 population (2004)	CDR/000 population (2004)	IMR/000 Live Birth (2004)	Literacy Rates 2001	Per-capita Expenditure on Health in Rs. 2001-02		Per-capita GSDP 2001-02
						Public	Private	
BETTER LEVELS OF LIVING STATES								
1.	Kerala	Kerala	Kerala	Kerala	Kerala	HP	Kerala	Punjab
2.	Punjab	Tamil Nadu	WB	Maharashta	MP	Punjab	Haryana	Haryana
3.	Maharashta	WB	HP	Tamil Nadu	HP	Kerala	Punjab	Maharashta
4.	Haryana	Maharashtra	Punjab	WB	TN	Karnataka	UP	HP
5.	Tamil Nadu	AP	Gujarat	Punjab	Punjab	TN	AP	Gujarat
AVERAGE LEVELS OF LIVING STATES								
6.	HP	Punjab	Haryana	Karnataka	Gujarat	Maharashta	Maharashta	Tamil Nadu
7.	Karnataka	Karnataka	Maharashta	HP	WB	AP	HP	Kerala
8.	WB	HP	Karnataka	Bihar	Haryana	Rajasthan	MP	Karnataka
9.	AP	Orissa	TN	Gujarat	Karnataka	WB	Bihar	AP
10.	Gujarat	Gujarat	AP	AP	Maharashta	Assam	Gujarat	WB

LOW LEVELS OF LIVING STATES								
11.	Rajasthan	Assam	Rajasthan	Haryana	Assam	Haryana	TN	Rajasthan
12.	Bihar	Haryana	Bihar	Assam	Orissa	Gujarat	WB	MP
13.	UP	MP	Assam	Rajasthan	AP	Orissa	Karnataka	Assam
14.	Orissa	Rajasthan	MP	UP	Rajasthan	MP	Orissa	Orissa
15.	Assam	Bihar	UP	MP	UP	Bihar	Rajasthan	UP
16.	MP	UP	Orissa	Orissa	Bihar	UP	Assam	Bihar

closet latrine and other types of latrine in total availability of latrines. Out of 191.96 million HHs in the country 70.50 million (36.5%) HHs are availing toilet facilities within the house in this country. In rural areas out of 138.29 millions only 20.29 million (21.92%) HHs availing toilet facilities within the house and Urban HHs counted 53.69 million in the country, only 39.57 million (73.72%) HHs are availing toilet facilities within the house. Inter-State disparities among the HHs availing toilet facilities with the house is observed within the twenty major states. Kerala (84.01% HHs) is number one followed by Assam (64.64%) and Punjab (56.84%) where HHs availing more than 55 per cent of toilet facilities within the house. A cluster of quite big area of plain land in Orissa (14.89%), Bihar (19.19%), UP (31.43%), Jharkhand (19.67%), Rajasthan (29.00%) and MP (23.99%) show low percentage HHs using toilet facility with the house. Some UTs like Dadar Nagar Haveli (0.70%) and Daman and Diu (2.08%) shows lowest and very low percentage of HHs availing toilet facilities within the house. Details are in Table 13

On the basis of summary indicators, 16 major states of India have been categorised into three categories. The ranking is done with the help of various health indicators like CDR, CBR, IMR, Life expectancy, etc. In the task of categorisation some other indicators have also been considered. These are some social and economic indicators like Literacy rates, per-capita expenditure on health, per-capita GSDP, etc. As per these indicators better level of living states are Kerala, HP, Punjab, Haryana, Maharashtra and Tamil Nadu. On the other hand states like Rajasthan, Assam, Bihar, Orissa, UP find place only inlow level of living states.

References

Baran, Paul (1957), The Political Economy of Growth, Monthly Review Press, New York.

Bairoch, Paul (1981), "The Main Trends in National Economic Disparities Since the Industrial Revolution" in Paul Bairoch and Levy-Leboyer (eds.), Disparities in Economic Development Since the Industrial Revolution, St. Martin's Press, New York.

Census of India (2001), Housing Atlas of India 2001, Office of the Registrar General, Government of India.

Emmanuel, A. (1972) Unequal Exchange: A Study of the Imperialism of Trade, New Left Books, London.

Frank, A.G. (1967) Capitalism and Underdevelopment in Latin America, Monthly Review Press, New York.

GOI (2007), National Health Profile 2007, Government of India, Central Bureau of Health Intelligence, Director General of Health Services, Ministry of Health and Family Welfare, Nirman Bhawan, New Delhi

Haq (2004), Human Development in South Asia-2004, The Health Challenge, Mahbub ul Haq.

Human Development Centre, Oxford University Press, Pakistan.

Hirschman, Albert O. (1958), The Strategy of Economic Development, New Haven: Yale University Press.

IBN Live (2008), Stink Record: Indians Lead in Defecating in Open, Published on Friday 18, 2008 in Health section.

Myrdal, Gunnar (1957), Economic Theory and Under-developed Regions, London: Duckworth.

Rao Veena S. (2008), Malnutrition, An Emergency: What it Costs the Nation, Council for Advancement of People's Action and Rural Technology (CAPART), New Delhi

Sen, Amartya (1998), Mortality as an Indicator of Economic Success and Failure, *Economic Journal*, 108 (446):1-25.

Solow, Robert M. (1956), "A Contribution to the Theory of Economic Growth", *Quarterly Journal of Economics*, Vol. 70.

UNICEF (2008), 'The State of the World Children 2008: Child Survival', United Nations Child Emergency Fund, New York, pp. 118-28.

WHO (2003), The World Health Report: Shaping the Future, Washington, D.C., World Health Organisation.

Williamson, J.G. (1965), "Regional Inequality and the Process of National Development: A Description of the Patterns", *Economic Development and Cultural Change*, Vol. 13, No. 4, p. 2.

4

Regional Disparities in Levels of Living in India

H.C.L. Das

India is a vast country having different regions with different natural resources and socio-economic structure. Its political and economic map has been characterized by disparities and divergencies among the potential or the performance of the various states. The states in India are differing from one another not only in being bigger or smaller in area or population, but also in terms of social and economic development in such areas like levels of living, progress of agriculture, industrialization, development of transport and communication, public health services, spread of literacy, human development, quality of life and work, etc. Hence, it is necessary to measure the degree of development of different sectors in different regions.

In economic literature, the problem of regionalism has developed from the theory of location of industries which took its birth in Germany where the works of Von Thunen[1] and Weber[2] were among the most important contributions.

In India the convention of dividing the country into some sorts of regions seems to have started with the preparation of the census reports. After the Independence, the first major attempt at regionalization of the country was made at the time of of 1951 Census (Paper No. 2 of 1952).[3] Daniel Thorner,[4] M.S. Randhawa,[5] O.H.K. Spate,[6] Ashod Mitra,[7] P. Sengupta,[8] P.S. Sharma,[9] Abel and Easter,[10] M.N. Pal,[11] and Hemlata Rao[12] made significant contributions towards the development of economic or agricultural regionalization of the Indian economy. In almost all the studies mentioned above, the terms 'region' and 'state' have been used interchangeably.

In the present study an attempt has been made to identify the degree of inter-state disparities in respects of levels of living mainly in the context of quality of life and work in India.

LEVELS OF LIVING

'Level of living' is the American version of 'standard of living'. Standard of living with reference to a person, family or a body of people means the extent to which they can satisfy their wants. Thus, if they can afford only the minimum of food, clothing and shelter, their standard of living is very low. If, on the other hand, they are able to enjoy a great variety of food, a good supply of good clothing and live in a well-furnished houses and in addition are able to satisfy a wide variety of other wants, then clearly such people are said to be enjoying a high standard of living.

The standard of living of people depends, in the first place, on the size of national income, and secondly, on the manners of distribution of the national income. People in a developing region of the world are poor, because the national income as an average per head is low; wide differences in the standard of living of people in the same country are the result of unequal distribution of the national income. The higher standard of living of the people in the advanced economies is due to these countries having large stocks of up-to-date capital and well-trained labour, and the willingness of the people themselves to work for a higher standard of living. Today there is less inequality of income in the economically more advanced countries than that in many of the underdeveloped parts of the world. A great deal is being done to raise the standard of living in the economically less developed countries, since the accumulation of capital proceeds more rapidly the more a country has of it, and this, therefore, otherwise tends to widen the gap between the developed and the underdeveloped nations.

The problem of measuring the level or standard of living has been engaging the attention of research institutions, universities, governments and the specialized agencies of the United Nations for a fairly long time. The UN Committee of Experts under the chairmanship of Prof. V.K.R.V. Rao released in 1954 its pioneering report on the 'International Definition and Measurement of Standards of Living' discussed the fundamental problem of methodology facing researchers in this field. Since then the UN agencies have tried to operationalise the concepts the concepts and suggested certain standard procedures.[13]

METHODOLOGY

The present paper is based purely on the secondary data available from the government and non-government publications. First Ginn's coefficient of concentration in respect of net state domestic product has been calculated on the basis of the following formula:[14]

1. $$GCC = [(X_1 \cdot Y_2 - X_2 \cdot Y_1) + (X_2 \cdot Y_3 - X_3 \cdot Y_2) + \ldots + (X_n \cdot 100 - 100. Y_n)]/100$$

where GCC = Ginni's coefficient of concentration,

$X, X_2, \ldots Xn$ = Subsequent cumulative percentages of population distributed over states in India., and

$Y_1, Y_2, \ldots Y_n$ = Subsequent cumulative percentages of population net state domestic product distributed over states in India.

The Ginni's coefficient of concentration has been calculated for 1991 and 2001 mainly to find the trend in concentration of net state domestic product.

The weighted index of regional inequality in respect of different variables has been calculated on the basis of the following formula:[15]

$$2. \quad V_w = \sqrt{\frac{(Si - N)\frac{2.Pi}{P}}{P}}$$

where Vw = Weighted index of regional inequality in respect of a variable.
Si = Per-capita value of a variable for the ith state.
N = Per-capita value of variable for the nation as a whole.
Pi = Population of ith state.
P = Population of the nation.

The weighted indices of reignal inequalities have been calculated in respects of per-capita net state domestic product for 1991 and 2001, per-capita availability of k calorie (rural and urban) for 1993-94 and 1999-00, per-capita availability of food grains (rural and urban) for 1988 and 2002, per-capita consumption expenditure for 1993-94 and 1999-00, and per-capita domestic consumption of electricity for 1992-93 and 1999-00.

INDICES OF ECONOMIC DEVELOPMENT

Economic development is a process—a quantitative change between two levels of development or levels of development at two points of time. Development is basically an inter-temporal comparison. It is a well-known fact that development is a process and the process is multi-dimensional. When any process is conceived as multi-dimensional, it becomes difficult to adequately capture its character through any index. However, some attempts have been made to measure the level of development, namely per-capita Income, Physical Quality of Life Index, Human Development Index and Quality of Life Index.

Per-capita Income

Net national income at factor cost divided by population is popularly known as per-capita income of a country. Similarly, net state domestic product divided by population is known as per captained state domestic product which is an important indicator for measuring and comparing the development of regional units of an economy.

Physical Quality of Life Index

Moriss David Morris pursuing the variables adopted by several UN Committees, United Nations Research Institute for Social Development (UNRISD) and the Organization for Economic Co-operation and Development (OECD) has developed the Physical Quality of Life Index (PQLI) based on the three variables—life expectancy at age of one year, infant mortality rate per thousand and basic literacy. In the case of positive indicators of life expectancy and basic literacy the best is demonstrated by the maximum and the worst is demonstrated by the minimum. But in the case of negative indicator of infant mortality the best is demonstrated by the minimum and the worst by the maximum. By the use of the following formulae[16] the achievement levels of positive variables, negative variables and the physical quality of life index are calculated:

$$3.\quad AL(+) = \frac{\text{Actual Value - Minimum Value}}{\text{Maximum Value - Minimum Value}}$$

$$4.\quad AL(-) = \frac{\text{Maximum Value - Actual Value}}{\text{Maximum Value - Minimum Value}}$$

$$5.\quad PQLI = \frac{1}{3}\cdot(LEI + IMI + BLI)$$

where AL(+) = Achievement level for positive indicator
AL(–) = Achievement level for a negative indicator
PQLI = Physical quality of life index
LEI = Life expectancy index
IMI = Infant mortality index
BLI = Basic literacy index

In the present paper the state-wise PQLI has been calculated for 1991 and 2001

Human Development Index

Since 1990 an agency of the United Nation, Viz., the United Nations Development Programs (UNDP) has been publishing every year a Human Development Report (HDR). This Report, besides discussing various aspects of Human development, has been ranking the different countries according to the level of human development index. In India, the Planning Commission has published in 2002 the National Human Development Report (2001), in which the human development index has been calculated for 1981, 1991 and 2001 for India as well as the major states of the country.[17]

Quality of Life Index

Dasgupta and Weals[18] have computed the quality of lire index (QLI) based on six parameters what they have called 'living standard' indicators or 'constituents of well-being'. These parameters are: (a) per-capita income, (b) life expectancy at birth in years, (c) infant morality rate in per thousand live births, (d) adult literacy rare in per cent of adult population, (e) index of political rights, and (f) index of civil rights. It may be noted that while political rights are citizens' rights to play a part in governance of their country, civil rights are rights of individual *via-a-vis* the state.

In the present paper, the quality of life index has been calculated for 1991 and 2001 for the 15 major states in India based on the first four indicators.

Further, the final index of development for the 15 major states have been computed for 2001 on the basis of seven indicators namely—life expectancy at age of one year, infant mortality rate per thousand live births, percentage of literacy, per-capita net state domestic product, motor vehicles per lakh of population, daily circulation of newspapers per thousand of population, and coverage of televisions (per cent of population).

Again the correlation coefficients of rank differences among the final ranking of index of development, ranking of human development index and ranking of quality of life and work index[19] have been computed, The student's t-distribution has been applied to test the significance of correlation coefficients.

ANALYSIS

The state-wise distribution of net state domestic product for 1991 and 2001 has been presented in the Table 1. It is evident from the table that in 1991 Maharashtra had the highest net state domestic product (Rs. 15961 crore), followed by Utttar Pradesh (Rs. 14012 crore) and West Bengal (Rs. 9594 crore). On the other hand, Assam had the lowest

TABLE 1

State-wise Distribution of Net State Domestic Product (1991 and 2001)

State	*Net State Domestic Product (Rs. Crore at Current Prices)*			
	1991	*1*	*2001*	*1*
	Amount	*Rank*	*Amount*	*Rank*
1	*2*	*3*	*4*	*5*
1. Andhra Pradesh	7324	4	126321	4
2. Assam	2298	15	28262	15
3. Bihar	6349	8	42224	13
4. Gujarat	6547	7	89877	7
5. Haryana	3032	14	48581	12
6. Karnataka	5287	9	93386	6
7. Kerala	3223	12	65732	10
8. Madhya Pradesh	7012	6	64553	9
9. Maharashtra	15961	1	210193	1
10. Orissa	3443	13	33906	14
11. Punjab	4449	10	58787	11
12. Rajasthan	4126	11	69898	8
13. Tamil Nadu	7218	5	125970	5
14. Uttar Pradesh	14012	2	150676	2
15. West Bengal	9594	3	128975	3
India	450280		1804819	

Sources: *Economic Survey,s* (2000-01 and 2005-06)

net state domestic product (Rs. 2298 crore) followed by Haryana (Rs. 3032 crores) and Orissa (Rs. 3443 crores).

Almost the same trend emerges for 2001. Again Maharashtra is found to have the highest net domestic product (Rs. 210193 crores), followed by Uttar Pradesh (Rs. 150676 crores) and West Bengal (Rs. 128975 crores). Assam, on the other hand, has been found with the lowest amount of net state domestic product (Rs. 28262 crore), followed by Orissa (Rs. 33906 crores) and Bihar (Rs. 42224 crores).

The Ginni's coefficient of concentration has been found to be 74.16 in 1991 which fell down to 13.79 in 2001. This significant decline in the coefficient of concentration may be regarded as the result of the planned efforts for the balanced regional development of the country.

Table 2 present some important weighted indices of regional inequalities in India at two points of time. The table reveals that the weighted index in respect of per-capita net state domestic product in 1991 was 23274.89 which came down to 11297.54 in 2001.

The weighted index of regional inequality in respect of per-capita availability of k-calorie in 1993-94 for rural area was 350.61 and for urban areas it was 6.45. While the index for rural area declined to 52.77 in 1999-00, the same for urban area increased to 9.52 in 1999-00.

The weighted index of regional inequality in respect of per-capita availability of foodgrains in 1988 was observed to be 0.5079 for rural area and it was 0.0224 for urban areas. The corresponding figures declined to 0.2301 and 0.0121 respectively in 2002.

The Weighted indices of regional inequality in respect of per-capita consumption expenditure were found to be 4.18 and 13.50 in 1993-94 and 1999-00 respectively.

The Weighted indices of regional inequality in respect of per-capita domestic consumption of electricity declined from 293.09 in 1992-93 to 17.28 in 1999-00.

There has been a marked decline in the consumption of all the cereals over the period 1987-88 through 2001-02 in almost all the states in both rural as well as in urban areas with the reduction being particularly sharp in the case of smaller cereal items, i.e., barley maize and cereal substitutes

TABLE 2

Weighted Indices of Regional Inequalities in India

	Weighted Indices of Regional Inequalities	*Year*	
1.	Weighted index of Regional Inequalities in respect	1991	2001
	of Per-capita Net State Domestic Product	23274.89	11297.54
2.	Weighted index of Regional Inequalities in	1993-94	1999-00
	respect of Per-capita Availability of K-calories:		
	Rural	350.61	52.77
	Urban	6.45	9.52
3.	Weighted index of Regional Inequalities in	1988	2002
	respect of Per-capita Availability of Food grains:		
	Rural	0.5079	0.0224
	Urban	0.2301	0.0121
4.	Weighted index of Regional Inequalities in	1993-94	1999-00
	respect of Per-capita Consumption of Expenditure	4.18	13.56
5.	Weighted index of Regional Inequalities	1992-93	1999-00
	in respect of Domestic Consumption of Electricity	293.09	17.28

such as tapioca. There has been a switch over in preference towards non-cereal items such as meat, fish, eggs and fruits/ vegetables. Whatever the underlying factors causing these changes, these have led to a significant decline in calorie intensive cereal items to non-cereals which are more expensive source of calorie.

However, malnutrition occurs also in many families which are not poor, because people do not always know what food or feeding practices are best for their children or for themselves, and, because people cannot easily tell when their children are becoming malnourished, since faltering growth rates and micro-nutrient deficiency are not easily visible to the untrained eyes. The need to correct these informational asymmetries suggests intervention on the part of the government. Such interventions through specific channel can help improving nutrition and reduce the spread of contagious diseases. With respect to the public distribution system, it is suggested that the system of dual prices which encourages leakages, may be replaced by uniform price policy along with a system of food coupons for the below poverty line facilities.[20]

Considering the standard calorie requirements of 2400 and 2100 respectively for rural and urban people, the estimates of available calorie are well within the prescribed limit of balanced diet, which emphasizes 50 per cent of calorie to be derived from the consumed cereals. Fifty per cent of the required calorie means 1200 out of 2400 and 1050 out of 2100 calorie. To get 1200 calories 10.44 kg cereal per-capita per 30 days or 348 gm per-capita per day are required by the rural people Similarly, 9.12 kg cereal per-capita per 30 days or 304 gm per-capita per day are required by the urban people to get 1050 calories in urban areas.

It is also estimated that 5 per cent of the people and 2.85 per cent household belonging to MPCE class in rural areas may not be able to get the required caloric from their consumed cereals, The similar percentage for urban areas were 5 and 2.5 per cent respectively. Of course, how far the remaining calories to be estimated from food items containing protein and fat by different MPCE classes is yet to be estimated. But the quantitative data for such items are not readily available from NSS Reports. Pulses data although available, the quantum of pulse consumption was insignificant. Net production and availability of pulses were not increasing, but decreasing over time.[21]

The state-wise distribution of per-capita net state domestic product at current prices for 1991 and 2001 has been presented in the Table 3. It is evident from the table that in 1991 per-capita net state domestic product was the highest (Rs. 8318) in Punjab, followed by Haryana (Rs. 7508) and Maharashtra (Rs. 7439). The corresponding figure was the lowest (Rs. 2600) in Bihar, followed by Orissa (Rs. 3077) and Uttar Pradesh (Rs. 3590).

Almost the same pattern reveals for 2001 in respect of the distribution of per-capita net state domestic product. Again Punjab has been found having the highest amount of per-capita net state domestic product (Rs. 24185), followed by Haryana (Rs. 23194) and Maharashtra (Rs. 21883). Further,

TABLE 3

State-wise Distribution of the Per-capita Net State Domestic Product in India (1991 and 2001)

State	Per-capita Net State Domestic Product (In Rupees at Current Prices)			
	1991 Amount	1 Rank	2001 Amount	1 Rank
1	2	3	4	5
1. Andhra Pradesh	4531	7	16708	9
2. Assam	4261	9	10718	12
3. Bihar	2600	15	5157	15
4. Gujarat	5891	14	17938	6
5. Haryana	7508	2	23194	2
6. Karnataka	4508	8	17816	7
7. Kerala	4200	10	20107	5
8. Madhya Pradesh	4049	12	10777	11
9. Maharashtra	7439	3	21883	3
10. Orissa	3077	14	9281	13
11. Punjab	8318	1	24183	1
12. Rajasthan	4191	5	12514	10
13. Tamil Nadu	4983	4	20346	4
14. Uttar Pradesh	3590	13	9162	14
15. West Bengal	4673	6	17499	8
India	7323		16223	

Source: Government of India, *Economic Survey,s* (2000-01 and 2005-06).

the per-capita net state domestic product has been observed to be the lowest (Rs. 5157) in Bihar, followed by Uttar Pradesh (Rs. 9162) and Orissa (Rs. 9281).

The State-wise distribution physical quality of life index (PQLI) for 1991 and 2001 has been presented in the Table 4 which receals that the value of PQLI was the highest (1) for Kerala in 1991, followed by Punjab (0.6095) and Maharashtra (0.5611). On the other hand the lowest value of PQLI was found to be lowest in Orissa (0.1115), followed by Uttar Pradesh (0.1721) and Assam (0.2263). Almost the same pattern reveals for 2001. Kerala has been observed as having the highest value (1) of the PQLI, followed by Maharashtra

(0.6223) and Punjab (0.6183). Similarly, Uttar Pradesh has been found with the lowest value of PQLI (0.1681), followed by Orissa (0.1767) and Madhya Pradesh (0.1801).

TABLE 4

State-wise Distribution of Physical, Quality of Life Index (1991 and 2001)

State	*1991*		*2001*	
	Rank	*Index*	*Rank*	*Index*
1	2	3	4	5
1. Andhra Pradesh	0.3138	9	0.3522	9
2. Assam	0.2263	13	0.2144	11
3. Bihar	0.2311	12	0.2069	12
4. Gujarat	0.4303	7	0.4341	8
5. Haryana	0.4396	6	0.4726	6
6. Karnataka	0.4161	8	0.4588	7
7. Kerala	1.0000	1	1.0000	1
8. Madhya Pradesh	0.2544	10	0.1801	13
9. Maharashtra	0.5611	3	0.6233	2
10. Orissa	0.1115	15	0.1767	14
11. Punjab	0.6095	2	0.6185	3
12. Rajasthan	0.2329	11	0.27850	10
13. Tamil Nadu	0.5000	4	0.5286	4
14. Uttar Pradesh	0.1721	14	0.1681	15
15. West Bengal	0.4680	5	0.4873	5

The state-wise distribution of quality of life index (QLI) has been given in the Table 5. It is very much evident from the table that the highest value of the QLI (53) was, followed by Kerala (51) and Maharashtra (50). The lowest value of the QLI, on the other hand, was seen to be with Orissa (12), followed by Uttar Pradesh (13) and Rajasthan (16) in 1991.

In 2001, Kerala was observed to have the highest value of QLI (56), followed by Maharashtra (54) and Tamil Nadu (48). In contrast, Uttar Pradesh was observed with the lowest value of QLI (11), followed by Orissa (12) and Madhya Pradesh (14).

TABLE 5

State-wise Distribution of Quality of Life Index in India (1991 and 2001)

State	1991		2001	
	Rank	Index	Rank	Index
1	2	3	4	5
1. Andhra Pradesh	27	9	26	9
2. Assam	19	11	18	11
3. Bihar	16	12	15	12
4. Gujarat	40	6	37	7
5. Haryana	39	7	42	5
6. Karnataka	33	8	36	8
7. Kerala	51	2	56	1
8. Madhya Pradesh	24	10	14	13
9. Maharashtra	50	3	54	2
10. Orissa	12	15	12	14
11. Punjab	53	1	43	4
12. Rajasthan	16	13	19	10
13. Tamil Nadu	46	4	48	3
14. Uttar Pradesh	13	14	11	15
15. West Bengal	41	5	39	6

Sources: 1. Government of India, Economic Survey, (2000-01 and 2005-06)
2. Tata Economic Services Ltd., Mumbai Statistical Outline of India (2000-01, 2000-02 and 2002-03)

Table 6 presents the state-wise distribution of human development index (HDI) for 1991 and 2001. Kerala was observed to have the highest value of HDI (0.591), followed by Punjab (0.475) and Tamil Nadu (0.466). Bihar on the other hand has been found with the lowest value of HDI (0.308), followed by Uttar Pradesh and Madhya Pradesh (0.314 and 0.328) respectively in 1991.

In 2001, the highest value of HDI was observed with Kerala (0.638), followed by Punjab (0.537) and Tamil Nadu (0.531). Again, on the other hand, Bihar has been found to have the lowest value (0.361) of HDI. Followed by Assam (0.386) and Uttar Pradesh (0.388).

TABLE 6

State-wise Distribution of Human Development Index in India (1991 and 2001)

State	*1991*		*2001*	
	HDI	*Rank*	*HDI*	*Rank*
1	2	3	4	5
1. Andhra Pradesh	0.377	9	0.416	10
2. Assam	0.348	10	0.386	14
3. Bihar	0.308	15	0.367	15
4. Gujarat	0.431	6	0.479	6
5. Haryana	0.443	5	0.509	5
6. Karnataka	0.412	7	0.478	7
7. Kerala	0.591	1	0.638	1
8. Madhya Pradesh	0.328	13	0.394	12
9. Maharashtra	0.452	4	0.523	4
10. Orissa	0.345	12	0.404	11
11. Punjab	0.475	2	0.537	2
12. Rajasthan	0.307	11	0.424	9
13. Tamil Nadu	0.466	3	0.531	3
14. Uttar Pradesh	0.314	14	0.388	13
15. West Bengal	0.404	8	0.472	8

Source: Planning Commission (2002), National Human Development Report (2001), p. 25.

The quality of life and work index (QLWI) as estimated by India Today's (2003 and 2004 combined) has been presented in the Table 7. This table clearly shows that Punjab has got the first rank with 4.98 value of QLWI, followed by Kerala (4.57) and Tamil Nadu (4.02). On the other hand, Bihar has got the last (15th) rank with 0.65 value of QLWI, followed by Orissa (1.17) and Uttar Pradesh (1.37).

The final development index (FDI) which may be regarderd as the level of living as well, prepared on the line of Morris David Morris has been presented in the Table 8. It is apparently clear from the table that Kerala has obtained the first rank with 0.8185 value of FDI, followed by Punjab (0.8031) and Maharashtra (0.6196). Orissa, on the other hand has been observed with the lowest value of FDI (0.2040) followed by Bihar (0.2137) and Madhya Pradesh (0.2185).

TABLE 7

India Today's Index of Quality of Life and Work (2003 and 2004 Combined)

State	*2003 and 2004 Combined*	
	Index	*Rank*
1	*2*	*3*
1. Andhra Pradesh	2.78	8
2. Assam	1.55	12
3. Bihar	0.65	15
4. Gujarat	3.62	5
5. Haryana	3.77	4
6. Karnataka	3.06	7
7. Kerala	4.57	2
8. Madhya Pradesh	1.94	11
9. Maharashtra	3.55	6
10. Orissa	1.77	14
11. Punjab	4.98	1
12. Rajasthan	2.14	9
13. Tamil Nadu	4.02	3
14. Uttar Pradesh	1.37	13
15. West Bengal	1.95	10

Source: Living Media Ltd. (2004), *India Today*, August 16, 2004, p. 32, New Delhi

From the analysis of the Tables 1 to 8, it is clear that Kerala, Punjab, Maharashtra, Tamil Nadu, Gujarat and Haryana Have emerged as the six advanced states holding first to sixth ranks. On the other hand, Uttar Pradesh, Bihar, Madhya Pradesh, Assam, Orissa and Rajasthan have emerged as six backward states holding 10th to 15th ranks.

The correlation coefficients among the three indices namely, final development index, human development index and quality of life and work index have been computed. Further, Student's t-distribution has been applied to test the significance of correlation coefficients among these indices. The result of the correlation analysis has been presented in the Table 9.

The Correlation coefficient between final development

TABLE 8

State-wise Distribution of Final Development Index in India (2001)

	State	*Index*	*Rank*
	1	*2*	*3*
1.	Andhra Pradesh	0.3710	9
2.	Assam	0.2137	14
3.	Bihar	0.2267	12
4.	Gujarat	0.5210	6
5.	Haryana	0.5575	5
6.	Karnataka	0.4119	8
7.	Kerala	0.8185	1
8.	Madhya Pradesh	0.2815	13
9.	Maharashtra	0.6156	3
10.	Orissa	0.2040	15
11.	Punjab	0.8031	2
12.	Rajasthan	0.4121	10
13.	Tamil Nadu	0.5671	4
14.	Uttar Pradesh	0.2476	11
15.	West Bengal	0.5032	7

index and human development index has been found to be +0.936 which is significant at 0.001 level of probability. The correlation coefficient between final development index and quality of life and work index has been found to be +0.914 which is significant at 0.001 level of probability. Again the correlation coefficient between human development index and quality of life and work index has been observe to be +0.944 which has been found significant at 0.001 level of probability. Thus, all the three correlation coefficients among these indices have been found highly significant.

All the six backward states are termed as BIMARU states—Bihar, Madhya Pradesh, Assam, Rajasthan, Orissa and Uttar Pradesh. State specific development strategy is required for the development of the BIMARU states.

The basic weakness of the steps taken so far under the different plans to tackle the problem of inter-state/regional disparities is that they have been largely in financial terms,

TABLE 9

Correlation Cofficients of Rank Differences among Different Indices of Development

State	FDI Rank	HDI Rank	ITI Rank
1	2	3	4
1. Andhra Pradesh	2	10	8
2. Assam	14	14	12
3. Bihar	12	15	15
4. Gujarat	6	6	5
5. Haryana	5	5	4
6. Karnataka	8	7	7
7. Kerala	1	1	2
8. Madhya Pradesh	13	12	11
9. Maharashtra	3	4	6
10. Orissa	15	11	14
11. Punjab	2	2	1
12. Rajasthan	10	9	9
13. Tamil Nadu	4	3	3
14. Uttar Pradesh	11	13	13
15. West Bengal	7	8	10

1. Rank Correlation Coefficient between FDI and HDI
   = + 0.936 t = 9.5867 (Significant at 0.001 level of Probability)
2. Rank Correlation Coefficient between FDI and ITI
   = + 0.914 t = 9.3625 (Significant at 0.001 level of Probability)
3. Rank Correlation Coefficient between HDI and ITI
   = + 0.944 t = 10.1817 (Significant at 0.001 level of Probability)

i.e., additional finance and location of heavy investment projects in the backward regions. Central assistance should, however, be linked with specific programs for the development of relatively backward states. Besides, the financial approach should be replaced, as far as possible, by the planning approach, under which the backward regions should be clearly identified along with their capabilities so that separate strategies may be adopted for each type of backward regions/states. In view the peculiar nature of some backward districts as draught-prone, industrial development in some of the districts cannot spread to the rest of the districts due to the in-built constraints. Naturally, incentives alone are not adequate to bring about dispersal of industrial development. Instead, agricultural development become significant in the growth process. There is, therefore, the necessity to coordinate the dispersal process and the development of agriculture through a scheme of agro-based industries.

Notes and References

1. Von Thunen, J.N. (1966), Isolated States, (Translated from German into English by C.N. Wentenberg, Penguin Books Ltd., London.
2. Weber, Alfred. (1965), Theories of Industries, (Translated from French into English by C.J. Fredrich), Fifth Edition, Chicago University Press, Chicago.
3. Census of India, (1952), Population Zones, National Regions, Sub-Regions and Divisions. (Paper No. 2 of 1952).
4. Thorner, Daniel (1957), Demarcation of Agricultural Regions in India, Indian Society of Agricultural Economics, Bombay.
5. Randhawa, M.S. (1969), Farming in India, (quoted by C.B. Memorial) in Agricultural Problems in India, Kitbag Mahal, Allahabad.
6. Spate, O.H.K. (1964), India and Pakistan, Oxford Univerity Press, London.
7. Mitra, Ashok. (1964), "Levels of Regional Development in India", Census of India, New Delhi.
8. Sengupta, P. (1964), "Planning Region for Resource Development in India", Paper contributed to 20th International Geographers Union Congress, New Castle, UPON-TYNE.
9. Sharma, P.S. (1964), "Regional Approanh to Agricultural Development in India", *Indian Journal of Agricultural Economics,* Vol. 19, No. 1, Sharma, P.S. (1968), "Quantitative Delimitation of Agricultural Regions in India", *Indian Journal of Agricultural Economics,* Vol. 23, No. 1.
10. Abel, Martin E. and K.W. Easter (1971), "Agricultural Planning Process Evaluation: Focus on National Restraints", *Economic and Political Weekly,* Special Nos. 30, 31, and 32, July.
11. Pal, M.N. (1968), Regional Analysis of National Development: Technique and Case Study, Doctoral Dissertation, University of Delhi, Delhi.
12. Rao, Hemlata. (1977), "Identification of Backward Regions and the Trends in Regional Disparities", *Arthavijnan,* Vol. 19, No. 4,
13. Ganguli, B.N. and D.B. Gupta (1976), Levels of Living in India, S. Chand and Company, New Delhi.
14. Gupta, B.N. (1990), Statistics, Sahitya Bhawan, Agra.
15. Williamson, J.G. (1965), "Redgional Inequality and Process of

National Development: A Description of Change", *Economic Development and Cultural Change*, Vol. 13.

16. Chaubey, P.K. (2002), Indian Economic Development, National Council of Educational Reseatch and Training, New Delhi.
17. Planning Commission (2002), National Human Development Report (2001), Government of India, New Delhi.
18. Dasgupta, P. and Martn Weal (1985), Measuring the Quality of Life, Oxford University Press, London.
19. *India Today*, May 19, 2003, and *India Today*, August 16, 2004.
20. Goliath, Ramesh and N.C. Pradhan (2006), "Changing Food Consumption Pattern in Rural India: Implications on Nutrition and Security", *Indian Journal of Agricultural Economics*, Vol. 61, No. 3, p. 186.
21. Giri, A.K. (2006), "Cereal Consumption over Time in the Country Across the States", *Indian Journal of Agricultural Economics*, Vol. 61, No. 3, p. 197.

5

Inter-State Disparities in India under Liberalised Regime: Extent, Trends and Sources

KULWANT SINGH PHULL

Since 1951, balanced regional development has remained one of the major planks for adopting planning process in India. In the Constitution, the basic objectives were set forth as "The Directive Principles of State Policy". Among these 'Directive Principles' one such principle is that "The State shall strive to promote the welfare of the people by securing and protecting, as effectively as it may, a social order in which justice, social, economic and political, shall inform all the institutions of national life" (Government of India, 1951, pp. 1-2; 1961: p. 3). These Directive Principles were given a more precise direction in December 1954, when Parliament adopted the 'socialistic pattern of society' as the major objective of country's socio-economic policy. The same was strongly endorsed by the Industrial Policy Resolution of 1956. Accordingly, the process of planned development remained biased towards the growth of public sector with overall approach of mixed economy. However, excessive centralization, nationalization, protection and subsidy regime encouraged permanent dependence, which hampered development, and created stagflation in India by the end of eighties. Consequently, mixed economic approach was evaluated, and it was realized that the country should improve productivity by adopting modern sophisticated technology and by optimally utilizing available resources. Consequently, New Economic Policy, popularly known as Policy of LPG was introduced on July 24, 1991 involving market friendly policies of Liberalization, Privatization and Globalization. Since then the economy has been experiencing structural changes, thereby according greater role to the private sector, relaxing government controls, encouraging private investment both domestic as well as foreign and integrating the domestic economy with global economy by following a rationalized custom regime.

Apart from massive investments in backward regions, various public policies directed at encouraging private investments in such regions have been pursued during the first three decades of planned development. Though the efforts to reduce regional disparities were not lacking, yet the achievements were not often commensurate with such efforts. The accelerated economic growth since the early eighties appeared to have aggravated inter-state disparities in the country. The on-going economic reforms since 1991 with stabilization and deregulation policies as their central themes seem to have further widened the regional disparities. The seriousness of the emerging acute inter-state imbalances has not yet received the public attention, it deserved. Therefore, it becomes essential to examine the pattern of inter-state development in the Indian economy, especially in the light of liberalized regime. In the present paper, an attempt has been made in this regard with the help of some available important indicators, keeping the following specific objectives in view:

1. To analyze the extent and trends of inter-state disparities in the overall economic development of India, particularly under the liberalized policy regime,

2. To identify and examine the sources of inter-state disparities in the overall economic development of the country, and
3. To draw policy implications with a view to explore effective corrective measures for the future balanced regional development in India.

DATA BASE AND METHODOLOGY

The study being country specific is based on the secondary data, which have been collected and compiled from various authentic reports such as: Census of India, published by the Registrar General and Census Commissioner of India; Statistical Abstract India, Annual Survey of Industries and Estimates of State Domestic Products, each published by the Central Statistical Organization, Ministry of Statistics and Programme Implementation; Agricultural Statistics at a Glance published by The Directorate of Economics and Statistics, Ministry of Agriculture, Government of India; Statistical Abstract of Punjab published annually by the Government of Punjab; and different publications of the Centre for Monitoring Indian Economy (CMIE), Mumbai.

The scope of this study has been confined to the comparative analysis of the emerging trends in fifteen major states of the country in respect of some key parameters, which have an intrinsic bearing on their socio-economic development. The selected fifteen States: Andhra Pradesh, Gujarat, Haryana, Karnataka, Kerala, Maharashtra, Punjab, Tamil Nadu, Assam, Bihar, Madhya Pradesh, Orissa, Rajasthan, Uttar Pradesh and West Bengal (three states viz: Uttrakhand, Jharkhand and Chhattisgarh have not been included in the analysis as these have been created in November 2001 and comparable data for 1990-91 were not available) together account for more than 95 per cent of the population and 85 per cent of the area of the country in 2001. The remaining five per cent of the population has been spread out in 13 other smaller states and seven Union Territories including the National Capital Territory of Delhi. Leaving out these states and UTs from the detailed study is mainly due to their special characteristics, and also to keep the data sets analytically and logistically manageable as well as comparable. Depending upon the availability of statistical information, following 12 indicators have been selected and used for analysis:

1. Per-capita Net State Income (in Rs.) at 1993-94 Prices (PCY).
2. Average Yield of Food grains (Per Hectare in Quintals) (AYF).
3. Irrigation Intensity (IRI).
4. Cropping Intensity (CRI).
5. Per-capita Milk Production (in Kgs.) (PMP).
6. Number of Factory Units Per Lakh of Population (NF/L).
7. Per-capita Net Value Added in Manufacturing Sector (in Rs.) (PVM).
8. Per-capita Invested Capital in Factory Sector (in Rs.) (PIC).
9. Pe-capita Bank Credit (in Rs.) (PBC).
10. Per-capita Consumption of Electricity (in Kwhs.) (PEC).
11. Per-capita Actual Annual Plan Outlay at 1993-94 Prices (in Rs.) (PAP).
12. Per-capita Income from Tertiary Sector at 1993-94 Prices (PTI).

Owing to the massive discrepancies in area and population of the selected states, indicators of development were not comparable in aggregate and hence do not reveal the genuine scenario regarding inter-state disparities in the country. Accordingly, data has been customarized on the basis of population/area and thereafter standardized by using the formula of Gender-related Development Index (UNDP, 2004: p. 261):

$$Z_{ij} = \frac{X_{ij} - X_L}{X_H - X_L}$$

where Z_{ij} indicates the standardized value of the ith indicator for the jth State,

X_{ij} is the actual value of ith indicator for jth State,
X_L stands for the lowest value of each indicator, and
X_H represents the highest value of each indicator.

'Composite Index of Economic Development' (CIED) has been constructed using the technique of Factor Analysis, to estimate the dimensions of inter-state disparities in the country. For this purpose, method of Principal Component Analysis has been used to identify the critical 'Factors'. In order to decide, how many 'Factors' were required for the analysis, Eigen values have been calculated and the Varimax Factor Rotation method has been applied to enhance the interpretability of the factors. All the 'Principal Components' (Factors derived) were taken into account while determining the relative weights of the selected variables, so as to reflect the maximum possible variation in the inter-state development. The relative weights of variables were:

$$W_i = F_{ik} V_k$$

where W_i = Weight of ith variable,
F_{ik} = Factor loading of ith variable and kth factor, which reflect the highest correlation between variable X_i and Factor F_k, and
V_k = Variation explained by the kth factor.

Higher weights were assigned to those variables which contributed more towards inter-state variations and *vice versa*. 'Composite Index of Economic Development' (CIED) has been calculated as under:

$$CIED_j = \frac{\sum W_i Z_{ij}}{\sum W_i}$$

where $CIED_j$ = Composite Index of the jth state for time period t

Z_{ij} = Standardized value of ith variable for the jth state, and

ΣW_i = Sum of the weights.

Coefficient of Variation (C.V.) of CIED has been estimated to examine the degree of inter-state disparities in the country. While, in order to identify the most important sources of inter-state variations, Karl Pearson's coefficients of correlation for the selected variables with CIED have been calculated, and to test their significance Student's t-ratio has been applied. The high degree of association among the explanatory variables was expected to create the problem of multicollinearity in the analysis. Hence, Step-wise Backward Regression technique has been used to overcome the problem of multicollinearity. Adjusted R^2 has been calculated for comparing the explanatory power of different sets of regression equations. Explanatory variables were dropped from the Step-wise Backward Regression Model in accordance with the calculated value of Student's t-ratio along with taking into account the collinearity. For this purpose SPSS was rigorously used.

The next part of the paper has been organized in three sections. Section-I scans the extent and trends of inter-state disparities in the economic development of India, particularly under the liberalized regime, while in Section-II an attempt has been made to identify and examine the sources of inter-state disparities in the economic development of the country. Section-III concludes the discussion and presents certain policy implications for the future balanced regional development of India.

Section I

In order to estimate the extent and trends of inter-state disparities in India, the 'Composite Index of Economic Development' (CIED) has been constructed by using the technique of 'Factor Analysis' at three different time periods: 1990-91, 2000-01 and 2004-05.

Table 1 amplifies the results of Factor Analysis and weights calculated for the year 1990-91 for the selected 12 variables indicating inter-state disparities in India. Communality values of all the variables, except two, ranged between 0.7993 and 0.9358 (higher than the required level of 0.7000) demonstrating that the two 'factors' derived were sufficient to account for most of the variations. It has been observed that 82.824 per cent of inter-state variations during 1990-91 were explained by the two 'Factors' taken together. The first 'Factor' explained 51.387 per cent of the total variations, while the second explained 31.436 per cent variations. Almost all the primary sector variables were significantly associated with the second 'Factor', hence the same were termed as 'primary sector', while the first 'Factor' has been named as 'non-primary sector' since all the remaining variables were reported to be highly correlated with the first 'Factor'. The components of the first 'Factor' were: Per-capita Net Value Added in Manufacturing Sector (PVM), Per-capita Income from Tertiary Sector (PTI), Per-capita Invested Capital in Factory Sector (PIC), Per-capita Bank Credit (PBC), Per-capita Consumption of Electricity (PEC), Per-capita Income (PCY) and Number of Factories per Lakh of Population (NF/L). The variables, which contributed more toward inter-state variations in the development process, have been assigned higher weights. All the variables representing the 'non-primary sector' have higher weights, while the 'primary sector' variables have relatively lower weight values. Per-capita Net Value Added in Manufacturing Sector (PVM) has the highest (49.38) weight value, while the Cropping Intensity (CRI) has the lowest (24.71) weight value in 1990-91. Thus, it can be concluded that most of the inter-state variations during 1990-91 were mainly due to 'non-primary sector' factors.

Factor Analysis results for the year 2000-01, delineated in Table 2, illustrates that again two 'Factors' came out from the 12 selected indicators that explained 83.272 of the total variations in the inter-state disparities in the country. Communality values ranged between 0.9572 and 0.7124 (i.e., 95.72% and 71.24%), suggesting that the two 'Factors' derived were sufficient to account for most of the variations. A perusal of the table shows that all the variables of the secondary and tertiary sectors were the component of the first 'Factor', which explained 53.63 per cent of the total variations and hence the same has been labeled as 'non-primary sector'. PVM, PTI, PCY, and NF/L were observed to be the important variables in the 'non-primary sector' and so had

TABLE I

Results of Factor Analysis and Derived Weights for 1990-91

Variables	*Factor 1*	*Factor 2*	*Commu-nalities*	*Weights*	*Weights (in %)*
Per-capita Income (PCY)	0.8415	0.4670	0.9262	43.24	9.44
No. of Factories per Lakh Pop. (NF/L)	0.8372	0.3136	0.7993	43.02	9.40
Per-capita Net Value Added in Manuf. (PVM)	0.9610	-0.0008	0.9235	49.38	10.78
Per-capita Invested Capital (PIC)	0.9186	0.1889	0.8795	47.20	10.31
Per-capita Bank Credit (PBC)	0.9116	-0.0674	0.8356	46.84	10.23
Per-capita Electricity Consumption (PEC)	0.8624	0.4382	0.9358	44.32	9.68
Per-capita Annual Plan Expenditure (PAP)	0.5555	0.5275	0.5868	28.54	6.23
Per-capita Income from Tertiary Sector (PTI)	0.9354	0.1642	0.9019	48.07	10.50
Average Yield of Food grains (AYF)	0.1822	0.8921	0.8290	28.04	6.12
Irrigation Intensity (IRI)	0.1804	0.8852	0.8162	27.83	6.08
Cropping Intensity (CRI)	-0.0875	0.7859	0.6253	24.71	5.40
Per-capita Milk Production (PMP)	0.3981	0.8493	0.8799	26.70	5.83
Percentage Variance Explained	51.3870	31.4360	Total	457.90	100.00
Cumulative Variance	51.3870	82.8240	C.V. (%)	26.00	---

Extraction Method: Principal Component Analysis, Rotation Method: Varimax with Kaiser Normalization.

Rotation converged in 3 iterations.

the relatively higher weights. The primary sector variables: Average Yield of Food grains Per Hectare (AYF), Irrigation Intensity (IRI), Cropping Intensity (CRI), and Per-capita Milk

TABLE 2

Results of Factor Analysis and Derived Weights for 2000-01

Variables	*Factor 1*	*Factor 2*	*Communalities*	*Weights*	*Weights (in %)*
Per-capita Income (PCY)	0.9198	0.3334	0.9572	49.331	10.22
No. of Factories per Lakh Pop. (NF/L)	0.8750	0.3351	0.8779	46.928	9.73
Per-capita Net Value Added in Manu. (PVM)	0.9424	0.0105	0.8883	50.543	10.47
Per-capita Invested Capital (PIC)	0.8485	-0.0666	0.7243	45.504	9.43
Per-capita Bank Credit (PBC)	0.8608	0.0813	0.7475	46.163	9.57
Per-capita Electricity Consumption (PEC)	0.8544	0.4385	0.9223	45.820	9.50
Per-capita Annual Plan Expenditure (PAP)	0.8266	-0.1793	0.7154	44.329	9.19
Per-capita Income from Tertiary Sector (PTI)	0.9275	0.0367	0.8617	49.743	10.31
Average Yield of Food grains (AYF)	0.0716	0.9373	0.8836	27.783	5.76
Irrigation Intensity (IRI)	0.1120	0.9069	0.8351	26.883	5.57
Cropping Intensity (CRI)	-0.2007	0.8495	0.7620	25.182	5.22
Per-capita Milk Production (PMP)	0.3787	0.8209	0.8173	24.333	5.04
Percentage Variation Explained	53.63	29.642	Total	482.540	100.00
Cumulative Variance	53.63	83.272	C.V. (%)	26.49	----

Extraction Method: Principal Component Analysis, Rotation Method: Varimax with Kaiser Normalization.

Production (PMP) were highly associated with the second 'Factor', which explained 29.642 per cent variations. Hence, the second 'Factor' has been denoted as 'primary factor'. Therefore, it can be concluded that again the 'non-primary sector' was the most important factor responsible for the inter-state variations in 2000-01 in the country.

TABLE 3

Results of Factor Analysis and Derived Weights for 2004-05

Variables	*Factor 1*	*Factor 2*	*Commu-nalities*	*Weights*	*Weights (in %)*
Per-capita Income (PCY)	0.9275	0.2914	0.9452	44.969	10.472
No. of Factories per Lakh Pop (NF/L)	0.8371	0.3312	0.8104	40.582	9.451
Per-capita Net Value Added (PVM)	0.8883	0.0022	0.7890	43.066	10.029
Per-capita Invested Capital (PIC)	0.8822	-0.0495	0.7807	42.771	9.961
Per-capita Bank Credit (PBC)	0.7545	-0.1442	0.5900	36.578	8.518
Per-capita Electricity Consumption (PEC)	0.8504	0.4565	0.9317	41.231	9.602
Per-capita Annual Plan Expenditure (PAP)	0.6665	-0.3483	0.5655	32.313	7.525
Per-capita Income from Tertiary Sector (PTI)	0.8770	0.0526	0.7719	42.519	9.902
Average Yield of Food grains (AYF)	0.1358	0.9236	0.8714	27.820	6.479
Irrigation Intensity (IRI)	-0.0293	0.8874	0.7884	26.731	6.225
Cropping Intensity (CRI)	-0.2205	0.8555	0.7806	25.770	6.001
Per-capita Milk Production (PMP)	0.3403	0.8317	0.8076	25.053	5.834
Percentage Variance Explained	48.482	30.122	Total	429.404	100.000
Cumulative Variance	48.482	78.604	C.V. (%)	21.61	-----

Extraction Method: Principal Component Analysis. Rotation Method: Varimax with Kaiser Normalization

For the year 2004-05, Table 3 illustrates the Factor Analysis results in terms of factor loadings and communalities for the selected 12 variables, and the objective weights worked out for the same. A glance at the table reports that the communality values for all the selected variables, except two, varied between 0.9452 and 0.7719. The resulting two 'Factors' explained together 78.604 per cent of inter-state variations in terms of the original indicators. The first 'Factor' explained 48.482 per cent, while the second explained 30.122 per cent of the total variations. All the primary sector variables had a higher association with the second 'Factor', while the remaining variables were highly correlated with the first 'Factor'. Therefore, the second 'factor' may be referred to as 'primary sector', while the first 'Factor' as 'non-primary sector'. The constituents of first Principal Component were: PCY, PVM, PIC, PTI, and PEC as they had higher weights nearing 10 per cent or more. Whereas the primary sector variables had lower weights. Per-capita Income (PCY) had the highest (10.472) weight value percentage, while the Per-capita Milk Production (PMP) had the lowest (5.834%) in 2004-05. Consequently, it can be concluded that in 2004-05 again the 'non-primary sector' was the most imperative factor responsible for the inter-state variations in the country.

Table 4 presents the Composite Index of Overall Economic Development (CIED) of 15 selected states at three different points of time viz.: 1990-91, 2000-01 and 2004-05. An examination of the table indicates that in 1990-91, only five states: Punjab (0.86812), Maharashtra (0.65227), Haryana (0.64209), Gujarat (0.54118) and Tamil Nadu (0.50605) were above the national average (All-India Index=0.50000). On the worst side, Bihar was at the bottom with index value 0.08148, which was more than 10 times lower as compared to the top ranking Punjab. Other bottom line states were Assam (0.10659), Orissa (0.14610), Rajasthan (0.16762) and Uttar Pradesh (0.17612). The range of CIED (0.78664) as well as the Coefficient of Variation (C.V.) of CIED (68.12) was very high in 1990-91, which is suggestive of a very high level of disparities in the development levels. However, in 2000-01 no significant change was observed in the category of above average states as well as below average states, except some changes in their relative rankings. Although the index value of Punjab (0.75145) has declined in 2000-01, yet it remained at the top among these 15 selected states, followed by Haryana (0.64561) which improved its standing from third to second, closely followed by Maharashtra (0.64545), Gujarat (0.63216) and Tamil Nadu (0.63099). No change has been observed in

TABLE 4

Composite Index of Economic Development

(Base: All-India = 0.50000)

State	Index Values			Index Ranks		
	1990-91	2000-01	2004-05	1990-91	2000-01	2004-05
Andhra Pradesh	0.34200	0.40914	0.40976	6	8	7
Gujarat	0.54118	0.63216	0.62165	4	4	3
Haryana	0.64209	0.64561	0.64491	3	2	2
Karnataka	0.27617	0.45440	0.46664	7	6	6
Kerala	0.24303	0.41159	0.36972	9	7	8
Maharashtra	0.65227	0.64545	0.58545	2	3	4
Punjab	0.86812	0.75145	0.67963	1	1	1
Tamil Nadu	0.50605	0.63099	0.54235	5	5	5
Assam	0.10659	0.14364	0.13125	14	14	14
Bihar	0.08148	0.05981	0.05857	15	15	15
Madhya Pradesh	0.22148	0.19936	0.19836	10	11	11
Orissa	0.14610	0.16875	0.19345	13	13	12
Rajasthan	0.16762	0.25892	0.24519	12	10	10
Uttar Pradesh	0.17612	0.19241	0.18897	11	12	13
West Bengal	0.24797	0.32653	0.33522	8	9	9
All-India	0.50000	0.50000	0.50000	---	---	---
C.V. (%)	68.12	56.47	54.07	---	---	---

the position of bottom line states: Bihar (0.05981), Assam (0.14364), and Orissa (0.16875) during 1991-2001. Only Rajasthan improved its rank from 12th to 10th during this period. The range of CIED (0.69164) and the C.V. of CIED (56.47) declined in 2000-01, but it remained quite lofty indicating thereby still a high level of inter-state variations in the country.

In 2004-05, Punjab again was at the top among these 15 states, though with a declined index value (0.67963), followed by Haryana (0.64491), Gujarat (0.62165), Maharashtra (0.58545) and Tamil Nadu (0.54235). Gujarat has improved its ranking over Maharashtra among the five forward states during 2001-05. On the flip side, Bihar (0.05857), Assam (0.13125), Uttar Pradesh (0.18897) and Orissa (0.19345) remained at the lowest level. Position of UP, Madhya Pradesh and Bihar worsened, perhaps, due to their bifurcation (i.e. due to the creation of new states: Uttrakhand, Chhattisgarh and Jharkhand). Even though the range of CIED (0.62106) declined further in 2004-05, but the same was still reasonably high signifying the existence of wider degree of inter-state disparities in the economy. Accordingly, the C.V. of the CIED for all the 15 States has declined from 68.12 per cent in 1990-91 to 56.47 per cent in 2000-01 and further to 54.07 per cent in 2004-05. The decline in the range as well as the C.V. of CIED indicates that the extent of inter-state disparities in India have decreased during the study period of liberalized regime, since 1991. This happened not because of development in the bottom line states, albeit the same attributes to the slow growth rate of the some top ranking states, particularly like: Punjab and Maharashtra, during the foresaid period. Otherwise, no major change has been observed in the index ranking of these 15 states.

Thus, in general, the relative position of almost all the states did not change significantly during the 15 years study period of 1990-2005. This has also been confirmed by the coefficients of correlation worked on the Composite Index of Economic Development (CIED) and ranks based on the index values, mentioned in Table 5.

TABLE 5

Correlation between CIED Values and State Ranks

Correlation between Index Values			*Rank Correlation*		
1991-2001	*2001-05*	*1991-05*	*1991-2001*	*2001-05*	*1991-05*
0.944** (10.306)	0.992** (28.278)	0.931** (9.20)	0.968* (13.908)	0.989* (24.040)	0.964* (13.071)

N.B. **Indicates significant at 0.01 level.

The high, positive and significant coefficients of correlation (0.944 and 0.931) as well as of rank correlation (0.968 and 0.964) indicate that no significant change has been observed in the development pattern of the states during the periods 1991-2001 and 1991-2005. However, a rising trend in the coefficient of correlation (0.992) and rank correlation (0.989), during the short span of 2001-05, indicate some minor changes in the relative positions of the states and their development pattern.

Section II

An endeavor has also been made to identify the major sources of inter-state variations in the country. For this purpose, Karl Pearson's coefficients of correlation for the selected 12 variables with Composite Index of Economic Development (CIED) have been calculated.

Table 6 outlines the correlation matrix of the CIED and the selected 12 indicators of development for the period 1990-91. The results indicate that all the variables, except CRI, were significantly correlated with the CIED. At least four variables: PCY, PEC, PTI and PIC were highly correlated with the CIED. However, high value of correlation amongst some of the explanatory variables implied the presence of multicollinearity. Consequently, Multiple Regression Analysis including all the variables could not be expected to provide the reliable results. Hence, to overcome this problem, Step-wise Multiple Backward Regression Analysis has been applied and results have been presented in Table 7. The results show that explanatory power of the regression model (Adj. R^2) has improved with the dropping of each successive variable from the model, after checking the collinearity. The results connote that the factors like: PIC, PMP, PVM, PBC, PAP and AYF were found to be the most significant sources of inter-state variations in the overall economic development of the country during 1990-91.

For the period 2000-01, correlation matrix of the CIED and selected 12 indicators has been amplified in Table 8. A perusal of the table points out that all the indicators, except AYF, IRI and CRI were significantly correlated with the CIED. Nevertheless, the variables such as: PCY, PEC, NF/L, and PTI were highly significantly correlated with the CIED. Accordingly, the results of Step-wise Multiple Backward Regression Analysis, applied to overcome the problem of

TABLE 6

Correlation Matrix (1990-91) for the Indicators of Overall Economic Development

	Composite Index	PCY	AYF	*IRI*	*CRI*	*PMP*	*NF/L*	*PVA*	*PIC*	*PBC*	*PEC*	*PAP*	*PTI*
Composite Index	1.000	.959**	.585*	.569*	0.308	.736**	.886**	.854**	.902**	.785**	.959**	.723**	.909**
PCY		1.000	.549*	.521*	0.299	.797**	.807**	.812**	.829**	.725**	.916**	.682**	.893**
AYF			1.000	.836**	.687**	.767**	.519*	0.158	0.278	0.218	0.498	0.386	0.370
IRI				1.000	0.509	.815**	0.492	0.177	0.374	0.076	.544*	0.499	0.269
CRI					1.000	.536*	0.051	-0.012	0.065	-0.014	0.203	0.358	0.138
PMP						1.000	.556*	0.361	0.498	0.253	.752**	.686**	0.503
NF/L							1.000	.742**	.845**	.721**	.873**	.547*	.778**
PVA								1.000	.889**	.887**	.791**	.541*	.903**
PIC									1.000	.742**	.881**	.665**	.837**
PBC										1.000	.717**	0.319	.925**
PEC											1.000	.791**	.832**
PAP												1.000	.518*
PTI													1.000

** Correlation is Significant at the 0.01 level (2-tailed).

** Correlation is Significant at the 0.05 level (2-tailed).

TABLE 7

Determinants of CIED: Results of Step-wise (Backward) Multiple Regression Analysis (1990-91)

Constant	Regression Coefficients											R^2 (F-value)	Adj. R^2
	PIC	*NF/L*	*PMP*	*PVM*	*PBC*	*PAP*	*AYF*	*PCY PEC PEC PEC*	*IRI*	*PTI*	*PEC*		
-0.288* -4.703	.00004 2.33	.0015 0.61	.00022 0.28	.00007 1.05	.00005 0.97	.00021 1.46	.0056 2.13	.00002 0.93	.0004 8 0.75	.00002 0.54	.0001 1 0.28	.999 254.63	.995
-0.281* -5.676	.00004* 3.78	.0021 1.71	.00040 1.06	.00006 1.17	.00006 2.75	.00025* 3.91	.0050* 3.32	.00002 1.03	.0004 5 0.82	.00002 0.55	----	.999 364.19	.996
-0.285* -6.276	.00004* 4.42	.0018 1.77	.00032 0.99	.00005 1.13	.00007* 5.16	.00026* 4.44	.0051* 3.68	.00002 1.88	.0005 0 0.99	---	---	.999 470.64	.997
-0.260* -6.996	.00005* 5.08	.0020 2.00	.00054 2.29	.00007 0.181	.00006* 5.11	.00024* 4.38	.0060* 5.63	.00001 1.63	----	----	----	.999 531.81	.997
-0.207* -10.090	.00005* 4.62	.0023 2.14	.00087* 6.49	.00010 2.57	.00007* 5.49	.00022* 3.73	.0056* 4.85	---	---	---	---	.998 491.94	.99 6

N.B.: Figures in parentheses are T-values.

* Indicates significant at 0.05 level.

multi-collinearity, delineated in Table 9, confirm that the explanatory power of the regression model has increased with each additional variable dropping from the model, after checking the collinearity. In Step-wise Backward Regression Equations, indicators like: PCY, NF/L, PIC and PMP were observed to be the major causes of inter-state variations during 2000-01 in the economy.

Correlation matrix of CIED and selected 12 indicators of development for the period 2004-05 has been presented in Table 10, a perusal of which shows that almost all the variables, except AYF, IRI, CRI and PAP were significantly correlated with the CIED. The variables like: PCY, PEC and NF/L were highly significantly correlated with the CIED. The results of Step-wise Multiple Backward Regression Analysis described in Table 11 explicate that the explanatory power of the regression model has improved with the dropping of each additional variable from the model, after checking the collinearity. In Step-wise Backward Regression Equations, indicators such as: PEC, PTI, PVM and PMP were reported to be the significant sources of inter-state variations during 2004-05 in the economy.

Thus, the variables such as: PIC, PVM and PMP were found to be the significant sources of inter-state disparities in the economic development during the overall (1990-2005) study period as well as during the period 1991-2001, while others like: PVM and PMP were found to be significant during the period 2001-05

Section III

On the whole, it can be concluded that no major change has been observed in the relative position of almost all the selected 15 states during the 15 years study period of 1990-2005. However, the range as well as the C.V. of the CIED for these selected states has shown a declining trend during this period. The range of CIED has diminished from 0.78664 in 1990-91 to 0.69164 in 2000-01 and further to 0.62106 in 2004-05, while the C.V. of CIED has declined from 68.12 per cent in 1990-91 to 56.47 per cent in 2000-01 and then to 54.07 per cent in 2004-05. This indicates that the

TABLE 8

Correlation Matrix (2000-01) for the Indicators of Overall Economic Development

	Composite Index	*PCY*	*AYF*	*IRI*	*CRI*	*PMP*	*NF/L*	*PVA*	*PIC*	*PBC*	*PEC*	*PAP*	*PTI*
Composite Index	1.000	0.980**	0.428	0.441	0.153	0.649**	0.932**	0.877**	0.759**	0.831**	0.947**	0.699**	0.881**
		1.000	0.403	0.354	0.149	0.619*	0.875**	0.839**	0.694**	0.844**	0.899**	0.762**	0.921**
			1.000	0.820**	0.794**	0.700**	0.415	0.017	-0.091	0.149	0.428	-0.022	0.173
				1.000	0.623*	0.773**	0.436	0.175	0.124	0.120	0.517*	-0.134	0.056
					1.000	0.561*	0.017	-0.169	-0.215	-0.040	0.116	-0.282	-0.062
						1.000	0.568*	0.364	0.286	0.339	0.747**	0.175	0.309
							1.000	.827**	0.742**	0.716**	0.932**	0.621*	0.783**
								1.000	0.929**	0.774**	0.799**	0.655**	0.829**
									1.000	0.569*	0.708**	0.605*	0.664**
										1.000	0.761**	0.644**	0.881**
											1.000	0.579*	0.743**
												1.000	0.807**
													1.000

** Correlation is Significant at the 0.01 level (2-tailed).

* Correlation is Significant at the 0.05 level (2-tailed).

TABLE 9

Determinants of CIED: Results of Step-wise (Backward) Multiple Regression Analysis (2000-01)

	Regression Coefficien									R^2 (F-value)	Adj. R^2
	PCY	*NF/L*	*PBC*	*PIC*	*PMP*	*PEC*	*PAP*	*PVM*	*PTI*		
-0.09296	.00003	.0072	.00001	.00001	.00043	-0.00018	-0.00006	-0.00002	0.0000	.996	.988
(-2.94)	(2.32)	(2.46)	(1.58)	(1.73)	(1.24)	(-0.78)	(-2.67)	(-0.67)	(0.06)	(131.31)	
-0.09328	.00004	.0072	.00001	.00001	.00042	-0.00017	-0.00006	-0.00002	—	.998	.990
(-3.28)	(3.91)	(2.70)	(1.74)	(1.92)	(1.55)	(-0.86)	(-0.74)	(-0.74)	—	(177.14)	
-0.9000	.00003	.0087	.00001	.00001	.00041	-0.00013	-0.00004	—	—	.995	.991
(-3.315)	(3.98)	(2.69)	(1.63)	(2.98)	(1.55)	(-0.69)	(-0.57)	—	—	(216.57)	
-0.08674	.00003	.0073	.00001	.00001	.00050	-0.00017	—	—	—	.995	.992
(-3.415)	(5.68)	(3.32)	(2.30)	(3.28)	(2.51)	(1.02)	—	—	—	(275.84)	
-0.09693	.00003	.0054	.00001	.00001	.00032	—	—	—	—	.995	.992
(-4.137)	(6.38)	(4.32)	(2.21)	(3.21)	(3.280)	—	—	—	—	(328.99)	

N.B.: Figures in parentheses are T-values.

* Indicates significant at 0.05 level.

TABLE 10

Determinants of CIED: Results of Step-wise (Backward) Multiple Regression Analysis (2000-01)

	Composite Index	*PCY*	*AYF*	*IRI*	*CRI*	*OMP*	*NF/L*	*PVA*	*PIC*	*PBC*	*PEC*	*PAP*	*PTI*
Composite Index	1.000	.969*	0.506	0.328	0.167	.641*	.887**	.815**	.782**	.634*	.955**	0.462.	832**
PCY		1.000	0.413	0.189	0.123	.536*	.821**	.800**	.783**	.705**	.882**	0.491	.924**
AYF			1.000	.743**	.767**	.749**	0.471	0.050	0.000	-0.056	0.512	-0.15	0.237
IRI				1.000	.664**	.702**	0.281	0.034	0.006	-0.177	0.408	-0.313	-0.071
CRI					1.000	.562	-0.546	-0.151	-0.58	-0.169	0.123	-0.527	0.000
PMP						1.000	.553	0.303	0.255	0.061	.725**	0.036	0.229
NF/L							1.000	.649**	.691**	.539*	.920**	0.458	.683**
PVA								1.000	.966**	.556*	.725**	0.509	.711**
PIC									1.000	0.512	.736**	0.506	.656**
PBC										1.000	.534*	0.364	.827**
PEC											1.000	0.463	.673**
PAP												1.000	0.480
PTI													1.000

** Correlation is Significant at the 0.01 level (2-tailed).

* Correlation is Significant at the 0.05 level (2-tailed).

TABLE 11

Determinants of CIED: Results of Step-wise (Backward) Multiple Regression Analysis (2000-01)

Constant	*Regression Coefficients*								R^2	*Adj*R^2
	PEC	*PTI*	*PVM*	*PMP*	*PBC*	*PCY*	*PIC*	*NF/L*	*(F-value)*	
-0.0055	.00049	.00004	.00003	.00038	-0.0000	0.00001	-0.0000	.0006	.994	.985
(-0.138)	(2.39)	(1.32)	(1.77)	(1.13)	(-1.10)	(-0.48)	(-0.63)	(0.24)	(115.33)	
-0.0020	.00053	.00005	.00003	.00040	-0.0000	0.00002	-0.0000		.993	.987
(-0.058)	(4.57)	(1.87)	(1.91)	(1.29)	(-1.47)	(-0.75)	(-0.62)	—	(152.36)	
0.00010	.00051	.00006	.00002*	.00053	-0.0000	0.00002			.993	.988
(0.003)	(4.81)	(2.47)	(3.03)	(2.52)	(-1.50)	(-1.12)	—	—	(192.35)	
-0.0315	.00042	.00003	.00002*	.00035	-0.0000				.992	.988
(-1.757)	(6.19)	(6.19)	(3.05)	(2.52)	(-1.05)	—	—	—	(224.09)	
-0.0242	.00040	.00003	.00002*	.00041					.991	.987
(-1.458)	(6.11)	(7.31)	(3.29)	(3.08)	—	—	—	—	(227.18)	

N.B.: Figures in parentheses are T-values.

* Indicates significant at 0.05 level.

extent of inter-state disparities in India have been eased to some point during this period of liberalized regime. Although this decline in the extent has not been due to the development of bottom line states, yet the same attributes to the slow growth of the top ranking states, particularly Punjab and Maharashtra. So far the major sources of these disparities are concerned; the study observed that variables like: Per-capita Income from Tertiary Sector (PTI), Per-capita Net Value Added in Manufacturing Sector (PVM) and Per-capita Milk (PMP) were the most significant sources of inter-state variations during the overall (1990-2005) study period

Therefore, it can be implied that there is need to encourage the investment in manufacturing sector along with diversification of agriculture in the backward states, to reduce the inter-state disparities in the country. For this purpose, private investment, both domestic as well as foreign, should be encouraged, especially in the backward states together by the central and state governments. There is also need to strengthen the financial position of almost all the states; for the forward states, it is essential to accelerate the growth of the CIED and for the bottom line states, the same is necessary to abridge the gap with forward states. Majority of the states were facing a crisis of expenditure composition. Growth-inducing and socially productive investments have been shrinking, while other items, particularly interest obligations and subsidies in the form of freebies, were absorbing a growing share of their resources. Most of the states have remained slower in implementing economic reforms during the study period. Hence, it also becomes essential for these states that they should reduce their fiscal deficits through the developmental effort accompanied by good governance and institutional reforms as the central assistance alone do not count. More financial powers can also be given to the states to encourage the state level planning in order to minimize the inter-state disparities in the country.

References

CMIE (2007), Energy, Different Issues, Economic Intelligence Service, Centre for Monitoring Indian Economy, Mumbai.

Government of India (2006), *Statistical Abstract,* India, Different Issues, Ministry of Statistics and Programme Implementation, Central Statistical Organization, New Delhi.

Government of India (2005), *Annual Survey of Industries,* Different Issues, Ministry of Statistics and Programme Implementation, Central Statistical Organization, New Delhi.

Government of India (2008), *Economic Survey,* Different Issues, Ministry of Finance, Economic Division, New Delhi.

Government of India (2008), Estimates of State Domestic Product: 1993-94 Series, Ministry of Statistics and Programme Implementation, Central Statistical Organization, New Delhi.

Government of India (2007), Indian Public Finance Statistics, Different Issues, Ministry of Finance, Economic Division, New Delhi.

Kurian, N.J. (2000), "Widening Regional Disparities in India", *Economic and Political Weekly,* February 12-18, pp. 1-23.

Mundinamani, P.S. (1983), Regional Disparities in India, *Yojana*, New Delhi, pp. 17-20.

Reserve Bank of India (1998), Report on Currency and Finance, 1996-97, Vol. I; Bombay.

Reserve Bank of India (2007), Handbook of Statistics on the Indian Economy, Mumbai.

UNDP (2004), Human Development Report, 2004, Oxford University Press, New Delhi.

6

Inter-Regional Disparities: Threats and Challenges

S.K. Pant, Firdaus Fatima Rizvi and D.C. Pathak

Whenever the history of India's development is written, it will surely be remembered as a saga of triumph and disappointments, successes and failures and integration and marginalization. While the triumphs, successes, and integrations were achieved in many core areas of the economy like the agriculture, science, medicine, technology, etc., disappointments, failures, and marginalization were witnessed largely in the field of literacy, health, poverty, regional disparities to name few.

No doubt, the decades of planned efforts has pushed the nation into the frontiers in many areas, helped her to emerge from being a net importer to being an exporter in many fields, from being a dependent and despondent nation to becoming a self reliant and independent country and from being a poor, impoverished and deprived nation to becoming a vibrant, thriving and power economy.

However, the inability of the planning to address many critical issues and more specifically its failure to distribute the fruits of development uniformly to all segments and sections of the society has come as a big set back to the planners because it has triggered off a process of chain reactions that has lead to a lop-sided or skewed development, resulting into the emergence of developed pockets in some of the regions. The subsequent models tried out later, by the planners, have so far not succeeded to stem the wrought.

These developed pockets, which later metamorphosed into urban centers, became the nodal points of development, which instead of acting as the catalyst of growth, as was envisaged of them, stifled the growth process and development activities in other areas by attracting both physical and non-physical resources (Pant, 2002).

The commensuration of skewed development also heightened other socio-economic angularities, speeded up the process of rural to urban migration and started exerting tremendous pressure on the fragile urban resources thereby threatening to destabilize the very process of growth. Hence reduction of regional disparities also became essential from the point of view of maintaining national integration, political stability and unity (Rao, 1984).

The situation had come to such a pass that the nation had to pledge its gold to international agencies in the early nineties of the twentieth century to avoid becoming a defaulter. The international help did arrive but with stringent conditions and the country had to initiate structural reforms better known as structural adjustment programme (SAP), besides opening the core sectors of the economy, which till the yester years were a restricted zone for the private-players partnership.

Thus, the onset of globalization heralded a new era in the history of planning in the country. That also brought a major shift in the development paradigm. The process of liberalization, privatization and globalization (LPG), which were the main plank of the new economic policy (NEP), brought forth major upheaval in many sectors which till then had experienced no competition at all.

As globalization places premium on skills rather than resources, it rewarded the developed regions/growth pockets favourably while the developing regions were left behind. Thus, the problem of regional imbalances subsequently got accentuated, which in turn, adversely affected the growth process of less developed regions. Besides this, the plan allocation of the government on vital sectors viz. economic and social also declined substantially and that also hit the growth process of these sectors in the developing regions hard. These imbalances have not remained confined to regions only but have percolated across the caste and occupation lines as well. (Table 1, Figure 1)

TABLE 1

Pattern of Profile of Poor along Caste and Occupation

(%age)

Category	*Rural*				*Urban*			
	Very Poor 1993-94	*Poor 1993-94*	*Very Poor 1999-2000*	*Poor 1999-2000*	*Very Poor 1993-94*	*Poor 1993-94*	*Very Poor 1999-2000*	*Poor 1999-2000*
Caste								
ST	22.1	50.2	17.0	44.2	24.0	43.0	17.5	37.5
SC	21.7	48.3	11.5	35.3	26.1	50.9	16.4	39.1
OBC	NA	NA	7.0	25.5	-		10.7	30.2
Occupation								
Ag. Lab.	26.2	54.4	14.1	39.7	-		-	-
Non-Ag. Lab.	15.2	42.2	8.7	27.2	-		-	-
Casual Lab.	-	-		-	36.6	64.5	26.0	53.0

Source: India Development Report, 2004-05, Oxford University Press.

Though, it could be stated that there has been an all round decline in the levels of poverty in both the rural and urban areas, however it could also be stated that the incidence of poverty has been still very high amongst the SC and ST households. Further, it can also be stated that on the occupational front, the incidence of poverty has been high among the agricultural labourers and non-agricultural classes in rural areas and among the casual labourers in urban areas. The fact is subsequently depicted in the Figure 2 below:

FIGURE 1

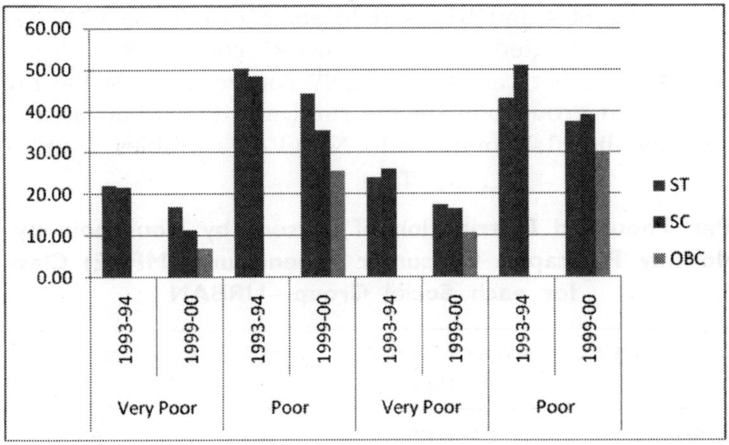

FIGURE 2

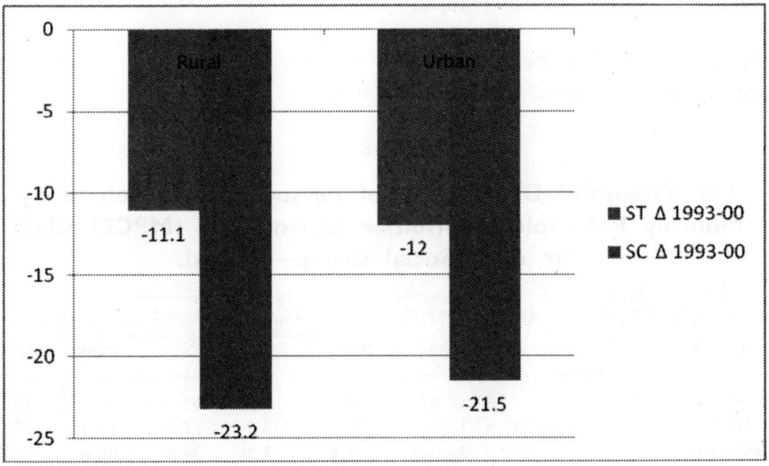

Figure 2 above shows that the SCs have benefited more by the growth process as they have shown a greater reduction in poverty compared to STs which are even more disadvantaged class than the SCs.

Similarly, the study of monthly per-capita expenditure also reflects the consumption disparities among the social groups. The SCs and STs and to some extent the OBCs are mostly concentrated in the lowest consumption group whereas the other castes are highly concentrated in the high consumption group both in the rural and the urban areas as shown by the 61st round of to NSSO data (Tables 2 and 3).

TABLE 2

Per Thousand Distribution of Persons by Household by Monthly Per-capita Consumer Expenditure (MPCE) Class for each Social Group—URBAN

Household MPCE class (Rs.)	*Average MPCE class (Rs.)*	*Household Social Group (%)*				
		ST	*SC*	*OBC*	*Other*	*All*
Less than 485	242.5 (6.17)	21.9	24.8	16.4	7.7	13.8
485-790	637.5 (16.24)	28.1	37.2	34.3	21.0	28.3
790-1380	1085.0 (27.64)	33.3	26.9	31.1	31.9	30.9
1380-2540 and above	1960.0 (49.93)	16.8	11.2	17.9	39.5	27.0
Total	3925.0 (100.0)	100.1	100.0	99.7	100.0	100.0

Note: Parenthesis shows percentage of income.
Source: NSSO Report, 2004-05, 61st Round.

TABLE 3

Per Thousand Distribution of Persons by Household by Monthly Per-capita Consumer Expenditure (MPCE) Class for each Social Group—RURAL

Household MPCE class (Rs.)	*Average MPCE class (Rs.)*	*Household Social Group (%)*				
		ST	*SC*	*OBC*	*Other*	*All*
Less than 320	160 (7.83)	26.6	17.2	11.4	6.5	13.0
320-455	387.5 (18.97)	31.7	33.6	27.9	20.4	27.6
455-690	572.5 (28.02)	28.4	33.3	36.9	35.6	35.0
690-1155 and above	922.5 (45.16)	13.1	15.7	23.8	37.6	24.4
Total	2042.5 (100.0)	99.8	99.8	100.0	100.0	100.0

Source: NSSO Report, 2004-05, 61st round.
Note: Parenthesis shows percentage of income.

How acute has been the incidence of poverty could better be gauged when we analyze the NSSO data, which states that there were about 14 per cent of the total households in the rural areas who were languishing at the lowest strata of the society, having an income of less than Rs. 485 per month. Of which, about 22 per cent of the households belonged to ST, about 25 per cent to SCs while the proportion of other (high caste groups) was reported to be hardly 8 per cent. Likewise, is the case of urban areas where the proportion of SC and ST households in the lowest stratum was found to be about 27 per cent and 17 per cent respectively while it was hardly 7 per cent for the other caste households. Similarly, as we .move up the ladder the proportion of SC, ST and even OBC households starts declining both in the rural as well as the urban settings, thereby upholding the fact that poverty alleviation and other social welfare programmes of the government have, so far, failed to mitigate the incidence of poverty.

It is against this background that the paper attempts to study and explore the nature, magnitude and trend of inter-regional imbalances on some already specified indicators. The paper has broadly been divided into three sections. The first sections traces the pattern and magnitude of regional imbalances at some broad socio-economic indicators of the developed and developing states, the second section studies the plan allocation of government in the pre and post-liberalization period and its subsequent impact on social sector while the third section proposes the strategy to address the issue associated with the problem of regional-imbalances.

I

REGIONAL IMBALANCES: TRENDS AND MAGNITUDE

The problem of regional imbalances or regional disparities is not only confined between states but within the states, castes, and regions as well. The decades of planning has, no doubt, succeeded in mitigating the intensity of it at the macro-level and however sharp differences not only prevail at micro-levels but even has grown and become sharp with the passage of time. An attempt has been made to study the level of regional imbalance at the following indicators: (a) Poverty, (b) Gender disparity, and (c) State Domestic Products, etc.

(a) Imbalances in the Poverty Levels

Poverty alleviation has been a core issue which makes the attention of planners to shift to the problem of regional imbalances. For instance, the 'states' poverty' has been a major criterion for fund disbursement by Finance Commissions in India.

The issue of poverty has always remained at the core of planners since the inception of planning and concerted efforts were made to address it. The decade's efforts bore fruits and there has been an overall decline in the level of poverty both at the urban and rural areas at the macro-level. However, sharp differences exist through the subsequent plans (Table 4).

TABLE 4

Incidence of Poverty and Inequality

Year	*Head Count Ratio (HCR)*		*Poverty Gap Index (PGI)*		*Gini Coefficient at 1993-94 price structure*		*Urban-Rural Disparities*
	R	*U*	*R*	*U*	*R*	*U*	
1973-74	56.4	49.0	16.2	15.5	28.7	31.9	1.39
1977-78	53.1	45.2	17.6	18.4	29.5	33.7	1.46
1983-84	45.7	40.8	13.4	12.9	30.0	34.1	1.52
1987-88	39.1	38.2	10.1	11.2	29.4	34.5	1.63
1993-94	37.3	32.4	7.8	8.4	28.5	34.4	1.63
1999-2000	27.1	23.6	5.3	5.0	26.7	34.8	1.80

Source: Handbook of Poverty Perspective, Policies and Programmes (2005):3.

It could be seen that though there has been a declining tendency of poverty, measured in terms of head count ratio (HCR), the incidence in rural areas has been much higher in contrast to the urban regions. The poverty gap index (PGI) have shown a decline in both rural and urban areas, however, it is still considered to be abnormally high after the reforms had been sat in. Similarly, the ratio of urban income to rural income which was just about 1.6 in 1951 and continued to remain within reasonable limit during the first three decades of development planning to reach 2.1 in 1980-81, worsened during the last two decades to a record a level close to 4.5. While the share of agriculture in the national income declined from 30 per cent to almost half, the share of population dependent on agriculture remains the same.

Likewise, despite all this, the Gini's coefficient index, a popular measure of measuring regional discrepancies, has remained significantly high for both rural and urban areas. Similarly, there has been an increase of about 29 per cent in the urban rural disparities between 1973-74 and 1999-2000, which reflects that the development efforts have not yet succeeded to address the issue of poverty adequately.

Incidentally, the period which had experienced divergent economic growth has also seen divergent trend in poverty reduction. During the period 1983 to 2004-05 the share of the poor in the population at the national came down from 45 to 28 per cent. However, in terms of absolute numbers the decline was only marginal from 324 million to 315 millions (Dev and Ravi, 2007). While all the major states experienced reduction in the percentage of the poor to varying degrees, five major states experienced increased in the number of poor during this period. These are Bihar (46.4 to 50.5 million), Madhya Pradesh (from 27.3 to 33.0 million), Maharashtra (from 28.5 to 31.7 million), Orissa (from 16.2 to 18.4 million) and Uttar Pradesh (from 55.2 to 63.9 million).

Therefore, it could be said that while poverty level has, by and large, fallen during the 1990s, it is increasingly getting concentrated in certain states and there has been considerable variation in the incidence of poverty across states -spreading from as low as 6-8 per cent for the states like Punjab and Haryana to as high as 47 per cent and 43 per cent for Orissa and Bihar (Panda, 2005), We hereby, present the profile of poverty in some of the developed and developing states (Table 5).

(b) Gender Disparity

Gender discrimination is evident even in the

TABLE 5

Head Count Ratio of Rural Poverty for Major States in India: 1999-2000

State	*HCR 1993-94*	*HCR 1999-2000*	*Est. number of Poor in 1999-2000 (million)*	*Percentage contribution to total poor in 1999-2000*
Bihar	54.96	42.7	39.02	16.18
Madhya Pradesh	45.52	37.52	28.79	11.94
Orissa	48.56	47.38	16.64	06.90
Rajasthan	27.41	14.78	06.89	02.86
Uttar Pradesh	40.85	30.99	49.92	20.70
Gujarat	24.21	13.13	05.67	02.35
Kerala	25.43	12.12	03.32	01.38
Maharashtra	36.86	24.58	22.00	09.12
Punjab	11.77	05.83	01.28	00.53

Source: India Development Report, 2004-05, Oxford University Press, New Delhi.

demographic indicators of the country. Not only that, child sex-ratio has been moving inexorably against the gird child in the recent decades. The 2001 Census figures indicate that illegal sex-selection is more prevalent in some of the prosperous parts of the country, like Punjab, Haryana and Delhi.

Though the gender gap in literacy is declining, still there exists a considerable difference. Census 2001 says while male literacy is 76 per cent, female literacy is as low as 54 per cent at the national level. For the states like Bihar, UP, Rajasthan, MP and Orissa, the gender gap in literacy is even more pronounced. Low level of female literacy is often associated with poor access to health and family planning facilities, poor awareness of proper childcare and other hygienic practices.

Poverty is a complex and multi-dimensional phenomenon. The ultimate solution to it cannot be just on just doling-out aid and help to the poor in need, but enable them to join and participate in the mainstream of economic activities. This is only possible if they are empowered and their capacities suitably enhanced (Hashim, 2007).

Female constitute an important significant and integral part of the workforce. Their participation in the main stream activities is, therefore, seen as a positive fall out of developmental planning. Because of low literacy and educational attainments, the ratio of estimated female to male earned income in India is 31 per cent, which is one of the lowest in the world. Though, the women constitute a third of the labour force in India, they account for less than one-fifth of the employees in the organized sector. Often they are engaged in activities which are characterized as drudgery. The study of work participation for women is, therefore, taken a crucial indicator of development (Table 6).

TABLE 6

Work Participation Ratio of Women, 1983 to 1999-2000

Year	*Female WPR as Percentage of Male WPR*	
	Rural	*Urban*
1983	62.2	29.5
1987	60.0	30.0
1993-94	59.3	29.8
1999-2000	55.3	26.8

Source: Hand Book of Poverty, Oxford University Press, 2005:30.

Similarly, the profile of women work participation rate (WPR) between 1983 and 1999-2000 also provides a very discouraging and disappointing scenario, both in the urban and rural settings. The striking feature has been a steady decline of female workforce in the country as a whole; however, the fall has been much steeper among the females as compared to that of the males, thereby implying that the post-reform period has affected the WPR more adversely that also contributed to the heightening of gender disparities. Though, the women earners often have to bear the double burden of work as a traditional house-maker and at workplace and the socially high valued activities like supplemented with their poor child caring are not assigned any economic value in national income accounting, their poor literacy, vocational skills also makes them on highly vulnerable class that needs urgent attention of the planner.

(c) State Domestic Product (SDP)

Another important indicator for measuring and comparing the growth differentials between the two regions, commonly used, has been the per-capita state domestic product (SDP). However, the experts also agree that SDP alone cannot be taken to be an absolute reliable and satisfactory measure of development because it does not accounts income from all sources, for example, the remittances of the migrant workers are not included with the SDP. However, in the absence of other alternatives, SDP is conventionally used.

The data on per-capita SDP shows that not only the gap between the maximum and minimum ratio has inclined but even the coefficient of variation has widened over the last four decades. What has been an area of concern is that there has been further rise in the ratio in the post-reform period (Bagchi and Kurian, 2005). An attempt has also been made to study the growth profile of population and net state domestic product in the pre and post-reforms period (Table 7).

TABLE 7

Share of States in the Population Net State Domestic Product

(In %)

States	*1970-71*	*1980-1981*	*1990-1991*	*1998-99*
High Income				
Population	19.9	20.0	20.3	20.0
NSDP	27.6	30.8	33.0	33.8
Middle Income				
Population	33.4	32.7	31.9	29.0
NSDP	34.6	32.5	31.0	32.9
Low Income				
Population	43.8	44.1	45.1	45.0
NSDP	34.7	33.8	33.4	30.0

Source: Bagchi (2001).

The data shows that while the populations of high income states have risen marginally, the increase in case of low income state was about 1.2 percentage points. The enhancement in the share of high income states was over 6 percentage point while, the middle and low income states registered a decline of 4 to 5 percentage point during the same period. Needless to say that the post-reform periods have benefited the developed states.

Similarly, the monthly per-capita expenditure shows that during 2004-05, compared to 30 per cent at the all-India level, 57 per cent of rural population in states like Orissa, Chhattisgarh (55%), Madhya Pradesh (47%), Bihar and Jharkhand (46% each) was living below the monthly per-capita expenditure (MPCE) level of Rs. 365 or about Rs. 12 per day! As against this, 57 per cent of rural population in Kerala and 51 per cent of Punjab and 47 per cent in Haryana had MPCE of Rs. 690. At the all-India level this corresponds to the top 20 percentile of MPCE distribution. During 2004-05, as compared to 30 per cent at the all-India level, 55 per cent of Bihar and 50 per cent of Orissa's urban population was below the MPCE level of Rs. 580 or Rs. 19 per day. As against the top 20 per cent at the all-India level, 28 per cent of Kerala's and 27 per cent of Punjab's urban population were having an MPCE level of at least Rs. 1,380 (*Economic Survey*, 2007-08).

Further, even the comparison of health indicators like life expectancy at birth shows a marked dichotomy between the developed and developing states. For example, we know that the life expectancy is highest in Kerala followed by Punjab, Maharashtra, Himachal Pradesh and Tamil Nadu, while it has been least in Madhya Pradesh followed by Assam, Orissa, UP and Bihar. As on March 2006, 100 per cent of Primary Health Centers (PHCs) had labour room in Andhra Pradesh, Karnataka and Tamil Nadu while its proportion was low in UP, Bihar, and MP. As on March 2006, proportion of PHCs with operation theatres was 87 per cent in Andhra Pradesh followed by Rajasthan (83%), Maharashtra (74%), Haryana (71%) and Gujarat (67%). It was low in UP, West Bengal, Chhattisgarh, Kerala and Bihar (*Economic Survey,* 2007-08). Thus, mode of unsafe delivery coupled with prevalence of low literacy levels and dominance of superstitious practices contributes to the plan performance of health indicators in developing states, which is not the case with developed ones.

Likewise, it can also be shown for other indicators like the female literacy, levels of urbanization, etc. that it is only the developed states that have taken advantage of the new economic policy or have prospered in the new scenario and in the process contributed into the heightening of regional inequalities. In 2004-05, the Gross Enrolment Ratios for elementary education, i.e., I-VIII Class (6-14 years) was highest in Madhya Pradesh (114.1%), followed by Tamil Nadu (114%) and Chhattisgarh (112.6%). It was lowest in Bihar (65.2%) followed by Punjab (72.6%) and Jharkhand (75.8%). Gross Enrolment Ratio for Secondary education (IX-X Class) was high in Himachal Pradesh (134.9%) followed by Kerala (93%), and Tamil Nadu (80.7%). It was lowest in Bihar (22.5%), Jharkhand (26.5%) and West Bengal (41.5%). For Senior Secondary level (XI-XII Class), Gross Enrolment Ratio was least at 2.5 per cent in Jharkhand followed by 9.8 per cent in Bihar and highest at 127.7 per cent for Himachal Pradesh followed by 43.9 per cent in Tamil Nadu (*Economic Survey*, 2007-08).

Similarly, another important indicator of development could be the per-capita consumption of electricity. The study shows that there also has been a wide range of variation across the states. 'For instance', in 1998-99, the maximum minimum ratio of per-capita electricity consumption was worked out to be 7 which, no doubt, was a marked improvement over what had prevailed earlier, in the mid-eighties, however sharps inequalities prevailed. If we accept the All-India average to be 100, the index of per-capita electricity consumption stood at 34 for Assam, 42 for Bihar contrasting with 239 for Punjab and 201 for Gujarat (Bagchi and Kurian: *Ibid*.).

Likewise, it could be seen that while the states like Himachal Pradesh, Punjab, Haryana, Kerala, Karnataka, Gujarat, Tamil Nadu and Andhra Pradesh have much larger percentage of households having electricity than is the case in Bihar, Assam, Jharkhand, UP and Orissa. Households having access to toilet facilities are high in Kerala, Assam and Punjab and low in Chhattisgarh, Jharkhand, Bihar and Madhya Pradesh (*Economic Survey*, 2007-08).

Therefore, mere decline in the overall level of poverty at the macro-level does not spells good unless the issues of regional inequalities are not adequately addressed (Deaton and Dreze, 2002; Thamarajakashi, 2003).

II

PLAN ALLOCATION AND ITS IMPACT ON SOCIAL SECTORS

It could be stated that earlier under the federal system, the issue of development wrested solely with the government, though private sector was invited to participate but only in few selected sectors. In core sectors like economic and social, all investment allocations were made by the government—central and state, depending upon the subject. These allocations were guided, largely, on the recommendations of experts groups, commissions, task force, etc. that the government constituted from time to time.

In view of time and space constraints only two sectors viz. Education and Health have been taken up for analysis and discussion. Incidentally both fall under the state government's jurisdiction. Therefore, it will be worthwhile to see how these two sectors have performed in the pre and post-reforms periods. Further, these two sectors are also considered to be crucial sectors whose close inter-play decides the course and level of human and region's development.

(i) Education

Education, on account of its highly pervasive nature has always remained an area of importance and concern since time immoral. The plausible reason for this could be its ability to transgress, influence and mould the human capability from very low levels to unprecedented heights, from being an unknown and unproductive class to becoming a highly competitive unit and from being a raw and uncultivated class to a highly refined value added finished product. (Pant, 2005) Unfortunately the performance of education in developing region is far from satisfactory. High drop-out rates, marginalization of socially disadvantaged groups, dilution in the quality of education, lack of supervision and monetary support are some of the concerned areas that have afflicted the overall performance of education all this had held back the development in developing states while developed state-have marched ahead in this adding to the on going problem of regional disparities.

Though the government has been concerned about it as exemplified by the setting up of various commission to look after its working and suggest appropriate remedial measures, however, it has receives scant attention as far as the allocation to it is concerned.

For example the Kothari Commission was set-up to look into the working of education came up with the recommendation that allocation to the tune of 6 per cent of the Gross Domestic Product (GDP) should be made in education. However, the government has failed to honour these recommendations since the inception of five year plans for whatever reasons, however, the level has subsequent been enhanced in various plans (Table 8).

TABLE 8

Plan Allocation on Education against GDP

Years	*% of GDP*
1950-59	1.2-2.3 (1.8)
1960-69	2.5-3.0 (2.8)
1970-80	3.1-3.5 (3.1)
1980-90	2.9-4.5 (3.2)
1990-96	4.9-4.0 (4.1)

Note: Figures in brackets denotes the average value.
Source: India Education Report (2002), Oxford University Press, New Delhi.

Thus, it could be said that depletion of allocation in this sector is only going to compound the things for developing states unless utilization of resources is not taken up on optimum levels.

(ii) Health

In the case of health too, the government seemed to be very concern. The announcement of National Health Policy in the early fifties of twentieth century and followed up by setting of various commissions are testimony to the fact that health sector remained a priority area.

The setting up of the first commission under Bhore was setup in 1946 to look into the working of health services in rural India shows the concern of the government how much seriously it was taking this sector; however, its recommendations of allocating one per cent of GDP on health sector once again, could not be implemented. Later the National Health Policy (NHP) subsequently enhanced the allocation to 2-3 per cent of GDP by 2010. However, on the contrary, this amount has remained static at 0.9 per cent for almost two decades and whatever actual increase has occurred, it has largely been because of increase in GDP.

Therefore, it could be said that when the plan allocations have not been honoured, for whatever reasons, the development process is likely to be affected. In the post-liberalisation period when the government's allocation is being severely curtailed, the development of these sectors is likely to be adversely affected. Unfortunately both education and health fall under the state list, which now will get lesser amount to invest; the developing states will be more severely affected (Table 9).

Thus, it becomes quite clear that with the drastic reduction in the allocation of health and education sector, the process of human development and consequently the quality of life is all likely to be affected in both developed and developing states but as the developed states have more resources, they are in a better position to compensate for it. However, in the case of developing states, their position will become more vulnerable which with only help in increasing the regional imbalances, a situation that will only be a drag in the overall development process of the country because the developed states, with their higher levels of income and consumption and stronger revenue base are in a bitter position to raise their resource for development (Bagchi and Kurian: *Ibid.*).

TABLE 9

Expenditure on Education and Health in Pre- and Post-Reform Periods

(Rs. crore)

Year	*Education*	*Health*
Pre-Reform Period		
1980-81	3859 (3.2)	943 (0.8)
1989-90	16905 (4.1)	3767 (0.9)
1990-91	19791 (3.9)	4508 (0.9)
Post-Reform Period		
1991-92	21914 (3.7)	4888 (0.8)
1992-93	24722 (3.7)	5621 (0.9)
1993-94	27530 (3.5)	6218 (0.8)
1994-95	32107 (3.5)	6920 (0.7)
1995-96	37097 (3.5)	7880 (0.7)
1996-97	43035 (3.5)	9231 (0.7)
1997-98	49200 (3.6)	10544 (0.7)

Note: Figures in brackets denote percentage to GDP.
Source: Central Statistical Organisation, Selected Socio-economic Statistics for Indian, 2000.

III

FUTURE STRATEGY: DISTRESSING SIGNALS

The problem of regional imbalances or regional disparities is a complex phenomenon. It has precipitated not only an account of the failure of one or some institutions but points out towards collective failure of the institutions, the machinery meant for delivering goods, programme and functionaries supposedly meant for facilitating the execution of programmes. This is truer in case of developing states. If the situation is allowed to persist, it will not only heighten the regional imbalances but will also pose a severe threat to our national integrity, security and above all the very development process.

Thus, in order to address the issue; multi-pronged strategy that addresses the problem at multiple levels, simultaneously, needs to be evolved. It is true that development needs infrastructure and developing states possess poor infrastructure, thus developing it poses a severe challenge because under the changed scenario, the onus of developing solely cannot lie on the government hence some alternative option of viable and sustained to provide local leadership considered vital for vibrancy of the programme nature needs to be searched. Similarly, mobilization of grass-root institutions is also required to be undertaken and finally the re-organization of grass-root committees and organisation also needs to be taken up. An attempt has been made to address these issues here:

(A) Development of Infrastructure: Onus lies with whom?

There can be no denying that infrastructure plays a very vital role in the socio-economic development of the region. Inadequate or lack of infrastructure does not invite private participation and under the liberalization era, government's role has also been redefined and therefore cannot be depended upon. The problem of developed states will not be as acute as the developing states would face. Thus, in the new set-up, developing states have to devise their own planning models. Fortunately, the decades of planned efforts have succeeded in erecting grass-root institutions, through which the government executes and monitors rural development and other development programmes. The 73rd and 74th Constitutional Amendment Act has empowered the Panchayatraj and other local body institutions through devolution of powers. Each year they identify the works to be carried about. It has been found that, in most of the cases, the work identified by block panchayatraj functionaries does not gets the peoples' consent or the approval of the people, and they, by and large remain ignorant and thus do not participate or get involved in the programme. In other words, the rural development work generally lacks people participation and this is particularly true in case of developing states. Thus, the problem for them is to device such a strategy that sensitizes, motivates and encourages them to participate.

The problem here lies, as has been brought out various studies, that the programme functionaries along with public representatives at some point of time in the course of disbursing their duties strike an unholy alliance with other local a influential groups/parties that isolates the people in general and marginalized people in particular. So the programme, which it is meant for construction of infrastructure or for the welfare of the people, is promulgated without people consent and worst without their knowledge. Their arbitrary way of operation not only annoys the people but also develops an element of distrust and lack of credibility for them. This jinx needs to be broken!

Therefore, in order to facilitate development, the role and working of block and panchayats, the two most important administrative and legislative units at the grass-roots levels, needs to be re-defined. The people's trust could only be restored once their working becomes transparent. This will only be possible when the people are informed or made aware of the programmes that the block office intends to launch or initiate. The unholy collusion between programme functionaries and people's representative could only be broken when all transaction whether related to selection of sites for implementing any project or beneficiaries under any welfare programme are undertaken in the Gram Sabha's open meetings. It has also been alleged that these meetings, many a times, are manipulated—a practice that needs to be curbed. The venue of such meetings also needs to be changed so as to enable more and more people to participate. Thus, when the meetings are held in open and all transactions take before the eyes of people, the chances of manipulation and forging of unholy alliances diminish considerably.

(B) Mobilization of Grass-root Institutions

The role of grass-root institutions in the rural transformation is second to none. Often it has been found that they are under staffed. It has also been observed that the vacancies have not been filled for quite some time and the block personnel have not been received relevant training, which leaves most of them in a dejected and de-motivated state. On account of shortage of staff, they are also required to do multiple functions which they fail to perform.

In order to honour the directives of their bosses, they try to resort to short-cut methods and invariable indulge in unholy alliances with those public representatives who have dubious records. This alliance one hand isolates them with the masses and on the other develops disliking for them in the eyes of the public. All this ultimately has a bearing in their efficiency level and adversely affects the performance of the programme.

The solution, therefore, lies by mobilizing these grass-root institutions by rejuvenating their functionaries. It is therefore recommended that all the vacancies of these institutions especially the blocks be filled on priority basis. Each functionary is assigned the job for which he/she needs to be made accountable. Their training aspects needs not only be strengthened but even be repeated periodically. The concept of providing one time training needs to be abolished as training giving in succession, over a period of time, helps them to keep abreast of the latest happening in the field and makes them sharp, committed and more focused.

Further, it has also been observed that period of training generally is of very short or short period, which is thoroughly insufficient to address the apprehensions of the participants/functionaries or allow the functionaries to grasp subtle intricacies of the programme. The shorter period of training, it is generally alleged, is organized for fulfiling the mandatory conditions imposed in the programme by the implementing authorities and is of perfunctory nature. Therefore, it is suggested that training component needs to be taken up more seriously and its period be decided according to the needs of the area and status of programme functionaries since as it has a very significant bearing on improving the quality of functions.

(C) Reorganization of Grass-root Committees and Organisations

The third important component of regional/rural development is the grass-root committees and organizations. In order to make the planning process more democratic and participative in nature, the concept of grass-root organizations and committees was envisaged. They have subsequently been empowered by constitutional amendments and acts also. Provision of including members of the marginalised committees as well female has also been made to enable this section to have a say in decision-making process.

Unfortunately, it has been found that a good majority of these organisations and committees are lying in a defunct state, and this is particularly true for developing states. Their non-participation emboldens the programme functions and public representative to strike unholy alliances and indulge in nefarious activities at the cost of development. The nomenclature of the committees often shows that they have been infected by sizeable proportions of beaurocrats, and people's representatives who have no stake in the development of the region and hence evince no interest. Therefore, the need of the hour is to replace all such personnel irrespective of their position and class, who fail to live up to the expectations of the people by those who have some state in show commitments.

Similarly, there should also been a provision with constitutional legality to call back the peoples' representatives or the member of committee who fails to deliver the goods or show lack of inclination towards his duties. Likewise an element of social accountability also needs to be incorporated in the system of working. All this will go a long way not only to make the system vibrant but also provide credibility in the eyes of the people who will also participate in the programmes in enmass.

REFERENCES

Bagchi, Amresh and John Kurian (2005), Regional Inequalities in India. Pre and Post-reform Trends and Challenges for Policy in the Politics of Economic Reforms in India (Ed) by Jos Moij, Sage Publication, New Delhi.

Deaton, Angus and Jean Dreze (2002), Poverty and Inequality in India, A Re Examination, *Economic and Political Weekly*, No. 36, September 7, Mumbai: 3729-48.

Dev, S.M and Ravi, C. (2007), Poverty and Inequality: All-India and States, 1983-2005, *Economic and Political Weekly*, Feb. 10, Vol. 42, No. 6, pp. 509-21, 2007.

Economic Survey, 2007-08, Government of India.

Hashim, S.R. (2007), Poverty and Inclusive Growth, *Indian Economic Journal*, Vol. 55, No. 2, July-September

Panda, Manoj (2005), Macroeconomic Scene Growth and Equality Perspectives in India Development Report (Ed) by Kirit S. Parikh and R. Radhakrishnan, Oxford University Press, New Delhi.

Pant, S.K. (2002), Gender Bias in Girl Child Education, Kanishka Publishers, Distributors, New Delhi.

Pant, S.K. (2005), Final Evaluation of Total Literacy Campaign in District Gumla, Jharkhand, Project Report, sponsored by National Literacy Mission, New Delhi and Directortate of Adult Education, Ministry of Human Resource Development, New Delhi and Funded by Biri Argana Zila Saksharta Samiti, Gumla.

Rao, Hemlata (1984), Regional Disparities and Development in India, Ashish Publication House, New Delhi

Thamarajakashi, R. (2003), Growth and Poverty in India in the 1990s, *Economic and Political Weekly*, April 26, Mumbai: 1721-24.

7

Inter-Regional Disparities with Multi-dimensional Aspects in India

V.L. LAVANYA AND B. KARTHIKEYAN

INTRODUCTION

Disparities in economic and social development across the regions and intra-regional disparities among different segments of the society have been the major planks for adopting planning process in India since independence. Apart from massive investments in backward regions, various public policies directed at encouraging private investments in such regions have been pursued during the first three decades of planned development. While efforts to reduce regional disparities were not lacking, achievements were not often commensurate with these efforts. Considerable level of regional disparities remained at the end of the Seventies. The accelerated economic growth since the early Eighties appears to have aggravated regional disparities. The on-going economic reforms since 1991 with stabilisation and deregulation policies as their central pieces seem to have further widened the regional disparities. The seriousness of the emerging acute regional imbalances has not yet received the public attention it deserves.

Development is a multi-dimensional phenomenon. Some of its major dimensions include: the level of economic growth, level of education, level of health services, degree of modernization, status of women, level of nutrition, quality of housing, distribution of goods and services, and access to communication. In India, the progress of socio-economic development among major states is not uniform.

The states in India are marked with wide disparity in socio-economic development. The factors, which are found out to be more important for the overall development process, relate to basic needs like education, availability of food, minimum purchasing power and facilities like safe drinking water, health care infrastructure, etc. It is also found that enrolment ratio cannot be raised unless minimum needs of the common people are satisfied. Therefore, true development requires government action to improve elementary education, safe drinking water facilities and health care, and to remove barriers against social minorities, especially women. The role of social development such as literacy (and particularly of female literacy) in promoting basic capabilities emerges as the prerequisite to overall development.

LAND INEQUALITY DISTRIBUTION

One of the most important aspects of India's development progress is its remarkable regional disparity in eliminating basic deprivations. The economy suffers from large and incessant inequalities. The majority of the poor people lives in rural areas and belongs to the category of landless labourers and the land continues to be highly inequitably distributed.

CONCEPT OF INTER-REGIONAL DISPARITIES

Regional inequality is a major concern in a large number of developing countries. Growth pole dynamics and inverted-U hypothesis sustain that regional inequalities within developing countries will be eventually reduced through factor mobility. "Reduction of socio-economic disparities is essential from the point of maintaining National integration, political stability and unity also. If neglected and unchecked these disparities may assume menacing dimension, and threaten the very existence of this nation.

Neo-classical growth theory highlights the mobility of supply side factors, in particular capital stock, technical change and labour, as the reason for the eventual reduction of such disparities. On the other hand the opposing theories, in particular dependency and structural change theories, postulate that regional inequality is an inevitable outcome of capital accumulation and profit maximisation.

The proposition of convergence in recent growth literature has been of much appeal to the analysis of disparities amongst developed countries. Would it be equally applicable to the analysis of regional disparities within a developing country? Following Barro and Sala-i-Martin (1995) in the context of regions there are two views on how the process of catching up and convergence can take place: b-convergence, where poor regions will tend to grow faster than the more developed regions (as the diminishing marginal returns to capital prevails in the latter regions) and s-convergence concerning cross-regional dispersion (inequalities) which would tend to decrease over time.

Economic growth is essential for improvement in the living standards of the population and to reduce absolute deprivation (poverty). It is through the process of trickle down that growth benefits percolate to the lowest strata of the society. The increased disparities in the distribution of income both across the population groups and between different regions, which are widely experienced in the developing countries reflect the failure of the trickle down process. Income inequality is an outcome of skewed distribution of factors of production both in terms of quantity and quality, strategy of economic growth, inappropriate social and political institutions, lack of or inadequate capabilities and functioning of the population, etc. A.K. Sen (1984) maintained that absolute deprivation in terms of personal capability relates to relative deprivation in terms of commodities, income and resources.

Along with faster economic growth and reduction in

poverty, there has been accelerated improvement in various indicators of human development since the early Eighties whether it is in the case of demographic characteristics or social development indicators. During the last two decades, the country has made major strides in health and education sectors. The economy got diversified significantly and the share of the service sector in employment and incomes improved considerably. While there is a broad consensus on the overall improvement of the economy and quality of life during the period under consideration, there are significantly differing perceptions about the distributional impacts of these gains.

Disparities in economic and social development across the regions and intra-regional disparities among different segments of the society have been the major planks for adopting planning process in India since independence. Apart from massive investments in backward regions, various public policies directed at encouraging private investments in such regions have been pursued during the first three decades of planned development. While efforts to reduce regional disparities were not lacking, achievements were not often commensurate with these efforts. Considerable level of regional disparities remained at the end of the Seventies. The accelerated economic growth since the early Eighties appears to have aggravated regional disparities. The on-going economic reforms since 1991 with stabilisation and deregulation policies as their central pieces seem to have further widened the regional disparities. The seriousness of the emerging acute regional imbalances has not yet received the public attention it deserves. The purpose of this study is to initiate a debate on the various issues involved with a view to explore effective corrective measures without any further delay.

Most of the studies on inter-country and inter-regional differences in levels of living and income are done within the theoretical framework of neoclassical growth models. These models, under plausible assumptions demonstrate convergence of incomes. Three notable recent studies, however, indicate that in the Indian context these convergence theories do not explain the ground realities. The scope of this study is restricted to a comparative analysis of the emerging trends in fifteen major States in respect of a few key parameters which have an intrinsic bearing on social and economic development. The variables chosen for examination include those which will have a bearing on gender and equity issues. The fifteen States together account for 96 per cent of the population of India. The remaining 4 per cent of the population is spread out in 10 smaller States and seven Union Territories including the National Capital Territory of Delhi. Leaving out these States and UTs from detailed study is mainly due to non-availability of all relevant data and also to keep the data sets analytically and logistically manageable. The fifteen States taken up for the detailed study have been grouped into two—a forward group and a backward group. The forward group consists of Andhra Pradesh, Gujarat, Haryana, Karnataka, Kerala, Maharashtra, Punjab and Tamil Nadu. The backward group comprises of Assam, Bihar, Madhya Pradesh, Orissa, Rajasthan, Uttar Pradesh and West Bengal.

Geographically, the forward group of States fall in the Western and Southern parts of the country and are contiguous except for Punjab and Haryana which are separated by Rajasthan from the rest of the States in this group. The group of backward States are in the Eastern and Northern parts of the country and are geographically contiguous. Another notable geographical feature is that while six out of eight States, except Haryana and Punjab, in the first group have vast sea coasts, only two out of the seven in the second group viz., Orissa and West Bengal are littoral. While the forward group of States accounts for about 42 per cent of the national population, the backward group accounts for as much as 54 per cent of the population of the country. In terms of natural resources including mineral wealth, water resources and quality of soil, the latter has definite edge over the former. A limitation of inter-regional analysis using States as units is the fact that this may not be able to capture the significant intra-State disparities in economic and social development which exists today. The larger States in both the groups have regions within themselves, which are vastly different in terms of various indicators of development. There are identifiable distinct regions, at different stages of development, in several States. After discussing the inter-regional disparities in development, treating States as units, we will take up intra-State disparities for a brief analysis in the latter part of the present study.

The National Human Development Report 2001 for India (2002) reveals vast differences in human development and poverty between the States of India in 1981. The report notes that "At the state level, there are wide disparities in the level of human development."

CONCLUSION

In India too, area disparities in the level of poverty, unemployment, income infrastructure, agriculture industry and above all the level of living of the people exist substantially across the regions. Numerous measures have been undertaken in the last forty years of planning to achieve balanced regional development of the country. Yet, wide disparities in area development continues in this country. The most pitiable situation is that the most resources rich states such as Orissa, Bihar, Madhya Pradesh, Assam, and Uttar Pradesh are the regions with high poverty pockets.

A limitation of inter-regional analysis using States as units is the fact that this may not be able to capture the significant intra-State disparities in economic and social development which exists today. The larger States in both the groups have regions within themselves, which are vastly different in terms of various indicators of development. There are identifiable distinct regions, at different stages of development, in several States.

References

Akita, T. (1988), "Regional Development and Income Disparities in Indonesia", *Asian Economic Journal*, Vol. 2, pp. 165-91.

Akita, T. and Lukman, R.J. (1995), Interregional Inequalities in Indonesia: A Sectoral Decomposition Analysis for 1975-92", *Bulletin of Indonesian Economic Studies*, Vol. 31, No. 2, pp. 61-81.

Barro, Robert and Sala-I-Martin, Xavier (1991), "Convergence Across States and Regions", Brookings Papers on Economic Activity, I, pp. 107-81.

Barro, Robert and Sala-I-Martin, Xavier (1995), Economic Growth, New York: McGraw-Hill.

Bhagwati, Jagdish N. and T.N. Srinivasan (1975), Foreign Trade Regimes and Economic Development: India, New York: Columbia University Press.

Bhalla, G.S. (1995) "Globalisation and Agricultural Policy in India", *Indian Journal of Agricultural Economics*, Vol. 50, pp. 8-26.

Birdsall, Nancy, David Ross, and Richard Sabot (1995), "Inequality and Growth Reconsidered: Lessons from East Asia", *World Bank Economic Review*, Vol. 9, pp. 477-508.

Breton, Albert (1996), Competitive Governments, Cambridge: Cambridge University Press.

Chhibber, Pradeep (1995), "Political Parties, Electoral Competition, Government Expenditures and Economic Reform in India", *Journal of Development Studies*, Vol. 32, pp. 74-96.

Chong Alberto and Cesar Calderon (2000), "Institutional Quality and Income Distribution", *Economic Development and Cultural Change*, Vol. 48, pp. 761-86

Mathur, A. (1983), "Regional Development and Income Disparities in India: A Sectoral Analysis", *Economic Development and Cultural Change*, Vol. 31, No. 3, pp. 475-505.

Mahajan, O.P. (1982), Regional Economic Development in India. (New Delhi, Ess Ess Publishers).

World Bank (2000), World Bank Development Indicators, The World Bank Group, Washington DC.

Noorbakhsh, F. (1999), 'Standards of Living, Human Development Indices and Structural Adjustments in Developing Countries: An Empirical Investigation', *Journal of International Development*, Vol. 11, 151-75.

8

Inter-Regional Disparities in India

PRADEEP PUNJABI AND PRASHANT BHARDWAJ

India has had a glorious past. Our cultural heritage is comparable to that of China or Egypt. We had great kings and kingdoms. Half of the major world religions had their origin in India. We had produced great thinkers and philosophers who contributed to several branches of knowledge.

But most of our history before 1500 AD is in oral traditions. Indians, by and large, were not good at record keeping. This is especially true about hard facts and data relating to various aspects of life. Even for the period 1500 to 1750 AD data are rudimentary. The historical trends discussed in this section, by and large, are based on Cambridge Economics History of India edited by Dharma Kumar with editorial assistance by Meghnad Desai and Tapan Raychaudhuri and Irfan Habib.

India during Akber's time was considered as prosperous a country as the best in the world. Though mainly agrarian, India was a leading manufacturing nation at least at par with pre-industrial Europe. She lost her relative advantage only after Europe achieved a revolution in technology.

The economy was village based. Though under Muslim rule for over 500 years, the society continued to be organized in Hindu traditions. Caste system was intact. The social disparity often added another dimension to economic exploitation. While the Jajmani system ensured social security, the caste system ensured social immobility.

However, flexibility of the Jajmani system ensured that the artisans working under it were not completely cut off from the market. They were free to sell outside the village the surplus goods left after the fulfilment of community obligations. The traditional economic system based on agriculture and small scale industries were not disrupted either by the activity of native capital or by the penetration of the foreign merchant capital.

Domestic trade was facilitated by a fairly developed road network. Sher Shah Suri during his short regime laid the foundation of a highway system in India. He alone had built 1700 sarais for the convenience of travellers, mainly traders, on the highways.

The Indian village was highly segmented both socially and economically. There was significant inequality in distribution of farm land, though there was plenty of cultivable waste land available which could be brought under plough if capital, labour and organization were forthcoming.

In comparison to the rural rich, the urban rich especially the merchants in coastal towns were much wealthier. Some of the merchants of Bengal and Gujarat had stupefying wealth. The pattern of life of the nobility and the upper class in Mughal India has become a byword for luxury and ostentation. There is hardly any evidence to show that the puritan style set-up by Aurangzeb had any marked effect on the lives of the nobility. Of course, this consumerism created demand for a horde of luxury items, which generated employment, income and general prosperity.

The debate concerning the level of India's economic development in the pre-colonial era is unlikely to ever reach a satisfactory conclusion, as the basic quantitative information is absent.

Dadabhai Naoraji was the first one to make an attempt to estimate national and per-capita income in India. He placed per-capita income of India at Rs. 30 in 1870 compared to that of England of Rs. 450. However, since necessities in India cost only about one-third as compared to England at that time, the real difference in terms of purchasing power parity was not fifteen times but only five times.

The statistical reporter of the "Indian Economist" ran a series of articles on the standard of living in India in 1870. One of the items which was given region-wise was value of per-capita agricultural output for 1868-69. According to that it varied from Rs. 21.7 in Central Province to as low as Rs. 11.1 in Madras. Others were Bombay (Rs. 20.0). United Privinces (Rs. 12.1), Punjab (Rs. 17.4) and Bengal, including Bihar and Orissa (Rs. 15.9).

Region-wise birth rates, death rates and life expectancy at birth are given in the table below for the period 1901-11:

TABLE I

Region	*Birth rate*	*Death rate*	*Life expectancy*	
			Male	*Female*
East	52.8	45.8	22.4	22.8
West	48.1	42.1	24.8	23.8
Central	46.6	31.1	31.7	32.7
North	48.6	48.7	21.7	19.2
South	40.3	32.2	29.8	32.3
All-India	47.7	41.7	24.7	24.4

Source: Census of India.

In 1901, there were 2093 towns in the Indian Sub continent and about ten per cent of the population was urban. There was considerable variation in the level of urbanization across the country, it varied from 18.8 per cent in Bombay Presidency to five per cent in Bengal Presidency, including Bihar and Orissa.

The dependence on agriculture for livelihood varied considerably across the regions. While the share of cultivators in the male working force in Assam, Bihar, Orissa and Uttar Pradesh was 55 per cent or more, it was less than 40 per cent in Gujarat, Maharashtra, Kerala and West Bengal in 1911.

Industrialization in India, from the beginning, had been experiencing a duality. European entrepreneurs invested more and more in industries, which were mainly export-oriented whereas Indian entrepreneurs concentrated on industries mainly for the Indian markets. Thus jute, tea, etc. were mainly in European hands whereas textile, sugar, etc. were mainly Indian. Apart from other factors, one main reason was that Indian market offered higher profit margins which Indian industrialists found easier to penetrate. Not surprisingly this tendency continues even today.

The benefit of irrigation development was mainly concentrated in northern, western and southern provinces during British period. Central and Eastern India were relatively neglected. This had had serious implications in the post-independence period also. While the former areas were ripe for benefiting from the green revolution package, the latter could not.

From its beginning in 1853, India's railway system expanded rapidly to become, by 1910, the forth-largest in the world. This network which covered most of the Sub-continent, radically altered India's transportation system.

Railways vastly increased the speed, availability and reliability of transportation, reduced the cost, allowed regional specialization and expansion of trade. For attracting private investors, Government of British India assured guaranteed return. Under this scheme, which was used in other parts of the world to build railways, if a company did not attain a minimum rate of return of five per cent, it received compensation for the difference from the Government. Stimulated by an assured rate of return, British investors swiftly made their capital available to the private railway companies. By 1947 all but a few remote districts in far-flung remote regions were served by railways.

INDEPENDENCE INDIA

The State-wise details of banking operations in the country as on March 31, 2000 are presented in Table 2, column two gives the State-wise distribution of bank branches in the country. It is obvious that, by and large, the bank

TABLE 2

Bank Branches, Deposits and Bank Credit

(As on 31st March, 2000)

S. No.	State	Bank branches	Share of bank deposits	Rank	Share of bank credit	Rank	Credit-deposit ratio	Rank
1	2	3	4	5	6	7	8	9
1.	Andhra Pradesh	5102	5.3	7	6.9	3	63.8	3
2.	Gujarat	3626	5.9	5	5.1	6	49.8	5
3.	Haryana	1492	2.1	12	1.6	12	41.4	10
4.	Karnataka	4697	5.4	6	6.6	4	61.0	4
5.	Kerala	3231	4.6	8	3.7	7	42.3	9
6.	Maharashtra	6205	19.9	1	25.9	1	83.8	2
7.	Punjab	2498	4.6	8	3.2	9	39.1	12
8.	Tamil Nadu	4736	6.6	4	11.5	2	88.0	1
	Sub-Total (1 to 8)	31587 (48.3)	54.4		64.5			
9.	Assam	1229	1.0	14	0.6	14	31.5	13
10.	Bihar	4992	4.3	9	2.1	11	22.5	15
11.	Madhya Pradesh	4472	3.9	10	3.6	8	49.2	6
12.	Orissa	2216	1.5	13	1.2	13	39.8	11
13.	Rajasthan	3306	2.8	11	2.4	10	46.7	7
14.	Uttar Pradesh	8855	9.9	2	5.1	6	27.5	14
15.	West Bengal	4382	7.5	3	6.2	5	45.2	8
	Sub-Total (9 to 15)	29452 (45.1)	30.9		21.2		57.1	
All-India		65340	100		100			

branches are fairly distributed across the States without any major bias towards the group of forward States. It may need mention that this could be attributed to the banking sector policies pursued after nationalization of the major commercial banks in the country in 1969.

INTRA-STATE DISPARITIES

A number of States included in out analysis have clearly identifiable regions which are at different stages of development and which have distinct problems to tackle. Creation of new States, certainly, may not be a solution to such regional disparities. At the same time, it is important to recognize such intra-State regional disparities explicitly and tackle them through special efforts. As we have noted in an earlier section, Maharashtra is a typical example of a State where overall development is quite good in terms of almost all indicators, but extreme regional disparities exist. Andhra Pradesh has three distinct regions which are at different stages of socio-economic development, viz. Coastal Andhra, Telangana and Rayalaseema. Similarly, North Bihar and South Bihar before State reorganization in 2000 were at different stages of development with entirely different problems. Uttar Pradesh, even after caving out Uttaranchal, has at least three regions with varying problems and different levels of socio-economic development. Other States like Gujarat, Karnataka, Madhya Pradesh, Orissa, Rajasthan and West Bengal also have regions with distinct characteristics of backwardness.

A closer examination of the nature of backward regions in each State will indicate specific regions for their backwardness. The major cause of backwardness of Vidharba and Marathwada in Maharashtra, Rayalaseema and Telangana in Andhra Pradesh and Northern Karnataka is the scarcity of water due to lower precipitation and lack of other perennial sources of water. On the other hand, backwardness of certain regions in Gujarat, Madhya Pradesh, Bihar and Orissa can be associated with the distinct style of living of the inhabitants of such regions who are mostly tribals and the neglect of such regions by the ruling elite. Topography of a region could also constrain the development of that region; the desert region of Rajasthan is an example of such a case. Historical factors like the attitude of rulers of the former Princely States towards development could have significantly affected the development of a region. For example, the distinctly higher level of social development of the

Travancore and Cochin regions of Kerala can be traced back to the enlightened attitude of the former rulers of the Princely States of Travancore and Cochin. On the other hand, the poor social development of Telangana region of Andhra Pradesh and certain other parts of the Deccan could be traced back to the absence of visionary rulers in the respective princely States.

We may mention a few successful cases, where intra-state regional disparities have been reduced considerably through public policies. First, in 1956 when Kerala was formed at the time of State re-organization, there was substantial disparity in the social development of Malabar region *vis-a-vis* the Travancore-Cochin region. Over the last four decades, there has been remarkable improvement in the social indicators of Malabar to catch up with the rest of Kerala as a result of appropriate public policies. The development of the drought prone districts of Haryana through irrigation is another remarkable example of reduction in economic disparities across the regions within a State. Provision of educational, health and communication facilities even in the remotest villages of Himachal Pradesh is a third example of successful public policies in reduction of regional disparities within a State. Overall, Tamil Nadu could be considered as one State, which is most successful in reducing regional disparities in economic and social development even when there was substantial variation in the natural endowments in different parts of the State. This was achieved by a combination of public policies and private initiatives. In other States, especially in Maharashtra, Gujarat and Rajasthan, there are a number of successful cases of NGOs, which succeeded in transforming pockets of destitution into areas enjoying very high levels of socio-economic development.

PROFILE OF REGIONAL DISPARITIES FOR DIFFERENT GROWTH SCENARIOS, 2025

During the first four decades of development planning, most of the large units in basic and heavy industries were set-up in the public sector in a regionally well-balanced manner. Indeed, their location, other things being equal, was biased towards backward regions, as natural endowments such as mineral deposits were concentrated in those regions. Massive public investments have been made to provide economic and social infrastructure in the backward regions to accelerate their overall development.

Economic reforms initiated in 1991 implied among, other things, that the private sector would be the principal engine of economic growth. Most of the restrictions on private investment have been removed. Mounting debt burden of the government has imposed a cap on public investment. As a result, while there was significant increase in the quantum of private investment, there was a sharp fall in the public investment over the last decade.

The flow of private investment, both domestic and foreign, has been extremely biased in favour of the more developed regions of the country. This has enabled the developed regions to achieve accelerated economic growth during the 1990s. On the other hand, backward regions of the country, which were unable to attract any significant private investment flows, experienced decelerated economic growth during this period.

The net result of this divergent growth performance of the developed and backward regions has been a widening of the regional disparities in the country in terms of per-capita income and other indicators of well-being of the people.

The adverse impacts of the deteriorating State finances are much more severe for the backward States as compared to the developed States, where investments of the past have created adequate social and economic infrastructure to attract private investments. The backward States are facing multiple dilemma. They are not able to attract investments due to lack of infrastructure. They are not in a position to provide these facilities on their own due to lack of investible funds. Unlike in the past, Centre is not in a position to help them either as the Centre itself has a serious fiscal constraint.

Alongwith social and economic infrastructure, efficiency of administration and the quality of governance including law and order situation are important factors in attracting private investment. Studies conducted by NCAER and some of the apex associations of industries have indicated that prospective investors give higher weight-age to these factors than various incentives, including fiscal incentives offered by the State governments. Indeed, there are enough evidences to the effect that the investors don't mind paying speed money to get things done fast. In other words, a corrupt but efficient regime is preferred to an honest but inefficient regime in the context of investment decisions. Other aspects of governance like the law and order situation, trade union activism, etc., are also important factors affecting the flow of private investments.

It will be appropriate to state that there are hardly any signs of reversing the recent trend of accentuating regional disparities in the country in the coming decades. Indeed, almost all the relevant forces are such that the disparities are likely to widen deriving the next quarter century. It will require Herculean tasks on the part of the Centre and the leadership in the concerned regions to ensure that the gap does not widen further.

Lastly, with divergent trends in various sectors of development, there emerges a resistance to vertical and horizontal fund transfers to the backward regions by forward regions. Immediately after the report of the Eleventh Finance Commission there was an uproar from the so-called "Performing States" against increased tax revenue devolution to the backward States. One of the main arguments was that non-performing States are rewarded for their non-performance. It is imperative that Centre and the leadership of the backward States should evolve institutional arrangements to ensure that funds transferred result in the best use in terms of development.

CONCLUSION

In the conclusion over the fast three decades the share of revenue expenditure in the plan expenditure has been steadily increasing due to various reasons to reach an adverse level of about 60 per cent for all States together. As a result there has been persistent demands from the States to the Centre to raise the grant component of Central assistance to atleast 50 per cent.

An important characteristic of Maharashtra's development is its regional concentration. Most of the high-income activities are concentrated in Mumbai-Pune region. Further, a substantial share of income accrues to migrants who transfer part of their earnings to their places of origin. These factors may partly explain the paradox of high per-capita NSDP and high share of population below poverty line in Maharashtra.

A recent report by National Commission on Population titled "District-wide Social Economic Demographic Indicators" rank 569 districts in the country on the basis of a composite index based on 12 indicators. While almost all the districts (95%) in the developed region have ranks above 300, half of the districts in the backward region have their ranks below 400. Indeed, the socio-demographic distance between the two regions is frighteningly large.

In current trend continues, Punjab and Haryana are likely to have a higher level of dependence on agriculture. However, since the present system of foodgrain management based on procurement at support prices is likely to collapse soon on its own weight policy changes are imminent. This will lead to a significant reduction of dependence on agriculture in these States.

With the recent reorganization of the States, there are a total of 28 States, besides 7 Union Territories in the Indian Union now. In the absence of the relevant data, for the purpose of the present study, we consider the undivided States of Bihar, Madhya Pradesh and Uttar Pradesh.

It is well known that Punjab and Haryana with their heavy dependence on agriculture (44% and 38% of GSDP respectively) could not gain significantly from deregulation and liberalization which helped the other States in the forward group to grow faster through accelerated growth of industry and service sectors.

The Tenth Finance Commission recommended an alternate formula for devolution of a fixed share of the pooled tax revenues from all major taxes, including customs duty and corporation tax. This was to be made effective from April, 1996 which required an amendment to the Constitution. Though the Government had accepted alternate formula, in principle, the required Constitutional amendment was carried out only in May, 2000.

The formula recommended by the Eleventh Finance Commission gives the following weight: Population 10.0 per cent, per-capita income—6.25 per cent, Area—7.5 per cent, Index of infrastructure—7.5 per cent, Tax effort—5.0 per cent and Fiscal discipline—7.5 per cent. While State-wise allocation is inversely related to per-capita income, it is directly related to all other variables.

References

Convergence of incomes across Indian States—A Divergent View by M.G. Rao, R.T. Shand and K.P. Kalirajan.

Economic and Political Weekly.

India Today.

Manorama Year Book, 2000-07.

See for detail: S. Sivasubramanian: The National Income of India in the Twentieth Century, Oxford University Press, New Delhi, 2000.

The Cambridge Economic History of India, Vol. I and II. General Editors: Dharma Kumar and Tapan Ray Chaudhuri, Orient Longman, Third Edition, 1991.

The Indian Plans.

Trends in Inter-State Inequalities of Income in India by Nirupam Bajpai and Jeffery D. Sachs.

Widening Inter-State Economic and Social Disparities in India by Fahrettin Yagci. The first study was published in *EPW*, March 27, 1999. The other two were presented in a seminar organized jointly by the World Bank and the Institute of Social and Economic Change at Bangalore in May 1999.

World-wide website

Yojana.

9

Inter-Regional Disparities in India's Development

MANDAKINI R. MAHORE AND A.S. MOHAMMAD

Regional disparity is a ubiquitous phenomenon in both developed and developing economies. But in the latter it is more acute and glaring. National economies are often composed of sets of smaller and localized economies. If the national economy is to prosper then its constituent regional economies must be brought into some sort of harmony.

The period since 1980 has seen the introduction/ expansion of several anti-poverty programmes and public intervention policies in favour of the poor including public distribution of subsidised food grains. The reduction in poverty in the recent period is attributed to anti-poverty programmes by their protagonists and to accelerated economic growth by market friendly experts.

Along with faster economic growth and reduction in poverty, there has been accelerated improvement in various indicators of human development since the early Eighties During the last two decades, the country has made major strides in health and education sectors. The economy got diversified significantly and the share of the service sector in employment and incomes improved considerably. While there is a broad consensus on the overall improvement of the economy and quality of life during the period under consideration, there are significantly differing perceptions about the distributional impacts of these gains. Disparities in economic and social development across the regions and intra-regional disparities among different segments of the society have been the major planks for adopting planning process in India since independence. Apart from massive investments in backward regions, various public policies directed at encouraging private investments in such regions have been pursued during the first three decades of planned development. While efforts to reduce regional disparities were not lacking, achievements were not often commensurate with these efforts. Considerable level of regional disparities remained at the end of the Seventies. The accelerated economic growth since the early Eighties appears to have aggravated regional disparities. The on-going economic reforms since 1991 with stabilisation and deregulation policies as their central pieces seem to have further widened the regional disparities. The seriousness of the emerging acute regional imbalances has not yet received the public attention it deserves.

Most of the studies on inter-country and inter-regional differences in levels of living and income are done within the theoretical framework of neoclassical growth models. These models, under plausible assumptions demonstrate convergence of incomes. The fifteen States together account for 96 per cent of the population of India. The remaining 4 per cent of the population is spread out in 10 smaller States and seven Union Territories including the National Capital Territory of Delhi.

The fifteen States taken up for the detailed study has been grouped into two—a forward group and a backward group. The forward group consists of Andhra Pradesh, Gujarat, Haryana, Karnataka, Kerala, Maharashtra, Punjab and Tamil Nadu. The backward group comprises of Assam, Bihar, Madhya Pradesh, Orissa, Rajasthan, Uttar Pradesh and West Bengal.

While the forward group of States accounts for about

42 per cent of the national population, the backward group accounts for as much as 54 per cent of the population of the country. In terms of natural resources including mineral wealth, water resources and quality of soil, the latter has definite edge over the former. A limitation of inter-regional analysis using States as units is the fact that this may not be able to capture the significant intra-State disparities in economic and social development which exists today. The larger States in both the groups have regions within themselves, which are vastly different in terms of various indicators of development. There are identifiable distinct regions, at different stages of development, in several States.

Among the fifteen States considered in our study eight have sex ratio above the national average and seven have below national average. The international experience indicates that as a society develops economically the sex ratio turns more favourable to women. Within India, however, this does not appear to hold good. Though only two out of the eight States in the forward group have sex ratio below national average, they happen to be the two of the richest States (first and third) in the country in terms of per-capita income. Further, their sex ratios happen to be the lowest (Haryana) and the third lowest (Punjab) in the country. Even the second and fourth richest States in the country viz., Maharashtra and Gujarat have sex ratios only marginally higher than that of the nation. The highest sex ratio is that of Kerala. Indeed, Kerala is the only State in the country which has a sex ratio favourable to women. While a sex ratio favourable to women is considered the norm in the developed world and is quite logical in view of the biological advantage `women have for longevity, in India, it is a rare occurance.

The share of urban population in India was 25.7 per cent in 1991. While all the States except Haryana in the first group had higher share of urban population, all States except West Bengal in the second group had urban population share below the national average. The most urbanised State in the first group is Maharashtra and the least urbanised one is Haryana. In the second group the corresponding States are West Bengal and Assam. While the most urbanized State in the first group is a little more than 1.5 times urbanised as compared to the least urbanised, in the second group the most urbanised West Bengal is about 2.5 times urbanised as compared to Assam. Indeed, West Bengal has a number of characteristics of a forward State, the level of urbanisation being one of them. This is because of the historical background of Bengal and especially Calcutta which used to be the second most important city of the British Empire. Another aspect of the level of urbanisation is the fact that all those States with higher level of urbanisation have a metro-city each which accounts for a considerable share of urban population in the respective States.

The level of literacy is, perhaps, the most important index of development of a society. Invariably, male literacy is higher than female literacy in any society. Often there may be significant gender gap in literacy. The gap between Kerala and the rest of the country in female literacy is, indeed, phenomenal. Rajasthan is the least literate State where female literacy is as low as 20 per cent, which implies that out of every five females in Rajasthan four are illiterate. The female literacy rates in the other three 'BIMARU' States viz., Bihar, Madhya Pradesh and Uttar Pradesh are also below 30 per cent. The empirically well-established positive relationship between female illiteracy and TFR is quite evident in the case of these States. It is quite evident that the critical precondition for stabilisation of Indian population is to raise the female literacy in the 'BIMARU' States.

Life expectancy at birth or longevity is an overall indicator of the economic and social well-being of a people. As a society advances, the life expectancy of its people also increases. The highest life expectancy for a nation reported so far is that of Japan, which is 80. For most societies, especially developed ones, female life expectancy is higher than male life expectancy. In India, however, female life expectancy at birth remained below male life expectancy till recently mainly due to high infant and child mortality among the females and substantial loss of female life associated with child birth due to lack of health care. This trend has been reversed in recent years.

INCOME AND POVERTY

The most common indicator of the economic development of a society is the per-capita annual income generated by it. An important structural change in the economy in the process of development is the decline of income generated in the agriculture sector and the increase in the income generated in the manufacturing sector. The level of poverty or the share of population which do not have minimum income to meet its basic requirements is an indicator of the level of economic development as well as the inequality in the income distribution.

Resource Transfer from the Centre to the States

There is an inbuilt imbalance between the expenditure responsibilities and the revenue sources of the State governments. The founding fathers of the Indian Constitution were aware of this fact and ensured a comprehensive scheme of devolution of Central Tax revenues through the mechanism of Finance Commissions. The sharing of Personal Income Tax and Excise duties collected by the Centre with the States is periodically reviewed by the Finance Commission appointed every five years. The Commission also decides the principles and the formula by which the allocable funds are to be distributed among the States.

An important aspect of the devolution of Central tax revenues under Finance Commission dispensation is that it has inbuilt bias in favour of fiscally weak States. Population and per-capita income of the State get high weightage in the distribution formula. A State with larger population and lower per-capita income gets a higher share in the Central tax revenues. The gap between revenue receipts (other than the Central tax revenues) and revenue expenditure is another parameter which decides the level of a State's share. As a result the Central tax share constitutes a major revenue source for the backward States. While it constitutes about one-third of the total tax revenues of all the States taken together; it accounts for more than 50 per cent of the total tax revenues of less developed States like Bihar and Orissa; but its share is less than 20 per cent of the total tax revenues of more developed States like Gujarat, Haryana, Maharashtra and Punjab.

Pattern of Private Investment

In the wake of economic reforms initiated in 1991, the role of private investment has acquired a special significance in the context of economic development of various States of the Indian Union. Indeed, there has been an element of competition among States for attracting private investment, both domestic and foreign. Some of the States have been offering various tax concessions and other special facilities to new investors on a competitive basis. The percentage share of different States in these investment proposals differs. Hence occurance of disparities is obvious. The group of forward States accounted for about two-third of the amount while the group of backward States accounted for just about 28 per cent of the amount. Indeed, Gujarat and Maharashtra received together 36.7 per cent of the investment proposals which is significantly more than the total investment proposals received by all the States in the second group. While Gujarat which accounted for less than 5 per cent of the population of the country received about 19 per cent of the private investment proposals, Bihar which accounts for more than 10 per cent of the population of the country received just little over one per cent of such proposals. This is a clear pointer to the direction of private investment in the coming years.

Level of Infrastructure Development

Availability of adequate infrastructure facilities is an important pre-condition for sustainable economic and social development. Broadly, infrastructure can be physical, social or financial in nature. Energy, transport, irrigation, finance, communications, education and health are some of the more important infrastructural facilities. While private sector may provide some of these facilities, market forces may not always ensure adequate supply of a variety of infrastructure facilities. The share of irrigated area in gross-cropped area is an important indicator of the level of agricultural development of a region. Assured irrigation being a pre-condition for modern agricultural practices, the level of labour absorption and productivity will critically depend on the quality of irrigation. As compared to all-India average of 36.5 per cent, six States have higher percentage share and 9 States have lower percentage share. Punjab has the highest share of about 95 per cent irrigated area, followed by Haryana (77.9%) and Uttar Pradesh (62.6%). It is to be noted that some of the forward States like Gujarat, Karnataka and Maharashtra, have lower level of irrigation mainly because of the comparatively lower irrigation potential in these States. Similarly, though the irrigation level in Tamil Nadu is only about 50 per cent, the State has almost exhausted its irrigation potential. The situation in AP is not much different. On the other hand, in States like Assam, Bihar, Orissa and UP, much more irrigation potential remains unexploited. Since a significant increase in productivity of agriculture in these States is essential for reduction of rural poverty, the importance of fully exploiting the irrigation potential in these States need special mention. Indeed, removal of rural poverty in most areas of eastern India critically depends on raising the productivity of agriculture, especially the productivity of rice from one to one-and-a-half tonnes per hectare to 3 to 4 tonnes per hectare. This requires considerable public and private investment in irrigation.

Intra-State Disparities

In the foregoing sections, we have examined the various dimensions of interstate disparities. An important aspect of regional disparities in India, which could not be covered by this approach, is the significant level of regional disparities which exist within different States. An important cause of regional tensions which lead to popular agitations and at times militant activities is such regional disparities in economic and social development which exist within some of the States. Indeed, creation of some of the States in the past was in the wake of popular agitations based on perceived neglect of certain backward regions in some of the bigger States. The best examples of such cases are the creation of Andhra Pradesh and Gujarat in the Fifties and creation of Punjab, Haryana and Himachal Pradesh in the Sixties. The past experience, by and large, is that when two or more States are carved out from an existing one or a new State is created by combining parts from more than one State on the basis of some homogeneity criterion like language or some other common heritage, the newly created States develop faster than the pre partition States.

Before concluding this Section, we may mention a few successful cases where intra-State regional disparities have been reduced considerably through public policies. First, in 1956 when Kerala was formed at the time of State re-organisation, there was substantial disparity in the social development of Malabar region *vis-a-vis* the Travancore-Cochin region. Over the last four decades, there has been remarkable improvement in the social indicators of Malabar to catch up with the rest of Kerala as a result of appropriate public policies. The development of the drought prone districts of Haryana through irrigation is another remarkable example of reduction in economic disparities across the regions within a State. Provision of educational, health and communication facilities even in the remotest villages of HP is a third example of successful public policies in reduction of regional disparities within a State. Overall, Tamil Nadu could be considered as one State which is most successful in reducing regional disparities in economic and social development even when there was substantial variation in the natural endowments in different parts of the State. This was achieved by a combination of public policies and private initiatives. In other States, especially in Maharashtra, Gujarat and Rajasthan, there are a number of successful cases of NGOs which succeeded in transforming pockets of destitution into areas enjoying very high levels of socio-economic development.

The data presented in the earlier Sections and the analysis so far clearly establish that there are considerable disparities in socio-economic development across the Indian States. Efforts through the planning process during the first three decades of the Indian Republic had only partially succeeded in reducing regional disparities. The accelerated economic growth since the early Eighties with increased participation by the private sector appears to have aggravated regional disparities. The on-going economic reforms since 1991 with stabilisation and deregulation policies as their prime instruments and a very significant role for the private sector seem to have further aggravated the inter-State disparities.

A marked dicotomy between the forward and backward groups of States has been emerging. The forward States are characterised by better demographic and social development higher per-capita incomes and more developed economies, lower level of poverty, higher level of revenue receipts and State government expenditure on plan and non-plan, higher per-capita resource flows and private investment and significantly better infrastructural facilities. On the other hand, the backward States are characterised by lower level of demographic and social development, lower per-capita incomes and backward economies, higher level of poverty, lower level of revenue receipts and lower State government expenditure on plan and non-plan, lower per-capita resource flows and private investment and underdeveloped infrastructural facilities.

The pressing requirement of the backward States is more investment in their social and infrastructural sectors. To improve the level of social services massive investment in primary education and primary health services are required. Improvement in literacy especially female literacy and health indicators like infant mortality and expectation of life at birth will bring down the rate of growth of population. Stabilisation of population, especially in the 'BIMARU' States is an important pre-condition for the sustained economic growth of that region.

Improvement in the basic infrastructural facilities like power, irrigation, transport and telecommunication in the backward States is a precondition of improving the quality of life of the people and to usher in sustainable economic development in those States. Availability of assured power supply, developed transport system and modern telecommunication facilities are important factors to attract private investments into these States. Similarly, development of the irrigation potential fully will go a long way in improving the productivity of agriculture and fully engaging the underemployed rural labour productively which in turn will improve the rural incomes substantially and reduce the rural poverty significantly.

To conclude, if the existing trends in differential rate of socio-economic development continue, regional disparities in India are bound to accentuate. Therefore, it is imperative that the present trends are arrested and preferably reversed. This will require concerted efforts on the part of the concerned State governments and the Centre. Resources may be a major constraint, but not necessarily the only or not even the most important one. The determination on the part of the State government, the ruling elite and the people at large is even more important. Centre's helping hand in the form of focused investment, especially in social sectors and key infrastructural sectors will facilitate the tasks of the concerned States. Meaningful decentralisation of decision-making and financial powers with appropriate accountability at all levels will facilitate faster socio-economic development of the backward regions where people are likely to take up considerable share of the developmental responsibilities

One of the studies has suggested that the state must endeavor to achieve short-term objectives of maximum income and employment by promoting the income and employment intensive agro-based sectors of the economy for improving upon the general under development in the region. At the same time, the study has suggested that the policy-makers of this poor state should not discourage the producers who may be interested in undertaking production risk in the heavy sectors because a complete neglect of growth oriented sectors can create supply bottlenecks and may cause a decline in the production base for this poor economy. Resources must be allocated efficiently on the basis of total and indirect income and employment performances within this under developed Orissa state.

The exploratory exercises here at explaining inter-state disparities in the levels of economic and social development seem to throw up some interesting hypotheses, which need much more detailed and in-depth examination. Evidence here suggests that growth in NSDP has been accompanied at the regional level by much higher growth in employment in the pre-reform era than in the post-reform one. To the extent that growth in employment is related to the development of agriculture, this seems a natural outcome because while there are some indications of inter-state convergence in the pre-reform era, there is no evidence of this in the post-reform one.

The evidence here also suggests that at the regional level in India, reduction of poverty has a beneficial impact on per-capita NSDP though the same is not true if we consider human development as a whole. Infrastructural development seems to have beneficial effects on human development in particular and there are some indications that the impact was similar at the regional level on per-capita NSDP too, specially in the pre-reform period. In view of this, a very welcome finding of the study is the tendency of interstate convergence in terms of the index of infrastructural development in both the pre and the post-reform periods. There is an evidence in the study to suggest that infrastructural development is of great help in promoting regional development. This is particularly true if we consider an indicator of level of living like HDI and seems true to some extent also in the case of per-capita NSDP. A detailed analysis of the development of industry at the state level in India also indicates that infrastructural development is particularly helpful for the development of both registered . and unregistered manufacturing There are also two other indications with interesting policy implications. One is the already accepted finding that agricultural development is beneficial for the development of unregistered manufacturing at the regional level. The other is the interesting hint here that measures to reduce poverty in a region do not always go against the objective of improving the relative position of a region in terms of its per-capita net domestic product. Much more work possibly with the help of causality tests and along the lines also of Datt and Ravilion (2002) to be done before more definite policy inferences can be drawn in this needs regard.

The preliminary analysis here on the basis of the latest available data gives some broad indications regarding India's regional development experience in the two decades since the eighties. It seems to substantiate the view that the pattern of regional economic change depends upon the indicator of economic development considered as has been argued in the multi-pattern hypothesis in this regard. As regards per-capita NSDP, while there are no definite indications of either divergence or convergence at the regional level

in the pre-reform era whereas if we consider indicators of levels of living, there are signs of inter-state convergence in the pre-reform period. If we consider the post-reform period, the evidence here points towards some indications of inter-state divergence in terms of per-capita NSDP along with very definite evidence in this regard in terms of the indicators of levels of living. It has of course to be borne in mind that we have looked at convergence and divergence in a non-econometric sense and not examined sigma or beta convergence which involve inter-temporal analysis of sinle rates of growth and base year values of the indicator under study for the summary measures of inter-regional dispersion and relationship between rates of growth and base year values of the indicator under study for the different regions respectively. Besides lending credence to findings on the basis of much earlier data by many including Nair (1982) from the fifties to the eighties, the evidence here seems to be in line also with the results of some detailed studies using data for recent years like the ones by Dholakia (2003), Shetty (2003) and Bhattacharya and Sakthivel (2004).

Recent econometric studies using data for much longer periods also seem to lead to similar inferences. Das (2002) compares inter-state movements in real wage rates in agriculture between the years 1956-57 to 1992-93 to infer that there are no indications of continued divergence with some indications also of convergence. Shaban (2002) on the other hand finds clear indications of divergence on the basis of his analysis of data on per-capita NSDP between the years 1960-61 to 1996-97.

Measures to Narrow Down these Differentials

During the XIth Plan, the Government proposes to set-up 30 central universities-16 in uncovered states and 14 aiming at world-class standards; eight IITs; 10 National Institutes of Technologies; 20 Indian Institutes of Information

Technology (IIITs); three Indian Institutes of Science Education and Research (IISERS); seven IIMs and two Schools of Planning and Architecture. Apart from this central assistance will be provided for 1,000 polytechnics: 300 in public private partnership mode and 400 in the private sector. Assistance for setting up of polytechnics in the government sector shall be extended to those states that do not have one at present. The aim of the Government is also to take of infrastructure shortages and faculty shortages that hamper education at present.

The Government also aims to provide $ 10 laptops to students so that they can benefit from the telecommunication revolution. Efforts and research in this direction are on at the Indian Institute of Science, Bangalore and the Indian Institute of Technology, Madras. Apart from this, the Government wishes to network each department of about 400 university level institutions and 20,000 colleges through broadband connectivity and make available suitable e-learning material. The National Policy on Education (1986) had set a goal of expenditure on education to be of the order of 6 per cent of GDP. However, the actual expenditure on education as a percentage of GDP has remained about 3 per cent of GDP till 2007-08 (fiscal year). The National Knowledge Commission's recent report on higher education has recommended that the present support for higher education should be at least 1.5 per cent of GDP, from a total of 6 per cent of GDP for education. The Government has to keep this in mind if it wants to accelerate the level of progress for the country and expand the knowledge base.

We have a long road to travel before we can claim to have fulfiled Mahatma Gandhi's prayer to wipe the last tear from the poorest of the poor. The Government has been committed to making the growth process more socially inclusive. A great part of the effort in the past three years has been precisely in this direction.

The Government has launched a number of initiatives to step up investment in agriculture and rural development, in education and health care, in urban renewal and poverty removal, in rural infrastructure and in rural employment generation. These initiatives are bearing results and will certainly make the growth process more inclusive.

The inter-regional disparities in development are major obstacles in balanced growth. The 9 per cent growth rate is an average of over 10 per cent in some parts of India and under 3 per cent in others. Large continental economies are bound to have inter-regional disparities. However, we cannot afford to see this gap between our developed and backward regions persist. And we are not yet seeing the catching-up effect as should be the case. This is a cause for serious concern.

This is where the role of State Governments comes into focus. The implementation of many of the social and human development programmes is in the hands of State Governments. The capacity of State Governments to effectively plan and implement these programmes varies from state to state.

If Centre Government can improve the administrative capacity of State Governments, then it would be possible in making the growth process more socially inclusive. Therefore, while there is still an unfinished agenda of economic reforms awaiting our attention at the Centre, the real action will have to be at the level of states.

In this context, we must compliment McKinsey for the initiatives it has taken in India to work with State Governments. It would be appropriate to think that such effort at the State level will create greater awareness in our political leadership and within Government of the challenges and opportunities that lie ahead. Such exercises have given us a good idea of what we need to do to accelerate the tempo of social and economic development. There is also fairly wide recognition of the importance of this agenda. However, given the nature of competitive politics and the very fractured mandates given to Governments, it has become difficult sometimes to the Government to do what is manifestly obvious. The main problem is implementation of various schemes of the Government.

References

Bhattacharya, B.B. and S. Sakthivel (2004), Regional Growth and Disparity in India, *Economic and Political Weekly* (*EPW*), March 6, pp. 1071-77.

Booth, E.J.R (1964), " Inter-Regional Income Differences", *Southern Economic Journal (SEJ)*, Vol. 31, No. 1, July, pp. 44-51.

Cassen, R.H. (2002), "Well-Being in the 90's: Towards a Balance Sheet", *EPW*, Vol. 37, No. 27, pp. 2789-94.

Das, T.K. (2002), "Convergence Across Indian States: Cross-Sectional and Panel Estimations", *South Asia Economic Journal*, Vol. 3, No. 2, pp. 227-39.

Datt, G. and M. Ravallion (2002), "Is India's Economic Growth Leaving the Poor Behind?", Mimeographed paper at World Bank Workshop on Poverty Estimates, New Delhi, January.

Dholakia, R.H. (1985), Regional Disparity in Economic Growth in India, Himalaya, New Delhi.

Dholakia, R.H. (2003), Regional Disparity in Economic and Human Development in India, RBI Chair Lecture, IIM, Ahmedabad.

Hanna, F.A. (1959), State Income Differentials, 1919-54, Duke University Press, Durham.

Hirschman, Albert. O (1961), The Strategy of Economic Development, Yale University Press, New Haven.

Hughes, R.B. (1961), "Inter-Regional Income Differences: Self-Perpetuation", *Southern Economic Journal*, Vol. 28, No. 1, July, pp. 41-45.

Kurian, N.J. (2000), "Widening Regional Disparities in India: Some Indicators", *EPW*, Vol. 35, No. 7, pp. 538-55.

Prime Ministers' Address at the McKinsey Meet (2007), New Delhi, October 23.

10

Inter-Regional Disparities in India's Development

Rama J. Shah and Rita N. Patel

INTRODUCTION

Indian economic development is initially a function of the social process of growth in production. But, Development is not balanced in the country. In India balanced growth is essential for the harmonious development of the country economy having a federal political structure in all the states. In India, a few regions have acquired relatively a high level of development in comparison to those which have experienced a slow rate of growth and display a low level of development. The large number of regions having, the low level of development in productive forces and unfavourable social conditions to introduce in the process of production, the highest the regional disparities in the level of development in a country.

Balanced regional development has been one of the central objectives for reducing regional disparities in the development of Indian Economy

The First Plan conceived balanced regional

development as an integral part of the process of growth. The problem of regional imbalances has become a world wide phenomenon today. In the five year plans, a perfect approach was spelt out for development of backward area as a policy instrument to reduce regional disparities. There were four major problems facing the Indian economy. when the First Five Year Plan launched in 1951. They were poverty illiteracy unemployment and a vide gap between the haves and the have nots.

The concept of balanced regional development as conceived in planning means reduction in the existing or growing regional inequalities in the development of the Indian economy. Some programmes and plans launched for relation of production to promote and accelerate the process of development in the regional backward areas and creating favourable social condition. The problems of nations was growth in material production. The problem is threatening the peace and security of various economics. The regional variation is also threatening the integrity of the nations various studies in regional progress show that regional disparities in development have not declined but on the contrary have been increase through time during the period of planning in India. The inter-state disparities in the levels of development measured in terms of change in per-capita national domestic product across the states by way of social process of growth in production varies from developed to backward regions in the country. The inter-states variation in growth on the assumption that per-capita income inequalities are major source for regional disparities of development.

The regional structure of development in Indian agriculture is not uniform. The reason is that the levels of development in productive forces such as area under HYV, mechanization, lack availability of rural credit facility institution, irrigation, consumption of fertilizer per hectare techniques of farming, etc. vary from one state to another. Some states are found to be agriculturally well developed in terms of high levels of growth in agriculture production and productivity. But some other states are not found to be well, developed in agriculture in terms of production and daring technology. The existence of regional disparities in Indian agriculture implies. Prevalence of unevenness in the process of capitalist development in agriculture.

Industrialization plays an important role in the process of economy. India on its path of economic development has adopted industrialization. Indian economy development has emerged as one of the most industrialized economics of the world. But its industrial structure is not uniformally developed in all states nor the process of growth in industrial productions is the same. The role of finance institution in the promotion of industrial entrepreneurship and industries in backward states or region is extending and intensifying in recent years. Mostly in all the states the industrial units of the manufacturing sector are concentrated in urban areas, specially, more so in metropolitan cities. Industrial disparities caused by the production inefficiency negligence and shortage of raw material in backward regions. In another way disparities due to better performance and proper resource utilization in industrially advanced regions.

The female participation rates and employment are not uniform in the states. The rates vary from one state to another because the levels of agricultural development and cropping pattern, social status and caste education and literacy are different in various states. The states with higher percentage of SC and ST population also exhibit, higher participation rates of females in rural areas. Agriculture and unorganized sectors do not provide employment opportunities on a continuing basis to female employers. Thus the position of women is found to be precarious.

NET STATE DOMESTIC PRODUCT

Table 1 shows the Net State Domestic Products of 10 states in India taken of year 1990-91 to 2001-02. The total NSDP of all 10 states to gather increased from Rs. 215842 crores to Rs. 888691 crores in the period under of 1990-91 to 2001-02. This shows that the total NSDP of all 10 states to gather increased 312 per cent in 10 years. When we compare the performance of individual states in the rank of NSDP, We note that Maharashtra, Andhra Pradesh, Gujarat, Punjab, Karnataka had the rank-wise growth in their NSDP, higher

TABLE I

Net State Domestic Product of the States in India

(Rs. in Crores)

Sr. No.	*State*	*NSDP 1990-11*	*Rank*	*NSDP 2001-02*	*State Rank*	*Growth rate in percentage*
1.	Andhra Pradesh	29867	2	135597	2	354.00%
2.	Assam	9498	10	29198	10	207.41%
3.	Bihar	22787	4	51345	8	125.32%
4.	Gujarat	24180	3	105023	3	334.18%
5.	Haryana	12238	7	57937	7	373.42%
6.	Karnataka	20551	5	97253	4	373.22%
7.	Kerala	12173	8	69602	5	471077%
8.	Maharashtra	58137	1	241877	1	316.05%
9.	Orissa	9664	9	37891	9	292.098%
10.	Punjab	16378	6	62968	6	276.19%
		215842		888691		311.73%

Source: Statistical Outline of India, 2004-05.

than other states. When in other states had the rank-wise growth in their NSDP less than the other states. In Kerala the rank was eight in 1990-91 and its comes in five ranks in 2001-02 on growth of NSDP. But in Bihar states the NSDP of Rs. 22787 crores in 1990-91 and its rank was four. But it comes down in 2001-02 up to eight ranks. total NSDP was Rs. 51345 crores as compare to other states. This is an important disparity in the economic performance of the states in India.

PER-CAPITA INCOME

We see the impact of inter-state differentials in rate of growth on regional per-capita income inequality in Table 2. Table 2 presents classification of 10 states according to the level of per-capita income at current prices in 1990-91 to 2001-02. The relatively high developed states of Andhra Pradesh Gujarat Haryana, Karnataka and Kerala shows high per-capita income at current prices compared average per-capita income of India (247.87%). Whereas Maharashtra, Punjab, Orissa fall in the medium developed states per-capita in come variables. Among the low developed states. Assam and Bihar shows low per-capita income at current prices from the year 1990-91 to 2001-02. This shows that per-capita income inequality varies from state to state in India

TABLE 2

Per-capita Income at Current Prices of the States of India

(in rupees)

States	*Per-capita Income*		*Average increased rate of per capita income*
	1990-91	*2001-02*	
1. High Developed States:			
Andhra Pradesh	4513	17642	289.36%
Gujarat	5891	21276	261.16%
Haryana	7508	26632	254.71%
Karnataka	4598	18324	298.52%
Kerala	4200	21310	407.38%
2. Medium Developed States:			
Maharashtra	7439	24736	232.51%
Orissa	3077	10103	228.34%
Punjab	8318	25652	208.39%
3. Low Developed States:			
Assam	4281	10951	155.80%
Bihar	2660	6015	126.13%
Total of 10 states of India	52503	182641	247.87%

Source: Tata Statistical Outline of India, 2004-05.

The analysis of inter-state measures taken to remove regional differentials in per-capita income have not been such as to reduce, inter-state income disparities, raises a number of interesting policy issues. It may be pointed out that we are barking up the wrong tree and are unnecessarily confusing issues since what should interest us is the removal of poverty and not the mere lessening of inter-state inequalities in per-capita income.

LITERACY RATE

Table 3 shows the literacy rate of 10 states of India according to census 2001.In Kerala literacy rate was highest in the (90.90%) comparison to other states. But the literacy rate was lowest in the Bihar (47.00%) as compared to other states in India. In males the literacy rate is higher than the female literacy rate in all the states in India. Females was highest compare to males.

CONCLUSION

TABLE 3

Literacy Rate of India According to Census 2001

States	*Literacy Rate 2001*		
	Persons	*Males*	*Females*
Andhra Pradesh	60.47	70.32	50.43
Assam	63.25	71.28	54.61
Bihar	47.00	59.68	33.12
Gujarat	69.14	79.66	57.80
Haryana	67.91	78.49	55.73
Karnataka	66.64	76.10	56.90
Kerala	90.90	94.24	87.12
Maharashtra	76.90	85.97	67.03
Orissa	63.08	75.35	50.51
Punjab	69.65	75.23	63.36
All-India	64.84	75.26	53.67

Source: Socio-economic Review of Gujarat, 2004-05.

The study here on the basis of available data indicates that inter-regional disparities in per-capita income are on the increase in the period 1990-91 to 2001-02. The important problem of the removal of poverty provided care is taken to see that the poorer per-capita income states take necessary steps to improve their large per cent of people below the poverty line as per-capita income increase. It is necessary that literacy rate also increase in females to reduce the disparities in growth of Indian economy.

References

Susheela Subrahmamya, Regional Economic Development in India, Deep & Deep Publications, New Delhi.

G.P Mishra (1985), Regional Structure of Development and Growth in India, Ashish Publishing House, New Delhi.

Dr. C.B. Mamoria, Agriculture Problems of India, Kitab Mahal, Delhi.

India 2008: A Reference Annual, Government of India.

Mahajan, O.P. (1982), Economic Planning and Regional Development in India, Ess Ess Publication, New Delhi.

Tata Statistical Out Line of India, 2004-05.

Pal, M.N., Regional Disparities in the Level of Development in India, *Indian Journals of Regional Science*, Kharagpur.

Socio-economic Review of Gujarat State, Gandhinagar, 2004-05.

11

Industrial Disparity in India: An Analysis of UP vis-a-vis Maharashtra and Gujarat

RAJESH KUMAR SINGH AND VIJAY NATH DUBEY

INTRODUCTION

Geographically the vast countries like India face the problem of regional disparity because natural endowments, climate and physical conditions significantly differ across their regions. As a result, economic opportunities are not uniformly available to population residing in different regions. The regional problem gets manifest through several symptoms like significant differences among regions in levels of per-capita income, levels of unemployment rates, physical quality of life, human development, property prices and so on.

We shall initiate the discussion on initiatives for balanced regional growth by illustrating two instances of initiatives in the past. One relates to agriculture and the other relates to industry, the two most important sectors of our economy.

The strategy to boost agricultural production and to ensure food security was evolved in the mid-Sixties when the country faced a grim situation following two consequent years of severe draught. The strategy consisted of various incentives to farmers to adopt high yielding seeds of wheat and paddy along with complimentary inputs, assured minimum support prices for the output, buffer stocking of the food grains and supplying the same to the States to distribute through the public distribution system (PDS) to the consumers, especially in the deficit regions. To back up this strategy, institutions like Agricultural Prices Commission (APC), Food Corporation of India (FCI) and Warehousing Corporation of India and other ancillary institutions were established. Arrangements were made to spread the message of high yielding seeds and the associated package of inputs and practices.

The above strategy ushered in a green revolution, which resulted in doubling of wheat and rice production in the country over a short period. Adequate food grains surpluses were generated to build up the needed buffer stock. India was no more a 'basket case'. The initial success of green revolution strategy was restricted to Punjab, Haryana and western Uttar Pradesh where assured irrigation networks already existed. Subsequently, it was extended to a few irrigation commands in the South and West also. It was, however, expected that with the expansion of assured irrigation the green revolution would spread to other parts of the country soon. In the event this did not happen. Even today almost the entire food grain surpluses are generated by the small region, which benefited initially

The other example of a major public policy, which had gone sore after initial success is the industrial policy. In the Fifties, when India initiated a policy of import substitution by starting various industries in key sectors there were very few critics both within the country and abroad. Indeed, the industrial policy embedded in the Second Five Year Plan, giving emphasis to basic and heavy industries, was lauded equally by Russian experts as well as western experts. That policy enabled the country to lay the foundations of an industrial base.

Gradually the ills of public sector undertakings and the stifling effects of a market without competition became more and more evident. By late Sixties and early Seventies, several perceptive observers noted that there was need to deregulate the industrial sector to allow competition. Government, instead, went ahead with nationalization of more and more key sectors of the economy and also further throttling of private sector to control concentration of wealth and industrial power. The result was further retrogression and immiserization of the economy.

The economic reforms initiated in 1991 were also essentially crisis driven. It was the international payment crisis which forced the country to carry out deregulation of trade and industry. Again, once the crisis was overcome reforms also slowed down. There are several vital areas of reforms, which we have been talking about for the last one decade without doing much—public sector reforms, reform of labour laws, reform of the legal system, establishment of effective regulatory bodies and so on. Again, it is the politicians, the bureaucrats, the 'Deshi' industrialists and the trade union leaders who are standing in the way. They do not want to give up the powers, perks and monopoly profits, which they have been enjoying.

The main interest of the foreigners in India is its large potential market. Unless the rural incomes grow, especially in the backward regions this potential market will not be realized. Corporate India must realize that its future lies with the masses. Raising rural incomes should no longer be looked upon only as a philanthropic objective.

Also reduction of regional disparities should be looked upon as a national objective. The strength of a building depends on the strength of its weakest pillar. In a similar way the strength of the Indian economy depends on the strength of the economy of Bihar. Similarly, the bottom line of India's human development will depend on the incomes and socio-demographic indicators of development in northern and eastern India.

OBJECTIVES OF THE STUDY

The overall objective of the present study is to enquire into the industrial disparity across the states in India. This has been initiated with the following sub-objectives;

1. to analyse the number of factories, invested capital, employment and output of factories across the states in India, and
2. to peep into the input-output ratio, output per rupee of invested capital, and employment per rupee of invested capital in factories across the states in India.

NEED OF THE STUDY

In the past, Government of India has taken two important initiatives for balanced regional growth. The first initiative relates to green revolution in agricultural sector and the second relates to industrial policy initiative, i.e. policy of nationalization emphasized in Second Plan and the Policy of Industrial Deregulation Initiated after 1991. But the policy initiatives of the past could not reap the desired results of balanced regional development. Hence it is imperative to conduct a comparative study of backward and forward states to derive fruitful inferences for the balanced regional development of India.

METHODOLOGY OF THE STUDY

The study is based mainly on secondary data and information. The data and information have been collected from three important sources, viz. Annual Survey of Industries, Report on Currency and Finance, and Economic Survey of India. Various websites like www.econstats.com, www. Indiastats.com, www.capitalmarket.com, etc. have also been used for the collection of data and information. For preparation of present study various journals and magazines like *Indian Journal of Commerce, Vikalpa, Capital Market, Economic and Political Weekly*, etc. have also been used. The study covers the period from 1998-99 to 2004-05. However, the period varies according to availability of data and nature of subject dealt with. The states covered under the study are UP, Maharashtra and Gujarat. The period and states have been chosen on the ground of consistency of available data and information. The study has been initiated with relevant percentages, statistical averages and trend analysis, etc.

FINDINGS OF THE STUDY

The number of factories, invested capital, employment and output of the factories in India, UP, Maharashtra and Gujarat have been analysed in Tables 1, 2, 3, and 4 covering the period from 1998-99 to 2004-05. The analysis revealed the following facts:

1. The number of factories in UP is very much lower than that in Maharashtra and Gujarat. On an average, Uttar Pradesh accounts for only 7.35 per cent factories whereas Maharashtra and Gujarat accounted for 14.04 per cent and 10.67 per cent factories of India respectively during the period of analysis (Table 1).
2. The average share in Invested capital of factories in Maharashtra and Gujarat accounted for 17.98 per cent and 16.62 per cent of all-India during the period covered. Whereas UP accounted for only 8.23 per cent during the same period (Table 2).
3. During the period covered under study, factories in Maharashtra and Gujarat provided, on an average, 14.78 per cent and 9.44 per cent of total employment provided by factories in India. Whereas factories in UP have provided only 6.95 per cent of total employment in factories in India (Table 3).
4. The analysis of output of factories revealed that factories in UP have registered only 7.0 per cent of total output of factories in India during the period from 1998-99 to 2004-05. The relative share of Maharashtra and Gujarat, on an average, was recorded as 19.82 per cent and 14.95 per centrespectively during the same period (Table 4).

The input-output ratio, output per rupee of invested capital, and employment per rupee of invested capital of factories in India, UP, Maharashtra and Gujarat have been analysed in Tables 5, 6, and 7 covering the period from1998-99 to 2004-05. The above analysis revealed the following facts;

1. Table 5 depicts that the input-output ratio of factories in UP is similar to that of India, Maharashtra and Gujarat.
2. The output per rupee of invested capital in UP has been found similar to that of Gujarat but lower than Maharashtra and India (Table 6).
3. Table 7 highlights that employment per rupee of invested capital of factories in UP has been more than Gujarat during the period covered. It was just equal to Maharashtra but lower than India during the said period.

CONCLUSION

The planned development in India aiming at reducing various imbalances across the states has been only partially successful. At best, they have ensured that regional disparities in terms of various indicators of development are not aggravating. Of course, this is no mean achievement. In order to encounter the disparity across the states, the following measures are essential on the part of backward states:

1. Ensuring better developed economic and social infrastructure as well as more efficient and investor friendly state governments,
2. Efficiency of administration and the quality of governance including law and order situation are important factors for balanced and sustainable development across the regions,
3. The number of factories/industries and amount of invested capital should be accelerated in backward states which will, in turn, augment the employment and output of the industries in the concerned states, and

4. The backward states should adhere to the policies of developed states regarding social and economic growth pattern. In this connection, advice of Government as well as private and foreign experts should be availed.

References

Abramovitz, M. (1986). "Forgoing Ahead, Falling Behind." *Journal of Economic History*, 46(2): 385-406.

Balasubramanyam, V.N. and Y. Wei (2005). "Textile and Clothing Export from India and China." *Journal of Chinese Economic and Business Studies.*" 3(1): 23-37.

Benhabib, J. and M. Spiegel (1994). "The Role of Human Capital in Economic Development." 34(2): 143-74.

Bhanumurthy, N.R. and A. Mitra (2004). "Economic Growth, Poverty and Inequality in Indian States in Pre-Reform and Post-Reform Periods." *Asian Development Review*, 21(2): 79-99.

Bhattacharya, B.B. and S. Sakthivel (2004). "Regional Growth and Disparity in India: Comparision of Pre and Post-Reform Perods." *Economic and Political Weekly*, 6 March: 1071-77.

Harrision, A. (1996). "Openness and Growth: A Time Series, Cross Country Analysis for Developing Countries", *Journal of Developing Economies*, 48 (2): 419-47.

Jain, T., J.D. Sachs and A.M. Warner (1996). "Trends in Regional Disparity in China.", *China Economic Review*, 7(1): 1-21.

Mitra, A. (1992). "Growth and Poverty: The Urban Legend", *Economic and Political Weekly*, 28 March: 659-65.

Sachs, J., D.N. Vajapai and A. Ramiah (2002). "Understanding Regional Economic Growth in India", *Asian Economic Papers*, 1(3): 32-62.

Zhang, X. and K. Zhang (2003). "How does Globalisation·Affect Regional Inequality within a Developing Country? Evidence from China." *Journal of Development Studies*, 39 (4): 47-67.

APPENDIX

TABLE 1

Number of Factories

(Numbers)

Year	*All-India*	*UP*	*Maharashtra*	*Gujarat*
1998-99	131706	10508(7.98)	19390(14.72)	15455(11.73)
1999-00	131558	10303(7.83)	19009(14.45)	14710(11.18)
2000-01	131268	9635(7.34)	18528(14.11)	14090(10.73)
2001-02	128549	9157(7.12)	17853(13.89)	13950(10.85)
2002-03	127957	8980(7.02)	17570(13.73)	13180(10.30)
2003-04	129074	9237(7.06)	17474(13.54)	12795(9.90)
2004-05	136353	9582(7.03)	18912(13.87)	13603(9.98)
Average		7.35	14.04	10.67

Note: Figure in brackets are percentages of All-India.
Source: Annual Survey of Industries, Government of India, Various Issues.

TABLE 2

Invested Capital

(Rs. Lakh)

Year	*All-India*	*UP*	*Maharashtra*	*Gujarat*
1998-99	53706813	6457333(12.02)	8618508(16.05)	8761928(16.31)
1999-00	56663430	5085709(8.98)	10469124(18.48)	8580412(15.14)
2000-01	57179940	4901000(8.57)	10363120(18.12)	9300141(16.26)
2001-02	60591285	4423859(7.30)	10508270(17.34)	11106001(18.33)
2002-03	63747308	4399806(6.90)	11891264(18.65)	10956152(17.19)
2003-04	67959786	4761440(7.01)	12401930(18.25)	11502721(16.93)
2004-05	75869399	5160774(6.80)	14368443(18.94)	12257791(16.16)
Average		8.23	17.98	16.62

Note: Figure in brackets are percentages of All-India.
Source: Annual Survey of Industries, Government of India, Various Issues

TABLE 3

Employees

(Number)

Year	*All-India*	*UP*	*Maharashtra*	*Gujarat*
1998-99	8588581	621155(7.23)	1393688(16.23)	815986(9.50)
1999-00	8172836	571719(7.0)	1217260(14.89)	822884(10.07)
2000-01	7987743	539737(6.76)	1172782(14.68)	752013(9.41)
2001-02	7750366	513190(6.62)	1162542(15.00)	712804(9.20)
2002-03	7935948	542160(6.83)	1170461(14.75)	717055(9.04)
2003-04	7870081	569603(7.24)	1114070(14.16)	729310(9.27)
2004-05	8453628	587702(6.95)	1162346(13.75)	808618(9.57)
Average		6.95	14.78	9.44

Note: Figure in brackets are percentages of All-India.
Source: Annual Survey of Industries, Government of India, Various Issues.

TABLE 4

Output

(Rs. Lakh)

Year	*All-India*	*UP*	*Maharashtra*	*Gujarat*
1998-99	78377081	5811990(7.42)	16115975(20.56)	11319078(14.44)
1999-00	89793835	6104692(6.80)	18133252(20.19)	11855115(13.20)
2000-01	92690185	6485418(7.0)	18497146(19.96)	12797728(13.81)
2001-02	96245663	6703704(6.97)	18122281(18.83)	14755010(15.33)
2002-03	113056111	8052063(7.12)	21759551(19.25)	18269979(16.16)
2003-04	128740055	9340116(7.26)	23832495(18.51)	20733426(16.10)
2004-05	167256142	10913874(6.53)	35887957(21.46)	26074860(15.59)
Average		7.0	19.82	14.95

Note: Figure in brackets are percentages of All-India.
Source: Annual Survey of Industries, Government of India, Various Issues.

TABLE 5

Input-Output Ratio

Year	*All-India*	*UP*	*Maharashtra*	*Gujarat*
1998-99	1.28	1.29	1.29	1.26
1999-00	1.27	1.27	1.29	1.27
2000-01	1.24	1.24	1.26	1.22
2001-02	1.24	1.23	1.25	1.20
2002-03	1.23	1.21	1.24	1.21
2003-04	1.24	1.20	1.26	1.22
2004-05	1.23	1.19	1.20	1.21
Average	1.25	1.23	1.26	1.23

Source: Computed From Data Given in Annual Survey of Industries, Government of India, Various Issues.

TABLE 6

Output per Rupee of Invested Capital

Year	*All-India*	*UP*	*Maharashtra*	*Gujarat*
1998-99	1.46	0.90	1.87	1.29
1999-00	1.58	1.20	1.73	1.38
2000-01	1.62	1.32	1.78	1.38
2001-02	1.59	1.52	1.72	1.33
2002-03	1.77	1.83	1.83	1.71
2003-04	1.89	1.96	1.92	1.80
2004-05	2.20	2.11	2.50	2.13
Average	1.73	1.55	1.91	1.57

Source: Computed From Data Given in Annual Survey of Industries, Government of India, Various Issues

TABLE 7

Employment per Rupee of Invested Capital

Year	*All-India*	*UP*	*Maharashtra*	*Gujarat*
1998-99	0.16	0.10	0.16	0.09
1999-00	0.14	0.11	0.12	0.10
2000-01	0.14	0.11	0.11	0.08
2001-02	0.13	0.12	0.11	0.06
2002-03	0.12	0.12	0.10	0.07
2003-04	0.12	0.12	0.09	0.06
2004-05	0.11	0.11	0.08	0.07
Average	0.13	0.11	0.11	0.08

Source: Computed From Data Given in Annual Survey of Industries, Government of India, Various Issues

12

Regional Disparity in Indian Development

BHAVESH N. DESAI, ASHOK B. TRIVEDI AND DIPAK R. CHAUDHARI

INTRODUCTION

The Phenomenon of disparity in Indian development was found during colonial period. Government's economic policies during the colonial period were more to protect the interests of the British economy rather than for advancing the welfare of the Indians. The primary concerns of the Government were law and order, tax collection and defense. As for development, Government adopted a basically *laissez-faire* attitude. Of course, Railways Irrigation systems, road network and modern education system were developed during this period. Railways and road network were more to facilitate movements of goods and defense personal and to futilities better administrative control Irrigation canal system was mainly to fight repeated droughts and famines and to boost land revenue. Education to begin with, was developed mainly to train lower-ranking functionaries for the colonial administration.

After independence, India is a large federal nation and it is well-known that there are widespread disparities in the levels of economic and of social development between the different regions of the Indian nation. It is generally recognized that inter-regional economic dispraise increase, at least in the initial stages of national economic development. As a result, governments everywhere including India used to initiate deliberate policy measures to reduce these disparities. But with the reaffirmation of faith in the market mechanism in the liberated economic scenario the world over now, there is a tendency to withdraw such measures under the implicit assumption that the invisible hand will deliver the goods in this regard.

India has also witnessed a change has its economic policy in recent years. India has now become a highly liberalized and globalized economy with great faith in the hence a matter of considerable research interest to know the manner in which inter-regional dispararities in the levels of economic development have changed in India over time in the past decade. A comparison of India's regional development experience over the past decade would therefore give at least a broad idea of the impact, if any, of these changes on the regional aspect of India's development.

In such a scenario, widespread inter-state disparities in levels of economic and social development can political consequences, this being particularly. Therefore, it is necessary to find out the remedies to alleviate disparity in Indian nation.

[I} Poverty

Poverty estimates by the planning commission show that the percentage of population below the poverty lie has fallen form 55 per cent in 1973-74 to 36 per cent in 1993-94 and further to 27 per cent in 2004-05 for rural and urban areas taken together.

Poverty ratio in Table 1 reveal substantial variation across the states in India Among the major states, Orissa, Bihar, and Madhya Pradesh (including the new states of Jharkhand and Chhattisgarh have substantially higher poverty ratio than all-India, while Punjab has single digit poverty ratio. Here, it is note that the high poverty states are contiguous, lying in the central and eastern parts of India.

TABLE I

Poverty in Major Indian States

States	*Rural*		*Urban*		*Total*	
	1993-94	*2004-05*	*1993-94*	*2004-05*	*1993-94*	*2004-05*
Andhra Pradesh	15.9	11.2	38.3	28.0	22.2	15.8
Assam	45.0	22.3	7.7	3.3	40.9	19.7
Bihar	58.2	43.0	34.5	28.7	55.0	41.1
Gujarat	22.2	19.1	27.9	13.0	24.2	16.8
Haryana	28.0	13.6	16.4	15.1	25.1	14.0
Karnataka	29.9	20.8	40.1	32.6	33.2	25.0
Kerala	25.8	13.2	24.6	20.2	25.4	15.0
Madhya Pradesh	40.6	37.9	48.4	41.9	42.5	39.0
Maharashtra	37.9	29.6	35.2	32.2	36.9	30.7
Orissa	49.7	46.8	41.6	44.3	48.6	46.4
Punjab	12.0	9.1	11.4	7.1	11.8	8.4
Rajasthan	26.5	18.7	30.5	32.9	27.4	22.1
Tamil Nadu	32.5	22.8	39.8	22.2	35.0	22.5
Utter Pradesh	42.3	33.7	35.4	31.0	40.9	33.1
West Bengal	40.8	28.6	22.4	14.8	35.7	24.7
India	37.3	28.3	32.4	25.7	36.0	27.5

Source: Government of India

The data revealed that the poorer states of Bihar, Madhya Pradesh, Orissa and Utter Pradesh have not exhibited any significant increase in the rate of reduction of poverty over the periods 1993-2005. Poverty has increased single become concentrated in these states. While 46 per cent of India's poor lived in the states of Bihar, Madhya Pradesh, Orissa and Uttar Pradesh in 1993, over 54 per cent lived in these states in 2004-05. Moreover rural poverty has also become concentrated in these four states which accounted for 56 per cent of all-India rural poor in 1983 and 61 per cent in 2004-05. It is risky to ignore this problem as it could potentially become a source of social conflict.

North-Western states (Punjab, Haryana, Himachal Pradesh and Jammu & Kashmir had made substantial progress in poverty reduction even by the early 1980, and their combined share in all-India poor was 2.7 per cent in 1983, this further declined to 2.2 per cent in 2004-05.

(2) Employment

According to the estimation of Indian government's special cell regarding employment opportunity. The employment rates varied in various states of Indian nation after the economic reforms.

TABLE 2

Annual Employment Growth Rate

(Percent)

Sr. No.	States	1980-90			1990-2005		
		Rural	Urban	Combined	Rural	Urban	Combined
1.	Andhra Pradesh	4.38	2.59	3.64	2.27	1.16	1.85
2.	Assam	N.A.	N.A.	N.A.	3.18	3.42	3.26
3.	Bihar	1.30	3.23	2.20	0.80	-0.95	-0.02
4.	Gujarat	2.84	2.44	2.61	1.61	1.22	1.39
5.	Haryana	3.56	3.21	3.34	4.90	2.13	3.33
6.	Himachal Pradesh	2.85	3.73	3.13	2.64	1.82	2.38
7.	Karnataka	2.60	2.96	2.77	1.67	0.43	1.09
8.	Kerala	1.66	5.13	2.98	4.55	1.97	3.56
9.	Madhya Pradesh	3.97	4.09	4.03	1.33	1.05	1.19
10.	Maharashtra	2.87	2.87	2.87	3.29	1.10	1.87
11.	Orissa	3.22	2.51	2.97	2.73	0.76	2.11
12.	Punjab	3.40	2.60	2.85	4.10	2.11	2.82
13.	Rajasthan	1.48	2.57	2.05	3.69	1.74	2.71
14.	Tamil Nadu	2.26	1.68	1.94	4.00	2.24	3.11
15.	Utter Pradesh	1.19	2.40	1.87	2.99	1.15	1.99
16.	West Bengal	4.95	2.09	3.38	2.04	0.96	1.51
All-India		2.88	2.81	2.84	2.72	1.49	2.08

Source: Government of India.

It is observe that the overall India's unemployment rates in year of 1993-94, it was reported 5.99 per cent while in the year of 1999-2000 it was marked 7.32 per cent.

In 1993-94, the highest unemployment rate in India was found in kerala and the unemployment rate was the lowest in Rajasthan. Similarly, it was also found in year 1999-2000.

In 1993-94, Gujarat, Karnataka, Madhya Pradesh, Maharashtra, Punjab, Rajasthan and Uttar Pradesh status was found the lower unemployment rate rather than average of

India. While during 1999-2000 in the eight status of India namely Gujarat, Haryana, Karnataka, Madhya Pradesh, Maharashtra, Punjab, Rajasthan and Uttar Pradesh the unemployment rate in Bihar was the similar with the average of overall India.

The unemployment rates in the year of 1999-2000 decreased In comparison to the year of 1993-94. in Gujarat, Haryana and Karnataka states. During this period domestic production growth rated also increased in these three states. While in the other twelve states, the unemployment rates increased during this period. It is noteworthy, that during this period though The domestic production growth rates in Rajasthan, Tamil Nadu and West Bengal were more than 7 per cent, the unemployment rates increased.

To the large extent during the first decade of the economical reforms, the unemployment rates increased in most of the states in India.

(3) Growth Rate of GSDP

The data on growth rate of GSDP has been given by Ahluvaliya. The data is available for two period that is before a decade or economic reforms and after a decade of economic reforms This data is limited only for main eight states of India (Table 3).

The average growth rate of GSDP in India was 5.47 per cent during 1980-81 to 1990-91. Thereafter it has been increased by 6.23 per cent during the period of 1993-94 to 2003-04 it means that it is increase sharply after the decade of new economic reforms.

The average growth rate of GSDP in Maharashtra, Andhra Pradesh, Haryana and Rajasthan were higher than the average of India before new economic reforms but three states out of four except Rajasthan have been decreased then the average of India after new economic reforms.

The average growth rate of GSDP in Gujarat, Bengal and Karnataka was lower than the average rate of India before new economic reforms but it was higher in all three states than the average rate if India after new economic reforms. While the growth rate of Punjab was lower than the average rate of India before and after new economic reforms.

TABLE 3

Development Rate in Major Indian States

State	1993-94 to 2003-04	1991-92 to 1998-99	1980-81 to 1990-91
Gujarat	7.77	8.15	5.08
West Bengal	7.07	6.97	4.71
Rajasthan	6.99	5.85	6.60
Haryana	6.13	5.13	6.43
Karnataka	6.97	5.87	5.29
Andhra Pradesh	5.90	5.20	5.65
Maharashtra	5.31	8.01	6.02
Punjab	4.29	4.77	5.34
All India	6.23	6.50	5.47

Source: Government of India

There is only two states like Gujarat and Bengal where the growth rate now been passed more then 7 per cent after new economic reforms.

It is show that the averages growth rate of GSDP in Rajasthan was the highest in averages India before new economic reforms and in Bengal was the lowest growth rate but latter new economic reforms this growth rate is higher in Gujarat and lowest in Punjab

(4) Per-capita Income

Central Statistical Organization has been given the data on per-capital income.

The growth rate of per-capital income in various status has been given by Central Statistical Organization. Central Statistical Organisation has been given the data on per-capita income.

The growth rate of per-capita income in various states has been given by Central Statistical Organisation. This data has been used to compare this growth rate among various states between period of 1993-94 to 2003-04. It is try to know that the result of economic reforms in various states of India in terms of growth rate of per-capita income.

TABLE 4

Per-capita Income in Major Indian States

Sr. No.	*States*	*1993-94 (Rs.)*	*2003-04 (Rs.)*	*Average Growth Rate*	*Population (2003-04) (Lakh)*	*Population Growth Rate (1991 to 2001)*
1.	Delhi	18,166	29,231	4.87	1.5	3.88
2.	Gujarat	9,796	16,779	5.53	5.4	2.05
3.	Maharashtra	12,183	16,479	3.07	10.3	2.06
4.	Punjab	12,710	15,800	2.20	2.6	1.82
5.	Haryana	11,079	15,721	3.56	2.2	2.50
6.	Karnataka	7,838	13,141	5.30	5.6	1.60
7.	Tamil Nadu	8,955	12,976	3.78	6.6	1.07
8.	Kerala	7,983	12,328	4.44	3.4	1.07
	All-India	7,690	11,799	4.37	10.88	1.95

Source: Central Statistical Organization, Census of India.

The average growth rate of per-capita income in India is 4.37 per cent during this period.

It is reported that some states like Karnataka, Delhi, Gujarat and Kerala have higher growth rate of India. Whereas Maharashtra, Punjab, Haryana and Tamil Nadu states has lower growth rate than the average growth rate of India. It is surprise that the lower growth rate states has been known as a developed state in India. It is observed that the growth rate of per-capita income has become slow after new economic reforms. During this period it is show that grow rate of per-capita income in Gujarat is the higher growth

(5) Human Development Index

The data on HDI in various states of India is published in Social Development Report, 2006. This data has compare the rural and urban HDI during the year 1991 and 2001 shows that Kerala state was stood at first rank in terms of HDI during 1991 and 2001 in rural area and it was also first rank during 1991 in urban area but not during 2001. Surprisingly, it was a third rank during 2001 in urban area.

While Bihar state was stood at last rank during 1999 and 2001 in both rural and urban area of India.

TABLE 5

Human Development Index in Major Indian States

State	*Rural*				*Urban*			
	Human Development Index		*Number*		*Human Development Index*		*Number*	
	1991	*2001*	*1991*	*2001*	*1991*	*2001*	*1991*	*2001*
Andhra Pradesh	29.99	40.22	12	09	35.06	52.37	13	06
Assam	36.43	38.83	06	12	42.64	53.49	06	05
Bihar	16.03	16.13	20	20	22.45	27.10	20	19
Chhattishgarh	20.86	28.87	15	15	28.35	36.35	14	16
Gujarat	38.85	39.68	05	11	44.84	51.56	07	08
Haryana	35.36	44.85	09	05	44.09	48.83	08	10
Himachal Pradesh	52.84	63.55	02	02	65.32	70.37	02	01
Jammu & Kashmir	47.80	52.29	04	04	60.34	-	03	-
Jharkhand	16.85	16.22	19	19	22.48	33.96	19	17
Karnataka	32.34	41.30	10	08	40.48	54.90	11	04
Kerala	69.55	68.73	01	01	67.32	62.94	01	03
Madhya Pradesh	19.76	26.56	16	17	27.51	41.63	15	14
Maharashtra	36.26	40.16	07	10	47.23	46.48	05	12
Orissa	24.50	27.29	14	16	27.44	37.37	16	15
Punjab	49.92	57.59	03	03	50.84	64.49	04	02
Rajasthan	31.06	34.93	11	13	35.77	46.09	12	13
Tamil Nadu	35.90	44.08	08	06	42.70.	47.68	09	11
Uttar Pradesh	17.81	23.65	18	18	23.61	33.94	18	18
Uttaranchal	18.44	42.48	17	07	23.84	49.59	17	09
West Bengal	29.80	33.82	13	14	40.61	52.31	10	07

Source: Social Development Report, 2006.

Kerala and Jharakand states have been decreased the HDI during 2001 than the year of 1991, in rural area while rest of states have been increased. The HDI has also decreased In Kerala during 2001 than year of 1999 in urban area. And, The Maharashtra state where this rate is decrease during 2001 than the year of 1991 in urban area. Rest of the state has been increased the HDI during 2001 than the year of 1991 in urban area.

It is shows that Kerala is only single state where the HDI of rural area was higher than the urban area during 1991 and 2001 also. Remaing states the HDI of rural area was the lower than the urban area during 1991 and 2001.

The Gujarat state was stood at rank 5 and 11 respectively at year of 1991 and 2001 in rural area and rank 7 and 8 respectively during year of 1991 and 2001 in urban area.

CONCLUDING REMARKS

The above study has find out some concluding remarks given below.

- The disparity had been found out since colonies period. It was long period in Indian development.
- The poverty ratio has fallen out in rural and urban both area during last four decades.
- It was also found out that ratio has also fallen after new economic reforms.
- Orissa, Bihar and Madhya Pradesh lying in the central and eastern parts of India have substantially higher poverty ratio.
- Bihar, Madhya Pradesh, Orissa, and Uttar Pradesh have not exhibited any significant increase in the rate of reduction of poverty over the periods 1993-05.
- North-western States had made substantial progress in poverty reduction even by the early 1980 and after economic reforms.
- The unemployment rates have been increased during the period of economic reforms in India.
- In given data, highest unemployment rate was found in Kerala state which is well known state regarding human development in India.
- Unemployment rate of Gujarat and Karnataka state became lower than the average of India due

to increased domestic production growth rate during same period.

- The domestic production growth rates in Rajasthan, Tamil Nadu and West Bengal were more than 7 per cent however the unemployment rates increased.
- The average growth rate of GSDP in India has been increased after new economic reforms.
- It is surprise that well develop state Punjab was found lower growth rate of GSDP rather than the average of India before after new economic reforms.
- The average growth rate of GSDP was found high before reforms in Maharashtra, Andhra Pradesh and Haryana than the average of India. But not same position after reforms. While the average growth rate of GSDP was found lower in Gujarat, Karnataka and West Bengal rather than the average of India but it was high after economic reforms.
- It is surprise that Punjab, Haryana and Tamil Nadu were found lower growth rate of per-capita income rather than the average of India. Which states are known as a develop states in Indian nation.
- It is seen that Kerala was stood at first rank in most of cases in terms of HDI except urban area HDI in 2001. It is also noted that Kerala state was found decreased HDI during 1991 and 2001 in rural and urban both areas.
- It is show that all of the states of India except Kerala were found lower HDI in rural area with the compare of urban area.
- There was not found the inverse relationship between growth rate of GSDP and poverty ratio in Punjab. The growth rate of GSDP and poverty ratio both were lower in Punjab.

References

H. Indira and M. Darshini (2004), "Gujarat Human Development Report, 2004", 'Mahatma Gandhi Shram Sansathan, Ahmedabad.

———(2006), "Arthsankalan", Arthsankalan Charitable Trust, Ahmedabad.

K.R.G. Nair (2004), "Regional Disparity of Indian Development", Centre for Research, Delhi.

R. Radhakrishna (2008), "Indian Development Report, 2008", Indira Gandhi Institute of Development Research, Mumbai.

———(2005) "Human Development Report, 2005", Oxford University Press, Delhi.

13

Regional Disparities Across Indian States: A Sector-wise Analysis

Pooja Sikka

INTRODUCTION

The pattern of growth across states within India has been a subject of interest both to academics as well as policy-makers. The existence of wide inter-regional variations in a vast country like India is well recognized. Reducing such disparities is essential for the success of a federal structure. This has been an important challenge now for federal structure like India.

No doubt, considerable disparities in the level of development across the regions existed even 50 years ago. Indeed, one of the principal justifications for introduction of five year plans and the establishment of the Planning Commission was to ensure a process of regionally balanced and socially equitable development. Through public and directed private investments, as well as various other interventions and public policies, balanced development across the regions was pursued during the first four decades of planning. But the role of government in the economic activities of the nation changed substantially since the initiation of economic reforms in 1991. (Kurian: 2002)

Economic reforms have been initiated at different levels across states. Most of the economic reforms have been pursued in the industrial sector, the spread and growth of which show considerable regional variations. In the post-reform period, due to deregulation, the degree of control of the Central Government declined in many sectors. The private sector, which was controlled and contained in various ways, has since then been encouraged to play a more important role. Now, market forces, rather than government directions, decide the investment decisions—where to invest, what to produce, whom to sell to, and so on. State Governments can now take more initiatives for economic development than ever before. Also, the role of private sector is becoming more important as compared to the public sector. In the changed economic scenario, it would be interesting to examine the economic performance in the post-reform period at state level.

This paper examines the sectoral composition of growth performance of 14 major states in the post-reform period on the basis of available data from CSO (Central Statistical Organisation). The Central Statistical Organisation has revised the GDP series with base 1993-94. The SDP series for states have also been revised accordingly. It may be noted that 1993-94 base GDP (and corresponding SDP series) are based on the United Nations System of National Accounts (SNA) 1993. The new GDP and SDP series not only changed base year in terms of price, but also revised the production boundary in a number of sectors, notably, agriculture, real estate and finance. It has also shifted the occupation force database from the census to the National Sample Survey (NSS). Finally, it has incorporated some new dynamic economic activities, such as software, which were not included in the earlier series (Bhattacharya and Sakthievel: 2004).

To examine the post-reform economic performance of states, the study period has been taken from 1993-94 onwards (based on new series) upto 2004-05. Accordingly, this paper has been divided into two sections.. Section I describes sectoral composition of state domestic product of 14 major states. In Section II, sectoral growth rates of SDP in primary, secondary and tertiary sector has been worked out.

SECTION I

SECTORAL COMPOSITION OF STATE DOMESTIC PRODUCT

When an economy progresses, the share of the primary sector declines and that of secondary sector and tertiary sector increases. At the later stage, however, the tertiary sector overtakes the secondary sector. It happens when the economy attains a fairly high level of development, typically when it becomes a middle-income country. This is the general pattern of development seen, especially in East Asia. For example, in China, the secondary sector now contributes almost 50 per cent of GDP. However, in India, at the aggregate level, and also at the regional level, the tertiary sector became the largest sector even before the secondary sector pre dominated the economy (Bhattacharya and Mitra: 1990).

Table 1 exhibits the sectoral composition of state domestic product of 14 major states (in percentage) at constant prices (1993-94) for three point of time, i.e., 1993-94, 1999-00 and 2004-05. From the glance at the table one thing is very clear that the tertiary sector, rather than the secondary sector has become the engine of growth in most of the states. Almost in all the states, the share of tertiary sector now exceeds 50 per cent of SDP. Indeed, this reflects a poor pace of industrialization in India at regional levels. It may be seen that the share of primary sector in state GDP has decreased for all the states during the period from 1993-94 to 2004-05. While, the share of secondary sector has decreased for all states except Tamil Nadu, West Bengal, Maharashtra and Orissa.

On the other hand, the share of tertiary sector has increased for all the states for the period from 1993-94 to 2004-05. In this way, Indian states are also experiencing restructuring of economic activity with a shift from primary

Table 1

Sectoral Composition of SDP (Per Cent) at Constant Prices (1993-94)

States	*Sectors*	*1993-94*	*1999-00*	*2004-05*
ANDHRA PTRADESH	PRIMARY	35.73	29.95	27.11
	SECONDARY	21.91	23.47	22.96
	TERTIARY	42.36	46.58	49.93
BIHAR	PRIMARY	48.78	40.85	40.19
	SECONDARY	9.93	12.09	11.73
	TERTIARY	41.29	47.06	48.08
GUJARAT	PRIMARY	25.46	18.37	18.46
	SECONDARY	35.77	39.99	39.09
	TERTIARY	38.77	41.64	42.45
HARYANA	PRIMARY	42.44	33.88	28.19
	SECONDARY	26.24	28.24	27.45
	TERTIARY	31.32	37.88	44.36
KARNATAKA	PRIMARY	36.32	29.86	18.22
	SECONDARY	25.4	25.55	27.28
	TERTIARY	38.28	44.59	54.5
KERALA	PRIMARY	30.59	24.51	14.71
	SECONDARY	20.61	20.01	20.7
	TERTIARY	48.8	55.48	64.59
MADHYA PRADESH	PRIMARY	43.19	35.46	32.91
	SECONDARY	21.14	28.01	25.79
	TERTIARY	35.67	36.53	41.3
MAHARASHTRA	PRIMARY	20.17	16.61	11.93
	SECONDARY	32.77	32	29.22
	TERTIARY	47.06	51.39	58.85
ORISSA	PRIMARY	44.95	37.28	35.83
	SECONDARY	19.78	21.26	19.58
	TERTIARY	35.27	41.46	44.59
PUNJAB	PRIMARY	46.13	40.24	37.07
	SECONDARY	21.77	23.48	23.48
	TERTIARY	32.1	36.28	39.45
RAJASTHAN	PRIMARY	36.27	30.32	28.82
	SECONDARY	24.96	30.19	27.57
	TERTIARY	38.77	39.49	43.61
TAMIL NADU	PRIMARY	24.78	18.33	15.03
	SECONDARY	33.69	33.45	32.31
	TERTIARY	41.53	48.22	52.66

UTTAR PRADESH	PRIMARY	39.8	37.24	33.4
	SECONDARY	21.45	23.13	23.62
	TERTIARY	38.75	39.63	42.98
WEST BENGAL	PRIMARY	33.84	28.3	23.12
	SECONDARY	23.02	22.85	20.2
	TERTIARY	43.14	48.85	56.68

Source: Calculations made from CSO data.

sector to tertiary sector. In Tamil Nadu, Maharashtra and Kerala more than 50 per cent of SDP came from tertiary sector in 2004-05. The well known agriculturally prosperous states, Punjab and Haryana, have also faced the reduction of share of primary sector from 46.13 per cent to 37.07 per cent and from 42.44 per cent to 28.19 per cent respectively in total SDP. Even in the poorest states- Bihar, Madhya Pradesh, Orissa, Rajasthan and Uttar Pradesh, the share of primary sector has declined significantly during the period between 1993-94 to 2004-05. For instance, the share of primary sector in Bihar which was 48.78 per cent of SDP in 1993-94 has now come down to about 40.19 per cent in 2004-05.

In industrial states such as Gujarat, Maharashtra and Tamil Nadu, the share of primary sector in SDP has declined significantly. This happened due to faster growth in tertiary sector. The share of primary sector in SDP comes down from 24.78 per cent to 15.03 per cent, from 20.17 per cent to 11.93 per cent and from 25.46 per cent 18.46 per cent in Tamil Nadu, Maharashtra, and Gujarat respectively. On the other hand, the share of secondary sector has also declined moderately from 33.69 per cent to 32.31 per cent and from 32.77 per cent to 29.22 per cent in Tamil Nadu and Maharashtra respectively. The other two more states in which the share of secondary sector has been reduced during the period of analysis are Orissa and West Bengal. Among all the 14 States, Gujarat is contributing highest percentage of SDP in secondary sector, i.e. 35.77 per cent (in 1993-94), which further rose to 39.09 per cent in 2004-05 and Bihar is contributing lowest percentage of SDP in secondary sector, i.e. only 9.93 per cent, which however rose to 11.73 per cent in 2004-05.

SECTION II

SECTORAL GROWTH RATES OF STATE DOMESTIC PRODUCT

In the last section, one thing which was missing is the rate of growth at which the state is growing ahead. The need for a separate section to fill this gap then arises naturally because sometimes it may happen that certain states are good at aggregate income criterion, but they are not able to maintain the same high growth rate in the following period. It may then become more likely that some states which were lagging behind earlier are now performing better in terms of growth rates.

Therefore, in this section, sectoral growth rates of 14 States have been calculated for the period from 1993-94 to 2004-05. For more accurate analysis, this period has been further subdivided into two parts, i.e. period from 1993-94 to 1998-99 and from 1999-00 to 2004-05. These sectoral rates of growth are based on State's SDP.

From a glance at the Table 2, it is evident that, all the states have experienced positive growth rate in primary, secondary and tertiary sector. Karnataka received the highest growth rate of 11.5 per cent in primary sector and Kerala received the lowest growth rate of only 0.94 per cent. The agriculturally prosperous states like Punjab and Haryana recorded comparatively low growth rate in primary sector, i.e. 1.43 and 1.14 respectively.

To talk about secondary sector growth rate, most of the states experienced more than 6 per cent growth rate except Orissa with 2.14 per cent, Kerala with 4.94 per cent and Tamil Nadu with 5.17 per cent. The highest growth rate, i.e. 17.6 per cent in secondary sector is again enjoyed by Karnataka and lowest growth rate, i.e. 2.14 per cent has been received by Orissa. The growth rate of tertiary sector during this period has remained more than 6 per cent except few states (Bihar and Uttar Pradesh). In the category of those states which received more than 9 per cent growth rate comes Haryana, Karnataka, Rajasthan, Tamil Nadu and West Bengal. Karnataka, in tertiary sector also enjoyed highest growth rate

TABLE 2

Sectoral Growth Rate of SDP (Per Cent Per Annum) at Constant Prices (1993-94)

States	*Sectors*	*1993-94 to 1998-99*	*1999-00 to 2004-05*	*1993-94 to 2004-05*
ANDHRA PRADESH	PRIMARY	1.92	3.32	3.54
	SECONDARY	6.79	6.55	5.83
	TERTIARY	6.64	7.97	7.58
BIHAR	PRIMARY	1.33	2.3	2.38
	SECONDARY	6.07	4.66	6.99
	TERTIARY	5.88	4.38	6.3
GUJARAT	PRIMARY	7.75	9.38	1.57
	SECONDARY	9.59	7.08	7.08
	TERTIARY	8.96	7.36	8.04
HARYANA	PRIMARY	1.14	2.85	2.04
	SECONDARY	7.43	6.07	6.43
	TERTIARY	9.44	10.1	9.96
KARNATAKA	PRIMARY	11.5	-3	4.89
	SECONDARY	17.6	11.5	12.5
	TERTIARY	18.8	13.5	15.7
KERALA	PRIMARY	0.94	-2.1	-1.61
	SECONDARY	4.94	7.39	5.54
	TERTIARY	6.99	9.81	8.93
MADHYA PRADESH	PRIMARY	2.62	2.47	-1.14
	SECONDARY	8.26	0.6	5.84
	TERTIARY	7.16	4.84	5.67
MAHARASHTRA	PRIMARY	2.25	-1.4	-1.11
	SECONDARY	6.95	4.18	3.36
	TERTIARY	6.77	8.37	7.79
ORISSA	PRIMARY	2.25	5.26	-2.24
	SECONDARY	2.14	4.92	3.58
	TERTIARY	6.46	7.33	7.08
PUNJAB	PRIMARY	1.43	1.81	2.23
	SECONDARY	7.37	3.9	5.04
	TERTIARY	7.22	5.84	6.45
RAJASTHAN	PRIMARY	8.54	5.04	2.55
	SECONDARY	10	3.47	6.58
	TERTIARY	9.77	6.93	7.74
TAMIL NADU	PRIMARY	1.35	-3.8	-0.52
	SECONDARY	5.17	1.25	3.65
	TERTIARY	9.91	4.9	7.48

UTTAR PRADESH	PRIMARY	2.55	1.85	-2.69
	SECONDARY	7.3	4.49	4.15
	TERTIARY	5.35	5.65	5.06
WEST BENGAL	PRIMARY	4.45	2.68	-3.31
	SECONDARY	6.95	4.55	5.82
	TERTIARY	9.35	10.4	9.86

Source: Calculations made from CSO data

of 13.5 per cent. So in this way Karnataka is the only state which received highest growth rate in each sector during this period.

During the period from 1999-00 to 2004-05, four states (Karnataka, Kerala, Maharashtra and Tamil Nadu) experienced negative growth rate in primary sector. Surprisingly, Karnataka also experienced negative growth rate in primary sector, in spite of receiving highest growth rate during the period 1993-94 to 1998-99. On the other hand, six states (Andhra Pradesh, Bihar, Gujarat, Haryana, Orissa and Punjab) managed to increase their primary sector growth rates in this period in comparison with the previous one. The secondary sector growth rates decreased in all states except two states, i.e. Kerala and Orissa where it increased by 2.24 points and 2.78 points respectively. Karnataka during this period also, received the highest secondary sector growth rate of 11.5 per cent, followed by Kerala with 7.39 per cent growth rate. Madhya Pradesh received the least growth rate of only 0.6 per cent. The tertiary sector growth experienced mixed trends. Half of the states (Andhra Pradesh, Gujarat, Haryana, Kerala, Maharashtra, Orissa, Andhra Pradesh and West Bengal) expeienced rise in tertiary sector growth rates. Rest of the states had to undergo decline in tertiary sector growth rate during this period. Bihar received the least growth rate of 4.38 during this period followed by Madhya Pradesh with 4.84 per cent growth rate.

During the whole period, i.e. from 1993-94 to 2004-05 half of the states (Kerala, Madhya Pradesh, Maharashtra, Tamil Nadu, Uttar Pradesh and West Bengal) received negative growth rates in primary sector. Further among these states West Bengal received highest negative growth rate (-3.31%) followed by Uttar Pradesh (-2.69%). However, two agriculturally prosperous states, Punjab and Haryana received low but positive growth rates in primary sector of 2.23 per cent and 2.04 per cent respectively. It simply means that economic activity is now shifting from primary sector to secondary and tertiary sector. In all the states except two (Bihar and Madhya Pradesh) growth rate of tertiary sector exceeds secondary sector. In BIMARU states also, the growth rate of tertiary sector exceeds 5 per cent.

On the other hand, during this aggregate period also, Karnataka received highest growth rate in secondary (12.5%) as well as tertiary sector (15.7%). In the three leading industrial states (Gujarat, Maharashtra and Tamil Nadu), only Gujarat performed fairly well as its secondary sector grew at more than 7 per cent. Maharashtra and Tamil Nadu received only marginal growth of 3.36 per cent and 3.65 per cent in secondary sector. In tertiary sector, except Punjab, Madhya Pradesh Bihar and Uttar Pradesh, all the states grew with more than 7 per cent growth rate. Notably, Haryana, Karnataka and West Bengal grew at more than 9 per cent growth rate. Therefore, it is quite likely that in the periods ahead other states would also receive more growth rate in tertiary sector, and would face declining growth rate in primary sector.

CONCLUSIONS

India accounts for a meager 2.4 per cent of the world surface area yet it sustains a whooping 16.7 per cent of the world population, a little over 1 billion people residing in 29 States and 6 Union Territories. The variation across these states and territories is enormous in regard to physical geography, culture and economic condition. Some states have achieved rapid economic growth in recent years, while others have languished.

Indian states are also experiencing restructuring of economic activity with a shift from primary sector to tertiary sector. Almost in all the states, the share of tertiary sector now exceeds 50 per cent of SDP. Indeed, this reflects a poor pace of industrialization in India at regional levels. It is a matter of serious concern that, well known agriculturally prosperous states, Punjab and Haryana, have also faced the reduction of share of primary sector. As the livelihood of most of the population of India is based upon agriculture, the reduction of primary sector contribution to total SDP will make poor people poorer. Therefore, in the context of Indian economy, it would not be exaggeration to say that, indeed, economic growth has taken place but somehow development is lacking. This is really true, especially as is the case with key geographical regions especially the BIMARU (Bihar, Madya Pradesh, Rajasthan, and Uttar Pradesh) states.

References

Bhattacharya, B.B, Sakthivel, S. (2004), "Regional Growth and Disparity in India: Comparison of Pre- and Post-Reform Decades," *Economic and Political Weekly*, Vol. XXXXIX, No. 10, pp. 1071-77.

Bhattacharya, B.B. and Arup Mitra (1990): 'Excess Growth of Tertiary Sector in Indian Economy: Issues and Implications', *Economic and Political Weekly*, Vol. XXV, No. 44, pp. 2445-50.

Kurien, C.T. (2002), "Poverty and Inequality Again", *The Hindu*, dated November 11, 2002.

14

Reforms and Regional Disparities in India

UPENDRA SAH, HIRA LAL RAM AND UMA SHANKAR BHARTI

I. INTRODUCTION

Reduction in disparities in economic and social development across the regions and intra-regional disparities among different segments of the society have been among the major objectives of economic planning in India. Apart from massive investments in backward regions, various public policies were directed at encouraging private investment in such regions. But despite these efforts regional disparities did not lessen. Considerable level of regional disparities remained at the end of 1970s. The accelerated economic growth since the early 1980s appears to have aggravated regional disparities. The ongoing economic reforms since 1991 with stabilisation and deregulation policies as their central themes seem to have further widened the regional disparities.

The purpose of this paper is to reveal the widening regional disparities in India using some indicators of development, mention the causes of widening regional disparities and explore corrective measures for reducing regional disparities.

II. REVIEW OF STUDIES

Dandekar (1993) claimed that the economic disparity between Indian States have been increasing rather than decreasing over time. Marjit and Mitra (1996) examined the issue of regional convergence in 24 States over the period from 1961-62 to 1989-90 and on the basis of real per-capita net State domestic product (PCNSDP), the authors concluded that there is no *prima facie* evidence in favour of convergence of PCNSDP among the States in India. Subsequently, Ghosh, Marjit and Neogi (1997) constructed a measure of real PCNSDP with the help of State level deflators. Their finding indicated that Indian states have significantly moved apart during the last 30 years. Other studies which have analysed the levels, trends and causes of such inequalities in India are Das and Barua (1996), Rao and Kaliranjan (1999), Shand and Bhide (2000); Nagaraj Varadouski and Veganzones (2000), Shetty (2003), Bhattacharya and Sakhivel (2004), among others.

III. METHODOLOGY

This paper mainly focuses on the analysis of growth and disparity among major states of India in the pre-reform and post-reform period. The study is restricted to a comparative analysis of the emerging trends in 15 major states in respect of a few key parameters which have an intrinsic bearing on social and economic development. The 15 states together account for 95 per cent of the population of India in 2001. The remaining 5 per cent of population is spread in 10 smaller States and 7 Union Territories. These states and UTs have been left out of the study to keep the analysis simple and manageable. The 15 states have been classified into two major groups: Forward States and Backward States. The forward states consists of Punjab, Haryana, Gujarat, Maharashtra, Karnataka, Kerala, Andhra Pradesh and Tamil Nadu. The Backward States comprises of Assam, West Bengal, Bihar, Madhya Pradesh, Uttar Pradesh, Orissa and Rajasthan. While the forward group of states account for about 50 per cent of the national population the backward states account for about 45 per cent of the population of the country.

III. SYMPTOMS OF REGIONAL DISPARITY

The most widely preferred measure of regional economic disparity is the estimates of per-capita income. The level of regional development as measured through the level of PCNDP across the state is presented in Table 1.

TABLE I

Levels of PCNSDP Across Selected States

(In Rs. at 1993-94 prices)

States	*1980-81*	*1985-86*	*1990-91*	*1995-96*	*2000-01*
Maharashtra	8754	9623	12396	15893	18166
Punjab	8450	10267	11785	13008	15390
Haryana	7549	9213	11175	11702	14331
Gujarat	6607	7446	9022	11746	12975
Kerala	5635	5634	6786	8964	10627
Andhra Pradesh	5470	6063	7050	8048	9982
Tamil Nadu	5298	6360	7911	10276	12779
Karnataka	5004	5411	6709	8497	11902
West Bengal	4984	5421	6028	7562	9778
Assam	4611	5422	5543	5711	5867
Rajasthan	4284	4692	6842	7335	7937
Madhya Pradesh	4260	4468	5376	5688	5760
Orissa	4066	4463	4282	5021	5187
Uttar Pradesh	3817	4108	4936	5111	5770
Bihar	3363	3939	4391	3552	4087
All-India	5352	6082	7321	8498	10254
Mean	5555	6193	7314	8449	9933
SD					
CV (%)	28.32	31.05	33.76	38.27	40.43

Source: *Indian Economic Journal*, Vol. 54, No. 2.

The per-capita net domestic product at all-India level has increased from Rs. 5352 in 1980-81 to Rs. 7321 in 1990-91 and further to Rs. 10254 by 2000-01. The average PCNSDP of selected States has increased from 5555 to Rs. 7314 and to Rs. 9933 during the corresponding years. This is due to the fact that some of the well performing regions like Delhi, Goa, Pondicherry and Chandigarh are outside the selected States. The table shows that PCNSDP has been steadily increasing both at the national level as well as at the level of states.

On comparison of all-India PCNSDP with individual states, we find that Punjab, Maharashtra, Haryana and Gujarat had higher PCNSDP throughout, indicating that they continue to remain at higher ladder of development. But Tamil Nadu since 1985-86 and Kerala since 1995-96 have raised their PCNSDP above the national level Karnataka raised their level of PCNSDP above the national level since 2000-01. Thus, looking at the level of PCNSDP Punjab, Haryana, Maharashtra, Gujarat, Tamil Nadu and Kerala may be considered as advanced regions. Karnataka too recorded greater than average PCNSDP for the post-reforms period. Thus Karnataka can also be included in the better off states. Andhra Pradesh had higher than the all-India PCNSDP in 1980-81 and had PCNSDP nearer to the average PCNSDP though never crossed it thereafter. It can be treated as intermediate income state and may be included in the category of advance states for the sake of classification and analysis. The remaining states, Assam, West Bengal, Bihar, Orissa, Madhya Pradesh, Rajasthan and Uttar Pradesh can be said to form the category of poorer states.

The above results obtained from the analysis of PCNSDP are confirmed by the analysis of ranks of the states based on respective PCNSDP (Table 2). Maharashtra, Punjab, Haryana, Gujarat and Tamil Nadu have been at the top five states throughout the period with only minor changes in their rankings. On the other hand, Bihar, Orissa, Uttar Pradesh, Madhya Pradesh, Rajasthan and Assam have been the bottom five states with minor changes in their rankings. This indicates that rankings have more or less remained the same. Developed states have been moving ahead and the backward states continued to lag behind.

TABLE 2

Ranks of PCNSDP of Selected States

States	*1980-81*	*1985-86*	*1990-91*	*1995-96*	*2000-01*
Maharashtra	1	2	1	1	1
Punjab	2	1	2	2	2
Haryana	3	3	3	4	3
Gujarat	4	4	4	3	4
Kerala	5	7	8	6	7
Andhra Pradesh	6	6	6	8	8
Tamil Nadu	7	5	5	5	5
Karnataka	8	10	9	7	6
West Bengal	9	9	10	9	9
Assam	10	8	11	11	11
Rajasthan	11	11	7	10	10
Madhya Pradesh	12	12	12	12	13
Orissa	13	13	15	14	14
Uttar Pradesh	14	14	13	13	12
Bihar	15	15	14	15	15

Source: Based on Table 1.

Growth Rates of NSDP and PCNSDP

Widening inter-state economic disparity may be cross-examined by the analysis of comparative growth rates of NSDP and PCNSDP of selected states . The average growth rate in NSDP of selected states (Table 3) has increased from 4.71 per cent p.a. in the 1980s to more than 5 per cent p.a. in the 1990s. But the average growth rate has been less than 5 per cent p.a. for the overall period. The co-efficient of variation (C.V.) of growth rates increased from about 25 per cent in the 1990s indicating growing disparity in the growth rates of NSDP of selected states. It may be seen that during the period between 1980-81 to 1990-91 Rajasthan recorded the highest growth rate of 6.57 per cent p.a. in ASDP followed by Haryana at 6.55 per cent p.a. Other than Rajasthan and Haryana, Maharashtra, Punjab, Tamil Nadu and Karnataka registered a growth rate of above 5 per cent during this period. Assam, Kerala and Orissa were the poor performers with a growth rate of below 4 per cent p.a. while rest of the states recorded a growth rate between 4 per cent and 5 per cent but below the average growth rate.

TABLE 3

Growth Rates in NSDP

(per cent per annum)

States	*1980-81 to 1990-91*	*1991-92 to 2000-2001*	*1980-81 to 2000-2001*
Andhra Pradesh	4.25	5.48	4.62
Assam	3.32	2.00	2.96
Bihar	4.77	3.18	2.79
Gujarat	4.87	6.65	5.80
Haryana	6.55	5.15	5.66
Karnataka	5.20	7.40	6.15
Kerala	3.15	5.89	5.10
Madhya Pradesh	4.18	4.51	4.44
Maharashtra	5.98	6.19	6.61
Orissa	3.95	2.78	3.12
Punjab	5.38	4.89	4.81
Rajasthan	6.57	6.56	6.32
Tamil Nadu	5.33	6.16	6.06
Uttar Pradesh	4.95	3.81	4.17
West Bengal	4.59	6.97	5.61
All-India	5.52	6.31	5.68
Average	4.71	5.20	4.88
CV (%)	24.68	29.91	25.43

Source: Computed from National Accounts Statistics, various issues.

During the post-reforms period between 1991-92 to 2000-01, there was acceleration in average growth rate and the highest growth of 7.40 per cent p.a. in NSDP was achieved by Karnataka. West Bengal, Gujarat, Rajasthan, Maharashtra, Tamil Nadu, Kerala and Andhra Pradesh had the growth rate higher than the average growth rate. Andhra Pradesh, Kerala and West Bengal which had below average growth rate in the 1980s improved their growth rates to above the average level. The growth rate of Bihar, Haryana, Punjab and Uttar Pradesh was below the average rate.

For the entire period from 1980-81 to 2000-01, the average growth rate has been 4.36 per cent. Maharashtra was the fastest growing state with 6.61 per cent p.a. followed by Rajasthan (6.32), Karnataka and Tamil Nadu with 6.15 and 6.06 per cent p.a. rates of growth respectively. Gujarat, Haryana and Kerala grew at more than 5 per cent. The poorer states viz., Bihar (2.79% p.a.), Assam (2.96% p.a.), Orissa (3.12% p.a.) and Uttar Pradesh (4.17% p.a.) were poor performer with lower growth rates.

Thus the overall growth rate has been impressive and it accelerated in the post-reforms period. But barring exceptions like Haryana in the forward category and Rajasthan in the backward category, the growth rates in NSDP has been of the type which has accentuated the inter-state disparities. Coefficient of variation (C.V.) of growth rates has increased in the post-reforms period. Thus the reforms seem to have favoured the advanced regions. It is also clear from the fact that growth has decelerated in all the backward states except Madhya Pradesh.

Growth Rate of PCNSDP

Growth rates of PCNSDP need not coincide with those of NSDP due to varying growth rates of population. Nonetheless, it is the most important indicator of identifying achievements of different regions so far as economic growth and levels of living of different regions are concerned. Table 4 reveals that on an average PCNSDP has grown at less than 3 per cent (2.81%) p.a. for the period 1980-81 to 2000-01. The growth rate of PCNSDP has increased from 2.72 per cent per annum in the pre-reforms period to 3.26 per cent p.a. in the first decade of the post-reforms period. The growth rates of Andhra Pradesh, Gujarat, Karnataka, Kerala, Tamil Nadu and West Bengal have not only been above the average growth rate, growth rates of PCNSDP of these states in the post-reform period has been higher than in the pre-reforms period. Growth rates of Haryana and Maharashtra decelerated in the post-reforms period and was less than the average rate but for the entire period from 1980-81 to 2000-01, growth rates of their PCNSDP remained higher than the average growth rate. On the contrary, growth rates of PCNSDP of backward states

TABLE 4

Growth Rates of PCNSDP

(per cent per annum)

States	*1980-81 to 1990-91*	*1991-92 to 2000-2001*	*1980-81 to 2000-2001*
Andhra Pradesh	1.93	3.99	2.68
Assam	1.14	0.34	0.90
Bihar	2.59	0.81	0.59
Gujarat	2.88	4.83	3.86
Haryana	4.01	3.07	3.27
Karnataka	3.12	5.64	4.27
Kerala	1.71	4.69	3.77
Madhya Pradesh	1.80	2.78	2.34
Maharashtra	3.53	2.34	3.01
Orissa	2.14	1.39	1.43
Punjab	3.46	2.95	2.87
Rajasthan	3.94	3.87	3.77
Tamil Nadu	3.76	5.11	4.74
Uttar Pradesh	2.52	2.04	2.21
West Bengal	2.33	5.17	3.52
All-India	3.79	4.22	3.46
Average	2.56	3.25	2.79
CV (%)	44.05	50.48	45.78

Source: Computed from National Accounts Statistics, various issues.

of Assam, Bihar, Orissa, Rajasthan and Uttar Pradesh decelerated and remained well below the average growth rate. Growth rates of Assam, Bihar and Orissa have been particularly dismal at 0.34, 0.81 and 1.39 per cent p.a. respectively in the post-reforms period. Though Madhya Pradesh improved its performance from 1.80 per cent in 1980-81 to 2.78 per cent in 1991-2001, yet its growth rate was below the average growth rate. Among the backward states only Rajasthan had a growth rate (3.87) higher than the average growth rate.

It can be observed that out of the selected states Andhra Pradesh, Gujarat, Karnataka, Kerala, Madhya Pradesh, Tamil Nadu and West Bengal improved their growth in PCNSDP in the post-reforms period. Even for the entire period PCNSDP of Assam and Bihar grew at less than 1 per cent p.a. while that of Orissa grew at 1.43 per cent p.a. only. Thus we see that poorer states have not only grown slowly but most of them have decelerated also. Thus the regional disparity in incomes is not only continuing, the process has aggravated in the post-reforms period.

A clear idea of regional inequalities can be found by considering the levels and trends in the co-efficient of variation (C.V.) of PCNSDP. As can be seen from Table 1, Table 3 and Table 4, C.V. of PCNSDP increased from 28.32 per cent in 1980-81 to 33.76 per cent in 1990-91 and further to 40.43 per cent in 2000-01. Similarly, the C.V. of growth rates of NSDP increased from 24.68 per cent for the period 1980-81 to 1990-91 to 29.29 per cent for the period 1991-92 to 2000-01 and C.V. of growth rates of PCNSDP increased from 44.05 per cent to 50.48 per cent for the same period. Thus, the inter-state disparities in economic development are increasing.

IV. REFORMS AND DISPARITY

In the wake of economic reforms initiated in 1991, the role of private investment has acquired a special significance in the context of economic development of various states of India. Consequent to reforms, public investment is expected to decline and that of private investment to increase. But the private investment naturally flows into already better off regions that have better infrastructural facilities and also overall congenial investment climate. The poorer regions are, thus, doubly constrained. Firstly, due to lack of investible resources and compulsion of investing whatever they have in more pressing needs such as poverty alleviation or provision of minimum basic necessities, they are unable to invest on their own. Secondly, their investment also suffers due to the cut in the flow of grants and assistance from the centre. The evidence for India reveals that a major share of foreign direct investment has flown into developed states. Similarly financial assistance by all-India developed financial institutions have gone more to developed states and less to poorer states (Table 5). The group of forward states accounted for about two-third amount of the investment while the group of backward states accounted for just about 28 per cent of the amount. In fact only Gujarat and Maharashtra taken together received 36.7 per cent of the investment proposals which is significantly more than the total investment proposals received by all the states in the second group. While Gujarat which accounts for less than 5 per cent of the population of the country received about 19 per cent of the private investment proposals, Bihar which accounts for more than 10 per cent of the population received just little over 1 per cent of such proposals. The disparities in the direction of private investment is obvious.

The great divide between forward and backward states is also very clear in the case of cumulative share of financial assistance distributed by all-India financial institutions upto March end 1997. Maharashtra alone received almost as much financial assistance as all the states in the second group put together. Here again the share of states like Assam, Bihar and Orissa are for below their respective population shares. The pattern is not any different from the other sources of financing private investment as far as the statewise distribution is concerned. While over two-thirds of such assistance is provided by the financial corporations in the forward states, just 29.1 per cent is shared by all the states in the backward group.

This is not to say that larger flow of private investment in better off regions of the country and disproportional distribution of assistance by financial institutions are the only reason for growing disparity among states. There are many other factors also responsible for this. Historically, the British helped the development of only those regions which possessed facilities for prosperous manufacturing and trading activities. Maharashtra and West Bengal were the states preferred by the British industrialists and three metropolitan cities, Calcutta, Bombay and Maharashtra attracted all the industries leaving rest of the country to lag behind. Even though balanced regional development was one of the major

TABLE 5

Investment Proposals and Disbursal of Financial Assistance for Investment

States	*Percentage Share of Investment Proposals August 1991-December 1998*	*Cumulative Share of Financial Assistance Disbursed by All-India Financial Institutions (Upto March end 1997)*	*Cumulative Financial Assistance Disbursed by State Financial Corporation (Upto March end 1997)*
(1)	*(2)*	*(3)*	*(4)*
Forward States:			
Andhra Pradesh	8.3	7.2	7.8
Gujarat	18.7	13.5	9.3
Haryana	3.6	2.5	4.8
Karnataka	5.6	6.1	15.5
Kerala	1.1	1.7	4.4
Maharashtra	18.0	21.0	11.5
Punjab	3.4	2.4	3.6
Tamil Nadu	7.2	9.0	10.6
Sub-total	65.9	63.4	67.5
Backward States:			
Assam	0.7	0.5	0.5
Bihar	1.2	1.4	2.0
Madhya Pradesh	7.4	5.1	3.2
Orissa	2.2	1.8	3.7
Rajasthan	3.9	4.5	6.1
Uttar Pradesh	9.4	7.9	11.1
West Bengal	3.3	3.9	2.5
Sub-total	28.1	25.1	29.1
All-India	100.0 (757316.0)	100.0 (312502.0)	100.0 (20896)

Notes: (1) Investment proposals include Industrial Enterprises Memorandum (IEM) filed for items under delicensed sectors and letters of intent in respect of items under licensed sector.

(2) All-India financial institutions include IDBI, IFCI, ICICI, UTI, LIC, GIC, IRBI and SIDBI.

Sources: (1) Annual Report, 1998-99, Ministry of Industry, Government of India.

(2) RBI, Report on Currency and Finance, 1997-98, Vol. 1.

objectives of planning in India, it was completely ignored by the planners and regional disparity was accentuated by disproportionate plan allocations in favour of advanced sates. This resulted in uneven availability of infrastructure among different states which had adverse effect of regional balance. The adoption of new technology in agriculture during the 1960s also aggravated regional economic disparities. All these generated cumulative process and increased regional disparities. A detailed analysis of all these is not possible in this paper. We need to emphasise that the reforms process has strengthened the forces which increase regional disparity.

V. CONCLUSION AND SUGGESTIONS

The reform process underway in our country since 1991 has led to a path of structural changes in the Indian economy through deregulation of both domestic and foreign investment, liberalisation of trade, exchange rate, interest rate and prices. India is gradually transforming into a market friendly economy. But the play of market forces normally tends to increase rather than to decrease the inequalities between the regions. The better off regions get a competitive advantage. Even the movements of labour, capital and other services generate ever-increasing internal and external economics in the preferred regions which has strong 'backwash effects' on the poorer regions. There is no natural smooth tendency towards inter-regional transmission of growth from the richer to the poorer ones. The trend of growing inequalities can not be arrested without containing the market forces and giving it the desired direction through proper governmental intervention.

Balanced regional development of the country is a long cherished goal of our planners and policy markers. This is essential not only for the healthy functioning of our federal polity but also for overall rapid economic growth of the whole country. Backward States need special attention to accelerate their growth and bring them somewhat at par with developed states of the country. Action programme on the following lines will help achieve this task.

1. Improvement in basic infrastructural facilities like power, irrigation, transport and telecommunication in the backward regions is a pre-condition to step up the rate of growth and to usher in sustainable development in those states.
2. The pressing requirement of backward states is mere investment in their social and infrastructural sectors. To improve the level of social services, massive investment in primary education and primary health services is required.
3. Service sector has emerged as the new driver of the growth process. Banking and insurance have contributed to acceleration in many states. There is a need to promote these sectors on priority basis in backward states.
4. Investment in agriculture needs to be stepped up in the lagging regions. The backward and forward linkages of agriculture in poorer states need to be emphasised more.
5. The governments of backward states are fiscally weak and lack resources. Liberalisation process has further weakened their financial position. Resource flows to the states via Finance Commission awards and Planning Commission dispensation should continue to remain positively discriminating in favour of backward states.
6. An important factor which influences the speed of socio-economic progress of a state is the quality of governance. A better administered state is more efficient in raising resources and putting them to better use. Hence governance needs to be given immediate attention in the backward states.

To conclude, if the existing trends in differential rate of socio-economic development continues, regional disparities in India are bound to accentuate. Hence, it is imperative that the present trends are not only arrested but reversed. This will require concerted efforts on the part of the concerned state governments and the central government. The centre's helping hand in the form of focussed investment will facilitate the task of the concerned states.

References

Dandekar, V.M. (1993): 'Forty Years after Independence' in B. Jalan (ed.), *The Indian Economy: Problems and Prospects.*

Nagraj, N. (2002): 'Virtuous Growth or Polarisation' in Uma Kapila (ed.), *Indian Economy since Independence.*

Dholakia, R.H. (1994): 'Spatial Dimensions of Acceleration of Economic Growth in India', *EPW*, Aug. 27..

Sarkar, P.C. (1994): 'Regional Imbalances in Indian Economy over Plan Periods', *EPW*, March 12.

Kurian, N.J. (2000): 'Widening Regional Disparities in India: Some Indicators', *EPW*, February 12.

Bhattacharya, B.B. and Sakhtivel, S. (2004): 'Regional Growth and Disparity in India—Comparison of Pre- and Post-Reform Decades', *EPW*, March 6.

Dasgupta, Dipankar, P. Maiti, R. Mukherjee, S. Sarkar and S. Chakrabarti (2000): 'Growth and Inter-State Disparities in India', *EPW*, July 17.

Ric., Shand and S. Bhide (2000): 'Sources of Economic Growth: Regional Dimension of Reforms', *EPW*, Oct. 14.

Shetty, S.L. (2003): "Growth of S.D.P. and Structural Changes in State Economics: Inter-State Comparison", *EPW*, Dec. 6.

15

Inter-Regional Disparities in India

S.K. Dhage, B.G. Lobo and S.N. Nukale

INTRODUCTION

Disparities in economic and social development across the regions and intra-regional disparities among different segments of the society have been the major planks for adopting planning process in India since independence. Apart from massive investments in backward regions, various public policies directed at encouraging private investments in such regions have been pursued during the first three decades of planned development. While efforts to reduce regional disparities were not lacking, achievements were not often commensurate with these efforts. Considerable level of regional disparities remained at the end of the Seventies. The accelerated economic growth since the early Eighties appears to have aggravated regional disparities. The on-going economic reforms since 1991 with stabilisation and deregulation policies as their central pieces seem to have further widened the regional disparities. The seriousness of the emerging acute regional imbalances has not yet received the public attention it deserves. The purpose of this study is to initiate a debate on the various issues involved with a view to explore effective corrective measures without any further delay.

Since it may lead to disparities and divide among rural-urban regions and between specific groups of population in different states, explaining the differences in standards of living (measured in per-capita income) across states in India has been a matter of serious concern among development economists, planners and policy-makers, administrators, and social scientists. In spite of considerable research made on the subject, much more remains to be understood to explore the nature and causes of differences in growth rates in order to calibrate appropriate policies and institutions to achieve balanced regional growth and hence, regional convergence in terms of per-capita income, and to combat poverty by spreading the benefits of growth processes in different regions of India. So this paper gives an idea and tried to give some extent of theoretical analysis of the problem.

REGIONAL DISPARITIES

One of the main objectives of the planning process initiated in the early 1950s was to reduce these regional differences and to achieve, regionally balanced development. Various policy instruments including direct public investment by the Centre in infrastructure, guided private investment and building up of capacity enhancing institutions have been tried to achieve this objective. These policies were continued during the first three decades of planning. Though these measures were not highly successful, they ensured that disparities were not getting aggravated during this period. With the initiation of economic reforms in the early 1980s which culminated in full-fledged deregulation, liberalization and globalization in the early 1990s, the role of the government in investment decisions has diminished.

States with better physical and social infrastructure, adequate forward and backward linkages and other conducive environment attracted the lion's share of private investment over the last two decades. The year-wise and state-wise private investment proposals since August 1991 indicate that the major share was accounted for by Maharashtra, Gujarat, Tamil Nadu, Andhra Pradesh and Karnataka. Only recently some of the backward States like Chhattisgarh, Jharkhand and Orissa started attracting large private investment proposals mainly in mining and industries based on mineral extraction.

As a result of higher economic growth and better tax compliance resulting from tax reforms, there has been some improvement in the finances of the Centre and the States. However, the fiscal responsibility enactments of the various States following the 12th Finance Commission recommendation impose constraint on borrowings and expenditures. Currently most States have revenue balances, while expenditures are severely curtailed. This includes some of the most backward States where sectors like education, health, drinking water, sanitation, road connectivity, etc., are crying for investment. Differential economic performance of the last two decades has increased the regional disparities in the country. Broadly-speaking, while the western and southern States have experienced faster economic growth, the northern and eastern States lagged behind. On the other hand, population growth continues to be significantly higher in the lagging regions as compared to the forward regions. As a result, the per-capita income differentials have been widening even further. Thus, while the economic centre of gravity has been shifting in the south-westerly direction, the demographic centre of gravity has been moving in the opposite direction.

ISSUES RELATED TO ECONOMIC DISPARITIES

Employment opportunities are created in the developed regions of the country, the labour force growth is much higher in the backward regions. Large scale migration in search of employment will take place from the backward regions to the developed regions While the remittances of the migrant may add to the purchasing power back at home, a larger economic issue is that often migration depletes the availability of skills in the home market which will impede the development of the region. The period which had experienced divergent economic growth has also seen divergent trend in poverty reduction. During the period 1983 to 2004-05 the share of the poor in the population at the national level came down from 45 to 28 per cent. However, in terms of absolute numbers the decline was only marginal from 324 million to 315 millions. While all the major States experienced reduction in the percentage of the poor to varying degrees, five major States experienced increase in the number of poor during this period. These are Bihar (from 46.4 to 50.5 million), Madhya Pradesh (from 27.3 to 33.0 million), Maharashtra (from 28.5 to 31.7 million), Orissa (from 16.2 to 18.4 million) and Uttar Pradesh (from 55.2 to 63.9 million). In terms of social development also the regional divide has aggravated during this period. Traditionally, the levels of literacy and health indicators, and other social amenities have been better in the economically progressive States.

Public expenditure on socially relevant programmes continues to be significantly higher in these States. Again, compared to the rest of the country these States have better public expenditure efficiency on account of better governance and law and order situation. Accelerated private investments also generate their multiplier effects on social development. Better quality educational and health facilities have been financed by the private sector which reduced the pressure on public facilities. The boom in professional education, especially in engineering which started in Maharashtra and Karnataka in the early 1980s spread to other States in the region and still continues unabated. More than 70 per cent of the engineering graduates are coming out from the colleges of just four States, viz. Andhra Pradesh, Karnataka, Maharashtra and Tamil Nadu. The case of Maharashtra is somewhat puzzling. Though it has been one of the most prosperous State, the level of poverty remains above the national average both in rural and urban Maharashtra. Though urban Maharashtra was in the forefront of reform led economic growth, there was a significant increase in the number of urban poor in the State which accounts for the entire growth in the number of poor in the State. The IT boom in these States can be explained, to a large extend, by the explosion of engineering education in these States.

High quality private health care facilities have been coming up in the cities in the south and the west which have been attracting patients, not only from other parts of the country but also from abroad. Another interesting aspect of the contrast between the forward and backward regions is the divergent trends in the social and political dynamics. While regional parties in the backward States have been, by and large, engaged in identity politics based on castes and communal considerations, the regional parties in the forward regions have been taking up development issues which are more inclusive in nature. One reason for this could be the fact that various social movements in the south and west during earlier periods had weakened the caste-based exclusions and hence the benefits of development could be more equitably shared in these regions.

A closer examination of the nature of backward regions in each State will indicate specific reasons for their backwardness. The major cause of backwardness of Vidharba and Marathwada in Maharashtra, Rayalaseema and Telangana in Andhra Pradesh and Northern Karnataka is the scarcity of water due to lower precipitation and lack of other perennial sources of water. On the other hand, backwardness of certain regions in Gujarat, Madhya Pradesh, Bihar and Orissa can be associated with the distinct style of living of the inhabitants of such regions who are mostly tribal and the neglect of such regions by the ruling elite. Topography of a region could also constrain the development of a region; the hills of UP and the desert region of Rajasthan are examples of such cases. Historical factors like the attitude of rulers of the former Princely States towards development could have significantly affected the development of a region. For example, the distinctly higher level of social development of the Travancore and Cochin regions of Kerala can be traced back to the enlightened attitude of the former rulers of the Princely States of Travancore and Cochin. On the other hand, the poor social development of Telangana region of AP and certain other parts of the Deccan could be traced back to the absence of visionary rulers in the respective princely States.

DISPARITIES IN RESOURCE TRANSFER FROM THE CENTRE TO THE STATES

There is an inbuilt imbalance between the expenditure responsibilities and the revenue sources of the State governments. The founding fathers of the Indian Constitution were aware of this fact and ensured a comprehensive scheme of devolution of Central Tax revenues through the mechanism of Finance Commissions. The sharing of Personal Income Tax and Excise duties collected by the Centre with the States is periodically reviewed by the Finance Commission appointed every five years. The Commission also decides the principles and the formula by which the allocable funds are to be distributed among the States. An important aspect of the devolution of Central tax revenues under Finance Commission dispensation is that it has inbuilt bias in favour of fiscally weak States. Population and per-capita income of the State get high weightage in the distribution formula. A State with larger population and lower per-capita income gets a higher share in the Central tax revenues.

The gap between revenue receipts and revenue expenditure is another parameter which decides the level of a State's share. As a result the Central tax share constitutes a major revenue source for the backward States. While it constitutes about one-third of the total tax revenues of all the States taken together; it accounts for more than 50 per cent of the total tax revenues of less developed States like Bihar and Orissa; but its share is less than 20 per cent of the total tax revenues of more developed States like Gujarat, Haryana, Maharashtra and Punjab. A second channel of resources flow from the Centre to the States is Central Assistance for State Plans. The State plans are financed partly by State's own resources and the balance by Central Assistance. Central assistance is provided as a block assistance of which 30 per cent is grant and the remaining 70 per cent is a long-term loan. The rationale for this grant-loan proportion is imbedded in the fact that about 30 per cent of the plan expenditure was of revenue nature and 70 per cent was of capital nature when this proportion was decided in the late Sixties. Since plan expenditure of revenue nature is not expected to yield any financial returns for servicing the loan, this share was provided as grant by the Centre. In the case of fiscally weak States categorised as 'Special Category States' the grant component is, indeed, 90 per cent.

The distribution of Plan assistance to the States has been governed by 'Gadgil Formula' since the Fourth Five Year Plan (1969-74). As in the case with Finance Commission devolution, 'Gadgil Formula' which is administered by the Planning Commission also has its built in bias in favour of backward States. Population and per-capita income together account for 85 per cent of the weight in the formula. The remaining 15 per cent weightage is equally divided between State performance in the achievement of certain priority national objectives and the special problems of the States. Central assistance constituted about 45 per cent of the State Plans when all States are taken together. While the share of Central assistance constitutes less than 25 per cent of the Plan finances of the more developed States, it accounted for the major share of Plan finances of the backward States. Indeed, the Plans of the most backward States, especially the Special Category States, have been fully financed by the Central Assistance. In the wake of the foreign exchange crisis, the Centre has been encouraging States to seek and absorb more and more external aid for development projects.

The external aid to the States is routed through Central budget and devolved as additional Central Assistance for State plan. From the early Nineties, there has been a substantial increase in aid flows to the States. However, the major share of such flows have been absorbed by a few developed States. As a result, during the Eighth Plan period, there has been an apparent increase in the Central assistance to the more developed States. While 'Gadgil Formula' based normal Central assistance continued to be positively discriminating towards backward States, additional Central assistance for externally aided projects was skewed towards better-off States. Indeed, external aid accounted for 40 to 60 per cent of Central Plan assistance to some of the developed States, while such assistance contributed less than 20 per cent of the Central Plan assistance to most of the backward States.

Resource flows through the Finance Commission and

Planning Commission account for a substantial share of State resources. Though their overall effects are highly beneficial to the fiscal health of the States, there are certain adverse effects of such flows on the State finances. First, since the Finance Commission approach to revenue deficit is basically a gap-filling approach, this diminishes the incentive of the States to raise revenue receipts and reduce revenue expenditure. In other words, there is an implicit premium on fiscal profligacy. Second, continuing expenditure on plan schemes beyond the Five Year Plans became the committed expenditure of the States and add to their fiscal burden. Since there is a premium on plan expenditure, State governments have a tendency to under-fund maintenance expenditure to inflate the plan size. This results in poor maintenance of public assets created in the past and poor quality of public services which are outside the plan. A further complication is due to steep increase in the revenue component of plan expenditure over the years. While the grant-loan ratio of Central assistance is still 30:70, the revenue share of State Plan expenditure has crossed 50 per cent. As a result, the debt servicing burden of the States has gone up significantly.

GENERAL FINDINGS OF ANALYSIS

The increase in rural poverty during the 1990s is not surprising considering the gross neglect of agriculture during this period. Because of the big drop in the annual growth rate of public investment in agriculture during the decade as also the substantial decline in the growth of banks' lending to the sector, the agricultural growth rate witnessed a substantial deceleration over this period. However, while the share of agriculture in our country's GDP has witnessed a substantial decline, the proportion of population dependent on this sector in the total population has not shown any significant drop. Not surprisingly, the people dependent on agriculture are getting increasingly impoverished.

It is thus evident that reduction of rural poverty is closely linked with agricultural growth. The moderate pick-up in the growth of the economy during the decade of the 1990s was largely driven by manufacturing and services sectors, the activities that are concentrated in urban areas. The challenges before the country in the context of the widening socio-economic disparities between states and regions as also the growing.

More than half of India's poor live in just four states. Over two-thirds of poor live in rural areas and depend largely on agriculture. The highest incidence of poverty is found among people of scheduled castes and scheduled tribes, who face major social barriers that exclude them from opportunity. With the concentration of poor people in these areas, there is a concentration of problems poor people face: Lower access to, and lower quality of public services, lack of leverage to gain fair treatment from public institutions, and greater vulnerability to corruption and abuse. Accelerating national growth, reducing poverty, and achieving national social targets will not be possible without strengthening the performance of, and access to, services in these lagging states, sectors and communities.

It is evident that if this trend of widening regional disparities and growing rural-urban divide is not arrested and reversed soon, it will not only continue to pull down the overall growth rate of the economy, but will lead to serious social strife in the country. It is, therefore, time the policy-makers viewed the situation with a new sense of urgency and initiated measures to contain the damage. There is a need for the Planning Commission, Centre and the States to jointly formulate strategies and play a pro-active role in developing infrastructure facilities in the less developed regions and in utilisation of resources more efficiently.

As the World Bank Report observes, for growth to improve in lagging states, implementation of reforms is essential to reduce fiscal imbalances and improve the composition of public expenditure and investment climate. Of particular importance for poverty reduction and increasing rural incomes are policies aimed at increasing agricultural productivity and rural employment. Taking a leaf out of the recent Asian experience, suitable modifications are needed in the development strategies of laggard states. The major thrust will have to be on the development of human capital through education, health and nutrition apart from increased flow of funds to agriculture and rural infrastructure. To ensure this, the role of state intervention would be crucial in the medium-term. Subsequently, the market will start playing its role.

CONCLUSION

The above analysis gives an idea of disparities in socio-economic development across the Indian States. Efforts through the planning process during the first three decades of the Indian Republic had only partially succeeded in reducing regional disparities. The accelerated economic growth since the early Eighties with increased participation by the private sector appears to have aggravated regional disparities. The on-going economic reforms since 1991 with stabilisation and deregulation policies as their prime instruments and a very significant role for the private sector seem to have further aggravated the inter-state disparities.

There is need for higher level of investment in social services and infrastructure in backward States as compared to forward States. The governments of backward States are fiscally weak and as such they are unable to find enough resources to meet these investment requirements. Forward States are fiscally better off to improve their comparatively better social and economic infrastructure further. The better off States are able to attract considerable amount of private investment, both domestic and foreign, to further improve their development potential because of the existing favourable investment climate including better socio-economic infrastructure. The backward States are unable to attract private investments because of unfavourable investment climate including poor infrastructure. They are unable to improve the investment climate by improving the existing poor infrastructural facilities due to lack of resources. Their lack of resources is linked to their poor development. Thus, they are truly in a vicious circle. The solution lies in breaking this vicious circle.

To conclude, if the existing trends in differential rate of socio-economic development continues, regional disparities in India are bound to accentuate. Therefore, it is imperative that the present trends are arrested and preferably reversed. This will require concerted efforts on the part of the concerned State governments and the Centre. Resources may be a major constraint, but not necessarily the only or not even the most important one. The determination on the part of the State government, the ruling elite and the people at large is even more important. Centre's helping hand in the form of focused investment, especially in social sectors and key infrastructural sectors will facilitate the tasks of the concerned States. Meaningful decentralisation of decision-making and financial powers with appropriate accountability at all levels will facilitate faster socio-economic development of the backward regions where people are likely to take up considerable share of the developmental responsibilities.

References

Annual Report (2006-07). New Delhi: Department of Industrial Policy and Promotion, Government of India, 2007.

Council for Social Development. India—Social Development Report, 2006. New Delhi: Oxford University Press.

Dasgupta, D., P. Maiti, R. Mukherjee, S. Searcher, and S. Chakraverti (2000): "Growth and Interstate Disparities in India", *Economic and Political Weekly*, July 1.

Dev, S.M., Ravi, C. Poverty and Inequality: All-India and States, 1983-2005. *Economic and Political Weekly*, 2007, 42(6), Feb. 10: 509-21.

Dholakia, Ravindra H. (2003): "Regional Disparity in Economic and Human Development in India", *Economic and Political Weekly*, Vol. 38, No. 39, pp. 4166-72.

Economic Survey, 2006-07. New Delhi: Ministry of Finance, Government of India, 2007.

National Human Development Report, 2001. New Delhi: Planning Commission, Government of India, 2002.

Reserve Bank of India. State Finances: A Study of Budgets of 2006-07. Mumbai: RBI, 2006.

Tenth Five Year Plan Document, Vol. 1, 2003. New Delhi: Planning Commission of India.

16

Disparities within India's Different Regions

Why does the same Countries Government Work Differently in Different States?

G. Vanithamani and Shiny Thankachan

"An Indian in which the poorest shall feel that it is their country in whose making they have an effective voice; an India in which there shall be no high class and low class of people; an India in which all communities shall live in perfect harmony, in such an India, there will be no place for the bane of untouchability and drinking. Both men and women shall have equal right. No one will exploit anyone nor anyone be exploited."

—*Mahatma Gandhi*

INTRODUCTION

India is a federal nation, regional balanced development is quite necessary for integrated development of the nation. Despite of this the problem of regional imbalances is quite complicated and serious in India. If we study on the basis of important indicator like per-capita income, population below the poverty line, population engaged in agriculture, population engaged in manufacturing activities, and then we find a very dangerous picture. Relatively some states of the country are most prosperous and developed, whereas others are relatively are in quite backward position. Besides even in states some regions are more developed whereas in other regions there are even scarcities of minimum requirement for survival. Relatively Co-existence of developed and economically backward states and difference in status of economic development in various states or various regions of the state is called region imbalance.

The recent problem is why the same government acts in each state in different manner? If the widening regional disparities and the growing rural-urban divide are not arrested and reversed soon, they will not only continue to pull down the overall economic growth rate, but also lead to serious social strife in the country. It is time policy-makers viewed the situation with a new sense of urgency and initiated measures to contain the damage. India will be a highly uneven nation in terms of various dimensions of public life. Incomes and living standards will vary considerably across the nation. People in most of the southern and western parts of the country will be enjoying fairly high per-capita incomes, which may be comparable to those of middle income developed countries today. More than half of India's poor live in just four states. Over two-thirds of poor live in rural areas and depend largely on agriculture. The highest incidence of poverty is found among people of scheduled castes and scheduled tribes, who face major social barriers that exclude them from opportunity.

The disparity between rich and poor to a greater extent affecting overall socio-economic development causes tension that may be reckoned within political system in India. So, more attention is needed for poverty alleviation; food security and health care facilities for the poor section of the society are of prime importance of planning. The problem of health care system remained same both in urban and rural areas for last three decades. But income of private industries increased by the advocacy and subsidies allotted by the Government of India. A disparity of GDP was also grown within the developing countries because of natural phenomenon that a static GDP growth enhances disparity. 75 per cent of GNP is taken as sum of the rest total population after taking away 25 per cent by 36 families. According to National Sample Survey daily income of 10 per cent Indian rural population is 0.225 dollar, 1/3 rural population live upon income of 0.285 dollar. In urban area in India daily income of 30 per cent population 0.452 dollar and another 10 per cent earning is only 0.309 dollar. Maximum poverty exists in the states of Bihar, Orissa, Uttar Pradesh, Madhya Pradesh, Jharkhand, Rajasthan, Maharashtra and Karnataka respectively. As existence of black money is there, it is very difficult to calculate actual income of lower range of poverty (D.R. Sachdeva, 2000).

With the concentration of poor people in these areas, there is a concentration of problems poor people face: Lower access to, and lower quality of public services, lack of leverage to gain fair treatment from public institutions, and greater vulnerability to corruption and abuse. Mr Stern concluded: "Accelerating national growth, reducing poverty, and achieving national social targets will not be possible without strengthening the performance of, and access to, services in these lagging states, sectors and communities."

Regional disparity is a ubiquitous phenomenon in both developed and developing economies. But in the latter it is more acute and glaring. National economies are often composed of sets of smaller and localized economies. If the national economy is to prosper then its constituent regional economies must be brought into some sort of harmony. In India too, area disparities in the level of poverty, unemployment, income infrastructure, agriculture industry and above all the level of living of the people exist substantially across the regions. Numerous measures have been undertaken in the last forty years of planning to achieve balanced regional development of the country. Yet, wide disparities in area development continue in this country. The most pitiable situation is that the most resources rich states such as Orissa, Bihar Madhya Pradesh, Assam, and Uttar Pradesh are the regions with high poverty pockets. In this regard, regional scientist in India has ascribed area disparities to the top to bottom approach of national level planning process. The national level planning process lacks specific and local assessment of the problems, resources and productive potentials of the micro-level regions in general and of the backward regions in particular.

Diagram Shows Now Where We are and Where We Want to Go

Past	*Present*	*Future*
Colonial	Independent	Federal
Alien	Confused	Comprehensible
Imposed government	Centralized government	Decentralized government
Exploitation	Individual profit	Community satisfaction
Divide and rule	Social fragmentation	Social cohesion
Local growth denial	Rapid growth	Equity with growth
Resource export	Resource development	Resource conservation
Export-led growth	Export trade	Balanced trade
Imperial trade	North-South trade	South-South trade
Profiteering	Optimizing	Satisfying
Mercantile investment	National investment	Local investment
Exploitative	Quantitative	Qualitative
Labour-intensive	High technology	Appropriate technology
Rural-rustic	Industrial-urban	Agro-industrial
Unemployment	Underemployment	Useful employment
Discrete projects	Large projects	Small projects

Here, in a construct which attempts a representation of the organizational dimensions to development, some indication of the motives involved are brought into relief (Robert Riddell, 1985).

Some governments cleave to central unity ('balanced progresses for distributional equity, social harmony and environmental equilibrium) and from their experience we can perceive and become informed about a number of policy conflicts.

Moving clockwise around the construct gives rise, at two o'clock, to the view that even if central 'balanced progress' is acceptable to the public sector it is interpreted variously by the other institutions of society (ethnic groups,

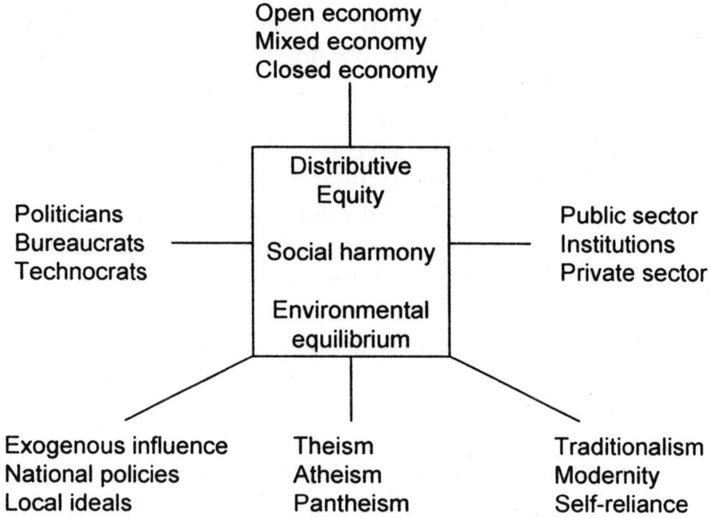

statutory bodies, religious organizations) and is markedly incompatible with the ambitions of the private sector (Robert Riddell, 1985)

POVERTY CONDITION

1. The Planning Commission as the Nodal agency in the Government of India for estimation of poverty has been estimating the number and percentage of poor at national and state levels. Since, March 1997 it has been using the Expert Group Method (Expert Group on Estimation of Proportion and Number of Poor) to estimate poverty. According to this method the estimates of poverty are made from the large sample survey data on household consumer expenditure conducted by the National Sample Survey Organization (NSSO) of the Ministry of Statistics and Programme Implementation. While releasing the estimates of poverty for 1999-2000, it had been noted that these estimates were not strictly comparable with the estimates for the previous years.

2. The NSSO has now released the result of the latest large sample survey data on household consumer expenditure (NSS 61st Round), covering the period July 2004 to June 2005.

From this data, two different consumption distributions for the year 2004-05 have been obtained.

(a) The first one from the consumption data collected using 30-day recall period (also known as reference period) for all the items.

(b) The other distribution is obtained from the consumer expenditure data collected using 365-day recall period for five infrequently purchased non-food items, namely, clothing, footwear, durable goods, education and institutional medical expenses and 30-day recall period for the remaining items.

These two consumption distributions have been termed as Uniform Recall Period (URP) consumption distribution and Mixed Recall Period (MRP) consumption distribution respectively. The Planning Commission, using the Expert Group methodology has estimated poverty in 2004-05 using both the distributions.

3. The URP-consumption distribution data of the 61st Round yields a poverty ratio of 28.3 per cent in the rural areas, 25.7 per cent in the urban areas and 27.5 per cent for the country as a whole in 2004-05. The corresponding figures obtained from the MRP-consumption distribution data of the 61st Round are 21.8 per cent in the rural areas, 21.7 per cent in the urban areas and 21.8 per cent for the country as a whole.

4. The poverty estimates in 2004-05 based on URP consumption distribution (27.5%) is comparable with the poverty estimates of 1993-94, which was 36 per cent. The poverty estimates in 2004-05 based on MRP consumption (21.8%) is roughly (but not strictly) comparable with the poverty estimates of 1999-2000, which was 26.1 per cent.

From the diverse experience of India's states, we can identify two routes to rural poverty reduction.

- One is (farm and non-farm) economic growth. In some states, robust growth in rural areas (fuelled in part by state development spending and

combined with beneficial effects of good initial conditions in physical and human infrastructure) appears to have been the main factor in poverty reduction; Punjab-Haryana is the prime example.
- The other route is human resource development. This can reduce poverty even if there is little output growth in the domestic economy, by enhancing the ability to export relatively skilled labour and so benefit from the consequent remittances.

Kerala is the prime example. Unfortunately some states, such as Bihar, were unsuccessful on both counts; there was too little growth, and human and physical resources were underdeveloped. And no state can reasonably be said to have got both rights—if it had the rate of poverty reduction would have been rapid.

INDICATORS OF REGIONAL DISPARITY

Regional disparities may be measured in terms of following parameters.

- Percentages of villages electrified;
- Per-capita electricity consumption;
- Literacy;
- Literacy among women;
- Crude death rate or birth rote;
- Infant mortality rate;
- Percentage of school going children in the 6-14 age group;
- Percentage of population below the poverty line; and
- Per-capita net domestic product (NDP).

Out of these various indicators, the per-capita Het domestic product is considered the single most satisfactory indicator. Various Extent of Regional Disparity in India on the basis of per-capita NDP different states in India have been grouped into three following categories.

(a) *Higher Income States.*: Gujarat, Goa, Punjab, Haryana, and Maharashtra.
(b) *Middle Income States*: West Bengal, Himachal Pradesh, J & K, Karnataka, Andhra Pradesh, Kerala, Tamil Nadu and Arunachal Pradesh.
(c) *Lower Income States*: Rajasthan, UP, Assam, Tripura, Tamil Nadu, Orissa, Madhya Pradesh, Manipur, Bihar.

In 1988-89, Goa and Punjab had the highest and Bihar the lowest per-capita NDP. The difference between their per-capita NDP was about 3:1. This shows the degree of uneven regional development in India. Even in a state, there are large variations in the level of development of different regions; uneven development is thus both an inter-state and an inter-state problem (B.N.P. Singh, 1995).

REMEDIAL MEASURES TO REDUCE REGIONAL UNEVEN

Following important measures have been taken up in recent years to bring about a more even regional development:

- Central grants to states for upgrading standards of administration;
- Weightage to backwardness in working out the scheme of financial transfers from the Center to the States;
- Weightage to backwardness in distributing central assistance to state plans;
- Special area programmes for the disadvantageous regions;
- Evolution and propagation of improved dry farming technology, and the special Rice Production Programme in the Eastern states;
- Progress to backward district in the grant of industrial finances; and
- Construction of road by the Centre in remote and inaccessible border regions.

REGIONAL DISPARITIES FOR DIFFERENT GROWTH SCENARIOS: 2025

An analysis of the historical trends, especially the more recent trends, leads to the inevitable inference that regional disparities are bound to aggregate in the coming decades. Regions, which are characterized as backward in our foregoing discussions, have very weak growth impulses.

Their demographic disadvantage is implicit in the fact that major States in this region, viz., Bihar, Madhya Pradesh, Rajasthan and Uttar Pradesh are likely to have fertility rates exceeding the replacement level well beyond 2025, a level which some of the forward States like Kerala and Tamil Nadu have already achieved and others are expected to achieve within a decade or so. We have noted that if the current trend is projected, Madhya Pradesh will reach replacement level only by 2060, and Uttar Pradesh only by 2100.

The implications of these divergent demographic trends on population density, employment opportunities, social sector investments and the overall development can be extremely grave. One of the major objectives of development planning initiated immediately after Independence has been, among others, reduction of regional disparities in social and economic development. Direct investment by the Central Government and Centrally directed investment of the private sector have been two powerful instruments to achieve this objective.

During the first four decades of development planning, most of the large units in basic and heavy industries were set-up in the public sector in a regionally well-balanced manner. Indeed, their location, other things being equal, was biased towards backward regions as natural endowments such as mineral deposits were concentrated in those regions. Massive public investments have been made to provide economic and social infrastructure in the backward regions to accelerate their overall development.

Economic reforms initiated in 1991 implied among, other things, that the private sector would be the principal engine of economic growth. Most of the restrictions on private investment have been removed. Mounting debt burden of the government has imposed a cap on public investment. As a result, while there was significant increase in the quantum of private investment, there was a sharp fall in the public investment over the last decade.

The flow of private investment, both domestic and foreign, has been extremely biased in favour of the more developed regions of the country. This has enabled the developed regions to achieve accelerated economic growth during the 1990s. On the other hand, backward regions of the country, which were unable to attract any significant private investment flows, experienced decelerated economic growth during this period.

The ability of the governments at the Centre and in the States to counter this trend by effecting countervailing public investment also has been reduced considerably. In the context of macro-economic stabilization policies initiated in 1991, the ability of the Centre to finance public investment by borrowings has been severely constrained. Revenues of the Centre also experienced reduced buoyancy in the wake of tax reforms especially due to reduction in customs tariff to levels comparable to those of our trading partners.

The factors which attracted more and more private investments to developed regions have been their better developed economic and social infrastructure as well as more efficient and investor friendly State governments. The backward regions, to be attractive to the private investors, have to improve their infrastructure facilities, both economic and social, considerably. This needs substantial public investment. The State governments in the backward regions are, however, strapped for funds even to meet the current expenditure.

Almost all the State governments in the backward regions find that their entire revenues are not sufficient to meet even the committed revenue expenditure like interest liability, salaries and pensions. A sizable share of their borrowings is diverted to fill the gap between the revenue receipts and revenue expenditure. There are several States where borrowings have been steadily increasing, but investments have been decreasing secularly. The adverse impacts of the deteriorating State finances are much more severe for the backward States as compared to the developed States, where investments of the past have created adequate social and economic infrastructure to attract private investments. The backward States are facing multiple dilemma. They are not able to attract investments due to lack of infrastructure. They are not in a position to provide these facilities on their own due to lack of investible funds. Unlike in the past, Centre is not in a position to help them either as the Centre itself has a serious fiscal constraint (V.P. Singh, 2006).

Along with social and economic infrastructure, efficiency of administration and the quality of governance including law and order situation are important factors in attracting private investment. Studies conducted by NCAER and some of the apex associations of industries have indicated that prospective investors give higher weight-age to these factors than various incentives, including fiscal incentives offered by the State governments. Indeed, there are enough evidences to the effect that the investors don't mind paying speed money to get things done fast. In other words, a corrupt but efficient regime is preferred to an honest but inefficient regime in the context of investment decisions. Other aspects of governance like the law and order situation, trade union activism, etc., are also important factors affecting the flow of private investments.

On almost all indicators of governance discussed above, the backward States are at a disadvantage. Indeed, even perceptions about the governance issues based on past may haunt the States in such matters. The cases of Kerala and West Bengal are typical in this regard. All the efforts of these two States during the last decade to woo the investors, both domestic and foreign, have not yielded any significant results. This was mainly on account of the general perception of investors that these States are dens of militant trade union activism, though in reality such militancy, of late, has been significantly subdued in these States.

To conclude this section, it will be appropriate to state that there are hardly any signs of reversing the recent trend of accentuating regional disparities in the country in the coming decades. Indeed, almost all the relevant forces are such that the disparities are likely to widen deriving the next quarter century. It will require Herculean tasks on the part of the Centre and the leadership in the concerned regions to ensure that the gap does not widen further.

CONCLUSION

Whatever efforts have been made in India in the direction of removing regionable imbalances has yet to see light of the day. The basic weaknesses of these plans have been that these emphasize on mere availability additional financial resources. No relevant efforts have been made for linking of central financial assistance with special development programmes. It is necessary to replace financial attitude with planning attitude, but no serious efforts have been made in this direction. It will be appropriate to take proper account of resource available in backward state so that appropriate special plan can be prepared in favour of individual states. The problem is why the same government act in each states in different manner? The economy will not get sustatainable development without giving proper impotance to poor regions. The government should give more considerations to poor region than rich regions. Through this our economy will evenly improve.

REFERENCES

Abdul Aziz, Sudhir Krishna (1996), Regional Development Problems and Policy Measures, Concept Publishing Company, New Delhi.

Andre Philip (1932), India's Social and Political Aspect.

Barro, R.J. and X. Sala-i-Martin (1995), *Economic Growth*, McGraw Hill, New York.

Bell, Clive, and R. Rich (1994), Rural Poverty and Agricultural Performance in Post-Independence India, *Oxford Bulletin of Economics and Statistics*, 56(2): 111-133.

Bhadouria, B.P.S. (1986), Regional Economic Development, Anmol Publications, Delhi.

Bhattacharya, B.B. and S. Sakthivel (2004), Regional Growth and Disparity in India, *Economic and Political Weekly* (*EPW*), March 6, pp. 1071-77.

Bhattacharya, N., D. Coondoo, P. Maiti, and R. Mukherjee (1991), Poverty Inequality and Prices in Rural India, Sage Publications, New Delhi.

Booth, E.J.R. (1964), "Inter-Regional Income Differences", *Southern Economic Journal (SEJ)*, Vol. 31, No 1, July, pp. 44-51.

Cassen, R.H. (2002), "Well-Being in the 90's: Towards a Balance Sheet", *EPW*, Vol. 37, No. 27, pp. 2789-94.

Datt, G. and M. Ravallion (2002), "Is India's Economic Growth Leaving the Poor Behind?"

Dholakia, R.H. (1985), Regional Disparity in Economic Growth in India, Himalaya, New Delhi.

Ghosh, R.N., Melotte, Y.M., Siddique, M.A.B. (1996), Economic Development and Change—South Africa and the Third World, New Age International Ltd. Publishers, New Delhi.

Michael Roemer, Joseph T. Stern (1981), Cases in Economic Development Projects, Policies and Strategies, Butterworths' Advanced Economics Texts.

"Mimeographed paper at World Bank Workshop on Poverty Estimates, New Delhi, January Panel Estimations", *South Asia Economic Journal*, Volume 3, No. 2, pp. 227-39.

Reeta Mathur (2006), Challenges Facing Indian Economy, RBSA Publishers, Jaipur.

Robert Riddel, Regional Development Policy, St. Martine Press, New York.

Sachdeva, D.R. (2000), Social Welfare Administration in India, Kitab Mahal Publishers.

17

Estimating Regional Disparities in Economic Growth: A Case Study of Indian States

ACHAL KUMAR GAUR

I. INTRODUCTION

The nexus in between and inequality has been debated extensively by the scholars in terms of theory as well as empirical investigators. For example, starting with the classical economists, Ricardo's two sector model which mainly concentrated on growth and distribution within agriculture and industry addressed the shares of rent and profits and growth process eventually approaching the steady state of zero growth due to diminishing returns in agriculture (Boyer, 1996). Karl Marx also believed that capitalist development would inherently result in unenven distribution of wealth and capitalist have an incentive for pushing wages to the subsistence level (Martin and Sunley, 1998, Dunford and Smith, 2000). The neo-classical growth models for closed economies [Solow (1956, 1957, 1970), Cass (1965), and Koopmans (1965)] state that per-capita growth rate tends to be inversely related to the starting level of output/income per head and if economies are similar in respect of preferences and technologies, then poor economies grow faster than rich ones. The neoclassicals, however, were more optimistic about market forces and postulated that regional inequality is a passing phase and that market forces would ensure that the returns to all factors of production would approach their marginal products (Smith, 1975). Neo-Keynesians such as Kalechi (1954, 71), Steindl (1952), Kaldor (1955-6, 60) and Pasinetti (1962, 77, 81) have explained the inter-relationship between income distribution and economic growth. By and large, Neo-Keynesian growth models have concluded that reduction in concentration raises the real wage and provides a redistribution of income which leads to higher capacity utilization and higher rate of economic growth.

The link between inequality and average well-being for two sector economy is known as Kuznets Hypothesis (1955, 1963) which maintains that given a two-sector economy with not too distinct degrees of sectoral mean incomes, a perennial shift of population from one sector to another will initially raise aggregate inequality and it will decrease at later stage. This formulation has been labeled as the "Inverted U" (I-U)1 Hypothesis or Kuznets Cycle (Branlke, 1983). Regional concentration/diversification has also been examined through 'convergence hypothesis' which has primarily emerged due to seminal theoretical contributions on endogenous growth models by Romer (1986, 1987, 1990, 1992, 1993) and Lucas (1988). The hypothesis asserts that differences in contemporaneous per-capita income between any pair of regions will be transitory so long as the two regions contain identical technologies, preferences and population growth (Bernard and Durlauf, 1966). The bulk of the new theoretical literature on growth and inequality has focused on models which generate divergence across nations. The theoretical as well as empirical presentation by Barro, Robert J. (1990, 1991, 1999), Borro, Robert J. and Jong-Wha Lee (1994), Barro, Robert J., N. Gregory Mankiw, and Xavier Sala-i-Martin (1991, 1992a, 1992b, 1992c, 1997, 2007), Baumol (1986), Cashin (1995), Cashin and Sahay (1996), Delong (1988), Dowrick and Nguyen (1989), Easterlin (1960a, 1960b), Quah (1993, 1995,

1996a, 1996b), etc. deal with process of convergence/ divergence at national as well as international level.

In India, inter-state/region inequality has been one of the major concerns before policy-makers and planners. There had been a huge gap between active and vibrant region and the hinterland during the pre-independence period in terms of availability of facilities and this manifested itself in the form of unequal levels of development both in terms of economic and human. After independence, reduction in inter-state/region disparities has been emphasized during the successive five year plans. Apart from that, the issue has been examined, in depth, by the scholars like Chattopadhyaya, R.N. and M.N. Pal (1972), Rao, S.K. (1973), Nair, K.R.G. (1973, 1982), Sampat, R.K. (1977), Mohapatra, A.C. (1978), Mathur, Ashok (1983, 1987, 1992), Datt and Ravallion (1993, 1998, 2002), Dreeze and Sen (1995), Dreeze and Srinivasan (1996), Marie-Ange Veganzones (1998), Rao, M. Govinda, Ric Shand and K.P. Kalirajan (1999), Ramiah (2002), Ahluwalia, M. (2002), Ravindra H. Dholakia (2003), Majumdar, R. (2004), Shatakshee Dhongde (2006), Dev, S.M. and Ravi, C. (2007), N.J. Kurian (2007). For example, according to Dreze and Sen (1995), enormous variations in regional experiences and achievements coupled with the even sharper contrasts in some fields of social development have resulted in remarkable internal diversities in India. Furthermore, the long-term progress in raising rural living standards has been diverse across Indian states (Datt and Ravallion, 1998). Such disparities are responsible for various states having different capacities for poverty reduction (Datt and Ravallion, 2002). Similarly, Rajarshi Majumdar (2004) in his paper entitled, "Human Development in India: Regional Pattern and Policy Issues" has observed that states like Kerala, Maharashtra and Himachal Pradesh put up consistently good performance regarding social and human development indicators, however, Kerala has not been able to convert its social development into economic progress. On the other hand, Gujarat, in spite of its having low Human Development (HD) ranks, have consistently good ranking in per-capita Net State Domestic Product (PCNSDP).

The National Human Development Report-2001 for

India reveals considerable differences in human development among Indian states during 1981-2001. The report notes that in the early eighties, states like Bihar, UP, MP, Rajasthan and Orissa had HDI close to just half that of Kerala's. The inter-state differences in human poverty are quite striking and report notes that while there have been improvements in the human development index and human poverty index during the 1980s, the inter-state disparities and the relative position of the states has practically remained the same. Facts show that inter-state disparity as measured in terms of standard deviation in human development index stood 0.083 for 1981 which further increased and stood at 0.100 in 1991 [Tenth Five Year Plan (2002-2007), Vol. III]. The World Bank (2006) in its report entitled, "India-Inclusive Growth and Service delivery: Building on India's Success" has observed sharp differentiation across states since the early 1990s reflects acceleration of growth in some states but deceleration in others. The report further adds that more worryingly, growth failed to pick up in states such as Bihar, Orissa and Uttar Pradesh that were initially poor to start with, with the result that the gap in performance between India's rich and poor states widened dramatically during the 1990s. An approach to the 11th Five Year Plan (Planning Commission, Government of India, 2006) has also acknowledged regional backwardness as an issue of concern. The differences across states have long been a cause of concern and therefore, we cannot let large parts of the country be trapped in a prison of discontent, injustice and frustration that will only breed extremism. The World Bank (2008) in its recent release "The Growth Report Strategies for Sustained Growth and Inclusive Development" has mentioned that disparity in income distribution in India has risen during 1993-2005. The report (pp. 125-26) further adds that Gini-coefficient in this connection stood at 0.3152 during 1993-94 which increased later on and was recorded at 0.3676 in the year 2004-05.

It is against this backdrop, the present study has bee undertaken. The data on State Domestic Product (Total as well as Per-capita) for twenty major Indian States has been taken for the period 1980-2002. Interstate disparity in SDP has been examined with the help of several inequality indices that are based on properties of Lorenz Curve, Atkinson's Social Welfare Function, Herfindahl's indices followed by traditional measures like, CV and Log Normal Distribution. In addition, 'convergence hypothesis' as σ-convergence and β-convergence has been tasted to detect inter-state disparities during the period 1980-2002. Section II deals with data and methodology (technical note) while empirical results are contained in Section III. Concluding remarks and policy observations are contained in Section IV.

II. DATA AND METHODOLOGY

The present study attempts to examine inter-state disparities in terms of state domestic product (SDP) and per-capita state domestic product (PC SDP) over the period 1980-81 to 2001-02. Significant to mention that state income and per-capita income have their limitations in any study of inter-state comparisons (Bhattacharya and Sakthivel, 2004). Inter-State comparison of SDP is also hampered by the quality of statistics provided by different states and the CSO has revised the base year from 1980-81 to 1993-94. The modifications in the new GDP and SDP series have been done in terms of price, production boundaries for many sectors, etc. and hence any comparison of inter-state income levels and growth rate based on 1980-81 base series upto 1993-94 base series may not yield the correct picture. In view of this, an important task before analyzing the trends in income disparities is to evolve a comparable income series with a single base year. This has been done through the technique of base shifting and SDP data onwards 1998-99 up to 2001-02 at the base 1993-94 has been converted at the base 1980-81 in order to prepare inter-state SDP from 1980-81 to 2001-02 at the base 1980-81. In the present paper, Net State Domestic Product (at current prices-base 1980-81) and per-capita Net State Domestic Product (at current prices-base 1980-81) for twenty major Indian states have been taken for the period 1980-81 to 2001-02.

Measures of Income Inequality

There exists plethora of literature on measures of

income and wealth inequality. The conventional inequality measures (Atkinson, 1970, 83) that are most frequently used in empirical research are (a) the coefficient of variation, i.e.

$$\sigma / \mu \tag{1}$$

and (b) the standard deviation of logarithms, i.e.

$$\int_0^{\bar{Y}} \{\log(y/\mu)\}^2 f(y).dy \tag{2}$$

where Y, σ and μ are in usual notations.

Dalton's Principle of transfer (1920) has established that measure of inequality should increase when income is transferred from a poor person to a richer person. Chapernowne (1974) argues that coefficient of variation is most sensitive to inequality of extreme income that procedures a flat response to the transfers. The variance of logarithms of income may be interpreted as a measure of concentration of incomes since it can be estimated through the framework of Lorenz's measures of concentration (Aitchinson, J. and Brown, J.A.C., 1957).

An attractive way to measure income inequality without imposing a functional form of statistical distribution on income graduation is to use Lorenz-based inequality measures. In the Lorenz diagram (Figure 1), the proportion of income receivers having income less than x is measured along x-axis and the proportion of total income accruing to the same income receivers along the y-axis. The points plotted for the various values of x trace out a curve below the line sloping 450 from the curve explains the relation between the distribution function F(x) and the first-moment distribution function $F_1(x)$, given by

$$F_1(X) = \int_0^X tdF(t) / \int_0^\infty tdF(t) \tag{3}$$

It is obvious form the Lorenz diagram that the measure of income concentration is the ratio of the shaded area between the Lorenz curve and the 450 line. The income

FIGURE I

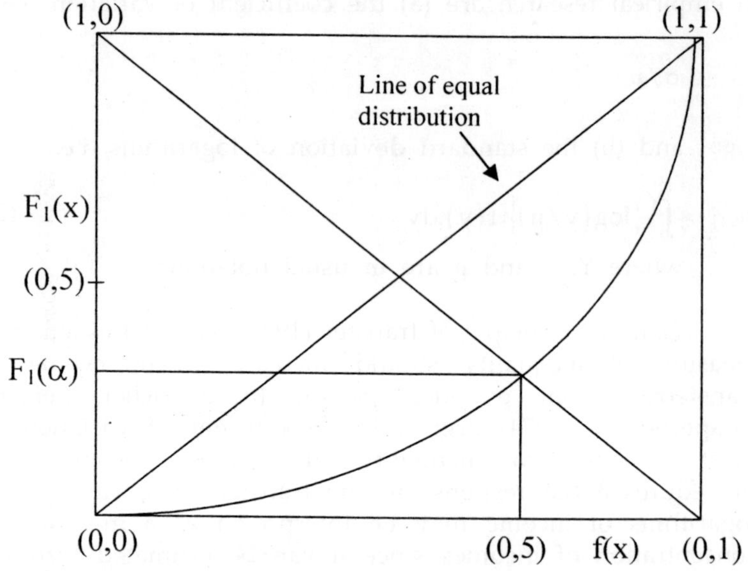

concentration (L) for the log normal hypothesis is defined as:

$$L = 1 - 2\int_0^\infty F_1(x)dF(x) \qquad (4)$$

substituting the value of $F_1(X)$ in Eq. (4), we get

$$L = \left[2N\left\{\frac{\sigma}{\sqrt{2}}|0,1\right\} - 1\right] \qquad (5)$$

Obviously, the measure of concentration (L) is monotonically related to value of 2 and thus the parameter 2 (variance of logarithms of the income) may well be interpreted as a measure of income inequality.

The Lorenz curve may again be generated by defining the income earner units, say, quintile shares where q_i, i=1,2,.. n reveals the share of ith income earner. Let, incomes are arranged in ascending order, i.e.

$$O \le q_1 \le q_2 .... \le q_i ..... \le q_n \le 1 \tag{6}$$

From the order of the incomes as shown by Eq. (6), several well known income inequality measures may be derived (Slottje, D.J., Basmann, R.L. and Nieswiadomy, M., 1989).

For example, the Gini (1912) measure of income inequality is given by

$$G = 1 - \frac{1}{n} - \frac{2}{n} . \sum_{i=1}^{n-1} (n-i) q_i ... \tag{7}$$

and the relative mean deviation (Cowell, 1980)

$$R = \frac{1}{2} . \frac{n}{n-1} \left[\sum_{i=1}^{n} \left| q_i - \frac{1}{n} \right| \right] \tag{8}$$

Theil's (1967) entropy measure (normalised) is given by

$$T = 1 + \frac{1}{\ln(n)} \left[\sum_{i=1}^{n} q_i . \ln(q_i) \right] \tag{9}$$

Kakwani's (1980a, 80b) measure is defined by

$$K = \frac{\left\{ \sum_{i=1}^{n} \left[\sqrt{q_i^2 + 1/n^2} \right] - \sqrt{2} \right\}}{2 - \sqrt{2}} \tag{10}$$

The survey of literature on income inequality reveal that Gini coefficient suffer with serious drawbacks. For instance, the simple aging of a populations will raise income inequality (Morgan, 1962). The Gini Coefficient is also insensitivity to non-money components and differential price indices between states which exaggerate income inequality in rural areas. It is found that Gini ratio is more responsive to changes in income of the middle class rather than among the rich or poor (Allison, 1978 and Osberg, 1984), and despite of major changes in taxation and welfare during 1950-70 in United States, inequality as measured by Gini Coefficient remained unchanged. It is obvious that the Kakwani measure and the Gini ratio measure every different properties of the Lorenz Curve (Basmann, R.L. Slottje, D.J., 1987). The Gini ratio measures a property of distribution inequality that varies in direct proportion to the area of the closed geometric representation (Figure 1) and bounded below by the horizontal axis on the right by the Lorenz Curve itself while the Kakwani measure correlates a property of distributional inequality that varies directly with the perimeter if the closed geometric area (Figure 1).

The relative mean deviation violates the principle of transfer since it is insensitive to transfer between income units on the same side of the mean. Theil (1967) proposed a decomposable measures based upon the Lovenz Curve that satisfy Dalton's Principle of Transfer (Allison, 1978). Theil index is similar to the Gini index since it is too sensitive to movements in the middle part of the income distribution (Osberg, 1984).

Atkinson (1970) developed a new measure of income inequality and argued that there should be social welfare function with each measured of income inequality. The index is defined as.

$$\text{Atkin}(I) = 1 - \left[\sum_i \left[\frac{Y_i}{\mu} \right]^{1-\epsilon} .f(Y_i) \right]^{\frac{1}{1-\epsilon}} \quad \epsilon \geq 0 \tag{11}$$

The value of ϵ, which is clearly a measure of the degree of inequality-aversion reveals the relative sensitivity to transfers at various income levels. As ϵ increases, inequality is emphasized much among the poors. Aktinson observed that if we take ϵ=1.0 which implies a lower degree of inequality aversion then the ranking is closer to that of the Gini ratio. A wide range of values of inequality aversion emphasized the inequality at the top of the distribution ($\in$=0.5) and at the bottom ($\in$=1.0).

Apart from aforesaid measures of income/wealth inequality, Herfindah's index (1950) is one that measures the concentration in income/wealth and more specifically in industrial sector. This index contains the feature of decomposability (Gaur, A.K., 2002). Let respective income (total per-capita) of n federating units are given by S_i= i=1, 2,.......n, then, the Herfindahl's index of concentration is given by:

$$H_i = \sum_{i=1}^{n} \left\{ \frac{S_i}{\sum_{i=1}^{n} S_i} \right\}^2 = \frac{1}{\left\{\sum_{i=1}^{n} S_i\right\}^2} \sum_{i=1}^{n} S_i^2 \tag{12}$$

The Herfindahl's index of concentration can again be generated by defining the expenditure gainer units on, say quintile shares, where q_i, i=1, 2, ...n represents the ith quintile expenditure share, letting,

$$0 \le q_1 \le q_2 \le q_3 \ldots\ldots\ldots\ldots\ldots q_1 \le 1 \tag{13}$$

from this simple ordering, the Herfindah;s index may be written as

$$H_i = \sum_{i=1}^{n} \left\{ \frac{q_i}{\sum_{i=1}^{n} q_i} \right\}^2 \tag{14}$$

since $\sum_{i=1}^{n} q_i = 1$, Eq. 14 may written as

$$H_i = \sum_{i=1}^{n} (q_i)^2 \tag{15}$$

The properties as well as alternative forms of the Herfindahl's index have been reviewed by Theil (1967),

Srivastava and Aggarwal (1979), Gaur, A.K. (2002). For instance, the other two form of the Herfindahl's index are:

$$H_2 = \frac{n}{n-1}\sum_{i=1}^{n}(q_i)^2 \tag{16}$$

$$H_3 = \frac{1}{3}\left[n\sum_{i=1}^{n} q_i^2 - 1\right] \tag{17}$$

The range of variation of the alternative form of the Herfindahl's index are:

$$\frac{1}{n} \le H_i \le 1$$

$$\frac{1}{n-1} \le H_2 \le \frac{n}{n-1} \tag{18}$$

$$0 \le H_3 \le 1$$

It is obvious that when only comparison over time is desired, one would fine H_3 better H_2 (since the extreme valves of H_3 are independent of number of observations) and H_2 better than H_i. However, when decomposing is needed, H_1 and H_2 are better than H_3.

In the present study, the following measures of inequality have been employed in order to measure the inter-state inequality in state domestic product (SDP) (total as well as per-capita, both) among Indian states during the period 1980-81 to 2001-02: (i) the Gini coefficient, (ii) Relative mean deviation (RMD), (iii) Theil's measure, (iv) Kakwani's measure, (v) Herfindahl's-H_i, (vi) Herfindahl's-H_2, and (vii) Herfindahl's-H_3, (viii) C.V., (ix) Variance of Logarithms, (x) Atkin ($\in$=0.5), (xi) Atkin ($\in$=1.1), (xii) Atkin ($\in$=1.5), (xiii) Atkin ($\in$=1.9), (xiv) Atkin ($\in$=2.1), and (xv) Atkin ($\in$=2.5).

Convergence Hypothesis

Two concept of convergence exist in the discussions of economic growth across the nations/states/regions (Barro and

Sala-i-Martin, 1991, 1992a, 1992b, 1992c, 1997, 2007). They are: (i) β-convergence, and (ii) σ-convergence. β-convergence emerges if a poor economy tends to grow faster than a rich one, so that the poor economy tends to catch up to the rich one in terms of levels of income/product. Let, Y_i stands for SDP of ith state and Y_{it}+T=[log (Y_i, t + T/Y_{it})] be the annualized growth rate of SDP of ith state between t and (t + T) period and log (Y_i, T) be the logarithm of SDP of ith state at time t then in order to detect β-convergence, following type of regression equation has been fitted in the present study.

$$(1/T) \log (Y_i, t + T/Y_i, t) = \alpha + \beta \log (Y_i, t) + U_{it} \quad (19)$$

Equation (19) is also known as Barro regressions (Quah, 1995) and β < 0 indicates absolute β-convergence. In other words, a valve of β in the range of -1<β<0 would be an evidence of β-convergence i.e nearer the valve of β to -1, the higher the speed of convergence and the nearer to zero the lower the speed to convergence. By implication zero means no convergence and a positive valve for β indicates a divergence.

The second concept relates to cross sectional disparison (Baumol, 1986; Dowrick and Nguyen, 1989; Barro and Sala-i-Martin, 1991, 1992a, 1992a, 1992b, 2007). In this context, convergence occurs if the dispersion measured, for example, by standard deviation of the logarithm of per-capita income across a group of regions-declines over time. This process is known as σ-convergence. That is σy(t+T) < σyt indicates the existence of σ-convergence and *vice versa*, where σyt is the time 't' standard deviation of log (y_i, T) across ith region.

III. RESULTS AND INTERPRETATION

In order to examine inter-state disparities in economic growth, total as well as per-capita State Domestic Product (SDP) at current prices for the period 1980-2002 has been taken. State income are available from 1980-81 to 1998-99 at 1980-81 base and later on it is available at 1993-94 base year. Thus, in order to evolve a comparable SDP with a single base year, technique of base shifting has been applied for SDP data onwards upto 1998-99 upto 2001-02 and SDP data for this period at base 1993-94 has been converted at the base 1980-81 in order to prepare inter-state SDP from 1980-81 to 2001-02 at the base 1980-81. Total SDP (at current prices) for the period 1980-02 have shown in Table 1 while relevant statistics are presented in Table 2. Similarly, per-capita SDP (at current prices) for 1980-02 are shown in Table 3 while relevant statistics are presented in Table 4.

Average annual growth in total SDP for 1980-02 has been examined in the semi-log model with the help of slope-dummy and intercept-dummy technique with dummy variable for year 1991, in order to detect any Kink, if any, in per annum growth in SDP around year 1991, i.e. the period when economic reforms where introduced in India. Regression result for per annum growth in Total SDP are shown in Table 5 while average annual growth during pre-reform (1980-90) and reform-era (1990-02) are presented in Table 6. Facts show that per annum growth in total SDP has fallen for 20 states during reform period (1990-02). Disparity in total SDP during this period has widen as per annum growth for relatively developed states like Gujarat (11.6%), Haryana (10.5%), Maharashtra (10.9%) has been found higher than poor states like Bihar (7.4%), MP (9.4%), Orissa (8.7%) and UP (8.8%). Similarly, during reform period, per annum growth in total SDP were found lower for hill states as Assam (7.6%), HP (7.2%), J & K (7.4%), Manipur (9.9%) and Tripura (7.8%) as compared to developed states like Gujarat, Haryana and Maharashtra. Estimated regression results for per annum growth in per-capita SDP (1980-02) are presented in Table 7 while per annum growth trends are shown in Table 8. It is evident from Table 8 that per annum growth in per-capita SDP during reform period (1990-02) has fallen for all twenty states under consideration. Significant to mention that per annum growth in this regard for relatively well-off states as Gujarat (8.62%), Haryana (7.31%), Maharashtra (7.95%) and Punjab (7.03%) were found higher than poor states like Bihar (6.16%), Orissa (6.07%) and UP (5.86%) and hill states like Assam (5.27%), HP (4.99%), J & K (4.52%), Manipur (5.39%) and Tripura (5.38%) during the reform era, i.e. 1991-2002. This has certainly aggravated the inter-state disparity in per-capita SDP among states during the reform period.

Widening economic disparities among states in terms of total as well as per-capita SDP is corroborated through enhancement in inequality indices over the period. Facts reveal that Gini index, RMD index, Theil's index and Kakwani's index for total SDP during 1980-81 stood at 0.4409, 0.3372, 0.1147 and 0.1804 respectively and they remained almost stagnant upto 1990-91. But later on, these indices have risen and were recorded at 0.4558, 0.3459, 0.1237 and 0.1929 respectively during 2001-02. Similarly, for per-capita SDP, Gini index, RMD-index, Theil's index, Kakwani's index stood at 0.1493, 0.1177, 0.0124 and 0.0215 respectively in 1980-81 and with mild enhancement these indices stood at 0.1596, 0.1164, 0.0144 and 0.0248 respectively in 1990-91. Later on, a surge was found among these inequality indices and finally these stood at 0.2171, 0.1660, 0.0249 and 0.0429 respectively in 2001-02. Inequality indices pertaining to total as well as per-capita SDP for 1980-2002 reveal the harsh reality, that income inequalities at aggregate as well as per-capita level have increased with is evident in increasing values of inequality indices as mentioned above. These inequalities have been much more prominent during the reform (1991-2002) period.

Different measures of convergence/divergence, for instance σ-convergence and β-convergence, have also been estimated for the period 1980-2002 in order to examine the trends and issues pertaining to inter-state income disparities among twenty major Indian states. σ-convergence results for total SDP as well as per-capita SDP are shown in Table 11 and Table 12 respectively. The estimated beta-coefficient are found positive and significant for all three periods, i.e. 1980-81 to 1990-91, 1991-92 to 2001-02 and 1980-81 to 2001-02. Beta coefficients for reform period (1991-2002) as compared to pre-reform (1980-91) period suggest that economic reforms have resulted in widening of inter-state disparities. In order to detect β-convergence, estimated Barro-regressions are presented in Table 13 and Table 14. Facts show that β-coefficient for total as well as per-capita SDP were found negative (insignificant) during pre-reform (1980-91) period indicating weak convergence in state income during this period. However, Beta coefficient were found positive and significant for total as well as per-capita SDP during reform (1991-2002) period revealing the fact that divergence in state income (total/per-capita) resulting in increasing inter-state disparities has occurred after the reforms of 1991 have been introduced.

IV. SUMUP

The empirical results pertaining to interstate disparity in terms of total as well as per-capita for 20 major Indian states during the period 1980-2002 are quite pathetic and alarming. Inequality indices for total SDP in terms of Gini ratio, RMD, Theil's index and Kakwani index stood at 0.4409, 0.3372, 0.1147 and 0.1804 respectively during 1980-81 and these indices have risen, however moderately, and stood at 0.4558, 0.3459, 0.1237 and 0.1929 respectively is 2001-02. These indices for per-capita SDP were noted at 0.1493, 0.1177, 0.0124 and 0.0215 respectively during 1980-81 and these indices have risen drastically later on and were observed at 0.2171, 0.1660, 0.0249 and 0.0429 in the year 2001-02. Widening gap in terms of income among rich and poor states, especially after 1991 has also been established through empirical results based on β-convergence and σ-convergence. This is indeed an alarming situation and a potential threat for stability of a federation like India. Redressel of horizontal economic disparity happens to be an important objective in any scheme of federal devolution of funds among federating states. In India, this task is done by the Planning Commission and Finance Commission. The Thirteenth Finance Commission (2010-15) should assign due weightage to this factor in its scheme of devolution of taxes/grants for states such that inter-state economic disparities may be rectified effectively.

NOTES

1. There exists difference of opinion as to what the I-U hypothesis actually stands for. Sometimes, it is argued that inverted shape is merely a technical property of some inequality measures [Knight,

1976] while Robinson (1976) showed the same to hold true if the variance is taken as a measure of inequality. The other group of scholar [Oshima (1962), Adelman and Morris (1973), Paukert (1973), Della Valle and Oguchi (1976)] have interpreted as a theory about the nexus between economic development and inequality. There have been several attempts [Ahulwalia (1976), Sen (1984), Harris (1986), Braun (1988), Deaton (1989), Anand and Kanbur (1990), Hadd and Kanbur (1992), Alperovich (1992), Braulke (1983), and Shreman Robinson (1976)] to test this hypothesis empirically in case of only two sector. However, it would be more realistic to explore the possibility of existence of "I-U hypothesis" in case of multi-sector/region economy (Gaur, A.K., 2004).

2. Chatterji (1992) and Chatterji and Dewhurst (1996) distinguish between weak convergence where $\beta<0$, and strong convergence where $-2<\beta<0$.

References

Adelman, Irma and Morrris, C.T. (1973), Economic Growth and Social Equity in Developing Countries, Stanford: Stanford University Press.

Ahluwalia, M.S. (1967), "Inequality, Poverty and Developmental", *Journal of Development Economics*, Vol. 3(4), 307-42.

Ahluwalia, Montek (2002), "State Level Performance Under Economic Reforms in India", in Anne Krueger (eds.), Economic Policy Reform and the Indian Economy Chicago: University of Chicago Press.

Aitchinson, J. and Brown, J.A.C. (1957), "The Log Normal Distribution", Cambridge: Cambridge University Press.

Allison, P.D. (1978), "Measure of Inequality", *American Sociological Review*, 43, 865-80.

Alperovich Gershon (1992), "Economic Development and Population Concentration", *Economic Development and Cultural Change*, Vol. 41, No. 1, 66-74.

Anand, S. and Kanbur, R. (1990), "Inequality and Development: A Critique", *Journal of Development Economics*.

Atkinson, A.B. (1970), "On the Measurement of Inequality", *Journal of Economic Theory*, 2, 244-263.

Atkinson, A.B. (1983), "The Economics of Inequality (2nd Edition), Oxford: Clarendon Press.

Barro, Robert and Xavier Sala-i-Martin (1997), "Technological diffusion, Convergence, and growth", *Journal of Economic Growth*, 2, March 1-26.

Barro, Robert J. (1990), "Government Spending in a Simple Model of Endogenous Growth", *Journal of Political Economy*, 98, October, Part-II, S103-S125.

Barro, Robert J. (1999), "Lisbon Meets Ramsey in the Neo-classical Growth Model", *Quarterly Journal of Economics*, 114, Nov. 1125-1152.

Barro, Robert J. and Xavier Sala-i-Martin (1922c), "Public Finance in Models of Economic Growth", *Review of Economic Studies*, 59, October, 645-661.

Barro, Robert J. and Xavier Sala-i-Martin (1992a), "Convergence", *Journal of Political Economy*, 100, April, 223-51.

Barro, Robert J. and Xavier Sala-i-Martin (1992b), "Regional Growth and Migration: A Japan-United States Comparison", *Journal of Japanese and International Economies*, 6, December, 312-46.

Barro, Robert J. and Xavier Sala-i-Martin (2007), "Economic Growth (2nd ed.)", New Delhi:. Prentice-Hall of India, Pvt. Ltd.

Barro, Robert, J. (1991), "Economic Growth in a Cross Section of Countries", *Quarterly Journal of Economics*, 106, May 407-43.

Barro, Rovert J., and Jong-Wha Lee (1994), "Sources of Economic Growth", Carnegie-Rochester Conference Series on Public Policy.

Barro, Rovert J., N. Gregory Mankiw, and Xavier Sala-i-Martin (1995), "Capital Mobility in Neo-classical Models of Growth", *American Economic Review*, 85, March, 103-115.

Barro, Rovert, J. and Xavier Sala-i-Martin (1991), "Convergence across States and Regions", Brookings Paper on Economic Activity, No. 107-182.

Basmann, R.L. and Slottje, D.J. (1987), "A New Index of Income Inequality—The B Measure", *Economic Letters*, 4, 385-389.

Baunol, William J. (1986), "Productivity Growth Convergence and Welfare: What the Long-run Data Show", *American Economic Review*, Vol. 76, No. 5, 1072-15.

Bernard, A. and Durlanf S. (1996), "Interpreting Tests of the Convergence Hypothesis", *Journal of Econometrics.*

Bhattacharya, B.B. and Sakhtivel, S. (2004), "Regional Growth and Disparity in India—Comparison of Pre- and Post-Reform Decades", *Economical Political Weekly*, Vol. 29 (10), March 6, 1071-1077.

Boyer, R. (1996), "The Convergence Hypothesis is Revisited: Globalization but still a century of Nations?" in S. Gerger and R. Dore (eds.) National Diversity and Global Capitalism, Cornell University Press, London.

Brankle, Micheal (1983), "A Note on Kuznet's U", *The Review of Economics and Statistics*, 135-39.

Braun, Denny (1988), "Multiple Measurements of U.S. Income Inequality", *The Review of Economics and Statistics*, 70(3), 398-405.

Cashin, Paul A. (1995), "Economic Growth and Convergence Across the Seven Colonies of Australia: 1861-1991", *Economic Record*, Vol. 71, June, 132-44.

Cashin, Paul A. and Sahay, Ratan (1996), "Internal Migration, Center-State of India", *IMF Staff Papers*, Vol. 43, No. 1 March, 123-71.

Cass David (1965), "Optimum Growth in an Aggregative Model of Capital Accumulation", *Review of Economic Studies*, 32, 233-40.

Champernowne, D. (1974), "A Comparison of Measures of Inequality of Income Distribution", *The Economic Journal*, 84, 787-816.

Charterji, M. (1992), "Convergence Clubs and Endogeneous Growth", *Oxford Review of Economic Policy*, 8, 57-69.

Charterji, M. and Dewhurst, J.H. (1996), "Convergence Clubs and Relative Economic Performance in Great Britain, 1977-91", *Regional Studies* 30, 31-40.

Chattopadhyaya, R.N. and Pal, M.N. (1972), "Some Comparative Studies on the Composition of Composite Regional Indices", *Indian Journal of Regional Sciences*, 4(2).

Corrado, Gini (1912), Variability Mutabilita (Olonga).

Cowell, F.A. (1980), "On the Structure of Additive Inequality Measures", *The Review of Economic Studies*, 47, 521-32.

Dalton, H. (1920), "The Measurement of the Inequality of Income", *Economic Journal*, 30.

Datt, G. and Ravallion, M. (1993), "Regional Disparities, Targeting and Poverty in India", in Michael Lipton and J. Van Der Gaag (eds.) Including the Poor, World Bank: Washington, D.C.

Datt, G. and Ravallion, M. (1998), "Why have Some Indian States Done Better than Others at Reducing Rural Poverty?", *Economica*, Vol. 65.

Datt, G. and Ravallion, M. (2002), "Why has Economic Growth been More Pro-poor in Some States in India than others?, *Journal of Development Economics*, 68.

Deaton, Angus (1989), "Looking for Boy-Girl Discrimination in Household Expenditure Data", *World Bank Economic Review*, Vols. 1-15.

Della Valla Philip, A and Noriyoshi Oguchi (1976), "Distribution, The Aggregate Consumption on Function and the Level of Economic Development: Some Cross-Country Results", *Journal of Political Economy*, 84, 1325-34.

DeLong, J. Brodford (1988), "Productivity Growth Convergence and Welfare: Comment", *American Economic Review*, Vol. 78, No. 5, 1138-54.

Dev, S.M. and Ravi, C. (2007), "Poverty and Inequality:all-India and States, 1983-2005", *Economic and Political Weekly*, 42(6), Feb. 10.

Dowrick-Steve and Nguyen, Dcu Tho (1989), "OECD Comparative Economic Growth 1950-80 Catch up and Convergence", *American Economic Review*, Vol. 79, 1010-30.

Dreze, J. and Sen, A. (1995), India: Economic Development and Social Opportunity, New Delhi: Oxford University Press.

Dreze, J. and Srinivasan, P.V. (1996), "Poverty in India: Regional Estimates", Discussion Paper No. 70, London School of Economics.

Dunford, M. and A. Smith (2000), "Catching up or Falling Behind? Economic Performance and Regional Trajectories in the New Europe", *Economic Geography*, 76(2), 169-95.

Easterlin, Richard A. (1960b), "Inter-Regional differences in Pre capita Income, Population and Total Income, 1840-1950: Trends in the American Economy in the Nineteenth Century", Vol. 24, NBER Studies in Income and Wealth, *NBER*, pp. 73-140

Easterlin, Richard A. (1960a), "Regional Growth Income: Long-term Tendencies", in Simon Kuznets, Ratner Miller and Richard A. Easterlin (eds.) Population Redistribution and Economic Growth: United States, 1870-1950, Vol. II, Philadelphia: American Philosophical Society, pp. 141-203.

Gaur, A.K. (2002), "Industrial Disparity Among Indian States: A Decompositon of Herfindahl Index", *Indian Journal of Regional Science*, Vol. XXXIV, No. 2.

Gaur, A.K. (2004), "Detection of Inter-State Kuznets Cycle Through Neo-Classical and Noe-Keznesian paradigms: Indian Experience", Paper Presented at the International Seminar on the Theme entitled, "Third Annual Conference on Models and Methods in Economics" Organized by Economics Research Unit (ERU), Indian Statistical Institute, Kolkata during Jan. 15-17, 2004.

Hadd, I. and Kanbur, R. (1992), "Is there an Intra-Household Kuznets Curve? Some Evidence From the Philippines", Public Finance Supplement to Vol. 47, 77-93.

Harriss, Barbara (1986), "The Intra-Family Distribution of Hunger in South Asia" in J. Dreze and Sen, A.K. (eds.), Hunger and Public Policy, New Delhi, Oxford University Press.

Herfindahl, O.C. (1950). Concentration in the Steel Industry, Unpublished Ph.D. Dissertation, Columbia University.

Kakwani, N. (1980a), "On a Class of Poverty Measures", *Econometrica*, 48, 437-46.

Kakwani, N. (1980b), "Income Inequality and Poverty", Oxford University Press.

Kaldor, Nicholas (1955-56), "Alternative Theories of Distribution", *Review of Economic Studies*, 23(2), No. 61:81-100.

Kaldor, Nicholas (1960), Essays on Economic Stability and Growth, London: Duckworth.

Kalecki, Michal (1954), Theory of Economic Dynamics, London: Allen and Unwin.

Kalecki, Michal (1971), Selected Essays on the Dynamics of the Capitalist Economy, 1933-70, Cambridge: Cambridge University Press.

Knight, J.B. (1976), "Explaining Income Distribution in Less Developed Countries: Framework and an agenda", *Oxford Bulletin of Economics and Statistics*, 38, 161-177.

Koopmans, TC (1965), "On the Concept of Optimal Economic Growth"-The Econometric Approach to Developmental Planning, Amsterdam: North Holland.

Kurian, N.J. (2007), "Widening Economic and Social Disparities: Implications for India", *Indian J. Med Res.* 126, October 2007.

Kuznets, Simon (1955), "Economic Growth and Income Inequality", *American Economic Review*, 45, 1-28.

Lucas, Robert E. Jr. (1988), "On the Mechanic of Economic Development", *Journal of Monetary Economics*, 22, July, 3-42.

Majumdar, Rajarshi (2004), "Human Development in India: Regional Pattern and Policy Issues" Munich Personal RePec Archive (MPRA) Paper No. 4821, (online at http://mpra.ub.uni-muenchen.de/4821/).

Marie-Ange Veganzones (1998), "Long-Run Growth Trends and Convergence Across Indian States, OECD Technical Paper No. 131.

Martin, R. and Sunley, P. (1998), "Slow Convergence? The New Endogenous

Growth Theory and Regional Development", *Economic Geography*, 74, 201-27.

Mathur, Ashok (1983), "Regional Development and Income Disparities in India: A Sectoral Analysis", *Economic Development and Cultural Change*, 31 (April).

Mathur, Ashok (1987), "Why Growth Rates Differ within India-An Alternative Approach", *Journal of Development Studies*, 23(2).

Mathur, Ashok (1992), "Regional Economic Change and Development Policy in India", *Indian Journal of Applied Economics*, 1(2).

Mohapatra, A.C. (1978), "An Alternative Model of Measuring Divergence-Convergence Hypothesis: A Study of Regional Per-capita Incomes in India", *Indian Journal of Regional Science*, 10(2).

Morgan, J. (1962), "The Anatomy of Income Distribution", *The Review of Economics and Statistics.*

Nair, K.R.G. (1973), "A Note on the Inter-State Income Differentials in India, 1950-51 to 1960-61", *Journal of Development Studies*, 9th July.

Nair, K.R.G. (1982), Regional Experience in a Developing Economy New Delhi: Wiley Eastern Ltd.

Osberg, L. (1984). Economic Inequality in the United States, New York, M.E. Sharpe.

Oshima, Harry T. (1962), "The International Comparison of Size Distribution of Family Income with Special Reference Asia", *The Review of Economics and Statistics*, 44, 439-45

Pasinetti, Luigi (1962), "The Rate of Profit and Income Distribution in Relation to the Rate of Economic Growth", *Review of Economic Studies*, 29, 267-79.

Pasinetti, Luigi (1977), Lectures on the Theory of Production, London: Macmillan.

Pasinetti, Luigi (1981), Structural Change and Economic Growth, Cambridge: Cambridge University Press.

Paukert, Felix (1973), "Income Distribution at Deferent Levels of Development: A Survey of Evidence", *International Labour Review*, 108, 97-125.

Planning Commission (2006), "An Approach to the 11th Five Year Plan—Towards Faster and More Inclusive Growth", Government of India, June 14, 2006.

Planning Commission, Government of India (2002), National Human Development Report-2001, New Delhi: Oxford University Press.

Quah, D.T. (1993), "Empirical Cross-section Dynamics in Economic Growth", *European Economic Review*, Vol. 37, April, 426-434.

Quah, D.T. (1995), "Galton's Fallacy and Tests of the Convergence Hypothesis", *The Scandinavian Journal of Economics*, Vol. 95, No. 4, 427-43.

Quah, D.T. (1996a), "Convergence Empirics with Capital Mobility", *Journal of Economic Growth*, Vol. 1, No. 1, March, 95-124.

Quah, D.T. (1996b), "Twin Peaks: Growth and Convergence in Models of Distribution Dynamics", The Economics Journal, Vol. 106, July, 1045-1055.

Ramiah (2002), "Understanding Regional Economic Growth in India", CID Working Paper No. 88, Harvard University.

Rao, M. Govinda, Ricshcand and Kalirajan, K.P. (1999), "Convergence of Income Across Indian States: A Divergent View", *Economic and Political Weekly*, March 27, April 2.

Rao, S.K. (1973), "A Note on Measuring Economic Distances Between Regions in India", *Economic and Political Weekly*, 8 April.

Ravindra, H. Dholakia (2003), "Regional Disparity in Economic and Human Development in India", *Economic and Political Weekly*, Sept. 27.

Robinson, Sherman (1976), "A Note on the U Hypothesis Relating Income Inequality and Economic Development", American Economic Review, 66, 437-40.

Romar, Paul M. (1990), "Endogenous Technological Charge", *Journal of Political Economy*, 98, October, Part-II, S71-S102.

Romer, Paul M. (1986), "Increasing Returns and Long-Run Growth" *Journal of Political Economy*, 94, October, 1002-37.

Romer, Paul M. (1987), "Growth Based on Increasing Returns Due to Specialization", American Economic Review, 77, May, 56-62.

Romer, Paul M. (1992), "Two Strategies for Economic Development: Using Ideas and Producing Ideas", In World Bank, Annual Conference on Economic Development, Washington D.C.

Romer, Paul M. (1993), "Idea Gaps and object Gaps in Economic Development", *Journal of Monetary Economics*, 32, December, 543-573.

Sampath, R.K. (1977), "Inter-State Inequalities in Income in India: 1951-1971", Indian Journal of Regional Science, 9(1).

Sen, Amartya (1984), "Family and Food: Sex Bias in Poverty in A.K. Sen(eds.) Resources, values and Development", Oxford: Blackwell Publishers Ltd.

Shatakshee Dhongde (2006), "Decomposing Spatial Differences in Poverty in India", in Ravi Kanbur, Anthony J. Venables and Guanghua Wan (Eds.) Spatial Disparities in Human Development, Tokya: United Nations University Press (http://www.unu.edu)

Slottje, D.J., Basmann, R.L. and Niewwiadomy, M. (1989), "On the Empirical Relationship Between Several Well Known Inequality Measures", Journal of Econometrics, 42, 49-66.

Smith, D.(1975), "Neoclassical Growth Models and Regional Growth in the US", *Journal of Regional Science*, Vol. 15, 165-81.

Solow, R.M. (1970): Growth Theory: An Exposition, Oxford University Press: Oxford

Solow, R.M. (1956), "A Contribution to the Theory of Economic Growth", *Quarterly Journal of Economics*, 65-94.

Solow, R.M. (1957), "Technical Change and the Aggregate Production Function", *Review of Economics and Statistics*, 312-20.

Srivastava, D.K. and Aggarwal, P.K. (1979), "Measuring Tax Revenue Centralization in Federal Fiscal Systems: A Case Study of India", *Public Finance*, No. 3, pp. 414-33.

Steindl, Josef (1952), Maturity and Stagnation in American Capitalism. Oxford, Basil Blackwell.

Tenth Five Year Plan (2002-2007), Vol. III, Planning .Commission, Government of India, New Delhi.

Theil, H. (1967). Economics and Information Theory, Amsterdam, North-Holland.

World Bank (2008), "The Growth Report—Strategies for Sustained Growth and Inclusive Development", Commission on Growth and Development, Washington: The World Bank, May 2008. (www.growthcommission.org).

TABLE I

State Domestic Product (at Current Prices) of States (1981-2002)

(Rupees Crores)

Year	AP	Assam	Bihar	Gujarat	Haryana	HP	J&K	Karnataka	Kerala	MP	Maharashtra	Manipur	Nagaland	Orissa	Punjab	Rajasthan	Tamilnadu	Tripura	UP	WB
1981	7324	2298	6349	6547	3032	723	1050	5587	3823	7012	15163	200	105	3443	4449	4126	7218	264	14012	9594
1982	8974	2966	7391	8205	3498	846	1195	6423	4050	7596	16993	242	131	3844	5285	4850	8677	313	15036	10667
1983	9702	2359	8289	8675	4004	897	1362	7137	4742	8680	18304	256	160	4070	5838	5531	8821	354	17600	12002
1984	11516	4016	9479	11283	4351	1023	1549	8617	5523	10151	21152	304	185	5253	6456	7043	10222	390	19533	14121
1985	11962	4715	11371	11740	4747	1031	1747	9697	6141	10224	22890	344	215	5191	7381	6983	12028	433	21514	16319
1986	13412	5175	12366	12103	5788	1237	1929	10218	6503	12092	26467	372	240	6226	8317	7669	13682	474	24669	17415
1987	14242	5601	14182	14022	6081	1363	2134	11733	7354	12491	28431	426	268	6748	9174	8341	15305	522	27237	18946
1988	17375	6330	15358	13908	6743	1539	2086	13435	8258	16112	33770	542	349	6853	10816	9436	18166	601	30481	23012
1989	22089	6780	18533	19496	8878	1933	2548	15671	9182	18994	40472	606	424	8681	12495	12892	20423	771	36601	24686
1990	25423	8064	19408	21425	9919	2184	2688	17798	10668	21119	50139	634	477	9917	15055	13836	23935	840	41664	27790
1991	31165	9498	22787	24180	12238	2521	2908	20551	12173	26515	58137	723	579	9664	16788	18281	27674	917	49496	31500
1992	37344	10632	25099	26068	14639	2975	3250	26738	15102	27849	65808	868	691	12505	20245	20062	32584	1030	57206	36433
1993	39131	11543	26820	35018	15416	3411	3565	29162	17176	31070	82076	958	811	13416	23280	23671	37023	1079	62066	38768
1994	48048	13095	31250	39190	18347	3744	4416	33924	19688	38500	99729	1156	1045	15481	27547	24727	46152	1244	69846	44460
1995	55844	14580	34912	52013	21863	4340	4901	40427	23236	42901	113197	1306	1209	18156	31543	30420	54131	1307	79135	53819
1996	66780	16385	33705	57861	24652	4931	5329	45133	27909	49118	136119	1412	1442	21463	35504	33708	59718	1557	88511	62462
1997	75410	17480	41188	66883	30363	4676	5812	51360	32387	55872	155388	1571	1727	20636	40585	41872	69042	1703	102864	71555
1998	76705	18865	46219	75335	33275	4971	5599	59752	38002	61019	164577	1695	1541	24105	44789	46846	77302	1863	113105	80665
1999	76606	18588	43467	69499	30645	5266	5905	53935	33850	57830	158196	1828	1647	23112	42223	42497	71963	1785	106351	73719
2000	81311	19601	45792	73867	32538	5561	6210	57206	35940	61243	168130	1961	1752	24401	44763	45100	76368	1882	112455	78004
2001	88453	20877	48152	81173	36316	5698	6439	62691	40583	66963	184306	2094	1867	25943	48947	50575	83705	2055	123440	86419
2002	93038	21821	50516	85534	38438	5910	6666	66031	43068	70477	194322	2227	1957	27076	51532	53570	88168	2161	130021	91099

Source: Figures have been taken from (i) Handbook of Statistics of the Indian Economy, RBI, 2006-07, Mumbai, and (ii) C.S.O., Government of India.

TABLE 2

State Domestic Product of States (1981-02) at Current Prices: Some Relevant Statistics

States	*Mean*	*Median*	*Maximum Value*	*Minimum Value*	*Standard Dev.*	*Skewness*	*Kurtosis*	*Jerque-Bera*	*Probability*	*No. of Obs.*
AP	41447.9	34254.5	93038	7324	29954.3	0.40513	1.61805	2.35245	0.30844	22
Assam	10966.8	10065	21821	2298	6595.27	0.23658	1.61092	1.97397	0.3727	22
Bihar	26028.8	23943	50516	6349	14924.1	0.26405	1.64633	1.93538	0.37996	22
Gujarat	37001.1	25124	85534	6547	27711.3	0.50385	1.66592	2.56227	0.27772	22
Haryana	3035.46	2748	5910	723	1856.05	0.19938	1.47857	2.26762	0.3218	22
HP	16626	13438.5	38438	3032	12224.4	0.48253	1.72086	2.35358	0.30827	22
J&K	3604	3079	6666	1050	1933.81	0.25097	1.53267	2.20459	0.33211	22
Karnataks	29692.1	23644.5	66031	5587	21124.1	0.43014	1.64993	2.34921	0.30894	22
Kerala	18425.4	13637.5	43068	3823	13497.2	0.55078	1.78311	2.46973	0.29088	22
MP	32446.7	27182	70477	7012	22003.6	0.39491	1.64599	2.25238	0.32427	22
Maharashtra	84262.1	61972.5	194322	15163	63401	0.44491	1.62613	2.45603	0.29287	22
Manipur	987.5	795.5	2227	200	669.27	0.47854	1.83011	2.09426	0.35094	22
Nagaland	855.546	635	1957	105	663.61	0.39917	1.56324	2.47651	0.28989	22
Orissa	13462.9	11211	27076	3443	8215.96	0.33811	1.5862	2.25143	0.32442	22
Punjab	23318.7	18516.5	51532	4449	16340.6	0.40576	1.63674	2.3073	0.31548	22
Rajasthan	23274.4	19171.5	53570	4126	16920.9	0.47613	1.73969	2.28723	0.31867	22
Tamil	39195.8	30129	88168	7218	28246.3	0.43543	1.64784	2.37116	0.30557	22
Tripura	1070.23	973.5	2161	264	629.83	0.31534	1.69181	1.93337	0.38034	22
UP	61038.3	53351	130021	14012	39635	0.38091	1.67549	2.14015	0.34298	22
WB	41975.2	33966.5	91099	9594	27720.9	0.47103	1.7274	2.29807	0.31694	22

Note: Relevant Statistics are based on figures as shown in Table 1.

TABLE 3

Per-capita State-Domestic Product (at current prices) of States (1981-2002)

(Rs.)

Year	AP	Assam	Bihar	Gujarat	Haryana	HP	J&K	Karnataka	Kerala	MP	Maharashtra	Manipur	Nagaland	Orissa	Punjab	Rajasthan	Tamilnadu	Tripura	UP	WB
1981	1358	1144	901	1906	2325	1677	1747	1493	1493	1334	2397	1258	1329	1298	2630	1192	1483	1275	1254	1745
1982	1629	1428	1024	2334	2622	1922	1949	1672	1560	1419	2639	1401	1578	1432	3051	1355	1761	1455	1309	1902
1983	1731	1594	1127	2422	2903	2002	2161	1824	1776	1580	2771	1503	1882	1480	3311	1513	1754	1623	1509	2098
1984	2017	1865	1262	3088	3068	2243	2401	2156	2043	1808	3134	1696	2078	1876	3590	1877	1998	1741	1642	2420
1985	2057	2142	1483	3152	3258	2217	2646	2377	2230	1799	3324	1899	2336	1820	4031	1812	2312	1890	1772	2743
1986	2264	2300	1579	3190	3874	2615	2857	2456	2321	2063	3773	2111	2500	2144	4482	1939	2588	2025	1991	2873
1987	2362	2334	1772	3630	3977	2833	3092	2765	2583	2088	3985	2325	2680	2283	4851	2054	2852	2184	2153	3067
1988	2831	2689	1878	3539	4316	3147	2963	3107	2854	2640	4661	2747	3388	2279	5642	2265	3337	2453	2360	3657
1989	3357	2814	2218	4880	5573	3889	3543	3558	3126	3051	5506	2908	3962	2838	6437	3016	3701	3084	2775	3853
1990	4002	3272	2274	5279	6107	4324	3662	3970	3578	3328	6724	3728	4297	3188	7661	3155	4280	3294	3095	4263
1991	4660	4210	2625	5815	7372	4820	3723	4540	4165	3975	7319	4123	4745	3035	8200	4120	4933	3286	3529	4599
1992	5481	4606	2820	6158	8626	5613	4088	5818	5091	4093	8121	4677	5484	3852	9780	4427	5753	3626	4014	5230
1993	5643	4893	2948	8126	8890	6316	4384	6248	5711	4476	9932	5046	6238	4058	11080	5114	6473	3707	4277	5470
1994	6812	5433	3362	8937	10359	6794	5307	7161	6457	5439	11834	5722	7798	4599	12926	5233	7993	4174	4732	6168
1995	7787	5924	3678	11659	12099	7736	5759	8413	7517	5946	13177	6197	8697	5297	14603	6311	9286	4285	5271	7345
1996	9203	6588	3601	12644	13204	8163	5927	9103	8976	6580	15642	7162	9809	6208	15793	6734	10008	4675	5613	8329
1997	10279	6914	4324	14408	15963	7178	6276	10212	10294	7350	17603	7665	11287	5904	17792	8203	11451	4936	6400	9399
1998	10611	7354	4766	15994	17205	7387	5676	11367	11957	7883	18407	6456	8886	6828	19389	8910	12697	5203	6894	10442
1999	10286	7024	4269	15184	16546	9142	6619	10688	10489	7655	17853	8218	10424	6475	19105	8003	11762	5613	6531	9645
2000	10793	7281	4414	15947	17372	9554	6854	30794	11004	8007	18151	8544	10748	6753	20037	8322	12355	5826	6780	10080
2001	10885	7618	5709	14533	15559	9424	6335	11001	11264	10338	18043	7679	8883	6791	18749	7893	12459	6085	6937	9845
2002	11017	7894	4882	15640	16881	9488	6732	11426	11394	8436	19213	7837	10425	6970	19980	8347	12851	5732	7026	10148

Note: State-wise Net Domestic at factor cost (At Current Prices) for the period 1980-81 to 2001-02 have been taken from Handbook of Statistics on the Indian Economy, RBI 2006-07, Mumbai, and C.S.O., Government of India.

TABLE 4

Per-capita State Domestic Product of States (1981-2002) (Current Prices): Some Relevant Statistics

States	Mean	Median	Maximum Value	Minimum Value	Standard Dev.	Skewness	Kurtosis	Jerque-Bera	Probability	No. of Obs.
AP	5575.68	5070.5	11017	1358	7675.19	0.286	1.4604	2.4728	0.2904	22
Assam	4423.68	4408	7894	1144	2345.29	0.10382	1.466	2.1966	0.3334	22
Bihar	2859.82	2722.5	5709	901	1432.99	1.911	1.4384	1.4384	0.4871	22
Gujarat	8112.05	5986.5	15994	1906	5308.47	0.3771	1.4904	2.6105	0.2711	22
Haryana	9004.5	7999	17372	2325	5623.17	0.3183	1.522	2.3739	0.3051	22
HP	5385.63	5216.5	9554	1677	2828.32	0.1381	1.5332	2.0421	0.3602	22
J&K	4304.59	3905.5	6854	1747	1734.8	0.1025	1.5395	1.9938	0.369	22
Karnataks	6915.86	5179	30794	1493	6414.84	2.4068	9.7483	62.9832	0	22
Kerala	5812.86	4628	11957	1493	3828.26	0.4138	1.5611	2.5257	0.2828	22
MP	4604	4034	10338	1334	2761.74	0.4496	1.9192	1.812	0.4041	22
Maharashtra	9736.77	7720	19213	2397	6365.82	0.3121	1.4547	2.5461	0.2799	22
Manipur	4586.46	4400	8544	1258	2557.85	0.1509	1.5134	2.1095	0.3483	22
Nagaland	5884.27	5114.5	11287	1329	3499.61	0.1883	1.4745	2.2632	0.3225	22
Orissa	3973.09	3520	6970	1298	2077.87	0.2271	1.4823	2.3005	0.3166	22
Punjab	10596.4	8990	20037	2630	6498.27	0.2656	1.4794	2.3781	0.3045	22
Rajasthan	4627.05	4223.5	8910	1192	2766.64	0.2485	1.4952	2.302	0.3163	22
Tamil Nadu	6549.41	5343	12851	1483	4283.56	0.3119	1.4794	2.4764	0.2899	22
Tripura	3553.27	3460	6085	1275	1581.98	0.1208	1.6768	1.6558	0.4364	22
UP	3993.82	3771.5	7026	1254	2127.72	0.1817	1.4954	2.1962	0.3335	22
WB	5696.41	4914.5	10442	1745	3134.47	0.32	1.5546	2.291	0.318	22

Note: Relevant Statistics have been computed on the basis of data as given in Table 3.

TABLE 5

Inter-State Growth in Total SDP of Indian States (1980-81 to 2001-02): Regression Results

States	*Intercept*	*t*	D_1	D_2t	*Adj.* R^2	*RSS*	*SER*
AP	8.784	0.128 (13.006)	0.593 (4.225)	-0.029 (-2.365)	0.989	0.145	0.089
Assam	7.631	0.14 (13.043)	0.779 (5.102)	-0.064 (-4.808)	0.982	0.171	0.098
Bihar	8.655	0.127 (20.495)	0.629 (7.167)	-0.052 (-6.819)	0.993	0.057	0.0561
Gujarat	8.732	0.119 (9.079)	0.211 (1.125)	-0.003 (-0.169)	0.98	0.259	0.119
Haryana	7.88	0.127 (13.679)	0.477 (3.606)	-0.022 (-1.905)	0.99	0.128	0.085
HP	6.443	0.118 (14.088)	0.742 (6.227)	-0.046 (-4.339)	0.989	0.104	0.076
J&K	6.903	0.103 (12.116)	0.379 (3.145)	-0.029 (-2.719)	0.985	0.107	0.077
Karnataks	8.513	0.126 (13.258)	0.489 (3.619)	-0.025 (-2.116)	0.989	0.134	0.086
Kerala	8.124	0.113 (11.677)	0.187 (1.355)	-0.0001 (-0.011)	0.988	0.139	0.088
MP	8.692	0.123 (14.089)	0.524 (4.233)	-0.029 (-2.699)	0.989	0.112	0.079
Maharashtra	9.449	0.127 (11.416)	0.473 (2.989)	-0.018 (-1.293)	0.987	0.183	0.101
Manipur	5.18	0.131 (20.842)	0.421 (4.697)	-0.032 (-3.994)	0.995	0.059	0.057
Nagaland	4.535	0.163 (13.154)	0.823 (4.656)	-0.055 (-3.546)	0.986	0.229	0.113
Orissa	8.023	0.114 (11.774)	0.381 (2.769)	-0.027 (-2.197)	0.984	0.139	0.088
Punjab	8.273	0.129 (14.513)	0.525 (4.158)	-0.03 (-2.715)	0.99	0.117	0.081
Rajasthan	8.227	0.127 (13.372)	0.536 (3.959)	-0.026 (-2.202)	0.989	0.135	0.087
Tamil Nadu	8.739	0.132 (13.541)	0.488 (3.527)	-0.028 (-2.269)	0.989	0.141	0.088
Tripura	5.465	0.123 (19.672)	0.546 (6.118)	-0.045 (-5.668)	0.993	0.058	0.057
UP	9.396	0.121 (18.493)	0.536 (5.77)	-0.033 (-4.048)	0.993	0.063	0.059
WB	9.055	0.119 (14.144)	0.3 (2.505)	-0.02 (-1.927)	0.989	0.105	0.077

Note: Regression results have been calculated on the basis of data as given in Table 1. Figures in the parenthesis are t values.

TABLE 6

State Domestic Product (Total) of Indian States (1981-2002): Per Annum Growth Rates

States	*Growth rate (in percentage) during*	
	Pre-economic reform era (1980-81 -1990-91)	*Economic reform era (1991-92 -2001-2002)*
AP	12.8	9.9
Assam	14	7.6
Bihar	12.7	7.4
Gujarat	11.9	11.6
Haryana	12.7	10.5
HP	11.8	7.2
J&K	10.3	7.4
Karnataka	12.6	10.1
Kerala	11.3	11.29
MP	12.3	9.4
Maharashtra	12.7	10.9
Manipur	13.1	9.9
Nagaland	16.3	10.8
Orissa	11.4	8.7
Punjab	12.9	9.9
Rajasthan	12.7	10.1
Tamil Nadu	13.2	10.4
Tripura	12.3	7.8
UP	12.1	8.8
WB	11.9	9.9

Note: Per annum growth has been calculated on the basis of regression coefficients at t and D_2.t as given in Table 5.

TABLE 7

Per-capita Growth Rate of SDPs at Current Prices (1981-2002): Regression Results.

States	*Intercept*	*t*	D_1	D_2t	R^2	*Adj.* R^2	*RSS*	*SER*
AP	7.0932	0.1156 (12.8626)	0.7121 (4.2647)	-0.0411 (-3.2331)	0.986	0.9835	0.16	0.0943
Assam	7.0235	0.1127 (18.3419)	0.8463 (7.4157)	-0.06 (-6.9078)	0.991	0.9891	0.0747	0.0644
Bihar	6.7243	0.1049 (17.6172)	0.5173 (4.676)	-0.0433 (-5.1379)	0.989	0.9874	0.0702	0.0625
Gujarat	7.5042	0.1032 (8.6433)	0.4331 (1.9519)	-0.017 (-1.0067)	0.975	0.9708	0.2825	0.1253
Haryana	7.6081	0.109 (11.7014)	0.6574 (3.7993)	-0.0359 (-2.7276)	0.984	0.9811	0.1718	0.0977
H.P	7.2851	0.104 (15.9701)	0.8266 (6.8358)	-0.0541 (-5.8788)	0.989	0.9871	0.0839	0.0683
J & K	7.4503	0.0761 (11.3639)	0.4374 (3.5186)	-0.0309 (-3.2627)	0.978	0.9744	0.0887	0.0702
Karnataka	7.2001	0.1082 (4.9627)	0.3504 (0.8649)	-0.0108 (-0.3513)	0.93	0.918	0.9419	0.2288
Kerala	7.1841	0.0997 (11.1328)	0.4561 (2.7430)	-0.0151 (-1.1955)	0.986	0.9836	0.1587	0.0939
MP	7.0309	0.1068 (13.6283)	0.4163 (2.8595)	-0.0267 (-2.4099)	0.987	0.9846	0.1216	0.0822
Maharashtra	7.6027	0.1123 (11.5308)	0.644 (3.5592)	-0.0328 (-2.3818)	0.984	0.9815	0.1879	0.1022
Manipur	6.9757	0.1182 (16.0414)	0.9211 (6.7325)	-0.0643 (-0.1730)	0.988	0.986	0.1074	0.0772
Nagaland	7.111	0.1247 (11.4296)	1.0639 (5.2497)	-0.0715 (-4.6342)	0.977	0.9737	0.2357	0.1144
Orissa	7.0854	0.0911 (12.4925)	0.5272 (3.8935)	-0.0304 (-2.9477)	0.985	0.9826	0.1052	0.0765
Punjab	7.7525	0.1132 (15.7346)	0.7239 (5.4173)	-0.0429 (-4.2163)	0.99	0.9886	0.1025	0.0755
Rajasthan	6.9709	0.1105 (11.0325)	0.7742 (4.1623)	-0.0463 (-3.2727)	0.98	0.9767	0.1985	0.105
Tamil Nadu	7.1616	0.1185 (14.1066)	0.7052 (4.5186)	-0.0398 (-3.3533)	0.988	0.9865	0.1398	0.0881
Tripura	7.0651	0.0978 (22.1409)	0.5015 (6.1126)	-0.0440 (-7.0421)	0.993	0.9913	0.0386	0.0463
UP	6.988	0.1033 (19.1601)	0.6733 (6.7232)	-0.0447 (-58616)	0.992	0.9912	0.0576	0.0565
WB	7.3741	0.0985 (12.5162)	0.4072 (2.7857)	-0.0266 (-2.3896)	0.984	0.9814	0.1226	0.0825

Notes: (1) Regression results have been calculated on the basis of data as given in Table 3.
(2) Figures in the parenthesis are t values.

TABLE 8

Average Annual Growth in Per-capita State Domestic Products of States (1981-2002)

States	*Growth rate (in percentage) during*	
	Pre-economic reform era (1980-81 -1990-91)	*Economic reform era (1991-92 -2001-2002)*
AP	11.56	7.45
Assam	11.27	5.27
Bihar	10.49	6.16
Gujarat	10.32	8.62
Haryana	10.9	7.31
HP	10.4	4.99
J & K	7.61	4.52
Karnataka	10.82	9.47
Kerala	9.97	8.46
MP	10.68	8.01
Maharashtra	11.23	7.95
Manipur	11.82	5.39
Nagaland	12.47	5.32
Orissa	9.11	6.07
Punjab	11.32	7.03
Rajasthan	11.05	6.42
Tamil Nadu	11.85	7.87
Tripura	9.78	5.38
Uttar Pradesh	10.33	5.86
WB	9.85	7.19

Note: Growth rates for Pre-economic and Reform era have been calculated on the basis of coefficients of t and D_2t as given in Table 7.

TABLE 9

Family of SDP (Total) Inequality Indices of Indian States (1981-2002)

Year	Inequality Indices Based on														
	Traditional Measures		Properties of Lorenz Curve				Herfindahl's Index			Atkinson's Social Welfare Function					
	C.V.	Variance of Log	Gini Coefficient	RMD	Theil Index	Kakwani index	H_1	H_2	H_3	Atkin (ϵ=0.5)	Atkin (ϵ=1.1)	Atkin (ϵ=1.5)	Atkin (ϵ=1.9)	Atkin (ϵ=2.1)	Atkin (ϵ=2.5)
1980-81	0.8106	1.3900	0.4409	0.3372	0.1147	0.1804	0.0829	0.0872	0.0346	0.1958	0.4994	0.6933	0.8178	0.8548	0.8990
1981-82	0.7872	1.3700	0.4340	0.3347	0.1109	0.1707	0.0810	0.0852	0.0326	0.1910	0.4931	0.6849	0.8105	0.8483	0.8936
1982-83	0.7886	1.3600	0.4319	0.3313	0.1107	0.1753	0.0811	0.0854	0.0327	0.1901	0.4873	0.6786	0.8040	0.8421	0.8881
1983-84	0.7727	1.3800	0.4282	0.3295	0.1088	0.1733	0.0799	0.0841	0.0314	0.1889	0.4893	0.6827	0.8077	0.8403	0.8905
1984-85	0.7754	1.3700	0.4292	0.3334	0.1094	0.1745	0.0801	0.0843	0.0316	0.1895	0.4879	0.5785	0.8026	0.8403	0.8860
1985-86	0.7845	1.3600	0.4304	0.3308	0.1100	0.1744	0.0808	0.0850	0.0324	0.1894	0.4864	0.6770	0.8018	0.8397	0.8858
1986-87	0.7803	1.3500	0.4297	0.3321	0.1095	0.1741	0.0804	0.0847	0.0320	0.1888	0.4846	0.6745	0.7993	0.8375	0.8838
1987-88	0.7960	1.3400	0.4395	0.3395	0.1131	0.1798	0.0817	0.0860	0.0333	0.1933	0.4871	0.6709	0.7919	0.8296	0.8767
1988-89	0.7868	1.3500	0.4334	0.3360	0.1113	0.1774	0.0810	0.0852	0.0326	0.1911	0.4850	0.6703	0.7926	0.8306	0.8775
1989-90	0.8109	1.3400	0.4411	0.3368	0.1147	0.1808	0.0829	0.0872	0.0346	0.1946	0.4874	0.6699	0.7667	0.8283	0.8751
1990-91	0.8144	1.3500	0.4441	0.3389	0.1162	0.1835	0.0832	0.0875	0.0349	0.1975	0.4930	0.6746	0.7932	0.8300	0.8757
1991-92	0.8041	1.3500	0.4391	0.3333	0.1142	0.1804	0.0823	0.0867	0.0340	0.1949	0.4901	0.6728	0.7921	0.8291	0.8748
1992-93	0.8299	1.3600	0.4454	0.3360	0.1181	0.1848	0.0844	0.0889	0.0363	0.1996	0.4965	0.6779	0.7953	0.8316	0.8765
1993-94	0.8430	1.3600	0.4512	0.3428	0.1203	0.1876	0.0855	0.0900	0.0374	0.2019	0.4976	0.6765	0.7926	0.8288	0.8737
1994-95	0.8298	1.3800	0.4486	0.3421	0.1192	0.1871	0.0844	0.0889	0.0362	0.2022	0.5533	0.6850	0.8008	0.8362	0.8796

1995-96	0.8542	1.3600	0.4557	0.3484	0.1224	0.1904	0.0865	0.0910	0.0384	0.2047	0.5011	0.6784	0.7930	0.8286	0.8730
1996-97	0.8563	1.3800	0.4580	0.3472	0.1244	0.1937	0.0867	0.0912	0.0386	0.2097	0.5120	0.6889	0.8000	0.8342	0.8764
1997-98	0.8405	1.4500	0.4536	0.3438	0.1234	0.1927	0.0853	0.0898	0.0372	0.2117	0.5302	0.7150	0.8250	0.8541	0.8954
1998-99	0.8459	1.3900	0.4538	0.3443	0.1223	0.1909	0.0858	0.0903	0.0377	0.2067	0.5103	0.6899	0.8029	0.8373	0.8796
1999-00	0.8787	1.4300	0.4757	0.3703	0.1318	0.2055	0.0886	0.0933	0.0406	0.2209	0.5348	0.7122	0.8195	0.8515	0.8904
2000-01	0.8494	1.3900	0.4555	0.3459	0.1235	0.1925	0.0867	0.0913	0.0386	0.2087	0.5144	0.6934	0.8148	0.8587	0.8904
2001-02	0.8501	1.4000	0.4558	0.3459	0.1237	0.1929	0.0868	0.0913	0.0387	0.2092	0.5154	0.6942	0.8253	0.8691	0.9606

Note: Inequality indices have been calculated on the basis of data given in Table 1.

TABLE 10

Family of Per-capita SDP Inequality Indices of Indian States (1981-2002)

Year	Inequality Indices Based on														
	Traditional Measures		Properties of Lorenz Curve				Herfindahl's Index			Atkinson's Social Welfare Function					
	C.V.	Variance of Log	Gini Coefficient	RMD	Theil Index	Kakwani index	H_1	H_2	H_3	Atkin (ϵ=0.5)	Atkin (ϵ=1.1)	Atkin (ϵ=1.5)	Atkin (ϵ=1.9)	Atkin (ϵ=2.1)	Atkin (ϵ=2.5)
1980-81	0.2816	0.0688	0.1493	0.1177	0.0124	0.0215	0.0569	0.0599	0.0073	0.0181	0.0385	0.0513	0.0635	0.0693	0.0806
1981-82	0.2864	0.0708	0.1520	0.1192	0.0128	0.0222	0.0571	0.0601	0.0075	0.0187	0.0397	0.0528	0.0652	0.0712	0.0827
1982-83	0.2770	0.0658	0.1463	0.1138	0.0119	0.0207	0.0568	0.0598	0.0072	0.0174	0.0370	0.0492	0.0608	0.0664	0.0772
1983-84	0.2677	0.0623	0.1403	0.1087	0.0110	0.0191	0.0564	0.0594	0.0067	0.0161	0.0345	0.0463	0.0576	0.0631	0.0738
1984-85	0.2677	0.0625	0.1441	0.1107	0.1130	0.0195	0.0565	0.0595	0.0068	0.0164	0.0350	0.0467	0.0578	0.0631	0.0733
1985-86	0.2757	0.0642	0.1455	0.1111	0.0118	0.0204	0.0567	0.0597	0.0071	0.0171	0.0363	0.0482	0.0595	0.0649	0.0752
1986-87	0.2726	0.0634	0.1457	0.1109	0.0116	0.0200	0.0566	0.0596	0.0069	0.0169	0.0357	0.0475	0.0587	0.0640	0.0742
1987-88	0.2804	0.0667	0.1481	0.1105	0.0121	0.0209	0.0569	0.0599	0.0073	0.0177	0.0375	0.0499	0.0617	0.0673	0.0783
1988-89	0.2865	0.0695	0.1509	0.1149	0.0128	0.0219	0.0571	0.0601	0.0075	0.0185	0.0392	0.0520	0.0641	0.0699	0.0810
1989-90	0.3108	0.0799	0.1602	0.1203	0.0148	0.0252	0.0579	0.0610	0.0084	0.0214	0.0451	0.0597	0.0735	0.0801	0.0928
1990-91	0.3042	0.0802	0.1596	0.1164	0.0144	0.0248	0.0577	0.0608	0.0082	0.0210	0.0447	0.0595	0.0736	0.0804	0.0935
1991-92	0.3163	0.0871	0.1669	0.1228	0.0156	0.0267	0.0582	0.0612	0.0086	0.0227	0.0482	0.0643	0.0871	0.0800	0.1010
1992-93	0.3447	0.1055	0.1847	0.1388	0.0186	0.0319	0.0592	0.0623	0.0096	0.0271	0.0578	0.0771	0.0954	0.1043	0.1214
1993-94	0.3577	0.1131	0.1925	0.1455	0.0199	0.0342	0.0597	0.0628	0.0102	0.0291	0.0619	0.0824	0.1019	0.1112	0.1291
1994-95	0.3715	0.1286	0.2030	0.1541	0.0219	0.0379	0.0603	0.0634	0.0108	0.0322	0.0691	0.0924	0.1146	0.1253	0.1458

1995-96	0.3804	0.1418	0.2086	0.1579	0.0232	0.0402	0.0607	0.0639	0.0112	0.0344	0.0745	0.1004	0.1255	0.1377	0.1615
1996-97	0.4066	0.1572	0.2239	0.1741	0.0263	0.0456	0.0618	0.0651	0.0125	0.0388	0.0833	0.1113	0.1377	0.1503	0.1742
1997-98	0.4275	0.1697	0.2352	0.1861	0.0289	0.0499	0.0628	0.0661	0.0135	0.0425	0.0905	0.1201	0.1476	0.1605	0.1846
1998-99	0.4023	0.1508	0.2188	0.1653	0.0255	0.0439	0.0616	0.0648	0.0122	0.0375	0.0804	0.1073	0.1329	0.1452	0.1686
1999-00	0.5330	0.2150	0.2695	0.2098	0.0407	0.0664	0.0683	0.0718	0.0192	0.0578	0.1184	0.1537	0.1854	0.2000	0.2271
2000-01	0.3660	0.1204	0.2006	0.1539	0.0211	0.0365	0.0601	0.0632	0.0106	0.0309	0.0657	0.0821	0.1076	0.1173	0.1354
2001-02	0.3980	0.1450	0.2171	0.1660	0.0249	0.0429	0.0614	0.0647	0.0120	0.0365	0.0779	0.1037	0.1281	0.1396	0.1616

Note: Inequality indices have been calculated on the basis of data given in Table 3.

18

Inter-State Disparities in India: A Similarity Matrix Approach

MAHALAYA CHATTERJEE

I. INTRODUCTION

Since independence in 1947, India has made enormous strides towards the progress of the nation. The concerted and coordinated efforts of the national governments through various five year plans, starting from 1951, have changed the economic scenario of the country considerably. Agricultural production has risen steadily; the progress of industrialization has increasingly played a role in India's economic development. There are indeed many areas of economic and social development in which India's achievements have been creditable. However, overall success in reducing poverty, ignorance and inequality has been quite limited. A large proportion of population falls short of minimum basic needs. At the same time, the enormous size of the country, its cultural, ethnic and religious traditions, social backwardness, its paucity of communication, the variety of climate, geographical and socio-economic activities, make nation-wide solutions incomparably difficult to implement.

Various factors, such as the level of literacy, infant mortality, political commitments, etc. and their corresponding interactions contribute to these striking variations among states in the livelihood of common people. Here, state level indicators are of prime importance as the state is an accepted political unit. A wide range of relevant fields of actions, including health and education are constitutionally defined as "state subjects", to be handled by the individual states rather than the central government, or as "concurrent subjects", involving both state and central government. This provides a strong motivation for studying the variability of inter-state development and thereby identifying the indicators responsible for existing diversity in development. In this context, any state level policy action on the issues relating to human life necessarily depends on the proper measurement of development process and the suitability of the choice of the indicators affecting development. In this paper we have focused on the derivation of a composite index of developmental process and thereby studying the variability existing among major Indian states.

The paper is organized as follows: the second section is devoted to the selection and sources of variables and the limitations of the data. The methodology for similarity matrix is briefly discussed in this section, followed by the analysis of the findings in the third section. The similarity/dissimilarity of the progress of development among states have also been discussed in sub-section, presenting various charts to give an instant impression. The final section concludes with some policy implications.

2. DATA SOURCE AND METHODOLOGY

Our analysis concentrates on 25 states and 1 union territory. We have left newly created/recently bifurcated states and the Union Territories except Delhi as for them data for 1991 for most of the variables were not available creating difficulties in comparative analysis, or having negligible value.

We have identified and collected data on 18 variables in 5 different categories for 25 States and 1 Union Territory.

Then we prepare similarity matrices (Cooper and Weekes, 1988, pp. 299-303) for each of the five indicators for both the years (1991 and 2001). A composite index of development is constructed using variables which denote following mentioned 5 indicators of development chosen here for our purpose:

(a) Economic indicator.
(b) Demographic indicator.
(c) Educational indicator.
(d) Infrastructural indicator.
(e) Health indicator.

VARIABLES CHOSEN AS ECONOMIC INDICATOR

(1) Per-capita State Net Domestic Product (PCSNDP)
(2) Percentage of Labourers in Household industry (LBHSIND)
(3) Work Participation Rate (WRKPRT)
(4) Cultivators and Labourers per 100 hectare of sown area (AGLBR)
(5) Gross irrigated area as percentage of net area sown (IRRIGN)
(6) Land under Multicropping (LNDMLCR)
(7) Percentage of immigrant (IMGRNT)

Of the variables available for measuring economic progress, per-capita state-level NDP is the most widely accepted and commonly available indicator. Data for these are taken from statistical abstract-2004. Using this single variable, a particular ranking of state can be created which can be compared with ranking of the basis of composite indexation. Another important indicator for economic development is the employment situation, which has been represented by LBHSIND, WRKPRT and AGLBR. It is an indicator of the ability of the economy to create and cater jobs. These particular variables are not only an index of the overall economic development but also serve as a crucial link between social and demographic determinants. Percentage of immigrants in search of jobs and multi-cropped area and more irrigated land are generally features of developed states, which also signify level of economic development of state and can work as economic indicators.

VARIABLES CHOSEN AS DEMOGRAPHIC INDICATOR

1. Sex ratio (SEXRTO)
2. Population Density (POPDEN)
3. Percentage of Urban Population (POPURBN)
4. Percentage of SC and ST of the total Population (SC/ST)
5. Percentage of Religious Minorities (MINORT)
6. Percentage of Increase in Population (POPGRTH)

At one side, where Population Density gives an idea about the portion which is actually inhabitable (particularly climate, civic facilities), sex ratio gives an idea of gender bias. The other three variables (POPURBN, SC/ST, and MINORT) signify demographic transition during a period and composition of population.

VARIABLES CHOSEN AS EDUCATION INDICATOR

1. Crude Literacy Rate (LITRCY).

Education is one of the principle attributes of the quality of a population. It plays an important link between social and economic development processes. For this component, the general indicator is one which is cumulative and measures the proportion of the population with certain characteristics relating to educational attainment, such as the percentage of literate population, which is here denoted by (LITRCY)

VARIABLES CHOSEN AS INFRASTRUCTURAL INDICATOR

1. Kilometers of surfaced roads (KMSRFRD).
2. Consumption of electricity (CSMELC).

This indicator tries to encompass the extensiveness of

communication and infrastructure. The role of this indicator is to evaluate the degree of percolation throughout the community of those goods and services, which particularly relate to communication network, of this, the most important variable is KMSRFRD. Other than this, one major component of daily amenities is household electricity, which serves as the indicator of infrastructure in an economy. It may be mentioned that availability of these two infrastructure facilities is mainly dependent on the public (government) actions and political commitments.

VARIABLES CHOSEN AS HEALTH INDICATOR

1. Infant mortality rate (INFMR)
2. Number of hospital beds (HSPBED)

One vital component of human development is the access and availability of primary health service. Decline in infant mortality is directly related to the level of existing health standard. Indicator for the availability of health services related to the number of hospital beds. Accordingly, hospital beds per lakh population are taken as an indicator of health service facilities specifically characterizing the level of infrastructure and accommodation facilities of health available in state.

It is worthwhile to mention specifically data on all 18 variables corresponds to 1990-91 and 2000-01, except for consumption of electricity which is available for 2003-04 and number of hospital beds which is for 2002. Corresponding to 90s, INFMR corresponds to 1980-81, LNDMLCR—for 1993-94, consumption of electricity CSMELC 1994-95, KMSRFRD for 1992-93.

METHODOLOGY

To derive a composite index from a set of variables, a wide variety of multivariate techniques are available. Actually the choice of the most appropriate method depends upon the type of the problem, the nature of the data and the objective of analysis. One such simple technique which we have applied to our analysis is ranking through similarity matrix.

It is very closely related to the concept of distance. If the distance between two individuals (objects) or variables is relatively large they may be said to be dissimilar and this suggests that we may define a measure with respect to two individuals which is similar and small if they are dissimilar or distant. Such a measure is called similarity coefficient. The similarity matrix consist of these coefficients measure pair-wise similarity of objects, the greater the similarity of two objects, the greater the value of the measure. To be more precise, a similarity coefficient is a number whose value lies between 0 and 1 with the upper limit implying that the two variables are identical in terms of the respective values of the data variables. To facilitate visual inspection, similarity coefficients may also be expressed in percentage terms, thereby giving perfect similarity value of 100. In our analysis, this same concept has been applied with respect to 26 states (which include one union territory) and 18 variables.

To start with the numerical case, our 26 states (by 2001, Delhi has become a state from UT) and 18 variables constitutes the basic data set divided into 5 different categories as mentioned earlier. We have worked upon all 5 indicators separately for all the 26 states, in both the years, 1991 and 2001, i.e. in all we have 10 similarity matrixes. Here, we will elabourate procedure for one indicator and similar procedure follows for other too.

Economic indicator set consists of 7 variables. We combine data regarding them in a single worksheet. Range of each variable over 26 states has been calculated separately using formula (max. value of a variable over 26 states—min. value of a variable over 26 states).

We divide each variable by this range calculated, to standardize them. This process of standardization make the variables comparable across states, i.e. if we compare two states like West Bengal and Goa, size of these two states differ enormously, so the values of the variables cannot be compared as such; but when we standardize them, we are actually making them comparable. This standardization has been done for all 7 variables in this group.

Proceeding from here, absolute difference for the variables among any two states has been calculated. Summing the differences over variables and dividing by number of variables (7 in this case) and finally, subtracting this from 1 gives similarity, which has been expressed in percentage term by multiplying this value with 100. Dimension of this matrix is 26×26, where each coefficient measures similarity between any two states, e.g. Andhra-Arunachal, Andhra-Bihar and so on. To be also noticed here, that all diagonal element will be 100, as they measure similarity of a state with itself, i.e. (Andhra-Andhra), (Kerala-Kerala), etc. which logically give a 100 per cent result, and statistically we have found so in our case. Similar procedure follows for data regarding 2001 also. This completes our similarity matrix for the economic indicators.

Calculations on similar footsteps have been done for other four indicators with difference in number of incorporated variables, e.g. the demographic indicator contains 6, educational indicator incorporates 1, infrastructure and health indicator encompass 2 variables each.

Thus the formula for the Similarity Coefficient is as follows:

[1–{sum (ABS difference between 2 states for all the variables)}/No. of variables]*100

After forming the similarity matrix, the question of comparison can be resolved with the help of the similarity coefficients obtained. We also divide the 18 variables used into 5 groups of indicators as mentioned before.

Here we find a state which is a base for each indicator group and find the similarity coefficients of all the states with respect to base. To answer the question of which base is suitable, one method which we followed, was to look for a state which dominates in each indicator group. To illustrate further on this, we find among the set of variables in economic indicator, Delhi performs the best in 4 out of 7 variables in 1991. This gives a signal that Delhi can be taken as a base in economic indicator group, with respect to which similarity coefficients of all the states can be seen from the similarity matrix prepared.

Coming on to the demographic indicator set, we see, Delhi again dominates in 3 out of 6 variables, therefore again qualifying Delhi to work as a base.

In terms of education indicator, Kerala is the best as well as the consistent performer in both years 1991 and 2001. Therefore in this case, base changes to Kerala and similarity coefficients are now seen on the basis of Kerala.

Having a quick look on infrastructural and health indicator we find Maharashtra ranks 1 in both infrastructural indicator and health indicator and hence similarity is to be find with respect to Maharashtra as base for both the year.

We have considered four clusters of coefficient values; (0-25), (25-50), (50-75), (75-100). Now the states have been bunched according to their coefficient values in these clusters. This is done for both 1991 and 2001. Then we interpret the changes, if any of their coefficients over the decade. Thus we consider the inter-cluster as well as intra-cluster changes in our analysis.

Then we classify the states for each group of indicators into these 4 ranges as per their values for both the years 1991 and 2001. After that, we see the change in the similarity coefficients for all the states for each group of indicators and see whether they move from 1 cluster to another or whether their values change significantly and they remain in the same cluster. We analyze the causes for such changes. The analysis is done on the basis of our observations and considering the variables for each group of indicators.

3. AN ANALYSIS OF THE EMPIRICAL FINDINGS

In this section, we first show the similarity matrices and then proceed to analyse the findings.

As per economic indicator is concerned, Delhi is the best performer. First we consider the inter-clustural changes. There is only one state which moves from (25-50) to (50-75) registering a marginal increase in the similarity coefficients of 3 per cent. This is Meghalaya, for which all the economic variables have improved at a faster rate than that of Delhi. Therefore, similarity has increased. Ten states have moved from the cluster (50-75) to (25-50). Among these, Punjab stands out with a fall in the coefficient by 20 per cent. The reason behind this can be traced from the drastic rise in gross irrigated area as percentage of gross area sown by (16.35%)

and land under multi-cropping. In comparison to Delhi these changes have been larger. Therefore, the coefficient might have fallen.

Maharashtra is another state whose coefficient fell by 13 per cent. However, all the variables show an improving trend, even if not very significant. This fall in coefficient is plausibly explained by some external factors such as the 1993 Bombay blast; which had totally disrupted the economic activities in the region. Many business houses shifted base from Maharashtra after this and these attributed to growing dissimilarity with respect to Delhi. The 6 states of Assam, Gujarat, Himachal Pradesh, Jammu & Kashmir, Karnataka and Sikkim register a fall in the coefficient ranging from 10-12 per cent.

In case of Assam, gross irrigated area as percentage of gross area sown falls by 8 per cent, which can be traced as the only reason for this fall. For Gujarat, the fall can be attributed to the decrease in land under multicropping. Coming to Himachal Pradesh, we find insignificant changes in cultivators and labourers per 100 hectare of sown area and percentage increase in population and a fall in Land under multicropping over the decade. Thereby dissimilarity with Delhi increased. For Jammu & Kashmir, Work Participation Rate had failed to improve, also, a number of external factors ranging from small internal conflicts to the Kargil war in 1999 created confusion in the state's economy. This led to a fall in the coefficients. Karnataka registers an improvement in all seven variables but the rate of improvement is slower than that of Delhi. Therefore, this results in a fall in coefficient. In case of Sikkim, percentage of labourers in household industry and land under multi-cropping both decrease, while other variables show marginal improvement causing a fall in the similarity coefficients.

Now coming to the intra-clustural changes, we find that in cluster (25-50), we have four states which register a significant fall in the coefficient. Madhya Pradesh shows a 7 per cent fall in the coefficient. Three variables, land under multi-cropping, percentage of immigrants and percentage of labourers in household industry experience a fall over the decade, among which the fall in land under multi cropping is

TABLE 1

Similarity Matrix for Economic Indicators (1991)

States	*A. Pr.*	*Ar. Pr.*	*Assam*	*Bihar*	*Goa*	*Gujarat*	*Haryana*	*HP*	*J&K*	*Karnataka*	*Kerala*	*MP*	*Maharashtra*	*Manipur*	*Meghalaya*	*Mizoram*	*Nagaland*	*Orissa*	*Punjab*	*Rajasthan*	*Sikkim*	*Tamil Nadu*	*Tripura*	*UP*	*WB*	Delhi
1	*2*	*3*	*4*	*5*	*6*	*7*	*8*	*9*	*10*	*11*	*12*	*13*	*14*	*15*	*16*	*17*	*18*	*19*	*20*	*21*	*22*	*23*	*24*	*25*	*26*	*27*
A. Pr.	100																									
Ar. Pr.	73	100																								
Assam	74	77	100																							
Bihar	74	55	78	100																						
Goa	51	71	73	58	100																					
Gujarat	72	73	88	70	80	100																				
Haryana	55	57	71	74	78	79	100																			
HP	76	80	89	75	77	89	69	100																		
J&K	81	77	86	76	77	84	72	90	100																	
Karnataka	82	77	95	71	76	91	73	86	86	100																
Kerala	73	77	89	74	75	83	72	94	82	82	100															
MP	77	64	73	66	68	80	87	74	76	87	73	100														
Maharashtra	75	71	75	64	74	85	76	77	75	88	72	84	100													

(Contd.)

TABLE 1 (*Contd.*)

1	2	3	4	5	6	7	8	9	10	11	12	13	14	15	16	17	18	19	20	21	22	23	24	25	26	27
Manipur	73	58	53	69	54	59	47	69	74	66	62	58	54	100												
Meghalaya	78	84	81	70	67	77	57	87	81	81	74	69	72	74	100											
Mizoram	76	82	79	70	63	73	53	84	77	78	74	65	70	74	92	100										
Nagaland	81	87	78	66	69	78	62	85	84	79	71	68	73	69	91	87	100									
Orissa	79	59	80	78	70	79	70	75	78	81	80	84	78	63	66	62	55	100								
Punjab	59	49	67	68	68	74	88	63	66	67	64	67	76	42	52	48	57	70	100							
Rajasthan	74	64	85	75	77	87	78	80	79	87	83	85	83	55	69	66	67	87	76	100						
Sikkim	74	88	82	60	76	84	66	85	83	87	78	74	82	64	88	85	87	69	59	75	100					
Tamil Nadu	90	70	74	75	63	74	64	79	81	80	74	71	71	80	82	78	82	73	58	68	75	100				
Tripura	71	75	92	73	84	83	70	90	85	80	90	69	71	66	81	80	77	76	63	80	81	71	100			
UP	76	60	83	85	66	75	79	77	82	75	82	68	63	67	68	64	68	78	74	76	65	77	83	100		
WB	82	61	81	79	66	75	70	80	77	77	82	78	74	66	69	65	69	87	69	85	66	78	79	79	100	
Delhi	43	51	56	48	70	59	68	57	61	51	53	41	51	38	48	43	53	47	69	51	56	47	58	60	46	100

TABLE 2

Similarity Matrix for Economic Indicators (2001)

States	A. Pr.	Ar. Pr.	Assam	Bihar	Goa	Gujarat	Haryana	HP	J&K	Karnataka	Kerala	MP	Maharashtra	Manipur	Meghalaya	Mizoram	Nagaland	Orissa	Punjab	Rajasthan	Sikkim	Tamil Nadu	Tripura	UP	WB	Delhi
1	2	3	4	5	6	7	8	9	10	11	12	13	14	15	16	17	18	19	20	21	22	23	24	25	26	27
A. Pr.	100																									
Ar. Pr.	71	100																								
Assam	75	77	100																							
Bihar	81	62	81	100																						
Goa	59	77	69	56	100																					
Gujarat	80	83	83	73	75	100																				
Haryana	74	68	69	72	69	78	100																			
HP	74	84	75	65	69	84	64	100																		
J&K	72	71	81	82	65	76	65	73	100																	
Karnataka	89	79	81	75	68	87	73	80	77	100																
Kerala	70	78	87	77	69	83	66	81	79	76	100															
MP	80	79	82	76	66	88	75	76	70	85	75	100														
Maharashtra	75	74	74	68	69	83	79	73	62	82	71	88	100													

(Contd.)

TABLE 2 *(Contd.)*

1	2	3	4	5	6	7	8	9	10	11	12	13	14	15	16	17	18	19	20	21	22	23	24	25	26	27
Manipur	77	69	70	71	60	72	57	73	88	73	69	66	58	100												
Meghalaya	76	87	82	75	74	89	68	88	84	80	84	83	74	82	100											
Mizoram	75	80	76	66	61	83	63	90	68	81	79	78	73	65	82	100										
Nagaland	78	90	82	69	77	92	70	88	79	83	84	84	78	77	95	83	100									
Orissa	78	71	85	87	66	83	74	69	85	88	75	83	74	78	79	71	78	100								
Punjab	69	55	64	70	60	70	87	55	63	68	60	71	80	52	60	55	62	70	100							
Rajasthan	84	72	80	81	65	86	77	70	75	84	70	93	86	71	80	72	79	86	78	100						
Sikkim	73	92	77	61	74	83	66	90	70	80	78	78	74	68	86	85	90	71	56	72	100					
Tamil Nadu	88	70	72	75	60	80	70	76	87	83	74	70	67	82	78	73	78	80	65	74	71	100				
Tripura	73	85	91	77	75	83	67	82	85	78	90	78	73	76	90	77	89	80	62	76	84	73	100			
UP	78	60	79	84	54	71	70	59	86	73	74	67	59	75	69	61	67	83	68	72	59	82	74	100		
WB	83	58	72	82	53	70	68	61	84	75	69	75	73	78	69	63	67	81	73	81	58	79	71	78	100	
Delhi	39	48	45	48	62	46	55	47	51	39	52	34	38	47	51	38	49	41	48	39	44	47	51	52	39	100

TABLE 3

Similarity Matrix for Demographic Indicators (1991)

States	A. Pr.	Ar. Pr.	Assam	Bihar	Goa	Gujarat	Haryana	HP	J&K	Karnataka	Kerala	MP	Maharashtra	Manipur	Meghalaya	Mizoram	Nagaland	Orissa	Punjab	Rajasthan	Sikkim	Tamil Nadu	Tripura	UP	WB	Delhi
1	2	3	4	5	6	7	8	9	10	11	12	13	14	15	16	17	18	19	20	21	22	23	24	25	26	27
A. Pr.	100																									
Ar. Pr.	65	100																								
Assam	85	79	100																							
Bihar	69	74	92	100																						
Goa	84	69	85	89	100																					
Gujarat	93	67	88	89	86	100																				
Haryana	89	74	83	89	74	87	100																			
HP	91	62	82	86	77	86	82	100																		
J&K	88	75	88	90	79	87	89	83	100																	
Karnataka	96	65	85	90	87	94	87	89	88	100																
Kerala	79	65	79	75	86	76	69	73	74	80	100															
MP	93	70	87	91	78	93	92	88	92	91	73	100														
Maharashtra	91	69	88	91	87	94	87	81	91	92	76	92	100													

(Contd.)

TABLE 3 (*Contd.*)

1	2	3	4	5	6	7	8	9	10	11	12	13	14	15	16	17	18	19	20	21	22	23	24	25	26	27
Manipur	84	74	84	79	83	79	79	79	87	84	81	82	83	100												
Meghalaya	75	65	78	71	74	70	71	70	81	75	69	74	74	87	100											
Mizoram	70	57	65	70	63	72	71	65	77	72	52	73	75	70	83	100										
Nagaland	77	73	76	81	64	77	83	72	81	76	58	81	77	69	64	70	100									
Orissa	94	65	84	89	81	89	84	96	84	92	76	91	85	78	70	65	75	100								
Punjab	81	75	86	85	84	83	86	77	85	84	79	81	83	87	77	67	72	77	100							
Rajasthan	90	74	85	91	75	89	96	84	92	88	70	94	89	81	72	73	86	86	85	100						
Sikkim	70	85	93	88	79	81	86	78	87	79	72	83	83	81	73	64	80	79	88	88	100					
Tamil Nadu	94	59	79	85	87	92	84	88	88	94	81	87	88	79	70	68	71	91	80	85	73	100				
Tripura	90	74	86	91	77	87	87	86	91	90	72	92	88	82	77	75	85	89	77	91	83	85	100			
UP	87	75	87	94	76	86	94	82	91	87	72	89	89	80	72	70	83	84	89	94	89	83	88	100		
WB	88	71	90	92	82	87	88	82	93	89	79	89	91	86	78	72	76	82	90	89	85	85	85	92	100	
Delhi	46	43	43	50	40	48	57	38	52	48	32	48	53	41	35	48	60	40	48	54	47	45	51	55	51	100

TABLE 4

Similarity Matrix for Demographic Indicators (2001)

States	*A. Pr.*	*Ar. Pr.*	*Assam*	*Bihar*	*Goa*	*Gujarat*	*Haryana*	*HP*	*J&K*	*Karnataka*	*Kerala*	*MP*	*Maharashtra*	*Manipur*	*Meghalaya*	*Mizoram*	*Nagaland*	*Orissa*	*Punjab*	*Rajasthan*	*Sikkim*	*Tamil Nadu*	*Tripura*	*UP*	*WB*	*Delhi*
1	*2*	*3*	*4*	*5*	*6*	*7*	*8*	*9*	*10*	*11*	*12*	*13*	*14*	*15*	*16*	*17*	*18*	*19*	*20*	*21*	*22*	*23*	*24*	*25*	*26*	*27*
A. Pr.	100																									
Ar. Pr.	71	100																								
Assam	82	84	100																							
Bihar	84	79	87	100																						
Goa	81	74	86	75	100																					
Gujarat	91	75	82	88	78	100																				
Haryana	86	77	79	89	72	90	100																			
HP	91	71	82	85	73	86	80	100																		
J&K	79	90	90	86	82	83	87	74	100																	
Karnataka	95	74	85	87	85	92	86	89	81	100																
Kerala	76	67	80	70	80	67	65	67	75	75	100															
MP	90	80	81	87	74	95	89	89	82	88	66	100														
Maharashtra	86	78	86	89	84	94	88	80	86	92	71	89	100													

(Contd.)

TABLE 4 (*Contd.*)

1	*2*	*3*	*4*	*5*	*6*	*7*	*8*	*9*	*10*	*11*	*12*	*13*	*14*	*15*	*16*	*17*	*18*	*19*	*20*	*21*	*22*	*23*	*24*	*25*	*26*	*27*
Manipur	90	82	83	86	79	86	83	87	84	91	73	90	88	100												
Meghalaya	74	87	78	74	71	70	70	73	79	75	65	75	73	84	100											
Mizoram	74	77	66	73	68	80	76	71	70	77	52	80	79	78	83	100										
Nagaland	65	73	60	69	48	69	70	66	65	63	41	74	64	68	76	78	100									
Orissa	92	73	80	82	73	85	79	96	73	88	68	90	80	89	76	73	69	100								
Punjab	85	74	76	82	72	91	90	87	79	86	62	91	85	81	65	73	67	85	100							
Rajasthan	89	81	82	91	73	93	92	88	86	88	66	95	89	90	77	81	75	87	88	100						
Sikkim	72	86	88	83	74	75	81	74	91	74	71	76	78	78	76	64	64	71	75	81	100					
Tamil Nadu	94	66	78	80	83	89	83	85	74	92	75	84	88	84	68	75	59	85	82	84	66	100				
Tripura	89	81	84	85	76	85	81	89	77	90	69	89	84	89	80	79	73	92	82	88	74	84	100			
UP	85	84	86	0\94	77	89	91	82	90	88	71	89	92	89	76	74	70	81	86	91	84	81	85	100		
WB	87	82	91	86	84	86	83	83	87	90	78	87	89	88	79	73	62	82	83	87	81	82	86	89	100	
Delhi	46	42	44	55	47	54	60	40	53	51	32	49	58	48	36	45	41	39	52	52	49	49	43	57	49	100

TABLE 5

Similarity Matrix for Educational Indicators (1991)

Statesw	A. Pr.	Ar. Pr.	Assam	Bihar	Goa	Gujarat	Haryana	HP	J&K	Karnataka	Kerala	MP	Maharashtra	Manipur	Meghalaya	Mizoram	Nagaland	Orissa	Punjab	Rajasthan	Sikkim	Tamil Nadu	Tripura	UP	WB	Delhi
1	2	3	4	5	6	7	8	9	10	11	12	13	14	15	16	17	18	19	20	21	22	23	24	25	26	27
A. Pr.	100																									
Ar. Pr.	96	100																								
Assam	86	82	100																							
Bihar	91	95	77	100																						
Goa	50	46	64	41	100																					
Gujarat	73	69	87	64	78	100																				
Haryana	81	78	95	73	69	91	100																			
HP	69	65	83	60	82	96	87	100																		
J&K	72	76	58	81	23	45	54	41	100																	
Karnataka	81	77	95	72	69	92	100	87	54	100																
Kerala	28	24	42	19	77	55	46	59	0	46	100															
MP	100	96	86	91	50	73	82	69	72	81	28	100														
Maharashtra	67	63	81	58	83	94	86	98	39	86	61	67	100													

(Contd.)

TABLE 5 (*Contd.*)

1	*2*	*3*	*4*	*5*	*6*	*7*	*8*	*9*	*10*	*11*	*12*	*13*	*14*	*15*	*16*	*17*	*18*	*19*	*20*	*21*	*22*	*23*	*24*	*25*	*26*	*27*
Manipur	75	71	89	66	75	98	94	94	47	94	53	75	92	100												
Meghalaya	92	88	94	83	58	81	89	77	64	89	36	92	75	83	100											
Mizoram	39	36	53	31	89	87	58	71	12	58	88	40	72	65	47	100										
Nagaland	72	68	86	63	78	100	91	96	45	91	55	72	95	97	80	67	100									
Orissa	92	88	94	83	58	81	89	77	64	89	36	92	75	83	100	47	80	100								
Punjab	77	73	91	68	73	95	96	91	50	96	50	77	90	98	85	62	95	85	100							
Rajasthan	91	95	77	100	42	64	73	60	81	72	19	91	58	66	83	31	64	83	68	100						
Sikkim	80	76	94	71	71	93	98	89	52	99	48	80	87	95	88	60	93	88	97	91	100					
Tamil Nadu	71	67	84	82	80	98	89	98	43	89	57	71	97	96	78	69	98	78	93	62	91	100				
Tripura	74	70	88	65	76	99	93	94	47	93	53	74	93	99	82	65	98	82	97	85	94	96	100			
UP	96	100	82	95	46	69	78	65	76	77	24	96	63	71	88	36	68	88	73	95	76	87	70	100		
WB	78	74	92	70	72	94	97	90	51	97	49	79	89	97	86	61	94	86	99	70	99	92	96	74	100	
Delhi	51	47	65	42	199	78	69	82	23	69	77	51	84	76	58	89	78	58	73	42	71	80	76	47	72	100

TABLE 6

Similarity Matrix for Educational Indicators (2001)

States	*A. Pr.*	*Ar. Pr.*	*Assam*	*Bihar*	*Goa*	*Gujarat*	*Haryana*	*HP*	*J&K*	*Karnataka*	*Kerala*	*MP*	*Maharashtra*	*Manipur*	*Meghalaya*	*Mizoram*	*Nagaland*	*Orissa*	*Punjab*	*Rajasthan*	*Sikkim*	*Tamil Nadu*	*Tripura*	*UP*	*WB*	Delhi
1	*2*	*3*	*4*	*5*	*6*	*7*	*8*	*9*	*10*	*11*	*12*	*13*	*14*	*15*	*16*	*17*	*18*	*19*	*20*	*21*	*22*	*23*	*24*	*25*	*26*	*27*
A. Pr.	100																									
Ar. Pr.	85	100																								
Assam	93	78	100																							
Bihar	69	83	61	100																						
Goa	51	36	58	20	100																					
Gujarat	80	65	87	48	72	100																				
Haryana	83	68	90	51	68	97	100																			
HP	63	48	70	32	88	83	80	100																		
J&K	85	99	77	84	36	64	67	48	100																	
Karnataka	86	72	94	55	65	93	96	77	71	100																
Kerala	31	17	39	0	80	52	49	68	16	45	100															
MP	93	78	100	62	58	86	90	70	78	93	38	100														
Maharashtra	63	48	70	31	88	83	80	100	47	76	69	70	100													

(Contd.)

TABLE 6 (*Contd.*)

1	2	3	4	5	6	7	8	9	10	11	12	13	14	15	16	17	18	19	20	21	22	23	24	25	26	27
Manipur	82	67	89	51	69	97	99	81	67	96	49	89	81	100												
Meghalaya	95	80	98	64	56	85	88	68	80	91	36	98	68	87	100											
Mizoram	37	22	44	6	86	57	54	74	22	51	94	44	74	55	42	100										
Nagaland	86	71	93	55	65	93	97	77	71	100	45	93	77	96	91	51	100									
Orissa	95	80	98	64	58	85	88	68	80	91	36	98	68	87	100	42	91	100								
Punjab	80	65	87	48	71	100	97	83	64	93	52	87	83	98	85	57	93	85	100							
Rajasthan	100	86	93	69	51	79	83	63	85	86	31	93	63	82	95	37	86	95	79	100						
Sikkim	80	66	88	49	71	99	97	83	65	94	51	87	83	98	85	57	94	85	99	80	100					
Tamil Nadu	72	57	79	40	80	92	89	92	56	85	60	78	91	89	71	65	85	77	92	71	91	100				
Tripura	71	56	78	40	80	91	88	92	56	85	60	78	92	89	76	66	85	76	91	71	91	100	100			
UP	91	94	84	77	42	71	74	54	93	78	23	84	54	73	86	28	78	86	71	92	72	63	62	100		
WB	81	67	89	50	70	98	99	82	66	95	50	88	81	99	86	56	95	86	98	81	99	90	90	73	100	
Delhi	52	38	60	21	99	73	70	89	37	66	79	59	90	70	57	85	66	57	73	52	72	81	81	44	71	100

TABLE 7

Similarity Matrix for Infrastructural Indicators (1991)

States	*A. Pr.*	*Ar. Pr.*	*Assam*	*Bihar*	*Goa*	*Gujarat*	*Haryana*	*HP*	*J&K*	*Karnataka*	*Kerala*	*MP*	*Maharashtra*	*Manipur*	*Meghalaya*	*Mizoram*	*Nagaland*	*Orissa*	*Punjab*	*Rajasthan*	*Sikkim*	*Tamil Nadu*	*Tripura*	*UP*	*WB*	Delhi
1	*2*	*3*	*4*	*5*	*6*	*7*	*8*	*9*	*10*	*11*	*12*	*13*	*14*	*15*	*16*	*17*	*18*	*19*	*20*	*21*	*22*	*23*	*24*	*25*	*26*	*27*
A. Pr.	100																									
Ar. Pr.	43	100																								
Assam	46	97	100																							
Bihar	63	80	83	100																						
Goa	43	99	97	80	100																					
Gujarat	99	44	47	64	44	100																				
Haryana	58	85	88	95	85	59	100																			
HP	47	96	98	84	96	48	89	100																		
J&K	45	98	99	82	98	46	87	98	100																	
Karnataka	88	55	58	75	55	89	70	59	57	100																
Kerala	62	81	84	95	82	63	95	85	84	74	100															
MP	83	34	38	54	35	83	49	38	37	79	53	100														
Maharashtra	58	1	5	21	2	57	17	6	4	46	20	67	100													

(*Contd.*)

TABLE 7 (*Contd.*)

1	2	3	4	5	6	7	8	9	10	11	12	13	14	15	16	17	18	19	20	21	22	23	24	25	26	27
Manipur	42	99	96	79	99	43	84	95	97	54	81	34	1	100												
Meghalaya	43	99	96	79	99	43	84	95	97	54	81	34	1	100	100											
Mizoram	42	99	96	79	99	43	84	95	97	54	80	33	0	100	99	100										
Nagaland	42	99	96	79	99	43	84	95	97	54	81	34	1	100	100	100	100									
Orissa	60	83	86	95	83	61	95	87	85	72	98	51	18	83	83	82	83	100								
Punjab	74	69	72	89	69	75	84	73	71	86	88	65	33	68	68	68	68	86	100							
Rajasthan	78	65	69	85	66	79	81	70	68	90	84	69	36	65	65	64	65	82	87	100						
Sikkim	42	99	95	79	98	43	83	94	96	54	80	33	0	99	99	100	99	82	67	84	100					
Tamil Nadu	87	30	33	50	30	86	45	34	32	75	49	96	71	29	29	29	29	47	61	65	29	100				
Tripura	43	99	97	80	99	44	85	96	97	55	81	34	1	100	100	99	199	83	69	65	99	30	100			
UP	97	40	43	60	40	96	55	44	42	85	59	82	62	39	39	39	39	57	71	75	39	85	40	100		
WB	63	80	83	95	80	64	95	84	82	75	90	54	22	79	79	79	79	90	89	86	78	50	80	60	100	
Delhi	42	98	95	79	98	43	83	94	96	54	80	33	0	99	99	99	99	82	68	64	100	29	99	39	79	100

TABLE 8

Similarity Matrix for Infrastructural Indicators (2001)

States	A. Pr.	Ar. Pr.	Assam	Bihar	Goa	Gujarat	Haryana	HP	J&K	Karnataka	Kerala	MP	Maharashtra	Manipur	Meghalaya	Mizoram	Nagaland	Orissa	Punjab	Rajasthan	Sikkim	Tamil Nadu	Tripura	UP	WB	Delhi
1	2	3	4	5	6	7	8	9	10	11	12	13	14	15	16	17	18	19	20	21	22	23	24	25	26	27
A. Pr.	100																									
Ar. Pr.	38	100																								
Assam	42	96	100																							
Bihar	49	90	93	100																						
Goa	40	99	99	91	100																					
Gujarat	95	33	37	44	35	100																				
Haryana	56	82	86	89	84	51	100																			
HP	44	95	98	95	96	39	88	100																		
J&K	43	96	98	94	97	38	87	97	100																	
Karnataka	86	52	56	63	54	81	70	58	57	100																
Kerala	58	81	84	91	82	53	91	86	85	72	100															
MP	72	66	70	77	68	67	84	71	70	86	85	100														
Maharashtra	63	1	5	12	3	68	19	6	5	49	20	35	100													

(Contd.)

TABLE 8 (*Contd.*)

1	2	3	4	5	6	7	8	9	10	11	12	13	14	15	16	17	18	19	20	21	22	23	24	25	26	27
Manipur	38	99	96	89	98	33	82	94	95	52	80	66	1	100												
Meghalaya	39	99	97	90	99	34	83	95	96	53	81	67	2	99	100											
Mizoram	38	99	96	89	98	33	82	94	95	51	80	65	0	100	98	100										
Nagaland	38	100	97	90	99	34	83	95	96	52	81	66	1	99	99	99	100									
Orissa	57	82	85	92	83	52	88	87	86	71	97	84	19	81	82	81	82	100								
Punjab	71	67	70	77	68	67	84	72	71	85	86	87	34	66	68	66	67	85	100							
Rajasthan	74	64	68	75	66	69	82	70	69	88	84	96	37	64	65	64	65	83	83	100						
Sikkim	37	99	95	89	98	32	81	94	95	41	80	65	0	99	98	100	99	81	66	63	100					
Tamil Nadu	95	33	37	44	35	98	51	39	38	81	53	67	68	33	34	32	33	52	66	69	32	100				
Tripura	38	99	96	89	98	33	82	95	96	52	81	66	1	100	99	99	99	82	67	64	99	33	100			
UP	83	36	39	46	37	81	53	41	40	84	55	70	65	35	37	35	36	54	69	71	35	78	36	100		
WB	66	72	76	83	73	61	90	77	76	80	91	90	29	72	73	71	72	89	95	86	71	61	72	64	100	
Delhi	44	95	96	95	95	39	88	97	94	57	85	71	6	94	96	94	96	87	72	70	94	38	95	41	77	100

TABLE 9

Similarity Matrix for Health Indicators (1991)

States	*A. Pr.*	*Ar. Pr.*	*Assam*	*Bihar*	*Goa*	*Gujarat*	*Haryana*	*HP*	*J&K*	*Karnataka*	*Kerala*	*MP*	*Maharashtra*	*Manipur*	*Meghalaya*	*Mizoram*	*Nagaland*	*Orissa*	*Punjab*	*Rajasthan*	*Sikkim*	*Tamil Nadu*	*Tripura*	*UP*	*WB*	*Delhi*
1	*2*	*3*	*4*	*5*	*6*	*7*	*8*	*9*	*10*	*11*	*12*	*13*	*14*	*15*	*16*	*17*	*18*	*19*	*20*	*21*	*22*	*23*	*24*	*25*	*26*	*27*
A. Pr.	100																									
Ar. Pr.	70	100																								
Assam	74	95	100																							
Bihar	89	80	85	100																						
Goa	85	80	76	77	100																					
Gujarat	81	72	77	89	66	100																				
Haryana	88	78	79	80	97	69	100																			
HP	76	94	93	87	84	79	85	100																		
J&K	81	89	88	89	88	78	90	85	100																	
Karnataka	90	77	81	97	75	91	78	84	87	100																
Kerala	81	51	55	70	70	78	72	57	62	73	100															
MP	58	71	76	69	53	61	56	69	65	66	39	100														
Maharashtra	55	42	46	62	40	70	43	49	52	65	61	31	100													

(Contd.)

TABLE 9 (*Contd.*)

1	2	3	4	5	6	7	8	9	10	11	12	13	14	15	16	17	18	19	20	21	22	23	24	25	26	27
Manipur	74	70	65	66	88	55	86	72	77	63	67	41	28	100												
Meghalaya	75	95	90	86	86	78	84	97	94	82	56	66	47	75	100											
Mizoram	86	82	77	78	98	67	97	84	88	75	69	53	40	88	87	100										
Nagaland	85	81	76	77	99	66	97	83	88	74	70	52	39	89	86	99	100									
Orissa	58	79	84	69	61	61	64	77	73	66	39	92	31	49	74	61	60	100								
Punjab	85	85	89	95	82	84	85	91	94	93	66	71	58	71	90	83	82	73	100							
Rajasthan	82	87	92	93	73	85	76	89	85	90	63	76	55	61	86	73	72	76	90	100						
Sikkim	84	85	80	81	95	70	93	87	91	78	65	56	43	84	90	96	95	64	86	76	100					
Tamil Nadu	93	63	67	82	80	87	82	69	74	85	88	51	60	68	68	80	79	51	78	75	77	100				
Tripura	74	96	91	85	85	77	83	98	93	82	55	67	47	74	99	86	85	75	89	87	89	67	100			
UP	71	75	80	79	56	90	59	72	68	81	69	71	60	45	69	56	55	71	74	83	59	77	70	100		
WB	89	85	69	84	74	92	77	71	76	88	88	54	66	62	70	74	73	53	80	77	77	95	69	82	100	
Delhi	93	76	80	84	93	74	96	82	87	82	75	60	47	81	81	93	92	65	89	80	90	87	80	63	81	100

TABLE 10

Similarity Matrix for Health Indicators (2001)

States	*A. Pr.*	*Ar. Pr.*	*Assam*	*Bihar*	*Goa*	*Gujarat*	*Haryana*	*HP*	*J&K*	*Karnataka*	*Kerala*	*MP*	*Maharashtra*	*Manipur*	*Meghalaya*	*Mizoram*	*Nagaland*	*Orissa*	*Punjab*	*Rajasthan*	*Sikkim*	*Tamil Nadu*	*Tripura*	*UP*	*WB*	*Delhi*
1	*2*	*3*	*4*	*5*	*6*	*7*	*8*	*9*	*10*	*11*	*12*	*13*	*14*	*15*	*16*	*17*	*18*	*19*	*20*	*21*	*22*	*23*	*24*	*25*	*26*	*27*
A. Pr.	100																									
Ar. Pr.	58	100																								
Assam	69	74	100																							
Bihar	87	69	82	100																						
Goa	54	94	70	65	100																					
Gujarat	98	58	67	85	54	100																				
Haryana	73	82	93	85	78	70	100																			
HP	73	85	89	84	81	73	97	100																		
J&K	60	98	76	71	94	60	83	87	100																	
Karnataka	88	70	72	90	66	88	75	78	72	100																
Kerala	56	41	25	43	46	59	29	31	41	54	100															
MP	59	61	86	72	57	57	79	76	62	62	16	100														
Maharashtra	53	32	22	40	28	55	26	28	33	50	57	12	100													

(*Contd.*)

TABLE 10 (*Contd.*)

1	2	3	4	5	6	7	8	9	10	11	12	13	14	15	16	17	18	19	20	21	22	23	24	25	26	27
Manipur	46	88	63	58	93	46	70	73	87	59	52	49	20	100												
Meghalaya	63	95	79	74	89	63	86	90	95	75	36	65	33	84	100											
Mizoram	45	87	61	56	91	45	68	72	85	57	53	47	18	98	82	100										
Nagaland	66	92	82	77	86	66	89	93	91	78	32	68	29	80	96	79	100									
Orissa	57	62	87	70	57	55	80	77	63	60	13	98	10	50	66	48	69	100								
Punjab	74	84	81	85	80	74	84	87	86	86	45	71	41	72	89	71	88	69	100							
Rajasthan	77	60	86	90	56	75	78	75	62	80	33	82	30	48	65	47	68	80	76	100						
Sikkim	62	94	78	74	89	62	86	89	94	74	35	65	32	83	99	82	96	66	88	64	100					
Tamil Nadu	86	72	67	85	68	86	71	73	73	95	58	57	55	60	77	58	74	55	86	75	76	100				
Tripura	61	97	77	72	91	61	84	88	96	73	37	63	34	85	98	84	95	64	87	63	98	74	100			
UP	88	47	73	78	43	85	85	62	49	77	44	72	41	35	52	34	55	70	63	87	51	75	50	100		
WB	90	68	63	81	64	90	67	69	70	91	62	53	59	56	73	55	70	51	82	71	72	96	70	79	100	
Delhi	73	85	78	85	81	73	81	84	86	85	48	68	44	73	88	72	85	66	97	75	88	87	87	62	83	100

TABLE 11

Changes in Similarity Coefficients for Economic Indicators

States	*0-25*	*25-50*	*50-75*	*75-100*
Andhra Pradesh		42.51 (38.80)		
Arunachal Pradesh		(47.73)	51.20	
Assam		(45.06)	55.83	
Bihar		48.10 (48.38)		
Goa		69.79 (62.29)		
Gujarat		(46.30)	58.56	
Haryana		67.76 (54.59)		
Himachal Pradesh		(47.40)	57.44	
Jammu & Kashmir			60.69 (50.85)	
Karnataka		(39.35)	51.31	
Kerala			53.41 (52.19)	
Madhya Pradesh		41.11 (34.09)		
Maharashtra		(37.77)	51.01	
Manipur		37.53 (47.43)		
Meghalaya		47.51	(50.76)	
Mizoram		43.18 (37.70)		
Nagaland		(49.24)	53.11	
Orissa		46.54 (41.41)		
Punjab		(48.33)	68.56	
Rajasthan		(38.62)	50.56	
Sikkim		(43.51)	55.56	
Tamil Nadu		47.27 (47.43)		
Tripura			56.20 (51.40)	
Uttar Pradesh			60.07 (51.76)	
West Bengal		45.38 (38.88)		
Delhi				100(100)

NB: Figures in parenthesis indicate similarity coefficients of 2001 and the rest indicate coefficients of 1991.

by 18, 82,000 hectares. This can be due to the separation of Chhattisgarh from the state; nevertheless they act in favor of decreasing the similarity. Manipur gives an unexpected increase in similarity by 9 per cent which can be explained by the rise in per-capita net domestic product but specific conclusions cannot be drawn. For Mizoram, the coefficient fell by 5 per cent due to the marginal of five variables out of seven. Rajasthan shows an 11 per cent fall in the coefficients in spite of improvement in all variables. This can be explained by saying that Delhi might have improved at a faster rate as compared to Rajasthan. In case of Haryana, the percentage increase in population is at a greater rate than the increase in per-capita state net domestic product at current prices. This might have a deteriorating effect overall, which had tended to increase the states dissimilarity with Delhi. The states of Bihar, Kerala, Tamil Nadu and Uttar Pradesh have performed consistently with no change in their coefficients.

TABLE 12

Changes in Similarity Coefficients for Demographic Indicators

States	*0-25*	*25-50*	*50-75*	*75-100*
Andhra Pradesh		46.43 (45.84)		
Arunachal Pradesh		42.71 (42.48)		
Assam		42.56 (43.96)		
Bihar		49.73 (54.99)		
Goa		40.36 (46.62)		
Gujarat		48.12 (53.73)		
Haryana			56.55 (59.96)	
Himachal Pradesh		38.16 (39.96)		
JammuKashmir			52.01 (52.94)	
Karnataka		48.16 (51.07)		
Kerala		38.51 (31.73)		
Madhya Pradesh		48.44 (48.97)		
Maharashtra		(58.26) 52.58		
Manipur		41.22 (48.03)		
Meghalaya		35.40 (36.02)		
Mizoram		48.22 (45.12)		
Nagaland		(41.24)59.88		
Orissa		40.46 (39.21)		
Punjab		47.76 (52.12)		
Rajasthan			53.71 (51.94)	
Sikkim		46.91 (48.87)		
Tamil Nadu		45.42 (48.94)		
Tripura		(43.19) 51.19		
Uttar Pradesh			54.77 (56.90)	
West Bengal		(49.25) 51.28		
Delhi				100(100)

NB: Figures in parenthesis indicate similarity coefficients of 2001 and the rest indicate coefficients of 1991.

In this case also Delhi performs best. The similarity coefficients with respect to Delhi for this indicator range from 31.51 per cent to 59.96 per cent. It covers two clusters (25-50) and (50-74). The values do not lie in the other two clusters (0-25) and (75-100). Delhi is the base thereby, its coefficients is 100 which is very obvious. Therefore, we can say that initially and over the decade there had been a moderate similarity and the changes had also been moderate except for a few states.

First, we consider the inter-cluster changes. The five states of Bihar, Goa, Gujarat, Karnataka and Punjab have shown an increase in their similarity coefficients ranging from 5 per cent-6 per cent with respect to Delhi. This led to their cluster change from (25-30) to (50-75) over the decade. This phenomenon can be explained by a significant increase in population density for all these states which is similar to Delhi. Also, the sex ratio for these states have either fallen or increased very marginally which is similar to Delhi.

Three states show a decrease in similarity and move from (50-75) to (25-50). They are Tripura, West Bengal and Nagaland. While Tripura shows similar performance with that of Delhi in most of the variables except for percentage of SC/ST which increased significantly over the decade (16% to 48%). This change in composition explains the fall in the coefficient by 8 per cent. For, West Bengal, it's a nominal 2 per cent fall in the coefficient which is considered normal change over the decade. Now, coming to Nagaland its coefficient falls by 19 per cent over the decade. This fall is attributed to the significant growth of Population by 8 per cent. Otherwise all the other variables do not show many dissimilar performances.

Now, we come to states which have maintained their coefficients with respect to Delhi. They are Andhra Pradesh, Arunachal Pradesh, Assam, Haryana, Himachal Pradesh, Kerala, Madhya Pradesh and Orissa. All these states show a significant increase in population density and lower population density growth which is similar to Delhi. Although they show an increase in sex ratio, except for Haryana, the other variables compensate for this dissimilarity and they maintain their positions. The remaining states show

TABLE 13

Changes in Similarity Coefficients for Educational Indicators

States	*0-25*	*25-50*	*50-75*	*75-100*
Andhra Pradesh		27.60 (31.29)		
Arunachal Pradesh	23.64 (16.61)			
Assam		41.54 (38.60)		
Bihar	18.73 (0)			
Goa				77.34 (80.17)
Gujarat			54.85 (51.71)	
Haryana		46.14 (48.53)		
Himachal Pradesh			58.97 (68.21)	
Jammu & Kashmir	0 (15.97)			
Karnataka		46.45 (44.76)		
Kerala				100 (100)
Madhya Pradesh		27.76 (38.21)		
Maharashtra			60.55 (68.54)	
Manipur		(49.18) 52.63		
Meghalaya		35.52 (36.36)		
Mizoram				88.11 (94.39)
Nagaland		(45.12) 55.33		
Orissa		35.52 (36.36)		
Punjab			50.41(51.67)	
Rajasthan	18.89	(31.11)		
Sikkim		47.88 (51.04)		
Tamil Nadu			57.07(59.780)	
Tripura			53.42 (60.22)	
Uttar Pradesh	23.64 (22.65)			
West Bengal		49.15 (49.98)		
Delhi				77.03 (79.02)

NB: Figures in parenthesis indicate similarity coefficients of 2001 and the rest indicate coefficients of 1991.

intra-cluster changes of 2 per cent to 3 per cent which is considered normal over a decade.

Under this indicator, we consider only one variable which is the crude literacy rate. Kerala had been the best performer in both 1991 and 2001; so it forms the base. Hence we find the similarity of the other states with respect to Kerala.

Considering the inter-cluster movement, we have Rajasthan showing considerable improvement as it crosses the boundary from (0-25) to (25-50). Its co-efficient increases by 12 per cent, which can be explained by the increase in literacy from 38.6 per cent to 61.03 per cent. Sikkim has also crossed the same range with an increase in the co-efficient by 4 per cent. The inter-clustural movement is not always unidirectional as we see in the case of both Manipur and Nagaland which moved from the range (50-75) to (25-50).

Manipur deteriorated by 3 per cent and Nagaland by 10 per cent. The conspicuous fall in case of Nagaland can be explained by the fact that there has been a substantial increase in population growth but the increased population has not been aptly educated.

Now we come to the intra-clustural changes. In the range (0-25), Bihar shows a significant fall in the co-efficient by 18 per cent which can be explained in terms of its low per-capita income. Low per-capita income entails low preference for education and therefore the loss in the similarity. Jammu & Kashmir registers a 15 per cent increase in the co-efficient which is explained by a drastic increase in the literacy rate (26% to 54%). In the cluster (25-50) we observe that MP is the only state that has increased significantly with an increase in the co-efficient by 11 per cent, which can be attributed to the increase in the crude literacy rate from 44.2 per cent to 64.11 per cent. In the range (50-75), the states Madhya Pradesh, Maharashtra and Tripura show improvement in the co-efficients. For all the three states, the crude literacy rate increased by around 12 per cent. In the range (75-100), Mizoram is the only state which shows an increase of 6 per cent due to increase in literacy from 82.3 per cent to 88.49 per cent.

The overall performance of all the states as far as this indicator is concerned is not very impressive but consistent leaving a few states like Rajasthan, Himachal Pradesh, Madhya Pradesh and Jammu & Kashmir which have improved considerably.

Under this we have two variables and Maharashtra is the best performer. Therefore, it forms the base of our analysis. Here, we can locate only two inter-cluster changes.

TABLE 13

Changes in Similarity Coefficients for Infrastructural Indicators

States	*0-25*	*25-50*	*50-75*	*75-100*
Andhra Pradesh			58.45 (62.78)	
((62.78)(62.78)				
Arunachal Pradesh	1.47 (1.05)			
Assam	4.70 (4.60)			
Bihar	21.48 (11.55)			
Goa	1.77 (2,52)			
Gujarat			57.50 (67.62)	
Haryana	16.66 (18.60)			
Himachal Pradesh	5.65 (6.37)			
Jammu & Kashmir	3.83 (5.41)			
Karnataka		46.48 (48.82)		
Kerala	20.21 (20.43)			
Madhya Pradesh		(35.01) 67.18		
Maharashtra				100(100)
Manipur	0.85 (0.65)			
Meghalaya	0.97 (1.85)			
Mizoram	0.43 (0.32)			
Nagaland	0.88 (2.26)			
Orissa	18.35 (19.45)			
Punjab		32.63 (34.25)		
Rajasthan		36.09 (36.65)		
Sikkim	0.07 (0.06)			
Tamil Nadu			71.48 (67.84)	
Tripura	1.23 (1.01)			
Uttar Pradesh			61.50 (65.20)	
West Bengal	21.61	(29.04)		
Delhi	0.13 (6.30)			

NB: Figures in parenthesis indicate similarity coefficients of 2001 and the rest indicate coefficients of 1991.

Madhya Pradesh registers a drastic fall in the co-efficient by nearly half its previous value which may be due to the decrease in kilometers of surfaced roads from 121999 kilometers to 19135 kilometres, probably due to the separation of Chhattisgarh. West Bengal moved from (0-25) to

(25-50) with an increase in the co-efficient by 8 per cent. This is due to a rise in kilometers of surfaced roads from 22350 kms to 48419 kms over the decade, also consumption of electricity rose from 1164.3 GwH to 17841.9 Gw.

Most of the states have intra-cluster changes in their indicators in the range (0-25) we have the states of Arunachal Pradesh, Assam, Bihar, Goa, Haryana, Himachal Pradesh, Jammu & Kashmir, Kerala, Manipur, Meghalaya, Mizoram, Nagaland, Orissa, Sikkim, Tripura and Delhi for 1991. The most important observation is that except West Bengal, all the states remained in their clusters in 2001. Most of them have minor changes in co-efficient except for Bihar and Delhi. Delhi registered an increase of 6 per cent in the co-efficient which can be explained by a significant rise in kilometers of surfaced roads (1299 kms to 23274 kms). And increase in electricity consumption (17 GwH to 917.4 GwH). Bihar has shown a significant fall of 10 per cent. This change cannot be explained directly from data as all the variables considered, show an improvement. External factors might be at work or the relative performance of Maharashtra might have been better then Bihar. In the range (25-50) we have the states of Karnataka, Punjab, Rajasthan in 1991. In 2001 Madhya Pradesh and West Bengal joins in. The changes in co-efficients for the first three states are insignificant.

In the range (50-75) we have the states Andhra Pradesh, Tamil Nadu and Uttar Pradesh. Gujarat shows a significant increase in similarity by 10 per cent, which is due to the rise in both the variables, kilometers of surfaced roads (83994 kms to 123420 kms) and consumption of electricity (2339 GwH to 37971 GwH).

The overall performance is not so impressive since for most of the states the co-efficient lies in (0-25) range. Apart from Delhi and West Bengal, most of the states show fall or insignificant change in the co-efficient.

Under the health indicator there are two variables. Maharashtra is the best performing state as per the data on both the years. Therefore, it is taken as the base and all the other states are compared to it. Considering the similarity coefficients we can observe that all the states have moved away from Maharashtra in the sense that they could not keep up to the pace of development.

TABLE 14

Changes in Similarity Coefficients for Health Indicators

States	*0-25*	*25-50*	*50-75*	*75-100*
Andhra Pradesh			54.62 (53.02)	
Arunachal Pradesh		42.24 (31.59)		
Assam	(22.08)	46.43		
Bihar		(40.20) 61.85		
Goa		40.20 (27.50)		
Gujarat		40.04 (55.42)		
Haryana		(25.60) 69.76		
Himachal Pradesh		42.85 (28.25)		
Jammu & Kashmir		48.52 (33.38)		
Karnataka			51.86 (50.41)	
Kerala			65 (56.64)	
Madhya Pradesh	(12.46)	61.09		
Maharashtra		30.90		
Manipur	(20.01)	28.42		
Meghalaya		47.46 (32.81)		
Mizoram	(18.39)	40.33		
Nagaland		39.38 (29.22)		
Orissa	(10.27)	30.71		
Punjab		(41.49) 57.66		
Rajasthan		(30.05) 54.80		
Sikkim		43.33 (32.02)		
Tamil Nadu			60.47 (50.04)	
Tripura		46.52 (34.25)		
Uttar Pradesh		(40.64) 60.09		
West Bengal			65.95 (58.97)	
Delhi		47.14 (44.44)		

NB: Figures in parenthesis indicate similarity coefficients of 2001 and the rest indicate coefficients of 1991.

First we consider the inter-clustural changes from (50-75) to (25-50). The five states Bihar, Jammu & Kashmir, Punjab, Rajasthan, and Uttar Pradesh experience fall in their coefficient ranging from 18 per cent to 20 per cent. For these states the fall in infant mortality has been less than that of Maharashtra, which could be the only explanation for the poor performance of the states with respect to Maharashtra. Considering the cluster change from (25-50) to (0-25) we have five states with the fall in coefficient ranging from 20 per cent to 24 per cent. These are Assam, Orissa, Mizoram, Madhya Pradesh, and Manipur. For the first four there is a decline in the infant mortality rate, however, the number of hospital beds have either remained same or increased very marginally. For Madhya Pradesh, the number has actually fallen due to the separation of Chhattisgarh. This attributes be the increase in dissimilarity with the best performer.

Considering the intra-cluster changes, there are seven states which have shown a significant change in the coefficient. These are Arunachal Pradesh, Gujarat, Goa, Haryana, Karnataka, Meghalaya, and Tripura. A general trend can be traced for all these states that is a very marginal increase in the number of hospital beds compared to the population growth. This has indeed negative impacts on health and thus resultant fall. Andhra Pradesh is a consistent performer which shows no change in the coefficient.

4. CONCLUSION

After analyzing which state is at what distance from the best performer in each indicator group, a critical question arise. That is what should be the policy implications for the regions which have not performed impressively over the decade. It is important to emphasize that the states are quite diverse in their size, population, culture and entitlements and historical process of economic development; therefore, it is very unrealistic to expect that all states would perform equally consistently. Some states might be particularly well-placed to exploit some new opportunities while others might not have such favorable conditions. So, the mere fact that states grow at different rates should not be viewed as a failure of policy. Keeping in view all these facts, we try and formulate certain befitting policies and strategies for the currently poor performing states; so as to break the specific constraint that prevents these states from replicating the success of the better performer.

- More emphasis on spread of primary education through incentives as mid-day meals and free books should be given specially for sates showing dismal performance as Bihar.
- Provision of heath facilities should be increased as that it can keep pace with the increasing population.
- Checking infant mortality rates through public awareness especially in state of Haryana.
- Public investment should be stepped up in infrastructure which is stuck at a low level.

References

Cooper, P.A. and A.J. Weekes (1988), Data, Models and Statistical Analysis, Heritage Publishers, New Delhi.

Dasgupta, Biplab (1971), Socio-economic Classification of Districts—A Statistical Approach", *Economic and Political Weekly*, 6(31).

Government of India, Ministry of Finance and Company Affairs, Economic Affairs Division, *Economic Survey* of various years, New Delhi.

Government of India, Ministry of Statistics and Programme Implementation, Central Statistical Organisation, "Statistical Abstract 2004", "Statistical Abstract 1998", "Statistical Abstract 1997", New Delhi.

Kapila Uma (2006), Indian Economy since Independence, Academic Foundation, New Delhi

Soft Sources:

www.censusindia.gov.in

www.en.wikipedia.org/wiki/Encyclopedia

www.jstor.org

www.agricoop.nic.in

Government of India, Office of the Registrar-General and Census Commssioner, Census of India 1991, computerized tables in CD.

19

Regional Development and Locational Dynamics in Andhra Pradesh

K. MADHU BABU

There has been considerable debate in several international for a about the regional imbalances between the developed countries and the developing countries in recent times. GATT, UNCTAD and other international organizations have provided extensive discussions about the various measures necessary to implement a more rational transfer of resources from developed countries to developing countries and for reduction in global imbalances arising on account of maldistribution of natural and human resources. The developed countries have all along taken measures by introducing restrictions on transfer of resources to the poor countries on one pretext or the other. In reality not much headway has been made in motivating the developed countries to share their resources with poor nations, despite the economic advantage accruing to developed countries themselves in the process, which is at the root of the problem of world-wide disparities.

In India, the uneven distribution of natural resources has itself created large under developed regions in the country, which have been recently brought into sharp focus. The problem needs to be addressed by well-thought out strategies including deliberate transfer of resources to under-developed regions. This is vital because proper growth of all regions of the country is essential for its prosperity in terms of political and social systems, and for the economic viabilities of the nation itself. The need for industrialization needs no emphasis. Having realized the importance of industrial development, our country has been launching various programmes from time to time with a determined effort to achieve sustained industrial development. No period in the industrial history of India has attached more importance to industrialization than that of the present period.

In the context of industrialization, the concept of regional development of industries has been assuming great significance in current economic thinking. This is because regional method of industrial development is the *sine qua non* of rational economic planning. The extremely localized character of industrial activity puts forth a serious stumbling-block to the smooth performance of a national plan. There must be a regional plan in each area for dealing specifically with the large local residue of unemployment. In the locational dynamics of industrial growth, it is essential to study the economic forces which go to constitute a theory of location.

Sargant Florence offers an inductive method[1] of analysis, which has assumed a great practical significance during recent years, that the "relation of an industry to an area is not so important as the relation of the industry to the distribution of the occupied population as a whole."[2] The location quotient can be computed by two different methods. (I) by dividing (a) the percentage share of the region in the total workers employed in the industry by (b) the percentage share of the region in the total working population, (II) by dividing (a) the percentage share of the industry in the total workers employed in the region by (b) the percentage share of the industry in the total working population. Both the methods yield the same results. The difference between the two methods can, however, be explained by the following formula:[3]

$$A/C \times B/D = A/B \times C/D.$$

where

A – Represents the share of the region in the total workers employed in the industry,

B – Represents the total workers employed in the industry,

C – Represents the share of the region in the total working population, and

D – Represents the total working population.

It is true that a study of locational dynamics is essential not only for analyzing the present framework of industrial activity but also for formulating a realistic policy of locational planning. In short, the present study is an attempt in this direction.

Andhra Pradesh reflects India in terms of climate, soils, water, agricultural and industrial and ecology excepting that of the Icy Himalayans. Therefore, whatever happens in Andhra Pradesh has implications for the country as a whole.

The state of Andhra Pradesh came into existence on 1st November, 1956. Andhra Pradesh has three well-defined regions, viz., Telangana, Rayalaseema and Coastal Andhra. The Telangana region is made up of ten districts, Rayalaseema region consists of four districts and Coastal Andhra region consists of nine districts. In view of the importance of balanced regional development, regional planning is essential.

In this paper an attempt is made to examine the concentration of medium and small scale industries, fixed investment and employment in the regions of Andhra Pradesh. As the study is mainly intended to examine the locational dynamics of the medium and small scale industries in the state of Andhra Pradesh, two time periods have been selected to facilitate comparative analysis, viz., 1995 and 2005. Simple percentages have been calculated besides using simple statistical techniques like annual compound growth rate for two periods.

TABLE I

Small and Medium Registered Units, Fixed Investment and Employment in Andhra Pradesh, Region-wise

Region/State	*No. of Units*			*Fixed Investment (Rs. in crores)*			*Employment*		
	1995	*2005*	*CAGR 1995-2005*	*1995*	*2005*	*CAGR 1995-2005*	*1995*	*2005*	*CAGR 1995-2005*
CoastalAndhra	54293 (43.7)	59299 (41.6)	2.5	820 (38.2)	1658 (39.0)	12.5	469356 (43.9)	532371 (42.1)	2.1
Rayalaseema	14957 (12.0)	16487 (11.5)	1.3	228 (10.6)	418 (9.8)	10.6	128696 (12.1)	144934 (11.5)	2.0
Telangana	54959 (44.2)	66508 (46.8)	3.3	1097 (51.2)	2171 (51.2)	12.1	470430 (44.0)	586741 (46.4)	3.8
Andhra Pradesh	124209 (100)	142294 (100)	2.7	2144 (100)	4247 (100)	12.1	10684821 (100)	1264046 (100)	2.8

Source: (1) Office of the Commissioner of Industries, AP
(2) Various issues of statistical abstract of Andhra Pradesh.
(3) Fifty years of Andhra Pradesh 1956-2006. Centre for Documentation, Research and Communication—Hyderabad, Andhra Pradesh.

Note: Figures within parentheses indicate percentage to the total.

This study is based on the secondary data. The data have been collected from the directory of large and medium industries in Andhra Pradesh, 1997 published by All-India Manufacture's Organization, Andhra Pradesh State Office of the Commissioner of Industries, for the reference period 2005. For the year 1995, data have been obtained from Andhra Pradesh Industry Hand Book—1998.

Notes and References

1. Sargant Florence (1973): Economic Research and Industrial Policy, in *Economic Journal,* No. 188, December, Vol. XLVII, p. 623.
2. Sargant Florence (1948): Investment, Location and Size of Plant, Cambridge University Press, Cambridge, p. 34.
3. Meha, M.M. (1948), "Theory of Location, a Critical and Analytical Study", Allahabad, p. 622.

References

Anthony, R.N. (1942), "Effect of Size on Efficiency," Harvard Business Review, Spring, Vol. XX, No. 3, pp. 290-306.

Balakrishna, R. (1958), "Measurement of Productivity in Indian Industry, Madras", University of Madras, (Madras University Economics Series.

Chand, Mahesh and Puri, Viney Kumar (1983), "Regional Planning in India" Allied Publishers, Delhi.

Kuchhal, S.C. (1991), "The Industrial Economy of India", Chaitanya Publishing House, Allahabad.

Lakshmana Rao, V. (1985), "Industrial Development of Andhra Pradesh," B.R. Publishing Corporation, Delhi.

Mehta, M.M. (1948), "Theory of Location, a Critical and Analytical Study" Allahabad, p. 622.

Sargant Florence (1937): Economic Research and Industrial Policy, in *Economic Journal,* No. 188, December, Vol. XLVII, p. 623.

Sargant Florence (1948): Investment, Location and Size of Plant, Cambridge University Press, Cambridge, p. 34.

Siva Prasad, K. and Sree Rama Murty, K. (1993), "Regional Planning and Industrial Development", Chugh Publications, Allahabad.

Sivayya, K.V and Das, V.B. (1972), "Indian Industrial Economy." Maruthi Book Depot, Guntur-3.

20

Regional Socio-economic Disparities in India: With Special Reference to Assam Economy

KUMUD BHAGAWATI

INTRODUCTION

The problem of regional disparities has enveloped both the developed and the underdeveloped countries in the world. In Indian economy too this problem of regional disparities has been considered as a crucial problem .It is fact that Indian economy has made lots of achievements in the field of socio-economic aspects covering education, public health and sanitation , social security measures, percapita income, standard of living of the people since the inception of its economic planning in 1951. However, on the threshold of the 21st century, millions of people have yet been deprived of getting their minimum necessities of life. Millions of people have remained unemployed and living below the poverty line. It is because of the fact that the development that the country has made so far is not equally shared by all sections of the people in the society. Regional differences have been on rise in different parts of the country. Regional differences may be inter-state and intra-state in character and again it may be sectoral or total. Disparities between states in development outcomes can largely be attributed to governance and delivery of services. In spite of improvement in quality of health care, wide inter-state and rural-urban disparities in outcomes and impacts continue to persist in the health sector. These socio-economic differences have made some states richer than others, which ultimately stand in the way of rapid economic development of the country. Hence, considering the gravity of the problem of the regional disparities in India; there is an urgent need to study about the regional economic disparities in India for the harmonious development of the economy.

Objectives

The objective of this paper is to investigate into the depth of regional disparities in India with special reference to Assam Economy and to find out reasons and provide suggestions to solve this crucial problem.

Methodology

The investigation under study is purely based on secondary data collected from different books, journals, magazines and newspapers and government records.

FACTORS OF REGIONAL DISPARITIES IN INDIA

There are multiple factors responsible for socio-economic disparities in India, some of which are due to differences in natural endowments and some are man made. The factors of regional differences include the following:

(a) Historical factors,
(b) Geographical factors,
(c) Locational advantage,
(d) Inadequacy of economic overheads,
(e) Failure of planning machinery,
(f) Impact of Green revolution, and
(g) Lack of motivation on the part of the backward states

POLITICAL INSTABILITY AND MANY MORE

Socio-economic Indicators of Regional Disparities

The socio-economic indicators of regional differences comprise of per-capita income, the proportion of population living below the poverty line, the percentage of urban population to total population, people engaged in agricultural activities and industries, infrastructural development, urbanization, per-capita consumption of electricity, etc. According to Prof. Raj Krishna there are six categories of state disparities that include the following: (i) Indices of income, poverty and unemployment, (ii) Agricultural indicators, (iii) Industrial indicators, (iv) Infrastructural indicators, (v) Social service indicators, and (vi) Resource allocation indicators.

Regional Disparities and its Magnitudes in India and Assam

Regional differences can be understood by considering the following indicators:

(a) Per-capita Net State Domestic Product (NSDP)

One of the most vital indicators of regional differences in India is the differences in the per-capita income. The following table reflects the per-capita State Net Domestic Product (NSDP) in 15 major states of India including Assam at current prices. Data pertaining to NSDP can be used for assessing the degree of regional disparities as well as measuring structural transformations of these states.

This Table 1 reveals that states like Punjab, Maharashtra, Gujarat, Kerala, Tamil Nadu, Karnataka are the richer states as the per-capita NSDP is much higher in these states in comparison to other states in India. It also shows that Punjab is far ahead of other states. According to 2000-01 estimates its per-capita income was 33 per cent higher than the national average. During 2000-01 the per-capita income of Punjab was the highest, i.e., Rs. 25,048 while the second and third position was occupied by Haryana and Maharashtra with their per-capita income of Rs. 23,742 and Rs. 23,726 respectively. But in 2003-04 the per-capita income of Haryana was the highest with Rs. 29,963 the second and the third

TABLE I

SL No.	State	1960-61	1971-72	1980-81	1990-91*	2003-04
1.	Andhra Pradesh	314	627	1467	4816	20757
2.	Assam	349	548	1329	4432	13339
3.	Bihar	216	415	1022	2966	5780
4.	Gujarat	380	827	2089	6343	20797
5.	Haryana	359	960	2437	7721	29963
6.	Karnataka	292	698	1644	4975	21696
7.	Kerala	278	592	1835	5110	24492
8.	Madhya Pradesh	274	534	1609	4798	14011
9.	Maharashtra	419	808	2492	7612	29204
10.	Orissa	226	473	1352	3166	12388
11.	Punjab	271	560	1424	4883	15486
12.	Tamil Nadu	344	648	1666	5541	23358
13.	Uttar Pradesh	244	497	1402	3937	10817
14.	West Bengal	386	779	1925	5072	20896
	Average	305@	660@	1741@	5365@	21142@

* Advance estimate.

@ Per-capita NNP at current prices.

Source: Directorates of Economics and Statistics of respective state governments.

position were occupied by Maharashtra and Punjab respectively with their per-capita income of Rs. 29,204 and Rs. 27,851. Rajasthan has improved slightly but the per-capita income of Bihar, Orissa and UP have remained very low. Assam is one of the backward states situated in the North East India. The per-capita income at constant prices (1999-2000) stood at Rs. 14,950 and Rs. 18,598 at current prices in the year 2005-06 which accounts for 4.2 per cent growth rate. So, it has shown a steady improvement over the previous years.

(b) Differences in Growth Rates

Differences in growth rates of various states also reveal the inter-state disparities in India. The annual growth rates of the richer states like Punjab, Haryana, Maharashtra and Gujarat were higher than the poorer states during 1970-71 to

1995-96. The annual growth rate in the poorer states varies from 1.4 per cent to 1.9 per cent. The national average of growth rates during that period was 2.1 per cent. Karnataka, Tamil Nadu and West Bengal were edged over this percentage. So, the disparities between the rich and the poor states have been widening. The following table shows the annual percentage growth rate of per-capita SDP for the 14 major states including Assam at 1980-81 prices. The annual percentage growth rates in Assam were 1.7 per cent which was much below the richer states in India. The high growth rate of the four major states, moderate growth rates in two middle income states and very slow growth rates in the rest of the states have increased the problem of regional disparities in India.

TABLE 2

Estimated Annual Percentage Growth Rates of Per-capita SDP for 14 Major States at 1980-81 prices

Sl. No.	*State*	*Annual Percentage Growth Rates 1970-71 to 1995-96*
1.	Andhra Pradesh	1.9
2.	Assam	1.7
3.	Bihar	1.8
4.	Gujarat	2.7
5.	Haryana	3.1
6.	Karnataka	2.2
7.	Kerala	1.7
8.	Maharashtra	3.0
9.	Orissa	1.4
10.	Punjab	3.0
11.	Rajasthan	1.9
12.	Tamil Nadu	2.4
13.	Uttar Pradesh	1.8
14.	West Bengal	2.3
	All-India	2.1

Source: *Economic and Political Weekly*, July 1, 2000, p. 2414.

(c) Population Living Below the Poverty Line

Another vital indicator of regional differences is the percentage of people living below the poverty line. The incidence of poverty in the richer states is less than the poorer states. The incidence of poverty was 6.2 per cent in Punjab, 15.8 per cent in Andhra Pradesh and 8.7 Per cent in Haryana in 1999-2000. Bihar, Orissa and UP and MP are the four states which have the highest percentage of population below the poverty line and in addition they have the lowest per-capita income in the country. The states like Andhra Pradesh, Karnataka, Tamil Nadu and West Bengal have registered a comparatively high per-capita income but these states are to bear the burden of large percentage of people living below the poverty line. Poverty in such states is the result of large inequalities of income and wealth and deprivation of the underprivileged section of the society. Punjab is the only state which is maintaining the higher growth rate of the economy with lowest incidence of poverty, i.e., 6.2 per cent as compared to 42.6 per cent in Bihar, 47.2 per cent in Orissa, 37.4 per cent in Madhya Pradesh and 36.1 per cent in Assam and 26.1 per cent for all-India 1999-2000. So, it is seen that poor states have largest concentration of poor people with low incomes.

(d) Disparities in Agricultural Development and Industrial Development

Widespread regional disparities can be seen as regards to the production of agricultural goods. The States of Punjab, Haryana and the parts of Uttar Pradesh were highly benefited by the Green revolution in agriculture through the application of high yielding verities (HYV), modern technology and better irrigation system. The combined share of Punjab and Haryana in total output of foodgrains was 17.8 per cent in 2003-04. The per-capita output of food grains in the states like Bihar, Orissa and UP and MP were very much less than Punjab and Haryana,

Assam and the other North-Eastern regions are severely lagging behind in agricultural productivity. Productivity in these states has been much less due to poor agricultural infrastructures including the scanty use of fertiliser, less coverage of net irrigated area, poor marketing facilities and credit facilities and transport bottlenecks. In Punjab and Haryana, in 2002-03 gross irrigated area as percentage of gross cropped area were 97.8 per cent and 86.2 per cent as against national average of 40.2 per cent. Similarly fertiliser consumption per hectare of cropped area was 184.1 kgs. In Punjab and 167.1 kgs. In Haryana in 2003-04 as against the national average of 89.8 kgs. in that period. Agricultural productivity has remained very low in Assam. The index of agricultural production (base triennium ending 1981-82=100) for the state stands at 153.27 in 2004-05.

The pace of industrialization is also an important indicator of regional differences. West Bengal and Maharashtra had experienced robust growth in industrialization before independence. But after independence Gujarat, Punjab and Tamil Nadu have developed the industrial sector considerably by developing different industrial units. The states like Bihar, Orissa and UP, MP and Assam have been lagging far behind in respect of industrialization. Only few small-scale and medium-scale industries are in working. The number of large-scale industries is too few and also some are running with losses. The general index of industrial production of the state moved up to 159.10 in 2005-06 from 142.21 in 2004-05. The concentration of industries in the three states namely Maharashtra, Tamil Nadu and Gujarat gives the fool proof of regional differences in India. In 2002-03 these three states accounted for 45 per cent of gross output, 42.4 per cent of value added, 45.9 per cent of total invested capital and 37.9 per cent of employment in factory sector. The richer states are maintaining higher proportion of industrial labourers to total population than the poorer states.

(e) Degree of Urbanisation

The percentage of urban population to total population is also considered to be another indicator of regional differences. The proportion of urban population to total population in the states like Maharashtra (42.4%), Tamil Nadu (43.8%), Gujarat (37.4%), Karnataka (34%) Punjab (33.9%) and West Bengal (28.1%) have shown much more than the national average, i.e., 25.7 per cent in 2001. While the degree of urbanization in the backward states like Orissa (15%), Bihar (10.5%), HP (9.8%) and Assam (9.7%) has shown a very slow growth. The degree of urbanisation in Assam has been very discouraging. About 87.10 per cent of the total population of Assam is still living in villages, i.e. 12.90 per cent lives in urban areas, which again reflects vast regional differences in the country. According to 2001 Census there are only 125 towns in Assam. The urban population is the highest in Kamrup district, i.e., 9,08,217 while other districts have recorded only little number of urban populations.

(f) Per-capita Consumption of Electricity

There have been gross dissimilarities in the domestic consumption of electricity too. During 1999-2000 the per-capita domestic consumption of electricity was 161.3 kwh in Punjab and in Kerala it was 144.3 kwh as against all-India per-capita consumption of 70.1 kwh. But in Assam, Bihar, MP and UP it was about 49 kwh. This data again has reflected widespread regional disparities in India. Other backward states have also recorded less consumption of electricity than the national average. The overall power supply position in Assam is not encouraging as the people have the experiences of erratic power supply.

(g) Other Indicators of Regional Disparities

Gross regional differences can be seen in terms of other infrastructures like road length per 100 km^2, deposit mobilisation by the commercial banks, etc. Kerala topped in road length in 1997, i.e. 377 kms. which was five times higher than the national average. J & K ranked at the bottom with only 9 kms. Assam and the North-eastern states are quite backward so far as the network of the roads are concerned. The network of banking facilities is wide spread in Tamil Nadu and Maharashtra while Assam and the North-eastern states are much lagging behind in this regard too. So far as the level of literacy is concerned Kerala topped with 90.9 per cent as against the national average of 65.4 per cent in 2001 Census. Moreover the female literacy rate is also high in Kerala, i.e. 87.9 per cent while Bihar recorded a very low female literacy rate, i.e. 33.57 per cent. In Assam literacy rate was 63.25 per cent in 2001 out of which 56.03 per cent was female literacy rate. Plan expenditures in different states in India also exhibit vast regional discrepancies, as richer states get due importance in the economic plans. The sectoral contribution to the national economy shows that the contribution of agriculture has been declining during the plan period, while industry's contribution has been on rise. The tertiary sector, on the other hand has shown a robust growth. In Assam agriculture has been the mainstay of the people of Assam. As per the advance estimates the contribution of the Primary sector, Secondary sector and Tertiary sectors to the total NSDP of the state at constant (1999-2000) prices stands at 33 per cent, 18 per cent and 49 per cent respectively during 2006-07. It reveals that contribution from the industry sector is not encouraging, while service sector is improving a lot.

(h) Regional Disparities during Economic Reforms

The main objective of economic reforms in India is to bring rapid economic development in the country. Regional disparities increased at a slow pace during 1980-81 to 1990-91 but after the economic reforms in 1991, the developed states got stimulus by attracting foreign investment, consequently, regional disparities widened further because the developed states experienced a growth rate of 6.3 per cent per annum during 1990-91 to 2000-01, while the backward states showed a growth rate of only 3 per cent during that period. The vital reasons for these differences were due to refusal of the richer states to transfer resources to the poorer states, lack of integrated approach, lack of infrastructural facilities, failure of the central projects, lack of proper incentives from the state governments, non-utilization of plan outlays, etc.

(i) Inter-State Disparities

Above all intra-state disparities does also an indicator of regional imbalance exist within each particular state. It is seen that most of the developmental activities are concentrated in the more developed, urban and metropolitan areas of the states. In Maharashtra, Punjab and other developed states most of the developmental activities are concentrated in and around the city area. All these have resulted in wide regional disparities. In Assam too intra-state disparities are glare. While the city areas of the district head quarters are well developed, the remote villages are deprived of getting urban opportunities like better housing and sanitation facilities, improved medical and health facilities, better educational facilities, improved transport and communication system and other modern amenities.

GOVERNMENT POLICY MEASURES TO REMOVE REGIONAL DISPARITIES

During the plan period the government of India has undertaken various steps to remove regional disparities from the country. In the First Five Year Plan (FYP) it was mentioned that the pattern of development would take due considerations of regional balance and growth. But due to limitation of resources it could not reach the target. The regional disparities had increased due to the wide gap in the per-capita development expenditure of different states. The Second FYP adopted a series of programmes to tackle the problem of regional disparities which included location of new industries, the expansion of village and small scale industries and provision of drinking water, water supply, transport and irrigation facilities in backward areas. But the Third FYP had opened a separate chapter on balanced regional development. It emphasises that balanced regional development of different parts of the country, extensions of benefits of economic progress to less developed regions and widespread diffusion of industry are among the major aims of planned development. The IVth Plan introduced a number of schemes for the benefit of the rural poor such as SFDA, MFALDA, etc. The government also decided to setup industrial estates in the semi-urban and sub-urban areas to accelerate the growth of rural economy and to lessen overcrowding the towns. These policies continued in the Vth Plan too renewing the importance of backward area development. The VIth Plan undertook some valiant measures to remove regional differences that included the programmes like IRDP, NREP.ITDP and CSRE. The VIIth Plan had stressed on agricultural development, human resource development and reduction in regional disparities in the country. During the VIIIth Plan the government of India gave much emphasis on the generation of employment opportunities by adopting various programmes like JRY, IRDP, TRYSEM, PMRY, PMGY, PMGSY, etc. Some Special Area Development Programmes like Hill Area Development Programme, North Eastern Council, and Desert Development Programmes were undertaken to bridge the gap of regional differences. The IXth Plan proposed to continue the Special Area Development Programmes. To ensure balanced regional development the Xth plan emphasized on State-wise break-up of the broad developmental targets. The government of India gave high priority to social sector development through emphasising on education, science and technology development and identified some thrust areas like reduction of poverty and generation of employment opportunities through NREGA. This scheme is being implemented throughout the country since April 1st, 2008. The government of India has taken multifaceted actions like resource transfer to the backward areas, tax holiday concession, central investment subsidy scheme, promoting new financial institutions in backward areas, backward regions grant fund, etc. As a part of the planning process these schemes are also being implemented in Assam to remove the problem of regional imbalance in the country. Presently the government of Assam has undertaken multiple measures to bring rural areas closer to the urban like establishment of educational institutes, technical institutes and industries in the adjacent rural areas of Guwahati and in other semi-urban areas.

SUGGESTIONS

The problem of regional disparities is a complex problem which needs to be addressed with much attention. The following suggestions may be made for its solution:

(a) The Central government should give due attention to the development of backward regions and provide adequate funds for its development to meet the needs of those underprivileged areas.

(b) Agriculture being the primary livelihoods of the vast majority of the people much attention should be given on agricultural development in the backward regions of the country by providing them with HYV, modern technology, better irrigation facilities and credit facilities to farmers. The most important thing is the effective implementation of such programmes by ensuring the benefits to the targeted groups.

(c) By making proper identification of the backward regions the integrated programmes should be taken up for the development of small-scale and cottage industries which are cost effective as well as labour intensive.

(d) Infrastructures are the key for all-round development of an economy, so such facilities should be made available in the backward regions of our country. The geographical isolation of Assam and other States can be broken by ensuring improved transport and communication system in these areas.

(e) Planning expenditures for such underdeveloped regions should be enhanced and proper monitoring authority should be appointed by the government.

(f) Review of the programmes from time to time is also quite essential to meet the needs of different regions.

(g) Decentralization of economic plans would undoubtedly help in bridging the gap between the developed and the underdeveloped regions. For this purpose The Panchayati Raj System should be revitalized by ensuring political and economic empowerment to such institution.

(h) Rural development should get the topmost priority in the planning for backward regions of the country.

CONCLUSIONS

It can be concluded that the governmental efforts to remove regional disparities have failed to do much as a result of which regional disparities are growing rapidly. What needs is to undertake long-term multifaceted and comprehensive efforts along with effective economic plans. Unless the Central assistance is linked with certain specific programmes the problem of regional disparities can not be tackled. Agricultural development as well as industrial development coupled with infrastructural development in the underdeveloped regions can only bring a solution to the problem of regional imbalance. The backward regions of our country in general and Assam in particular should be given due weightage in the economic planning of our country, so that the problem of regional disparities be overcome. More governmental accountability in the implementation of planning programmes through e-governance is a must to remove regional disparities in India. Unless the problem of regional disparities is overcome by the concerted efforts of the central government and the state governments the goal of achieving a prosperous India will be difficult to attain.

References

Dutt, Ruddar and Sundharam, K.P.M. (1991), 'Indian Economy', pp. 368-78, S. Chand and Company Ltd., New Delhi.

Dhar, P.K. (2007), "Indian Economy its Growing Dimensions", pp. 85-98. Kalyani Publishers, Ludhiana.

Economic Survey, of Assam, 2006-07, Directorate of Economics and Statistics, Assam.

Jhingan, M.L. (1985), 'The Economics of Development and Planning', pp. 637-46, Vani Educational Books Pvt., UP.

Lekhi, R.K. and Choudhury, R.K., 'Economy of India Including Assam and North-East', pp. 57-66.

Misra, S.K. and Puri, V.K. (2006), 'Indian Economy', pp. 918-27.

Yojana, December 2007.

21

Economic Development and Disparities in Maharashtra

Kavita S. Sharma

Maharashtra has established strength in every sector including Engineering, Electronics, Hardware, Automobiles and Auto-components, Consumer durables, Chemicals, Petrochemicals, Pharmaceutical, Textiles, Information technology and Bio-technology and raises the per-capita domestic product of the state. Thus Maharashtra has a unique development experience. It is second most populous state after Utter Pradesh. Its per-capita income is 40 per cent higher than the all-India average. Although the state has the largest urban slum-dwelling population and serious intra-state differences both in the levels of attainment and poverty ratios.

Maharashtra is located on the west coast along the Arabian Sea. It is among the richer States of the country. It has an uneven natural resource endowment. Its rainfall from the South West Monsoon is subject to much variation, making some hinterland areas severely drought prone. Maharashtra's 35 districts are divided into 6 revenue divisions. Being more urbanized than most States in the country, almost 43 per cent of its population, much of it migrant, lives in towns and cities.

Maharashtra derives most of its income from the secondary and tertiary sectors and it is not yet self-sufficient in food grains. However, the tilt towards commercial crops like sugarcane and cotton, has given rise to a vibrant agro-processing industry. In recent times, fruits and vegetables have been added to this industry. Mumbai, the capital of Maharashtra, was once the icon of national industrialization but with the decline of manufacturing it is now the principal financial center and a major commercial hub of India.

In the matter of human development the state has performed miserably as per the Human Development Report 2002. The report considers that widespread inequalities in distribution of resources have led to glaring regional disparities, acute poverty and a high level of unemployment. The Human Development Report covers the study of population, education, gender, health and nutrition, these are the more accurate indicators of quality of life and progress made by the state. According to the report, Maharashtra's average HDI stands at 0.58 under the value of HDI range between 0 and 1. It ranks fourth in terms of HDI after Kerala, Punjab and Haryana. While district-wise study of HDI of Maharashtra highlights a grave disparity among districts. Only Mumbai, Thane and Pune stand at more than 0.75 in HDI. Hence severe disparities exist among districts and the regions of the state in the areas of health, education, population and economic development. The northern region of Marathwada and Vidarbha lag behind development. The study which was conducted for each district showed that Gadchiroli of Vidarbha region and Nandurbar of north Maharashtra region have lowest HDI and Mumbai has the highest.

POPULATION GROWTH AND ITS IMPACTS

The 2001 Census put Maharashtra's population at 96,752,247 which is 9.4 per cent of India's population. At the time of its formation as a separate State, 40 years ago, its population was 39.6 million. Hence the density of population

TABLE I

Human Development Index and Per-capita District Domestic Product

Sl. No.	Districts	HDI 2000	Rank	PCDDP (Rs.) 1998-99 (At Current Prices)	Rank
1.	Mumbai	1.00	2	45471	1
2.	Mumbai (Subn.)	1.00	1	45471	2
3.	Thane	0.82	3	33200	3
4.	Raigad	0.70	6	30364	4
5.	Ratnagiri	0.44	22	14354	25
6.	Sindhudurg	0.60	9	20016	10
7.	Nasik	0.51	13	20636	8
8.	Dhule	0.36	30	11789	34
9.	Nandurbar	0.28	32	11789	35
10.	Jalgaon	0.50	14	16449	17
11.	Ahmednagar	0.57	11	15251	22
12.	Pune	0.76	4	28000	6
13.	Satara	0.59	10	15563	20
14.	Sangli	0.68	7	20411	9
15.	Solapur	0.48	17	18097	13
16.	Kolhapur	0.64	8	20925	7
17.	Aurangabad	0.57	12	19365	11
18.	Jalna	0.27	33	12047	33
19.	Parbhani	0.43	24	13827	26
20.	Hingoli	0.43	25	13827	27
21.	Beed	0.47	18	15303	21
22.	Nanded	0.37	29	13068	31
23.	Osmanabad	0.38	28	12905	32
24.	Latur	0.47	19	13677	29
25.	Buldhana	0.41	27	13823	28
26.	Akola	0.44	23	16069	18
27.	Washim	0.36	31	16069	19
28.	Amravati	0.50	15	17168	14
29.	Yavatmal	0.22	34	13382	30
30.	Wardha	0.49	16	16952	16
31.	Nagpur	0.71	5	28878	5
32.	Bhandara	0.46	20	14467	23
33.	Gondiya	0.46	21	14467	24
34.	Chandrapur	0.41	26	19325	12
35.	Gadchiroli	0.21	35	17140	15
	Maharashtra	0.58	22763		

increased from 129 persons per sq. km. in 1961 to 314 persons per sq. km. in 2001. It has increased unevenly in rural and urban areas. An almost even mix of rural-urban population, with a large segment of slum-dwellers, has impacted on overall fertility rates. Population levels in the cities have also increased as a result of social norms such as a preference for sons, early marriages and teenage motherhood observed by migrants. Disparities in the availability of education, healthcare and employment has affected the infant mortality rates and resulted in a declining sex ratio. Only three districts—Ratnagiri, Sindhudurg and Gondiya have a sex ratio that is favourable to women.

The Konkan division of Maharashtra is by far the most urbanized region of the State. In contrast, the Marathwada division does not have a single district that is 40 per cent or more urbanised. A problem related to urbanisation, especially where affordable

Housing is limited, hence slums have increased at large scale and Mumbai is also known for hosting Asia's largest slum-Dharavi. Apart from Dharavi, Maharashtra has about 10.6 million people living in slums, the largest number among all the States. The census report of 2001 found that 31.7 per cent of the 33.6 million people of Maharashtra, living in 62 towns and cities, were slum-dwellers. Hence long-term measures are needed to decongest the cities in Maharashtra such as development of infrastructure agriculture and industries and education and medical facilities, creation of new employment access in rural areas.

ECONOMIC DEVELOPMENT AND RURAL-URBAN DISPARITIES

Maharashtra has done consistently well in terms of the State Domestic Product index despite of its poor quality of arable land, scanty rainfall and the uneven distribution of natural resources. Its State Domestic Product during the 90's was second only to Gujarat. In terms of per-capita income Maharashtra is only marginally behind Punjab. This economic growth has come largely from non-agricultural sectors, essentially in areas like Mumbai and Thane, resulting in both sectoral and regional imbalances of development. Wealth is unevenly distributed and wide disparities exist which affect human development.

The agriculture sector is heavily dependent on an uncertain monsoon leaving the rural population vulnerable to highly unstable incomes. It is also causes rural poverty and farmers' suicide in Maharashtra. To counter this instability more women (almost twice the men) work as marginal workers to supplement the family income. Estimates for 1999-2000 show that only 14.5 per cent of the net area sown in the State was irrigated, mainly by wells, resulting in insufficient food grain production. Though drought is the single major cause of low productivity, Maharashtra has chosen water intensive sugarcane as its principal cash crop which is resulted unequal distribution of water in various regions of the state.

The average landholding size has also decreased over the years, further intensifying the pressure of population on land and impacting adversely on productivity. Though two-thirds of the workforce in Maharashtra is dependent on agriculture as its primary source of livelihood, the low level of per-capita income in the rural areas highlights the scope of labour absorption and productive employment. This constraint that had led the State to the path of non-agricultural development has yet to satisfactorily address the problems of unemployment and poverty levels in the rural sector.

As regards the overall growth process, the primary sector's share declined from 42.14 per cent in 1960-61 to 27.69 per cent in 1980-81 and fell to 17.44 per cent by 1999-2000. The secondary sector as a whole increased its share from 26.13 per cent in 1960-61 to 31.70 per cent in 1970-71 and has maintained that level ever since keeping pace with the economy since the 70's. It is the tertiary sector that has grown consistently, maintaining a higher growth than the national average. Its share increased from 31.73 per cent in 1960-61 to 38.44 per cent in 1980-81 and upwards to 50.45 per cent in 1999-2000. Trade and transport account for much of the rising rate of growth.

It is clear then that though the primary sector has the

largest workforce, it is the least productive; in the secondary sector, manufacturing is the major employer with good productivity levels; the tertiary sector, which has increased its share of the workforce by only 7 per cent, has the highest productivity level. This gives rise to serious imbalances within the State and can become a major cause for concern. Furthermore, the incidence of rural poverty increased during the 70's, declined during the 80's and had fallen below the national average by 1999-2000. Urban poverty, however, decreased since the 70's, remained below the national average till the mid-80's, but, thereafter, crossed the national average. Primary sector therefore needs more concern to increase the productivity through better agricultural infrastructure and to reduce the disparity in the state.

Despite the intra-state imbalances, Maharashtra has demonstrated strong, overall growth. The uneven distribution of these gains needs to be addressed and the agricultural sector has to be encouraged. Improved irrigation facilities, water conservation programmes and the diversification of agriculture could help mitigate some of the problems of the rural poor, while new employment systems for the primary workers together with an improved public distribution system could improve their lives.

HEALTH INFRASTRUCTURE DISPARITIES

Improvement in health and access to healthcare, higher life expectancy levels and better nourishment standards are just as important indicators of human development. While Maharashtra has done fairly well-reducing the infant mortality rate (IMR) and raising life expectancy at birth. From 105 in 1971, the IMR declined to 48 per 1000 births in 1999 with a marginal differential between males and females.

The health infrastructure of Maharashtra has expanded rapidly in last few years. The bed-population ratio and doctors-population ratio in the state are significantly higher than the country as a whole. While nearly 50 per cent of doctors in Maharashtra work in Mumbai. According to available information, 88 per cent of hospitals and 91 per cent of dispensaries are in urban areas, and 12 per cent of hospitals and 88 per cent of dispensaries belong to the private sector.

There is a wide gap in the healthcare infrastructure available in the rural and urban areas. Public investment and health expenditure is not only inadequate but has declined since the 1990's, lowering Maharashtra's position *vis-à-vis* the other States of India. The private health sector in Maharashtra is the largest in the country and better developed, especially in Mumbai, but the issues of quality and minimum standards need to be assessed. As far as the public sector is concerned, the non-availability of doctors and medicines, lengthy bureaucratic procedures and inadequate medical staff add to the problems. More resources are required, therefore, in the public domain to achieve better equity in health services with a special focus on children and their needs.

The latest estimates of life expectancy at birth are 67.7 years and 61.7 years for urban and rural males respectively, and it is 71.2 years and 63.9 years for urban and rural females respectively. This is due to improved access to healthcare and facilities like immunization and nutrition. In the tribal areas or among the poorer sections in the cities, the high prevalence of diseases can be ascribed to poor living conditions like overcrowding and congestion. Nutrition standards also vary in the State and insufficient calorie intake at the formative stages of growth lead to higher mortality rates. About 57.4 per cent of rural and 54.8 per cent of urban households consume less than the required standard calorie intake of 2,700 per day. Nutritional deficiencies are more evident in women and children below 3 years and among the tribal populations. It is necessary, therefore, to improve the food security of the poorer people. Here the State could utilise and extend further the Integrated Child Development Services (ICDS) to cover more areas.

EDUCATIONAL DEVELOPMENT

Within the State education budget, the proportion allocated for elementary education was around 45 per cent from 1988-89 to 1995-96; secondary education received about 40 per cent and the balance went towards higher and technical education. An impressive growth of institutions over the last 40 years has been accompanied by a steady growth in access to basic education. The average number of students in each primary school has risen from about 140 in 1970 to 190 in 2000, while the ratio of teachers to students has remained remarkably stable. In the case of secondary schools, the increase in schools was almost 100 per cent during the years 1980-90, and almost all government teachers have received intensive training in the last 5 years. Educational opportunities have considerably widened for the youth of the State.

Enrolment levels of education have increased for both boys and girls, and the difference is much smaller than in most States until the higher levels of education. With access to education so easy the high dropout levels are disturbing. Data reveals that by Standard IV only 85 per cent of boys and 86 per cent of girls remain in school. These figures dip further for the higher classes and by Standard X only 47 per cent of boys and 40 per cent of girls remain in school. This gender-based dropout rate needs to be addressed speedily.

To upgrade the system of education a constant restructuring of expenditure in favour of districts with poor educational participation or attainment levels needs to be done. Accurate data on school attendance and reliable estimates of learning and achievement need to be collected so as to build a dynamic system that provides a strong basic foundation for human development.

GROWTH AND GENDER ISSUES

Historically, Maharashtra has a better track record on women's rights than many other States of India. There are also many Centrally Sponsored Schemes, beneficial to women, but because State resources have been spread thin they have failed to make an adequate impact on the economic situation of women. While the government of Maharashtra recognizes the need for special protection to women, the absence of sufficient data makes it difficult to monitor their policies and programmes.

Life expectancy for women in Maharashtra stands at

about 65.4 years, higher than for men, which is 63 years. Only in 2 other Indian States, Kerala at 74.7 years and Punjab at 67.6 years, do women have a higher life expectancy rate. However, the sex ratio records declining trends—in 1901 it was 978 women to 1000 men, in 1991 it fell to 934 and in 2001 even further to 922. A deficit of this nature confirms that socio-economic conditions are weighted against women. The combined effect of increased male migration, decline in the number of girl children born and a high mortality rate for girls and young women only aggravates the problem.

This imbalance needs focused attention as Mortality Rates reveal the neglect of women in general and the girl child in particular. Nutritional deficiencies are well documented, particularly anemia in girls and women. There is a higher mortality rate in the age group of 15-19 years for women than men in the same age group. Early marriage, often before the legally prescribed age of 18, and teenage pregnancies pose high risks to these young women. It is essential, therefore, to ensure good health by providing adequate food, proper nutrition, safe drinking water, improving personal hygiene as also promoting integrated health services that include curative, preventive and rehabilitative services.

To give women dignity, social identity and prestige it is important to provide them with work and an independent income. Agriculture, as elsewhere in the country, is the biggest employer of women in Maharashtra but their work is often undervalued, both by custom and perception. According to the 2001 Census, of the 12.7 million women working in rural areas 89 per cent are employed in agriculture, 41 per cent as cultivators and 48 per cent as agricultural labour. A small number of women work in the household industry and in other non-farm occupations. This significantly alters the popular image of the farmer as a man. It is also true that a larger proportion of women than men are employed in subsidiary and marginal work. More than half the women work as casual labour with no more than 1.5 per cent working on a regular basis. This results in great fluctuations between weekly and daily wages in the peak and lean seasons of agricultural activity. This impermanent and insecure employment attracts the illiterate rather than the educated women and discourages them from enhancing their qualifications and skills.

In the urban sector only about 13 per cent of the female population is part of the work force. A large urban-rural gap has always existed, reflecting the different working conditions faced by women. The agricultural sector allows women to combine home management with outside work and requires relatively low skills and easy job training. In contrast, urban markets demand literacy, greater specialised skills as well as organised job training. Distances between home and work place, childcare requirements and longer working hours makes it difficult for many women to meet these demands, forcing them to take up self-employment. These self-employed are mainly domestic workers, hawkers and rag pickers making up 45.3 per cent of the work force, while regular employees make up only 33.3 per cent. Until literacy levels are not improved it will be difficult for a woman to enhance her earning capacity, or fully realise her potential for empowerment. It is noted that more girls dropout of courses at the higher educational levels than boys, though they do excel in the Higher School Certificate exams.

For 87.5 per cent of the women of Maharashtra the only domain where their writ runs is their kitchen. Almost half of them cannot seek healthcare for themselves, or visit and stay with parents and siblings without the permission of their husbands or family members. For 35.8 per cent of the women their earned income is controlled by the husband or other senior members of their family. This underlines the fact that women are not yet fully integrated in the social structure of society, despite Maharashtra's legacy of women playing a leading role in freedom struggles and political protests.

It is not uncommon for a woman to just sign away her authority to the upa-sarpanch, even if she is an elected sarpanch to fill a reserved slot because the powerful males dictate the terms. This practice is seen in a pronounced manner in municipal councils and Samities, where the male functions as a proxy to the woman who thereby has her legitimate rights curtailed.

At the policy level, Maharashtra is way ahead of many

other States in the country, but gender development is not commensurate with the potential on account of the socio-political conditions. The benefits of growth must be shared equally among all people; the multiplier effect on society of an investment in women and their development must be accorded an important place in any strategy.

CONCLUSION

Maharashtra's per-capita income is 40 per cent higher than the all-India average. Yet sharp disparities exist across regions, districts and between the urban and rural areas in the fields of education, health and nutrition, income, infrastructure. Marathwada districts are the most backward and score low on the Human Development Index. The non-agricultural sector plays a major role in the economy of the state. Agriculture sector still depends on the uncertain monsoon and its share in income has declined from 42.14 per cent in 1960-61 to 17.44 per cent in 1999-2000. Wealth is unevenly distributed and wide disparities exist. Economic growth has come largely from non-agricultural sectors, essentially in areas like Mumbai and Thane districts and creates the imbalances of development. Largest urban slum-dwelling population and grave intra-state differences in level of attainment and poverty ratios indicates socio-economic inequality among the people. Hence appropriate water management to increase the proportion of arable land, more employment opportunities, better health, education and transportation infrastructures are required for improving rural economic condition and reducing migration of people in urban areas.

The health infrastructure of Maharashtra has expanded rapidly in last few years. The bed-population ratio and doctors-population ratio in the state are significantly higher than the country as a whole. While nearly 50 per cent of doctors in Maharashtra work in Mumbai. There is a wide gap in the healthcare infrastructure available in the rural and urban areas. Public investment and health expenditure is not only inadequate but has declined since the 1990's, lowering Maharashtra's position *vis-à-vis* the other States of India. The private health sector in Maharashtra is the largest in the country and better developed, especially in Mumbai. As far as the public sector is concerned, the non-availability of doctors and medicines, lengthy bureaucratic procedures and inadequate medical staff add to the problems. More resources are required, therefore, in the public domain to achieve better equity in health services with a special focus on children and women to mitigate the declining sex ratio.

There are several factors are responsible for disparity like over utilization of resources, under utilization of resources, unequal distribution of resources like water, agriculture output, industrial output, unequal development of infrastructures for health, education, transportation and banking in rural and urban areas. There is also regional imbalanced development which creates poverty and unequal access of employment. There is not any shortcut method to solve these problems. United efforts are required at large scale at all levels to improve the situation of the state.

References

Aunupama Katakam (2002), A State of Disparity, Maharashtra, June.

Maharashtra, Human Development Report, 2002.

Maharashtra, Integrated Population and Development Project, UNFPA, 1999.

Minocha, A.C. (1983), Regional Disparities in India—Some Basic Issues.

Ngadeve, D.A. (2004), Impact of an Irrigation Project on Demographic Behaviour of Rural Maharashtra.

Ravi Duggal and T.R. Tulip (2006), Health and Healthcare in Maharashtra, Healthcare Management, Feb.

22

Economic Growth and Regional Disparity in Uttar Pradesh

S.P. SINGH

I. INTRODUCTION

Since 1991, a number of studies have been conducted in India to examine what has happened to the regional disparity in the post-reform period. A perusal of these studies reveals that most of them are based on the data collected from 14 or 15 major Indian States (for instance, see Pradhan, *et al.*, 2000; Kurian: 2002; Alluwalia, 2002; Deaton and Dreze: 2002; Singh, *et al.*, 2002; Noorbakhsh, 2003; Shetty: 2003, Dholakia: 2003 and 2005; Jha, 2004; Singh and Nauriyal: 2006; Singh, *et al.*, 2007). Findings of most of these studies have conclusive evidence of rising economic disparity across States. Deaton and Dreze (2002) find evidence of rising regional disparities in the 1990s, with the southern and western regions doing much better than the northern and eastern regions. However, study by Singh, *et al.* (2002) does not find any conclusive evidence about the increasing inequalities in the post-reform period; though, they find some indications of rise in regional inequality, driven by the factors necessary for accelerated growth. Singh and Nauriyal (2006) observe that inter-State disparities in economic growth widened in 1990s, while inter-State disparities in human development narrowed down, thus providing an evidence of a slight divergence in economic development and convergence in human development. Dholakia (2005) finds that regional disparity in human and social development has declined over the last two decades. However, his study does not have any evidence of declining economic disparity across States over the period. Noorbakhsh (2003) observes a divergence, not convergence in the economic disparity among Indian States. Jha (2004) examines that regional disparity as well as disparity within the rural and urban areas have increased in the post-reform period. Dadibhavi and Bagalkoti (2006) also find evidence of rising income inequalities in terms of aggregate NSDP and PCNSDP across Indian States.

A perusal of literature on economic disparity shows that the issues related to the intra-State disparity have not been examined to a greater extent, probably due to inadequate accessibility of district-level data. It may be noted that aggregate PCNSDP, as a measure of economic development, is insufficient to throw light on the magnitude and pattern of disparity across districts. Therefore, study of the extent of disparity within the State and its determining factors is quite relevant. Keeping this in view, this paper is written to examine economic growth and regional disparity in Uttar Pradesh, which is one of the most backward States of India.

2. ECONOMIC GROWTH IN UTTAR PRADESH *VIS-À-VIS* ALL-INDIA

Uttar Pradesh comprises 16 per cent of the country's population, 7.3 per cent of the area and about 8 per cent of NDP. Among the major States, it ranks 14th in terms of per-capita income. The State is organized into 17 divisions, 70 districts, 300 Tehsils and 813 development blocks. It has 52028 Gram Panchayats, covering 97134 inhabited villages (Kumar, 2005). The State is divided into four economic regions, namely, Western Region (WR), Central Region (CR),

Bundelkhand Region (BKR) and Eastern Region (ER). As per the 2001 Census, cultivators and agricultural labourers together constituted 65.89 per cent of total workforce of the State whereas the corresponding percentage for all-India was only 58.4, indicating that the economy of the State is largely rural and agricultural based. Average size of holdings in the State was only 0.83 hectare in 2000-01 as against 1.32 hectares at all-India level.

Table 1 shows that the NSDP of the State has increased from Rs. 70935 crore in 1993-94 to Rs. 109768 crore in 2004-05, thus recording a 1.55 fold increase whereas the corresponding increase in India is estimated to be 1.97 times. PCNSDP of the State does not evince any growth over the years. The ratio of the State's PCNSDP to India's average steeply declined from 65.9 per cent in 1993-94 to 49.4 per cent in 2004-05. This implies that some other States achieved faster growth than Uttar Pradesh. During the last 12 years, State's PCNSDP increased only by 18 per cent as against 61 per cent in India. Due to slow growth, the State's share in India's NDP declined from 10 per cent in 1993-94 to 8.1 per cent in 2004-05.

The Table 1 shows sector-wise NSDP at constant prices for the years 1993-94 and 2004-05. Compound annual growth rates (CAGR) are estimated taking the data for the last 12 years (i.e., 1993-94 to 2004-05). It is evident from the table that share of agriculture in the State's total NSDP has significantly declined from about 40 per cent in 1993-94 to 32.69 per cent in 2004-05. However, if we compare it to the National average, which declined from about 30 per cent in 1993-94 to about 20 per cent in 2004-05, we find that the State's economy is still largely dependent on the agriculture. Percentage shares of manufacturing and electricity, gas and water supply have decelerated. In the secondary sector, only construction sector shows the remarkable rise in its share. Tertiary sector records 5.5 percentage points rise in its share. Transport, storage and communication have made significant contribution to this rise. Banking and insurance, public administration and other services have also positively contributed to the tertiary sector, while shares of trade, hotels and restaurants and real estate sector have declined.

TABLE I

Sector-wise Net State Domestic Product at Factor Cost in Uttar Pradesh at 1993-94 Prices

(Rs. crore)

S. No.	Sector	Uttar Pradesh			All-India		
		1993-94	2004-05	CAGR (1993-94 to 2004-05)	1993-94	2004-05	CAGR (1993-94 to 2004-05)
1.	Total of Primary	29607 (41.74)	39262 (35.77)	2.65*	244779 (35.07)	323331 (23.57)	2.35*
	1.1 Agriculture	28357 (39.98)	35880 (32.69)	2.07*	210919 (30.22)	269912 (19.67)	2.04*
2.	Total of Secondary	13613 (19.19)	21666 (19.74)	3.10*	151289 (21.67)	314193 (22.90)	5.84
	2.1 Manufacturing	9235 (13.02)	13302 (12.12)	1.59***	103739 (14.86)	204787 (14.93)	5.33*
	2.2 Construction	3221 (4.54)	7346 (6.69)	8.34*	38749 (5.55)	79922 (5.83)	6.62*
	2.3 Electricity, Gas and Water Supply	1157 (1.63)	1018 (0.93)	-3.30**	8801 (1.26)	16895 (1.23)	5.9*
3	Total of Tertiary	27715 (39.07)	48840 (44.49)	5.08*	301924 (43.26)	753880 (54.95)	8.53*
	3.1 Transport, Storage and Communication	3175 (4.48)	9389 (8.55)	10.51*	37721 (5.40)	138390 (10.09)	12.24*
	3.2 Trade, Hotels and Restaurants	10533 (14.85)	14410 (13.13)	2.73*	96627 (13.84)	236767 (17.26)	8.04*
	3.3 Banking and Insurance	1994 (2.81)	5787 (5.27)	9.81*	40110 (5.75)	102714 (7.49)	8.83*
	3.4 Real Estate, Ownership of Dwellings, etc.	4281 (6.03)	5511 (5.02)	1.86*	40431 (5.79)	78347 (5.71)	6.63*
	3.5 Public Administration	3029 (4.27)	5448 (4.96)	5.44*	38760 (5.55)	78590 (5.73)	7.2*
	3.6 Other Services	4704 (6.63)	8295 (7.56)	5.05*	48275 (6.92)	112467 (8.20)	8.24*
	Total (1+2+3)	70935 (100)	109768 (100)	3.73*	697992 (100)	1371957 (100)	6.04*

* Significant at 1 per cent level of significance.
** Significant at 5 per cent level of significance.
*** Significant at 10 per cent level of significance.
Note: Figures in parentheses are percentages to the total.

Tertiary sector observes the highest growth (5.08%) among all the three sectors. It is followed by the secondary sector. Primary sector experiences the lowest growth. Agriculture grew annually only by 2.06 per cent during the last 12 years. Its slow growth is worrisome because it is the backbone of the State economy. Within the secondary sector, it is the construction, which achieved remarkable growth rate of 8.34 per cent per annum. Manufacturing sector grew only by 1.59 per cent annually, which is even lesser than the agricultural growth. As manufacturing sector has greater forward and backward linkages, its dismal performance is of much concern. NSDP from the electricity, gas and water supply observed a decline of 3.30 per cent per annum. Negative growth in power sector is also a big concern as it is a critical component of economic infrastructure needed for accelerating the growth of the economy.

Within the tertiary sector, transport, storage and communication observed the highest growth (10.51%), followed by banking and insurance (9.81%), public administration (5.44%) and other services (5.05%). Real estates and trade, hotels and restaurants, which together constitute about 41 per cent of tertiary sector's NSDP, showed the poor performance in terms of growth.

In order to know how the economy of the State has performed *vis-à-vis* all-India, we also estimated the sectoral CAGR for India. As is indicated from the table, the growth of the State economy has been far below the national average. As against 6.04 per cent average annual growth rate in the NDP of India, the corresponding growth rate for the State was only 3.73 per cent. Non-agricultural sectors achieved higher growth rates in India than in the State, however, two sub-sectors, namely, construction and banking and insurance recorded relatively higher growth in UP. The growth differentials imply that the position of State economy *vis-à-vis* other major States has deteriorated during the last 12 years.

3. REGIONAL DISPARITY IN THE ECONOMIC DEVELOPMENT

Table 2 shows the region-wise trend in the PCNSDP in

Uttar Pradesh at 1993-94 prices. Region-wise PCNSDP is estimated taking average of all districts of each region. A perusal of the table reveals that there exists a wide disparity in the distribution of PCNSDP across regions. Western and Eastern regions have more or less equal share in the State's total area and population, but their level of development is quite different. On an average, PCNSDP in the ER is only about 58 per cent that of WR. Between 1993-94 and 2004-05, it increased by only Rs. 620 in the ER as against Rs. 1426 in the WR.

TABLE 2

Region-wise Per-capita NSDP in Uttar Pradesh

(at constant prices in rupees)

	Uttar Pradesh	*WR*	*CR*	*BKR*	*ER*	*Gap between WR and ER*
1980-81	784.29	979.47	714.63	762.28	586.20	393.269
1989-90	902.29	1162.27	841.32	835.39	631.86	530.41
1993-94	5154.19	6326.00	5134.80	5377.00	3872.26	2453.74
2001-02	5717.81	7194.15	5617.30	6019.00	4255.30	2938.86
2002-03	5633.24	7123.27	5564.40	6615.86	3969.15	3154.12
2003-04	6110.14	7556.38	5933.20	7055.71	4537.85	3018.53
2004-05	6243.28	7752.44	6170.02	7496.64	4492.20	3260.23

At 1980-81 prices up to year 1989-90 and at 1993-94 prices for remaining years.
Source: Indiastat.com.

In order to understand regional and intra-regional disparities in the distribution of PCNSDP, we have calculated coefficients of variation (CVs) taking the district-wise data from 1980-81 to 2004-05. Figure 1 shows that there is high magnitude of disparity across districts in the State. However, the value of CVs does not evince any steady trend; it rather fluctuates across the years. Between 1989-90 and 1993-94, disparity declined in the State and in its regions, only exception being the CR. On an average, disparity in the

PCNSDP has increased across regions since 1993-94. Magnitudes of CVs show that in 2004-05, variation in PCNSDP within the region was highest in the WR, followed by the CR. It was lowest in the ER. It is significant to observe that both average PCNSDP and value of CVs were observed highest in the developed WR and lowest in the backward ER. This clearly indicates that there are relatively higher variations in the PCNSDP across districts of the WR as compared to the variations across districts of the ER. For instance, in the WR, PCNSDP was as high as Rs. 19947 in Gautam Buddhanagar and as low as Rs. 3363 in Budaun. While in the ER it ranged from a maximum of Rs. 8688 in Sonbhadra to a minimum of Rs. 3115 in Shrawasti.

FIGURE 1

Region-wise Trends in COV in PNSDP of Uttar Pradesh

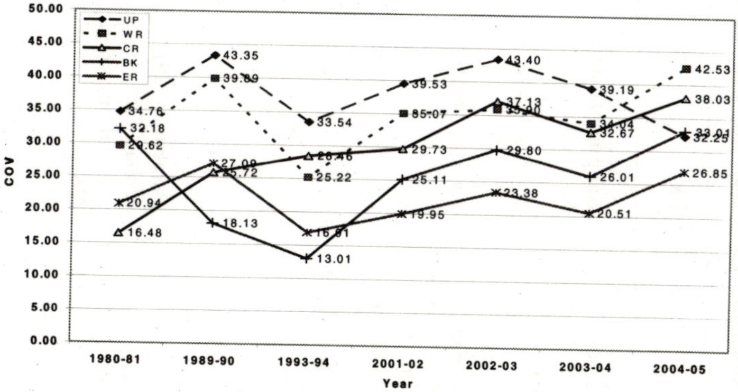

Disparity within the region can be examined by identifying the level of economic development of each district of the region. The State government has computed a composite index of development (CID) using 36 indicators of socio-economic development. Based on the value of CID, districts are categories into five categories, namely, Most Developed Districts (CID 125.00 and above), High Medium Developed Districts (CID 105.00-125.00), Medium Developed Districts (CID 90.00-105.00), Low Medium Developed Districts (CID 78.00-90.00) and Most Backward Districts (CID Below 78.00). Table 3 shows region-wise ranking of the districts.

TABLE 3

Inter-district Variation in the Level of Development

Category of district	*WR*	*CR*	*BKR*	*ER*
Most Developed Districts (CID) 125.00 and above	Gautam Buddha (1), Ghaziabad (2) Meerut (4); Agra (6)	Kanpur Nagar (5) Lucknow (3)	-	-
High Medium Developed Districts (CID 105.00-125.00)	Muzaffar Nagar (7) Mathura (8) Sahranpur (9) Jyotibaphule Nagar (10) Bulandshahar (11) Bijnore (13) Baghpat (16) Hathras (17) Moradabad (18)	Kanpur Dehat (14)	Jhansi (15)	Varanasi (12) Gorakhpur (19)
Medium Developed Districts (CID 90.00-105.00)	Firozabad (21), Rampur (22) Bareilly (23), Aligarh (25) Farrukhabad (26), Kannauj (28);	Barabanki (29) Unnao (32) Lakhimpur Kheri (38)	Jalaun (24) Mahoba (35)	Allahabad (20) Faizabad (27) Sonbhadra (30) Sultanpur (33)

	Pilibhit (31) Etawah (34); Mainpuri (36), Shahjahanpur (37)			
Low Medium Developed Districts (CID 78.00-90.00)	Etah (47) Auraiya (50) Budayun (40)	Sitapur (42) Raebareli (43) Fatehpur (48) Hardoi (52)	Hamirpur (44) Lalitpur (46)	Basti (39); Sant Ravidas Nagar (41); Ambedkar Nagar (45) Mau (49); Chandauli (51); Jaunpur (53); Deoria (54) Gonda (55)
Most Backward Districts (CID Below 78.00)			Banda (61) Chitrakoot (68)	Ghazipur (56); Bahraich (57) Pratapgarh (58); Ballia (59) Balarampur (60); Mirzapur (62) Azamgarh (63); Kushi Nagar (64); Maharajganj (65); Kaushambi (66); Santkabir Nagar (67); Shravasti (69) Siddharth Nagar (70)

Source: Compiled from Annual Plan, 2008-09, Government of Uttar Pradesh, Lucknow.
Note: Figures in parentheses are the ranks of individual districts.

It is obvious from Table 3 that four out of six most developed districts; nine out of 13 high medium development district and 10 out 20 medium developed districts of the State are in the WR; on the other hand, 13 out of 15 most backward districts and 8 out of 17 low medium districts are in the ER. BKR and ER do not have any district under the category of most developed districts, whereas WR and CR do not have any district under the most backward districts category. Within the WR, there is incidence of high disparity in the level of development. Districts located near to the National Capital Region and north-west part of the region are having relatively higher level of development as compared to their counterparts located in the south-east part of the region.

In the CR, Kanpur Nagar and Lucknow come under the category of most developed districts and Kanpur Dehat in the category of high medium district. Hardoi district is having lowest level of development within the CR. In the BKR, Jhansi stands first and Chitrakoot last in the level of development within the region. In the ER, Varanasi and Gorakhpur come under the high medium developed districts and Allahabad, Faizabad, Sonbhadra and Sultanpur under medium developed districts. Rest of the districts are under most backward and low medium developed categories. Thus, Table 3 clearly indicates the extent of intra-region and inter-region disparity in the CID.

Region-wise incidence of rural and urban poverty is depicted in Table 4. In rural areas, ER has the highest incidence of poverty (38.0%) among all the regions. It constitutes 44.7 per cent of total population but shares 55.2 per cent of total poor of the State. Relative incidence is also highest in the ER, followed by the CR. Incidence of urban poverty is higher than the rural poverty. As against 30.7 per cent poverty in rural areas, the corresponding percentage in the urban areas is 32.9. The incidence of urban poverty is highest (41.7%) in the ER and lowest (27.3%) in the BKR. The WR constitutes 51.5 per cent of total urban population and 48.4 per cent of urban poor of the State. Thus, there is high concentration of rural poor in the ER while urban poor has high concentration in the WR.

TABLE 4

Regional Poverty Profile in Uttar Pradesh (2004-05)

Region	Rural Areas				Urban Areas			
	Poverty incidence	Poor	Share population	Relative incidence	Poverty incidence	Poor	Share population	Relative incidence
WR	24.7	27.2	33.9	0.8	30.9	48.4	51.5	0.94
CR	27.8	14.9	16.5	0.9	30.6	20.5	22.1	0.93
BKR	16.8	2.7	4.9	0.55	27.3	4.6	5.6	0.83
ER	38.0	55.2	44.7	1.24	41.7	26.4	20.8	1.27
UP	30.7	100	100		32.9	100	100	

Source: Government of Uttar Pradesh (2007)

4. REGIONAL VARIATIONS IN THE DEVELOPMENT INDICATORS

Based on district-wise data on 27 development indicators, we have estimated region-wise averages and coefficients of variation (CVs) in these indicators to assess the regional variations (Table 5). Urbanization is one of the most important indicators of development. On an average, it was highest in the WR (28.25%) and lowest in the ER (11.78%). Disparity in the distribution of urban population within the region was found highest in the CR, followed by the ER. The ER was not only having low level of urbanisation but also a significant variation in the level across districts. Literacy rate was highest in the BKR and lowest in the ER. However, there was not much variation in it across regions. Population density was highest in the ER and lowest in the BKR. Concentration of SC population was highest in the CR and lowest in the WR. Variation in the distribution of SC population across districts was lowest in the BKR and highest in the ER. As SC households relatively have lesser access to land, education and other resources, their higher concentration in any region also reflects economic backwardness of the region. The ratio of main workers to the total population was highest (27.1%) in the BKR and lowest (22.0%) in the ER. However, there was not much variation in its across regions.

TABLE 5

Region-wise Averages and Coefficients of Variation in Development Indicators (2003-04)

Development Indicators	*Average*					*Coefficient of Variation*				
	UP	*WR*	*CR*	*BK*	*ER*	*UP*	*WR*	*CR*	*BK*	*ER*
1	*2*	*3*	*4*	*5*	*6*	*7*	*8*	*9*	*10*	*11*
% of Urban population	20.78	28.25	25.11	22.46	11.78	71.39	38.83	106.77	48.51	72.38
Literacy rate	5627	57.36	57.58	59.30	54.27	16.55	15.71	16.82	11.32	17.54
Population density	689	765	658	280	776	52.45	54.56	47.46	21.86	40.05
% of SC population	21.15	18.17	26.10	25.14	21.15	28.19	20.82	18.35	9.32	33.15
% of main workers to total population	23.7	24.3	25.5	27.1	22.0	11.26	5.70	4.69	6.53	13.78
Length of pucca road per 1000 sq. kms (kms)	751.87	839.00	894.89	329.94	724.40	57.09	55.53	69.85	14.98	39.13
Length of pucca road in kms per lac population	93.32	94.52	101.09	117.44	83.03	26.24	28.74	27.31	16.58	18.64

Per-capita bank loan in Rs.	2441	2916	3726	1293	1806	113.79	93.16	122.83	75.74	114.54
Population per bank (in 1000)	21.36	21.77	20.83	18.93	21.79	37.08	53.77	33.70	14.16	17.09
Per-capita plan exp. in Rs.	176.21	183.51	149.55	95.49	199.99	197.95	154.45	194.20	31.08	231.10
Credit-Deposit Ratio	39.03	47.51	36.38	46.20	29.99	37.24	34.64	21.17	26.92	28.05
No. of telephones per lac population	1544	1989	1867	1175	1091	92.40	92.36	94.54	58.58	63.34
Per-capita electricity consumption in kvh	160	213	179	127	111	100.49	93.02	116.70	44.69	87.81
Per employee output in registered factories in Rs. lac	15.39	15.79	18.31	26.16	11.13	63.01	44.87	50.79	70.68	56.09
Per ha. value of agri. output in Rs.1000	32.30	40.35	28.03	16.32	30.28	42.81	45.46	19.97	23.68	16.51

(Contd.)

TABLE 5 (Contd.)

1	2	3	4	5	6	7	8	9	10	11
Electricity consumption in Agri. per ha. of NSA (kwh)	369.56	501.82	273.45	126.17	340.90	81.18	67.54	83.88	84.46	77.45
% of village electrified	64.68	71.83	68.02	65.03	56.47	30.42	26.15	32.87	28.26	31.28
No. of Cold stores per lac kms of area	5.35	7.76	7.48	1.45	3.25	115.37	74.25	149.26	70.02	94.83
No. of credit societies per lac population	4.31	3.50	4.77	4.17	4.97	31.42	36.05	36.93	21.43	19.06
No. of agri. Mandi per lac ha. of area	1.73	1.96	1.64	1.37	1.62	43.91	35.20	38.69	23.71	55.07
Av. size of holding in ha.	0.99	1.16	0.84	1.73	0.68	41.54	30.14	13.92	9.26	27.04
Cropping intensity (%)	152	157	150	125	156	10.29	9.27	7.93	9.05	7.46

Av. yield of food grains in Qtls/ha.	22.49	26.43	21.93	12.81	21.40	21.71	13.07	10.21	20.47	11.80
Fertilizer use in Kgs per ha.	134	157	126	38	141	45.15	26.72	20.37	34.67	48.84
% of NIA to NSA	79.79	91.48	86.49	50.33	73.70	22.76	7.76	8.46	37.11	23.57
% of Area under com. crops	15.51	25.23	15.20	5.04	8.99	81.53	56.82	60.16	43.11	59.72
% of Non-agri. workers to main workers	34.02	43.2	33.5	25.5	28.08	44.42	34.90	61.77	27.48	47.81

Source: Based on District Level Data collected from Directorate of Economics and Statistics, Government of Uttar Pradesh

Access to road, electricity, water, and other socio-economic infrastructure is crucial for the development of a region. Variations in their magnitudes across regions also explain regional inequality in the level of economic development. The length of pucca road per 1000 square kms of area was highest in the WR and lowest in the BKR. However, if length of pucca road per lac of population is considered, the BKR occupies the top position, mainly due to the lowest population density. Variations in the length of pucca per 1000 square kms across regions were relatively higher than that in the length of pucca road per lac of population. The per-capita electricity consumption was highest (212 Kwh) in the WR and lowest (111 Kwh) in the ER. Similarly, percentage of electrified villages was also highest in the WR and lowest in the ER. Variations in the percentage of villages electrified across districts are more or less same in all the regions. Per-capita bank loan was highest in the CR, followed by the WR. There exists a significant disparity in the distribution of loan across districts in all the regions, as is apparent from the large magnitude of CVs. Population per bank branch was same in the WR and ER, but value of CVs was much higher in the WR than the ER. The CDR was lowest in the ER and highest in the WR. A quite low CDR in the ER may be one of the reasons of backwardness of the ER.

In case of other infrastructure facilities too, it was the WR which had better access than other regions. The WR stands first in number of telephones per lac population while the ER occupies the last position. Number of cold stores per lac population was also highest in the WR. Similar pattern is also observed in case of agricultural mandies. However, number of credit societies per lac population was lowest in the WR and highest in the ER. The extent of availability of these infrastructural facilities varies across districts in a region, as is evident from the magnitudes of CVs.

Land is the most important factor of production in any agrarian economy. Average size of land holding in the State is less than one hectare. It is as low as 0.68 in the ER. Although BKR possesses the largest average size of holdings among all regions, the productivity of land is lowest due to lack of adequate irrigation facilities. Food grain productivity in the BKR was lowest at 12.81 qt/ha. The WR, having productivity of 26.43 qt/ha., is agriculturally most developed region. Per hectare value of agricultural output was as high as Rs.40.35 thousand in the WR and as low as Rs. 16.32 thousand in the BKR. Availability of irrigation facility is a deciding factor for the growth of agriculture, as other inputs such as high yielding seeds and fertilizer, largely depend on the availability of irrigation water. The percentage of net irrigated area to net area sown was lowest in the BKR and highest in the WR. Per hectare fertilizer consumption was also highest in the WR (157 kgs/ha.) and lowest in the BKR (38 kgs/ha.). The WR occupies the first position among all the regions by having largest area under commercial crops. It is followed by the CR and the ER. The BKR has only 5 per cent of total area under commercial crops as against over 25 per cent in the WR.

The level of industrial development in the BK and ER was much lower than that in the WR and the CR. The number of persons in the registered factories per lakh of population during 2003-04 was 66 in the BKR and 105 in the ER, while corresponding numbers in the WR and the CR were 483 and 243 respectively (Government of UP, 2007). However, per employee output in the registered factory was highest in the BKR and lowest in the ER. But disparity in per employee output was highest in the BKR. Another important indicator of development is the percentage share of non-farm workers in the total main workers. In this regard, we find that about 43.2 per cent of total main workers of the WR were engaged in the secondary and tertiary sectors, while the corresponding percentage in the BKR was only 25.5.

It may be concluded from the above analysis that apart from the presence of regional disparity in the level of development, inter-district variations in the development indicators within the regions of the State are also significant.

5. FACTORS AFFECTING VARIATIONS IN THE LEVEL OF DEVELOPMENT

There are a number of variables that may explain the

variation in the level of economic development. Agricultural productivity, extent of commercialisation of agriculture, distribution and size of operational holdings, literacy rate, urbanisation, access to basic infrastructure, such as pucca road, electricity, irrigation and banking facilities, etc. may be the key factors in determining the level of economic development of any region. Initially we identified 27 explanatory variables for studying the variation in the PCNSDP (Table 5). However, some variables were found to be highly correlated with other explanatory variables, posing the problem of multicollinearity. Some others were not found to have any significant impact on the PCNSDP and their inclusion in the regression model did not make any improvement in R-2 and F-value. Therefore, we had to drop these variables from our set of explanatory variables. Finally, we have selected 7 explanatory variables, as shown in Table 6.

It is evident from the values of R-2 that the regression equation is statistically significant in terms of goodness of fit, as 72.2 per cent variations in the PCNSDP are explained by the explanatory variables. F-value is statistically significant at one per cent level of significance. The value of estimated regression coefficients show that the PCNSDP is significantly affected by the change in the level of urbanisation, average size of agricultural holdings, per hectare value of agricultural output, per-capita consumption of electricity and percentage share of workers in secondary and tertiary sectors. Density of population is found to be inversely related with the PCNSDP. However, per worker output in the registered factories does not have significant impact on the PCNSDP.

The regression results show that on an average, a one per cent point increase in the urban population would increase the PCNSDP by Rs.53.06; the PCNSDP increases by Rs. 2092 with one hectare increase in the average size of operational holdings; one unit change in the per-capita consumption of electricity raises the PCNSDP by 2.09 units; a one rupee increase in the value of agricultural output makes a 0.05 rupee increase in the PCNSDP; a one per cent point increase in the share of secondary and tertiary workers in the total main workers raises the PCNSDP by Rs. 51.18; and a

TABLE 6

Factors Affecting PCNSDP in Uttar Pradesh (Results of Regression Analysis)

Variables	*Coefficients*	*Std. Error*	*T-Stat*
Intercept	63.53	776.09	0.08
Urbanization	53.057*	21.08	2.52
Av. size of holding	2091.77*	528.73	3.96
Per ha. Value of agri. output	0.045*	0.01	3.81
Per-capita electricity consumption in Kvh	2.085**	1.06	1.96
Population density	-1.380**	0.66	-2.09
Per employee output in registered factories in Rs.	0.00024	0.0002	1.36
% share of non-agri. workers in total main workers	51.177*	19.26	2.66
R^{-2}			0.722
F-value			26.66*
No. of districts			70

unit increase in the density of population would make a reduction in the PCNSDP by 2.09 units.

6. CONCLUSION

In this paper we have examined economic growth and regional disparities in Uttar Pradesh. Sector-wise growth rates in the NSDP are estimated for the period 1993-94 to 2004-05. During this period, the NSDP of the State grew only by 3.73 per cent per annum, as against the all-India average growth of 6.04 per annum. The growth differentials imply that the position of State's economy *vis-à-vis* other States has deteriorated in the post-reform period. This is also evident from the State's contribution in the India's total NDP that declined from 10 per cent in 1993-94 to 8 per cent in 2004-05. During the period, the PCNSDP in the State increased only by 18 per cent while the corresponding increase in India was 61 per cent. Consequently, ratio of the State's PCNSDP to the India's average declined from 65.9 per cent to 49.4 per cent.

The region-wise analysis of data shows that there exists a wide disparity across regions. The WR and The ER have more or less equal share in the State's total area and population, but PCNSDP of the ER is only about 58 per cent that of the WR. The magnitudes of CVs in PCNSDP show that the disparity has increased across regions since 1993-94. The ranking of the districts based on the CID reveals that a large number of districts of the WR are under the categories of most and high-medium developed districts; on the other hand, most of districts of the ER are under the most backward and low-medium developed categories. Region-wise averages and CVs in the development indicators reveal that apart from presence of the regional disparity, the inter-district variations in the development indicators within the regions are also significant.

The regression results show that the PCNSDP is positively related with the level of urbanisation, average size of holdings, per hectare value of agricultural output, per-capita consumption of electricity and percentage share of workers in secondary and tertiary sectors. The paper suggests that region-specific and sector-specific policy interventions are required to achieve balanced and inclusive development of all the regions. As agricultural productivity, per-capita electricity consumption and percentage share of non-farm employment in total employment are found to have significant impact on the PCNSDP; concerted efforts are required to make to improving the level of these development indicators in the most backward districts of the ER and BKR.

References

Ahluwallia, M.S. (2000), 'Economic Performances of States in Post-Reforms Period', *Economic and Political Weekly*, 6 May.

Dadibhavi, R.V. and S.T. Bagalkoti (2006), 'Reforms and Regional Inequalities in India: An Analysis', *The Indian Economic Journal*, Vol. 54(2), pp. 21-38.

Deaton, A. and Jean Dreze (2002), 'Poverty and Inequality in India: A Re-Examination', *Economic and Political Weekly*, September 7.

Dholakia, R.H. (2003), 'Regional Disparity in Economic and Human Development in India', *Economic and Political Weekly*, September 27.

Dholakia, R.H. (2005), 'Trend in Regional Disparity in Human and Social Development', Working Paper No. 2005-09-07, IIM Ahmedabad.

Government of Uttar Pradesh (2007), The Eleventh Five Year Plan, State Planning Commission, Lucknow. http://planning.up.nic.in/

Jha, R. (2004), Reducing Poverty and Inequality in India: Has Liberalization Helped? in G.A. Cornia (ed.) Inequality, Growth and Poverty in an Era of Liberalization and Globalization. UNU-WIDER Studies in Development Economics, Oxford University Press, New York, for UNU-WIDER, Helsinki.

Kumar, S. (2005), 'Note on Farm Sector in Uttar Pradesh', Planning Department, Lucknow.

Kurian, N.J. (2000), 'Widening Regional Disparities in India: Some Indicators', *Economic and Political Weekly*, Vol. 35, No. 7, pp 538-55.

Noorbakhsh, F (2003), 'Human Development and Regional Disparities in India', Centre for Development Studies, Department of Economics, University of Glasgow.http://www.gla.ac.uk

Pradhan, B., P.K. Roy, M.R. Saluja, S. Venkatraman (2000), "Rural-Urban Disparities: Income Distribution, Expenditure Pattern and Social Sector", The *Economic and Political Weekly*, pp. 2527-34.

Shetty, S.L. (2003), Growth of SDP and Structural Changes in State Economies: Inter-State Comparisons, *Economic and Political Weekly*, Vol. 38, No. 49, December 6, pp. 5189-5200

Singh, Nirvikar, L. Bhanadari, A. Chen and A. Khare (2003), "Regional Inequality in India: A Fresh Look", *Economic and Political Weekly*, Vol. 38, No. 11, March 15, pp. 1069-73.

Singh, S.P. and D.K. Nauriyal (2006), "Human Development Disparities in India: Inter-State Scenario", *Indian Journal of Social Development*, 6(2), 289-311.

Singh, S.P., Nauriyal, D.K. and Behera, M.R (2007), "Regional Disparity in Agricultural Growth in India: Magnitude and Determinants", Paper presented in the National Seminar on "Making Growth Inclusive with Special Reference to Imbalances in Regional Development", Department of Economics, University of Jammu, Jammu, March 12-13, 2007.

23

Inter-Regional Disparities: A Study of Uttar Pradesh

Nidhi Sharma

Over last two decades, Indian economy has emerged as a steady economy marching on the path of high economic growth. World recognizing India as a formidable force and is using its rising economic strategic strength to enhance world welfare and peace. High rate of 8.5 per cent growth rate and external self reliance failed to establish an equitable society. Economists over the last two decades are attempting to analyse the nature and causes of distributional changes in the era of market oriented economic reforms. In India the variables of income and consumption are considered for studying income disparity. An important issue, often neglected is the rising disparities in wealth concentration across households, individuals regions and groups. Distribution of wealth plays an important role in the development process. It influences the productivity level, public goods provision and occupation choice. Further, several theoretical models have considered the impact of market upon wealth and income inequalities. Examination of wealth disparities is valuable in itself. Arjun Jayadev, using

NSS data, focuses on per-capita as opposed to household size into account. Access to wealth of one member of the household has no effect on the access of other members, as wealth is a public good within the unit. He attempts to focus upon the changes of wealth pattern during the reform period rather than casual linkages between reforms and the changing nature of wealth distribution. This study concludes that there has been increase in wealth across virtually all areas and wealth distribution has become more unequal. Regional and other group-wise indicators reflect sharp divergences (Jayadev, 2007).

Pulapre Balkishan has estimated the growth rates of aggregate and sect oral GDP by using the exponential function in $Y_t=a+g_t+u_t$, where Y_t, g_t and u_t denote the log of income, growth rate, time trend and random disturbance, respectively. The exponential growth contains m+1 growth regimes.

$$\ln Y_t = a_1 + g_{1t} + u_t$$
$$\ln Yt = a_2 + g_{2t} + u_t$$

$$\ln Y_t = a_{m+1} + g_{m+1} + u_t$$

Main feature of the methodology is that it allows the data to parameterize the model. The resulting estimates reveal that there are two growth regimes in India since 1950. He then decomposes sector by the contribution to the change in the growth rate across these regimes. By means of a simple econometric model, he tests a hypothesis that emerges from his estimation (Balkishan, 2007).

Ojha in his study on the poverty of UP state finds that poverty fall is a function of two opposite forces. Households got out of poverty that left the rural areas after getting some employment and income. While others living above poverty line fell into poverty due to heavy expenditure on sickness, social ceremonies, etc. and ultimately into bad debts. Reasons for upward and downward household mobility across the poverty line are asymmetric and require a re-prioritization of poverty alleviation programmes. Downward movement of non-poor households' along with an upward movement of some rural poor reduces the net effect of poverty (Ojha, 2007). Sen considers the process of development related not only to expanding the supply of goods and services but the enhancing of capabilities of the people. (Ghosh, 1996).

Chelliah finds a rise in regional disparities in growth rates, poverty levels and indices of social development during the long period of national planning. Worrisome issue is that the present growth pattern leads not only to disparities in income but also in several other indices of development such as poverty ratio, IMR, life expectancy, literacy rate, female literacy rate, etc. (Chelliah, 2007). Nayyar analyses that generally empirical works consist of running cross section regression with subsequent growth rate of income as the dependent variable and initial income level as the primary independent variable using econometric model. He analysed that per-capita private investment, literacy rate, IMR and per-capita public investment are also important variables in determining state's steady level of income. First three are greatly influenced by fourth variable, policy-driven variable, thus focusing upon state's role in accelerating growth process of a region (Nayyar, 2007). Present paper focuses upon Review of Literature, Comparative Status of state Uttar Pradesh, Identification of Disparities in the state, Urban Disparities, Agricultural Disparities and lastly conclusion.

COMPARATIVE STATUS OF STATE: UTTAR PRADESH

Levels of poverty in India have been affected by the affairs of the Indian agriculture itself dependent upon the vagaries as well as bounties of nature. Magnitude of effects of vagaries of nature varies from region to region. Density of population, extent and degree of urbanization, land tenure system, irrigation and power system may have contributed to the inter as well as intra-state regional disparities. Regions where green revolution made remarkable progress, there had been decline in poverty levels and rise in state domestic product. Conscious public policy and planned development programmes contributed in removing poverty and disparities, yet not succeeded much in totality (Hicks, 1986).

Uttar Pradesh is a state with rich resources of alluvial

soil and plentiful ground and surface water. With a net cultivated area of about 168 lakh hectares, UP is the largest producing state of many agricultural products. Once the pacemaker for the country's economic and social upliftment UP has rich potential both in physical and human resources. Till seventies the state has performed well in all fronts, but in nineties, especially after 1990s, economic growth of the state began to fall, as state was unable to take advantages of liberalization and globalization (World Bank, 2002).

Real GSDP of Uttar Pradesh is going down, while population growth is highest, resulting in low per-capita income as compared to all-India. Per-capita income (measured by real gross domestic product) recorded a growth of only 33.6 per cent (1980-81 to 2002-03) (from Rs. 4891 in 1980-81 to Rs. 6535 in 2002-03) as compared to a growth of 111.5 per cent at all-India level (from Rs. 5908 in1980-81 to Rs. 12496 in 2002-03). At current prices, PCI of Uttar Pradesh during 2002-03 was recorded as Rs. 11856 as against Rs. 21373 (all-India average).

Table 1 throws light upon the average growth rates of Gross State Domestic Product of Uttar Pradesh and some selected states. Agriculture-wise, Gujarat made tremendous growth from 2.77 to 22.78 per cent. Even one of BIMARU state, Rajasthan made progress from 3.18 to 12.76 per cent. While UP, Bihar, Maharashtra and TN recorded negative growth. Industry-wise, all the states recorded positive rates. Gujarat recorded highest growth rate from 7.61 to 9.82 per cent. Even UP has recorded growth rate of 5.29 per cent (quite close to all-India average). Service sector-wise, Gujarat (11.08%), Haryana (6.29), WB (7.06) and Maharashtra (6.21) made remarkable progress while UP, Bihar, TN and Rajasthan recorded declining growth rates. If GSDP growth rates are observed it is found that Rajasthan and Bihar (BIMARU) states have performed well during the period 1990-01. States like Gujarat, Maharashtra and WB have performed better in period 2001-04 and states like UP, Bihar Rajasthan and Tamil Nadu fared poorly. Performance of UP in both periods (1994-01 and 2001-04) has been lowest.

Even though enriched with human and physical resources, Uttar Pradesh has been performing poor. Gap

TABLE I

Average of the Growth Rates of GSDP at 1994-95 Prices: UP and Selected States Period from 1994-95 to 2003-04

State	*Agriculture*		*Industry*		*Services*		*GSDP*	
	1994-01	*2001-04*	*1994-01*	*2001-04*	*1994-01*	*2001-04*	*1994-01*	*2001-04*
UP*	2.89	-2.32	5.58	5.29	4.77	2.24	4.34	2.24
GJ	2.77	27.78	7.61	9.82	8.29	11.08	7.86	11.08
MH	1.86	-0.72	3.48	5.76	6.97	6.21	8.34	6.21
RJ	3.18	12.76	9.27	3.41	8.60	5.6	4.66	5.6
TN	2.14	-6.76	6.76	0.77	9.26	2.02	5.92	2.02
WB*	3.86	2.78	6.26	5.1	9.48	7.06	10.15	7.06
HY	2.2	3.01	7.06	5.99	9.60	6.29	9.08	6.29
BH	6.62	-2.67	8.37	3.99	8.29	1.21	4.44	1.21
India	2.53	2.98	6.89	5.6	8.35	6.09	7.91	6.09

Source: (basic data): CSO.
Note: *data up to 2002-03 only.

between UP and India as a whole has been widening especially after 1990' s. UP, once a pride of India's social and economic development, now exhibits poor promises. Share of UP economy in national economy fell from 13.8 per cent in 1980-81 to 10.5 per cent in 1999-01 to 8.48 per cent in 2002-03 which indicates that UP economy's growth rate has been much slower as compared to other states' performance. In none of the sectors, state's performance is remarkable. If classified growth pattern of industrial sector is observed, UP has performed well in the organized manufacturing, communication, and construction, banking and primary sectors. However, it fared badly in areas of infrastructure such as power, water supply, railways, hotels, restaurants, real estate and trade. In fact, state government must focus upon infrastructural development to create development linkages in rest of the economy. Fast growth rates of secondary and tertiary sectors in fast growing states such as Gujarat, Maharashtra, Haryana, WB and Rajasthan hold the tempo of growth. Consequently, Indian average growth rate has been higher than that of Uttar Pradesh (GOI).

Table 2 shows the demographic and geographic features of four regions of the state UP Western region's 36.78 per cent population has 33.13 per cent of area of the state. Central region occupies 19.03 per cent of area for its 18.17 per cent of population. Eastern region's 40.04% population is fed upon 35.36 per cent of area while Bundelkhand region has 12.21 per cent of area for 4.96 per cent of population. Clearly population density is highest in Eastern region (776) followed by Western region (767), Central region (658) and lastly Bundelkhand region (280).

TABLE 2

Region-wise Area and Population of UP (2001)

Region	*Population (000)*	*% of Population*	*Area (sq km)*	*% of area*	*Population density*
Western	61114	36.78	79831	33.13	767
Central	30201	18.17	45834	19.03	658
Eastern	66628	40.09	85845	35.63	776
Bu.khand	8232	4.96	29418	12.21	280
UP	166175	100	240928	100	690

Source: Directorate of Economics and Statistics, UP.

Western region's capacity for higher agricultural growth through green revolution strategy in 1960 and 1970s helped the state to reach a new equilibrium level. In 1970s Eastern and Central regions made remarkable strides in the fields of irrigation, technology, investment in research and marketing infrastructure, consequently, state's growth rate was higher than the average Indian growth rate. Especially, since 1990s state has failed to take opportunities and advantages of liberalization and economic reforms. Inter-district variation in poverty incidence are also astonishing (Ojha).

Identification of Inter-State Disparities

Under Rashtriya Sum Vikas Yojana (RSVY) Planning Commission, Govt. of India has used following three parameters to identify the backwardness of the 150 districts in the country, including 21 districts of UP.

- Value of output per agriculture worker.
- Agricultural wage rate.
- Percentage of SC/ST population of the district.

Under National Food for Work Programme (NEFW) the Planning Commission, Govt. of India has identified backwardness of the 15 districts of UP on the basis of prevalence of poverty indicated by SC/ST population, agricultural productivity per worker and agricultural wage rate. The backward districts identified by the Planning Commission under RSVY and NFFW programmes are more or less same as identified by using 29 indicators in the study of regional disparities conducted in 2003 and 2005 respectively by Planning Department, Govt. of UP.

To identify the magnitude of disparities, the coefficient of variation is the best statistical method, which reflects the magnitude in numerical way. On the basis of secondary data available in respect of 70 districts of the State, the composite index of development of the districts has been calculated. There are many disparities also among the districts within a region. For working out the numerical values of the selected indicators, the State value of that indicator has been assumed as 100. After this, getting the average value of all the numerical values worked out, the Composite Index of Development (CID) have been calculated for all the 4 sectors viz., agricultural, economic, social infrastructures, industry, along with unclassified indicators. Based on this CID, the coefficient of variations has been worked out and also inter-regional inter-districts disparities have been identified.

In the study conducted in 2003, on the basis of data available (1991-2000) it was found that 9 districts, namely, Hardoi, Jaunpur, Shrawasti, Gonda, Bahraich, Balrampur, Chitrakoot, Azamgarh and Santkabir Nagar were identified as most backward districts as per their CID. Out of these 9 districts only one district belongs to Bundelkhand region and rest of the districts fall in Eastern region.

In the study of March, 2005 based on 2001-02 data 14 districts namely Shrawasti, Sant Kabirnagar, Chitrkoot, Balrampur, Kaushambi, Jaunpur, Gonda, Azamgarh, Siddharthnagar, Mahrajganj, Banda, Ghazipur, Bahraich and

Hardoi were found to be most backward. Out of these 14 districts, 11 districts belong to Eastern, 2 districts belong to Bundelkhand and one district belongs to Central region.

Classification of the District's Level of Development According to the Composite Index of Development in Descending Order (2005)

Most Developed Districts (CID 120 or above): 6 Districts

1. GBuddha Nagar 405.13
2. Ghaziabad 185.63
3. Meerut 149.48
4. Kanpur Nagar 141.43
5. Lucknow 136.73
6. Muzaffar Nagar 125.05
7. Bijnor 121.92

High Medium Developed Districts (CID 100 to 120) 22 Districts:

8. Saharanpur 119.37
9. Mathura 119.05
10. Agra 116.00
11. J.P. Nagar 114.58
12. Varanasi 114.29
13. Jhansi 113.82
14. Rampur 113.44
15. Muradabad 110.73
16. Bulandshahar 110.66
17. Kanpur Dehat 106.95
18. Bareilly 106.84
19. Aligarh 105.71
20. Pilibhit 105.49
21. Sonbhadra 105.42
22. Bagpat 104.75
23. Farrukhabad 103.95
24. Etawah 102.70
25. Jalaun 101.56
26. Firozabad 101.51
27. Shahjahanpur 101.37
28. Kannauj 100.59
29. Hathras 100.32
30. Lakhimpur Kheri 98.71

Low Medium Developed Districts (CID 80 to 100): 33 Districts

31. Mahoba 98.40
32. Auraiya 96.57
33. Gorakhpur 95.60
34. Allahabad 94.11
35. Faizabad 93.35
36. Manpuri 92.87
37. Barabanki 92.23
38. Lalitpur 90.92
39. Sultanpur 90.71
40. Hamirpur 90.67
41. Sitapur 90.09
42. Etah 89.76
43. Fatehpur 88.46
44. Badaun 87.07
45. Raebareli 86.76
46. Unnao 86.68
47. Ballia 84.36
48. Basti 83.43
49. Pratapgarh 83.26
50. Mirzapur 83.03
51. Kushinagar 82.62
52. Ambedkarnagar 82.58
53. Deoria 82.32
54. Mau 81.58
55. Chandauli 81.43
56. Sant Rabidas Nagar 80.62

Most Backward Districts (CID 80 and below): 9 Districts

57. Hardoi 79.75	64. Gonda 76.92
58. Bahraich 79.01	65. Jaunpur 76.89
59. Ghazipur 78.87	66. Kaushambi 76.85
60. Banda 78.82	67. Balrampur 73.48
61. Mahrganj 78.78	68. Chitrakoot 69.44
62. Sidd Nagar 77.85	69. Sant Kabir Nagar 69.25
63. Azamgarh 76.95	70. Shrawasti 63.47

Source: Directorate of Economics and Statistics, UP.

Disparities in Urbanization levels

Region-wise, sharp disparities are visible in the state. Major pockets of poverty are concentrated in the Eastern part of Uttar Pradesh where per-capita income is far below state average. Most prosperous region is Western region, followed by Central and Bundelkhand regions. On the other hand, Meerut and Saharanpur circles of Western region compete with national average, composing about 11 per cent of state's population. This fact clearly shows the widening gap of income between various regions of state.

In fact, In eastern region, Azamgarh, Devipatan and Vindhyachal have falling rates of 5.4, 2.4 and 0.1 per cents respectively. 40 per cent of population resides in Eastern Uttar Pradesh, 33.4 per cent in western part, 18.5 per cent in central and rest of the population is there in Bundelkhand region (DES).

Western region took advantage of green revolution strategy in agriculture and proximity from national capital Delhi. But as compared to other states of the country, this region is still moving slow during reforms period. Regional disparities are highlighted by several indicators such as urbanization rate, per-capita income, per-capita power consumption, percentage of irrigation facilities, size of holdings, average emoluments, literacy rates and persons engaged in different activities.

Table 3 indicates that Eastern region with 40 per cent of population has only two mega cities with population above 10 lakh, while western and central regions with 18.5 and 33 per cent of population have two mega cities respectively.

Western and central regions have 23 and 8 towns with population above 1 lakh as compared to eastern region (only with 13 towns). In fact, rising urbanization is an indicator of economic development of a state, creating much scope for tertiary sector in the state.

TABLE 3

Regional Disparity in Urbanization Centres

Region	*Circle*	*Share in total Pop. of UP*	*No. of towns with Pop. above 10 lakh*	*No. of towns with Pop. above 1 lakh*
Bundelkhand	Chitrakoot	2.4		1
	Jhansi	2.5		2
Central	Kanpur	6.8	1	3+1
	Lukhnow	11.7	1	5+1
Eastern	Allahabad	6.8	1	1+1
	Azamgarh	5.1		2
	Basti	2.1		1
	Devipatan	1.0		2
	Faizabad	6.0		1
	Gorakhpur	7.0		2
	Varanasi	7.1	1	3+1
	Vindhyachal	4.9		1
Western	Agra	9.9	1	6+1
	Bareilly	6.5		4
	Meerut	7.0	1	6+1
	Moradabad	6.2		5
	Saharanpur	3.8		2

Source (basic data): Uttar Pradesh Statistical Diary.

In Table 4 some development indicators throw light upon the interregional disparities spread in the state. Central region (including capital city) has highest per-capita power consumption (201.4 kwh) and Bundelkhand region has lowest consumption (129.7 kwh). 70.08 per cent of population is engaged in agriculture in Bundelkhand region while Western region has 56 per cent population on agriculture. Highest growth rate of population in Western region indicates that faster rate of development and urbanization failed to lower

TABLE 4

Region-wise Comparative Status of Development

Development Indicators	*W*	*C*	*E*	*B*
Per-capita power consumption (kwh) 2002-03	198.7	201.4	109.6	129.70
% of main workers engaged in agriculture (2001)	56.08	66.14	66.14	70.08
Population growth rate (2001)	26.55	26.29	25.58	22.57
No. of persons employed in registered factories per lakh (2001-02)	413	229	112	64
Literacy rate (2001)	57.36	57.8	54.27	59.3
Female literacy (2001)	43.96	45.52	39	43.11
Per-capita income in 2001-02 (at 1993-94 prices)	6978	5720	4222	6159
Urbanization rate (2001)	28.25	25.11	11.78	22.46
% of net irrigated area to net sown area	89.4	81	73.2	46.7
% of holdings of less than 1.0 ha. area (1995-96)	68.8	75	83	72
Length of pucca roads in km per lakh of population (2001-02)	84.25	93	74.77	111.48
Per-capita annual emoluments in Rs. (2001-02)	97,400	70,960	55,500	72,900

Source: Directorate of Economics and Statistics, UP.

the birth rate in the fertile Indo-Gangetic plains. Urbanization rate is lowest in Eastern region (11.78%) and highest in Western region (28.25%). Literacy rate is lowest in Bundelkhand region (59%) due to Government's sustained efforts. Female literacy is lowest (39%) in Eastern region due to poverty and social and cultural factors. Per-capita income is highest in Western region (Rs. 6978) and lowest in Eastern region (Rs. 4222). Even in the era of liberalization and globalization, Eastern and Bundelkhand regions' dependence upon agriculture and low urbanization rate indicate the poor investment and industrial opportunities and atmosphere in the region—main reason responsible for the backwardness of the region.

Industrial disparity is also visible in terms of stark disparities in per-capita employee emoluments. Western region has highest annual emoluments per employee at Rs. 97,400 followed by Bundelkhand region with Rs. 72,900, central zone with Rs. 70,600 and in eastern region this emolument stands at Rs. 55,500. Meerut circle has the highest emolument, while Faizabad in eastern region has the lowest emolument of Rs. 19,500. In other words, workers (supervisory and staff members) are poorly paid in rest of Uttar Pradesh. It also depicts that activities in rest of state are semi skilled and low level in technology.

Investment-wise, again it is western region which attracts highest percentage of total investment of state, i.e. 66.8 per cent while Bundelkhand receives lowest share1.57 per cent of investment. In western region, alone Meerut circle attracts 39.68 per cent of investment. Some circles such as Varanasi, Gorakhpur, Basti, Azamgarh, Chitrakoot, Jhansi, etc. present least opportunities for investment. In Bundelkhand region length of pucca road per lakh of population is 111.4 km while in Eastern region it is only 74.77 km per lakh population.

About 60.6 per cent of emoluments are cornered by Western region while Bundelkhand has 1.6 per cent of total emoluments. Alone Meerut circle corners 37.9 per cent of emoluments and Chitrakoot circle has the lowest share of 0.1 per cent. It clearly indicates the rising concentration of wealth in small parts of state while other parts exhibit low income levels.

Agricultural Disparities

Agriculture, main mobilizer of state UP also indicates poor growth. Tenth Plan draft focused upon Uttar Pradesh to achieve a growth of 7 per cent, if India wants to grow at 8 per cent. Sectoral structure of an economy is equally significant in realizing the required growths. Since, all the sectors are not equally responsive to economic reforms process. States with high dependence upon industry and service sectors are performing much better. Table 4 shows that Western region has ample irrigation opportunities (89.4%) while Bundelkhand region has only 46 per cent of net irrigated area to net sown area. Sharp disparities are also visible in land ownership. In Western region only 68.8 per cent holdings is less than one hectare while in Eastern region 83 per cent cultivators have land holdings less than one hectare. Even in Western region itself there are sharp disparities in land ownership.

Table 5 gives an idea of agricultural pattern of four regions of Uttar Pradesh. Western region's important agricultural group is cereals (53%) and commercial crops (35%) and small amount of pulses and fruits and vegetables. Central region's main group is cereals and commercial. Eastern region mainly concentrates upon cereals (77%) and smaller amount of pulses, commercial crops fruits and vegetables. Bundelkhand region is the only region with highest share in pulses (54%) and cereals (38%). There is a need of change in crop pattern of Eastern Uttar Pradesh. Cultivators should reduce their share of cereals and enhance the share of commercial crops. This would help them to raise their remunerative rewards and strengthen their economic levels.

TABLE 5

Region-wise Diversification of Agriculture in UP (Year 1997-98)

Region	*Commodity groups*	*Share in value of output (%)*	*Share in total area (%)*
WESTERN	Cereals	53.00	67.00
	Pulses	4.00	5.00
	Comm. crops	35.00	22.00
	Fruits and veg.	8.00	5.00
CENTRAL	Cereals	66.00	72.00
	Pulses	9.00	11.00
	Comm. Crops	21.00	14.00
	Fruits and veg.	4.00	4.00
EASTERN	Cereals	77.00	81.00
	Pulses	8.00	11.00
	Comm. crops	8.00	2.00
	Fruits and veg.	7.00	4.00
BU. KHAND	Cereals	38.00	42.00
	Pulses	54.00	49.00
	Comm. crops	8.00	89.00
	Fruits and veg.	0.50	0.50

Source: GOI, Uttar Pradesh Development Report, Vol. 2.

Table 6 clearly shows that the agricultural productivity of western region is much higher than rest of the regions. Rice, wheat and sugarcane are the products where western region's productivity is remarkable. Table also shows that over a period of 1991-92 to 1999-00 eastern and central regions agricultural productivity growth rate has improved much specially in case of rice and wheat. In case of sugarcane and cotton central region has performed well. Bundelkhand region's productivity level is very low as compared to other regions.

TABLE 6

Region-wise Yield of Different Crops

Crops	*WESTERN*		*CENTRAL*		*EASTERN*		*BUNDELKHAND*	
	1991-92	*1999-00*	*1991-92*	*1999-00*	*1991-92*	*1999-00*	*1991-92*	*1999-00*
Rice	2191.7	2393.75	1746.61	2054.95	1632.97	2030.63	827.96	1066.45
Wheat	2596.26	3027.38	2162.65	2483.41	1951.19	2347.54	1513.78	1895.77
S. Cane	53553.65	63838	44274.29	53838.42	48497.48	46319.95	37946.93	41543.94
Cotton	208.85	482.10	222.22	1095.76	—	—	—	—
Potato	19824	15946	15826	18590	16730	10410	18098	12510
Onion	15201	4340	14990	10818	14887	7479	11525	2575

Source (basic data): Uttar Pradesh ke Krishi Ankare (Ag. Statistics of UP).
Note: Yield = kg/hectare.

Table 7 depicts the region-wise annual compound growth rates of yield of important crops. Only in Bundelkhand region growth rates of rice, wheat and total cereals have improved while in other regions of west, central and east growth rates of these regions have declined. Pulses growth rates improved for the three regions but in Bundelkhand region it has fallen from 0.11 to -0.89. Otherwise, annual compound growth rates of total food grains for all the regions have declined over a period of 1980-89 to 1999-00. In Western region it fell from 3.67 to 2.29 per cent, in Central region from 4.14 to 2.17 per cent, in Eastern region from 3.96 to 2.47 per cent and in Bundelkhand from 1.46 to 1.41 per cent during time period 1980-89 to 1999-00. Oilseeds are an important crop in Indian agricultural scenario where eastern region shows tremendous growth rate in 1999-00.

TABLE 7

Region-wise Annual Compound Growth Rates of Yield of Important Crops

Crops	*WESTERN*		*CENTRAL*		*EASTERN*		*B. KHAND*	
	1980-89	*1990-99*	*1980-89*	*1990-99*	*1980-89*	*1990-99*	*1980-89*	*1990-99*
Rice	5.48	1.49	5.72	2.72	5.65	2.83	2.64	2.94
Wheat	2.76	2.03	3.56	2.02	2.69	2.39	1.53	3.37
Total cereals	3.92	2.12	4.32	2.07	4.53	2.28	1.12	3.19
Total pulses	1.25	2.47	1.22	2.55	1.06	3.44	0.11	-0.89
Total foodgrains	3.67	2.29	4.14	2.17	3.96	2.47	1.46	1.41
Total oilseeds	3.92	0.99	1.29	1.34	2.75	5.48	4.21	1.80
Sugarcane	0.32	1.72	1.41	2.20	1.77	-0.86	1.41	-0.14

Source (basic data): Agricultural Statistics of UP (Various issues).

CONCLUSION

Thus it may be concluded that drastic steps are needed to be taken to fill up the gaps among different regions of the state. There is urgent need of industrialization in the Eastern and Bundelkhand regions especially. Service sector's growth rate is to be accelerated through urbanization process. Western region is the largest contributor to state exchequer while Eastern region is the biggest beneficiary of state planning. In fact, urbanization itself is the cause as well as effect of developmental activities in the backward regions. Agricultural sector needs serious attention through several institutional and non-institutional reforms such as land reforms, technological advancements, etc. Diversification and commercialization of agriculture is urgently required. Flexible credit accessibility, insurance of cultivators, advanced marketing system, etc. are the need of the hour. In fact along with mechanical and physical inputs, non-economic factors are equally responsible for accelerating the growth tempo of a region such as scientific temperament, optimistic attitude, non-fatalism, rationality and zeal for progress. There is need of generating linkages between different sectors and industries in these two regions. In fact, slow growth rates of a region directly or indirectly affects the utilization level of resources, poverty, employment levels, investment criteria, income generating capacity and ultimately capability building capacity of the economy.

References

Balkishan, P. (2007): 'Understanding Economic Growth in India: A Prerequisite', *Economic and Political Weekly,* Vol. XLII, Nos. 27-28, p. 2915.

Chelliah, R.J.S., K.R. Sundaram (2007): 'Strategy for Poverty Reduction and Narrowing Regional Disparites', *Economic and Political Weekly,* Vol. XLII, No. 34, pp. 3475-76.

Directorate of Economics and Statistics, Uttar Pradesh: Report on Regional Imbalances, Chap. 7.

Ghosh, A. (1996): 'Development Economics---Paradigms of Economic Development', p. 54.

GOI: Uttar Pradesh Development Report, Planning Commission, Vol. 1.

GOI: Uttar Pradesh Development Report, Planning Commission, Vol 2.

Hicks, J.R, Mukherjee, Ghosh (1986): 'The Framework of the Indian Economy', p. 257.

Jayadev, A., Motiram, S., Vakulabharanam, V. (2007): 'Patterns of Wealth Disparities in India during the Liberalization Era', *Economic and Political Weekly,* Vol. XLII, No. 38, pp. 3853-55.

Nayyar, G. (2008): 'Economic Growth and Regional Inequality in India', *Economic and Political Weekly,* Vol. XLIII, No. 6, pp. 58-65.

Ojha, R.K. (2007): 'Poverty Dynamics in Rural Uttar Pradesh', *Economic and Political Weekly,* Vol. XLII, pp. 1453-58.

World Bank (2002): 'Poverty in India—The Challenge of Uttar Pradesh'.

24

Inter-State Disparities in Marine Fisheries Development

K. Pazhani and S. Jesi Isabella

India is a country with unity in diversity. Interregional disparities and how to narrow the regional disparities are the topic of discussion in the academic circles and in the midst of policy-makers. In a large country like India, with substantial regional differences in physical endowments, climatic conditions, social traditions and differences in the initial levels of development, growth rates are bound to vary among regions. It is the task of the State policy to implement compensatory measures to push forward the laggard regions and spread growth and development more evenly. However, during almost the entire period of national planning, as well-known, a steady widening of regional disparities has taken place (Chelliah et. al, 2007). The fisheries development in the maritime States of our country is no exception to this state of affair.

The rapid development of an economy depends on the development of different sectors from different angle—in terms of employment generated, output produced, input consumed, extent of exports and also contribution to GDP. The marine fisheries sector development depends on the socio-economic conditions of fishermen households. But the producers of fish (fishermen) mostly remain in a state of abject poverty and pushed down in the social ladder. They are struggling hard even for their existence. It is because of the nature of their employment, the product they are producing, the quantity they catch, the price they get for their product and also the availability of the necessaries for existence in their villages.

The fisheries economy of our country has undergone rapid structural changes during the last few decades. The vast technological options available to fishers led them for a fast shift from traditional to mechanized and motorized fishing methods in marine fisheries and from traditional to improved seed production and culture practices in inland fisheries (Sathiadhas *et. al.* 2000). But the lots of the actual fishermen remain unaltered. They use traditional non-motorized fishing (43.67%) crafts, 61.71 per cent of the fishermen families have no crafts, 48.84 per cent families have no gears and 46.7 per cent have neither crafts nor gears.

THE PROBLEM

The fisherfolk are the neglected sections of the society remaining socially and economically most backward. Economic backwardness coupled with non-availability of technical education in almost all the coastal areas paved the way for low quality of human capital. They depend on traditional methods of fishing, which deprive them from enjoying their entitlements. Further, absence of fishing, financial and marketing infrastructures put the fishermen into debt trap and led to the exploitation of one group of fishermen by another through various credit linkages. In addition to this, there is a wide disparity in the allocation of funds for fisheries development at the district, State and National level. These situations remain as obstacles to the development fishing industry in general and marine fisheries sector in particular.

The development of fisheries sector depends on the availability of marine resources, human resource engaged in fishing operations, the crafts and gears they use and also the infrastructures available for fishing and marketing the produce. Fishery resources are a common property. The users of this resource use it without considering the effect of their activities on the available fish stock and also the marine fishery environment. But after the introduction of the process of motorization of traditional crafts and introduction of mechanized boats, the traditional fishermen felt much about the depletion of marine resources in the inshore area due to indiscriminate fishing by the mechanized boats. It led to class conflicts and also formation of separate unions to establish their rights. Further, it has led to inter-state migration of fishermen and fishing in the international waters and the subsequent bad incidences near Sri Lanka and Pakistani boarders. With this theoretical background, this paper is framed in such a way to analyze the inter-state disparities in marine fisheries development in India.

Among the challenges faced by mankind today is to synchronise development with environmental sustainability. It has become a difficult task in the coastal zone where the ecological processes are inadequately understood because of its complex nature brought about by the influence of land, water and air. Industrial development and modernization have attracted more and more people to the coastal area and due to this; the rich natural resources of the coastal zone are under very strong pressure now. If the coastal areas are not managed scientifically, man-made environmental problems will place an unbearable strain on sustainable development. Environmental problems are almost always associated with resources that are regenerative (that is renewable) but in danger of exhaustion from excessive use. (Karl-Goran Maler, 1997).

IMPORTANCE OF FISHERIES IN INDIA

Fisheries have an important place in the Indian economy. India is blessed with abundant fishery resources, both marine and inland. The vast unexploited natural resources, which are replenishable in nature, have helped to transform the fishing activities from a mere subsistence level during pre-independence to a commercial fishery under the planning era. The role and potential of fisheries in the economic development of the country is very significant on the following grounds:

- Fish gives a high nutritive food value at a cheaper rate;
- Fisheries contribute 1.07 per cent of total GDP;
- It provides employment and livelihood to lakhs of people in fishing, processing, preserving, marketing, net making, boat building and other allied activities; and
- It earns the much needed foreign exchange through exports to different developed countries like USA and Japan. Considering the importance of fisheries in the above respects the Central Government has been allotting funds for fisheries development.

The importance of making full use of global fishing resources is widely recognized. Fisheries development is essential both as a means of increasing levels of food production and as a means of improving the quality of diet in developing countries; as a source of protein, vitamins and essential minerals, fish provides an ideal supplement to the poor and monotonous diet which is the daily fare of the inhabitants of many tropical and sub-tropical countries (Bailey, 1988).

Table 1 shows that the gap between outlay for fisheries development and actual expenditures widens in course of time which remain as a severe challenge to fisheries development in India. Further, different studies reveal that the outlay has been remaining less than 0.5 per cent of the total plan outlay. The funds allotted are insufficient compared to the stage of development of fisheries sector compared to other countries of the world and the population depending on fisheries for their livelihood. Even the allotted funds are not fully utilized or evenly distributed between inland and marine sector and among maritime states of our country.

Table 2 reveals that fish production has increased from 7.52 lakh tonnes during 1950-51 to 63.99 lakh tonnes during 2003-04. The share of marine fish production has decreased from 71.01 per cent in 1950-51 to 45.96 per cent during 2003.04.Inland fish production has increased from 28.99 per cent to 54.04 per cent during the same period.

The trend fitted to the data is represented by the equations:

TABLE 1

Financial Outlay fot Fisheries Development

Plan	Outlay (Rs. in crore)	Change (in%)	Expenditure (Rs. in crore)	Change (in%)
I	5.13	-	2.78	-
II	12.26	138.99	9.00	223.74
III	28.27	130.59	23.32	159.11
IV	82.68	192.66	54.11	132.03
V	151.24	82.92	115.11	112.73
VI	371.14	145.40	286.95	171.84
VII	546.52	47.25	477.59	66.43
VIII	1205.39	120.56	1118.46	134.72
IX	2069.70	71.70	1414.41	26.46
X	2060.54	-00.44	N.A	--

Source: Hand Book on Fisheries Statistics, 2004, p. 69.

TABLE 2

Trends in Fish Production (1950-51 to 2003-04)

(in Lakh tonnes)

Year	Marine	Inland	Total
1950-51	5.34 (71.01)	2.18 (28.99)	7.52 (100.00)
1960-61	8.80	2.80	11.60
1970-71	10.86	6.70	17.56
1980-81	15.55	8.87	24.42
1990-91	23.00	15.36	38.36
1991-92	24.47	17.10	41.57
1992-93	25.76	17.89	43.65
1993-94	26.49	19.95	46.44
1994-95	26.92	20.97	47.89
1995-96	27.07	22.42	49.49
1996-97	29.67	22.81	53.48
1997-98	29.50	24.38	53.88
1998-99	26.96	25.66	52.62
1999-00	28.34	28.23	56.57
2000-01	28.11	28.45	56.56
2001-02	28.30	31.26	59.56
2002-03	29.90	32.10	62.00
2003-04	29.41(45.96)	34.58 (54.04)	63.99 (100.00)

Source: Hand Book of Fisheries Statistics, 2004, p. 5.
Figures in parentheses indicate percentage to total.

$$Y = 1.2223X + 11.968 \text{ (Marine) } R^2 = 0.6979$$

$$Y = 1.799X + 3.0049 \text{ (Inland) } R^2 = 0.6565$$

The trend lines depict that the growth trend in inland fish production is greater than that of the marine fish production. During the beginning of the planning era, marine fish production is greater than inland fish production. During the year 1999-2000, they become equal (28 lakh tonnes) and after that inland fish production exceeded marine fish production. A fall in marine fish production may be attributed to indiscriminate fishing by mechanized boats and also increase in the number of motorized crafts and the resultant decrease in marine fishery resource.

Table 3 shows the growth trends in the quantity and value of marine products exported from India. The growth rate of exports in quantity term was 18.53 whereas in value terms it was 41.91.While the quantity of fish export increased from 15732 tonnes during 1961-62 to 412,017 tonnes during 2003-04, the value of total export increased from Rs. 3.92 crore to Rs. 6091.96 crore during the same period. The average annual growth rate of export of fish has decreased from -21.30 per cent in physical terms during 1961-62 to -11.83 per cent during 2003-04 whereas in value terms it has decreased from -15.52 per cent to -11.47 per cent during the same period. This drastic decrease in fisheries export was due to:

- Fall in marine fish production;
- Import restrictions imposed by Western countries; and
- Absence of proper infrastructures for fish export in most of the maritime States.

Table 4 shows that there were wide fluctuations in the contributions of fisheries to total GDP. This situation may be attributed to the existing inadequacy in infrastructure facilities for fishing, the operation of traditional non-motorised crafts (43.67%) and also a fall in the importance given to marine fisheries development by planners when compared to inland fisheries.

TABLE 3

Trend in Exports of Marine Products

Year	*Quantity (tonnes)*	*Value (Rs. crores)*	*Annual Growth Rate (%)*	
			Quantity	*Value*
1961-62	15,732	3.92	--	--
1971-72	35,883	35.07	13.2	4.8
1981-82	70,105	286.01	-7.2	21.8
1991-92	171,820	1,375.89	23.2	54.0
1992-93	208,602	1.767.43	21.4	28.5
1993-94	243,960	2,503.62	16.9	41.7
1994-95	307,337	3,575.27	26.0	42.8
1995-96	296,277	3,501.11	-3.6	-2.1
1996-97	378,199	4,121.36	27.7	17.7
1997-98	385,818	4,697.48	2.0	14.0
1998-99	302,934	4,626.87	-21.5	-1.5
1999-00	343,031	5,116.67	13.24	10.59
2000-01	440,473	6,443.89	28.41	25.94
2001-02	424,470	5,957.05	-3.63	-7.56
2002-03	467,297	6,881.31	10.09	15.52
2003-04	412,017	6,091.95	-11.63	-11.83

Source: Handbook of Fisheries Statistics, 2004, p. 65.

DISPARITIES IN DEVELOPMENT

To analyse the disparities in the development of marine fisheries sector the total coastal area has been classified into three regions—West Region, Eastern Region, and Other Areas. The State-wise indices of economic development (2004-05) in terms of per-capita GSDP (in 1993-94 price) Maharashtra (1), Gujarat (2), Karnataka (6) and Kerala (7) were among the top while the Tamil Nadu (5), West Bengal (9), Andhra Pradesh (10) and Orissa (12) ranks at a lower level. This situation may be attributed to the existing disparities in factor and resource endowments and also the available infrastructures—basic, financial and marketing. Similar situation also prevails in the case of marine fishing industry in all the maritime states.

Table 5 exhibits wide variations in length of coast line, continental shelf, number of landing centres and number of fishing villages. It shows that the Western region has 40.39

TABLE 4

Trends in the Contribution of Fisheries Sector to Gross Domestic Product

(Current Prices 2003-04)

Year	*Total GDP*	*GDP from Agri Forestry and Fishing*	*GDP from Fisheries*	*GDP from Fisheries as % of*	
				Total GDP	*GDP from Agri., Forestry and Fishing*
1993-94	781345	241967	8679	1.11	3.59
1994-95	917058	278773	10602	1.16	3.80
1995-96	1073271	303102	11866	1.11	3.91
1996-97	1243547	362606	14083	1.13	3.88
1997-98	1390148	387008	17269	1.24	4.46
1998-99	1598127	442494	18156	1.14	4.10
1999-00	1761838	461964	20017	1.14	2.33
2000-01	1902998	468480	22535	1.18	4.81
2001-02	2081474	510568	24843	1.19	4.87
2002-03	2254888	507863	27093	1.20	5.33
2003-04	2519785	575283	27026	1.07	4.70

Source: Hand Book of Fisheries Statistics, 2004, Ministry of Agriculture, Government of India, New Delhi.

per cent of coast line and 70.38 per cent of continental shelf. This is one of the reasons for the major portion of fish production and export from this region. On the other hand, the Eastern region has 33.67 per cent of the coastline and 22.26 per cent of continental shelf. Further, this region has more than 50 per cent of fishermen villages and landing centres. Though the remaining areas have 25.94 of the coastline, they have only less than ten per cent of continental shelf, 3.92 per cent of landing centres and 2.27 per cent of fishermen villages. These situations have contributed much for the existing inter-state disparities in fisheries development.

Table 6 shows that Maritime States in the Eastern part were having 58.63 per cent (2063383) of fisherfolk population since they have maximum number of fishermen families (424672) which forms 56.16 per cent of the total. Tamil Nadu

TABLE 5

Marine Fisheries Resources—Coastal States and Union Terrotories of India

Sl. No.	State/Union Territory	Length of Coast Line (kms.)	Continental Shelf ('000 sq. kms.)	Number of Landing Centres	No. of Fishing Villages
A.	**Western Region**				
1.	Goa	104	10	88	72
2.	Gujarat	1600	184	286	851
3.	Karnataka	300	27	29	221
4.	Kerala	500	40	223	222
5.	Maharashtra	720	112	184	395
	Total (A)	3224	373	813	1716
		(40.39)	(70.38)	(42.48)	(45.37)
B.	**Eastern Region**				
6.	Andhra Pradesh	974	93	508	508
7.	Orissa	480	26	63	329
8.	Pondicherry	45	1	28	45
9.	Tamil Nadu	1076	41	362	446
10.	West Bengal	158	17	65	652
	Total (B)	2688	118	1026	1980
		(33.67)	(22.26)	(53.60)	(52.32)
C.	**Other Areas**				
11.	A & N	1912	35	57	45
12.	Daman and Diu	27	-	7	31
13.	Lakshadweep	132	4	11	10
	Total (C)	2071	39	75	86
		(25.94)	(7.36)	(3.92)	(2.27)
	Grand Total (A+B+C)	7983	530	1914	3782
		(100.00)	(100.00)	(100.00)	(100.00)

Source: Hand Book of Fisheries Statistics 2004, Ministry of Agriculture, Government of India, New Delhi.

TABLE 6

Number of Fishermen Families and Population—2005

States/Union Territories	No. of Families	Sex		Total	Family Size
		Male	Female		
West Bengal	53816	142022	127543	269565	5.01
Orissa	86352	235610	214781	450391	5.22
AP	129246	259918	250073	509991	3.95
Tamil Nadu	192152	405790	384618	790408	4.11
Pondicherry	11541	21733	21295	43028	3.73
Kerala	120486	304308	297926	602234	5.00
Karnataka	30176	86826	84088	170914	5.66
Goa	1963	5516	5152	10668	5.43
Maharashtra	65313	163363	156034	319397	4.89
Gujarat	59889	166814	156401	323215	5.40
Daman and Diu	5278	14905	14400	29305	5.55
Total	756212	1806805	1712311	3519116	4.65

Source: Marine Fisheries Census, 2005, Part-I, Government of India, New Delhi.

alone has 191152 (25.41%) fishermen families and 790408 (22.46%) fisherfolk. The family size ranges from a minimum of 3.73 in Pondicherry to the maximum of 5.66 in Karnataka. This disparity in human resource is also a cause for existing disparities in fisheries development in India.

FISHING CRAFTS

Due to lower priority given to fisheries in relation to industries, fishing industry in India has not developed much. Moreover, the equipment and methods used are very old as compared with those of developed countries (Baheer, 1990). The importance of developing fishery resources lies in the fact that they can act as substitute to our land resources. The use of mechanised methods can help to raise the productivity substantially (Devi, 1997).

Table 7 shows that there are 238772 fishing crafts in the coastal areas, of which 58911 (24.67%) are mechanized boats,

TABLE 7

Distribution of Fishing Crafts in States/Union Teritories

States/Union Teritories	*Mechanised Boats*	*Motorised Crafts*	*Non-motorised Crafts*	*Total*
West Bengal	6829	1776	10041	18646
Orissa	3577	4719	15444	23740
Andhra Pradesh	2541	14112	24386	41039
Tamil Nadu	7711	22478	24231	54420
Pondicherry	627	2306	1524	4457
Kerala	5504	14151	9522	29177
Karnataka	4373	3705	7577	15655
Goa	1087	932	532	2551
Maharashtra	13053	3382	7073	23508
Gujarat	13047	7376	3729	24152
Daman and Diu	562	654	211	1427
Total	58911	75591	104270	238772

75591 (31.66%) are motorised crafts and 104270 (43.67%) are non-motorised traditional crafts. Maharashtra and Gujarat account for 26100 (44.3%) of the mechanized crafts in operation. Out of the 75591 motorised crafts 22478 (29.74%) are operating in Tamil Nadu alone followed by Kerala 14151 (18.72%) and Andhra Pradesh 14112(18.67%). Even after five decades of planned development 104270 (43.67%) traditional crafts remain non-motorised. Further, the States in the Eastern part operates 59.6 per cent of crafts and the western States have only 39.8 per cent of the fishing crafts. This is one of the reasons why India is lacking behind many East Asian Countries in fisheries development. Andhra Pradesh (24386) and Tamil Nadu (24231) have maximum number of non-motorised crafts compared to other States and Union Territories. This is also one of the reasons for low level of fisheries production, export and contribution to GDP in India.

FISHING GEARS

Gears are the nets used to catch fish. There are also wide variations in the number of units of gears possessed by different maritime states of our country. Gillnets are mostly used by almost all the States. The other types of gears which are in operation are given in the following table.

Table 8 shows that there were wide variations in the varieties and number of gears possessed by different regions. Trawl nets and Gill nets are the most commonly used fishing crafts in all the states. Out of 69188 trawl nets, the States in the West coast owned 43799 (63.30%) nets. This situation may be attributed to the operation of more number of mechanized boats (62.91%) in that area. On the other hand, the States in the Eastern part owned 2967023 Gillnets (71.76%). This situation may be attributed to the operation of more number of traditional crafts (67.28%) in this area.

FISHERY INFRASTRUCTURES

One of the important factors that determine fisheries development is the availability of landing facilities and fishing harbours. Coastal infrastructure is crucial for fisheries and overall socio-economic uplift of coastal rural areas in general. Inadequate infrastructures leads to human loss while entering into the sea and returning back to the shore with the catches. Further it is one of the causes for inter-village, inter-district, inter-state and international migration of fishermen. Levis (1955) included public utilities, ports, water supply and electricity as infrastructure. In the fisheries sector, infrastructures may include the following: (i) Basic infrastructures—Roads, hospitals, community centers, (ii) Financial infrastructures—Banks, Fishermen and Fisherwomen Co-operatives, (iii) Fisheries infrastructures - Fishing harbours, fish landing centres, boat yards, (iv) Marketing infrastructures—ice factories, cold storages, freezing plants, curing yards peeling sheds and fishmeal plants and organized markets.

Table 9 shows that there are wide disparities in the construction of fishing harbours and landing centers in the maritime states of India. The east coast area which possesses maximum number of fishing crafts (59.6%) has only 18 (47.36%) minor ports and four (26.66%) minor ports are under construction and in the case of landing centres also it possess only 57 (40.14%) of the total (142). This is one of the reasons for the migration of fishermen from Tamil Nadu, especially

TABLE 8

Gears Owned by Fisherfolk in India, 2005

States	*Trawl nets*	*Purse Seine*	*Boat Seine*	*Fixed bag net*	*Drift net*	*Gillnet pieces*	*Hooks and Lines*	*Lone lines*	*Others*
West Bengal	1228	19	49	46528	1164	327769	2896	80	168
Orissa	1387	1166	1716	19303	5433	483586	18864	7189	37678
AP	2229	0	4557	16787	4013	712362	48317	14673	16287
Tamil Nadu	17011	79	2872	1357	36705	1410975	140069	12079	121794
Pondicherry	1598	0	1	14	1376	32331	918	16	875
Kerala	2900	43	1772	709	6575	202416	9943	2856	15469
Karnataka	5127	515	21	1790	6482	136069	13887	2917	7957
Goa	1338	283	5	0	144	26348	0	0	1218
Maharashtra	8550	174	964	21482	12588	277150	8365	192	39052
Gujarat	25984	9	259	34059	823	472434	3844	806	80443
Daman and Diu	1936	0	0	230	0	53486	4	0	864
Total	69188	2288	12216	142259	75303	4134926	247107	40808	321805

Source: Marine Fisheries Census, 2005, Part-I, Government of India, New Delhi, p. 41.

TABLE 9

Number of Minor Fishing Harbours and Fish Landing Centres Commissioned/Under Construction by States/Union Teritories, 2004

States	*Minor Fishing Harbours*		*Fish Landing Centres*	
	Commissioned	*Under-construction*	*Commissioned*	*Under-construction*
West Bengal	4	1	12	-
Orissa	3	2	21	7
AP	3	1	2	15
Tamil Nadu	7	-	21	10
Pondicherry	1	-	1	-
Kerala	8	5	23	5
Karnataka	6	3	10	3
Goa	-	-	2	2
Maharashtra	1	1	35	1
Gujarat	4	2	20	2
Daman and Diu	-	-	2	-
A & N Islands	1	-	-	1
Lakshadweep	-	-	3	-
Total	38	15	142	46

Source: Hand Book of Fisheries Statistics, 2004, Ministry of Agriculture, Government of India, New Delhi, p. 75.

from Kanyakumari district to the west coast upto Gujarat. Even after five decades of planned development the Central Government has failed to construct a Port at Colachel (in Kayakumari District) in Tamil Nadu, which was promised by the Central Governement for a very long period. Further, these facilities were provided by the Central Governments without considering the length of the coastline, number of fishing villages, number of people depending on fishing, number of fishing crafts in operation. These factors contribute much for the disparities in marine fisheries development in India.

Table 10 reveals that 112 boat yards (50%), 315 (34.81%) ice factories, 31 (28.7%) cold storages, 56 (49.56%) freezing plants, 414 (41.73%) curing yards, 153 (52.22%) peeling sheds available in Kerala only. In the case of curing

TABLE 10

Fisheries-related Infrastructures, 2005

States	*Boat yard*	*Ice Factories*	*Colding Storages*	*Freezing Plants*	*Canning Plants*	*Curing Yards*	*Peel-Sheds*	*Fish-meal Plants*
West Bengal	1	38	0	0	0	0	0	0
Orissa	12	27	6	5	0	11	6	0
AP	8	17	0	1	2	39	24	0
Tamil Nadu	29	101	8	4	0	9	30	2
Pondicherry	0	8	1	0	0	0	0	0
Kerala	112	315	31	56	0	414	153	4
Karnataka	32	152	9	7	10	1	8	11
Goa	0	5	0	0	0	0	0	0
Maharashtra	6	54	11	3	1	2	6	0
Gujarat	24	178	42	37	0	516	66	29
Daman and Diu	0	10	0	0	0	0	0	0
Total	224	905	108	113	13	992	293	46

Source: Marine Fisheries Census, 2005, Part-I, Government of India, New Delhi, p. 49.

yard 930 (93.75%) out of 992 yards were established in Gujarat and Kerala. Why not the same facilities provided to other States? It indicates that the State Governments have failed to provide the basic infrastructures necessary to safeguard the interest of fishermen to which they are entitled. This situation may be attributed to the absence of representatives of fisherfolk in these State governments.

OTHER INFRASTRUCTURES

The World Development Report (1994) considers the following as the infrastructures necessary for development: (i) Public utilities—power, telecommunications, piped water supply, sanitation and sewerage, solid waste collection and disposal and piped gas; (ii) Public works—roads, major dams and canal works for irrigation and drainage; (iii) Other transport sectors urban and inter-urban railways, urban transport, ports and waterways and airports. The important infrastructures available in the maritime states and union territories are given below:

Table 11 reveals that only 2719 (84.49%) fishermen villages have been connected by road, 2067 (64.55%) have hospital facilities, 1336 (41.72%) have banking facilities and 4781 co-operative societies. Out of 2067 hospitals, only 316 (15.28%) and out of 1336 banks only 193 (14.45%) are in the Eastern coast. This is one of the reasons for the low level of fisheries development in the East compared to the Western part of our country. But out of 4781 Fisheries Co-operative Societies 3596 (75.21%) are in the East coast area. These co-operatives were established with the aim of providing necessary credit and other inputs necessary for fisheries development and also to undertake marketing activities. But most of them are at the dormant stage and in Tamil Nadu they are acting only as fair price shops. They neither provide credit nor undertake marketing activities.

TABLE 11

Other Infrastructures Fishing Villlage, 2005

States	*Total Villages*	*Villages connected by road*	*Hospitals*	*Banks*	*Co-operative Societies*
West Bengal	346	99	24	24	46
Orissa	641	453	54	43	170
AP	498	430	43	22	2378
Tamil Nadu	581	538	186	93	967
Pondicherry	28	28	9	11	35
Kerala	222	219	357	306	381
Karnataka	156	153	304	284	199
Goa	39	30	123	52	23
Maharashtra	406	333	455	217	366
Gujarat	263	241	486	269	200
Daman and Diu	22	22	26	15	16
Total	3202	2719	2067	1336	4781

Source: Marine Fisheries Census, 2005, Part-I, Government of India, New Delhi, p. 48.

EMPLOYMENT OF FISHERFOLK

The fisheries sector in India provides employment to over one million people fully, partially or in subsidiary activities with an equally important segment of the population engaged in ancillary activities. The demand for fish is on the increase whereas its availability declines; in such a context productivity improvement is key to poverty alleviation (Manickam, 2006). Sen (2004) has given three different aspects of employment. They are:

- The income aspect, employment gives an income to the employed;
- The production aspect, employment yields an output; and
- The recognition aspect, employment gives a person the recognition of being engaged in something worth his while.

Generally, employment provides income to the employed. But, there are workers like palmarah tapers and fishermen, who receive nothing for their work on many occasions. Moreover, their employment is seasonal in nature and so unemployment and underemployment are inherent features of marine fishing industry. Production may be zero during the lean season due fish famine1 or migration of fish. Further, fishermen are in the lowest ebb of the social ladder and considered as economically most backward community.

The employment profile of fisherfolk is given in Appendix-II. It reveals that 16,45,919 (46.77%) fisherfolk are employed in fishing and fishery related activities. About 25.7 per cent of the fisherfolk are actively engaged in fishing and 80.7 per cent in fishery related activities. Out of the total employed, those who are employed in fishing comes to 51.45 per cent, fishery related activities 43.75 per cent and non-fishing employment only 4.8 per cent. Tamil Nadu accounts for 23.3 per cent of active fishermen in India followed by Kerala (15.8%). The maximum percentage (27.2) of fisherfolk actively engaged in fishing within a state is in Andhra Pradesh. Women account for 48.3 per cent of the fisherfolk engaged in fishery related activities, of these 73.6 per cent is engaged in marketing of fish. Out of those actively engaged in fishing, fishermen in the eastern part constitute 61.59 per cent (5,47,895). Out of the total employed (17,28,992), only 4.81 per cent were engaged in non-fishing activities. This situation may be attributed to the absence of non-fishing activities or industries to generate sufficient employment opportunities.

FISH CONSUMPTION

Fish food provides proteins and vitamins required for the body. All the essential amino acids are present in the fish flesh. However, crustaceans have higher protein content than fish and molasses. Calcium is required for the growth of bones, teeth and the muscles, along with phosphates. Both these minerals are found in the fish flesh. Potassium is required to maintain the osmo regulatory phenomenon in the body. Potassium is found in high amount in the fishes. The other minerals present are iron and copper, which are required for the production of hemoglobin and for synthesis of connective tissue (Basheer, 1990). But, people in both rural and urban areas consume insignificant quantity of fish. This situation may be attributed to the prevailing social and religious customs and the absence of proper marketing infrastructures.

Table 12 reveals that monthly per-capita consumption of fish is very low in both rural and urban areas of all the States in India. It is high in islands like Andaman and Nicobar, Daman and Diu. This situation may be attributed to the availability of fish and also non-availability of vegetable in adequate quantities in these areas. Among the coastal States fish consumption is high in Kerala. It is due to the food habits of the people and also nearness to coastal areas in almost entire Kerala State. The number of households consuming fish per 1000 houses ranges from a minimum of 64 (rural) and 59 (urban) in Gujarat to a maximum of 957 (rural) and 934 (urban) in Goa. These situations may be the causes for lower price for fish and fish products in India, which ultimately affects the income and livelihoods of fishermen in India.

TABLE 12

Monthly Per-capita Consumption of Fish in India

Sl. No.	State/Union Territory	Per-capita Consumption (Kg.)		No. of HHs Per 1000 HHs	
		Rural	Urban	Rural	Urban
1.	Andhra Pradesh	0.18	0.08	250	205
2.	Goa	2.26	1.90	957	934
3.	Gujarat	0.03	0.03	64	59
4.	Karnataka	0.13	0.12	116	139
5.	Kerala	1.75	1.88	916	838
6.	Maharashtra	0.10	0.15	196	287
7.	Orissa	0.31	0.35	701	717
8.	Tamil Nadu	0.17	0.18	322	379
9.	West Bengal	0.59	0.86	938	878
10.	A & N	1.24	1.14	920	878
11.	Daman and Diu	0.54	1.19	591	718
12.	Lakshadweep	2.39	4.04	882	896
13.	Pondicherry	0.44	0.43	829	757
	All-India	0.21	0.22	336	285

Source: Hand Book of Fisheries Statistics, 2004.
HHs—Households.

POLICY IMPLICATIONS

The analysis of data clearly reveals that there exist wide disparities in the availability of fishery resources, human resources, infrastructures for fishing and also other infrastructures necessary for the socio-economic uplift of fisherfolk in India. The following are the policy implications emerging out of the present study:

1. The length of the coastline may vary among the maritime states, but the continental shelf and establishment of fish landing centres should be made by considering the number of fishing villages, fishermen population and the number of fishing crafts in operation.

2. The overall family size came to 4.68 and population has been increasing year after year. This situation will necessitate the fuller utilization of available fishery resource and increase in the number of fishing days and fishing trip, which ultimately results in the speedy depletion for fishery resource. To avoid this unwanted situation steps should be taken to make the fisherfolk to aware of the need for family planning practices. To achieve good results in this respect the NSS and NCC volunteers and PHCs may be used.
3. To eliminate the disparities in the number of mechanized and motorized crafts in operation and also the number of fishing gear units the following steps have to be taken:
   - Establishment of a Fisheries Development Bank exclusively for financing fishermen and fisherwomen;
   - Encouraging the Nationalised banks to lend liberally for fisheries development;
   - Group lending to fishermen by NCDC should be continued without any halt; and
   - Fishermen and Fisheries Co-operatives should be revitalized by supplying more credit and supplying inputs for fisheries development.
4. The infrastructure facilities like jetty, link roads, ice and cold storages, transport and drying/curing yards are not found in most of the fish landing centres. By providing all these facilities we can reduce the amount of wastage of fish during post-harvest operations and increase the income of the fisherfolk.
5. Other infrastructure facilities like link roads, safety drinking waters, hospitals, banks and co-operative societies should be established in adequate numbers considering the population of a group of fishing villages if not individual villages.
6. There is too much of underemployed and unemployed fishermen in the coastal villages. They suffer like anything to meet even their daily

necessaries. To generate employment to fishermen during the lean season, (i) sea weed collection, (ii) training in repairing the outboard/inboard engines, (iii) collection of shellfish may be initiated, and (iv) engage in non-fishing activities.

7. Out of 11,23,924 adult female population only 3,65,463 (32.52%) are employed in fishery-related and other activities. To generate gainful employment to the unemployed fisherwomen the State Government should take the following steps:
   - The habit of making fish nets in the coastal villages itself may be encouraged in order to generate employment to fisherwomen;
   - Infrastructures such as fish processing units, cold storages should established in the coastal villages to provide employment opportunities to willing people and also avoid to much of wastages which may occur while handling to reap the full benefit of lucky catches.
   - Cottage and small scale industries producing coir and palm products may be opened in the coastal villages to increase the household income from non-fishing activities.
   - Self-Help Groups may be formed with financial support from the government to start income generating small enterprises.
8. Fixation of support prices for at least commercially important fishes and making the co-operative to involve in the field of marketing will help the fishermen to get higher prices and reduce the pressure to fish for long hours to catch huge amount of fish. To help this the following infrastructures (ice factories, cold storages, freezing plants, canning plants curing yards, peeling sheds and fishmeal plants) have to established to every cluster of villages considering the number of crafts in operation and the amount of daily landings.
9. It is claimed that a fishery that is free for all and exploited on a 'catch-as-catch-can' basis is on a sure path to over fishing (Yami, 1998). For the

sustainable management and use of marine resources, marine fisheries policies should be aimed at:

(i) Preventing the mechanized trawlers from fishing in the inshore areas to provide life to lakhs of traditional fishermen;

(ii) To avoid class conflicts which leads to loss of men and material;

(iii) Fixing uniform duration of ban on fishing considering the season prevailing in different region;

(iv) Ban on fishing affects the livelihood of crew members of mechanized boats and generation of alternate employment opportunities is a must to provide for at least minimum subsistence to the fisherfolk;

(v) Night trawling should be strictly prohibited to prevent speedy depletion of fishing resources; and

(vi) Deep-sea fishing produces only three per cent of total fish catch and so it should be encouraged to avoid class conflict in the inshore waters and to increase fish production.

10. The Central as well as the State Governments should take the following steps to increase fish consumption by the people of India:

(i) Create awareness among the people regarding the benefits of fish consumption;

(ii) Opening fish markets;

(iii) Link roads and transport facilities should be increased between coastal villages and urban areas; and

(iv) Various types of advertisements pointing the benefits of fish consumption may be made through different media.

11. The number of fishing harbours and landing centres should be constructed by taking into account the length of the coastline, number of fishing villages, number of people depending on

fishing, number of fishing crafts in operation. To establish these infrastructures the Central Government should take the following steps:

- Allocate more funds for fisheries development and the outlay should be fully utilized for the intended purposes;
- State governments should be encouraged to establish these facilities by obtaining necessary funds from the Centre; and
- Like other rural development projects, the NABARD may be encouraged to operate projects of various types for fisheries development also.

12. Above all, the unexploited marine resources in the Andaman and Nicobar Islands area may exploited either by increasing the fishing crafts and fishery infrastructures in that area or by encouraging migration of fishermen during the ban period in the other areas.

CONCLUSION

From the above analysis pertaining to fisheries development, one can conclude that there is wide spread disparities in the development of marine fisheries in India. In total, the maritime states in the western part are well ahead of eastern part with regard to fishery infrastructures, number of mechanized boats in operation, fish production, Ports for fish export and institutions (Central Marine Fisheries Research Institute and Marine Products Export Development Authority at Cochin and Central Institute for Fisheries Education, Mumbai) related to Research and Development. On the other hand, the eastern part is having maximum number of fishermen villages, fisherfolk population, traditional and non-motorised crafts. Considering these situations, the Central as well as the State governments should frame policies with the participation of representatives from fishermen communities for the equitable and sustainable use of marine resources with better infrastructures for the socio-economic uplift of the fisherfolk and fisheries development of our nation in the years to come.

REFERENCES

Anisha Basheer (1990), 'Marine Biology: Some Aspects of Marine Ecology and Marine Fisheries' Pointer Publishers, Jaipur.

Richard Bailey, (1988), "Third World Fisheries: Prospects and Problems", *World Development*, Vol. 16, No. 6, p. 751.

Hand Book on Fisheries Statistics, 2004.

Karl-Goaran Maler (1997), 'Environment, Poverty and Economic Growth' in Boris Pleskovic and Joseph E. Stiglitz (eds.), Annual Conference on Development Economics, 1997, *The World Bank*, p. 255.

Laxmi Devi (1997), "Planning for Economic Development" (1997) (edited), Institute for Sustainable Development and Anmol Publication Pvt. Ltd., New Delhi, p. 369.

Manickam, S. (2006), 'Economic Development of Tamil Nadu in Perspective', Uyirmmi, Chennai.

Marine Fisheries Census 2005, Part I, Government of India, Department of Animal Husbandry, Dairying and Fisheries, New Delhi.

Menakhem Ben-Yami (1998), 'Stealing the Common', Samudra, No. 19, January.

Pazhani, K. (2001), 'Child Labour in the Coastal Villages—A Case Strudy of Kanyakumari District' in K.P. Kannan (Editor), 'Economics of Child Labour' Deep & Deep Publications Pvt. Ltd., New Delhi, p. 247.

Pazhani, K. (2006), "Sen's Entitlement Approach and Fishing Economy", *Journal of Fisheries Economics and Development*, Vol. 7 No. 1, July-December.

Pazhani, K. and S. Jesi Isabella (2007), 'Formal and Informal Credit in the Coastal Villages of Kanyakumari District' in 90th Annual Conference of IEA, Vol. 2.

Raja J. Chelliah (2007), 'Strategy for Poverty Reduction and Narrowing Regional Disparities', *EPW*, August 25, p. 3475.

Sathiadhas, R. and Biradar, R.S. (2000), 'Fisheries in the Development of Indian Economy' in Proceedings of the National Seminar on Fisheries Economics, Extension and Management, January 5 and 6, 2000 held at CIFE, Mumbai, p. 1.

25

Inter-State and Inter-Regional Disparities in Production and Productivity of Foodgrains in India (1970-71 to 2006-07)

Amrita Nandi

Agriculture forms the backbone of the Indian economy and despite planned industrialization during the last few decades, agricultural sector occupies an important place in the Indian Economy .The importance of agricultural sector in the process of economic development is indispensable. Being the largest industry in the country, agriculture has significantly contributed in terms of income and employment generation along with its role in food supply.

Though the share of agriculture in the GDP has registered a steady decline from 36.4 per cent in 1982-83 to 18.5 per cent in 2006-07. Yet this sector continues to support more than half a billion people providing employment to 52 per cent of the work force and accounts for 13.4 per cent of India's export.

The decade of 1990s was a period of concern as

agriculture witnessed a sharp deceleration in growth. Economic reforms initiated in 1991 has no doubt placed Indian economy on a higher growth trajectory yet agriculture, which accounted for more than 30 per cent of the total GDP in the beginning of reforms failed to maintain its pre-reform growth. While the prime concern of the policy-makers of the country was to bring about fiscal correction in the national budget the real crisis perpetuated in agriculture which did not receive adequate attention in the economic reforms of the country. As a result, the growth rate in agriculture has been low and erratic causing frequent shortages and unequal distribution of foodgrains. Thus, the dismal performance of agriculture against the backdrop of an impressive growth of the economy posed serious implications.One of the implications being wide inter-state and inter-regional disparities in production and productivity of foodgrains as well as income.

The variation across the Indian states in terms of foodgrain production is enormous and the differential performance across the states has begun to raise important policy questions within the country. A country which comprises different states and in which each state significantly differs in physical characteristic, climate, resource endowments from the other; the differences in the production and productivity among states, particularly in agricultural commodities like rice, wheat, pulses, etc. is not an unusual phenomena. Differences arise also on account of the entrepreneurial abilities of the people living in those states like Punjab, Haryana and Western parts of UP where production and productivity is high as compared to other states. .Whensoever, there has been some change in the technique of production farmers with a dynamic attitude and better entrepreneurial skills have adopted it instantaneously and reaped the benefits of the new technology. This fact, along with better soil fertility leads to an increase in the production and productivity *vis-a-vis* over the others.

Reduction of regional imbalances is one of the key challenges in agricultural development in India. Equally important is improving the conditions of agriculturally low performing states, as most of India's foodgrains are produced only in a few states. Hence, on account of large inter-state disparities in the production, productivity and area under foodgrains in various states, it is pertinent to look at the state level growth scenario. It is against this backdrop, this paper analyses the trend in foodgrains at the state level and examines some of the factors responsible for the inter-state disparities and attempts to identify the high and low performing states.

NATURE AND SCOPE

The study of inter-state and inter-regional disparities in production and productivity of foodgrains is heavily based on secondary data. The period of analysis being 1970-71 to 2005-06, i.e. 35 years and 1970-71 has been taken as the base year as the results of the Green revolution were received around 1970-71, and it also happens to be the year which started a trend in productivity with stability. To address the question of regional disparities the focus has been narrowed to fifteen states regarding production, productivity and area of rice, wheat, cereals, pulses and foodgrains. The scope of the study is to cover India as a whole hence certain states from five different regions of the country have been considered for the purpose of analysis in general *vis-a-vis* Amongst the Eastern region the following states have been considered.

W. Bengal, Assam, Orissa, Bihar

The Western region: Maharashtra, Rajasthan and Gujarat.

From the Northern region: Punjab and Haryana.

As regards the Central region: UP and MP.

From the Southern region: Andhra Pradesh, Karnataka, Tamil Nadu and Kerala.

It is from the aforementioned states that a sample has been formed for analyzing cropwise trend and differentials in the production and productivity regarding foodgrains.

METHODOLOGY

In order to measure the extent of disparities in the production of foodgrains as well as of different crops the most standard practice is to calculate the coefficient of variation through time. However, I have dispensed away from this common practice and instead estimated Theil-T Statistic wherein an attempt has been made to measure the trend in disparities among different states regarding rice, wheat, pulses, cereals and foodgrains.

Since this statistic is estimated over time, i.e. 1970-71 to 2005-06 therefore it facilitates to throw light on the convergence, divergence or constancy in the disparities of the overall foodgrains and different food items among states. Theil-T statistic is also a pure number like coefficient of variation and is estimated by the following formula:

$$T = (1/n)\ \Sigma(Y_1/\mu)\ \log\ (Y_1/\mu),$$

where,

n is the number of observation,

Y_1 is each state's production level of foodgrains or of a crop, and

μ is average production of foodgrains or of a crop.

Notice that, when a group population consists of equal observations, the final terms in T all reduce to log (Y_1/μ) = Log (1). Thus, T overall is zero for the case of perfect equality, and since deviations of (Y_1/μ) below the mean have values between zero and one, whereas deviations above the mean are unbounded, T increases as deviations away from the average value increases.

MEASUREMENT AND ANALYSIS OF THE DISPARITIES AMONG STATES IN THE PRODUCTION OF RICE

Two important crops under cereals in India are rice and wheat which account for 80 per cent of the total cereal production. Rice, India's preeminent crop, is the staple food of the people of the Eastern and Southern parts of the country. In the case of rice fifteen states from different regions have been considered as these states contribute a major chunk of the total rice production in India and form a reasonable sample size *vis-a-vis* West Bengal, Assam, Orissa, Bihar, Punjab, Haryana, Andhra Pradresh, Tamil Nadu, Karnataka, Kerala, Maharashtra, Gujarat, Rajasthan, UP and MP. The Eastern zone produces approximately 50 per cent of

TABLE

Inter-State Disparities in the Production of Rice, Wheat, Pulses, Cereals and Foodgrains as Measured in the Value of Theil-T Statistic

Sl. No.	Years	Rice	Wheat	Cereals	Pulses	Foodgrains
1.	1970-71	0.1177	0.0809	0.0091	0.1111	0.0512
2.	1971-72	0.1192	0.0564	0.0092	0.1292	0.0504
3.	1972-73	0.1352	0.0619	0.0104	0.1582	0.0605
4.	1973-74	0.1141	0.0615	0.0088	0.0909	0.0371
5.	1974-75	0.1298	0.0709	0.0100	0.1114	0.0503
6.	1975-76	0.1062	0.0673	0.0082	0.0988	0.0414
7.	1976-77	0.0958	0.0727	0.0074	0.1065	0.0523
8.	1977-78	0.0961	0.0723	0.0074	0.1030	0.0452
9.	1978-79	0.1005	0.0747	0.0077	0.1004	0.0481
10.	1979-80	0.1075	0.0900	0.0083	0.0954	0.0450
11.	1980-81	0.0979	0.1055	0.0075	0.1251	0.0601
12.	1981-82	0.0928	0.0931	0.0071	0.1383	0.0580
13.	1982-83	0.0971	0.0965	0.0075	0.1544	0.0738
14.	1983-84	0.1014	0.0904	0.0078	0.1385	0.0626
15.	1984-85	0.0988	0.0973	0.0076	0.1425	0.0697
16.	1985-86	0.1090	0.0892	0.0084	0.1196	0.0711
17.	1986-87	0.1187	0.0889	0.0091	0.1361	0.0714
18.	1987-88	0.1270	0.0953	0.0098	0.1799	0.0747
19.	1988-89	0.1226	0.0910	0.0094	0.1291	0.0709
20.	1989-90	0.1224	0.0941	0.0094	0.1333	0.0652
21.	1990-91	0.1163	0.0769	0.0089	0.1425	0.0694
22.	1991-92	0.1211	0.0876	0.0093	0.1645	0.0705
23.	1992-93	0.1153	0.0794	0.0089	0.1541	0.0684
24.	1993-94	0.1144	0.0832	0.0088	0.1634	0.0711
25.	1994-95	0.1128	0.0746	0.0087	0.1630	0.0706
26.	1995-96	0.1163	0.0736	0.0089	0.1575	0.0740
27.	1996-97	0.1222	0.0701	0.0094	0.1635	0.0788
28.	1997-98	0.1208	0.0656	0.0093	0.1832	0.0768
29.	1998-99	0.1249	0.0651	0.0096	0.1702	0.0680
30.	1999-00	0.1215	0.0709	0.0093	0.2106	0.0800
31.	2000-01	0.1463	0.0927	0.0113	0.1708	0.0827
32.	2001-02	0.1458	0.0836	0.0112	0.1726	0.0770
33.	2002-03	0.1634	0.0927	0.0126	0.1824	0.0991
34.	2003-04	0.1512	0.0859	0.0116	0.1773	0.0902
35.	2004-05	0.1547	0.0789	0.0119	0.1924	0.0990
36.	2005-06	0.1399	0.0907	0.0108	0.1954	0.0746

the total output of Rice followed by the southern zone which ranks second. In 2005-06, West Bengal was the leading producer followed by Andhra Pradesh and UP.

It may be inferred that the resource endowment directly influences the production performance. The production condition is generally homogeneous under irrigated situation (as in Northern and Southern zones) whereas rainfed rice in Eastern India is grown to highly diverse acosystem and almost in natural conditions. The heterogeneity in the production environments is the primary source of disparity in production among the zones.

On the whole, the overall improvement in the growth performance of Eastern India has been an important development that has positively affected the overall performance of the Indian Agriculture during the late 1990s. The cropping intensity has been an important factor that increased in all the states although West Bengal led other states of Eastern India on this account.

The value of Theil-T in the case of rice shows a little different picture. It has remained more or less static from 1950-51 to 1966-67, i.e. during the pre-Green revolution phase disparities in the production of rice amongst the states have remained unchanged. It is indeed noticeable that in the Southern and Eastern states of India the productivity during this period has been comparatively high as compared to other states like Punjab, Haryana, Bihar, Orissa and UP. After the Green revolution (1966-67) the productivity in these states improved considerably and therefore the disparities have tended to decline until the year 1981-82. This is obvious from the value of Theil-T which declined from 0.12 in 1966-67 to 0.11 in 1971-72 to 0.09 in 1981-82.Thus expansion of area was the main source of growth in the pre-Green revolution period wherein a phenomenal expansion was observed in the area under rice in West Bengal. However, the scope for area expansion diminished considerably in the Green revolution phase and increase in productivity became the main source of growth. There was a significant acceleration in yield growth during the Green revolution period as, the main source of productivity increase was technological breakthrough in both rice and wheat. From 1981-82 and until 1987-88 the disparities increased from 0.09 to 0.12 on account of the fact that the productivity in Punjab and Haryana was much more than many other states under analysis. However, when the productivity in the other states improved during late 80s and 90s the disparities have tended to stabilize.

It is observed that the prosperous states particularly Punjab, Haryana, and Western UP concentrated significantly on wheat production and therefore the disparities remained more or less same until the beginning of Green revolution technology. Thereafter, with the advent of the Green revolution the disparities tended to decline particularly because of the prosperous states taking the lead in the adoption of the new technology. This resulted in the decline in disparities, as production in those prosperous states which was quite low during the pre-Green revolution era increased gradually until 1981-82 and more significantly after 1981-82 to 1987-88 during which the disparities tended to increase. It is a unique case in itself, unique in the sense that initially (during pre-Green revolution phase) the disparities were due to the substantial difference in the production levels of high producing rice states like Andhra Pradesh, Tamil Nadu, West Bengal and Assam on one hand and low producing states on the other hand like Punjab, Haryana, UP, etc.

However after 1981-82 to 1987-88 the disparities persisted and it is on account of the fact that the hitherto high producing states became low producing states and low producing states became high producing states. Thus disparities which narrowed after the introduction of Green revolution technology have tended to widen till 1987-88. During the next phase (1987-88 to 1994-95) disparities have stabilized which is brought out in Theil-T measure which tended to stabilize at the level of 0.12 precisely from 1987-88 to 1999-2000.

During this phase (1987-88 to 1994-95) the area under irrigation, use of fertilizer and electric power showed a moderate to high increase in various states. However, after 1995-96 net sown area showed a decline in all the states coupled with slowing down of irrigation and fertilizer use. As a result once again the disparities widened in 2002-03 being 0.16 and finally narrowed down to 0.13 in 2005-06 as area under rice showed a slight improvement in the southern states but not in W. Bengal.

MEASUREMENT AND ANALYSIS OF THE DISPARITIES AMONG STATES IN THE PRODUCTION OF WHEAT.

Another important item of foodgrains in India is wheat which occupies most of the Northern, western and Central India. The following states have been considered in the analysis which form the core of the wheat region and contribute about 90 per cent of the total wheat production in India *vis-a-vis* Punjab, Haryana, UP, MP, Bihar and Rajasthan. The analysis suggests that in Punjab, Haryana and UP the production of wheat has shown an increasing trend along with the productivity. Therefore, the effect of Green Revolution has proved beneficial in raising the production and productivity in these states. However, the area under wheat has not shown a tendency to increase much during the 1990s. Moreover, it is observed that the production of wheat in these states now mainly depends on whether we can sustain the effect of Green Revolution technology in the near future or else there may be a need to develop still a better variety of HYV seeds. The production and productivity in the other two states viz., Bihar and MP are much below Punjab and Haryana as well as that of UP and it appears that the Green Revolution technology has not effectively made its dent in these two states. Therefore, as in the case of rice similarly in the case of wheat too, it is not possible to raise the production through extensive cultivation (extending the area). Hence, there is a need to develop new seed technology.

The behaviour of the trend in the disparities amongst states regarding wheat production is almost similar to that of cereals or foodgrains and is consistent with the hypothesis. Prior to the Green revolution period the premise was that disparity should decline till 1962-63 (the value of Theil-T declined from 0.13 in 1950-51 to 0.06 in 1962-63.) but between 1962-63 and 1966-67 disparities have increased (Theil-T being 0.13) because of certain exogenous factors which were the two wars which India faced with China and Pakistan and the two consecutive droughts in 1965-66 and 1966-67 which had adversely affected the production in all the states and the worst impact was in the backward states which had caused the disparities to widen in the short period from 1962-63 to 1966-67 (refer figure)

The decline in disparities among states regarding wheat production during the period immediately after the Green Revolution and until 1973-74 (value of Theil-T=0.06) is on account of the fact that the productivity of wheat in Bihar, MP and Rajasthan which was far short of the productivity with that of UP has come very close during the period 1966-67 to 1973-74. After 1973-74 the disparities have increased until 1980-81 (value of Theil-T increased from 0.05 to 0.11) because of sharp rise in productivity in UP, Punjab and Haryana as compared to other states under analysis. After 1980-81, the productivity tended to stabilize (Theil-T remained 0.09 till 1989-90) because the increase in productivity in UP, Punjab and Haryana has slowed down. However, in the later years the disparities tended to stabilize which is evident from the value of Theil-T statistic which remained approximately 0.07 between 1990-91 to 1999-2000 because the area under HYV of wheat is almost 90 per cent of the total cropped area under wheat. Total area is not increasing and productivity has tended to increase at a very slow rate. Therefore, it is expected that the inter-state disparities in the future should neither converge nor diverge regarding wheat. Theil-T from 2000-01 to 2005-06 hovered around 0.09. In a nutshell it can be said that the analysis of wheat production amongst states is quite consistent with my basic hypothesis if the impact of exogeneous factors are eliminated. In the case of wheat, average annual growth in yield during 2002-06 was negative and the productivity of wheat in 2005-06 varies from a low of 1,393 kg per ha. in Maharashtra to a high of 4,179 kg in Punjab.

MEASUREMENT AND ANALYSIS OF THE DISPARITIES AMONGST STATES IN THE PRODUCTION OF PULSES

Pulses form an integral part of the vegetarian diet in the Indian subcontinent. Besides being a rich source of protein, they maintain soil fertility and play a vital role in furthering sustainable agriculture . In the analysis of pulses nine important pulse producing states have been considered *vis-a-vis* Andhra Pradesh,Maharashtra, Punjab, UP, Bihar, MP, Rajasthan and West Bengal. The initial effort of the government in raising the productior and productivity of pulses started during the end of the Fourth Five Year Plan when it launched the Intensive Pulses district Programme. This required the raising of the production of pulses in low yield districts, standardization of technique of fertilizer application, etc. Further some more steps were taken like launching of the National Pulses Development Programmed (NPDP) and inclusion of pulses under the Technology mission on pulses and oilseeds (TEMPO).

In the case of pulses the growth in production has declined substantially because of sharp decline in the productivity and also a negative growth in area. However, the behaviour in the disparities amongst states regarding production of pulses is different from that of cereals or foodgrains. In the case of pulses, the disparities have first stagnated until 1965-66, then declined until 1979-80 (the value of Theil-T in 1970-71 was 0.11 which fell to 0.09 in 1979-80) However, with the advent of the Green Revolution technology disparities have shown some downward drift along with wild fluctuations. Thus the effect of Green Revolution technology on pulses is not evident because of the fact that productivity in Punjab, Haryana as well as UP has not shown any significant increase during this period. While in the states of Rajasthan and Maharashtra there has been some increase in productivity. It is important to mention hat the main reason for decline in disparities during this phase was not so much because of productivity differentials but mainly on account of the significant decline in the area under pulses production especially in Punjab and Haryana.

After 1979-80 disparities have tended to increase until 1987-88 (value of Theil-T rose from 0.09 to 0.17) despite the fact that productivity in Punjab, Haryana and UP have declined, yet in other states like Andhra Pradesh, Bihar, Maharashtra, Rajasthan, etc. it has relatively increased. Hence, in this phase (1979-80 to 1987-88), it is not the changes in productivity which is the root cause of the increase in disparities regarding production of pulses rather, it is the area under pulses among different states which is responsible for the widening of the disparities.

The area under pulses in Punjab and Haryana during this phase has remained almost constant while in states where the production and productivity is low like in Bihar ,Rajasthan, etc. area under pulses has declined. Finally in the next phase (1987-88 to 1994-95) disparities have slightly narrowed down. This is not on account of the fact that productivity in some states like Punjab, Haryana and UP have improved a little as compared to other states but on account of the significant decline in the area under pulses production in Punjab and Haryana. However, disparities have further increased 1995 onwards till 2005-06 where the value of Theil-T has risen from 0.15 to 0.19.

Our analysis of different regions of India based on selected states clearly reveal that the area under production of pulses in UP, Punjab, Haryana and Bihar have shown a declining trend while in AP and Maharashtra area has shown some increase but the increase is not enough to compensate the sharp decline in area under pulse production in other states. As regards productivity there has been sharp fluctuations in all the nine states.

Pulses Acreage Drop

The difference in the behaviour of disparities regarding production of pulses amongst states is on account of inter-temporal change in the area under production which is a worrisome factor and a cause of serious concern for the nation as a whole.

The manner in which there has been a gradual decline in the area under pulses in almost all pulses producing states on the one hand and the trend in the productivity of pulses not showing any significant change, on the other, indicates the fact that in the near future if such a trend continues then there may be a shortage of pulses in the country. Presently only Maharashtra accounts for a significant area and output of pulses in the country. Thus in order to meet the domestic demand of pulses particularly that of Arhar, Moong and Masoor there is a need to have a major breakthrough in seed technology.

MEASUREMENT AND ANALYSIS OF THE DISPARITIES AMONG STATES IN THE PRODUCTION OF FOODGRAINS

The present food situation in the economy is a major cause for concern. There is a clear evidence of sharp deceleration in agricultural growth at the all-India level. During the fifties decade, i.e. the pre-green revolution phase most of the growth in aggregate crop output was the result of an increase in area under crops. However,one great impetus to national growth came via "Green revolution" during the mid sixties which led to sharp increase in foodgrain productivity and helped agriculture keep pace with population growth thereby leading to national self sufficiency. During that phase the scope for area expansion diminished considerably and increase in productivity became the main source of growth in crop output leading to significant acceleration in yield growth.

Nonetheless, this technological breakthrough could gain momentum only in selected regions of the country and in terms of some cereal crops like rice and wheat consequently created wide regional and inter-state disparities as the technological breakthrough increased the yields in few states like Punjab, Haryana and Western UP whereas in other states the results were negligible, leading to considerable variation in crop yields within these states. Infact, pulses and coarse cereals lagged far behind and have indicated a sluggish and erratic growth.

Thus, the regional development of foodgrain production had been uneven. There have also been regional variations in performance for individual crops which have accentuated existing regional disparities. Initial gains accrued to the northern states which were environmentally more favourable and better equipped to give returns to the new wheat technology package. Irrigated areas of Tamil Nadu were also able to exploit the new rice technology. Much poorer performance has been experienced in the states of Eastern India with predominantly rainfed agriculture and in the dryland agriculture of the states of AP, Karnataka, Maharashtra and MP characterized by instability in production and a high incidence of poverty. The behavior of the trend in the disparities amongst states regarding overall foodgrains production is consistent with my hypothesis that "prior to the spread of Green revolution technology the law of diminishing returns operates in agriculture therefore disparities will either stabilize or tend to narrow down during the pre-green revolution phase". The second hypothesis is concerned with the disparities in the production and productivity of foodgrains which tend to increase upto a certain extent after the green revolution technology and as the technology spreaded to other states too, the disparities will stabilize for a while before it tends to decline.

From the Theil-T statistic table it is evident that there are few phases regarding the pattern of disparities amongst states. The 1st phase is from 1950-51 to 1966-67 which is the pre-Green revolution phase where the disparities tended to decline from 0.07 to 0.03 thereafter, from 1970-71 it tends to increase until 1985-86 (where the value of Theil-T increases from 0.05 to 0.07) after which it tends to stabilize till 1997-98, i.e. approximately 0.07. Disparities increased between 2002 to 2005 marginally to 0.09 and again stabilized to 0.07 in 2005-06.

In the late 70s and early 80s a number of studies raised concerns about a possible deceleration in the growth of foodgrain production, indicating a decline in the momentum of the Green revolution and possible exhaustion of the potential of the technology. A significant section had also shown serious doubts about the productivity of modern inputs that are used in increasing quantities to sustain growth. This is on account of a geographic spread in the yield growth that led to a more broad-based growth in foodgrain production though, this has still left out several potential growth regions such as the Eastern region and Western region. It indicates that as much as 90 per cent of the growth was entirely technology-based involving substantial increases in the adoption and use of modern inputs by the farmers. Growth in foodgrain production had mainly concentrated in the Northern region which was partly related to natural endowments, infrastructure, suitability of seed-fertilizer technology breakthrough and concentration of government efforts in this region to raise foodgrain production rapidly. All these factors led to a predominance of the Northern region in growth.

Inclusion of the Eastern region would be critical to making a significant dent in elimination of national poverty because of potential for growth there. Accelerating growth in the Western region required special efforts to improve the productivity and stability of dryland crops through new varieties, better water management and tackling of the specific soil fertility constraints.

Declining production growth in the Southern region is also of concern but is found to be mainly due to the declining area allocated to foodgrains. The first signs of a slowdown in agriculture were visible in the mid 1990s mainly due to a decline in public investment in agriculture. The deceleration in agriculture and particularly the foodgrains sector, was much sharper after 1996-97. Almost all the crops have shown a stagnant or decelerating growth rates during the period 1996-97 to 2004-05. This was due to the sharp deceleration in usage of main inputs like irrigation, fertilizer, electricity consumption. This trend in deceleration after the mid-90s was widespread and uniform at the all-India level and across almost all the states.

During the 1990s (1989-90 to 1998-99) growth rate for both foodgrain and non-foodgrain declined from 3.72 per cent achieved during the 80s to 2.35 per cent per annum. Among the states Punjab, Haryana, UP, MP, Bihar and Orissa registered a decline in growth rate of foodgrains production during 90s. However, Gujarat, Rajasthan, Karnataka and Goa have performed better. In the case of Tamil Nadu and Maharashtra the production growth remained very low whereas in Kerala and Orissa it was negative.Slower growth in production in the poorer states of UP, MP, Orissa and Assam was a matter of concern specially because these states are ground water rich states hence, with a great deal of untapped potential.

However, the rate of growth in crop productivity in W. Bengal during 1977-95 was nearly 5 per cent due to spurt in private shallow tube well irrigation and increasing access to institutional credit Production growth rate of rice and wheat declined because of lower growth in productivity during 90s though there has been some expansion in area. The plateauing of yield of rice and wheat in high productivity areas under rice-wheat system and low yield levels in Central, Eastern and North-Eastern parts of the country have affected the growth of production. Coarse cereals production recorded a negative growth rate due to diversion of about 8 million hectares to other more remunerative crops and the productivity has remained nearly stagnant. In the case of pulses, production has declined substantially because of sharp decline in productivity and also a negative growth in area.

FACTORS AFFECTING GROWTH AT THE STATE LEVEL

It was hypothesized that the level of agricultural output overtime was affected by variables like Gross cropped area, Gross irrigated area, Area under HYV, fertilizer, prices, average size of farm holding, institutional credit and technology.

Some other factors affecting growth at the state level were weather influence, particularly monsoon, a decline or stagnation in public investment, supportive infrastructure, electric power, i.e. rural electrification, a poor network of input distribution, a lack of resources, non-availability of adequate credit for purchase of modern inputs improved technology and environmentally sustainable production practices that adversely effected the yields of principal crops.

Cropping pattern: The area under foodgrain has been declining continuously indicating that the cultivation of non-foodgrain crops has been increasing.

Net sown area: All the states either showed an increase or a stagnation during 1985-86 to 1995-96.After this period net sown area showed a decline in all the states except Bihar, Jammu & Kashmir, Punjab and remained stagnant in UP and in West Bengal.

Most of the states have witnessed either a slowdown in growth or a negative growth in the area under irrigation, application of fertilizer, electric power and cropping intensity.

From the analysis it is evident that the important factors causing inter-state variations in foodgrains production are: Gross cropped area, Average size of farm holding, Gross irrigated area and area under HYV.

Factors affecting wheat production across different Indian states reveals that the gross cropped area and area under HYV are the two important factors causing inter-state variations whereas in the case of rice gross cropped area and gross irrigated area are the two significant factors. As regads pulses the two most important factors are gross cropped area and gross irrigated area. However, there is an urgent need to increase the area under pulses or else we will have to depend largely on imports. Hence, in order to step up production along with mitigating the inter-state disparities in foodgrains production the policy implications is that the Gross irrigated area as well as yield should be increased. Moreover, efforts like watershed management programme should should be further strengthened.

Inter-State Disparities of Rice, Wheat, Cereals, Pulses and Foodgrains

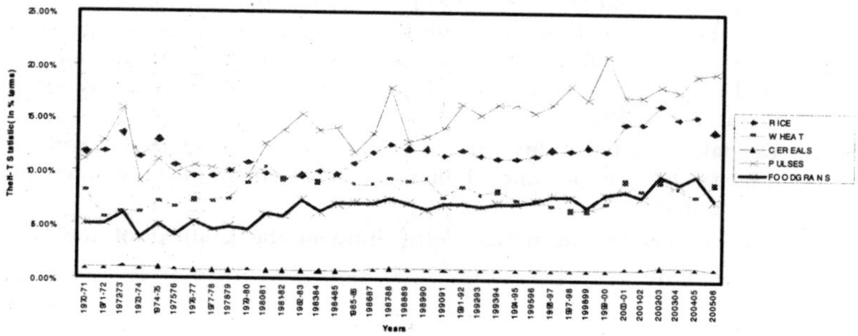

CONCLUSION

In the early 1990s, however signs of diminishing returns were observed as a result of decreasing fertilizer productivities. Moreover, the poorer villages which are dependent on rainfed coarse grains did not experience any "revolution" and here lies the challenge for the future. Thus reduction of regional disparities should be looked upon as a national objective as, the strength of the building depends on the strength of its weakest pillar. Moreover initial bias towards wheat, rice and towards certain states need to be balanced and ways sought to promote agricultural development in poorer rainfed areas.

References

Centre for Monitoring Indian Economy—CMIE database.

Chand, Ramesh, Pandey, L.M. and Raju, S.S. (2007), "Growth Crisis in Agriculture Severity and Options at National and State Levels", *Economic and Political Weekly*, June 30, 2007.

Economic Survey, Ministry of Finance, Government of India, New Delhi.

Manoj, S. Kamat, Manasvi Kamat and Tupe, N. Sanjay (2007), "Indian Agriculture in the New Economic Regime," 1971-2003.

Raju, K.V. (2004), Foodgrain Production: Towards an Explanation of Extremes.

Renuka Mahadevan, "Productivity Growth in Indian Agriculture: The Role of Globalization and Economic Reform."

Reserve Bank of India (2006-07), Handbook on Indian Statistics, Department of Economic Policy and Research, Mumbai.

Sachs, D. Jeffrey, Bajpai, Nirupamand, Ramiah, Anathi (2002-03), "Why Some Indian States have Grown Faster than the Other States", Centre for International Development, Harvard University.

Sarma, J.S. and Vasant, P. Gandhi (1990), "Production and Consumption of Foodgrains in India: Implications of Accelerated Economic Growth and Poverty Alleviation", International Food Policy Research Institute (IFPRI).

Shah, Deepak, "Sustainability of Slow Growth in Foodgrain Crops in Maharashtra: Issues and Options", Gokhale Institute of Politics and Economics.

Shakuntala, "Instability in Indian Agriculture in the Context of the New Technology."

26

Inter-Regional Disparities in India: A Comparative Study of Agricultural Development in each Zonal State

N.K. Thakur

Regional inequality continues to be a cause of deep concern and disparities, in the level of living manifest indifference in Agriculture production and productivity in different regions in the country.

In India Regional disparity in economic development an glaring as much as to cause anxieties. Some states are economically advance while other are almost primitive. There are some regions having good base of natural resources but economically backward while some regions are rich in resources and attracts,. investments. Even within state some district are much developed while other are almost primitive.

The co-existence of relatively developed and economically depressed states are known as regional imbalances which may be natural or due to unequal natural endowment or negligence by Authorities.

Regional disparities in India is a serious concern today in a large economy different regions have uneven growth path over the time.

Balanced regional growth is necessary for the harmonious development of a federal state such as India. Balance regional development does not mean equalization of all regions in every aspect of development.

Difference in Agro, climatic endowments, natural resources use of modern Agricultural imputs like hybrids, seeds and pesticides. Fertilizers Irrigation and availability of marketing facilities credit infrastructure are much more pronounced.

The maximum utilization of all the potentialities of an area and thereby giving its inhabitants the full benefit of possible progress in relation to overall economic growth.

AGRICULTURE

Agriculture is the backbone of our economy for livelihood, employment generation and antimigratery force. Agriculture contributes 18 per cent of GDP (2005-06) and occupies a place to pride in the countries progress.

It is the main stay of every developing country of the world and performances of other sectors are largely depending on the progress of Agriculture.

Agriculture provides social justice prosperity peace and harmony in the society apart from major sources of raw material for many industries.

Agriculture is still livelihood of 70 per cent of mass and 13 per cent of Indian foreign exchange comes from agricultural exports. Agriculture is powerful tools for poverty alleviation, employment generation and all economic development of country.

Nobel Laureate W. Arther Lewis focused on two sector model of Economic Development which emphasize on the structural transformation of primary substance economy.

According to this model Industrial expansion with an "AGFRICULTURAL SURPLUS" stimulating industrial growth by means of cheap food and surplus labour. Agriculture sector and rural economy are the dynamic path of development of rural area without which rural development can not sustain.

Agriculture is being the lifeline of our economy from very beginning and will remain so in future also. Agriculture provides 4Fs—Food, Fodder Fiber and Fuel.

"Adam Smith" has rightly said "No society can surely be flourishing and happy if great part of the numbers are poor and miserable." As such a strong frontal attack on rural poverty through accelerated "AGRICULTURAL DEVELOPMENT" is necessary to raise the living standard.

The accelerating growth in Agriculture bas become more importent today for narrowing the disparity between rural and urban population, the most burning problem being faced by every state. A robust growth in Agriculture is also essential for food and nutritional security for growing population and it has been proved that India has successfully come out from "SIP TO MOUTH" to "SELF SUFFICIENCY" at present through Green Revolution of 1960's.

FERTILIZERS

Fertilizers play a pivotal role in food production and contribute more than 50 per cent increase alone as a single input. Fertilizer use in India stared in 1920's and during 49s, synthetic ammonia plant developed during 60's the rapid growth of fertilizer production (Nitrogen, Phosphorus and Complexes) seen in India. All-India fertilizer consumption from 0.55 kg/ha. (1950s) to 117 kg/ha. (2007-08). Table 4 show the Fertilizer consumption state-wise.

REGIONAL DISPARITIES

Though there are different Agro climatic zones and difference in natural endowment among the state, some states are more performed item the rest of states in India.

According to Prof. C.H. Hanumantha Rao "After Green Revolution Implementation, Inter-personal, Inter-regional and Inter-site disparities have increased in India.

Year 2006-07

States	*Yield in Kg/ha.*	*All-India yield*
Punjab	4033	2020
Haryana	3497	
Uttar Pradesh	2266	
WB	2575	
Andhra Pradesh	2813	
Gujarat	1655	
Bihar	1749	
Maharashtra	1075	

Source: Fertilizer Statistics: 2007-08.

TABLE I

Key Figure of Indian Agriculture

Sl. No.	*Key Figure*	*(Area in Million ha. Consumption of Fertilizer in Kg/ ha. yield in Million ton)*
1.	Total Geographical Area	328.70
2.	Gross Cropped Area (2005-06)	192.70
3.	Net Irrigated	
4.	Gross Cropped Area	141.89
5.	Gross Irrigated Area	82.62
6.	Net Irrigated Area	60.19
7.	Drought Prone Area	260.00
8.	Flood Prone Area	40
9.	Area under High Varieties	119
10.	Fertilizers Consumption, 2007-08	117 kg/ha. 22..570 (NPK)
11.	Operational Holding	1.4%
12.	Contribution GDP (2006-07)	18%

Source: FAI Statistics (2007-08)

INTER-REGIONAL COMPARISON—ZONAL STATES

Inter-Regional comparison one state from each zone Northern (UP), Eastern Zone (Bihar), Southern Zone (Andhra

TABLE: 2

Compound Growth in Agriculture

Sl. No.	*Year*	*Compound growth rate*
1.	1951-61	2.62%
2.	1964-65	2.72%
3.	1971-81	1.7%
4.	1981-91	3.9%
5.	1995-96	1.65%
6.	1996-97	1.5%
7.	2003-04	3.13%
8.	2005-06	1.8%
9.	2006-07	2.3%
10.	2007-08	1.86%

Source: *Economic Survey*, G.O.I.

Pradesh), and West Zone (Gujarat) has been taken. In these states Agricultural development, Fertilizer Consumption. Agril. production, credit facilities weather fertilizer, sales outlets have been taken for study.

UTTAR PRADESH (Northern Zone)

The state of UP being the most populous and the fourth largest state in India. UP accommodates 16 per cent of population on 9 per cent land of the country. UP shares 13 per cent of Gross cropped area and 17 per cent of Food grains contributed by this state alone. The state produced 37.55 mt of food grains with an average productivity of 2057 kg/ha. (2006-07). If we compare Intra-state of this zone then Punjab is the highest.

Fertilizer consumption in the state ($N+P_2O_5+K_2O$) has increased 0.85 lakh tonnes (1966-67 Green Revolution Pd) to 19.73 lakh tonnes in 1985-86 and 37.25 lakh tonnes in 2006-07, a 44.5 times increase within four decades or 11 per cent increase every year. UP Consume 40 per cent of Total ($N:P_2O_5:K_2O$) followed by 42 per cent by Punjab and all-India 47 per cent.

TABLE 3

State-wise Consumption of Plant Nutrients per unit of Gross Cropped Area, 2006-07 and 2007-08 (Provisional)

Zone/State	*2006-07*				*2007-08*			
	N	*P_2O_5*	*K_2O*	*Total*	*N*	*P_2O_5*	*K_2O*	*Total*
East	59.4	23.0	15.0	97.4	63.5	24.2	15.8	103.5
Arunachal Pradesh	1.7	0.7	0.3	2.7	1.7	0.7	0.3	2.7
Assam	27.5	13.7	13.4	54.6	27.7	14.6	15.0	57.8
Bihar	109.3	24.2	11.2	144.7	125.5	25.9	11.4	162.8
Jharkhand	43.6	19.8	2.0	65.5	42.3	21.7	4.6	68.5
Manipur	63.6	16.1	5.8	85.5	64.3	15.1	5.8	85.2
Meghalaya	11.4	7.5	0.9	19.9	9.8	4.7	1.3	15.8
Mizoram	16.5	14.2	7.4	38.1	19.7	10.9	9.3	39.9
Nagaland	0.8	0.6	0.2	1.7	1.2	0.6	0.3	2.2
Orissa	29.4	10.6	6.1	46.2	31.2	13.4	7.2	51.8
Sikkim	1.7	0.9	0.2	2.8	-	-	-	-
Tripura	34.1	12.9	8.4	55.3	25.2	8.7	7.3	41.2
West Bengal	71.2	40.5	31.5	143.2	71.8	40.5	31.9	144.2
North	117.9	35.0	5.6	158.5	121.1	34.2	6.2	161.00
Haryana	132.6	37.5	2.8	173.0	144.4	39.6	3.6	187.6
Himachal Pradesh	32.8	10.9	8.5	52.1	34.4	9.5	9.3	53.1
Jammu & Kashmir	50.9	21.8	6.2	78.9	51.7	15.7	4.4	71.8
Punjab	160.7	43.7	4.8	209.2	162.7	42.5	4.7	210.0
Uttar Pradesh	108.2	33.8	6.4	148.4	109.6	32.7	7.3	149.6
Uttarakhand	85.7	20.2	7.1	113.1	91.2	19.5	8.1	118.9
Delhi	18.6	4.8	0.2	23.6	6.8	1.8	0.2	8.9
South	82.3	40.9	27.5	150.7	84.7	38.4	31.8	154.15
Andhra Pradesh	109.7	51.3	24.9	185.9	116.8	52.0	30.8	199.6
Karnataka	58.00	33.7	22.4	114.1	60.7	29.7	25.4	115.7
Kerala	29.7	15.3	25.0	70.0	31.2	14.3	24.2	96.8
Tamil Nadu	97.0	44.7	44.8	186.5	90.1	37.8	50.4	178.3
Pondicherry	699.4	316.7	210.0	1226.1	556.7	238.1	237.8	1032.5
A & N Islands	6.3	6.1	0.9	13.3	8.5	7.8	2.6	18.9
West	46.9	22.5	7.6	77.1	50.5	23.1	8.9	82.5
Gujarat	82.1	31.9	10.6	124.6	93.1	37.6	12.9	143.6
Madhya Pradesh	37.2	20.9	3.3	61.5	40.6	21.9	3.9	66.0
Chhattisgarh	47.4	20.2	8.4	75.9	47.4	20.4	9.2	76.9
Maharashtra	53.6	30.0	16.5	100.1	56.0	28.4	18.7	103.00
Rajasthan	30.6	11.9	0.6	43.1	32.5	12.0	1.0	45.0
Goa	16.8	8.4	9.8	35.0	20.4	10.8	10.7	41.9
Daman and Diu	140.0	20.0	3.3	163.7	126.7	20.0	10.00	156.7
D&N Haveli	25.7	16.8	2.1	44.6	20.4	14.3	1.8	36.0
All-India	71.4	28.8	12.1	112.3	74.8	28.6	13.7	117.1

TABLE 4

Consumption of Plant Nutrients in Major States (kg/ha.)#
($N+P_2O_5+K_2O$) (2006-07 and 2005-06)

States	*2007-08*	*2006-07*	*2005-06*
Punjab	210	209	209
AP	200	198	204
Tamil Nadu	178	186	187
Haryana	188	173	176
Uttar Pradesh	150	148	141
West Bengal	144	143	132
Bihar	163	145	118
Gujarat	144	125	116
Karnataka	116	114	119
All-India	117	113	107
Uttarakhand	119	111	94
Maharashtra	109	101	88
J & K	72	78	84
Chhattisgarh	77	76	66
Kerala	70	70	68
Jharkhand	69	65	65
MP	66	60	47
Assam	57	54	53
HP	53	52	49
Orissa	52	46	45
Rajasthan	45	43	42
Goa	42	35	33

#FAI-Statistics (2007-08).

Fertilizer consumption has increased to 37.55 lakh tonns at present (2007-08). Per hectare consumption of fertilizer is 150.9 (2007-08), NPK ratio is 16.0:5:1.

Agricultural Production

37.55 mt. of food grains and average productivity is 2057 kg/ha.

TABLE 5

Population/Total Cropped Area/Fertilizer Consumption and Food Grain Production

	1951-52	1960-61	1970-71	1990-91	2001-02	2006-07	2007-08
Population in Million	363	432	684	846	1027	110	117
Total Cropped Area in Million ha.	133.23	152.77	173	185	193	190	192
Fertilizer Consumption kg/ha.	0.55	1.93	31.9	67.55	90.12	113	117
Foodgrain Production (Million ha.)	52	82	129.6	176.39	212	217	233

Source: FAI Statistics: 2007-08.

Weather Condition

In the state eastern part received 701 mm and western 441 mm during south-west monsoon. During north-east monsoon rainfall was scanty and received 15 mm. in Eastern and 19 mm rainfall in western part of the state.

Credit Facilities

Agril. credit worth of 16.6 billion was provided to the farmers during 2006-07 as against 14.7 billion in 2005-06).

Sales Outlets

It has increased to 53.215 million from 53,200 of the previous year. The share of private co-operative is 60:40.

BIHAR (Eastern Zone)

Bihar is the most populous state moving 8.3 crores population (1991). Total geographical area is 780 lakh ha. The state Bihar having 2.8 per cent of country irrigated area. 59 per cent of Gross irrigated area to gross cropped area and area under foodgrain production is 646 lakh ha. and foodgrain production is 8140 (in '000 tonnes). Rice and Wheat are the main crop in Kharif and in Rabi. Average yield of rice is 792 kg/ha. and wheat 1617 kg/hevt which is low compare

TABLE 6

Share of Rice and Wheat to Total Area under Food Grains and Yield/ha., 2006-07

States	*Yield per hectare (Kg)*		*Share (%)*	
	Rice	*Wheat*	*Rice*	*Wheat*
Kerala	2390		96	5
Assam	1332	1117	92	3
West Bengal	2593	2282	89	6
Orissa	1534	1487	82	0.1
Chhattisgarh	1354	1002	74	2
Jharkhand	1828	1529	68	4
Tamil Nadu	3423		61	
Andhra Pradesh	2984	900	55	0.1
Bihar	1486	1908	50	31
Punjab	3868	4210	42	55
All-India	2131	2708	35	23
Uttar Pradesh	1879	2721	30	46
Uttarakhand	1979	2049	28	40
Jammu & Kashmir	2194	1893	28	29
Haryana	3238	4232	24	55
Karnataka	2470	762	19	4
Gujarat	1894	2498	16	26
Madhya Pradesh	824	1835	14	34
Maharashtra	1680	1325	11	9
Himachal Pradesh	1559	1385	10	45
Rajasthan	1577	2751	1	20

Note: Share of area under rice and wheat to total area under foodgrains

to other states like UP and Punjab. All-India sharing of Rice: Wheat the state is 48 per cent Rice and 31 per cent wheat.

Fertilizer Consumption

In the state is 1.095 million tonnes (2006-07) from 0.91 million tonnes (2005-06) which is an increase of 19.2 per cent per ha. consumption of Fertilizer has increased from 117.8 (2005-06) to 163 kg/ha. during 2007-08. Agril. Production total cereals 8840 (000 tonnes) and yield is 1368 kg/ha.

Weather condition of the States was normal at 910 mm during south-west monsoon (2006-07) about middle of 2006

TABLE 7

Target Growth Rate of GDP and Population and Agricultural Crops during 9th and 11th Plan Periods

Items	*Per Annum Growth (%)*		
	9th Plan 1996-97 to 2001-02	*10th Plan 2002-03 to 2007-08*	*11th Plan 2007-08 to 2011-12*
GDP	6.5	7.70	8.1
Population	1.57	1.57	1.45
Agricultural Crop	3.82	4.54	4.27
Rice	2.75	3.08	2.73
Course Cereals	2.20	2.40	2.43
Pulses	3.50	4.93	5.66
Oil Seeds	5.25	8.85	5.16
Sugarcane	4.00	6.16	6.07
Fruits and Vegetables	7.00	8.01	7.89
Tea	5.00	6.16	6.07
Coffee	5.00	6.16	6.07
Other Agri. Products	2.63	3.08	3.04
Total Agriculture	4.50	5.30	5.10

Source: FAI Statistics.

monsoon withdrew as a result a deficit only 24 mm rainfall received during north-east monsoon.

ANDHRA PRADESH (Southern Zone)

This is the second largest fertilizer consuming state of the country. The state of Andhra Pradesh is having 538 lakh ha., gross av. 49 per cent of the area comes under Rice cultivation, wheat cultivation is nominal.

Agricultural Production total cereals in the state is 1557 (000 tonnes) and average yield 2892 kg/ha. (2006-07).

Fertilizer Consumption

During 2006-07 the consumption of total nutrients is 2.556 million tonnes from 2.552 million tonnes (2005-06) to 200 kg/ha. in 2007-08.

N:P:K use ratio is 4.4:2:1 during 2006-07. Per hectare consumption of total nutrients has decreased from 204 during (2005-06) to 198 kg/ha. in 2006-07.

TABLE 8

Projected Population, Food Grains Production and Consumption, Input Use by the End of the 11th Plan

Item	2010-12
Population (Million)	1196.4
Per-capita foodgrains consumption (kg)	223.4
Foodgrains requirement (MT)	337.3
(a) Rice	128.2
(b) Wheat	130.4
(c) Course cereals	48.9
(d) Pulses	29.8
(e) Oil seeds	58.6
(f) Sugarcane	679.6
Gross area sown (Million ha.)	219.2
Net Area sown (Million ha.)	142.0
Gross Irrigated area (Million ha.)	105.5

Source: FAI Statistics.

Weather

The state of Andhra having Telengana region received 830 mm, costal area 5763 mm and Royalseema 320 mm rainfall during south-west monsoon in 2006-07.

In north-east monsoon, Telengana and Royalaseema received 70 mm and 164 mm respectively rainfall whereas costal area was 335 rainfall.

Credit Facilities

In the state a short-term disbursement of loan by co-operative increase for 29.82 billion (2005-06) to 31.4 billion during 2006-07.

Fertilizer Outlet

In the state increase was 17,756 (2005-06) to 17,931 during 2006-07.

GUJARAT (Western Zone)

The state Gujarat having gross area 319 lakh hectare and production of total cereals 5607 (000 tonnes) The average yield of Rice is 1806 kg/ha. and rice is having 17 per cent of country's share and 3 per cent is for wheat. The average yield of Rice is 1806 kg/ha. and wheat 2482 kg/ha.

Fertilizer consumption in the state (2007-08) is 1,444 million tonnes for 1280 millions tonnes (2007-08) having a 12.8 per cent Growth over the previous year.

NPK use ratio is 7.8:3:1 during 2007-08 per hectare Consumption of fertilizer nutrient has increased to 144 kg (2007-08).

Weather

In the state was excess rainfall during south west monsoon, 1449 mm rain recorded in 2006-07.

Credit Facilities

In the state Rs. 31.23 billion was spent during 2006-07.

Sales Outlets

In the state increase was 14,650 billion during 2006-07 from 14,290 billion during 2005-06.

CONCLUSION

Fertilizer has continued to play a vital role in enhancing cereal production. Fertilizer is the key input for achieving the higher target of growth in Agriculture. Land is a limiting factor at present hence it is most vital to maximise production in the economic use of fertilizer by the state (zone-wise) lagging behind in fertilizer consumption.

Regional imbalances in fertilizer is evident state-wise, UP is consuming about 22 per cent, of total fertilizer consumption of India followed by Andhra Pradesh, Bihar and Gujarat comes lower consuming states in comparison Northern and Southern zone.

Consumption fertilizer in nutrient per hectare consumption basis is 150 kg./ha. (UP), Andhra 200 kg./ha., Bihar 163 kg/ha. and Gujarat 144 kg./ha.

Similarly, Agril. production of all cereals in UP 38178 ('000 tonnes), Andhra Pradesh 15575 ('000 tonnes), Bihar 8140 ('000 tonnes) and Gujarat 5609 ('000 tonnes). Average yield in

UP 2266 kg./ha., Andhra 2813 kg/ha. Bihar 1749 kg./ha. and Gujarat 1655 kg./ha. (2007-08).

Natural resources, soil type and other conditions may be a limiting factor but the scope of reducing the imbalances in fertilizer consumption and enhancing the Agri. Production the scope is un-limited for narrowing the gap in inter-zonal states.

Regional disparities can overcome by the use of timely measures of modern package of practices in Agriculture and how best be economic use of plant nutrients (fertilizer) selection of HY seeds, irrigation, effective use of manure (organic+fertilizer) with a combination of Chemical Fertilizers, Farmers' education and easily availability credit to the farmers.

The present paper focuses on some key issues-like use of fertilizer by the UP, Andhra, Bihar and Gujarat states.

How best utilization of the land by applying minimum input and to get maximum Agril. production.

Though there may be temporary disturbances in the growth of Agril. production and weather, flood, draught and other natural factors may restrict on temporary basis but inspite of all the odds Agricultural growth has to be achieved to feed the mass as population is growing rapidly. The Government policies for promoting the fertilizer use and easily availability of fertilizer as door step at reasonable price are the main key area where Government attention is very much needed.

RECOMMENDATION/SUGGESTIONS

The stimulation in Agricultural growth of the states of each zone occupies a prime place in the overall Development of India.

To achieve the desired rates of growth in Agriculture we have to increase fertilizer consumption at par with the state like UP, Andhra (1st and 2nd state in the fertilizer consumption).

For increasing the fertilizer use we have to train farmers through village level extension workers who will be technically guided by the Block Agriculture officer. A training for extension workers for drawing soil samples, seed treatment, use of Irrigation facilities/pesticides and improved package of practices popular in that area, use of green manuring for the soil health extended free flow of credit facilities at lower interest rate, infrastructure for marketing agricultural produce/Government policy. Dry land farming and technical know-how extension by Agricultural Universities from Lab to Land is desirable for narrowing the gap.

The state like Bihar being flood prone area hence inter-linking of rivers, check dams and other related irrigation schemes, pertaining of water harvesting would be a boon for the Agricultural Development. Ponds can be utilized as Fisheries, Makhana cultivation for earning revenue by the villagers.

Rice cultivation in the state is more dominant hence scented rice/short duration rice cultivation scheme adopted to avoid the curse of the flood.

Land utilization in Bihar is limited to the fragmentation which can be best utilize by consolidation when modern package of practices can be adopted and more scope for Global produce. Several pockets of Bihar is growing Maize/vegetable/Fruits having ample scope for popcorn, "Sattu" and other edible items. With the help of Agril. process industries, vegetables and fruits like Mango/Litchi/Banana/Chhiku can be canned/exported for earning the foreign exchange. Good scope for Herbal farming in the state. Floriculture is much attractive and have ample future scope for earning revenue by adopting practices like scent, Rose, water essential fragrance and medical oils, etc.

In each state where the Agricultural production is low can be diversified with Pisciculture, Sericulture, Floriculture, Herbal farming and establishment of cottage industries like basket-making, Madhubani painting. Hexian (Jute) woving, Daring, Piggeries and Poultry farming and other related business by the use of computers for innovative ideas about the established of the industries/computers will also provide market rates for agricultural produce at door step level.

Application of Biotechnology in Agriculture has shown

a great promise particularly evolving genetically modified crop specially B.T. Cotton in Gujarat and Andhra.

Development of transgenic to improve nutritional quality of Rice, Potato with balance protein and oxalate free tomato are the few examples.

In nut shell each zonal state having potential to grow. Punjab is famous for scented rice, major produces of wheat, Andhra is famous for Tobacco and cotton, Bihar is famous for paddy, fruits and Gujarat is famous for cotton and sugarcane.

Regional imbalance can be minimized by adopting the recommendations given and Indian Agricultural produce have ample scope for Global marketing in the years to come.

27

Regional Disparity in Agri-Infrastructure with Particular Reference to Irrigation Development in the Post-Reform Period

R.K. Panda

INTRODUCTION

There is growing concern among the economists and policy-makers on the dismal growth of agriculture and its increasing regional disparity in the post-liberalization period. Studies measuring inter-state disparity in agricultural growth are many and the most recent are that of Sawant, 1997, Nagaraj, 2004, Landes and Gulati, 2004, Ghosh, 2006 and Dev, 2008. Most of the studies analyzing the regional disparity in agricultural growth have primarily discussed the inter-temporal and inter-crop trends in output growth with the possible attributes thereof. It is well acknowledged that in the context of agricultural growth the development of agricultural infrastructures particularly irrigation plays a crucial role. Studies of Dhawan, 1998, Chand, 2002, Dev, 2002, Bhattarai and Moorthy, 2003, Rao, 2005 and Moorthy and Hanjra, 2006 reveal strong positive association between irrigation development and agricultural growth. Also within irrigation, the ground water irrigation (lift irrigation) is found more efficient than canal irrigation in realizing higher cropping intensity and better yield (Narayanamoorthy, 1997, Marothia, 2003).

However, it is seen that since mid 1980s there has been a steady decline in public investment in agriculture with share of private investment increasing steadily (Mitra, 1996, Chand, 2000). Since investment on irrigation constitute a major item of farm investment and there is change in Government Policy towards encouraging private investment in agriculture through institutional credit support, it is apprehended that the relatively better-off regions will capture more private investment in developing irrigation potential (ground water irrigation) and thereby further widen the existing disparity in agricultural growth across states. On this backdrop the present study is an attempt to analyze the inter-state variation in the level and sources of irrigation development in the post-reform period, to measure the relationship between irrigation and agricultural development and to examine the inter-state inequity in the distribution of gross cropped area and credit deployment of commercial banks so as to suggest policy measures for reducing regional disparity in irrigational development and agricultural growth in the country.

DATA BASE AND ANALYTICAL TECHNIQUES USED

The study is based on secondary data obtained from the publications of Government of India, Reserve Bank of India and CMIE documents on agriculture. The study covers the period from 1992-93 to 1999-2000.

Log linear growth model ($Y= a + b^t$) is fitted to the data to calculate growth in gross irrigated area of 15 major states for the period from 1992-93 to 1999-2000. Gini Co-efficient of Concentration is worked out to measure the extent of inequality in the share of gross cropped area and credit distribution of commercial banks among the states.

RESULTS AND DISCUSSION

Inter-State Disparity in the Growth of Irrigation

Table 1 presents data on the gross irrigated area, ratio of gross irrigated area to gross cropped area and annual growth rate of Gross Irrigated Area (CAGR) of 15 major states during the period from 1992-93 to 1999-2000. Observation reveals that gross irrigated area in absolute terms has increased in 12 out of 15 states between 1992-93 to 1999-2000 excepting Assam, Haryana and Orissa. In case of Assam, while the gross irrigated area during this period has remained unchanged, for Haryana and Orissa it has

TABLE 1

Growth in Gross Irrigated Area Among Major States between 1992-93—1999-2000

(Area in '000 hectares)

Sl. No.	*States*	*Gross Irrigated Area*		*GIA/GCA*		*CAGR between 1993-2000*
		1992-93	*1999-00*	*1992-93*	*1999-00*	
1.	AP	50850	5746	39.87	44.12	2.19
2.	Assam	572	572	13.98	13.98	-10.38
3.	Bihar*	4040	4752	54.50	47.26	2.92
4.	Gujarat	3227	3840	29.33	37.83	2.83
5.	Haryana	5252	5124	89.75	84.99	0.69
6.	Karnataka	2802	3162	22.57	26.14	1.27
7.	Kerala	376	471	12.35	15.69	1.41
8.	MP	3834	5828	20.99	28.54	5.23
9.	Maharashtra	3262	3769	15.51	16.86	2.38
10.	Orissa	3112	2512	33.05	29.47	-2.62
11.	Punjab	7143	7487	94.58	90.86	0.60
12.	Rajasthan	5486	6934	27.20	35.95	3.66
13.	Tamil Nadu	3385	3585	47.89	54.99	0.58
14.	UP*	15996	17676	65.56	72.93	1.74
15.	WB	1911	2491	22.38	26.10	2.33
	All-India	66761	76336	35.99	40.23	1.96

*For Bihar and UP data are upto 1998-99.

registered a decline. The ratio of Gross Irrigated Area (GIA) to Gross Cropped Area (GCA) has shown a mixed trend across states. Of the total 15 states, the ratio of GIA to GCA has gone up for 10 states(Andhra Pradesh, Gujarat, Karnataka, Kerala, Madhya Pradesh, Maharashtra, Rajasthan Tamil Nadu, Uttar Pradesh and West Bengal). For Assam while it remained unchanged, for Bihar, Haryana, Orissa and Punjab it registered a decline. The compound annual growth rate of GIA between 1993-2000 has shown three distinct trends amongst the states. For states like Andhra Pradesh, Bihar, Gujarat, Karnataka, Kerala, Madhya Pradesh, Maharashtra, Rajasthan, Uttar Pradesh and West Bengal it has increased at more one per cent. For Madhya Pradesh it registered the highest growth rate (5.23%) followed by Rajasthan (3.66%) and Gujarat (2.83%). For states like Haryana, Punjab and Tamil Nadu the growth rate is positive but less than one per cent per annum. In case of Assam, and Orissa the annual growth rate is worked out to be negative. Particularly for Assam the negative growth rate is quite alarming (-10.38 per cent per annum). All these reveal that not only there is unequal distribution of irrigation facility across states but also this inequity has increased over time.

Sources of Irrigation

Inter-State disparity in agricultural growth is not only influenced by the varying growth rate in the spread of irrigational infrastructure as a whole but also by the source-wise irrigation spread in different regions. Studies have shown that input use is more efficient and crop yield is higher under ground water irrigation (lift irrigation) as compared to canal irrigation (flow irrigation) (Narayana-moorthy, 1997, Marothia, 2003). It has also been observed that over the years the farmers of better endowed regions are increasingly depending on lift irrigation in view of the various constraints coming up in canal irrigation. In contrast because of steady decline in government investment on agriculture and mostly on irrigation since mid-1980s the farmers of less endowed regions are experiencing falling agricultural performance. All these influence inter-state disparity in agricultural growth greatly. Taking all these into account, we have here discussed the source-wise development irrigation facility at the all-India and across states. Table 2 presents data in this respect. Observation reveals that at the all-India level acreage under canal irrigation has declined while that under ground water irrigation has gone up. Amongst the states, four types of trend results are noticed. While for states like Andhra Pradesh, Haryana, Karnataka, Kerala and Uttar Pradesh acreage under both canal and ground water irrigation has gone up, for Assam, Madhya Pradesh, Orissa, Rajasthan and Tamil Nadu area under canal as well as ground water irrigation has declined. In case of other states like Gujarat, Punjab and Wes Bengal area under canal irrigation has declined while that under ground water has increased. For Bihar and Maharashtra the area under canal irrigation has gone up while that under ground water has fallen. All these reveal that in case of the developed states like Gujarat, Haryana, Karnataka, Punjab, and moderately developed states like Andhra Pradesh, Uttar Pradesh and West Bengal there has been significant rise in ground water irrigation and this might be due to rise in private investment in agriculture and particularly on irrigation since mid-1980s. In contrast in states like Orissa, Bihar, Kerala, Maharashtra, Rajasthan and Tamil Nadu, ground water irrigation has not increased much and this might be due to high rate of poverty in the states like Orissa, Bihar and Rajasthan and less attention towards agricultural investment in case of Maharashtra and Tamil Nadu.

Relationship between Irrigation and Agricultural Development

As already observed, the growth rate in gross irrigated area across states has shown an uneven trend over time. The pattern of irrigation has also undergone rapid changes with ground water irrigation coming up increasingly in some states. It is well acknowledged that irrigation development increases the scope for multiple cropping and thereby raises the cropping intensity in the region. This makes the region more developed compared to others having poor irrigation development. In view of this we have here worked out the trend relationship between the irrigation intensity and cropping intensity across states for the triennium ending

TABLE 2

Source-wise Irrigation among Major States in Terms of Net Irrigation Area

('000 hectares)

Sl. No.	States	1997-98		1999-2000		2000-01		% Rise in 2000-2001 over 1999-00		% Rise in 2000-01 over 1997-98	
		Canal	Others	Canal	Others	Canal	Others	Canal	Others	Canal	Others
1.	AP	1538	2407	1634	2750	1649	2879	0.91	4.69	7.22	19.61
2.	Assam	362	210	362	210	148	22	-59.12	89.52	-59.12	-89.52
3.	Bihar	1072	2552	-	-	1136	2489	-	-	5.97	-2.47
4.	Gujarat	613	2429	602	2480	492	2487	-18.27	0.28	-19.74	2.38
5.	Haryana	1397	1396	1441	1447	1476	1482	2.43	2.42	3.58	6.16
6.	Karnataka	903	1460	994	1554	966	1677	-2.82	7.91	6.98	14.86
7.	Kerala	104	246	86	294	105	276	22.09	-6.12	0.96	12.19
8.	MP	1783	4521	1002	4659	808	3327	-19.36	-28.59	-54.68	-26.41
9.	Maharashtra	538	2029	1051	1921	1047	1912	-0.38	-0.46	94.60	-5.77
10.	Orissa	949	1141	949	1141	878	1055	-7.48	-7.54	-7.48	-7.54
11.	Punjab	1356	2491	1296	2708	676	2926	-47.84	8.05	-50.15	17.46
12.	Rajasthan	1525	3896	1619	3993	1384	3523	-14.51	-11.77	-9.29	-9.57
13.	Tamil Nadu	838	2107	868	2104	833	2055	-4.03	-2.33	-0.60	-2.47
14.	UP	3059	8953	-	-	3091	9725	-	-	1.05	8.62
15.	West Bengal	717	1194	717	1194	261	2093	-63.60	75.29	-63.60	75.29
	All-India	17092	37471	17995	39243	15988	38692	-11.15	-1.40	-6.46	3.26

1994-95 and 1999-2000. Observation reveals that (Table 3) states having higher irrigation intensity exhibit higher cropping intensity as compared to the states having low irrigation intensity with low cropping intensity. Besides states showing rise in irrigation intensity between period exhibit increase in the cropping intensity as compared others where a reverse trend is noticed. Only in case of a few states we find some exception to the above trend. While for Gujarat a rise in irrigation intensity has shown a decline in cropping intensity, for Haryana, Maharashtra and Karnataka we find a decline in irrigation intensity with a rise in cropping intensity.

TABLE 3

Relationship between Irrigation Intensity and Cropping Intensity Across States

Sl. No.	*States*	*Triennium ending 1994-95*		*Triennium ending 1999-2000*	
		Irrigation Intensity	*Cropping Intensity*	*Irrigation Intensity*	*Cropping Intensity*
1.	AP	128.7	116.1	132.09	123.38
2.	Assam	100.0	140.8	100.35	147.53
3.	Bihar	122.5	131.9	129.41	134.87
4.	Gujarat	121.8	114.9	123.59	110.32
5.	Haryana	179.3	167.2	175.93	170.98
6.	Karnataka	127.0	115.2	124.16	117.13
7.	Kerala	127.5	135.8	118.46	131.30
8.	MP	103.2	124.9	102.20	135.02
9.	Maharashtra	128.1	117.8	122.97	124.56
10.	Orissa	130.1	152.8	114.64	140.28
11.	Punjab	185.0	182.0	186.99	187.29
12.	Rajasthan	121.3	119.1	123.51	129.50
13.	Tamil Nadu	125.2	121.4	120.18	118.13
14.	UP	142.3	147.8	141.94	146.91
15.	West Bengal	120.2	158.0	130.35	171.54
	All-India	132.7	131.0	133.07	134.52

Inter-State Inequity in the Distribution of Gross Cropped Area and Agricultural Credit of Commercial Banks

Our earlier discussion on source-wise development of irrigation has amply brought out a considerable rise in irrigated area under ground water irrigation in several states, mostly better endowed states like Andhra Pradesh, Haryana, Karnataka, Kerala, Punjab, West Bengal Gujarat and Uttar Pradesh. Ground water development being a private investment affair, the determining factor that influences private investment in irrigation is the institutional credit support to the farmers. Studies have shown positive association between farm credit advanced by the institutional agencies, and agricultural growth (Desai *et al.*, 1988, Desai,

TABLE 4

Inter-State Sharing in Cropped Area and Credit Distribution of Commercial Banks

Sl. No.	*States*	*1995-96*		*1999-2000*	
		Percentage share of GCA	*Share in Outstanding Credit (per cent)*	*Percentage share of GCA*	*Share in Outstanding Credit (per cent)*
1.	AP	6.99	12.95	6.86	12.47
2.	Assam	2.11	1.11	2.16	0.63
3.	Bihar	5.37	4.95	5.26	3.12
4.	Gujarat	5.40	5.38	5.35	5.21
5.	Haryana	3.20	3.46	3.18	3.79
6.	Karnataka	6.41	9.82	6.37	11.57
7.	Kerala	1.64	4.46	1.58	4.66
8.	MP	10.33	6.05	10.76	7.01
9.	Maharashtra	11.43	9.79	11.78	10.41
10.	Orissa	5.18	2.37	4.49	2.05
11.	Punjab	4.15	5.80	4.34	6.78
12.	Rajasthan	10.54	3.98	10.16	5.92
13.	Tamil Nadu	3.36	11.58	3.43	9.48
14.	UP	13.15	10.00	13.12	11.01
15.	West Bengal	4.81	3.15	5.03	2.40
	Gini Ratios	0.323	0.322	0.327	0.350

1994, Panda, 2004). In view of this, we have here examined the relationship between share of different states in the total gross cropped area of the country (gross cropped area representing agricultural growth)and in the credit distribution of the commercial banks. To measure the degree of inter-state inequity in the distribution of gross cropped area and credit deployment of commercial banks we have worked out Gini Co-efficient of concentration. Observation shows that the relatively poor states like Assam, Bihar, Madhya Pradesh, Orissa, Rajasthan and West Bengal receive less credit from commercial banks as compared to their share in the total cropped area in the country. In contrast a few states like Andhra Pradesh, Karnataka, Maharashtra, Punjab, Tamil Nadu get disproportionately higher percentage of credit than what is warranted as per their share in the total cropped area of the country. The inter-state inequality in the credit distribution as calculated in terms of the value of Gini Co-efficients is found higher than that is observed in gross cropped area distribution among the states. The value of Gini Co-efficient of Concentration in regard to credit distribution among states has also found to have increased from 0.322 to 0.350 between 1995-96 and 1999-2000.

CONCLUSION AND POLICY IMPLICATIONS

The above findings reveal wide inequality prevailing in the irrigational development across states causing lop-sided development in agriculture. Since public investment in agriculture has been declining and more emphasis is now being given to private investment there is need for stepping up direct credit to farmers by the institutional agencies. The commercial banks have to shed their regional bias and explore the possibility of providing higher credit assistance to agriculturally laggard regions for raising investment in irrigation, increasing cropping intensity and agricultural production and thereby reduce the gap in agricultural growth across states.

References

Chand, Ramesh (2000) Emerging Trends and Regional Variations in Agricltural Investment and their Implications for Growth and Equity, Policy Paper 11, National Centre for Agricultural Economics and Policy Research, New Delhi.

Chadha, G.K. (2003) Indian Agriculture in the New Millennium: Post-Reform Behaviour of Investment, *Indian Journal of Agricultural Economics*, Jan-March

Desai B.M. *et al.*, (1988) Institutional Credit for Green Revolution Areas under Semi-arid Tropics in India, *Indian Journal of Agril. Economics*, Vol. XLIII(1).

Desai, Bhupat M. (1994) Contributions of Institutional Credit, Self Finance and Technology Change to Agricultural Growth in India, *Indian Journal of Agricultural Economics*, Vol. 49(3), July-September.

Dhawan, B.D. (1998), Studies in Agricultural Investments and Rural Savings, Common Wealth Publishers, New Delhi

Dev, S. Mahendra (2002) Bold Initiative Needed on Agriculture and Rural Employment, *Economic and Political Weekly*, March 23.

Dev, S. Mahendra (2008) Agriculture: Absence of a Big Push, *Economic and Political Weekly*, Vol. XLIII(15), April 12-18.

Ghosh, Madhusudan (2006) Regional Convergence in Indian Agriculture, *Indian Journal of Agricultural Economics*, October-December.

Landes Rip and Ashok Gulati (2004) Farm Sector Performance and Reforms Agenda, *Economic and Political Weekly*, August 7.

Marothia. D.K. (2003) Enhancing Sustainable Management of Water Resources in Agriculture Sector: The Role of Institutions, *Indian Journal of Agricultural Economics*, Vol. 58(3), July-Sept.

Narayanamoorthy, A. (1997a) Drip Irrigation: A Viable Option for Future Irrigation Development, *Productivity*, Vol. 38(3).

Narayanamoorthy and Munir A. Hanjra (2006) Rural Infrastructure and Agricultural Output Linkages; A Study of 256 Indian Districts, *Indian Journal of Agricultural Economics*, Vol. 61(3).

Panda, R.K. (2004) Farm Investment and Institutional Finance—A Study of Orissa, Project completed under Research Award Programme of the UGC, Dept. of A & A Economics, Utkal University. (unpublished)

Rao, C.H.H. (2005a) Agricultural Growth, Farm Size and Rural Poverty Alleviation in India in selected papers by C.H.H Rao, Academic Foundation, New Delhi.

28

Growing Inter-State Disparities in Indian Agriculture

NAZIA IQBAL HASHMI

INTRODUCTION

Regional disparity is a ubiquitous phenomenon in both developed and developing economies. But in the latter it is more acute and glaring. National economies are often composed of sets of smaller and localized economies. If the national economy is to prosper then its constituent regional economies must be brought into some sort of harmony. In India too, area disparities in the level of poverty, unemployment, income infrastructure, agriculture industry and above all the level of living of the people exist substantially across the regions. Numerous measures have been undertaken in the last forty years of planning to achieve balanced regional development of the country. Yet, wide disparities in area development continue in this country. The regional disparities and inequalities continue to be the main feature of Indian agriculture. The large part of growth in agriculture is contributed by relatively better endowed regions. Although the spread of growth performance has been better in the late 1980s and 1990s, it has not been uniform across regions and states. The central peninsular region continues to have slow growth and suffers from instability in production and productivity. Agriculture has always been in the forefront of policy deliberations in India. During the first two decades of planning era, the process of agricultural development was initiated through land reforms, public investments in creating irrigation, power and road infrastructure, setting up State Agricultural Universities for agricultural education, research and extension services, opening bank braches in small towns and rural areas for providing institutional credit to the farmers for purchasing modern technology, inputs, farm machines and electric and diesel pumps for and tube-wells. The Green Revolution (GR) Strategy that was started in the late 1960s, has transformed the Indian economy from a food-deficit to a self-sufficient one. But unfortunately, its benefits were distributed disproportionately in favour of the wealthier farmers, especially of agriculturally developed regions, bypassing the small and marginal farmers in particular and agriculturally under-developed regions in general. Although, the GR technology was size-neutral; it was not resource-neutral. Therefore, its benefits have largely been reaped by the large farmers of developed regions as they have better access to resources. There have, now, been ample evidences that inter-region and inter-farm disparities in the agricultural development has widened in the post-GR period.

India has made lot of progress in agriculture since independence in terms of growth in output, yields and area under many crops. It has gone through a green revolution, a white revolution, a yellow revolution and a blue revolution. Today, India is the largest producer of milk, fruits, cashew nuts, coconuts and tea in the world, the second largest producer of wheat, vegetables, sugar and fish and the third largest producer of tobacco and rice. The per-capita availability of food grains has risen in the country from 350 gm in 1951 to near about 400 gm per day now, of milk from less than 125 gm to 226 gm per day and of eggs from 5 to 30 per annum despite the increase in population from 35 crores to 95 crores. At present only 2330 per cent of the farmers are able to derive any benefits of extension services provided by various government agencies and every year about 20 per cent of the crop are lost due to mishandling, spillage, floods, droughts and pests and diseases. In fruits and vegetables the loss is around 30 per cent.

BACKGROUND

Disparities in the development have been a theme of great academic interest and practical significance during the post-world war second period. Although, economic reforms initiated in the Indian economy in 1991 did not directly target the agriculture; they did have indirect impact on it via reduction in the developmental role of the government and its capacity to generate resources for investment. A reduction in custom and excise duties owing to the process of tax liberalisation has reduced the tax-GDP ratio from 10.1 per cent in 1990-91 to 8.8 per cent in 2002-03. Due to fall in tax-GDP ratio and a rise in the non-plan expenditure, revenue deficit as percentage of the fiscal deficit increased from 49.4 per cent in 1990-91 to 82.2 per cent in 2002-03. These policies have also affected the State governments' fiscal resources as net transfer of funds from the Central Government to the State Governments has declined. Agriculture, being a State subject, and with dwindling State finances, the public investment in it has been adversely affected (Singh, 2005). Further, benefits of economic reforms did not evenly distributed across Indian States due to reasons such as, differences in the quality of infrastructure, governance, human capital, and the location of States. Several studies have been conducted on the subject of inter-state disparity in India. However, most of these studies are based on aggregate data of NSDP. These studies have conclusive evidence that in the post-reform period, economic disparity among states has increased (Kurian, 2000; Singh *et al.*, 2003; Bhattacharya and Sakthivel, 2004; Das, 2002; Shetty, 2003). But whether disparity is increased due to differences in agricultural or non-agricultural NSDP has not yet given due emphasis. Similarly, there are studies about inter-state disparities in agricultural development based on single crop or group of crops. These studies concluded that that agricultural growth has picked up in low productivity eastern states after the initial phases of green revolution, thus regional difference in agricultural income and productivity across states have narrowed down (Sawant and Achutan, 1995; Bhalla and Singh, 1997; Chand Ramesh, S.S. Raju, L.M. Pandey 2007). However, conclusions about inter-state disparities in agricultural development based on single crop, group of crops or even crop sector can be misleading. There has been progressive diversification towards livestock production within agricultural sector which implies that exclusion of livestock sub sector while evaluating growth performance is not justifiable (Sawant, 1997; Joshi, P.K. *et al.*, 2004; Singh and Sahoo, 2007). Thus, inter-state performance of agricultural sector should be analyzed based on state domestic product from the total agriculture. In the recent times attempts has been made to study inter-state variations over time in terms of performance of overall agriculture. It is found that in the short-run states exhibit a tendency to converge to a single rate of growth but in the longer-run there are two divergent patterns; states with better irrigation spread tend to converge to higher rate of growth whereas states with lower proportion of crop area under irrigation tend to converge to lower rate of growth (Bhide, Kalirajan and Shand, 1998). Even this study does not comment on convergence or divergence in agricultural performance when all states are considered together. Keeping this in backdrop, this paper examines the inter-state disparity in the agricultural productivity; identifies the major factors in explaining this disparity and suggests policy interventions to alleviate it.

OBJECTIVES

(a) To analyse inter-state disparities in area, production and yield of crops in major states of India during 1996-97 to 2005-06.

(b) To suggest suitable measures to reduce regional disparities in Indian agriculture.

METHODOLOGY

The study is mainly based on the secondary data collected from various published sources for the years 1995 to 2006. The main data sources are official websites of Ministry of Agriculture, Ministry of Statistics and Programme Implementation and Reserve Bank of India (RBI), Various Issues of *Economic Survey,*. Major Indian States, which together constitute about 90 per cent of total population of the country, are considered for studying the inter-state disparity in the agricultural performance.

TABLE I

All-India Area, Production and Yield of Foodgrains from 1990-91 to 2006-07 along with Percentage Coverage under Irrigation

Area—Million Hectares
Production—Million Tonnes
Yield—Kg/Hectare

Year	*Area*	*{roduction*	*Yield*	*% Coverage under Irrigation*
1990-91	127.94	176.39	380	35.1
1991-92	121.87	168.38	1382	37.4
1992-93	123.15	179.48	1457	37.4
1993-94	122.75	184.25	1501	38.7
1994-95	123.86	191.50	1546	39.6
1995-96	121.01	180.42	1491	40.1
1996-97	123.58	199.44	1614	40.0
1997-98	123.85	192.26	1552	40.8
1998-99	125.17	203.61	1627	42.4
1999-00	123.10	209.80	1704	43.9
2000-01	121.05	196.81	1626	43.4
2001-02	122.78	212.85	1734	43.0
2002-03	113.86	174.77	1535	42.8
2003-04	123.45	213.19	1727	42.2
2004-05	120.00	198.36	1652	NA
2005-06	121.60	208.60	1715	NA
2006-07*	124.07	211.78	1707	NA

*Advanced Estimatess on 4-4-2007.

Note: The yields rates given above have been worked out on the basis of production and area figures taken in '000 units.

Agriculture, and especially a variety of crops produced under diverse climatic situations in different cropping systems, supports 115.5 million farm families. Rice-Wheat is the main cropping system of Indo-Gangetic Plains in North-West and North-East Regions, while monoculture of rice is prevalent on the coastal belt of Eastern and Southern States. Cotton-based cropping system dominates in rain fed conditions of Central (Madhya Pradesh and Maharashtra), Southern (Karnataka, Andhra Pradesh and Tamil Nadu) and Western (Gujarat) regions and irrigated areas of Northern (Punjab and Haryana) and Western (Rajasthan) regions. Sugarcane is predominantly grown in Uttar Pradesh, Maharashtra, Tamil Nadu and Karnataka.

The above table (Table 1) shows all-India area, production and yield of Foodgrains during 1990-91 to 2005-06 with percentage coverage under irrigation. The percentage coverage under irrigation shows an increasing trend from 1991 to 2006 and also the production of foodgrains has increased from 2000.

The Annual Compound Growth Rates in agriculture and non-agriculture sector of the States is presented in Table 2. A perusal of the table reveals the gloomy performance of most of the States during the last two decades which is more pronounced in the later decade. To the dismay, none of the States achieved growth rates more than four per cent and seven per cent in agriculture and non-agriculture sector respectively, during 1991-92 to 2003-04. The best performing States (in both agriculture and non-agriculture sector) during 1981-82 to 1990-91 namely, Haryana, Maharashtra and Rajasthan are among the worst performers in agriculture sector during 1991-2003, though they retained higher growth rates in non-agriculture sector. Punjab, which experienced the highest growth rate in agriculture (4.91%) during 1981-1990 could achieve only a little more than two per cent during 1991-2003.

It is also evident from the table that all the States except Bihar and Andhra Pradesh have achieved much higher growth rates in agriculture sector during 1981-90 than in 1991-2003. The only welcoming fact that can be drawn from the table is Bihar's remarkable agricultural growth during

TABLE 2

Annual Compound Growth Rates of Agriculture and Bon-griculture NSDP at Factor Cost (Constant Prices, 1993-94)

	1981-82 to 1990-91		*1991-92 to 2003-04*	
Agri.	*Non-Agri. < 7%*	*Non-Agri. > 7%*	*Non-Agri. < 7%*	*Non-Agri. > 7%*
> 4%	Punjab, WB	Haryana, Maharashtra, Rajasthan	Bihar	-
3%-4%	Bihar, TN	-	-	WB
2%-3%	Assam, Kerala, MP	Karnataka, UP	AP, Punjab UP	Karnataka, Maharashtra
< 2%	-	AP, Orissa, Gujarat	Assam, MP, Orissa, T.N.	Gujarat, Kerala, Haryana, Rajasthan

Source: Based on data collected from Handbook of Statistics on Indian Economy, RBI (2005).

1991-2003 which is above four per cent. The table shows that during the pre-reform period, almost 50 per cent of the total States achieved over 3 per cent annual growth in agriculture while during the post-reform period, except for Bihar and West Bengal, all the other States could achieve less than three per cent agricultural growth.

AGRICULTURE IN THE INDIAN STATES

About 70 per cent of India is directly dependent on agriculture, which is the main component of most state economies in India. The Punjab region is suited for wheat-growing. The south Indian states of Andhra Pradesh, Tamil Nadu and Karnataka are also major producers of rice. These states are mostly irrigated by the rivers Krishna, Godavari and Cauvery.

Haryana is self-sufficient in food production and the

second largest contributor to India's central pool of food grains. Haryana contributed significantly to the Green Revolution in India in the 1970s. The high-altitude states of Himachal Pradesh and Jammu & Kashmirare ideal for production of apples. Arunachal Pradesh also has a large number of fruit orchards. Tea is the other produce of the high altitude regions of Assam, West Bengal (Darjeeling), Tripura, Tamil Nadu (Ooty), Himachal Pradesh and Kerala. Assam produces some of the finest and most expensive teas in the world (see Assam tea). However Assam tea is grown at elevations near sea level, giving it a malty sweetness and an earthy flavour, as opposed to the more floral aroma of highland (e.g., Darjeeling, Taiwanese). In mountainous states like Sikkim, farming is done on terraced slopes. The state has the highest production and largest cultivated area of cardamom in India. Karnataka is the largest producer of coffee in India and accounts for 59 per cent of the country's coffee production. The other state manufacturing silk is Tamil Nadu. Rajasthan is among the largest producers of edible oils in India and the second largest producer of oilseeds. The state is also the biggest wool-producing state in India. Kerala produces 96 per cent of national output of pepper. It is also the largest producer of spices which include cardamom, vanilla, cinnamon, and nutmeg. Kerala is also the largest producer of natural rubber in India (91%). The other state producing rubber is Tripura. 30 per cent of Mizoram is covered with wild bamboo forests, and accounts for 40 per cent of India's 80-million-ton annual bamboo crop. There has been an economic shift towards agriculture for some states like Bihar after the mineral rich areas were carved out to form the new state of Jharkhand.

State Disparities in Area, Production and Yield of Different Crops in India

Table 3 shows the area, production and yield of rice in different states of India. it can be noted that largest producing state is West Bengal with 15.2 million tonnes (mt) in 2005-06 followed by Andhra Pradesh (11.7 mt), UP (11.1 mt) and Punjab (9.7 mt). Largest area is also occupied by West Bengal followed by UP and Orissa but compared to

TABLE 3

Area, Production and Yield of Rice in Major States of India

*Area (A) ('000 ha.)**
*Production (P) ('000 tns) ***
Yield (Y) (Kg/ha.)

States	1996-97 to 2000-01			2001-02			2002-03			2003-04			2004-05			2005-06		
	A	P	Y	A	P	Y	A	P	Y	A	P	Y	A	P	Y	A	P	Y
Andhra Pradesh	20.1	54	13370	3.8	11.3	2978	2.8	7.3	2596	2.9	8.9	3010	3.0	9.6	3111	3.9	11.7	2939
Assam	12.6	17.5	6974	2.5	3.8	1524	2.5	3.7	1472	2.5	3.8	1534	2.3	3.4	1461	2.3	3.5	1541
Bihar	14.4	2.2	6090	3.5	5.2	1480	3.5	4.9	1387	3.5	5.3	1516	3.1	2.4	792	3.2	4.5	1415
Gujarat	2.9	4.2	6950	0.6	1	1549	0.5	0.6	1240	0.7	1.1	1891	0.6	1.2	1805	0.6	1.2	1799
Haryana	4.7	12.4	12945	1.0	2.7	2652	0.9	2.4	2714	1.0	2.7	2749	1.0	3.0	2941	1.0	3.1	3000
Karnataka	6.9	17.5	12458	1.4	3.2	2281	1.1	2.3	2070	1.1	2.5	2190	1.3	3.5	2712	1.3	3.4	2521
Orissa	22.2	26.6	5753	4.5	7.1	1588	4.2	3.2	759	4.5	6.8	1511	4.4	6.4	1446	4.4	6.4	1450
Punjab	12.1	40.9	16922	2.4	8.8	3545	2.5	8.8	3510	2.6	9.6	3694	2.6	10.4	3943	2.6	9.7	3700
Rajasthan	0.9	0.9	5768	0.2	0.1	1247	0.08	0.06	809	0.09	0.1	1653	0.1	0.1	1489	0.1	0.2	1458
Tamil Nadu	10.6	35.5	16323	2.0	6.5	3196	1.5	3.5	2359	1.3	3.2	2308	1.5	4.1	2627	2.8	7.5	2650
Uttar Pradesh	27.7	57.6	10371	6.0	12.8	2117	4.4	8.1	1836	5.7	12.4	2181	5.3	9.5	1789	5.5	11.1	1994
West Bengal	29.1	65.1	11190	6.0	15.2	2514	5.8	14.3	2463	5.8	14.6	2504	5.7	14.8	2574	5.7	15.2	2632
India	220.6	424.3	9610	44.6	93.3	2092	41.1	71.8	1744	42.4	88.5	2083	41.6	83.1	1995	44.2	91.7	2074

*values have been divided by 1000.
**values have been divided by 1000.
Source: CMIE, April 2007.

TABLE 4

Area, Production and Yield of Wheat in Major States of India

Area (A) ('000 ha.)
Production (P) ('000 tns)
Yield (Y) (Kg/ha.)

States	*1996-97 to 2000-01*			*2001-02*			*2002-03*			*2003-04*			*2004-05*			*2005-06*		
	*A**	*P@*	*Y*	*A*	*P*	*Y*	*A*	*P*	*Y*	*A*	*P*	*Y*	*A*	*P*	*Y*	*A*	*P*	*Y*
Andhra Pradesh	63.3	38.1	3001	14.0	9.0	643	11.0	14.9	1349	11.9	6.7	565	9.0	5.0	556	11.3	9.0	793
Assam	408.8	12.6	6139	72.2	85.3	1181	69.0	78.0	1130	70.0	73.2	1046	105.0	117.5	1119	78.0	85.6	1097
Bihar	10.1	21.6	10544	2.1	4.3	2056	2.1	4.0	1896	2.1	3.7	1783	2.0	3.9	1911	2.3	4.3	1863
Gujarat	2744.8	6.25	11482	470.1	1.1	2435	435.6	0.86	1966	759.5	2.0	2681	727.4	1.8	2482	922.0	2.2	2376
Haryana	11.8	43	19727	2.3	9.4	4103	2.3	9.2	4053	2.3	9.1	3937	2.3	9.0	3901	2.3	8.8	3844
Karnataka	1295.7	995.7	3826	260.5	198.8	763	246.9	147.7	598	231	111	480	237	145.5	614	223	125.8	564
Orissa	83.3	1119	6721	19.5	26.3	1348	4.6	5.8	1261	5.1	7.5	1471	-	-	-	-	-	-
Punjab	16.5	71.8	21676	3.4	15.4	4532	3.3	14.2	4200	3.4	14.4	4207	3.5	14.7	4221	3.5	14.5	4179
Rajasthan	12.7	32.6	12668	2.2	6.3	2793	1.8	4.9	2709	2.1	5.8	2794	2.1	5.7	2765	1.9	5.4	2756
Tamil Nadu	-	-	-			-			-			-			-			-
Uttar Pradesh	44.6	118.6	13304	9.2	25.4	2755	9.0	23.6	2596	9.4	26.5	2806	9.0	22.5	2502	9.2	23.5	2572
West Bengal	1876.2	4337.4	11534	434	961.5	2215	405.4	887.4	2189	425.7	985.7	2316	400	841.5	2104	450	773.5	1719
India	133	352.7	13240	26.3	72.7	2763	24.8	65.7	2645	26.5	72.1	2714	26.4	68.6	2600	26.8	69.3	2586

* Values (A and P) have been divided by 1000 of these states (Bihar, Haryana, Punjab, UP and India).
@production has been divided by 1000 of Gujarat.
Source: CMIE, April 2007.

area in production the highest yield of rice is in Punjab with 3700 kg/ha. followed by Andhra Pradesh and Haryana.

Table 4 shows the area, production and yield of wheat in different states of India, again West Bengal is the highest producing state of wheat followed by Karnataka and Assam. There is no growth of wheat in Tamil Nadu, there are large variations in area and yield of wheat in different states.

Table 5 shows the area, production and yield of maize in different states of India. Andhra Pradesh is a largest producing state of maize followed by UP and Punjab. The largest area is covered by Rajasthan while its production and yield is less than other states.

Table 6 shows the area, production and yield of food grains in different states of India. Uttar Pradesh is a largest producing state of food grains followed by West Bengal and Andhra Pradesh. The highest yield is in West Bengal as compared to Uttar Pradesh. There are large disparities in area and yield of other states.

Table 7 shows the area, production and yield of sugar cane in different states of India. Sugarcane is an important crop produced in India. The largest producing state is Andhra Pradesh followed by Uttar Pradesh and Tamil Nadu. The highest yield is in Tamil Nadu while its area covered is less than other states.

Table 8 shows the area, production and yield of cotton in different states of India. It can be noted from the above table that compared to other states growth of cotton is very less in Assam, Bihar and West Bengal. The largest producing state is Gujarat followed by Punjab and Andhra Pradesh. Gujarat has occupied large area compared to other states.

Table 9 shows the area, production and yield of rapeseed/mustard in different states of India. Rajasthan is a largest producer of rapeseed/mustard followed by Haryana and UP as compared to other states very less production is noted in Karnataka and Orissa. It is mainly produced in North western regions of India.

There are large disparities among India's states and territories in agricultural performance. A number of factors may be accountable for disparity in the agriculture output across States. Agriculture development depends on various

TABLE 5

Area, Production and Yield of Maize in Major States of India

Area (A) ('000 ha.)
Production (P) ('000 tns)
Yield (Y) (Kg/ha.)

States	*1996-97 to 2000-01*			*2001-02*			*2002-03*			*2003-04*			*2004-05*			*2005-06*		
	A	*P*	*Y*	*A*	*P*	*Y*	*A*	*P*	*Y*	*A*	*P*	*Y*	*A*	*P*	*Y*	*A*	*P*	*Y*
Andhra Pradesh	2136	6710	15754	429	1459	3401	526	1486	2827	721	2477	3436	624	2064	3308	758	3087	4073
Assam	98	71	3593	19	14	709	20	14	700	19	14	719	-	-	-	20	-	-
Bihar	2495	5427	8693	598	1565	2618	604	1350	2236	606	1440	2374	547	-	-	622	-	-
Gujarat	1981	2764	6944	444	885	1995	464	792	1706	484	832	1717	459	412	898	477	-	-
Haryana	106	213	10157	18	47	2611	16	29	1812	15	38	2533	16	40	2500	16	34	2125
Karnataka	2793	8306	14901	580	1451	2503	649	1343	2068	618	1244	2013	852	-	-	930	-	-
Orissa	269	352	6519	51	47	907	43	42	984	56	79	1417	185	244	1322	65	-	-
Punjab	813	1830	11868	165	449	2721	152	310	2039	154	459	2980	154	422	2740	148	403	2723
Rajasthan	4755	5276	5542	1017	1479	1454	984	871	885	1110	2068	1863	1043	1261	1211	1004	-	-
Tamil Nadu	360	586.9	8165	73	119	1624	121	192	1583	160	251	1567	190	294	1552	230	-	-
Uttar Pradesh	4857	6876	7088	931	1516	1628	762	839	1101	947	1318	1392	981	-	-	910	1041	1144
West Bengal	188	493	13049	33	86	2595	30	60	2000	41	97	2359	65	191	2949	59	-	-
India*	31.7	56.2	8841	6.6	13.1	1996	6.6	11.1	1681	7.3	14.9	2046	7.6	14.2	1846	7.7	14.7	1904

*Values of A and P of India has been divided by 1000.
Source: CMIE, April 2007.

TABLE 6

Area, Production and Yield of Foodgrains in Major States of India

Area (A) ('000 ha.)
Production (P) ('000 tns)
Yield (Y) (Kg/ha.)

States	1996-97 to 2000-01			2001-02			2002-03			2003-04			2004-05			2005-06		
	A	P	Y	A	P	Y	A	P	Y	A	P	Y	A	P	Y	A	P	Y
Andhra Pradesh	35.8	68.9	9562	7.1	14.8	2103	6.3	10.6	1694	6.8	13.7	2012	6.2	13.4	2138	-	-	-
Assam	13.5	20	7414	2.7	4.0	1465	2.8	3.9	1414	2.7	4.4	1474	-	-	-	-	-	-
Bihar	15.5	24.8	3756	7.1	11.9	1679	6.9	10.2	1493	7.1	11.2	1601	-	-	-	-	-	-
Gujarat	17.7	21.6	5970	3.4	4.9	1412	3.2	3.6	1127	4.0	6.5	1629	3.6	5.1	1408	-	-	-
Haryana	20.9	61	14590	4.2	13.3	3127	3.9	12.3	3100	4.3	13.2	3082	-	-	-	-	-	-
Karnataka	37.1	47.8	6428	7.1	8.6	1212	7	6.6	949	6.6	6.7	1008	-	-	-	-	-	-
Orissa	26.7	27.6	5168	5.4	7.5	1393	5.0	3.5	706	5.3	7.2	1341	6.5	7.5	1154	-	-	-
Punjab	30.5	119.3	19439	6.1	23.4	3832	6.3	24.7	3933	-	-	-	-	-	-	-	-	-
Rajasthan	62.1	50.5	4850	12.7	14	1099	8.6	7.5	875	13.9	17.9	1288	-	-	-	-	-	-
Tamil Nadu	18.5	42.2	11338	3.4	7.6	2228	2.8	4.4	1598	2.8	54.3	1520	3.3	6.1	1870	-	-	-
Uttar Pradesh	98.8	206.1	10420	20.2	44.0	2173	17.9	36.3	2029	20.0	44.1	2201	19.3	37.5	1943	19.5	39.8	2038
West Bengal	32.5	71	10930	6.8	16.5	2424	6.5	15.5	2374	6.6	16.0	2421	6.5	16.1	2480	-	-	-
India	616.5	1001.8	8117	121.9	212.8	1746	113.9	174.7	1535	123.3	213.9	1735	120.0	198.3	1652	-	208.6	-

* Values of A and P of all states has been divided by 1000.

TABLE 7

Area, Production and Yield of Sugarcane in Major States of India

Area (A) ('000 ha.)
Production (P) ('000 tns)
Yield (Y) (Kg/ha.)

States	*1996-97 to 2000-01*			*2001-02*			*2002-03*			*2003-04*			*2004-05*			*2005-06*		
	A	*P*	*Y*	*A*	*P*	*Y*	*A*	*P*	*Y*	*A*	*P*	*Y*	*A*	*P*	*Y*	*A*	*P*	*Y*
Andhra Pradesh	1082	820	3.7	8187	218180	82831	232	154	66190	209	150	72105	208	157	75668	230	187	81087
Assam	154	6	1.9	8903	2.7	1.1	37184	26	0.92	35231	25	0.98	38638	30	-	-	23	-
Bihar	395	17.7	180581	121	5.8	48165	107	4.5	42130	103	4.2	40990	97	-	-	102	-	-
Gujarat	906	63.6	351042	17.6	12.5	70902	203	14	69351	176	12.7	71820	171	14.5	85205	197	-	-
Haryana	711	39.3	276508	16.2	9.3	57593	189	10.6	56349	161	9.3	58012	243	8.1	33169	127	8.2	64409
Karnataka	1720	167.5	482997	40.7	33.0	81132	383	32.5	84880	237	15.8	66667	265	-	-	200	-	-
Orissa	103	5.9	293575	11	0.7	58351	14	0.7	53042	15	0.9	58774	34	2.3	68604	-	-	-
Punjab	631	3.8	302236	143	8.8	61664	154	9.3	60325	123	6.6	53821	87	5.2	59425	84	4.9	57857
Rajasthan	107	5	227782	9	0.4	47696	10	0.4	42170	6	0.3	53345	9	-	-	8	-	-
Tamil Nadu	1480	159.7	538367	321	37.2	115978	261	24.1	92446	192	17.7	91924	224	24.5	109184	333	-	-
Uttar Pradesh	9468	556.3	291145	2035	117.9	57980	2167	122.1	56331	2030	112.7	55541	3534	118.7	33592	2156	125.4	58196
West Bengal	123	8.8	362640	23	1.9	85124	19	1.3	65708	17	1.3	74118	16	1.0	66231	15	-	-
India	2072	11441	1047890	4410	297.2	67394	4520	287.3	63576	4023	233.8	58131	3760	237.1	63055	4280	281.1	65694

Values of P of all states have been divided by 1000.
Source: CMIE, April 2007.

TABLE 8

Area, Production and Yield of Cotton in Major States of India

Area (A) ('000 ha.)
Production (P) ('000 tns)
Yield (Y) (Kg/ha.)

States	*1996-97 to 2000-01*			*2001-02*			*2002-03*			*2003-04*			*2004-05*			*2005-06*		
	A	*P*	*Y*	*A*	*P*	*Y*	*A*	*P*	*Y*	*A*	*P*	*Y*	*A*	*P*	*Y*	*A*	*P*	*Y*
Andhra Pradesh	5262	7978	1302	1107	1877	288	803	1086	230	837	1889	384	1178	2190	316	1033	2108	347
Assam	-	-	-	-	-	-	-	-	-	-	-	-	-	-	-	-	-	-
Bihar	-	-	-	-	-	-	-	-	-	-	-	-	-	-	-	-	-	-
Gujarat	7849	12988	1404	1750	1702	165	1635	1685	175	1641	4027	417	1906	5443	485	2077	-	-
Haryana	2962	6171	1775	630	722	195	518	1038	341	526	1405	454	621	-	-	583	-	-
Karnataka	2897	4121	1197	609	612	171	393	331	143	313	321	174	398	-	-	450	-	-
Orissa	143	243	1476	36	60	280	30	50	288	37	88	409	46	111	412	57	-	-
Punjab	2975	5600	1611	607	1307	366	449	1083	410	452	1478	556	509	2087	697	557	2395	731
Rajasthan	3036	4223	1150	510	281	94	385	252	111	343	709	351	327	-	-	472	-	-
Tamil Nadu	1047	1746	1452	164	229	238	76	83	188	98	123	213	129	186	244	135	-	-
Uttar Pradesh	40	26	510	5	0.9	31	5	4.4	150	4	4	162	15	-	-	20	-	-
West Bengal	-	-	-	-	-	-	-	-	-	-	-	-	-	-	-	-	-	-
India	44575	58421	1117	9130	9997	186	7670	8623	191	7630	13729	306	8708	16429	321	8873	18499	354

Source: CMIE, April 2007.

TABLE 9

Area, Production and Yield of Rapeseed/Mustard in Major States of India

Area (A) ('000 ha.)
Production (P) ('000 tns)
Yield (Y) (Kg/ha.)

States	*1996-97 to 2000-01*			*2001-02*			*2002-03*			*2003-04*			*2004-05*			*2005-06*		
	A	*P*	*Y*	*A*	*P*	*Y*	*A*	*P*	*Y*	*A*	*P*	*Y*	*A*	*P*	*Y*	*A*	*P*	*Y*
Andhra Pradesh	-	-	-	-	-	-	-	-	-	-	-	-	-	-	-	-	-	-
Assam	1405	702	2499	272	137	503	261	130	498	264	138	524	245	129	528	257	-	-
Bihar	465	385	4093	96	78	815	90	62	688	94	78	830	83	67	805	85	-	-
Gujarat	1535	1821	5944	247	292	1182	161	172	1072	269	395	1469	291	405	1390	338	-	-
Haryana	2510	3013	6050	535	796	1488	607	697	1148	614	957	1559	702	826	1177	702	-	-
Karnataka	33	9	1317	7	2	286	4	1	266	6	2	333	6	2	333	-	-	-
Orissa	88	13	766	14	2	155	12	2	131	16	3	195	16	3	188	17	-	-
Punjab	346	375	5420	50	60	1200	66	60	909	51	61	1196	59	61	1034	-	-	-
Rajasthan	12395	10919	4448	1760	1908	1084	1518	1318	868	2062	2694	1306	3682	3971	1078	3559	-	-
Tamil Nadu	-	-	-	-	-	-	-	-	-	-	-	-	-	-	-	-	-	-
Uttar Pradesh	3782	3394	4464	537	536	998	582	524	900	528	532	1008	818	801	979	562	-	-
West Bengal	1772	1482	4151	440	337	766	408	328	805	452	419	928	457	342	749	421	383	909
India	30597	27001	4452	5070	5083	1003	4481	3880	866	5387	6291	1168	7316	7593	1038	7074	8131	1149

Source: CMIE, April 2007.

TABLE 10

Area, Production and Yield of Total Pulses in Major States of India

Area (A) ('000 ha.)
Production (P) ('000 tns)
Yield (Y) (Kg/ha.)

States	1996-97 to 2000-01			2001-02			2002-03			2003-04			2004-05			2005-06		
	A	P	Y	A	P	Y	A	P	Y	A	P	Y	A	P	Y	A	P	Y
Andhra Pradesh	7413	3322	4179	1624	772	934	432	150	348	521	218	418	483	219	453	565	301	533
Assam	578	322	6282	116	65	1257	7	5	714	7	5	700	6.7	4.8	716	-	-	-
Bihar	169	218	5153	42	54	1348	38	43	1141	38	45	1184	36	44	1235	100	-	-
Gujarat	3512	2137	5849	681	356	1047	313	197	630	297	258	870	254	236	928	285	-	-
Haryana	311	306	9130	38	26	1403	36	30	829	26	32	1266	31	32	1032	-	-	-
Karnataka	2443	873	1722	482	147	306	514	241	468	532	197	370	562	290	516	567	-	-
Orissa	3380	1107	3817	700	261	882	114	74	643	137	96	700	130	89	683	132	-	-
Punjab	331	231	7331	47	30	1445	9	8	864	48	37	1656	9	8	865	10	-	-
Rajasthan	9450	2414	5024	2388	691	862	17	4	236	20	16	815	17	13	746	18	-	-
Tamil Nadu	2646	1358	5122	673	285	1051	44	24	545	151	28	612	40	25	625	62	-	-
Uttar Pradesh	2214	2593	5877	394	456	1157	328	298	910	369	406	1101	387	380	982	437	378	865
West Bengal	1092	756	6904	198	132	1508	3	3	903	89	64	1621	81	55	1667	3	-	-
India	75942	39146	5788	15539	7900	1136	3520	6890	622	17473	9190	1141	3519	7660	668	3839	7790	714

factors, such as size of operational holdings, irrigation facilities, cropping intensity, application of new farm technology, HYVs seeds, fertilizers, pesticides, extension services, and rural infrastructure, including road, energy, credit and market. Besides these factors, quality of land, sunshine and rainfall can also explain the difference in the agricultural productivity. Above all, it is the capacity and willingness of individual State governments to investment in agriculture that determines the variation in the agricultural growth, as agriculture is a state subject. State policy related to the agricultural development, therefore, plays a vital role in explaining variation in agricultural productivity across state. The crop yield is heavily dependent on the rains. This was the main reason of decline in growth rate of agriculture sector in second half of 1990's. This uncertainty hits worst the small farmers and labourers, which are usually leading a hand to mouth lifestyle. In a country like our's, where people die of draughts and floods, every year, something must be done to support farmers and supply them enough water with electricity.

CONCLUSION AND SUGGESTIONS

The paper examines the extent of disparity that exists in the agricultural sector across the major States of India; identifies the factors in explaining this disparity; and finally suggests policy interventions to narrow down the inequality among regions. On the basis of data collected from various secondary sources for the period 1991-2006, the paper presents strong evidence of regional variations agricultural area, production and yield of major crops across States of India. It is also observed that the better performing States are mostly in the western and southern regions of the country. On the other hand, the non-performing or poorly performing States are in the northern and eastern regions.

There is a strong evidence of cyclical nature of the disparity across the States, implying that agriculture still is highly dependent of the nature and other stochastic factors that cause fluctuations in the agricultural output across time and space. It is also observed that agricultural growth has decelerated in the agriculturally developed States like Punjab, Haryana and Western Uttar Pradesh in the post-reform period and some agriculturally poor states such as Bihar and West Bengal have shown a significant improvement in their agricultural growth. As growth rate is pattering off in the green revolution regions and picking up in the other States, especially in eastern and north-eastern regions, there is likelihood that in the years to come inter-state disparity would be narrowed down provided that the state governments make sufficient investment in irrigation and flood control, power, road, agricultural R&D and extension services.

The disparity in the agricultural output is significantly and positively affected by the variations in fertilizer use and in length of pucca road. The variation in the number of tractor use and in the cropping intensity has positive impact on the variation in agricultural output.

SUGGESTIONS

The following suggestions are given to reduce regional inequalities in agriculture across Indian States:

- Agricultural disparity is found positively associated with the variation in the level of infrastructure (pucca road), fertilizer consumption and farm mechanisation. It is therefore necessary to improve the infrastructure in the infrastructure-deficit state and provide easy access to the farmers for short-term institutional credit facilities to the farmers to purchase fertilizer, seeds, etc. and long-term credit to procure farm machines such as tractor. As there is significant difference in the usage of modern farm inputs among states, efforts should be made to remove both the supply side and the demand side constraints in the access to these inputs.
- The cyclical pattern of agricultural disparity across states indicates that natural and other stochastic factors like flood and drought have significant

impact on the agricultural output. The state governments have to make substantial enhancement in watershed management, irrigation and flood control, especially in those state where frequency of such occurrences is very high.

- Promotion of "group farming" or "collective farming" among small and marginal farms through active support of government institutions, commercial banks and non-governmental organizations may go a long way in reducing the scale-disadvantages of these farms and in enhancing the farm productivity and profitability and reducing disparity not only across size of farms but also across regions.
- The public sector should concentrate on educational programmes for farmers, facilitating formation of farmers' groups, building linkages with other technology providers and initiating paid consultancy services by maintaining a cadre of qualified staff at the district and sub-district levels. The present concentration of subject-matter specialists at these levels does not match these needs.
- For growth to improve in lagging states, implementation of reforms is essential to reduce fiscal imbalances and improve the composition of public expenditure and investment climate. Of particular importance for poverty reduction and increasing rural incomes are policies aimed at increasing agricultural productivity and rural employment.

References

Ballabh, V. (2007). "Institutional Alternatives and Governance of Agriculture", Academic Foundation, New Delhi: pp. 46-58.

Bhalla, G.S. and Gurmail Singh (1997). "Recent Developments in Indian Agriculture: A State Level Analysis", *Economic and Political Weekly*, Vol. 32(13). March 29, pp. A2-A18.

Bhattacharya, B.B and S. Sakthivel (2004). "Regional Growth and Disparity in India", *Economic and Political Weekly*, (EPW), March 6, pp. 1071-77.

Bhide, Shashanka, K.P. Kalirajan and R.T. Shand (1998). "India's Agricultural Dynamics: Weak Link in Development", *Economic and Political Weekly*, Vol. 33 (39), September 26, pp. A118-A127.

Chand Ramesh, S.S. Raju, L.M. Pandey (2007). "Growth Crisis in Agriculture", *Economic and Political Weekly*, Vol. 42, No. 26, June 30 -July 6, 2007, pp. 2528-33.

CMIE, (2007). "Agriculture", April.

Das, T.K. (2002). "Convergence across Indian States: Cross-Sectional and Panel Estimation", *South Asia Economic Journal*, Vol. 3, No 2, pp. 227-39.

Government of India (2007). Agriculture Statistics at a Glance, Directorate of Economics and Statistics, Ministry of Agriculture, New Delhi.

Government of India, *Economic Survey*, Various issues, Ministry of Finance, New Delhi.

Joshi, P.K., Gulati, A., Birthal, P.S. and Tiwari, L. (2004). 'Agriculture Diversification in South Asia: Pattern, Determinants and Policy Implications'. *Economic and Political Weekly*, June 12, pp. 2457-67.

Kurian, N.J. (2000). "Widening Regional Disparities in India: Some Indicators", *Economic and Political Weekly* (*EPW*), Vol. 35, No. 7, pp. 538-55.

Naik, S.D. (2003). "Correct Regional Disparities, Rural-Urban Divide", *The Hindu*, Aug. 16, Saturday.

Sahoo, B.K. and S. Mohapatra (2008). "Agricultural Disparity Across Indian States: Determinants and Policy Implications", *The ICFAI Journal of Agricultural Economics*, Vol. 5, No. 2, April, pp. 64-82.

Sawant, S.D. (1997). "Performance of Indian Agriculture with Special Reference to Regional Variations", *Indian Journal of Agricultural Economics*", Vol. 52(3), July-September.

Sawant, S.D. and C.V. Achutan (1995). "Agricultural Growth Across Crops and Regions: Emerging Patterns and Trends", *Economic and Political Weekly*, Vol. 30(12). March 25, pp. A2-A13.

Singh, Nirvikar, L. Bhanadari, A. Chen and A. Khare (2003). "Regional Inequality in India: A Fresh Look", *Economic and Political Weekly*, (*EPW*), Vol. 38, No. 11, March 15, pp. 1069-73.

Singh, S.P. (2005). "Agriculture", in Disequalising Growth: Alternative *Economic Survey, India*, New Delhi: Daanish Books.

Singh, S.P. and B.K. Sahoo (2007). "Diversification of Agricultural Economy Towards Horticulture and Livestock: Regional Variation, Convergence and Determinants", *The Indian Journal of Labour Economics*, Vol. 50, No. 4.

Shetty, S.L. (2003). "Growth of SDP and Structural Changes in State Economies: Inter-State Comparisons", *Economic and Political Weekly*, (*EPW*), Vol. 38, No. 49, December 6, pp. 5189-5200.

29

Regional Disparities in Agricultural Development of Andhra Pradesh—A Factor Analysis

B. SUDHAKAR REDDY

Regional disparities are universal phenomenon. There is hardly any country, which does not face the problem of regional disparities in development certain regions enter the process of development earlier than the others may be due to historical reasons, or differences in natural resources or cultural and institutional factors. If differences persist over a period of time, political discontent is bound to emerge sooner or later. Regional problems becomes when income differences overlap with differences in race, religion, language, culture of people living in different regions. Interventions to correct regional disparities are justified not only socially, but also on economic grounds because development of backward areas can contribute to the utilization of unexploited resources.

Many development theories showed that regional disparities are inherent in the process of development, Myrdal (1975), the analysis of long-run data showed that income inequalities across Indian states have increased mildly till mid-eighties and rapidly afterwards (Subramanayam and Rajgopal, 2000 and Govind Rao *et. al.*, 1999).

The need for reducing regional disparities has been argued from various angles. The firs argument is in terms of social justice, it is believed that income inequalities can be reduced by way of reducing regional disparities. Hence, reduction in regional disparities is crucial from the point of accelerating the growth of the economy. There is complementary between reduction in regional disparities and the prosperity of the economy.

In a federal state like India the policies and strategies formulated under plans at the national level have their implications at state level also. Therefore, inter-regional and intra-regional disparities at the state level assumes paramount importance. In order to capture inter-and intra-regional disparities as well as influencing factors for agricultural development. The present paper made a modest attempt to examine the above aspects by taking the experience of Andhra Pradesh as case study.

The state of Andhra Pradesh is the fifth largest state in India both in terms of area and population came in to existence on November 1, 1956 under the State Re-Organization Act, which consists of 23 districts distributed over three geographical regions namely, Coastal Andhra (9 Districts), Rayalaseem (4 Districts) and Telangana (10 Districts). The state of Andhra Pradesh replicates growing inger-regional disparities in economic development, these disparities may be due to disparities in industry or agriculture. The three constituent regions of Coastal Andhra, Rayalaseem and Telangana represent unequal economic development since, Andhra Pradesh continues to predominately agricultural state. 68 per cent of population depending on agriculture and, over 70 per cent cropped area under production of food grains. A study on regional disparities is necessary. Apart from this the resource endowment differences among districts in a particular region also influence the regional disparities in agricultural development. Though, there are quite a number of studies dealing with regional disparities they have not focused on regions and factors contributing to crucial problem of regional disparities. Hence, the present study made a modest attempt to identify the different factors and assess their role across the regions of Andhra Pradesh during the period of 1981-82 (ending triennium) to 2005-06 to overcome the year-to-year fluctuations triennium average is taken for the analysis.

OBJECTIVES OF THE STUDY

1. To study the inter-regional and intra-regional disparities in the agricultural development of Andhra Pradesh.
2. To identify the factors causing the disparities in the agricultural development of Andhra Pradeh.

Towards the end of objectives mentioned, the following is the methodology adopted.

METHODOLOGY

There are two major problems in the construction of agricultural development index. First, related to the methodology to be used for deriving weights, second and more important problem is the selection of indicators. Keeping in view of the facts present study has considered 12 indicators. The various possible factors which 'apriori' likely affect the agricultural development. The selection of indicators is based on the premise that agricultural development of any region or district depends on the following factors:

- Water availability,
- Adoption of Modern Technology, and
- Availability of agricultural infrastructure facilities.

It is presumed that better irrigation facilities, and adoption of mechanization lead to faster agricultural development. Hence, the following indicators are selected in order to construct agriculture development index:

1. Irrigation Intensity.

2. Proportion of assured irrigated area.
3. Cropping intensity.
4. Total rainfall.
5. Pump sets per 100 ha.
6. Tractors per 100 ha.
7. Fertilizer consumption per 100 ha.
8. Agriculture credit per 100 ha.
9. Spread of HYV.
10. Agricultural workers.
11. Agricultural Production.
12. Literacy.

Consistent with the objectives of the study. Present study uses Principal component analysis for the benchmark years 1981-82 and 2005-06 in order to capture relative positions of individual districts/regions in terms of ranks have also been obtained. These ranks are to be understood in an inverse manner, to be precise, the lower the value of rank higher is the index of agriculture development and *vice-versa*.

PRINCIPAL COMPONENT ANALYSIS

Principal component method begins with normalizing the variables in such a way that mutual comparison is possible. Normalization is done by expressing the deviations from the original observations with regard to their arithmetical mean in their standard deviation. If the number of observations (districts) ranges from 1 to N and number of variables (indicators) from 1 to n, then X_1 be the Jth observed variable relating to ith observation.

For the purpose of normalizing the variables the following formulae is obtained;

$$Z = \frac{X_{ji}}{X_j} \qquad X = \frac{X_{ji}}{N}$$

$$X_j = 2_{xj} \qquad (X_{ji} - X_j)$$

where

$$X_{ji} = X_{ji} - X_j$$

(j = 1, 2.................n) (I = 1, 2.................N)

The expected value (i.e. the mean) of normalized variables like this equals 'O' and variance equals '1'. Each of the normalized variable Z_j is then related separately to the hypothetical variables, i.e., principal components. These relations are linear and have the following analytical expression.

$$Z_j = a_{jI} P_1 + a_{j2}P_2 + \ldots\ldots a_{ji} P_i + a_{jm} P_m \ldots\ldots(1)$$

The first principal component is the linear combination of weighted variables, which explains the maximum of variance. Then

$$P_i = a_{11} Z_1 + a_{21} Z_2 + \ldots a_{n1}Z_n$$

The composite index of agriculture infrastructure at the sectoral level or at aggregate level is nothing but the first principal component of the variables. Then the equation of composite index for the ith region is as follows:

$$I_1 = a_j Z_{ji}$$

where

I_1 = The composite index of infrastructure of ith region (I = 1, 2 ... N).

= (J = 1, 2, n) factor loading on the first principal component.

= (j=1, 2, ... n) j^{th} standard normal variable of ith region of (I = 1, 2 ... N).

= 2 ... n are the Co-efficients or factor loadings of
= 1, 2, ... m the jth variable relating to j^{th} component.

Thus each component explains certain portion of variance of ith variable. To put it in other word, each Principal component is a linear combination of weighted variables. This can also be written as:

where a_j = factor loading of 'j' variables.

J = 1, 2, ...n or

$P_i = a_{ji} \times ia_{2i} \times 2 + a_3 \times 3 \ldots . \; an_i \times n \ldots .(2)$

$P_i = 1, 2, \ldots ..m$ (components).

a_{ji} = factor loading of jth variable of ith component

x_j = Variables

In the above model, each of 'n' normalized observed variables is described linearly in terms of 'n' new uncorrelated components $P_1, P_{2 \ldots .} P_n$. Only one relationship of variables is derived from each separate component 'P_n' the coefficients of a_{jn} indicate to what extent and in which direction the normalized variables Z_j are related to the components of 'P_n'. For any individual observation (district). The same logic of the model applies and therefore, the mathematical sign 'i' (i = 1, 2, ...N) is ignored.

Generally in socio economic analysis, when the purpose is to a compare inter-regional development the 'First Principle Component' Method is used. The 'Principal Component Analysis' has been carried out in all the two-benchmark years to build up the composite index of agriculture development, after standardization of variables. The Principal component analysis shows that the first principal component failed to explain more than 60 per cent of total variance in the above said periods, i.e. 1981-82 and 2005-06. Therefore, it would not be proper to calculate component scores based on the first principal component alone, and compare the development of regions and districts for the different benchmark years. But if four components are taken together, they are able to explain 90 per cent of total variance. Hence, we have developed Combined Component Scores (CCS) based on four component scores, and to each set of scores in proportion to the variance explained by it, that is to say, CCS = $W_1S_1 + W_2S_2 + W_3S_3 + W_4S_4$, where $W_1 = V_1/(V_1 + V_2)$ is the proportion of variance explained by the first principal component with variance value V_1 and $W_2 = V_2/(V_1 + V_2)$ is the proportion of variance explained by the second component with a variance value V_2, whereas, S_1 and S_2 are the first and second component scores respectively and so on. The CCS thus, worked out is considered as composite index of agriculture development.

TABLE I

Combined Composite Index of Agricultural Development in Proportion to Variance

S. No.	*District*	*1981-82*	*Rank*	*2005-06*	*Rank*
1.	Srikakulam	-0.031	9	-0.025	9
2.	Visakhapatnam	-0.006	6	-0.060	16
3.	East Godavari	0.056	3	0.038	3
4.	West Godavari	0.086	1	0.094	1
5.	Krishna	0.063	3	0.052	5
6.	Guntur	0.008	5	-0.048	13
7.	Prakasam	-0.063	15	-0.063	17
8.	Nellore	0.065	2	-0.012	6
9.	Kurnool	-0.079	17	-0.091	20
10.	Ananthapur	-0.100	21	-0.123	21
11.	Cuddapah	-0.080	18	-0.068	18
12.	Chittoor	-0.024	7	-0.060	15
13.	Ranga Reddy	-0.031	8	-0.045	12
14.	Nizamabad	-0.037	10	0.065	2
15.	Medak	-0.077	16	-0.027	10
16.	Mahaboobnagar	-0.089	19	-0674	19
17.	Nalgonda	-0.061	14	0.016	8
18.	Warangal	-0.060	13	-0.014	7
19.	Khammam	-0.052	12	-0.047	11
20.	Karimnagar	-0.051	11	0.037	4
21.	Adilabad	-0.090	20	-0.050	14
	Coastal Andhra	0.196	1	0.138	1
	Rayalaseema	-0.002	3	-0.043	3
	Telanagana	0.080	2	0.102	2
	Andhra Pradesh	0.391		0.324	

FINDINGS OF THE STUDY

By following the above mentioned the 21 districts of AP are ranked on the basis of the agriculture development. As pointed out earlier 12 variables are taken for analysis. The districts are ranked on the basis of their aggregate scores over 12 identified variables. The ranking of the districts are done at two different points of time, i.e. 1981-82 and 2005-06.

As it is evident from the Table 1 that composite infrastructure index of the state as whole was 0.391, it is found that coastal Andhra occupied first place followed by Telangana and Rayalaseema during the two bench mark years. One can infer from the above that there is no change in the relative positions of regions which implied that the regional disparities in the agricultural development did not come down over a period of time, implying that developed region remained developed and backward remains backward in terms of agriculture agricultural development in Andhra Pradesh, in spite of considerable development that has taken place.

When we analyze intra-regional disparities, it is observed that West-Godavari stands first followed by Nellore, East Godavari and Krishna in the scale of agricultural development and least developed districts are Prakasam and Srikakulam in coastal Andhra region, Chittor stands first and Kurnool the least in Rayalaseema region. In Telangana region Nizamabad stood first followed by Karimnagar, Khammam and Warangal in 1981-82. When we compared disparities in the benchmark year 2005-06, West Godavari remained in the same position, i.e. it stands first in the scale of development followed by Nizamabad, East Godavari and Krishna.

FACTOR ANALYSIS

In order to identify the package of variables that can affect inter-regional and intra-regional disparities in agricultural development Regression Analysis may be applied. Due to various problems encountered in regression analysis, Factor Analysis is often applied to isolate the group of variables in to factors Adelman and Morries and others have recommended factor analysis as an appropriate technique in isolating the determents. The procedure for the factor analysis, which attempts to estimate the value of coefficient of regression where variables are regressed upon factors. The coefficient of regression are referred in5 factor analysis literature is Factor Loadings. In the present study the "Principal Axis Method" is used to get these coefficients.

The factor loadings are rotated in order to have better

explanation and interpretation of new factor loadings. While variety of criteria or methods are available in literature. The present paper applies "KISER'S VARIMAX CRITERIAN." The study also adopted Burt and Banks criteria to know the significance of factor loadings.

Table 2 presents the results of Rotated Matrix for 1981-82 the factors have been extracted on the basis of Kiser Varimax criterion, that is only factors with the latent roots greater than one are estimated. The table shows that the three factors with latent roots more than one could extract from the data together they could explain 82 per cent of variance of 12 indicators of agricultural development.

The first factor F1, explains nearly 48 per cent of total variance which consists of six significant factor loadings, that are well correlated these loadings include agricultural production, agricultural workers, and four indicators of capital used in agriculture, viz. agriculture credit, tractors, and fertilizer consumption. One can infer from the above analysis that agriculture output explains nearly about half of variance in agricultural development during 1981-82.

The second factor F2 explains 22 per cent of variance of indicators of agricultural development. This factor has only two significant factor loadings, i.e. high yielding varieties and irrigation. It is well known that the productivity of high yielding varieties depend on assured supply of water which is provided by irrigation. Thus we see that the new seed technology contributes about 22 per cent.

The third factor F3 explains nearly 12 per cent of total variance. It is unique factor having only one significant factor loading, i.e. rainfall. To summarize the results we could say that output, capital and labour contributed half of variations in the indicators of agricultural development. The new seed technology contributed about 22 per cent and rainfall 12 per cent.

Table 3 presents the results of the factor analysis of indicators of agricultural development during 2005-06. Four factors together explain about 90 per cent total variance of the indicators. The first factor F1, explains about 47 per cent of total variance. The six significant factor loadings comprising agricultural output, workers, and capital namely

TABLE 2

Factors in Agricultural Development the Rotated Factor Matrix 1981-82

Variables	Factors F1	F2	F3	Communalities
X12 Agril. Production	0.99845	0.01999	0.00715	0.99736
X5 Agril. workers	0.99627	-0.03159	0.01725	0.99384
X2 Fert. consump	0.98993	0.04978	0.00237	0.98245
X3 Agril. credit	0.98722	0.07981	0.04115	0.98267
X1 Tractors	0.98126	0.09756	0.01002	0.97250
X6 Pumpsets	0.91649	-0.06374	0.01280	0.84418
X9 HYV	0.03842	*0.89891*	0.18223	0.84273
X10 Irri. extent	0.05751	0.88310	0.19892	0.82274
X7 Cropp. intensity	-0.06367	0.71935	-0.18412	0.55542
X11 Literacy	0.10571	0.57582	0.47020	0.56593
X4 Rainfall	0.04416	0.39517	0.76902	0.74950
X8 Irri. intensity	0.00092	0.12806	-0.74558	0.57229
Latent Roots	5.768	2.633	1.477	
Per cent of variance	48.07	21.94	12.31	
Per cent cumulative Variance explained	48.07	70.01	82.32	
Critical value accor. to Burt and Bunks	0.714	0.732	0.751	

Note: Factor Analysis with Varimax Rotation was used.

agriculture credit, tractors, pump sets and fertilizer consumption, which implies that the four factors together explains about half of the variance in selected variables of agricultural development.

The second factor F2, accounts for about 20 per cent of variance in the variables. It has three significant factor loadings consists of high yielding varieties, irrigation extent and cropping intensity. Therefore, we see that high yielding varieties are well correlated with irrigation. However, in the year 2005-06 we found that these are combining with cropping intensity as well.

The third and fourth factors F3 and F4 have unique factor each which account for 12 and 10 per cent in that

TABLE 3

Factors in Agricultural Development the Rotated Factor Matrix 2005-06

	Variables	Factors F1	F2	F3	F4	Communalities
X3	Agri. credit	0.99835	-0.00573	0.05316	0.02444	0.99051
X1	Tractors	0.99001	-0.04522	0.05660	0.04075	0.98702
X12	Agri. prod.	0.98145	-0.09662	-0.00347	0.04302	0.97444
X2	Fert. consump.	0.98129	-0.07250	0.02968	0.03721	0.97046
X6	Pumpsets	0.94539	0.10745	-0.03166	0.05432	0.90929
X5	Agri. workers	0.93171	-0.09273	0.02525	-0.18902	0.91305
X11	Literacy	0.08718	-0.55722	0.62194	0.11270	0.71761
X8	Irri. intensity	0.02118	-0.14051	0.10777	0.93657	0.90897
X9	HYV	-0.02465	-0.76288	-0.41538	0.43460	0.90897
X10	Irri. intensity	0.00988	-0.87066	-0.13328	0.30497	0.86892
X7	Crop. intensity	0.00988	-0.83320	0.12530	-0.21667	0.76434
X4	Rainfall	-0.00293	-0.19622	-0.90984	-0.04585	0.86843–
Latent Roots		5.67	2.43	1.44	1.264	
Per cent of variance explained		47.26	20.33	12.54	10.54	
Per cent of cumulative variance explained		47.26	67.59	79.59	90.13	
Critical value according to Burt and Bunks		0.714	0.732	0.751	0.714	

Note: Factor Analysis with Varimax Rotation was used.

order. As stated above the third factor is rainfall and fourth factor is irrigation intensity. Irrigation intensity is the only significant loading and irrigation intensity and rainfall accounts for 10 and 12 per cent variations respectively.

To summarize the Rotated Factor Matrix results for the 2005-06, the major influencing factors are technological like tractors, fertilizer consumption, pump sets, irrigation extent. Institutional factors like agricultural credit and labour. These factors are continuously playing a predominant role in explaining disparities in agricultural development of Andhra Pradesh.

CONCLUSION

Balanced regional development is going to be the major issue in future, because of the sharp increase in inter-regional and intra-regional disparities. The remedial measures for achieving the balanced regional development, the solution is in the near future lies in the development of agriculture. Irrigation would play a critical role in the development process particularly public investment in surface irrigation; specifically canal irrigation should be increased. Priority should be given to backward regions and low rainfall regions. The most backward districts in respect of important and social variables have to identified and programmes should be implemented with close monitoring.

REFERENCES

Aldelman, I. and Morries, C.J. (1987), "Society Politics and Economic Development", A Qunatitative Approach, Joan Hopkins Press, Baltimore.

Burt, C. and Banks, C., "A Factor Analysis of Body Measurement for British Adult Males", Ann, Eugenics, 13, 238-256 (1947) as cited Child, Dennies", The Essentials for Factor Analysis, 2nd Edition, Cassell Limited, Villiers House, Londan (1990).

Canning David, Marriage Fay (1993), The Effects of Infrastructure an Economic Growth, Columbia University, New York, and World Bank, Washington D.C.

H.F. Kaiser, "The Varimax Criterian for Analytic Rotation in Factor Analysis", *Psychomatrics*, Vol. 23, No. 2, 1958, pp. 187-200.

Hagood, M.J. "Statistical Methods for the Purpose of Delineation of Regions Applied Data on Agriculture and Population", as Cited in Hemalatha Rao, Ashish Publishing House, New Delhi.

Jackson, J. William R. (1980), A Users Guide to Principal Components, Wisely and Sons Inc., New York, USA.

Roden, P.N. Rosentien (1965), Capital Formation and Economic Development, London, George Allen and Unwin.

Sarkar, P.C. (1989), Measurement of Imbalances in Regional Development in India: Graphical Approach, RBI, *OCCASSI OMAL Papers*, Vol. 10, No. 1.

Sarkar, P.C. (1994), Regional Imbalances in Indian Economy Over Plan Periods, *EPW*, March 12, pp. 621-33.

Subramanyam and N. Raj Gopal Rao (2000), "Liberalization and Income Convergence Across Indian States", *Working Paper No. 36*, January, CESS, Hyderabad.

Uchimura, K.V., Gao, H. (1993), Importance of Infrastructure on Economic Development, World Bank, Washington D.C.

30

Removing Regional Differences through Improved Irrigation Facilities in Andhra Pradesh (Jalayagnam)

K. RAJA BABU, M. SRIDEVI, R. ROHINI AND VENKATA NARAYANA

INTRODUCTION

In this paper, we have analysed existing regional disparities in general, in particular, the differences in irrigation facilities. This paper also examine the proposed Jalayagnam projects in eradicating regional disparities. The study also analysed the changes in the structure on the land-holding after the Jalayagnam.

HISTORY OF IRRIGATION FACILITIES IN ANDHRA PRADESH

Historically, the major sources of irrigation in Andhra Pradesh are tanks, canals and wells in the same order of importance. Till the early 1970s, tanks were the dominant sources of irrigation in the Telangana and Rayalaseema regions, while canals were the main source in the coastal Andhra region. After the 1970s, well irrigation emerged as a major source in Telangana and Rayalaseema regions. Over the period of four decades, the proportion of area under irrigation in the State has gone up from 27 per cent in 1963, to 40 per cent in 2002. The growth in the area under irrigation is more in the Telangana region (from 21 to 37 per cent between 1963 and 2002) when compared to the Coastal and Rayalaseema regions, resulting in substantial decrease in regional disparities.

The regional disparities in per-capita Gross State Domestic Product (GSDP) growth are even greater because the poorer States in general have experienced a faster growth in population. Although these disparities have accentuated in the post-reform period, they have been building up in the pre-reform period itself. For example, in the early 1960s, the per-capita GSDP of the richer States like Punjab, Maharashtra and Gujarat was, on an average, about 50 per cent higher than the average per-capita SDP of the bottom four States viz., Bihar, Uttar Pradesh, Orissa and Madhya Pradesh. This disparity increased to 125 per cent by the early 1970s (Rao, 2005) was contained at a little over 100 per cent during the eighties; and escalated steeply to 200 per cent towards the end of the nineties.

States whose per-capita GSDP is below the national average together account for over 60 per cent of the country's population and represent 75 per cent of the country's population below the poverty line. Further, these States account for nearly 60 per cent of the population belonging to the socio-economically disadvantaged sections like Scheduled Castes and Scheduled Tribes. There is thus a large potential for growth which needs to be exploited for sustaining development in the country over a long period. This is necessary for improving regional and social equity and for strengthening national integration.

Irrigation development or disparities are always viewed in a relative sense. Irrigation in a region is relatively developed or backward due to geographical/national conditions and historical reasons water scarcity is resulting in regional inequalities and political turmoil. In other words, water, especially irrigation has become the great divider across the communities and regions. Regional disparities in irrigation development are attracting attention at the political as well as policy levels.

Jalayagnam as the word speaks is a ritual for water utilisation. It has been implemented by Honourable Chief Minister of Andhra Pradesh, Dr. Y.S. Rajasekhara Reddy as a election promise to the cultivating people of State to bring 73 lakh acres under irrigation in five years. This project accords the highest priority for the development of irrigation infrastructure, particularly in backward and drought prone areas by taking up this programme in a big way. Jalayagnam programme to complete 30 major and 18 medium irrigation projects at a cost of Rs. 46,000 crores to provide irrigation to an extent of 73 lakh acres besides stabilisation of an existing ayacut of 21.32 lakh acres while providing drinking water to a population of 1.2 crore and generating power to the tune of 2700 MW.

In the past 50 years, a total ayacut of 65 lakh acres was developed in the State. Jalayagnam is expected to double the area under irrigation. Jalayagnam in Andhra Pradesh would constitute a major component of the Central Government programme National Irrigation Mission's (NIM) target of bringing one crore hectares of land (2.5 crore acres) in the country under the plough.

A case in point is Andhra Pradesh where distorted irrigation development has been central to the recent separatist movement in the State. In response, the new government has embarked on a massive irrigation development programme in the name of "Jalayagnam" with an estimated cost of Rs. 93,078 crore of which Rs. 46,000 crore for the 32 ongoing projects, Rs. 20,078 crore for eight pending projects and Rs. 27,000 crore for the four proposed projects. All these projects are expected to increase the gross area under irrigation from 44 per cent (57.97 lakh ha.) to 90 per cent (117.55 lakh ha.) with their completion through utilising the hitherto unutilised water in the State. Of the Rs. 46,000 crore on the ongoing project works worth of Rs. 30,000 crore have already been initiated. A lion's share of these investments is expected to be in the presently less irrigated regions of Telangana and Rayalaseema (Rs. 20,812 crore). The majority of projects are expected to be completed by 2008-09, as per the State Government Plans.

High levels of irrigation are often associated with high rainfall aggravating the problems of water scarcity and environmental degradation. The result is an imbalance in the distribution of and access to water resources across regions. On the other hand, regional development can be taken up in an absolute sense through appropriate policy initiatives. In the case of irrigation development, it is envisaged that at least a third of the net sown area should be provided with protective irrigation in order to make agriculture sustainable (GOI, 1976). Therefore, in the context of agricultural development, the first priority should be to bring at least 33 per cent of area under irrigation. While it is absolutely necessary to apply this principle at the household level to ensure the livelihoods of the communities.

The Main Objects of this paper are:

1. To examine the existing irrigation facilities in Andhra Pradesh,
2. Analyse the projects undertaken under Jalayagnam programme, and
3. To find out changes in irrigation facilities.

METHODOLOGY

To find out the existing irrigation facilities in various sources are consulted, i.e., statistical abstract of Andhra Pradesh, Government of Andhra Pradesh Yearbook, and other publications. Data on Jalayagnam is collected from various publications of Government of India and other important journals. Suitable cartographic techniques are used to depict the diagrams.

ADDITIONAL IRRIGATION FACILITIES (OR) JALAYAGNAM

The State Government has initiated a important irrigation projects and 4 major projects Jalayagnam programme at huge expenditure Rs.46,000 crore, which are envisaged to bring acres of lands under cultivation, including state 3.5 million acres of existing ayacut apart from providing drinking water to 12 million people in towns and village irrigation canals and generating 2700 MW of Power. It is planned to complete eight projects within 2 years, thus bringing 16.58 lakh acres under cultivation. These are Stage-2 Phase-1. Tatipudi Lift, Pushkaram Lift, Telugu Ganga, Somasila, Chokkarao Project (Godavari Lift), Alisagar Lift, Gupta Lift. It is prorammed to complete 18 projects within 5 years and provide irrigated water to a fresh ayacut of 5 million acres. Projects like Sripadasagar (Yellampalli), Chokkarao Project Stage-2 (Godavari Lift), Rajiv Sagar Lift (Dummugudem Link canal from Nagarjuna Sagar Project to its Reservoir, and Indira Sagar (Polavaram) are considered to be milestonnes in the history of State Irrigation. State Government is determined to complete modernization of Pulivendula Branch Canal and Mylavaram Projects as well as Lendi project within 2 years. Linking of Godavari and Krishna by constructing Indira Sagar Project and Rajiv Sagar Project across River Godavari would become a landmark achievement in the entire country, thus paving way to new era in water utility. By inaugurating the Janjhavati irrigation (Rubber Dam) project in Vizianagaram district, first of its kind to be built with Austrian Technology, during the last week of December 2005, the State Government proved that it is a performing government, giving priority to farmer's welfare. The State Government has sanctioned execution of 110 lift irrigation schemes to create an additional ayacut of 1.62 lakh acres. During 2004-05, 60 LI schemes were commissioned creating a potential of 43,000 acres, besides revival of 160 LI scheme with an ayacut of 80,000 acres. Rs. 5,200 crore Master Plan of huge number of minor irrigation scheme is being implemented for creating an additional ayacut of 1.5 million acres, and stabilisation of the existing ayacut of 5 lakh acres. The budgetary allocation to Irrigation was raised from Rs. 1,840 crore in 2003-04 to Rs. 10,400 (40 per cent of the State's own revenue) for irrigation sector during 2005-06. An amount of Rs. 1,200 crore is being spent by the State Government under AP Micro

Irrigation Project to properly utilise the water resources without any wastage. Under the Drought Prone Are Programme, construction of 3540 watersheds was taken up in 11 districts. In Ananthapur district where the drought conditions prevail in long spells of time, 772 watersheds are built to bring 3.31 lakhs under cultivation.

Some of the major irrigation projects have been discussed in the following few paragraphs for the benefit of readers. Majority of the irrigation proposed are in backward regions of the State (Table 1).

Ali Sagar Lift Irrigation Scheme: Chief Minister Sri Y.S. Rajasekhara Reddy dedicated the Ali Sagar Lift Irrigation scheme, the first project completed under ambitious Jalayagnam in Telangana, here on Sunday, the Chief Minister said an additional 1.04 lakh acres would be irrigated in the district by completing the Argul Rajaram Gupta and the Choutupally Hanumantha Reddy lift schemes in the next couple of months.

This long pending dream project of Nizamabad district will immediately provide irrigation to 54,000 acres in Navipet, Ramzal, Edpalli, Nizamabad, Dichpalli and Maklur mandals and cater to the drinking water needs of 89 villages. A press release issued by the Chief Minister's office said that 4 lakh acres out of the 11.9 lakh acres of ayacut created so far by the Jalayagnam projects lies in Telangana. The Chief Minister reiterated that his Government would take up Pranahita-Chevella Project.

Tadipudi Lift Irrigation Scheme: Chief Minister Sri Y.S. Rajasekhara Reddy dedicated the Tadipudi Lift Scheme on October 25th 2007. With this, the water-starved lands in the upland parts falling under 14 mandals in West Godavari district, are all set to receive the much sought after Godavari water. Besides, the river water is also set to quench the thirst of people from several upland villages. In this connection, Dr. Reddy addressed a massive rally of farmers at Annadevarapet 15 KM away from the site of lift project.

The Chief Minister released water from the lift scheme for 60,000 acres in the current kharif as against the target of 80,000 acres. It may be recalled that water was released for 12,300 acres during the kharif in 2006 in the first phase. The

TABLE I

The Major and Minor Irrigation Projects Taken-up in Jalayagnam

Sl. No.	*Name of the Project*	*Estimated cost (Rs. in crores)*	*Estimated Ayacut (in Acres)*	*Production of Electricity (MW)*	*Districts benefitting*
1	2	3	4	5	6
1.	Thotapalli Barrage	415.00	1,20,000	--	Vizianagaram, Srikakulam
2.	Jhanjhavathi	69.00	24,600	--	Vizianagaram
3.	Vamsadhara (Stage-2)	124.00	64,000	--	Srikakulam
4.	Pushkaram L.I.S.	300.00	1,81,168	--	East Godavari
5.	Tatipudi L.I.S.	240.00	2,06,000	--	West Godavari
6.	Pulichintala Project	566.00	--	60	Krishna, West Godavari, Guntur, Prakasam
7.	Gundlakamma Project	184.00	80,000	--	Prakasam
8.	Ramatirtha Balancing Reservoir	43.00	--	--	Prakasam
9.	Telugu Ganga (Somasila Project)	1821.00	6,70,000	--	Kurnool, Kadapa, Nellore, Chittoor
10.	Gururaghavendra L.I.S.	58.00	--	--	Kurnool
11.	KPCMP (KC Canal)	232.00	--	--	Kurnool, Kadapa
12.	GNSS (Galeru-Nagari)	2,800.00	3,25,000	--	Kadapa, Nellore, Chittoor
13.	HNSN (Handri-Nipa)	3,000.00	6,02,500	--	Kurnool, Anantapur, Chittoor
14.	Chitravali Balancing Reservoir	60.00	60,000	--	Kadapa

(Contd.)

TABLE 1 (*Contd.*)

1	2	3	4	5	6
15.	SLBC (AMR Project)	635.00	2,70,000	--	Nalgonda
16.	S.R.S.P. (Stage-2)	935.00	4,40,000	--	Warangal, Khammam, Nalgonda
17.	Flood Flow Canal	2,421.00	2,20,000	--	Warangal, Karimnagar, Nalgonda
18.	Bheema L.I.S.	1,570.00	2,03,000	--	Mahabubnagar
19.	Kalvakurthi L.I.S.	1,500.00	2,50,000	--	Mahabubnagar
20.	Alisagar L.I.S.	108.00	--	--	Nizamabad
21.	Gutsa L.I.S.	145.00	--	--	Nizamabad
22.	Godavari L.I.S.	900.00	1,23,000	--	Warangal, Khammam, Nalgonda
23.	Veligonda	1,660.00	4,38,000	--	Prakasam, Nellore, Kadapa
24.	Nettempadu L.I.S.	50.00	27,000	--	Mahabubnagar
25.	P.A.B.R. (Stage-2)	625.00	50,000	--	Ananthapur
26.	Polavaram	7,981.00	7,20,000	960	East Godavari, West Godavari, Visakhapatnam, Krishna
27.	Dummugudem:				
	(a) Hydro Electric scheme	3,166.00	--	360	--
	(b) Lift Irrigation scheme	3,458.00	3,29,000	--	Khammam
28	Itchampalli (FRL+112.77M)	4,500.00	3,30,000	975	Karimnagar, Warangal, Khammam
29	Ellampalli Project	4,088.00	--	--	Warangal, Khammam, Nalgonda
30	Bhupathipalem	77.00	24,000	--	East Godavari
	Total	43,731.00	57,57,268	2,355	

Source: Girish Sanghi, *Eenadu Daily* (Telugu), dt. 9-11-2004.

project is expected to create a total irrigation potential of 1.22 lakh acres under the ayacut of the lift scheme by the next kharif in 2008.

Brahmamsagar Reservoir: UPA Chairperson Sonia Gandhi released water from the left and right sluices of Brahmam Sagar reservoir on Wednesday, September 27th 2006 under Telugu Ganga Project to irrigate an ayacut of 50,000 acres on Wednesday, bringing joy to ayacutdars of Mydukur constituency who waited for over 23 years for their dream to come true.

Sonia Gandhi pressing a button to let-off water from the Brahmamsagar sluice under Telugu Ganga Project in Kadapa district on Wednesday, September 27th, 2006. Sonia Gandhi formally let-off 500 cusecs of water from each of the two sluices by pressing a button.

Alimineti Madhava Reddy Project: Chief Minister of Andhra Pradesh, Sri Y.S. Rajasekhara Reddy released water from the Alimineti Madhava Reddy Canal (AMR-Srisailam Left Bank Canal) to irrigate 50,000 acres in Nalgonda district on September 26, 2006.

Surampalem Reservoir Project: The Surampalem Reservoir Project in Gangavaram mandal of the East Godavari Agency area is dedicated to the State by Chief Minister Sri Y.S. Rajasekhara Reddy on September 11th, 2006. Constructed across Burada Kalava—a hill stream, the project is designed to provide irrigation facilities to 15,482 acres located n 9 tribal villages of Gangavaram mandal and 10 villages in drought-prone upland mandals of Gokavaram, Korukonda and Rajanagaram and drinking water to the population residing in the 19 villages enroute the alignment of the main canal. However, irrigation officials have made it clear that they are going to give water in the coming kharif season to only 9,000 acres as the reservoir is not full. This is the first project that is going to be inaugurated in the district after the Congress Government came to power.

Pedderu Medium Irrigation Project: Chief Minister, Sri Y.S. Rajasekhara Reddy on September 10th 2006 released water from the Pedderu medium irrigation project for irrigating 13,334 acres near Ravipalem, about 85 KM from Visakhapatnam. Of the revised project cost of Rs. 38 crores,

Rs. 35 crores has been spent. Another Rs. 5 crore will be spent to provide irrigation to 6,600 acres in Butchayyapeta mandal for next kharif. Dr. Reddy released water for irrigating 13,334 acres in the backward V. Madugula and Ravikamatam mandals in the district.

Jhanjhavathi Project: The first benefit of Jalayagnam is reaped by Vijayanagaram district, completed the Jhanjhavathi project before the targeted date this was pending for last 3 decades. From 1st January 2007, irrigation water is being provided to an extent of 9,000 acres in 5 mandals in Vijayanagaram district. In order to complete this project quickly Rubber Dam has been used. Government proud to inform that for the first time in Asia, this new technology is used in Jhanjharathi Project resulting in the completion of the project well before the Andhra Pradesh Chief Minister, Dr. Y.S. Rajasekhara Reddy inflated the dam to increase its height and released the impounded waters into the canal serving 9,000 acres both by pressing the button. Plans have been drawn up to achieve the ultimate target of 25,000 acres by June after excavating distributaries. The rubber dam on the Janjhavathi is the first to be created in Asia, said Werner Panhauser, manager, Hydro-construct of Austria, which fitted the pre-fabricated dam.

Polavaram Project: Indira Sagar, the Rs. 8,000 crore gigantic dam proposed at Polavaram in West Godavari district in Andhra Pradesh, promises to transfer 80 thousand million cubic feet (TMC) water to the Krishna basin via a 174 KM long right canal and to Visakhapatnam district via a 181.53 KM long left canal. The Project is promised will irrigate 7.21 lakh acres in Krishna, Godavari (East and West) and Visakhapatnam districts and generate about 960 MW of electricity.

In Table 2, Net Irrigated area in the years 2002 and 2010 are shown. The Net benefited areas are calculated. The most benefitted district is West Godavari having 3,08,243 and least benefitted is Rangareddy district with only 37,019 hectares.

Out of total area irrigated, coastal Andhra region accounts 15,21,904 hectares, Rayalaseema region accounts 5,03,618 hectares, while Telangana benefitted 8,89,313

TABLE 2

Net Irrigated Area (NIA) at a Glance in Andhra Pradesh

S. No.	*Name of the District*	*NIA 2002 (Hectares)*	*NIA 2010 (Hectares)*	*Net Benefit (Hectares) (Cols. 4–3)*
1	*2*	*3*	*4*	*5*
1.	Srikakulam	1,80,583	3,49,270	1,68,687
2.	Vizianagaram	1,31,223	2,75,085	1,43,862
3.	Visakhapatnam	1,08,551	2,38,573	1,30,022
4.	East Godavari	2,76,385	4,61,155	1,84,770
5.	West Godavari	2,95,991	6,4,234	3,08,243
6.	Krishna	3,13,846	3,77,012	63,166
7.	Guntur	3,69,546	5,05,863	1,36,317
8.	Prakasam	1,99,329	2,93,518	94,189
9.	Nellore	2,33,542	5,26,190	2,92,648
	Total of Coastal Andhra			15,21,904
10.	Kurnool	1,70,771	3,85,240	2,14,469
11.	Ananthapur	1,42,046	2,27,289	85,243
12.	Cuddapah	1,40,792	2,41,445	1,00,653
13.	Chittoor	1,70,675	2,73,928	1,03,253
	Total of Rayalaseema			5,03,618
14.	Rangareddy	75,260	1,12,279	37,019
15.	Nizamabad	1,71,697	2,42,981	71,284
16.	Medak	1,35,742	2,12,584	76,842
17.	Mahabubnagar	1,69,566	2,93,696	1,24,130
18.	Nalgonda	2,09,191	4,39,172	2,29,981
19.	Warangal	2,98,881	3,93,640	94,759
20.	Khammam	1,82,125	3,05,514	1,23,389
21.	Karimnagar	2,38,304	3,09,861	71,557
22.	Adilabad	78,073	1,38,425	60,352
	Total of Telangana			8,89,313
	Grand Total	42,92,119	72,06,954	29,14,835

Source: Economic and Political Weekly, 2007.

hectares. It appears most benefitted in coastal region 1,69,180 hectares per district, while Rayalaseema is having 1,25,904 and Telangana with 98,812 per district.

Overall picture shows that the jalayagnam benefitted already developed districts.

TABLE 3

Total Irrigated Area upto Years 2002 and 2010

S. No.	Name of the District	NIA 2002	Hectares (in lakhs)	NIA 2010	Hectares (in lakhs)
1.	Srikakulam	1,80,583	1.8	3,49,270	3.4
2.	Vizianagaram	1,31,223	1.3	2,75,085	2.7
3.	Visakhapatnam	1,08,551	1.0	2,38,573	2.3
4.	East Godavari	2,76,385	2.7	4,61,155	4.6
5.	West Godavari	2,95,991	2.9	6,04,234	6.0
6.	Krishna	3,13,846	3.1	3,77,012	3.7
7.	Guntur	3,69,546	3.6	5,05,863	5.0
8.	Prakasam	1,99,329	1.9	2,93,518	2.9
9.	Nellore	2,33,542	2.3	5,26,190	5.2
10.	Kurnool	1,70,771	1.7	3,85,240	3.8
11.	Ananthapur	1,42,046	1.4	2,27,289	2.2
12.	Cuddapah	1,40,792	1.4	2,41,445	2.4
13.	Chittoor	1,70,675	1.7	2,73,928	2.7
14.	Rangareddy	75,260	0.7	1,12,279	1.1
15.	Nizamabad	1,71,697	1.7	2,42,981	2.4
16.	Medak	1,35,742	1.3	2,12,584	2.1
17.	Mahabubnagar	1,69,566	1.6	2,93,696	2.9
18.	Nalgonda	2,09,191	2.0	4,39,172	4.3
19.	Warangal	2,98,881	2.9	3,93,640	3.9
20.	Khammam	1,82,125	1.8	3,05,514	3.0
21.	Karimnagar	2,38,304	2.3	3,09,861	3.0
22.	Adilabad	78,073	0.7	1,38,425	1.3
	Total	42,92,119		72,06,954	

Source: Economic and Political Weekly, 2007.

The Table 3 and Maps show overall development of irrigation after the year 2010 at a glance.

MAP 1

Total Irrigated Area, 2002

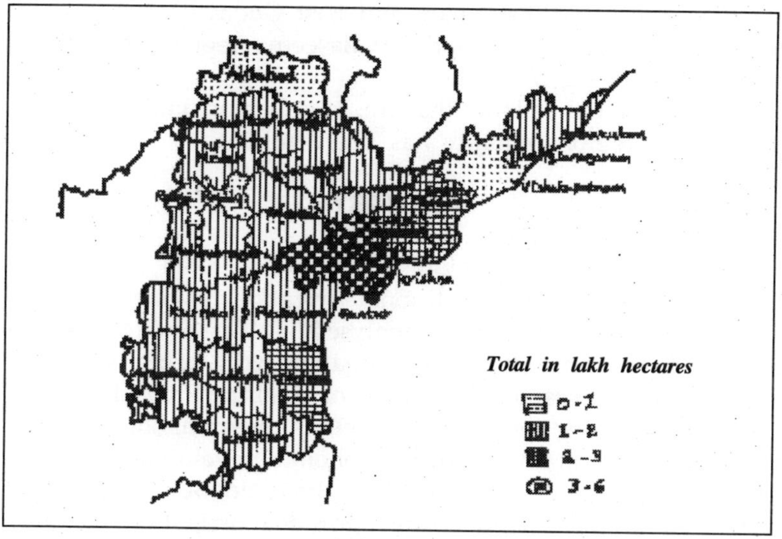

MAP 2

Total Irrigated Area, 2010

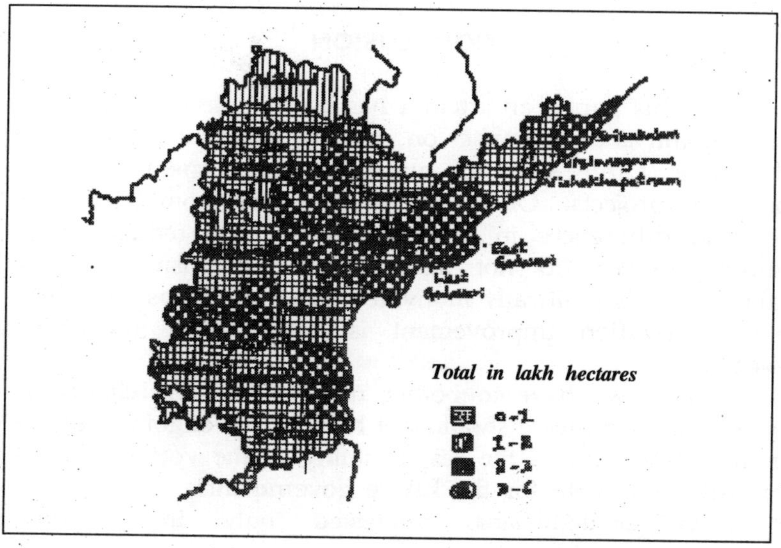

Comparative analysis supports the idea that the backward districts are benefitted much in Jalayagnam. In Coastal Andhra region, the backward districts of Srikakulam, Vizianagaram, Visakhapatnam and East Godavari districts are benefitted. In Telangana and Rayalaseema regions almost all districts are being benefitted.

This picture tells us that the idea behind Jalayagnam to develop all regions equally has been fulfiled.

SUMMARY

In this paper, developmental works taken up by the government in creating additional irrigation facilities all over Andhra Pradesh have been analysed. Tables and Maps are generated to show that the irrigation will bring sea saw change in the lives of the people of Andhra Pradesh.

The authors are in their previous research, showed that irrigation is the main source of economic development of any region. The present government is bold enough to take up such a huge exercise to create additional irrigation facilities all over the districts. This work is appreciated by States and Central Government in India. Even foreign countries are trying to imitate our experiments.

CONCLUSION

In this paper, an attempt has been made to analyse the Jalayagnam and its impact on creating potential irrigation in the State. Large sums of money is being spent on these ongoing projects. Once the projects are completed, the regional differences in development will be reduced to a minimum. We do not agree to the criticism that the Jalayagnam is politically motivated, since the maps show that entire irrigation improvement is spread over the space equally.

What we have to bother now is that any change in government in future should not hamper the ongoing projects in the State. This is the responsibility of the voters to think carefully and vote for the future governments.

As academicians, interested only in economic

development, must encourage such a bold step taken up by the present government to reduce the regional differences in development, where there is peace, there is development.

References

Raja Babu, K. (1977), "Spatial Variations in Levels of Development and Variations in Agriculture Production in Andhra Pradesh.

AP Year Book (2006), New Vision Publications, pp. 174, 177.

Economics and Political Weekly (2007), A Sameeksha Trust Publication, November, Vol. XLI, pp. 4613, 4620.

——— (2007), June 23, Vol. XLII, No. 25, A Sameeksha Trust Publication, p. 85.

——— (2007), Vol. XLII, No. 26, A Sameeksha Trust Publication, pp., 2679-80.

Kurukshetra (2006), A Journal on Rural Development, October, Vol. 54, No. 12, pp. 61, 72.

Statistical Abstract (2002-05), "Directorate of Economics and Statistics", Government of Andhra Pradesh, Hyderabad, pp. 165, 166.

31

Inter-district Variations in the Average Yield of Selected Crops in the State of Haryana

Anil Kumar and Inderjeet Singh

Agriculture is playing an important role in the economic development of the country. Majority of the population in the country directly and indirectly still depends on this sector to earn their livelihood. Therefore, agriculture development is a catalyst for economic growth and development of the country. Agricultures also links to the non-farm sector and generates considerable employment. Agriculture provides food for consumers and it also provides market for the industrial growth. Keeping in view the significance of this sector, attempt has been made to analyse the inter-district variations in the average yield of main crops in Haryana and comparison has also been made to compare average yield at all-India level.

OBJECTIVES AND METHODOLOGY

In this study an attempt has been made to pursue the

following objectives:

- to examine the average yield of selected crops at all-India as well as at the state level,
- to study the inter-district variations in the average yield of rice in the state of Haryana,
- to analyse the inter-district variations in the average yield of wheat in the state of Haryana,
- to investigate the inter-district variations in the average yield of Gram in the state of Haryana,
- to analyse the inter-district variations in the average yield of Barley in the state of Haryana,
- to examine the inter-district variations in the average yield of potatoes in the state of Haryana, and
- to determine the factors responsible for the increase in average yield in the state of Haryana.

To achieve these objective, Statistical Abstracts of Haryana, Report relating to use of fertilizers, Director of Agriculture, Haryana and various publications of ministry of agriculture during different time period have been used to analyse the data. To determine the factors responsible for the increase in average yield of crops in Haryana, multiple regression model of the following form has been used:

$$Y_i = b_0 + b_1X_1 + b_2X_2 + b_3X_3 + U_i$$

where

X_1 = Total Production,
X_2 = Area under Rice,
X_3 = Use of chemical fertilizer in the different districts of Haryana,
b_0 is the constant,
b_1, b_2, b_3 are the regression parameters, and
U_i is the error term.

RESULTS AND DISCUSSION

Table 1 shows the variations in the average yield of different crops among the states at the national-level during

TABLE I

Average Yield of Selected Crops in India by States during 2005-06

(in Kg. Per Hectare)

State	*Rice*	*Bajra*	*Wheat*	*Barley*	*Gram*	*Potato*
Andhra Pradesh	2939	1012	818	-	1591	9667
Arunachal Pradesh	1195	-	1525	-	-	7450
Assam	1468	-	1074	-	500	5082
Bihar	1075	1070	1617	1153	902	8663
Jharkhand	1150	500	1340	-	811	-
Goa	2822	-	-	-	-	-
Gujarat	1349	1169	2700	-	850	27500
Haryana	3051	1147	3844	2815	554	19705
Himachal Pradesh	1412	333	1894	730	538	6850
J & K	2150	600	1790	500	500	7250
Karnataka	3868	977	858	-	548	4452
Kerala	2284	-	-	-	-	-
Madhya Pradesh	999	1491	1613	1288	926	13140
Chhattisgarh	1337	-	886	842	706	4462
Maharashtra	1779	720	1393	500	691	4471
Manipur	2322	-	-	-	-	5204
Meghalaya	1508	-	1714	-	600	8170
Mizoram	1778	-	-	-	-	3900
Nagaland	1662	1000	1583	1780	1000	7324
Orrisa	1531	552	1364	-	646	9048
Punjab	3858	1000	4179	3316	750	16307
Rajasthan	1425	556	2762	2441	443	13488
Sikkim	1433	-	1385	1167	-	4347
Tamil Nadu	2546	1158	-	-	678	14920
Tripura	2260	-	2636	-	500	17642
Uttar Pradesh	1996	1434	2627	1925	893	22432
West Bengal	2509	2500	2109	1250	913	21051
All-India	2102	802	2619	1938	808	17058

Source: Ministry of Agriculture, Government of India.

2006-06. The average yield of Rice at all-India level has been 2102 kg/hectare. But there exist wide variations in the average yield of Rice among the different states. The highest average yield of Rice has been observed in the state of Karnataka (3868 kg/hectare) followed by Punjab (3858 kg/hectare) and Haryana (3051 kg/hectare). Similarly, 8 states have the average yield more than national level during the same period of time. The rest of the states have the average yield below the national average. The average yield of Bajra at the national level has been 802 kg/hectare. But the average yield of Bajra in the different states have much more than national average. The highest yield of Bajra has been observed in the state of West Bengal(2500 kg/hectare) followed by Madhya Pradesh (1491 kg/hectare) and Uttar Pradesh (1434 kg/hectare). Only 5 states have the average yield less than all-India average. The average yield of Wheat at the national level has been 2619 kg/hectare. The states are depicting different trends as compared to national average. The highest yield of Wheat has been observed in the state of Punjab (4179 kg/hectare) followed by Haryana (3844 kg/hectare). Information vividly reveals the different results so far as Wheat crop is concerned. The average yield of wheat shows a large variations at the states level. Only 6 states have the average yield more than national average. There is a need to formulate the policies to increase the average yield of the crop. Technological innovations and increase in the rate of capital formation can go a long way to enhance the average yield of wheat. The average yield of Gram per hectare more than all-India level has been found in the states of Andhra Pradesh, Bihar, Jharkhand, Gujarat, Madhya Pradesh, Nagaland, Uttar Pardesh and West Bengal. The average yield of Gram has remained highest in the states of Andhra Pradesh (1591 kg/hectare) and Nagaland (1000 kg/hectare). The average of Barley at all-India level has been 1938 kg/hectare. Its average yield has been found to be highest in the state of Punjab (3316 kg/hectare) followed by Haryana (2815 kg/hectare) and Rajasthan (2441 kg/hectare). Only 4 states have average yield less than 1000 kg/hectare. The average yield of potatoes at all-India level has been 17058 kg/hectare. But at state-level, its average yield presents different picture. The highest average yield has been observed in the state of Gujarat 27500 kg/hectare, followed by Uttar Pradesh 22432 kg/hectare and West Bengal 21051 kg/hectare.

Information vividly reveals that the state is leading in the average yield of wheat, Rice, Bajra and Barley when comparison is made with other states at the national level. State should formulate the suitable policies to further improve the average yield of these and other crops

Table 2 highlights the inter-district variations in the area under cultivation, production and average yield of rice in Haryana during 2005-06. Area under rice in the state has been1046.6 thousand hectares, whereas total production is

TABLE 2

District-wise Area, Production and Average Yield of Rice in Haryana

(Area in '000 hectares, Production in '000 tonnes and Yield in kg. per hectare)

State	*Area*	*Production*	*Average Yield*
Ambala	76.6	254.0	3,294
Panchkula	6.1	17.0	2,900
Yamunanagar	59.3	200.0	3,396
Kurukshetra	110.8	416.0	3,752
Kaithal	150.6	477.0	3,162
Karnal	169.1	521.0	3,080
Panipat	70.7	181.0	2,551
Sonipat	71.5	167.0	2,356
Rohtak	18.0	36.0	1,973
Jhajjar	17.0	29.0	1,699
Faridabad	26.4	70.0	2,701
Gurgaon	2.2	6.0	3,051
Mewat	8.6	27.0	3,051
Rewari	0.6	3.0	3,051
Mahendergarh	-	-	-
Bhiwani	12.5	25.0	1,909
Jind	96.7	258.0	2,661
Hisar	35.5	87.0	2,498
Fatehabad	68.4	254.0	3,735
Sirsa	46.0	166.0	3,616
All-Haryana	1046.6	3194.0	3,051

Source: Statistical Abstract of Haryana, 2005-06.

3194 thousand tonnes. The average yield of rice has been 3051 kg/hectare in the state. Karnal, Kaithal and Kurukshetra are leading districts in terms of area and production of rice. But the district-wise yield of rice depicts different trends. The average yield of rice more than average yield of state has been observed in the districts of Ambala, Panchkula, Yamunanagar, Kurukshetra, Kaithal, Karnal, Fatehabad, Sirsa, Gurgaon, Mewat and Rewari. The rest of district have the average yield less than the state average. The highest yield of rice has been observed in the districts Kurukshetra (3752 kg/hectare) followed by Fatehabad (3735 kg/hectare). Analysis of data reveals the wide variations in the average yield of rice in the different districts of Haryana. The reason to this has been assigned to different agro-climatic conditions, availability of irrigation facilities, average rainfall and type of technology utilized by farmers in the different districts

The results of the Regression model for Rice has been given in the following equation:

$$Y=2575.799 +14.893X_1 -43.504X_2$$

(5.062)* (–4.519)*

DW=1.777

R^2=.668

F=16.604

Note: Calculated from Table 2 and 8.

*Both are significant at 5 per cent level of significance.

Figures in the parentheses are the 't' values.

The above equation shows that, average yield of rice is influenced by total production positively and negatively by the area under rice in the different districts of Haryana. Both variables are independent and significant at 5 per cent level of significance. The equation has high R^2 value. The value of DW lies within the tolerance range. As per this model, third variable was found to be insignificant and not taken by the regression model. One may draw the inference that besides these variables, there might be some other variables such as adoption of technology, Fertility of soil, climatic conditions and entrepreneurial ability among the farmers, which may influence the yield of crop.

Table 3 reveals the variations in the area under cultivation, production and average yield of wheat at district level in the state of Haryana during 2005-06. Total area under wheat in the state has been 2302.7 thousand hectare. The average yield of wheat at the state level has been 3844 kg/hectare during this period of time. Sirsa, Jind and Hisar districts are having maximum area under wheat cultivation. The total production is highest in Sirsa and Jind. The average yield of wheat depicts a lot of variations at the district level. Nine districts have average yield more than 4000 kg/hectare

TABLE 3

District-wise Area, Production and Average Yield of Wheat

(Area in '000 hectares, Production in '000 Tonnes and Yield in kg. per hectare)

State	*Area*	*Production*	*Average Yield*
Ambala	83.0	314.0	3,789
Panchkula	17.0	32.0	1,881
Yamunanagar	72.3	265.0	3,682
Kurukshetra	109.2	499.0	4,582
Kaithal	172.9	726.0	4,197
Karnal	172.8	755.0	4,367
Panipat	83.1	365.0	4,397
Sonipat	142.0	571.0	4,024
Rohtak	87.9	303.0	3,441
Jhajjar	85.1	315.0	3,710
Faridabad	104.5	383.0	3,649
Gurgaon	47.7	168.0	3,495
Mewat	89.9	276.0	3,066
Rewari	41.0	172.0	4,187
Mahendergarh	38.3	157.0	4,119
Bhiwani	118.6	390.0	3,278
Jind	204.6	820.0	4,018
Hisar	203.2	752.0	3,704
Fatehabad	178.8	729.0	4,072
Sirsa	250.8	861.0	3,432
All-Haryana	2302.7	8,853.0	3,844

Source: Statistical Abstract of Haryana, 2005-06.

during this same period of time. The rest of districts have the average yield more than 3000 kg/hectare during this period of time. The highest average yield of wheat has been observed in the Kurukshetra district (4582 kg/hectare) followed by Panipat (4397 kg/hectare) and Karnal (4367 kg/hectare) during 2005-06. Analysis of data reveals that average yield of wheat depicts variations at district level in the state. The reason to this has been assigned to difference in climatic conditions and fertility of soil.

The results of the Regression model for Wheat has been given in the following equation:

$$Y=0.009 + .449X_3$$
(2.441)*
DW=2.009
R^2=.249
F=5.960

Note: Calculated from Tables 2 and 8.
* Significant at 1 per cent level of significance.
Figures in the parentheses are the 't' values.

The above equation shows that, average yield of Wheat is influenced by use of chemical fertilizer positively in the different districts of Haryana. This variable is independent and significant at 1 per cent level of significance. The value of R2 is .249. The value of DW lies within the tolerance range. As per this model, two variables, i.e. area and total production were found to be insignificant and not taken by the regression model. Model highlights that better quality of inputs are essential for the improvement in yield of wheat. More emphasis be given to availability of high quality of inputs foe the wheat to the farmers.

Potatoes, one of the main crops of the state and consumed by people of all walks of life. The area under cultivation, production and average yield of potatoes in the state of Haryana has been projected in the Table 4. The average yield of potatoes in the state had been 24804 kg/hectare during 2005-06. But at district level, the average yield of potatoes depicts a large variations. The average yield of

TABLE 4

District-wise Area, Production and Average Yield of Potatoes

(Area in '000 hectares, Production in '000 Tonnes and Yield in kg. per hectare)

State	Area	Production	Average Yield
Ambala	2.7	71.6	27,000
Panchkula	0.3	6.2	24,000
Yamunanagar	1.8	37.9	21,200
Kurukshetra	5.4	137.0	25,500
Kaithal	0.1	2.5	23,800
Karnal	0.8	17.7	23,240
Panipat	0.2	5.0	23,900
Sonipat	0.6	15.9	26,400
Rohtak	-	-	-
Jhajjar	-	0.1	16,600
Faridabad	0.2	4.7	19,000
Gurgaon	-	-	-
Mewat	-	-	-
Rewari	-	-	-
Mahendergarh	-	-	-
Bhiwani	-	-	-
Jind	-	0.4	26,100
Hisar	0.2	2.7	17,480
Fatehabad	0.3	9.3	25,600
Sirsa	-	1.5	25.880
All-Haryana	12.6	312.5	24,804

Source: Statistical Abstract of Haryana, 2005-06.

potatoes has been found to be highest in Ambala district (27,000 kg/hectare), followed by Sonipat (26,400 kg/hectare) and Jind (26,100 kg/hectare). On the other hand, lowest yield of potatoes has been observed in the Jhajjar district (16,600 kg/hectare). Efforts should be made to increase the area under this crop by following the suitable price policy for this crop. It will also increase the commercialization of this crop. Moreover, this crop is the main food item in the consumption basket of the common people.

Table 5 highlights the area under cultivation, production and average yield of Bajra in the state of Haryana and its different districts during 2005-06. It has been observed that crop of Bajra has been raised in all the districts of the state. 631.7 thousand hectares of land is used for the cultivation of Bajra in the state and total production in the state has been found to be 706 thousand tonnes. Area under Bajra crop has been highest in the district Bhiwani (225.5 thousand hectares).The average yield of Bajra in the state of Haryana has been (1117 kg/hectare) during this period of time. The highest yield of Bajra has been observed in Karnal district (2590 kg/hectare) followed by Kaithal(1892 kg/ hectare) and Panipat (1878kg/hectare). The lowest yield of Bajra has been found in Bhiwani (687 kg/hectare) and Rewari districts (872 kg/hectare). Analysis of data at state as well as national level reveals that state is doing well in the average yield of Bajra. But to remove disparities at the district level modern technology with innovative farming technique be adopted at the state level. Moreover, the demand for this food crop is enhancing rapidly due to more awareness about the nutritional value of this crop.

The results of the Regression model for Bajra has been given in the following equation:

$$Y=1216.589-0.459X_2+0.497X_3$$
$$(-2.581)^* \quad (2.801)^*$$
$$DW=1.909$$
$$R^2=.543$$
$$F=8.926$$

Note: Calculated from Tables 2 and 8.

*Both are significant at 2 per cent level of significance.

Figures in the parentheses are the 't' values.

The above equation shows that, average yield of Bajra is influenced negatively by area cultivated and positively by use of chemical fertilizer in the different districts of Haryana. Both variables are independent and significant at 2 per cent level of significance. The equation has high R^2 value. The value of DW lies within the tolerance range. As per this

TABLE 5

District-wise Area, Production and Average Yield of Bajra
(Area in '000 hectares, Production in '000 tonnes and Yield in kg. per hectare)

State	*Area*	*Production*	*Average Yield*
Ambala	0.3	-	-
Panchkula	0.7	1.0	1,147
Yamunanagar	0.9	1.0	1,147
Kurukshetra	0.1	-	-
Kaithal	11.8	23.0	1,892
Karnal	1.2	3.0	2,590
Panipat	0.6	0.2	1,878
Sonipat	7.0	11.0	1,504
Rohtak	14.3	20.0	1,434
Jhajjar	26.8	34.0	1,256
Faridabad	8.7	13.0	1,391
Gurgaon	32.6	35.0	1,049
Mewat	25.4	26.0	1,049
Rewari	55.4	48.0	872
Mahendergarh	98.7	110.0	1,111
Bhiwani	222.5	153.0	687
Jind	46.8	88.0	1,864
Hisar	58.4	102.0	1,757
Fatehabad	14.6	28.0	2,031
Sirsa	4.9	8.0	1,550
All-Haryana	631.7	706.0	1,117

Source: Statistical Abstract of Haryana, 2005-06.

model, second variable, i.e. production of Bajra was found to be insignificant and not taken by the regression model. According to this model, yield of Bajra can be enhanced by using latest technology. Information vividly reveals that Bajra is cultivated throughout in Haryana and its yield be increased by providing latest information regarding availability of latest inputs. Moreover, this crop has high nutritional value and consumed by poor people. There is a need to formulate policies for the further development of this crop.

Table 6 projects the area under cultivation, production and average yield of Barley in the state of Haryana and its different districts during 2005-06. Information in the table highlights that area under this crop is only 28.2 thousand hectares and total production is just 79 thousand tonnes in the state. The average yield of Barley in the state had been 2821 kg/hectare during this period of time. But large variations has been observed at districts level in the state. The highest average yield of Barley has been found in Fatehabad (3274kg/hectare) and Rewari (3102 kg/hectare).

TABLE 6

District-wise Area, Production and Average Yield of Barley

(Area in '000 hectares, Production in '000 tonnes and Yield in kg. per hectare)

State	*Area*	*Production*	*Average Yield*
Ambala	-	-	-
Panchkula	-	-	-
Yamunanagar	-	-	-
Kurukshetra	-	-	-
Kaithal	0.1	-	-
Karnal	0.1	-	-
Panipat	-	-	-
Sonipat	0.8	3.0	2,821
Rohtak	0.9	2.0	1,702
Jhajjar	1.2	3.0	3,117
Faridabad	1.2	3.0	2,551
Gurgaon	1.8	6.0	2,754
Mewat	1.9	6.0	2,821
Rewari	0.8	3.0	3,102
Mahendergarh	0.5	3.0	2,951
Bhiwani	4.9	12.0	2,368
Jind	0.8	3.0	2,635
Hisar	4.3	12.0	2,899
Fatehabad	3.4	10.0	3,274
Sirsa	5.5	13.0	2,595
All-Haryana	28.2	79.0	2,821

Source: Statistical Abstract of Haryana, 2005-06.

On the other hand, lowest yield of Barley has been observed in the Rohtak district (1702 kg/hectare).

Table 7 depicts the area under cultivation, production and average yield of Gram per hectare in the state of Haryana during 2005-06. The area under this crop has been 129.8 thousand hectares and total production is 72 thousand tonnes. The average yield of Gram in the state had been 554 kg/hectare during this period of time. Information in the table depicts that cultivation of Gram has been confined to only 10 districts of state. The average yield of gram at district

TABLE 7

District-wise Area, Production and Average Yield of Gram
(Area in '000 hectares, Production in '000 tonnes and Yield in kg. per hectare)

State	*Area*	*Production*	*Average Yield*
Ambala	0.1	-	-
Panchkula	0.5	1.0	554
Yamunanagar	0.3	-	-
Kurukshetra	0.1	-	-
Kaithal	0.2	-	-
Karnal	0.2	-	-
Panipat	0.1	-	-
Sonipat	0.2	-	-
Rohtak	1.6	2.0	862
Jhajjar	1.3	1.0	702
Faridabad	-	-	-
Gurgaon	-	-	-
Mewat	0.9	1.0	554
Rewari	0.2	-	-
Mahendergarh	8.1	4.0	553
Bhiwani	81.7	43.0	523
Jind	0.7	1.0	606
Hisar	23.1	13.0	552
Fatehabad	1.1	1.0	741
Sirsa	9.4	5.0	535
All-Haryana	129.8	72.0	554

Source: Statistical Abstract of Haryana, 2005-06.

level presents different results. The highest average yield of Gram has been observed in the Rohtak district (862 kg/ hectare), followed by Fatehabad (742 kg/hectare) and Jhajjar (702 kg/hectare).It has been further observed that only few districts are cultivating this crop and all these districts have average yield more than yield of the state. Moreover, the average yield also depicts a lot of variations.

Table 8 highlights the use of chemical fertilizer in the state of Haryana. In Haryana 11,24,974 tonnes of fertilizer has been used in agriculture sector . The information on fertilizer further depicts the different trend. Karnal (1,27,912 tonnes) and Sirsa (1.05,482 tonnes) districts are top in the list so far as use of fertilizer in the state is concerned.

TABLE 8

District-wise Utilization of Fertilizers in Haryana

(in Tonnes)

State	*Total*
Ambala	44774
Panchkula	6474
Yamunanagar	54346
Kurukshetra	80232
Kaithal	71488
Karnal	127912
Panipat	47360
Sonipat	78295
Rohtak	44456
Jhajjar	21001
Faridabad	62312
Gurgaon	13685
Mewat	17250
Rewari	31387
Mahendergarh	24623
Bhiwani	47146
Jind	78944
Hisar	86765
Fatehabad	81042
Sirsa	105482
All-Haryana	1124974

Source: Director of Agriculture, Haryana.

Total includes Nitrogenous, Phosphatic and Potassic.

SUGGESTIONS AND POLICY IMPLICATIONS

The foregoing analysis reveals that there exist wide variations in the average yield of selected crops at all-India as well as at state level. The average yield of major crops at national level vary significantly There is a need to strengthen the infrastructure relating to agriculture sector. More capital formation needs to be done in rural sector. Training among farmers be increased and there awareness in latest development in agriculture be strengthened. In the state of Haryana different districts have distinct advantage to raise various crops depending upon agro-climatic conditions. Suitable technology along with training to farmers be provided to increase the average yield of different crops. Analysis of information vividly highlights that some of the districts are moving at a very rapid rate but still more needs to be done to bring other districts at par with others. There is a need to formulate policies for the improvement of yield of different crops. Training among the farmers be intensified so that they may be able to utilize the latest development in the area of technology, availability of high yielding varieties of seeds, etc. Capital formation in agriculture be further increased. Quality inputs be made available to farmers at reasonable prices. Credit facilities should be provided to farmers at appropriate time.

References

Gujarati, N.D., Basic Econometrics, McGraw Hill Company, Singapore.

Statistical Abstract of Haryana, Various Issues.

Various Reports, Ministry of Agriculture, Government of India.

32

An Analysis of Inter-district Variations in the Level of Foodgrains Productivity in Rajasthan

MANJUSHRI GUPTA AND MANJU YADAV

I. INTRODUCTION

Agriculture is an important sector in the economy of Rajasthan. It contributes nearly 28.9 per cent (2006-07) of its NSDP employing nearly 65 per cent of total population.

Disparity in foodgrains production constitutes an important factor in explaining variations in regional pattern in Rajasthan. So, it is necessary to know the levels of foodgrains productivity in various regions because some of the areas have developed at faster rates while others have remained backward.

The present study is an attempt to measure the inter-district levels of foodgrain productivity in Rajasthan and the variations in it over the years between 1980-81 to 2004-05.

This is an important area of investigations because it is worthwhile to know why such variations exist, so that suitable measures can be undertaken to raise the level of productivity in the various regions.

Rajasthan is one such state in India where a lot of variations in agricultural productivity are found, because of the variations in physical endowments.

Development is a wholesome process. It not only implies increase in GDP/SDP, infrastructural development, improvement in human resource index, etc but also tends to reduce inter-district and inter-personal inequalities which are generated as an outcome of numerous factors such as variations in natural and physical endowments, differences in social and attitudinal parameters, institutional structures and to some extent discriminatory policies of the state.

These factors not only impede the process of development in some regions *vis-à-vis* other regions, but may also create wide gaps between the future prospectus of economic development in some regions over the other regions. While some regions continue to develop at high rate, others remain laggard. Such perpetuations of backwardness in certain regions is obviously an anti-thesis of study and balanced growth of a country.

II. NEED FOR THE PRESENT STUDY

In fact inter-district economic imbalance is a problem which was never addressed while formulating the five-year plans of Rajasthan. It was therefore considered appropriate to undertake a study on the magnitude of this problem and quantify the existing level of inter-district inequalities across the state.

The study analyses the inter-district variations in foodgrain productivity in Rajasthan from 1980-81 to 2004-05. The focus of the present study is to assess foodgrain productivity at district level in Rajasthan.

The rational behind choosing Rajasthan as the area of study is as follows:

1. The state is quite unique in the physical factor endowments, having nearly 60 per cent land in the dry region. So variations in productivity will be more marked.
2. The level of foodgrain productivity not only varies from region to region within the state but also over time because of unequal distribution of rainfall in the state.
3. The western part is quite different from the eastern part of the state for the view point of rainfall distribution, irrigation facilities and soil type.

III. OBJECTIVES

The present study has been undertaken with following objectives:

1. For ascertaining the level of development in foodgrains productivity.
2. For measuring inter-district variations in foodgrains productivity.
3. For suggesting measures to reduce inter-district variations in foodgrain productivity.

IV. SOURCES OF DATA AND METHODOLOGY

The study is mainly based on secondary data. The main sources of secondary data are Statistical Abstract, Rajasthan, Vital Agricultural Statistics (various issues) and Some Facts about Rajasthan.

The districts have been grouped in three major categories, viz. low, medium and high productivity on the basis of methods, equal weighted, composite ranking and deprivation.

The variations in foodgrain productivity have been discussed with respect to mean, standard deviation and coefficient of variation at five points of time viz., 1980-81 to 1984-85, 1985-86 to 1989-90, 1990-91 to 1994-95, 1995-96 to 1999-00 and 2000-01 to 2004-05. To neutralize weather effect five yearly averages are taken.

V. RESULTS

Grouping the consecutive years in five year periods the variation in food grain productivity have been discussed with respect to mean, standard deviation and coefficient of variation at five points of time.

TABLE I

District-wise Variations in the Level of Foodgrain Productivity in Rajasthan

Years	*Average of 1980-81 to 1984-85*	*Average of 1985-86 to 1989-90*	*Average of 1990-91 to 1994-95*	*Average of 1995-96 to 1999-2000*	*Average of 2000-01 to 2004-05*
Range	91-1307	78-1396	207-1688	158-2250	339-2110
Mean	663.41	704.26	927.61	1168.78	1260.19
S.D.	376.15	434.89	450.89	626.83	606.88
C.V.	56.70	61.75	48.61	53.63	48.16
Tatal No. of Districts	27	27	31	32	32
Above the Mean	12	12	17	17	15
Below the Mean	15	15	14	15	17

INTER-DISTRICT VARIATIONS IN FOODGRAIN PRODUCTIVITY DURING THE YEARS 1980-81 TO 2004-05

Year 1980-81 to 1984-85

Table 1 shows that the mean foodgrain productivity for the state as a whole was 663.41 kg/hectare in 1980-81 to 1984-85 and 15 districts recorded productivity below the state's average. Foodgrain productivity varying at district level, ranged from 91 kg/hectare (Bikaner) to 1307 kg/hectare (Bharatpur). The disparity of foodgrain productivity was 56.70 per cent in terms of coefficient of variation.

Table 2 shows that 8 districts were classified in the low productivity group in 1980-81 to 1984-85 and 11 and 8 districts were classified among medium and high productivity level districts respectively for the same period of time.

Year 1985-86 to 1989-90

The inter-district variations in foodgrain productivity

TABLE 2

District-wise Variations in the Level of Foodgrain Productivity in Rajasthan for the Years 1980-81 to 1984-85, 1985-86 to 1989-90, 1990-91 to 1994-95, 1995-96 to 1999-2000, and 2000-01 to 2004-05

Year	*No. of Districts*	*Name of the Districts*
		LOW PRODUCTIVITY DISTRICTS
1980-81 to 1984-85	8	Barmer, Bikaner, Churu, Jaisalmer, Jalore, Jodhpur, Nagore, Pali
1985-86 to 1989-90	9	Barmer, Bikaner, Churu, Jaisalmer, Jalore, Jodhpur, Nagore, Pali, Ajmer
1990-91 to 1994-95	14	Barmer, Bikaner, Churu, Jaisalmer, Jalore, Jhunjhunu, Jodhpur, Nagore, Pali, Sikar, Ajmer, Dungarpur, Sirohi, Bansawara
1995-96 to 1999-00	15	Barmer, Bikaner, Churu, Jaisalmer, Jalore, Jhunjhunu, Jodhpur, Nagore, Pali, Sikar, Ajmer, Dungarpur, Sirohi, Tonk, Bansawara
2000-01 to 2004-05	15	Barmer, Bikaner, Churu, Jaisalmer, Jalore, Jodhpur, Nagore, Pali, Sikar, Ajmer, Dungarpur, Rajasmand, Sirohi, Tonk, Bansawara
		MEDIUM PRODUCTIVITY DISTRICTS
1980-81 to 1984-85	11	Ganganagar, Jhunjhunu, Sikar, Ajmer, Bhilwara, Dungarpur, Jaipur, Sirohi, Tonk, Bansawara, Jhalawar
1985-86 to 1989-90	10	Jhunjhunu, Sikar, Bhilwara, Dungarpur, Jaipur, Sirohi, Tonk, Udaipur, Bansawara, Jhalawar
1990-91 to 1994-95	8	Bhilwara, Dausa, Jaipur, Rajasmand, Tonk, Udaipur, Baran, Jhalawar
1995-96 to 1999-00	9	Hanumangarh, Bhilwara, Chittore, Jaipur, Rajasmand, Sawaimadhopur, Udaipur, Baran, Jhalawar
2000-01 to 2004-05	7	Jhunjhunu, Bhilwara, Bundi, Jaipur, Sawaimadhopur, Udaipur, Jhalawar
		HIGH PRODUCTIVITY DISTRICTS
1980-81 to 1984-85	8	Alwar, Bharatpur, Bundi, Chittore, Dholpur, Sawaimadhopur, Udaipur, Kota
1985-86 to 1989-90	8	Ganganagar, Alwar, Bharatpur, Bundi, Chittore, Dholpur, Sawaimadhopur, Kota

1990-91 to 1994-95	9	Ganganagar, Hanumangarh, Alwar, Bharatpur, Bundi, Dausa, Dholpur, Sawaimadhopur, Kota
1995-96 to 1999-00	8	Ganganagar, Alwar, Bharatpur, Bundi, Chittore, Dholpur, Karouli, Kota
2000-01 to 2004-05	10	Ganganagar, Hanumangarh, Alwar, Bharatpur, Chittore, Dausa, Dholpur, Karouli, Baran, Kota

were found to be higher in 1985-86 to 1989-90. The coefficient of variation which was 56.70 per cent in 1980-81 to 1984-85 increased to 61.75 per cent in this period. The variability in foodgrain productivity was higher during this period because of a decline in the productivity of districts classified as 'low' and 'medium' while the productivity of some of the districts classified as 'high' increased.

Table 2 shows that 8 districts have high levels of productivity. The medium productivity group recorded 10 districts as against 11 in 1980-81 to 1984-85. Ajmer got downgraded to low productivity group.

Year 1990-91 to 1994-95

The inter-district variations in foodgrain productivity were less in 1990-91 to 1994-95 as compared to 1985-86 to 1989-90. The coefficient of variation was 48.61 per cent in 1990-91 to 1994-95 as against 61.75 per cent in 1985-86 to 1989-90. In high productivity group of districts there were 9 districts as Hanumangarh which was a new district came under this group.

The medium productivity group recorded 8 districts as against 10 districts in 1985-86 to 1989-90.

Year 1995-96 to 1999-2000

The inter-district variations in foodgrain productivity were high in this period as compared to previous period. The coefficient of variation was 53.63 per cent in 1995-96 to 1999-2000 as against 48.61 per cent in 1990-91 to 1994-95. There were 15, 9 and 8 districts under the low, medium and high productivity group respectively.

Year 2000-01 to 2004-05

The inter-district variations in foodgrain productivity were less in 2000-01 to 2004-05 as compared to 1995-96 to

1999-2000. The coefficient of variation was 48.16 per cent in 2000-01 to 2004-05 as against 53.63 per cent in 1995-96 to 1999-2000. There were 15, 7 and 10 districts under the low, medium and high productivity group respectively.

VI REASONS FOR INTER-DISTRICT VARIATION

Rajasthan is one such state in India where a lot of variations in agricultural production are found because of the variations in physical endowments, the production and productivity differs from district to district and region to region. The main reasons for the variations in productivity are as follows:

1. *Uneven Distribution of Natural Resources*: In a dry region like Rajasthan these factors play an important role. Average annual rainfall and soil facility are two main variables. Nature has behaved niggardly with the western districts, and agriculture has prospered only in these areas which have fertile soil and irrigation facilities have been made available.
2. *Adoption of New Technology*: New technology can be defined as "The employed or operative knowledge of means of production of a particular group of goods and services" and a technology change has been defined as "The incorporation of a new resource in the process of production as a partial substitute for some resources that is currently being used." New technology includes consumption of fertilizers, pesticides, HYV seeds and mechanical devices in agriculture. The technology changes have not been uniform across the districts, regions and classes, because The traditional drought prone regions had strong risk aversion among farmers and such risk averting attitude slowdown the adoption of technology. The livelihood system and culture of the communities also caused varied experience in adoption of technology. Small farmers were slow

to adopt new technology because the overall cost of cultivation went up with the inputs like seeds, fertilizers, pesticides and mechanical devices. The suitability of the technology parameter for the crop region dictated the process of accepting the technology. It is the resource endowments of various group that facilitated a few to adopt the technology more quickly than others.

3. *Literacy*: Backward districts have a lower level of literacy than advance districts. So the people from backward districts are resistance to any change and are generally not receptive to innovations.
4. Discrimination in the allocation of plan outlay has helped in aggravating in problem of inter-district disparities.
5. The emphasis on the food crops reduced gradually and commercial crops as well as non-foodgrains increased in their importance. The resources were also directed towards the high value and high yielding crops.
6. *Irrigation*: Lack of irrigational facilities retards the adoption of new technology and usages of modern inputs in agricultural sector for any farmer in any particular region.
7. *Economic Factors*: The allocation of government funds among districts is not based on their needs or priorities. Biases in allocation of plan outlays may aggravate inter-district variations, because higher plan outlays have been allocated to those districts which have performed well in relation to other district.
8. *Density of Population*: An inverse relationship between the density of population and cost of delivering services. The allocation of funds benefits the districts where the density of population is high.
9. *Institutional Factors*: Land ownership system, land tenancy system, farmers' property system, credit system and other services are also the most important factors in explaining variations in

agriculture production. The changes are not uniform throughout the state therefore, ' There are a few pockets of prosperity as against the regions, which lagged behind.'

VII. CONCLUSIONS AND SUGGESTIONS

It has been observed that the overall foodgrains productivity per-hectare is low in the districts Rajasthan, state. The majority of the districts have been accounted for low and medium productivity group. In 1980-81 to 1984-85 19 districts were accounted in this group, but 2000-01 to 2004-05 the number increased to 22 out of 32 in these two groups while the rest are in high productivity group.

Besides the above, variation in foodgrain productivity have become lesser in 2000-01 to 2004-05 as compared to 1980-81 to 1984-85. the yield level varied between 91 kg per hectare to 1307 kg per hectare in 1980-81 to 1984-85 and the coefficient of variation was 56.07 per cent. In 2000-01 to 2004-05 the yield level varied between 339 kg per hectare to 2110 kg per hectare and the coefficient of variation was 48.16 per cent. This shows that the disparity between low and high ranking districts has tended to decrease over this period.

On the whole, the spatial pattern reveals that all the high productivity districts except Ganganagar and Hanumangarh are situated in north-eastern and south-eastern part of the state which are characterized by high rainfall, fertile land, sufficient irrigation facilities and a cropping pattern favouring high valued crops. Due to sufficient irrigation facilities all the medium productivity districts located in central and southern part of Rajasthan but in the western part of state which is drought prone area, characterized by low rainfall the productivity level continue to remain low. Nature has behaved niggardly with the western districts and agriculture has prospered only in those areas which have fertile soil and irrigation facilities have been made available. The following measures have been suggested to reduce inter-district disparities:

1. The regions need to be studied in depth. The

structure, the existing level of development of regions needs to be studied in absolute and also in relative terms.

2. In the name of identification of backward regions vary crude and partial indicators of development are used at the district level.
3. A crop structure should be adopted as per recommendations of Indian Council of Agricultural Research (ICAR) and Central Arid Zone Research Institute (CAZRI). Greater attention should be paid to the inter-cropping and mixed cropping system regarding thereto.
4. Special attention should be paid to the optimum utilization of water resource available in the state through an advanced irrigational technology such as Drip-Irrigation and Sprinkler-Irrigation system. The farmers of the state should be promoted to use this advanced technology.
5. Small and marginal farmers should participate in new technology.
6. Special Drives were launched to diffuse improved technology in hitherto backward regions.
7. New crop varieties, technologies and enterprises are developed for rain-fed, dry-land and other ecological settings to improve agricultural productivity.
8. The strategy should be multi-pronged and convinced more or less all sectors of crop enterprises including interventions in correcting agrarian structure through various land reforms.
9. Regional dispensaries can be brought down in the real sense, when all regions are encouraging to exploit their own development potentials and formulate development plans suitable to their needs, potential and aspirations.
10. Education makes the cultivator capable of coping with a given situation more effectively so educated farmers are likely to become a curtail ingredient of dynamic agriculture.
11. The farmers belonging to weaker group in terms

of their land holdings and resource-base were induced to participate in the mainstream.

12. Disparities may be reduced in a deliberate attempt to allocate more funds to backward districts than advanced districts.
13. There should be a blanket policy intervention that covers all crops, all the classes of farmers and all crops enterprises.

REFEENCES

Bhattacharya, B.B. and Sakthivel, S. (2004), 'Regional Growth and Disparity in India; Comparison of Pre- and Post-Reform Decades', *Economic and Political Weekly*, 29(10), 6 March.

Dholakia, R.H. (2003), 'Regional Disparity in Economic and Human Development in India', *Economic and Political Weekly*, 27 September.

Rajput, M.S. (1985), "Agricultural Productivity in India; A District-wise Study of Rajasthan", Discovery Publication House, New Delhi.

Shastri, D.U. (1970), "Inter-State variations in industry in India (1951-61), A Tentative Explanation" *Indian Journal of Regional Sciences*, Vol. 2, No. 1.

Shastri, Siddarth (1997), "Analysis of Micro-regional Disparities in Rajasthan and Strategy for Development" Jaipur, Classical Publication.

Jalan, Bimal (1996), "Indian Economic Policy-Preparing for the Twenty-first Century", New Delhi, Viking.

Bhargav, P. and Bhaskar, R.R. (2003), "Growth and Fluctuation of Agricultural Products in Rajasthan", *Rajasthan Economic Journal*, Vols. 25 and 26 July 2001 and Jan. 2002 Published in 2003.

Dhaka, J.M. and Verma, R.C. (1989), "Agricultural Development in Rajasthan—A Zonal Analysis", Vol. 13, No. 1, Jan.

Mahendra Dev, S., "Growth and Instability in Foodgrains Production-An Inter-State Analysis", *EPW*, A-82 to A-92.

Mehta, B.S. (1986), "Regional Variations in Agrarian Relation in Rajasthan", *REJ*, Vol. 10, No. 1, Jan.

Parthasarthy, G. (1984), "Growth Rates and Fluctuation of Agricultural Production—A District-wise Analysis in Andhra Pradesh" *EPW*, A-74 to A-84.

33

Problem of Regional Imbalances— An Analysis of Social Sector

DASTGIR ALAM

INTRODUCTION

A 'region' is defined as a specific area posing a particular character all over the defined territory. The particular character may be of linguistic base, social differences, and diversity in the distribution of natural resources and above all the economic condition. A country can also be divided into different regions on the basis of climatic conditions. Hence, each and every nation of the world has some regional divisions irrespective of their level of economic development. Out of the above mentioned bases of regional division, the most important one is the resource endowments that is totally guided by the distribution of natural resources (Patnaik, 2006). Some part of a country may be well endowed with rich natural resources while the other part may have scarcity of resources. Such type of variations in the distribution of productive assets provide the basis for the regional disparities in terms of economic development. As the differences in the distribution of natural resources will be high and the means of production will be concentrated in a particular region, regional disparities will be more, since the level of economic development of an area depends on the availability of natural resources and *vice versa* (A. Kateja, 2005). Hence, in this respect, the concept of regional disparities represents an economic problem. It negates the economic development of each and every region at the same level. Natural imbalances that persist in every country, point out the man-made imbalance as a result of biased policies and negligence towards a particular region due to scanty resources. It exposes the inappropriate utilization of potentialities of an area irrespective of its capacity. In the present paper, therefore, an attempt is made to investigate the existence of regional imbalances, particularly with reference to social sector.

The problem of regional disparities was first recognized in the erstwhile USSR. The idea of regional development of Stalin (Tariq, 1984) was politically motivated, yet we can not ignore its importance in economic planning, today. His motivation was to develop economically each region of the country in such a way that in the event of an invasion and occupation of any region by the capitalist powers might not cripple the economic power of the country. While explaining the cause of regional inequality, Myradal (1957) established a contradictory view against the previous conviction and stated that the genesis of regional inequalities is not caused by the unequal distribution of the natural resources in the different regions. In his opinion regional inequalities within a country have a non-economic basis. It is the capitalist system with the single motive of profit maximization that is associated with regional inequalities. Only those regions are developed where the expectations of profits are high while other regions remain undeveloped. The gap between the two regions is ever increasing due to free play of market forces. He suggested, "If things were left to market forces unhampered by any policy interference, industrial production, commerce, banking, insurance, shipping and indeed almost all those economic activities which in a developing economy tend to give a bigger than average return and in addition, science, art, literature, education, culture generally—would cluster in certain localities and regions leaving, the rest of the country more or less in a back water" (Myradal, 1957).

The long-term existence of regional inequalities is dangerous from the view point of national solidarity and peace. The world has witnessed many events of disintegration of a nation because of the' growing regional inequality. Due to the growing regional inequalities, Pakistan was disintegrated in 1971 and the Eastern Pakistan got its independence with a new name, i.e. Bangladesh. The perpetuation of regional imbalances in underdeveloped economies is the main obstacle in the way of rapid economic development, because the progress of the entire economy depends on the full capacity utilization of factor endowments of the regions (G.K. Pal, 2005). If there is a widespread regional inequalities, the low level of per-capita income of backward region will badly affect the progress of the developed regions due to the lack of adequate demand for the products of developed regions. Again the evils of regional imbalance create the problem of low level of infrastructural development—a pre-requisite of economic development. The unbalanced growth of the economy opposes the utilization of resources to its maximum extent. The aim of regional development should be to secure maximum efficiency in the utilization of available resources (S. Shekhar, 2004). For a country, the concentration of industries in few regions has been a cause of serious concern. The ariel attack on the industrially developed region, by the enemy may easily create the fiscal problem for the government. Therefore, the existence of regional inequalities is also a problem from the nation's security and defence point of view. The localization of industries in an specified area causes a number of social evils like over crowding, congestion and noise, environmental pollution that undermine the health and efficiency of dwellers. The cost of living of these areas is very high that breeds poverty and increases discontent among the masses. In underdeveloped countries, the macro-economic variables like income, employment and output remain at their low ebb due to the presence of regional inequalities. The decentralized development of industries, not only increases the level of income and employment, but also improves the infrastructural facilities.

REGIONAL DISPARITIES IN INDIA

The problem of regional imbalances or regional disparities is a multi dimensional concept. It not only embodies the differences on economic basis, but also considers variation in cultural and social arrangement. The net domestic product of a region is often used to highlight the differences on regional basis. The drawback of this index in highlighting the regional imbalances is that this method only represents the income of a region in totality. It does not show anything about the distribution of income in that particular region. To check this limit, per-capita net domestic product of a region is used. Since the studies based on these indices reveals only inter-states differences in per-capita income that is alone not a sufficient indicator of human development. Differences in industrial growth, agricultural growth, level of literacy, poverty, life expectancy, etc. can be the other important indicators of regional imbalances. Thus measuring regional disparities is not an easy task. It will be difficult to consider each and every indicator for mapping inequalities in different regions. The other problem in such type of study is the recognition of a region. A country may be divided on the basis of a number of factors like location, resource endowment, climate, topography, language, race, etc. But the main constraint in these bases is the availability of data. In India data is available statewise. The present study will, therefore measure the regional imbalances in terms of inter-state disparities on the basis of following indicators.

(i) Poverty Ratio.
(ii) Literacy Rate.
(iii) Life Expectancy.
(iv) Infant Mortality Rate.

DISPARITIES IN TERMS OF POVERTY

From the very beginning, the perpetuation of poverty gap among the states has been recorded in Indian states. The alleviation of poverty in India has been the most important objective of the planners. Though various measures were taken through the implementation of different poverty alleviation programes to eradicate the incidence of poverty, some degree of success has also been attained, yet we failed to get the desired result. Still a large number of the people are living below the poverty line and a high degree of inter-state differentials persist among the states.

A secular decline has been witnessed by all states in the poverty ratio since 1973-74 to 1999-2000. The poverty ratio is calculated on the basis of state specific poverty lines and the distribution of group expenditure, released from NSSO data on consumption expenditure. The different survey of NSSO, revealed that the poverty ratio has declined at macro level. The rural, urban and inter-state disparities are clearly visible from the Table 1. The table represents the existence of poverty at state levels and national levels since 1973-74 to 1999-2000. Table 1 clearly reveals that the incidence of poverty in the rural as well the urban areas in different states has declined considerably, but there is an evidence of high degree of poverty differentials between backward states and developed states leading towards a mounting regional disparities.

In 1973-74 the highest poverty ratio in the rural areas was 73.16 per cent in West Bengal whereas the lowest ratio was 24.44 per cent in Delhi, showing a gap of 47.72 per cent and thus the highest poverty ratio in the rural areas was triple than the lowest. The states with highest poverty ratio in the rural areas in 1973-74 were, West Bengal, Orissa, Bihar, Madhya Pradesh and Kerala. In the case of urban poverty the scene is different. Kerala and Lakshadweep were providing shelter to 62.74 per cent of its population living below poverty line and ranked as the poorest.

The lowest urban poverty rate was 13. 17 per cent in Himachal Pradesh. Kerala, Uttar Pradesh, Madhya Pradesh, Orissa and Bihar were recognized as the states of the highest poverty incidence. In 1973-74, poverty ratio was 67.28 per cent in Orissa, 62.99 per cent in Bihar, 62.66 per cent in Madhya Pradesh and 52.67 per cent in Assam in the rural areas that declined to 48.9 per cent in Orissa, 44.30 per cent in Bihar, 37.06 per cent in Madhya Pradesh and 40.04 per cent in Assam during 1999-00. These present poverty ratios of

TABLE I

Poverty Ratio in the State

(per cent)

S. No.	State	Rural			Urban			Combined		
		1973-1974	1993-1994	1999-2000	1973-1974	1993-1994	1999-2000	1973-1974	1993-1994	1999-2000
1	2	3	4	5	6	7	8	9	10	11
1.	Andhra Pradesh	48.41	15.92	11.05	50.61	38.33	26.63	48.86	22.19	15.77
2.	Arunachal Pradesh	52.67	45.01	40.04	36.92	07.73	07.47	51.93	39.35	33.47
3.	Assam	52.67	45.01	40.04	36.92	07.73	07.47	51.21	40.86	36.09
4.	Bihar	62.99	58.21	44.30	52.96	34.50	32.91	61.91	54.96	42.60
5.	Goa	46.85	05.34	01.35	37.69	27.03	07.52	44.26	14.92	04.40
6.	Gujarat	46.35	22.18	13.17	52.57	27.89	15.59	48.15	24.21	14.07
7.	Haryana	34.23	28.02	08.27	40.18	16.38	09.99	35.36	25.05	08.74
8.	Himachal Pradesh	27.42	30.34	07.94	13.17	09.18	04.63	26.39	28.44	07.63
9.	Jammu & Kashmir	45.51	30.34	03.97	21.32	09.18	01.98	40.83	25.17	03.48
10.	Karnataka	55.14	29.88	17.38	52.53	40.14	25.25	54.47	33.16	20.04
11.	Kerala	59.19	25.76	09.38	62.74	24.55	20.27	59.79	25.43	12.72
12.	Madhya Pradesh	62.66	40.64	37.06	57.65	48.38	38.44	61.78	42.52	37.43
13.	Maharashtra	57.71	37.93	23.72	43.87	35.15	26.81	53.24	36.86	25.02
14.	Manipur	52.67	45.01	40.04	36.92	07.73	07.47	49.96	33.78	28.54
15.	Meghalaya	52.67	45.01	40.04	36.92	07.73	07.47	50.20	37.92	33.87

(Contd.)

TABLE I (Contd.)

1	2	3	4	5	6	7	8	9	10	11
16.	Mizoram	52.67	45.01	40.04	36.92	07.73	07.47	50.32	25.66	19.47
17.	Nagaland	52.67	45.01	40.04	36.92	07.73	07.47	50.81	37.92	32.67
18.	Orissa	67.28	49.72	48.01	55.62	41.64	42.83	66.18	48.56	47.15
19.	Punjab	28.21	11.95	06.35	27.96	11.35	05.75	28.15	11.77	06.16
20.	Rajasthan	44.76	26.46	13.74	52.13	30.49	19.85	46.14	27.41	15.28
21.	Sikkim	52.67	45.01	40.04	36.92	07.73	07.47	50.86	41.43	36.55
22.	Tamil Nadu	57.43	32.48	20.55	49.40	39.77	22.11	54.94	35.03	21.12
23.	Tripura	52.67	45.01	40.04	36.92	07.73	07.47	51.00	39.01	34.44
24.	Uttar Pradesh	56.53	42.28	31.22	60.09	35.39	30.89	57.07	40.85	31.15
25.	West Bengal	73.16	40.80	31.85	34.67	22.41	14.86	63.43	35.66	27.02
26.	A & N Island	57.43	32.48	20.55	49.40	39.77	22.11	55.56	34.47	20.99
27.	Chandigarh	27.96	11.35	05.75	27.96	11.35	05.75	27.96	11.35	05.75
28.	Dadra & Nagar Haveli	46.85	51.95	17.57	37.69	39.93	13.52	46.55	50.84	17.14
29.	Daman and Diu	N.A.	05.34	01.35	N.A.	27.03	07.52	N.A.	15.80	04.44
30.	Delhi	24.44	01.90	00.40	52.23	16.03	09.42	49.61	14.69	08.23
31.	Lakshadweep	59.19	25.76	09.38	62.74	24.55	20.27	59.68	25.04	15.60
32.	Pondicherry	57.43	32.48	20.55	49.40	39.77	22.11	53.82	37.40	21.67
	All-India	56.44	37.27	27.09	49.01	32.36	23.62	54.88	35.97	26.10

N.A.: Not available.

Source: Government of India, Planning Commission in *Economic Survey*, 2001-02, p. 239.

underdeveloped states are still very high as compared to relatively developed states like Punjab (6.35%) Gujarat (13.17%), and Kerala (9.38%). The rural poverty ratio is therefore still high in Orissa, Bihar and North Eastern states after four decades.

The combined poverty ratio of the backward states during the period 1973-74 to 1999-2000, gradually declined to 47.15 per cent from 66.18 per cent in Orissa, 42.60 per cent from 61.91 per cent in Bihar, 37.43 per cent from 61.78 per cent in Madhya Pradesh and 36.09 per cent from 51.21 per cent in Assam. In this regard the performance of some states have been quite satisfactory. The states like Kerala, West Bengal, Tamil Nadu and Uttar Pradesh have produced encouraging results in 1999-2000. The combined poverty ratio of Kerala was 59.79 per cent in 1973-74 that decreased to 12.72 per cent. Adopting the same trend, West Bengal, Tamil Nadu and Uttar Pradesh whose poverty ratios were 63.43 per cent, 54.94 per cent and 57.07 per cent in 1973-74, declined substantially to 27.02 per cent, 21.12 per cent and 31.15 per cent in 1999-2000.

The states, where the poverty ratio declined significantly are Kerala, Jammu & Kashmir, Goa, Lakshadweep, Delhi, Andhra Pradesh, Gujarat, Tamil Nadu, Karnataka, West Bengal and Andaman and Nicobar Islands. The monumental reduction in poverty ratio in these states is the result of economic growth and distribution, though the pattern of growth and its distribution is different in the different states. Kerala has focused on human resource development whereas West Bengal gave more stress on the implementation of land reform measures and empowerment of Panchayats. Andhra Pradesh distinguished herself in this regard by emphasizing on direct public intervention in the form of public distribution system of food grains.

In 1973-74, Orissa, Bihar, Madhya Pradesh, Uttar Pradesh, Kerala, West Bengal, Lakshadweep, Andaman and Nicobar, Tamil Nadu and Karnataka were the top ten states in the list of the incidence of poverty. This scene has changed in 1999-2000, Tripura, Meghalya, Arunachal Pradesh, Nagaland, Assam and Sikkim replaced Lakhshadweep, Andaman and Nicobar, Tamil Nadu, Karnataka, West Bengal and Kerala. Thus a new region or group of states emerged as poor states, i.e North Eastern states. Bihar, Orissa and Madhya Pradesh show the most discouraging trend. They were among the five states with the highest poverty ratio and still remained at the same position. Therefore, after four decades some states improved themselves in respect of the incidence of poverty but the level of disparities perpetuated in states, remain unchanged.

DISPARITIES IN SOCIAL SECTOR

In addition to disparities in incidence of poverty, it is necessary to consider regional disparities in other areas of human development as well. From this point of view the indicators chosen are literacy rate, life expectancy and infant mortality rate. In 1991 India's literacy rate was 52.4 per cent but this was not evenly distributed in each and every state. The state with the highest literacy rate was Kerala where 89.81 per cent people were literate. Maharashtra was on second position as revealed by the Table 2. The literacy rate of Maharashtra was 64.87 per cent nearly 25 per cent less than the Kerala. Thus, only between these two states there was a wide gap between the state at first position and state at the second position. Tamil Nadu and Gujarat followed Maharashtra by showing a literacy rate of 62.66 per cent and 61.29 per cent respectively. The lowest literacy rate was found in Bihar by the Census of India. Only 38.48 per cent people of Bihar were literate in 1991. Bihar was followed by Rajasthan. 41.60 per cent people got registered themselves as literate in Uttar Pradesh while the survey was being conducted. The other states, below the India's average literacy rate were Madhya Pradesh, Andhra Pradesh and Orissa as revealed from the given Table 2. The gap between the state of the highest literacy rate and state of the lowest literacy rate was 57.33 per cent in 1991 nearly equal to the national literacy rate for the given year.

According to Census of India (2001) after a period of ten years since 1991, the literacy gap among the states did not change. The statistics of the Census 2001 acknowledged that Kerala retains its position on top as it was in 1991. The literacy rate of Kerala touched the boundary of 90.00 per cent. The second position is captured by Maharashtra where 13 per cent increment is observed. The literacy rate of Maharashtra became 77.27 per cent in the year 2001. The most important fact as revealed by the Table 2 is that the gap between the state with the highest literacy rate and the literacy rate of the second highest literate state improved. Rajasthan registered the highest increment in the literacy rate over the whole decade. The literacy rate of Rajasthan increased to 61.03 per cent in 2001 from 38.55 per cent in 1991. The other three states out of five with a high literacy rate are Tamil Nadu, Gujarat and Punjab with a literacy rate of 73.47 per cent, 69.97 per cent and 69.95 per cent respectively. The literacy rate of Bihar revealed that the region is with lowest literacy rate. In 2001 only 47.53 per cent people of Bihar were literate. Uttar Pradesh followed it by literating 57.36 per cent of the total population. Rajasthan (61.03%), Andhra Pradesh (61.11%) and Orissa (63.61%) are on the third, fourth and fifth position from the bottom respectively. The difference between the highest literacy rate and the lowest literacy rate reduced to 43.39 per cent in 2001 against 51.33 per cent in 1991.

The infant mortality rate and the life expectancy rate are two other indices for measuring the physical quality of life. As the economy moved on the path of social and economic development, the death rate of child at birth has shown a tendency to decline. From this point of view Kerala is far ahead of the other states. In 1990 infant mortality rate in Kerala was 17 per 1000 against national infant mortality rate of 80 per 1000. Punjab, Maharashtra, West Bengal, Haryana and Tamil Nadu have infant mortality rates in the range of 59 to 69. The states registering high infant mortality rates in 1990 were Orissa (122), Uttar Pradesh (99), Madhya Pradesh (111), Rajasthan (84), Assam (76) and Bihar (75). In 1999, the death rate of child at birth declined to 14 per thousand representing an improvement in the quality of life. The states whose infant mortality rate is ranging between 60 to 70 are Andhra Pradesh, Gujarat, Bihar and Haryana. Orissa is in the worst condition where 97 children died at birth out of every thousand birth. A large difference in infant mortality

TABLE 2

Human Development Indices in Selected States

States	*Literacy Rate*[1]		*Life Expectancy*[2]		*Infant Mortality Rate*[3]
	1991	*2001*	*1989-93*	*1993-97*	*(1999)*
Andhra Pradesh	44.09	61.11	60.5	62.4	66
Assam	52.89	64.28	54.9	56.7	76
Bihar	38.48	47.53	58.4	59.6	63
Gujarat	61.29	69.97	60.0	61.9	63
Haryana	55.85	68.59	63.1	64.1	68
Karnataka	56.04	67.04	61.8	63.3	58
Kerala	89.81	90.92	71.7	73.3	14
Madhya Pradesh	44.20	64.11	53.9	55.5	90
Maharashtra	64.87	77.27	64.2	65.5	48
Orissa	49.09	63.61	55.5	57.2	97
Punjab	58.51	69.95	66.4	67.7	53
Rajasthan	38.55	61.03	57.9	60.0	81
Tamil Nadu	62.66	73.43	62.9	64.1	52
Uttar Pradesh	41.60	57.36	55.80	47.6	84
West Bengal	47.70	69.22	61.5	62.8	52

Sources: 1. Office of Registrar General in *Economic Survey*, 2001-02.
2. Government of India, Census 2001 in *Economic Survey*, 2001-02, pp, S-110-11.
3. Government of India, *Economic Survey*, 2001-02, p. 201.

rate between Kerala and Orissa represents the widespread disparities in the distribution of medical facilities and other social safety nets services. The other states with a high infant mortality rates are Uttar Pradesh (84), Rajasthan (81) and Assam (76).

Life expectancy—an index of quality of life, measures the average of life of an individual at birth. Data related with life expectancy is given in Table 2. The average life of an individual in Kerala was 71.7 years in 1989-93 that was the longest life expectancy of mankind in India. The state of second highest life expectancy was Punjab. The lowest life expectancy was 53.9 years in Madhya Pradesh for the same period. The state where life expectancy was between 60 to 70 years were Maharashtra (64.2), Haryana (63.1), Tamil Nadu

(62.9), Karnataka (61.8), West Bengal (61.5), Andhra Pradesh (60.5) and Gujarat (60.0). The expected life in Kerala was nearly 18 years more than the Madhya Pradesh where it was 53.9 years, representing the extent of regional disparities in terms of average life of an individual. The period of 1993-97, further improved the average life of Indians. An individual is expected to live for 67.7 years in Punjab for the period of 1993-97. The state where average life of human being is ranging between 60 to 70 years are Maharashtra (64.2), Tamil Nadu (62.9), Haryana (63.1), Karnataka (61.8) Andhra Pradesh (60.5), Gujarat (60.0) and West Bengal (61.5). Though an improvement is registered in the average life of Indians in all the states over the passage of time, yet the extent of gap between the states remained more or less same.

CONCLUSION

From the above analysis about the persistence of regional disparities among the states and the union territories of India, now we are able to state about the performance of the Indian economy in terms of regional imbalances. If we take the comparative study of incidence of poverty as a parameter to examine the disparities among the different states, we find that each and every state has improved in general but the differences among the states remain unchanged. We can't deny the opinion of the development of poor states but their rate of development has been less than the rich states particularly after 1991. There is an evidence of high degree of poverty differentials between backward states and developed states. The rural poverty ratio is still high in Orissa, Bihar and North Eastern States after four decades. However in case of urban poverty the scene is different. Kerala and Lakshadweep were providing shelter to 62.74 per cent of its population living below poverty line and ranked as the poorest. The study further acknowledged that in terms of literacy rate Kerala retains its position on top as it was in 1991. In the same manner Bihar remains at bottom with lowest literacy rate. Against this Rajasthan registered exceptionally highest increment in literacy rate over the whole decade. The same pattern is witnessed in case of life expectancy and infant mortality rate.

References

Ali, Tariq, Hamondsworth, etc. (1984) (ed.): The Stalinist Legacy: The Impact on Twentieth Century, World Politics, Penguin Books, London.

Alpna Kateja (2005): Regional Inequalities in Economic Development, J.V. Publication, Jodhpur.

Myradal (1957): Economic Theory and Underdeveloped Regions, Penguin Press, London.

Pal, G.K. (2005): Regional Disparities in Developing Economy, Deep and Deep Publications, New Delhi.

Pattnaik, K.C. (2006): Regional Economic Development, Somali Publication, New Delhi.

Sudhanshu Shekhar (2004) (ed.): Regional Planning in India, Anmol Publication, New Delhi.

34

Public Health Expenditure and Health Status in India: An Inter-State Analysis

KULDIP KAUR, SEOZY BHATIA AND PARAMJEET KAUR DHINDSA

INTRODUCTION

Development is a process of enlarging people's choices. Such choices tend to be very wide-ranging from the very basic ones like the option to stay healthy, acquire knowledge to greater social, economic and political freedoms including the opportunities to be creative and productive, enjoy personal self-respect and be assured of human rights. At all levels of development, however, especially from a viewpoint of poverty and inequality; three most essential choices for the people are to lead a long and healthy life, to acquire knowledge and to have access to resources needed for a decent standard of living. Human development has two sides—one is the formation of human capabilities such as improved health, knowledge and skills, another is to make people use their acquired capabilities for productive purposes, for leisure or for being active in social, cultural and political affairs. (UNDP, 1985)

Health as conceived by World Health Organization (WHO) is a "state of physical, mental and social well-being, and not merely the absence of disease or infirmity." In the terminology of Amartya Sen, health contributes to a person's basic capability to function to choose the life he/she has reason to value Sen, 1985). Health is not just an attribute of individuals; it is also a reflection of the social environment in which an individual experiences life. How a society values and understands health will determine in great part how the individuals in society experience health. Even more, it will determine what society and individuals can do about health—how health will be measured and how the society's medical care services will be evaluated. Health, in other words, is thought to be influenced by relative income, suggesting that levels of health can be regarded as a signal of the socio-economic development within which people live, as well as to how rich or poor the society is on an average. Inequality can affect health through a variety of social factors, such as access of life opportunities, levels of social cohesion and psychosocial explanations, such as hopelessness, lack of control, isolation, and chronic stress (Kawachi, 1999). Poor health, in turn, further contributes to these social factors, draining social capital and creating conditions where sections of a society become trapped in a cycle of self-reinforcing social exclusion. On a macro level, health is a major cornerstone of economic development, while at the micro-level, health is essential to ensure that people can achieve a more 'economically productive life'. Increasingly, research is showing that a healthy population is an engine for economic growth. This new thinking supplements and to a certain extent re-aligns, the traditional justifications of spending on health, which were rooted in humanitarian and equity arguments. Health, like any other good or service, is desired because it generates utility. Also like other goods and services, health is subject to the law of diminishing marginal utility. This law stipulates that each additional unit of health provides less marginal utility than the previous unit.

The classical view of the relationship between health and economic development is that wealth leads to health. This view is supported by the broad correlation between average GDP and life expectancy at the national level by a gain of only four years. Income growth has more impact in poor populations because additional resources buy basic necessities, particularly food and shelter, which yield especially large health benefits. Because poverty has a powerful influence on health, it is not just income per-capita that is relevant; the distribution of income and the number of people in poverty matter as well. In industrial countries life expectancy depends much more on income distribution than on income per-capita.

Alongside the intrinsic importance of health as a dimension of welfare, poor health can directly influence individual's opportunities—his or her earning capacity, performance at school, ability to care for children, participation in community activities, and so on. This important instrumental function of health implies that inequalities in health often translate into inequalities in other dimensions of welfare and these inequalities are reproduced over time. Education is of great intrinsic importance when assessing inequalities of opportunity. It is also an important determinant of individuals' income, health (and that of their children), and capacity to interact and communicate with others. Inequalities in education thus contribute to inequalities in other important dimensions of well-being.

The health system in India consists of a public sector, a private sector, and an informal network of providers of care operating within an unregulated environment. The Health Survey and Development Committee, known as Bhore Committee (1946) was established by the Indian government as the first policy statement on health in independent India. In India the evolution of health system can be categorized into 3 distinct phases:

Phase I (1947-83)

During this period, health policy was based on 2 principles—

(a) none should be denied care for want of ability to pay, and
(b) that it was the state's responsibility to provide health care to the people.

Phase II (1983-2000)

When the first national health policy of 1983 articulated the need to encourage private initiative in health care service delivery, while at the same time expanding access to primary health care.

Phase III (Post-2000)

Which is witnessing a further shift that has the potential to profoundly affect the health sector in three important ways:

(a) The desire to utilize private sector resources for addressing public health goals;
(b) Redefining the role of the state from being only a provider to a financier of health services as well; and
(c) Liberalization of the insurance sector to provide new avenues for health financing.

Public health expenditure and investment in India has increased substantially since independence but this has not been enough to secure a minimum decent standard of healthcare service in the country. The very social sector has been neglected by government since First Five Year Plan. The health sector's allocation was Rs. 98 crores for the first plan (5.6% of total), 226 crores (4.84%) for Second and (2.63%) for the Third Plan, Rs. 140 crores for the Annual Plans (2.12%), Rs. 336 crores for Fourth Plan (2.13%). Further, 761 crores for Fifth Plan (1.93%), Rs. 221.4 crores for Sixth Plan (1.83%), Rs. 3393 crores for Seventh Plan (1.69%), Rs. 75.76 crores for Eighth Plan (1.75%). Thus there has been a declining trend. Lack of expenditure on halth development reflects political, commercial and international priorities that are not focused on the health status of Indian people. India currently spends 0.9 per cent of GDP on public health sector programs compared to an average of 2.2 per cent GDP spent on health by lower income countries. (Market Rules, 2007) Meanwhile, India's total health expenditure as a percentage of GDP is 4.8 per cent of which 75 per cent is private health expenditure. Thus India ranks 171 out of 175 countries in percentage of

GDP spent on public sector health and ranks 17 in spending within the private sector. While most of the money spent on India's health system is in private sector, but more people rely on public health services.

Infant mortality is a commonly used indicator of the health status in poor countries, where 30 per cent of all deaths occur in childhood as against 11 per cent in richer countries (Cutler, 2006). The death rate declined from 48.6 per 1000 in 1910-20 period to 15 per 1000 in 1970's, and improved thereafter, reaching 10 per 1000 by 1990. India's high infant mortality rate was estimated to exceed 76 per 1000 live births in 1995. Thirty per cent of infants had low birth weights, and the death rate for children aged 1 to 4 years was around 10 per 1000 of population.

India has a poor record on health, with high infant mortality rates (IMR) and low levels of life expectancy (LE). There are also striking inter-state variations—Kerala's health indicators are comparable to developed countries, while Orissa has one of the highest maternal mortality rates (MMR) in the world. A major problem has been the consistent under-funding of public health services, by both central and state governments, which share responsibility for the provision and financing of health care in India.

In India health sector reforms are taking place under the broad umbrella of Structural Adjustment Programme (SAP) which is termed as the New Economic Policy (NEP). The two major aspects of SAP are privatization and globalization. Aim of privatization and globalization is to improve access and to enhance the quality of social services by supporting India's health sector reform initiatives. Due to liberalization, advanced techniques, instruments and medicines in the field of health sector are available now in India also. Further, India is now producing advanced equipments which have effectively reduced the cost price of items and drugs.

Thus India's dream of becoming "World Class" in health care system can be achieved by it, if it fulfils its two objectives: control of communicable and non-communicable diseases and to increase the budget allocation on health sector by government. Hence, India faces the daunting challenge of meeting health care needs of its vast population and ensuring efficiency, accessibility, equity and quality of health care and therefore achieving the objective of growth with equality and social justice.

REVIEW OF LITERATURE

It is important to review existing literature for conducting any meaningful research. The planning and execution of any study has to be proceeded by thorough review of literature in the related field. The review of the studies relating to health status of country has been done to assess the influence of health expenditure on the health status of the country. A brief review of some studies is being presented:

Reddy (2002) in his study has considered health indicators and determinants of health status of people for 21 states of India for the year 1921-81. He studied the relationship between percentage of literacy and expectation of life in India. Hence, it was pointed out that the spread of literacy must be paid due attention for the enhancement of health status.

Gupta, Monica Das, (2004) in her paper focused on health system in India and how well does it functions at national level. She underlined the fact that this is all because of misallocation of resources, inadequate focus on evaluation, deep management flaws and inadequate funds at state levels.

Bhatt and Jain (2004) in their study present analysis of public expenditures on health using state level public health expenditure data. Their findings suggest that state level government have target of allocating only about 0.43 per cent of state gross domestic product to health and medical care. This does not include the allocations received under central sponsored programmes such as family welfare. Given this level of spending at current levels and fiscal position of state governments the goal of spending 2 to 3 per cent of GDP on health looks very ambitious task. The analysis also reveals the elasticity of health expenditure in states and found that for every one per cent increase in state per-capita income, the per-capita health care expenditure increases by around 0.68 per cent.

Sankar and Kathuria (2004) in their paper attempts to analyze the performance of rural public health system of sixteen major states in India. The study concludes that investment in the health sector alone would not result in better health indicators, efficient management of investments is required. The analysis of variation across states in the health systems in the rural areas suggests that there are two critical ways to improve health outcomes. The first is to enhance the efficiency of health sector. The second is to create more infrastructure and thus provide better health access to rural health facilities and make more physicians available in rural areas. So, in order to cure what ails the health system in many Indian states, efforts need to be made in the direction not only of providing more infrastructure but also using them in the most efficient way.

METHODOLOGY AND RESEARCH DESIGN

After going through the literature on this aspect it was felt that there is a greater need for an in-depth analysis of the health status in India and correspondingly the public expenditure incurred by the centre and state governments respectively and how it influences IMR in India. In order to examine these aspects our study covers 12 major states of India covering time period from 1993 to 2003. We have tried to analyze the impact of public health expenditure on health status of India and have explained inter-state differences on this basis and worked out state level efficiency scores using Data Envelopment Analysis (DEA) model. DEA is an alternative as well as compliment to traditional production function approach. Methods like Cobb Douglas production function are used to study the technical and allocative efficiencies. However, method fails to estimate the relative efficiency of individual decision-making unit as it only identifies the central tendencies. DEA is a performance assessment tool useful for calculating patterns of dynamic efficiencies. Using only observed output and input data for observations, the DEA algorithm calculates an *ex-post*-measure of how efficient each observation was by converting inputs to outputs accomplished by the construction of an empirical-based Production Frontier, and by evaluating each observation against all others which are included in the data set. Thus the results that are arrived at in the present study evaluate which state is most efficiently utilizing its public health expenditure to decrease IMR, an important indicatior of health. In the study, DEA procedures have been used to generate efficiency scores for the 12 states of India for the time period from 1993 to 2003.

DISCUSSION AND FINDINGS

According to Indian Constitution, the health sector falls under the concurrent list and thus, the provision of public health in India is the responsibility shared by both the Central and State governments. For state government's health expenditure, the financing responsibility is primarily that of state government with some overlapping responsibilities in a series of centrally sponsored schemes. The total budgetary allocation of any state government on health in India mainly consists of expenditure on medical, public health and family welfare. We have analyzed the behaviour of the per-capita health allocations under these heads since 1993-94 to 2003-04 for 12 major states in India (Appendices 1, 2, 3 and 4). Based on this data technical efficiency scores have been worked out using Data Envelopment Analysis and the values are given in Table 1.

TABLE I

Efficiency Scores of Different States of India

States	*1993-94*	*1994-95*	*1995-96*	*1996-97*	*1997-98*	*1998-99*	*1999-2000*	*2000-01*	*2001-02*	*2002-03*
AP	.45	.36	.33	.40	.40	.50	.54	.58	.61	.60
Assam	.27	.13	0.33	0.07	0	0.14	0.29	0.30	0.38	.35
Gujarat	.56	0.48	0.53	0.45	0.52	0.62	0.62	0.67	0.59	.50
Haryana	0.44	.25	0.37	0.34	0.38	0.53	0.45	0.39	0.51	.50
Karnataka	0.	0	0.03	0	0.03	0	0.46	0.41	0.54	.53
Kerala	.86	0.82	0.85	0.83	0.85	0.85	0.80	0.9	0.95	.96
Maharashtra	.53	.34	.39	0.41	0.45	0.25	0.39	0.58	0.61	.60
MP	0	0	0	0	0	0.10	0.28	0	0	0
Punjab	.53	0.56	0.49	0.49	0.48	0.60	0.47	0.56	0.74	.76
Rajasthan	.11	0.09	0.24	0.21	0.14	0.17	0.54	0.38	0.48	.50
UP	0.04	0	0	0	0	0	0	0	0	0
WB	.37	.24	.37	.27	.25	.54	.57	.62	.68	.67

Worked out from Appendices 1, 2, 3 and 4.

There are wide variations across states and within each state on the health scenario. The health indicators of Kerala are comparable to those of middle-income countries, while those of UP, MP and Orissa are almost at the level of Sub-Saharan Africa.

Above table shows the calculated technical efficiencies for the 12 major states of India from 1993 to 2003-04. For a country like India, it is not surprising to pre-suppose that there are extreme regional variations in IMR and public health expenditure. Therefore, treatment at State level is an essential part of any detailed economic study of India.

We have divided 12 states into 4 major categories on the basis of their calculated technical efficiencies.

Highest TE	Kerala
Higher TE	AP, Punjab, WB, Haryana, Gujarat, Maharashtra
Lower TE	Karnataka, Rajasthan, Assam
Lowest TE	UP, MP

We have noticed that Kerala has retained its position with the lowest IMR and highest TE over the years. It was noted that its IMR is lowest in India (10) among all the states from 1993 to 2003, though public health expenditure has fluctuated over the years as compared to other states but it has worked efficiently to be on the top and has progressed enough on health front. Its efficiency level of working has reached near 100 per cent thus indicating that its health system is working properly and is able to reduce IMR.

Further there is second category of higher efficiency states like AP, Punjab, WB, Haryana, Gujarat and Maharashtra. These six states have their IMR falling in the range of 50 to 70 but the common good feature is that IMR has been reducing overtime in all these states. In these states TE has improved overtime and lies above 0.50. In all these states health expenditure has efficiently reduced IMR, thus indicating that these states of India are also taking care of people's health.

Among the lower efficiency category states are the

three states of, Karnataka, Rajasthan and Assam. They all have higher IMR and lower TE but the point to be noted is that although they all have increased their efficiency level overtime but Karnataka is the only state which has improved its position and has progressed the most on health front in these years.

Then in the last category are the states of UP and MP which come under the lowest category of technical efficiency overtime. Moving from 1993 to 2003 these two states have not been able to improve their Public Health system. There has been misinformation, disinformation, suppressing and manipulation of the tools of Public Health system in these two states.

Thus overall we notice that the efficiency scores of all the states has increased overtime, indicating improvement in health system of major states of India. We can say that it is a mixture of light and shade. There have been large gains in health status but these achievements present a rosy picture only when seen in isolation. If we compare them with the targets and goals that were put forth in various National Health policies, we can visualize the real picture. This certainly dilutes the gains. There is greater need for the efficient utilization of available resources of states particularly in relation to human resource development. Till now India has not leveraged her full potential of health sector to become a global player.

The following table gives areas of concern and relevant reform levers:

TABLE 2

Areas of Concern and Relevant Reform Levers

Area of concern	*Causes amenable to reforms*	*Relevant reform levers*
Non-availability of staff	Outdated policies and incentive structure Remote decision-making Role of paramedics limited	Organizational change and policy reforms Empowerment of nurses and paramedical staff Decentralization

Weak referral system	Lack of integration Ignorance of referral system	Strengthen communication and transport infrastructure Health awareness
Poor service delivery	Underutilization of resources	Data-based management planning and control
Funding shortfalls	Absolute shortfall Systematic inefficiencies	Public-private partnerships Increasing government health budgets Organizational change
Lack of accountability for quality of care	Lack of transparency	Overall performance of the health system

Source: Rama Rao, 2003.

Thus, to leverage full potentials that are available in health sector and to make the health sector accessible to common man the Government of India may initiate the following measures:

(1) Increase the expenditure on public health and education to minimum 6 per cent of GDP as against less than 4 per cent of GDP at present.
(2) Allow the private sector to establish medical, dental, nursing and Indian system of Medicine Colleges along with the centres of advanced medical technology by removing all the bureaucratic controls on their establishment
(3) Link up hospitality with health industry

CONCLUSIONS AND POLICY IMPLICATIONS

The growing inequalities in health and health care are taking its toll among various states in India. The Infant Mortality Rate in the poorest 20 per cent of the population is 2.5 times higher than that in the richest 20 per cent of the population. In other words, an infant born in a poor family is two and half times more likely to die in infancy, than an infant in a better off family.

In India, approximately 1.72 million children die each year before reaching their first birthday. Infant mortality has declined significantly in India from 129 in 1970 to 57 in the year 2005-06. The target for Millennium Development Goals 2015 is 27 per 1000 live births.

Drawing data from 12 major states of India over a time span of 10 years (1993-94 to 2003-04) and using Data Envelopment Analysis, this paper documents that how efficiently our public health expenditure is used to reduce Infant Mortality Rate in India. India's public expenditure on health, family welfare and medical facilities has been analyzed and its effect on Infant Mortality Rate has been considered overtime and further Inter-State comparison has been done. It has been observed that states like Karnataka, UP, MP, Rajasthan and Assam have their lower efficiency levels indicating that public expenditure on health has not been used efficiently to reduce IMR in India. In these states IMR lies in the range of 110 to 70 and their efficiency scores range from 100 to 50 over the time period; thus indicating that though per-capita health expenditure increased over time but it was not able to reduce IMR to that extent. If we consider states like Gujarat, Maharashtra, Punjab and Haryana then their efficiency scores lie in the range of less than 50 although their IMR is much on the lower side that is less than 50 per 1000 live births.

Further this paper suggests that Kerala is the state having maximum efficiency score that is its public health system is working with maximum efficiency and it has retained its position over the years. Thus, this paper concludes that overtime although IMR of all the states have reduced but some states lacks the efficiency to reduce it to the extent as public expenditure on it can do it. The public health infrastructure has changed overtime to provide the elements necessary for successful public health interventions: organized and systematic observations through morbidity and mortality surveillance, well-designed epidemiologic studies and other data to facilitate the decision-making process, individuals and organizations to advocate for resources and to ensure that effective policies and programs were implemented and conducted properly. In 20th century, public health is a complex partnership among federal agencies, state and local governments, nongovernmental organizations, academia, and community members. In the 21st century, the success of the Indian public health system will depend on its ability to change to meet new threats to the public's health.

The Eleventh Plan approach paper correctly notes that rural health care in most states in India is marked by absenteeism of doctors/health providers, low levels of skills, shortage of medicines, inadequate supervision/monitoring and callous attitudes. There are neither rewards for service providers, nor punishments to defaulters. As a result, health outcomes in India are worse than neighbouring countries like Sri Lanka and Southeast Asian countries like China and Vietnam

Further the approach paper suggests that the way out may be to empower Panchayati Raj Institutions to manage administer and be accountable for health services at community levels. The success of this strategy may hinge on whether health workers continue to have permanent government jobs, or get paid by the health care they provide and patients they see.

Thus India's dream of becoming "World Class" in health care system can be achieved by increasing the budget allocation on health sector by government and by efficiently utilizing its public and private resources. Hence, India faces the daunting challenge of meeting health care needs of its vast population and ensuring efficiency, accessibility, equity and quality of health care and therefore achieving the objective of growth with equality and social justice.

References

Agarwal, S.N., (1977), "Disinvesting in Health, New Delhi, Sage Publication.

Banerjee, J. (2004) "Planning and Management for Health Issues, Dilemmas and Challenges", *The Indian Journal of Public Administration*, XXVII, Jan.-March.

Bhatt and Jain (2004), "The Private/Public Mix of Health Care in India", Health Policy and Planning, pp. 43-56.

Bloom and Canning (2000) "National Health Policy and its Implementation", *Economic and Political Weekly*, XVIII, Jan., 105-08.

Bloom, D. (2005) "The Effect of Health on Economic Growth: A Production Function Approach, *World Development*, pp. 1-13.

Das, R.K. and Purnamita Das Gupta (2000), "Child Health and Immunisation" *Economic and Political Weekly*, XXXV, pp. 645-55.

Das Gupta, Monica (2004), "How well does India's Federal Government Perform: Its Essential Public Health Functions?", The World Bank Policy Research, Working Paper No. 3447, Washington, DC.

Gupta, I. (2007), "Economic Growth, Health and Poverty: An Exploratory Study for India", *Development Policy Review*, Vol. 22, March, pp. 193-206.

Gupta, Devendra B. (2002), "National Agencies and Centre-State Relationships in Public Health in India", World Bank, Washington, DC.

India Health Reports, 1993-2003.

Kawachi S. (1999), Rural Poverty in India: Data Base Issue, Vikas Publishing House, Pvt. Ltd, New Delhi.

Market Rules (2007), "The Changing Global Contexts of Public Health", *The Lacet*, Vol. 356, No. 9228, August 5, pp. 495-99.

Professor Rama Rao, The Role of Higher Education in Nation Building in India—My Dream: Agenda for Nation, Excel Books, New Delhi, 2003.

Appendix I

Per-capita Family Welfare Expenditure—State-wise (Rupees)

(in real terms—measured at constant prices)

States	*1993-94*	*1994-95*	*1995-96*	*1996-97*	*1997-98*	*1998-99*	*1999-2000*	*2000-01*	*2001-02*	*2002-03*
Andhra Pradesh	15.90	15.59	14.83	17.97	16.15	19.75	19.37	22.14	21.16	NA
Assam	14.41	10.11	12.95	10.15	9.59	10.17	11.50	14.80	13.11	11.05
Gujarat	14.14	14.41	14.50	13.59	16.46	18.64	18.12	18.62	11.80	15.70
Haryana	20.21	17.56	14.61	13.84	13.67	16.43	13.60	9.93	13.29	13.24
Karnataka	13.63	15.58	16.15	13.06	18.95	15.66	21.00	21.45	27.44	19.79
Kerala	16.81	17.77	15.50	15.10	14.97	15.65	19.52	15.47	17.44	15.34
Maharashtra	12.80	9.59	13.07	11.44	10.61	7.32	8.11	12.61	12.78	9.10
MP	11.53	11.09	11.29	12.34	11.66	12.22	13.33	8.01	4.35	9.04
Punjab	17.94	11.14	14.73	16.37	11.95	12.20	11.00	11.67	9.81	8.51
Rajasthan	17.26	21.36	20.38	21.22	22.98	21.81	19.86	17.97	23.93	15.46
UP	18.37	18.08	14.15	17.14	16.88	9.55	9.30	10.76	12.62	NA
WB	11.18	9.22	10.37	9.52	9.05	12.72	13.09	14.29	12.35	11.37

Source: India Health Reports.

Appendix 2

Per-capita Public Health Total Expenditure—State-wise (Rupees)

(in real terms—measured at constant prices)

States	*1993-94*	*1994-95*	*1995-96*	*1996-97*	*1997-98*	*1998-99*	*1999-2000*	*2000-01*	*2001-02*	*2002-03*
Andhra Pradesh	14.19	14.35	12.90	14.82	13.74	13.20	14.05	14.55	14.42	NA
Assam	11.00	10.58	10.46	8.39	13.57	8.57	10.85	11.08	9.35	9.16
Gujarat	14.88	16.17	16.56	17.15	19.51	19.30	21.43	16.76	12.28	14.72
Haryana	11.76	11.59	9.88	11.23	18.46	16.75	14.34	13.04	11.52	11.04
Karnataka	5.71	6.11	5.65	5.53	5.98	5.55	6.59	5.86	5.64	5.56
Kerala	7.85	8.15	8.75	8.55	8.58	9.74	11.58	10.26	8.83	9.79
Maharashtra	33.84	34.46	35.11	36.76	38.11	37.85	36.24	44.86	51.72	45.09
MP	10.84	10.20	8.78	10.30	10.36	16.43	13.60	8.44	3.92	10.00
Punjab	11.01	10.06	9.22	10.43	13.09	12.51	11.54	10.56	9.19	9.73
Rajasthan	8.71	8.79	9.91	11.30	10.65	9.67	10.99	7.49	7.31	6.69
UP	10.88	8.90	9.84	10.18	11.71	8.27	5.20	5.04	4.31	na
WB	9.05	8.45	8.58	9.59	8.44	11.66	10.92	10.61	9.72	8.97

Source: India Health Reports.

APPENDIX 3

Per-capita Expenditure on Medical—State-wise (in Rupees)

(in real terms—measured at constant prices)

States	*1993-94*	*1994-95*	*1995-96*	*1996-97*	*1997-98*	*1998-99*	*1999-2000*	*2000-01*	*2001-02*	*2002-03*
Andhra Pradesh	45.84	41.74	41.93	49.4	52.99	60.14	64.27	71.58	70.59	na
Assam	54.84	56.07	54.17	55.74	36.28	40.7	46.77	49.37	51.18	42.5
Gujarat	54.15	55.55	64.59	71.49	71.57	95.1	100.54	93.49	72.98	75.88
Haryana	49.33	49.15	49.92	53.07	53.77	70.14	64.22	63.22	62.07	63.94
Karnataka	67.09	68.06	65.84	66.02	79.93	90.21	99.80	101.88	101.98	93.76
Kerala	76.07	80.57	81.24	78.92	82.47	85.98	99.58	89.57	102.13	105.49
Maharashtra	41.12	37.99	38.38	40.34	43.21	46.13	54.58	54.34	50.88	50.74
MP	41.77	45.08	45.44	51.01	53.61	69.06	73.52	42.85	47.7	50.97
Punjab	82.14	78.72	76.39	85.93	100.5	127.3	130.44	144.3	131.57	126.04
Rajasthan	59.49	63.94	70.51	69.64	75.98	84.71	78.93	80.18	78.84	71.86
UP	38.46	32.37	34.88	33.89	39.92	39	38.09	38.44	31.36	NA
WB	54.08	51.01	52.86	59.32	60	72.92	82.19	90.95	80.24	77.86

Source: India Health Reports.

APPENDIX 4

Infant Mortality Rates in India

States	*1993-94*	*1994-95*	*1995-96*	*1996-97*	*1997-98*	*1998-99*	*1999-2000*	*2000-01*	*2001-02*	*2002-03*
Andhra Pradesh	64	65	67	65	63	66	66	65	66	62
Assam	81	78	77	74	76	76	76	75	74	70
Gujarat	58	64	62	61	62	64	63	62	60	60
Haryana	66	70	69	68	68	70	68	67	66	62
Karnataka	67	67	62	53	53	58	58	57	58	55
Kerala	13	16	15	14	12	16	14	14	11	10
Maharashtra	50	55	55	48	47	49	48	48	45	45
MP	106	98	99	97	94	98	90	87	86	85
Punjab	55	53	54	51	51	54	53	52	52	51
Rajasthan	82	84	86	85	85	83	81	79	80	78
UP	94	88	86	85	85	85	84	83	83	80
WB	58	62	58	55	55	53	52	51	51	49

Source: India Health Reports

35

Rural/Urban Health Disparity in India

NIGHAT AHMAD

"You must be the change you want to see in the world."

—*Mahatma Gandhi*

Health has been defined by the World Health Organization as a state of complete physical, mental and social well-being. It thus transcends the absence of death, disease and disability, and incorporates concepts of well-being and quality of life. Measures of health must likewise transcend mortality and morbidity.

However, health does not exist in isolation, but rather it is the product of the interaction of our natural and built physical environments, socio-economic status, psycho-social conditions and cultural norms and beliefs with our physiological and psychological selves and our genetic inheritance.

HEALTH DISPARITY

A health disparity should be viewed as a chain of events signified by a difference in: (1) environment, (2) access to, utilization of, and quality of care, (3) health status, or (4) a particular health outcome that deserves scrutiny. Such a difference should be evaluated in terms of both inequality and inequity, since what is unequal is not necessarily inequitable.

WHO (PAHOWHO, October 1999) has adopted the broad concept of health inequities developed by Margaret Whitehead as differences in health which are not only unnecessary and avoidable but, in addition, are considered unfair and unjust. The specific determinants of health disparity as per this criteria include: (1) natural, biological variations; (2) health-damaging behaviour that is freely chosen, such as participation in certain sports and pastimes; (3) the transient health advantage of one group over another when one group is first to adopt a health-promoting behaviour (as long as other groups have the means to catch up fairly soon); (4) health-damaging behaviour in which the degree of choice of lifestyles is severely restricted; (5) exposure to unhealthy, stressful living and working conditions; (6) inadequate access to essential health services and other basic services; (7) health-related social mobility, involving the tendency for sick people to move down the social scale. According to Whitehead (Whitehead, M., 1991), health inequalities determined by the first three categories are more likely to be considered unavoidable or fair, while those related to the last four categories are more likely to be considered avoidable and unfair. (Olivia Carter-Pokras, Claudia Baquet, 2002)

SIGNIFICANCE OF HEALTH DISPARITY

Investment in health along with education is an essential input in human resource development. It has been emphasized by Schultz as being the basis of an individual's economic productivity. Good health provides the capability to work and perform well in every sphere of economic activity. Health is important, both at the individual level as well as at the level of the economy. In any scheme of poverty reduction and long-term development in low income countries, health occupies an important place. Apart from economic considerations, humanitarian concerns also merit attention and aim at achieving the development goals adopted by the global community. WHO Commission on Macroeconomics and Health (2000) has observed that development would not occur automatically in the developing world without increased investment in health.

Some of the important categories of health disparities which have been given special attention world over include: (1) rich nation/poor nation health disparities; (2) rich/poor health disparities; (3) gender health disparities; (4) minority health disparities; (5) mother and child health disparities; (6) rural/urban health, etc.

Health as it prevails in India compares poorly with developed countries given below:

Maternal mortality rate (MMR) per 100,000 live births is high in India at 450, while in China it is 45, 58 in Sri Lanka and 320 in Pakistan (Economic Survey, 2007-08).

Likewise infant mortality rate (IMR) in India is 56 per 1000 live births against 12 in Sri Lanka and 23 in China. Even Bangladesh fares better with an IMR of 54.

Another parameter, under 5 mortality (U5MR) for India is 74 per 1000, as against 14 in Sri Lanka, 27 in China and 73 in Bangladesh.

With respect to life expectancy at birth (LEB) India at 62.9 yrs. fares better than Nepal (61.3) and Bangladesh (62) but lags behind China (72 yrs.), Pakistan (63.6 yrs.) and Sri Lanka (70.8 yrs.).

Although there has been some improvement in the quality of healthcare in India, wide disparities prevail between states, male-female and rural-urban in health outcomes and impact.

SIGNIFICANCE OF RURAL/URBAN HEALTH DISPARITY IN INDIA

In Indian context the rural-urban disparity is of significance because the village population forms more than

70 per cent of the Indian population. Any neglect of this will group will have an impact on overall development of the nation. The health disparity is wide and is of serious dimensions. The demands on the government for healthcare provision are great and the resources are meager. It is therefore important to tackle this problem with a well thought out strategy for next few decades to come.

The present paper therefore attempts to examine rural-urban disparities in health in India and to suggest strategy for tackling this mammoth problem.

The topic of health disparity has attained special significance recently. The USA has launched the so called 'Healthy People 2010', in January 2000 by which the Department of Health and Human Services (DHHS) committed the nation to an overreaching goal, to eliminate health disparities

In India, the National Health Policy (NPH), 2002 has set out the basic objective of achieving good health among all population of the country. Removal of health disparity is considered essential for national growth. The National Common Minimum Programme (NCMP) has also placed emphasis on raising public health investment with focus on primary health care and increased investment in programmes to improve the reproductive and child health care. It envisages an increase in public spending on health to 2-3 per cent of GDP by increased contributions from the Central and State Governments. Towards this end the Government has launched a National Rural Health Mission (NRHM). (Fikree, Fariyal F.; Pasha, Omrana, 2004)

MEASURING HEALTH DISPARITIES

Health Canada (Federal, Provincial and Territorial Advisory Committee on Population Health, 1999) considers 12 factors as determinants of health: (1) income and social status, (2) social support networks, (3) education, (4) employment and working conditions, (5) social environments, (6) physical environments, (7) personal health practices and coping skills, (8) healthy child development, (9) biology and genetic endowment, (10) health services, (11) gender, and (12) culture.

A number of these factors are similar to those enumerated by Whitehead. Many other lists of determinants exist, some of which address factors such as health promotion, environmental sustainability, globalization, and the role of media in health perception.

The Rockfeller Foundation (2002) suggests taking five steps to select measures to assess health inequalities: (1) define which aspect(s) of health to measure (e.g., death, disability, access to care); (2) identify the relevant population groups across which to compare health status (e.g., groups defined by gender, level of education, ethnicity); (3) choose a reference group against which to compare the health of different groups (e.g., in considering mortality rates within a country, the reference group might be the highest income group); (4) decide whether to measure inequality using the absolute or relative difference in health status between population groups; and, if examining more than one health measure, (5) select among alternative 'social weights' for preference that are built into health measures (e.g., adult morbidity may be 'weighted' to be more, less, or equally as important as child morbidity in a composite index of health. The Healthy People 2010 of USA with 467 objectives does use social weights to identify which objectives should be given attention first. All of the objectives are equally important since the goal is improvement in all of them. (Olivia *et al.*, 2003)

TACKLING THE HEALTH DISPARITY

The methods to be adopted depend upon (1) the factors causing the disparity; (2) the level of disparity; (3) the resources available; and (4) the psychological bent of mind, sincerity and determination to implement the decided course of action. These aspects attain special consideration in a developing country like India. Concept building is a special task for success of any undertaking in these situations.

The following figure shows the varied number of factors that influence the disparity in health, especially with respect to rural health in India.

A detailed account of the above factors is beyond the

scope of this paper. Each aspect requires an in-depth analysis in itself. In brief it can be mentioned that the government has great constraints of resources; the infra-structure facilities are deplorable in greater part of the 'village land'. In spite of the great emphasis on Community Medicine, both in medical curriculum and in government policies, the desired attitude and bent of mind which cares for the poor and the handicapped is little seen. The government policies are many a times affected by political consideration rather than the humanitarian approach. The implementing authorities have yet to develop the foresight the problem needs, and personal pecuniary and other benefits are obvious. The Private Health Service Providers are more business minded than humanitarian. Instances will be found in abundance of giving concessions to political persons and to men of importance rather than the needy and poor. Many policies are on paper only and actions reserved for the show cases. The NGOs have difficulties of operating in village situation. Some of these function even at the risk of their life and personal suffering. But even such sincere efforts would hardly serve to bridge this wide gap in healthcare provision between rural and urban areas. The dogmas and religions are important in acceptance of modern medical approach. People will go to quacks and to those who can advertise themselves better. Refusal to accept polio vaccination has been reported in many Muslim dominated localities. The crux of the problem is that we have to change ourselves. And what Mahatma Gandhi said in two words 60 years ago "You must be the change you want to see in the world" is most relevant in the present scenario as well.

RURAL/URBAN HEALTH DISPARITY IN INDIA

With the above background, I will try to project some aspects of the state of rural/urban disparity in India and suggest the course of action in the light of our strengths, weaknesses, opportunities and dimensions of the difficult task of bridging the rural/urban health disparity and its economic impact in India.

Norms for Rural Health Infrastructure

The infrastructural entitlements (for rural areas) under the Minimum Needs Programme started in the seventies are very minimal—a sub-center with two health workers for a population of 2500-5000, a 4-10 bedded primary health center (PHC) with one doctor and various paramedic staff for 10,000-30,000 population; and a 30 bedded Community Health Centre (CHC) with 6 doctors including basic specialists for every 5 PHCs. For secondary level reference there are sub district and district hospitals. Investments in primary health care have been very low and public expenditure is actually declining. Ever since India's commitment to the Structural Adjustment Programme (commonly referred to as SAP) in the nineties, public health expenditures have been declining, both in proportion to government spending as well as a ratio of GDP. Private investments have increased enormously and we are witnessing the 'corporatisation' of health care in India.

Rural-Urban Disparities in Health Outcomes

Before examining the extent of disparity in health, it is important to know the distribution of population in rural and urban areas. This is important for any meaningful comparison of the two areas. Table 1 below shows the distribution of population on the basis of the 1991 and 2001 census.

TABLE 1

Rural Population as per the 1991 and 2001 Census

	Total Population (in crores)	*Rural Population (in crores)*	*per cent of Rural Population*
1991	84.63	62.87	74.3
2001	102.86	74.25	72.2

Urbanisation is one of the features of development taking place in any country. The percentage of rural population has gone down by only 2 per cent during the period mentioned from 74.3 per cent to 72.2 per cent. We still have a large percentage of population living in rural areas. This makes the comparison between health outcomes in the two areas significant while exacerbating the inequalities that persist. Table 2 shows the health outcomes in rural and urban areas. Disaggregated data reveals severe disparities in both healthcare resources as well as health outcomes obtained in rural and urban areas. Health being a multidimensional concept, it is hard to define and measure the health status of a given population. The survival, morbidity and mortality rates (infant, children, maternal) are generally taken as indicators. To these have been added births attended by skilled staff and immunization of children. A large percentage of births in rural areas takes place at home with the local "dai" attending to the birth. Only about 25 per cent of deliveries are institutional (India Development Report 2004-05). Infections and complications are common as the births take place in an unhygienic environment. Likewise immunization of children against tuberculosis, polio, whooping cough, measles etc is essential because the incidence of these diseases is high in India. On both these counts, the rural areas (where majority of the population resides) fare very poorly. On examining Table 2 we find the extent of the differences in health outcomes of rural and urban population. Under 5 mortality of rural areas is high, at 133 while that in urban areas is considerably lower at 87. One possible reason is the low percentage of immunization at only 37 per cent compared to 61 per cent in urban areas. Only one third of deliveries are conducted by trained persons. Infant mortality is therefore rather high in rural areas (62 for 1000 live births) compared to urban areas (39 per 1000).With respect to LEB there is a difference of 7 years between rural and urban areas.

TABLE 2

Health Outcomes in Rural and Urban Areas

	Life Expectancy (1992-96)	*IMR*	*U5MR*	*Births attended (%)*	*Full immuni-zations*	*Median ANCs (%)*
Rural	59.4	62	133	33.5	37	2.5
Urban	66.3	39	87	73.3	61	4.2

IMR: Infant Mortality Ratio per 1000 live births
U5MR: Under 5 Mortality Ratio per 1000 live births

Disparities in Healthcare Resources

Poor health outcomes reflect disparity in infrastructure which is also very severe. The difference in availability of hospital beds is 15 times less in rural areas, while public expenditure is 7 times less. Out of pocket expenditure is higher for urban areas because diagnostic and related facilities are not available in rural areas and this is reflected in higher deaths at all levels.

TABLE 3

Healthcare Resources in Rural and Urban Areas

	Rural (per 1000 population)	*Urban (per 1000 population)*
Hospital Beds	0.2	3.0
Doctors	0.6	3.4
Public Expenditure	Rs. 80,000	Rs. 560,000
Out of pocket expenses	Rs. 750,000	Rs. 1,150,000

Investment of resources in health sector is rather low. Health expenditure as proportion of government expenditure is low, while in terms of GDP, public expenditure on health is not even 1 per cent of GDP. Rural areas are deprived of their rightful share in resources. This actually forms the basis of the "urban bias" theory of perpetuation of underdevelopment as given by Lipton. There is, as a result a considerable shortfall in health infrastructure in rural areas. Table 4 gives some information on this aspect.

TABLE 4

Shortfall in Health Infrastructure as per 2001 Population (as on March 2007)

	Required	*Existing*	*Shortfall*	*% shortfall*
Sub-centres	158792	145272	20855	13.13
PHCs	26022	22370	4833	18.57
CHCs	6491	4045	2525	38.90

PHC: Primary Health Centres; CHC: Community Health Centres.

Note: Requirement is calculated on the basis of Census 2001 in rural areas using the prescribed norms.

During the seventies and the late eighties a large expenditure in rural health infrastructure took place under the Minimum Needs Programme. Thus modern healthcare infrastructure was introduced in rural areas. Major responsibility of health expenditure is with the state governments. This is supplemented by public health programmes funded by the Centre, such as diagnosis and treatment of tuberculosis, AIDS, leprosy, polio, blindness control and family planning programmes, etc. Very often these are financed by international agencies like WHO and USAID. State government expenditures are mostly for urban healthcare while in rural areas emphasis is on family planning and on specific public health programmes like immunization, disease surveillance, ante-natal care rather than on curative care. All this puts a strain on the rural population whose out of pocket expenditures are high. Every bout of illness impoverishes the poor. Not only expenses have to be met, it also impacts adversely on earnings of the poor in rural areas. Out of pocket expenses in rural areas are ten times what the state spends on healthcare in rural areas while in urban areas the same are twice as high (Refer Table 3). These gross inequities in healthcare between rural and urban areas are evident in the health outcomes obtained. Large scale prevalence of poverty in rural areas acts as a handicap in accessing healthcare. It may also be pointed out that many of these public funded programmes are in the nature of plan grants often sponsored by the Centre and may not have a long-term commitment.

So far as private sector provision for health is concerned, it is curative in nature and is driven by profit considerations guided by the pharmaceutical industry. Further this sector is unregulated resulting in various type of malpractices. It is also expensive and beyond the reach of the rural poor.

As a result of low public investment in health, there are significant shortfalls in health infrastructure in rural areas as given in Table 4, with a shortfall of 13 per cent in the number of sub-centres, more than 18 per cent in Primary Health Centres and almost 39 per cent in Community Health Centres. Apart from this, medical and para-medical staff is also inadequate. As Table 3 reveals, per 1000 population, there are only 0.2 hospital beds in rural areas (i.e. 1 bed per 5000 population) while in urban areas, number of hospital beds are 3 (per 1000 population). Availability of doctors per 1000 population is 0.6 in rural areas (working out to roughly 1 doctor in 2000 population) while in urban areas, numbers of doctors is more than 3 (per thousand population).

Adding to this is inadequate supply of medicines and equipment and apathetic attitude of staff, the entire rural health infrastructure fails to deliver the necessary services in rural areas.

Certain other infrastructural factors that have a direct impact on health in rural areas are use of biofuels in cooking and lack of potable water supply and sanitation facilities available. It is estimated that more than 90 per cent of rural households use biofuels which emit a large number of pollutants causing acute respiratory and eye infections, chronic lung diseases and cancers. Unsafe drinking water and lack of sanitation facilities add to these diseases. It is estimated that 62 per cent of rural households do not have water supply in or near their homes while only 24 per cent have access to tap water in their homes. Only 7 per cent of households are connected with sewerage facility, 9 per cent have toilet facility in their house, 1 per cent use community toilets (India Development Report, 2004-05). This state of affairs existing in rural areas impacts on life expectancy and mortality rates. Women and children are prime sufferers. Adverse pregnancy outcomes like still births, premature births and low birth weights, high under 5 mortality rates and high maternal mortality rates prevail on account of indoor air pollution and poor sanitation facilities.

SUMMARY AND CONCLUSION

Although some improvements have taken place in health outcomes in India, rural-urban disparities are still significant. In view of the fact that more than 70 per cent of the population in India lives in rural areas, health disparities acquire a new meaning. Disparities breed discontent and dissatisfaction and along with other types of rural urban disparities are liable to act as a (sometimes powerful) destabilizing force. The large of factors affecting health disparity have to be tackle which is no easy task when the population is illiterate, tradition bound and not easily receptive to changes in their lifestyles. A significant departure in the government stance towards rural health spelling out government concern towards this is the launch of the National Rural Health Mission (NRHM) which proposes to raise public expenditure on health to 2 to 3 per cent of GDP as against less than 1 per cent of GDP being spent earlier. Let us hope this is not a political gimmick and the government takes up the matter with all the seriousness it deserves. With rampant corruption in bureaucracy, it will ultimately be a question of good governance.

REFERENCES

Fikree, Fariyal F.; Pasha, Omrana (2004): Role of Gender in Health Disparity: the South Asian Context: *British Medical Journal*, 3 Apr., http://www.accessmylibrary.com/coms2/summary_0286-21120562_ITM

Olivia Carter-Pokras, Claudia Baquet (2002): What is a Health Disparity: Association of Schools of Public Health. Public Health Reports, September-October, Volume 117, pp. 426-34.

Ravi Duggal (2003): Operationalising Right to Healthcare in India: Paper presented at the 10th Canadian Conference on International Health, Ottawa 28th October. www.cehat.org

PAHOWHO, Division of Health and Human Development (1999): Principles and basic concepgts of equity in health. October [cited 2020 Oct. 18]. Available from: URL.:http//www.paho.org/English/hdp/hdd/pahoho.pdf

Whitehead, M. (1999), The Concepts and Principles of Equity and Health. Copenhagen: WHO/Euro; 1991.

WHO Commission on Macroeconomics and Health (2000).

Federal, Provincial and Territorial Advisory Committee on Population Health (1999): Available from URI: http://www.hc-sc-gc-ca/hppb/phdd/report/toward/eng/report.html

Rockefeller Foundation and the Swedish International Development Cooperation Agency (2002), Challenging Inequalities in Health: From Ethics to Action. Summary [cited 2002. Nov 25]. Available from URL:http//www.rockfound.org/documents/435summary_challenging.pdf

Eonomic Survey, 2007-08, GOI, Ministry of Finance, Economic Division.

India Development Report, 2004-05, OUP, New Delhi.

India Infrastructure Report, 2007, Rural Infrastructure, OUP, New Delhi.

Ahmad, N. and Ansari, M.S. (2008), A Study of Inter-State Disparities in Health in India, *UPUEA Economic Journal*, Vol. 1, No. 1.

Ahmad, N. (2006), Health and Equity in *UPUEA Economic Journal*, Vol. 2, No. 2.

36

Inter-State Variation in Health Status in India: Significance of Nutritional Status and Health Awareness

BIPUL MALAKAR AND MONTU BOSE

Life expectancy at birth, infant and child mortality rate are all internationally accepted measures of Health Status of a country or region. All of them reflect the outcome of societal measures and focus on the socio-economic development level. Each of them individually or jointly are utilized for cross-country or interregional comparison of quality of life or more specifically health standard. All of these outcome variables if not directly, indirectly are being influenced by the state of health infrastructure. The interconnection between health infrastructure and health status is evident.

Special mention may be made regarding child mortality. Reduction of Child Mortality is a desired goal of every nation and is included in millennium development goal of United Nation. Reduce Child Mortality is the fourth

Millennium Development Goal—'Reduce by two-thirds, between 1990 and 2015, under five mortality.' Child mortality rate crucially depends on reproductive health and child health care facilities. On the other hand, prenatal and postnatal infant mortality rates with infant and child mortality help to evaluate the health condition and reproductive health and child health care.

Food intake or nutritional level, average daily calories intake per person, level of education or literacy rate are some mentionable components affecting the mortality, life expectancy and child health of an economy. Maternal malnutrition leads to premature birth, under weight babies. Consequently, the newborn becomes susceptible to various infections that ultimately reduce the nutrient absorption power of the baby. A child can be malnourished because of deficiency either of its own dietary nutritional level or for its mother's nutritional level and lactation. Chance of survival of a child is jeopardized. Moreover, the maternal health condition directly influences the child health and childcare. Health condition and health status of a mother are the two dominant factors, which reflect the social concern for women. Indeed, it cannot be denied that without improving the health condition of women it is very difficult to improve the health condition of children.

The health condition of a country depends on the level of nutrition, per head per day calories intake, vaccination, immunization, educational level, awareness and many more factors. Among these calories intake is singly most important influencing factor, nutritional level plays a big role in improving health condition of an individual and consequently uninterrupted supply of food to poorer section of the society should be given significance in understanding health condition of an economy. Thus, food security is an important gradient of Health Status of a region.

Inequality in the health condition within a country is an inevitable phenomenon. Intra-country variation in health status has been reported in almost every country in the world—in both developed and developing countries. India because of her geographical size cannot be an exception. Inequality in health within and between countries arises from inequalities within and between societies.

In what follows concern for health and health standard of a region are interrelated. Concern for health is better reflected by existing measures—a multi-dimensional vector and similarly health status is a multidimensional concept. Observed inter-state variation of physical indicator of health infrastructure in India can only partially explain the variation in Health Status measured by conventional concepts like Life expectancy.

Considerable variation in Life expectancy persists across India. While Life expectancy of a person residing in Kerala (73.6 years) is, almost 10 year more than 62.7 years an average Indian expected to live. According to available estimate people, living in Madhya Pradesh is having least life span 57 years. In the state, an average woman is expected to live less than an average male person. This unfortunate feature- life expectancy favouring male sex—is only observed in Hindi-speaking region—in UP and Bihar. In both the state Life expectancy for both sexes is also less than 60 years. Less than 60 years life expectancy is also observed in Assam and Orissa. Thus, it would be grossly unjustified to ignore the adverse state of Health status in India. Because the above-mentioned five states jointly accounts for more than 50 per cent of total population of India.

Available information suggests that average daily calorie intake by Indian is below the prescribed the minimum daily per-capita requirement of 2,250 calories. Situation in urban area is marginally better than rural areas. However, this inadequacy in calorie intake is not observed for all the states. The states where this average intake is above the minimum level are Haryana, Himachal Pradesh, Jammu & Kashmir, Punjab, Rajasthan, Uttar Pradesh, Delhi and Lakshadweep for the rural areas and Arunachal Pradesh, Himachal Pradesh, Jammu & Kashmir, Orissa, Andaman and Nicobar Islands, Chandigarh and Delhi in the urban areas. States suffering from calorie intake deficiency can be classified into three mutually exclusive categories. Deficiency observed across the states, i.e. both in rural and urban region, only in rural areas and only in urban areas. In major number of provinces 20 out of 32 belongs to first group (both in urban and rural area, per-capita daily calories intake falls

TABLE 1

Life Expectancy at Birth of Major States of India

State	Life Expectancy at Birth (1999-2003)		
	Male	Female	Person
Andhra Pradesh	62.2	64.8	63.7
Assam	57.8	58.3	58.0
Bihar	61.6	59.7	61.0
Gujarat	62.5	64.6	63.5
Haryana	65.0	65.6	65.4
Karnataka	62.9	66.4	64.6
Kerala	70.9	76.0	73.6
Madhya Pradesh	57.2	56.9	57.1
Maharashtra	65.2	67.6	66.4
Orissa	58.6	58.7	58.7
Punjab	67.6	69.6	68.6
Rajasthan	60.7	61.8	61.3
Tamil Nadu	64.3	66.5	65.4
Uttar Pradesh	59.6	58.7	59.3
West Bengal	63.5	65.0	64.1
All-India	61.8	63.5	62.7

Source: Office of the Register General India, Ministry of Home Affairs.

below the minimum level). Andhra Pradesh, Assam, Bihar, Goa, Gujarat, Karnataka, Kerala, Madhya Pradesh, Maharashtra, Manipur, Meghalaya, Mizoram, Nagaland, Sikkim, Tamil Nadu, Tripura, West Bengal, Dadra and Nagar Havali, Puducherry , Daman and Diu. Only in three states namely Arunachal Pradesh, Orissa and Chandigar adverse picture observed in the rural areas, i.e. second category of states. Calorie deficiency in urban region is observed in Haryana, Punjab, Rajasthan, and Uttar Pradesh.

The nutritional situation seems to be worst in southern states Tamil Nadu, Kerala, and Pondicherry and hilly states Sikkim, Meghalaya and Tripura and industrially advanced Maharashtra. The picture is disturbing—since in terms of life expectancy, Kerala tops the list and Tamil Nadu ranked 4th and Maharashtra comes 3rd. In all the mentioned states,

TABLE 2

Inter-State Difference in Calories Intake in India

[Calories Intake per day per person in Cal.]

States	*Rural*	*Urban*
Andhra Pradesh	2052	1992
Arunachal Pradesh	2130	2511
Assam	1983	2108
Bihar	2115	2188
Goa	1852	1996
Gujarat	1994	2027
Haryana	2491	2140
Himachal Pradesh	2324	2416
Jammu & Kashmir	2507	2392
Karnataka	2073	2026
Kerala	1965	1966
Madhya Pradesh	2164	2082
Maharashtra	1939	1989
Manipur	2157	2073
Meghalaya	1977	2066
Mizoram	2110	2200
Nagaland	2216	2169
Orissa	2199	2261
Punjab	2418	2089
Rajasthan	2470	2184
Sikkim	1892	2108
Tamil Nadu	1884	1922
Tripura	1924	2039
Uttar Pradesh	2307	2114
West Bengal	2211	2131
Andaman and Nicobar Island	N.A.	2268
Chandigarh	2100	2335
Daman and Diu	2230	1975
Dadra and Nagar Haveli	1594	1822
Delhi	2551	2383
Lakshadwip	2852	N.A.
Pondicherry	1968	1964
All-India	2153	2071

Note: N.A.—Not Available.
Source: NSSO 50th Round, July '93-June '94, Report-405.

estimates are above Indian average for both sexes. Thus, the forward movement in life expectancy at all-India level may not be positively associated with food intake.

However rank correlation between life expectancy and calorie intake is 0.66, i.e. food intake can at best explain 50 per cent of variation across the states in India.

Similarly, the observed interstate variation in child mortality rate may be related to supply of food. Science of Nutrition identified a series of diseases related to specific nutritional deficiencies and discovered the synergy between nutrition and infection (Nevin S. Scrimshaw *et al.*, 1968). It has been discussed earlier how the nutritional deficiency and subsequent death occurs. The interconnection between nutritional intake and child mortality can be understood form the correlation between them—the estimated correlation is 0.62. Such a low correlation is only apparently puzzling. The infant mortality rate in Kerala is low but the province suffers from nutritional deficiency. It is even more remarkable that Kerala, which is probably one of the world's poorest and most densely populated regions, had a total death rate of about 6.4 per thousand as in 2005—approximately equal death rate in the US, UK or Germany.

In Kerala, infant mortality for girl child or the female infant mortality rate is 12 per thousand live births and 11 for the male just followed by Manipur (FIMR-13, MIMR-18), Mizoram (FIMR-17, MIMR-16). Orissa has recorded highest infant mortality rate. The female infant mortality is 83 and the male infant mortality is 82 per thousand live births. Madhya Pradesh, Uttar Pradesh, Rajasthan, Assam, Bihar and Andhra Pradesh also has very high infant mortality rate

Perhaps regional imbalance is only partially related to nutritional level. Health awareness and medical facilities are dominant explanatory variables. A part of the explanation for the overtly paradoxical regional variation may be due to better private health practice and sanitation practices in Kerala compared to those in several other parts of the country. This is consistent too with the fact that the literacy rate (or any other index of general education) in Kerala is way above the Indian average. The literacy rate on the other hand is low in some of the nutritionally better-off states such

TABLE 3

Infant Mortality Rate of Different States and UTs of India

States	*Infant Mortality Rate (Per 1000 Live Birth), 2005*		
	Male	*Female*	*Person*
Andhra Pradesh	59	59	59
Arunachal Pradesh	31	38	34
Assam	69	65	67
Bihar	59	62	60
Goa	15	18	16
Gujarat	54	61	57
Haryana	54	65	59
Himachal Pradesh	54	44	49
Jammu & Kashmir	46	41	44
Karnataka	51	52	52
Kerala	11	12	11
Madhya Pradesh	77	86	82
Maharashtra	32	54	42
Manipur	18	13	16
Meghalaya	58	69	57
Mizoram	16	17	16
Nagaland	N.A.	N.A.	N.A.
Orissa	82	83	83
Punjab	46	52	49
Rajasthan	70	81	75
Sikkim	34	31	33
Tamil Nadu	44	41	43
Tripura	36	27	35
Uttar Pradesh	69	84	76
West Bengal	45	46	46
Andaman and Nicobar Islands	12	24	18
Chandigarh	21	32	26
Daman and Diu	43	34	39
Dadra and Nagar Havali	69	39	54
Delhi	28	29	28
Lakshadwip	21	32	26
Pondicherry	29	18	24
All-India	57	64	60

Note: N.A.—Not Available.
Source: Office of the Register General India, Ministry of Home Affairs.

as Haryana, Jammu & Kashmir, Rajasthan and Uttar Pradesh. Both life expectancy and child mortality are not favourably exposed in these states.

But a more important explanation may be the better access to medical facilities and public health services in states such as Kerala than in the other states. Health condition also depends on the supply and availability of health services. Per bed, population partially reflects the state of medicare facilities and persons undergoing treatment in hospital may

TABLE 4

Proportion (per 1000) of Persons Hospitalized in Rural and Urban Areas and Population per Bed in the Major States

Major States	*No. per 1000 Hospitalized*		*Popl. Per hospital bed*
	Rural	*Urban*	
Andhra Pradesh	22	28	1057
Assam	11	16	1782
Bihar	10	10	3029
Chhattisgarh	12	27	N.A.
Delhi	N.A.	11	493
Gujarat	29	26	709
Haryana	32	31	3026
HP	32	31	N.A.
J & K	18	20	4790
Jharkhand	9	22	N.A.
Karnataka	23	26	1319
Kerala	101	90	325
MP	18	29	5582
Maharashtra	30	36	920
Orissa	23	30	3064
Punjab	30	30	1623
Rajasthan	18	25	3175
Tamil Nadu	37	37	1135
Uttaranchal	17	19	N.A.
UP	13	20	2647
WB	23	35	1464
All-India	23	31	1503

Note: N.A.—Not Available.
Source: NSSO 60th Round, Jan.-June 2004, Published on March '06, p. 25.

be taken as an indirect measure of awareness. The proportion (per 1000) of persons in rural and urban areas and population per bed in the major states of India are given in Table 4.

Kerala is the state where the number per thousand hospitalized is maximum and population per hospital bed is lowest. Both awareness and health facilities in the state are praiseworthy. The favourable health conditions of Kerala owe more to these parameters rather than nutritional status. The adverse picture of Madhya Pradesh observed both in terms of life expectancy and child mortality rate can also readily be explained to inadequate availability of hospital bed—a bed is available for nearly about six thousand people.

We may thus surmise that health awareness and health facilities are the two dominant factors behind inter-state variation in health status in India. The health status scenario of Tamil Nadu and Karnataka in comparison to Kerala is unfavourable. Kerala is well known for high literacy rate and Life expectancy but daily calorie intake in the state is only moderate compared to other Indian provinces. On the other hand, during the past decades Chennai and Bangalore have emerged as supplier of qualitative health service centers in India. However, both of them lag far behind Kerala. It is thus difficult to ignore the significance of health awareness and health practices along with physical health infrastructure in explaining the variation. Influencing these factors will be more rewarding in ameliorating imbalance in health status.

References

P. Bardhan, (2003), Agrarian Structure and Political Economy in India, University Press.

Mark D. Hayward and David F. Warner (2005), The Demography of Population Health, Kluwer Academic/Plenum Publishers, NW, Boston, London, Moscow, Dordrecht.

W. Parker Frisbie, (2005), The Demography of Population Health, 4. Kluwer Academic/Plenum Publishers, NW, Boston, London, Moscow, Dordrecht.

Morbidity, Health Care and the Condition of the Aged—NSS 60th and 50th Round.

Malakar, B. (2000), Planning Health Sector of the State of West Bengal.

Malakar, B. and W. Habib, Concept of Human Health and Measurement at Individual and Community Level (in A. Roychoudury and J. Roy Edited Volume).

37

Regional Imbalances in Health Facilities in Costal Andhra Pradesh

M.V. Narasimha Sarma and D. Kailasa Rao

Historically, the right to health was one of the last to be proclaimed in the Constitutions of most countries of the world. At the international level, the Universal Declaration of Human Rights established a breakthrough in 1948, by stating in Article 25: "Everyone has the right to a standard of living adequate for the health and well-being of himself and his family." The Preamble to the WHO Constitution also affirms that it is one of the fundamental rights of every human being to enjoy "the highest attainable standard of health." Inherent in the right to health is the right to health or medical protection which is assured by a comprehensive system of Social Insurance that provides material security in cases of illness or accident, and free medical education, medicaments and other necessary materials and the right to be cared for by society in old age and invalidity.

In an increasing number of societies, health is no longer accepted as a charity or the privilege of the few, but demanded as a right for all. However, when resources are limited (as in most developing countries), the governments cannot provide all the needed health services. Under these circumstances the aspirations of the people should be satisfied by giving them equal right to available health care services.

The concept of "right to health" has generated so many questions, viz. right to medical care, right to responsibility for health, right to a healthy environment, right to food, right to procreate (artificial insemination included), the right not to procreate (family planning, sterilization, legal abortion), rights of the deceased persons (determination of death, autopsies, organ removal) and the right to die (suicide, hunger strike, discontinuation of life support measures), etc. Many of these issues have been the subject of debate. It is left to the lawyers, ethicists and physicians to formulate a general outline of what is acceptable and what is unacceptable in human society.

STATE RESPONSIBILITY

The responsibility for health does not end with the individual and community effort. In all civilized societies, the create assumes responsibility for the health and welfare of its citizens. The Constitution of India provides that health is a create responsibility. The relevant portions are to be found in the Directive Principles of State Policy, which are as below:

- The State shall, in particular, direct the policy towards curing.
- That the health and strength of workers, men and women and the tender age of children are not abused and that citizens are not forced by economic necessity to enter avocations unsuited to their age or strength.
- That childhoold any youth are protected against exploitation and against moral and material abandonment.
- The State shall, within the limits of its economic capacity and development, make effective provision for securing the right to work, to education and to public assistance in cases of unemployment, old age, sickness and disablement, and in other cases of underserved want.

- The State shall make provision for securing just and humane conditions of work and maternity relief.
- The State shall regard the raising of the level of nutrition and standard of living of its people and the improvement of public health as among its primary duties.

THE CONSTITUTION OF INDIA; PART IV

India is a signatory to the Alma-Ata Declaration of 1978. The National Health Policy, approved by Parliament in 1983 Nearly indicates India's commitment to the goal of Health for All by the year 2000 A.D. These trends have resulted in a greater degree of state involvement in the management of health services, and the establishment of nation-wide systems of health services with emphasis on primary health care approach.

Health and Development

The health is essential to socuo-economic development has gained increasing recognition. It was commonly thought in the 1960s that socio-economic progress was not essential for improving the health status of people in developing countries, and that substantial and rapid progress could be made through introduction of modern public health measures along. According to this way of thinking, the role of human beings in the development processes was grossly underestimated.

The period 1973-77 witnessed considerable rethinking on this subject. There was profound modification of the economic theory. It became increasingly clear that economic development alone cannot solve the major problems of poverty, hunger, malnutrition and disease. It its place, "non-economic" issues (e.g., education, productive employment, housing, equity, freedom and dignity, human welfare) have emerged as major objectives in development strategies.

The more recent experiences of a few developing countries (e.g., Sri Lanka, Costa Rica, and the state of Kerala in India) illustrate dramatically the way in which health forms part of development. This was because the efforts in the health field were simultaneously reinforced by developments in other sectors such as education, social welfare and land reforms. The link between health and development has been clearly established, the one being the starting point for the other and *vice-versa*.

Since health is an integral part of development, all sectors of society have an effect on health. In other words, health services are no longer considered merely as a complex of solely medical measures but a "sub-system" of an overall socuo-economic system. In the final analysis, human health and well-being are the ultimate goal of development.

REVIEW OF RESEARCH AND DEVELOPMENT

Indrani Gupta (2002) in his article titled "Private Health Insurance and Health Costs", examines the consequences of opening up of the health insurance sector to foreign and private investors. He was curious about the impact of privatisation on different sectors in India. He conveys that only part of the population is neither efficient nor equitable. The only way the entire population can be covered is by working out a market sharing mechanism, with a strong focus on quality improvement. It focuses on health insurance as distinct from other insurance and constitute a body that can go into the planning as well as implementation of health insurance, taking into account the objectives of equity and efficiency in health care.

Gita Sen, Aditi Iyer, Asha George (2002) in their article titled "Structural Reforms and Health Equity" presents morbidity and health care utilisation from two NSS surveys in 1980s and 1990s together with empirical results of other studies. They pointed out that the worsening factor is that class-based inequalities in access to health services for both men and women. Gender and economic classes are two major dimensions of socio-economic inequality and injustice. They conclude that health equity is a complex phenomenon with multiple determinates with various levels and dimensions. They focused that equity is needed by gender and economic class in access to health services.

Srinivasan (2002) in his article titled "Primary Health Care Services in Rural India: Current Status and Future Challenges" discussed various issues relating to primary health care, National Health Policies, Health financing achievements and limitations.

He has suggested various suggestions for effective discharging of health care services. Finally he concluded that in view of the experiences and difficulties faced in the provision of rural health services, it has been realised that acceleration of the pace of implementation of rural health programmes is an urgent imperative and concerted efforts need to be made by the State and Central Governments. Further, substantially large financial investment need to be made for rapidly improve the health profile of the country.

Sunil Nandraj and Anagha Khot (2003) in their article titled "Accreditation System for Health Facilities" addressed for establishing an accreditation system for health care facilities relates to purpose of accreditation for different stake-holders, defining who should be involved, mechanism for implementing monitoring systems, determining the role and levels of functioning of the accreditation bodies, dimensions of quality and the validity of such measurements and how to mobilise resources for this task. They conclude by writing that the design and performance of health systems is increasingly occupying centre space on the international health agenda. The heightened interest has created a unique climate for health care managers, policy-makers and decision-makers.

Ritu Priya's (2004) article entitled "Public Health Services Cinderella in the Social Sector", is an article on the changing priorities of health policy of India based on 2004-05 budget. She felt that well accepted epidemiological, Managerial and social dimensions of health service system need to be factored in if the financing of health care is to yield commensurate results. But she felt dissatisfaction over the budget because there is no evidence of this in the budget. She discussed various things and concludes that the issues of drug price control on one hand and of rational use of all available health technologies on the other, will hopefully get some attention.

OBJECTIVES

The following are the objectives set for the study:

1. To investigate into the causes for health care differentials in the three regions of Andhra Pradesh.
2. To examine the policies of Government in heath care in Andhra Pradesh.
3. To investigate into the attitude of the general public towards the government programmes with respect to health care.

TABLE I

Demographic and Health Profile of Andhra Pradesh State as Compared to India Figures

S. No.	*Item*	*Andhra Pradesh*	*India*
1.	Total Population (Census 2001) (in million)	76.21	1028.61
2.	Decadal Growth (Census 2001) (%)	14.59	21.54
3.	Crude Birth Rate (SRS 2007)	18.9	23.5
4.	Crude Death Rate (SRS 2007)	7.3	7.5
5.	Total Fertility Rate (SRS 2006)	2.0	2.9
6.	Infant Mortality Rate (SRS 2007)	56	57
7.	Maternal Mortality Ratio (SRS 2001-03)	195	301
8.	Sex Ratio (Census 2001)	978	933

Table 1 gives the demographic and health profile of Andhra Pradesh as a comparison to India. It may be observed form the table that in all the indicators Andhra Pradesh is better statistical performance. The decadal population growth is much lower than the national growth rate. The crude birth rate is much lower while the crude death rate is almost equal. Total fertility rate and Infant mortality rates are very near but lower to national growth rates. Hence, it may be concluded that Andhra Pradesh when compared to national rates is far better in its health statistics.

However, the picture is quite different. Within Andhra Pradesh State the health status and the facilities differ very widely with the three natural regions of Andhra Pradesh. As known, Andhra Pradesh is divided into three regions, viz., Costal Andhra, Rayalaseema and Telengana.

TABLE 2

Region-wise Growth Rates of Infant and Child Mortality Rate in Andhra Pradesh

S. No.	*Rate*	*Regions*			
		Costal Andhra	*Rayalaseema*	*Telengana*	*Andhra Pradesh*
Infant Mortality					
1.	1981-1991-39.86	-44.62	-40.64	-39.56	
2.	1991-200119.69	-27.27	-4.02	1.42	
3.	1981-2001-26.94	-59.73	-42.06	-39.54	
Child Mortality					
1.	1981-1991-34.28	-42.12	-35.59	-37.23	
2.	1991-2001-30.62	-30.74	-36.68	-30.51	
3.	1981-2001-54.41	-59.91	-59.34	-56.38	

Table 2 shows the growth rates of infant and child mortality rates in the tree regions. For a comparative purpose the study has been divided into two time periods. 1981 to 1991 which is the pre-reform period while 1991-2001 is the post-reform period. A total study is also given at the end.

In case of infant mordality there is a tremendous imporvemnent in the health care of infant mortality rate especially in the post-reform period. While there is an improvement in the other two regions the improvement is not as a match as in Costal Andhra region. In case of Andhra Pradesh as a whole there is an overall improvement in the situation.

Table 3 depicts the growth of hospitals and dispensaries in the three regions of Andhra Pradesh. It is clear from the table that there is negative growth in all the three regions. However, the negative growth rate is high in

TABLE 3

Region-wise Growth Rates of Hospitals and Dispensaries in Andhra Pradesh

S. No.	Rate	Regions		
		Costal Andhra	*Rayalaseema*	*Telengana**
1.	1981-1991	24.00	29.5	103.5
2.	1991-2001	-66.8	-69.8	-61.8
3.	1981-2001	-58.8	-60.9	-29.7

*Excluding Hyderabad.

case of Rayalaseema followed by Costal Andhra and Telengana regions. The overall growth rate of hospitals and dispensaries in Andhra Pradesh shows a negative growth rate during the study period.

TABLE 4

Region-wise Share of Doctors in Andhra Pradesh

S. No.	Rate	Regions		
		Costal Andhra	*Rayalaseema*	*Telengana**
1.	1981	38.4	17.5	23.8
2.	1991	37.4	19.1	25.5
3.	2001	38.8	19.4	26.7

*Excluding Hyderabad hence total not equal to 100.

In case of availability of doctors in the three regions, the highest share of doctors is in Costal Andhra region followed by Telengana and Rayalaseema Regions in 1981. The trend has continued even during the next two decades, i.e., 1991 and 2001. While the share has not changed much in case of Costal Andhra and Telengana, there is a slight change in the share of doctors of Rayalaseema region. It revels that the demand of doctors has not increased much in case of Costal Andhra and Telengana while the demand of doctors has increased in case of Rayalaseema region.

TABLE 5

Region-wise Growth Rates of Availability of Beds in Hospitals in Andhra Pradesh

S. No.	Rate	Regions		
		Costal Andhra	*Rayalaseema*	*Telengana**
1.	1981-1991	20.9	24.2	38.0
2.	1991-2001	17.10	20.62	35.7
3.	1981-2001	41.7	49.9	87.4

*Excluding Hyderabad.

Table 5 gives the details of growth rate of availability of beds in hospitals in the three regions of Andhra Pradesh. In the first decade, i.e., 1981-91, the growth rate of availability of beds in highest in Telegana region followed by Rayalaseema and Costal Andhra. The trend has continued even during the second decade that is 1991-2001, but the growth rates have decreased compared to first decade. There is a substantial change in the growth rate in case of Costal Andhra while the change is less in the other two regions. It may be implied from the statistics that during the reforms period there is a shift from heath care to some other sector in Andhra Pradesh.

TABLE 6

Region-wise Growth Rates of Primary Health Centers in Andhra Pradesh

S. No.	Rate	Regions		
		Costal Andhra	*Rayalaseema*	*Telengana**
1.	1987-1993	38.3	33.9	25.7
2.	1993-2003	14.5	15.1	16.9
3.	1987-2003	58.4	54.0	46.9

*Excluding Hyderabad.

Health care of any regions is mostly estimated basing on the Primary Health Centers available in a region. Two periods viz., 1987-93 and 1993-2003 are taken for the present study. Table 6 gives the growth rate statistics of Primary Health Centers in the three regions. During the first period the growth rate is highest in Costal Andhra followed by Rayalaseema and Telengana. However, in the post-reform period notonly the growth rates have decreased tremendously in all the three regions but also the rates growth have also changed among the three regions. In this period Telegana has a lead in growth followed by Rayalaseema and Costal Andhra which was first in the pre-reform period.

CONCLUSION

Basing on the above analysis it may be concluded that priorities in health are not given equal opportunities in the three regions of Andhra Pradesh. An over all study of all the variables leads to the conclusion that Costal Andhra has a better edge compared to Rayalaseema and Telengana.

The priority to health has shifted, as per the above study, from health to other sectors in Andhra Pradesh as a whole and regions in particular. Government has not taken steps during the post-reform period, to give a boost to the health sector during the post-reform period.

Health is the primary sector on which Human Development depends. In these days where human development is given top priority all over the world, it is very much necessary to give reasonable weightage for health care compared to other sectors. It is necessary to improve the percentage of doctors and beds increase in all the three regions for a better health care. It will reduce infant mortality rate and child mortality rate which are the basic indicators for calculating HDI. This will not only improve the status of our nation in the world map of health but also improves economic development in the country and in Andhra Pradesh in particular.

Notes and References

Gupta, Indrani "Private Health Insurance and Health Costs" (2002), *Economic and Political Weekly*, July 6-12, Vol. XXXVII, No. 27, A Sameeksha Trust Publications, Mumbai, pp. 2795-2802.

Nandraj, Sunil, Anagha Khot (2003), "Accreditation System for Health Facilities", *Economic and Political Weekly*, December 13-19, Vol. XXXVIII No. 50, A Samiksha Trust Publications, Mumbai, pp. 5251-55.

Priya, Ritu (2004), "Public Health Services", *Economic and Political Weekly*, A Sameeksha Trust Publication, Mumbai, Vol. XXXIX, No. 33, August 14-20, pp. 3671-73.

Sen, Gita, Aditi Iyer, Asha George (2002), "Structural Reforms and Health Equity", *Economic and Political Weekly*, April 6-12, Vol. XXXVII, No. 14, A Samiksha Trust Publications, Mumbai.

Srinivasan, S. (2002), "Primary Health Care Services in Rural India, Current Status and Future Challenges", *Kurukshetra*, A Journal on Rural Development, Annual Issue, Ministry of Rural Development, New Delhi, Vol. 50, No..12, October 2002.

38

Determinants of Health Disparities in Madhya Pradesh: Need for Region Specific Approach

MONA KHARE

INTRODUCTION

The debate between high growth *vs.* development continues to trouble the intelligentsia and the policy-makers alike, particularly in view of the distributive effect as well as the human resource based sustainable development effect of high economic growth. Studies have proved now and again that merely a high economic growth may not be able to achieve the desired goals of human capital formation and development with a human face. Performance in the social sector may have very little to do with growth but it is an important component of development. Thus, in the process of economic liberalization, though the State may withdraw from a number of economic activities, which may be left to the market forces, it has to play a vital role in creation of physical and social infrastructure. Dreze and Sen maintain that India is extremely poor in terms of non-income indicators like education and health. The irony lies in the fact that education and health are extremely important, not only for the improvement of the self but even for the society, yet expenditure on such items by the individuals does not occupy a high position in the list of their priorities in comparison with other consumption requirements of daily life, mainly due to their inadequate and in sufficient income. The role of state under such a situation assumes a significant position particularly during the transitional phase of the economy (Sengupta, 1998).

Madhya Pradesh is one such state in India, which is in this transitional phase. It continues to be reckoned among less developed states of the country, as is evident from the sheer fact that the gap between per-capita income of Madhya Pradesh and that of highest per-capita income state has increased from 1.93 times in 1993-94 to 2.32 times in 2003-04. Also, a look at the various budgets of the Madhya Pradesh Government reveals that expenditure on social and economic services have recorded a declining trend; the worst sufferer being public health. Good health is everybody's basic right irrespective of caste, class or region. But, the realities are very different from this ideology. Often, it is believed that just by improving the health facilities the problem can be taken care of. Though, overtly it appears that there is a direct relationship between increased expenditure, infrastructure creation and desired outcome but it may not necessarily be so. There is something more to just this simple hypothesis.

OBJECTIVES AND METHODOLOGY

It is with this background that the present paper makes an attempt to measure the levels of health status of major 45 districts of Madhya Pradesh and to identify the determinants and correlates of inter-district variations therein. The study is based on secondary data collected from various published sources on thirteen basic indicators of health standards, health infrastructure as well as other related indicators of education, employment and gender. Statistical packages such as Factor analysis, Multiple Regression, Correlation and simple descriptive statistics have been used to draw conclusions. The objectives of the study can be specified as;

1. To assess whether Madhya Pradesh fulfils the UNDP norms on social sector expenditure,
2. To study the district-wise status of health in Madhya Pradesh and measure the disparities existing therein,
3. To construct the multivariate composite index of Health (CHI) for the districts of Madhya Pradesh, and
4. To identify the determinants of disparities existing therein.

DISCUSSION: SOCIAL SECTOR EXPENDITURE

Madhya Pradesh has not only witnessed higher growth rates in recent years but also shown marginal improvement in terms of Human Development Index (HDI) with its rank increasing from 14th in 1981 to 13th in 1991 and further to 12th in 2001 among 15 major states in India. Now it is ahead of Uttar Pradesh, Bihar and Assam by improving its HDI from 0.328 in 1991 to 0.394 in 2001 (Ghosh, 2005). A look at Table 1 reveals that though there might have been an improvement in the HDI of Madhya Pradesh, it still lags behind the UNDP norms regarding four major human development ratios during the last decade covering a period from 1996-97 to 2007-08.

It is clear from the table above that not only are these ratios low in the State but have also declined in later period be it the Public Expenditure Ratio (PER)*, Social Allocation Ratio (SAR)*, or Human Expenditure Ratio (HER)*. The above observation may be attributed to the fact that while making efforts to reduce revenue expenditure, it is the social sector

*Note: (a) PER: Ratio of public expenditure to GSDP
(b) SAR: Percentage of total public expenditure on social services
(c) SPR: Expenditure on priority areas, i.e. education, health, drinking water and sanitation as a percentage of total public expenditure on social services.
(d) HER: Expenditure on education, health, drinking water and sanitation as percentage of gross state domestic product.

which has received the brunt of these cuts made by the state government. Studies have revealed that there had been a systematic reduction of expenditures on social sector (Sengupta, 1997). This is because reduction in this sector can be done easily and is less opposed by pressure groups, which seem to be weak in this area. However, it should be remembered that the impact of reduction in social sector expenditure would have a long-term damage on the State's economic growth in terms of slow down of human capital formation (Panchamukhi, 2000).

DISTRICT-WISE HEALTH STATUS AND DISPARITIES

Taking cue from the above when the inter-district data of major health indicators in Madhya Pradesh (Table 2) were analysed, it was found that conditions are poor not only in smaller and less developed districts of the State but also big and developed districts like Indore, Bhopal, Gwalior or Jabalpur. The multivariate composite index of health (CIH) prepared by making use of Factor Analysis (Table 3). reveals that Indore, Dewas, Mandsaur, Ratlam, Ujjain—the neighbouring districts in Indore-Ujjain divisions covering the rich and prosperous Malwa Belt are among the top while Panna, Tikamgarh, Satna, Damoh, Rewa lying in the underdeveloped Bundelkhand, Baghelkhand belts lie in the lower quartile. But, here too the low value of coefficient of variation (20) confirms that there is not much variation amongst the health index of various districts. Also the coefficients of variation of most individual indicators of health are either low or medium; which shows that the health disparities are not of a very high order.

Though, one cannot ignore the deplorable conditions prevailing in the hospitals and dispensaries for want of funds in MP, but more important than creation of infrastructure is the maintenance of quality infrastructure. In support of the above statement, it is important to note that the inter-district differentials in MP are higher in availability of infrastructure facilities, be it hospitals, immunization, safe deliveries or drinking water as compared to outcome indicators like Life Expectancy (LE), Maternal Mortality Rate (MMR), Birth rate

(BR), Infant Mortality Rate (IMR), etc. as revealed by lower values of their coefficients of variation.

This reinstates the fact that it is not just creation of facilities that can help improve health status but a number of other socio-economic, psychological factors may be as important. Until and unless the medical facilities are of good quality and people have the capacity and desire to use them no major dent can be made on the poor health status in the State as a whole.

FACTOR ANALYSIS

To identify the factors in order of their importance in explaining the existing variance, data reduction technique of Factor Analysis was applied to the 13 selected indicators, viz.,

1. Life Expectancy
2. Infant Mortality Rate
3. Maternal Mortality Rate
4. Birth Rate
5. Per cent Children Immunised
6. Per cent Safe Delivery
7. Sex Ratio
8. Child Sex Ratio
9. Per cent villages (Fully Covered) drinking water
10. Per cent villages (Partially Covered) drinking water
11. Allopathic institutions/village
12. Number of beds/hospital
13. Per cent Villages with aganwadi workers

Factor Analysis is a technique by which a large set of 'n' number of variables can be reduced to 'k' number of factors such that there is complete orthogonality between the factors so extracted.

The results of Factor Analysis as presented in Table 4. reveal that five factors cumulatively explain about 77 per cent of variance in health status, with the first three explaining 50 per cent of the variance. It is interesting to note that the first factor shows high correlations with longevity based indicators such as life expectancy, per cent immunized and per cent of safe deliveries—all of which are heavily dependant on access and ability as well as capacity to use quality health facilities. This is further confirmed by the first factor also having high correlation with number of allopathic institutions per village (Table 5).

Health care facilities do not simply mean fight against diseases but also good hygiene, proper sanitation, safe drinking water and clean surroundings (NCERT).The second factor that explains 16 per cent of variance and has high correlation with percentage of villages fully covered with safe drinking water facilities; supports the above thesis.

The third factor which has high correlation with Infant Mortality Rate and Maternal Mortality Rate point at the importance of Child and Maternal health care. Child care and maternal health care are both subject to a number of social and cultural taboos. Thus, one cannot deny the stark reality that other socio-psychological factors such as education, gender status, employment, customs and traditions are also important aspects affecting levels of Health.

DETERMINANTS

To testify the above observations multiple regression was carried out with Composite Health Index as the dependent and total literacy, workforce participation rates, sex-ratio, drinking water status as independent variables in addition to basic health infrastructure such as number of allopathic institutions/village, number of beds/hospitals and percentage of villages having Anganwadi workers. Studies have proved that there is a symbiotic synergy ,amongst the various components of the social sector. Education on the one hand, and health and medical care on the other are closely inter-linked (Panchamukhi, 2000). It is well known that birth rates are affected by the means of production (i.e. whether it is a subsistence economy or an industrialized economy), women's status and education, family structures and women's entry into the labour force (Murthy, 2002).

The results of the Multiple Regression are presented in Table 6. Most variables show very feeble impact (regression coefficients being very low) and hence cannot be regarded as major determinants of Health Status in the State. This can be explained as none of the chosen variables have been analysed for different levels of gradation. For all these variables to have any visible impact, there needs to be a threshold level beyond which they become effective, be it education, workforce participation or sex-ratio. It is not just literacy but education creating awareness and desire to change, it is not just employment but more than sustainable and continuous earning, not just improved sex-ratios but increased women autonomy regarding decision-making and conscious self-care. Similarly, quality of infrastructural facilities are more important than just creating them. For example not just availability of drinking water but availability of safe drinking water. It is interesting to note that areas such as Jhabua, Mandla have highest WPR but rank much low in Health Index. This indicates high degree subsistence level employability. Similarly, most districts which have higher Per cent of girls never enrolled in school rank lower in Health index. Jabalpur among the category of big and richer districts while Tikamgargh, Panna, Rewa, etc. among the category of underdeveloped regions are distinct examples.

CONCLUSION AND SUGGESTIONS

It can thus be concluded from the above analysis that health is a wider aspect which is closely associated with more important components of education, family welfare, sanitation, drinking water and welfare of economically and socially backward classes. Hence any effective policy of health improvement in the state should adopt a region-centric approach by identifying regional socio-economic-psychological characteristics. A blanket policy of simply creating health infrastructure will not help much. For example in prosperous and developed districts of Malwa plateau the approach should be on modernization and quality enhancement of Health care facilities, development of speciality centres; while in the lesser developed Vindhya region covering the Bundelkhand, Baghelkhand belt the emphasis should also be on awareness generation, health education, door to door services, training of local people in addition to creation of additional health care facilities. In tribal regions like Jhabua the problem may require rigorous methods of first bringing the area in the mainstream of development process, providing people with productive and gainful employment so as to ensure regular and threshold level income. Though public private participation can be encouraged in developed districts, government should take the responsibility of providing good quality health facilities at subsidized minimal rates or free of costs in lesser developed ones. Here too the policy of differential charges from individuals can be adopted depending on their paying capacities so as to make the government system more viable, sustainable and competitive.

References

Ghosh, M. (2006), "Economic Growth and Human Development in Indian States", *Economic and Political Weekly*, Vol. 41, No. 30, pp. 3321-29.

Ghosh, P.P. (2005), "Structure of Madhya Pradesh Economy Pre- and Post-Liberatlisation", *Economic and Political Weekly*, Vol. 40, No. 48, pp. 5029-37.

Jain, A. (2004), "Trends of Social Sector Expenditure in Pre and Post-Reform Era in India", Research Link-16, Vol. 111(6), pp. 76-78.

Murthi, M., A.C. Guio, and J. Dreze (1995), Mortality, Fertility, and Gender Bias in India, *Population and Development Review* 21(4): 745-82.

Madhya Pradesh Human Development Reports; various issues.

National Human Development Reports; (2001),. Planning Commission, Government of India, New Delhi.

Panchmukhi, P.R. (2000), "Social Impact of Economic Reforms in India: A Critical Appraisal", *Economic and Political Weekly*, Vol. 34, No. 10, pp. 836-37.

Rajeev, P.V. (1999), Planning for Social Reforms: the Key to Economic Progress, Deep & Deep Publications Pvt. Ltd., New Delhi.

Visaria, P. and L. Visaria, (1994), Demographic Transition: Acclerating Fertility Decline in the 1980s, *Economic and Political Weekly*, 24(51 and 52), 2381-92.

APPENDIX OF TABLES

Table I

Human Development Ratios in Madhya Pradesh (1997-98 to 2006-07)

Year	*Public Expenditure Ratio (PER)*	*Social Allocation Ratio (SAR)*	*Social Priority Ratio (SPR)*	*Human Expenditure Ratio (HER)*
1	*2*	*3*	*4*	*5*
Average of Ratios calculated on 5-yearly basis				
1997-2002	21.73	34.51	67.05	5.03
	(-3.27)	(-5.49)	(-+17.05)	(+0.03)
2002-07	21.37	28.75	62.75	3.84
	(-3.63)	(-11.75)	(+12.75)	(-1.165)
UNDP NORM	25%	40%	50%	5%

Figures in bracket show deviation from UNDP norm.

Source: Compiled from various Budget Documents of Madhya Pradesh Government.

TABLE 2

Health Indicators for Madhya Pradesh

Districts	*LE*	*IMR*	*MMR*	*BR*	*Immunised %*	*% of Safe Delivery*
1	*2*	*3*	*4*	*5*	*6*	*7*
Balaghat	58.5	90	786	24.4	90.4	29.4
Barwani	59.6	83	905	27.8	31.8	34.5
Betul	54.7	93	942	26.8	78.9	34.2
Bhind	59.9	110	965	28.01	53.8	18.9
Bhopal	64.9	74	747	31.04	78.5	69.7
Chattarpur	50.4	100	991	33.1	29.5	24.4
Chindwara	60.4	84	766	28.7	41.4	43.3
Damoh	54	95	962	27.3	27.2	29.1
Datia	55.2	86	837	23.53	35.1	32.9
Dewas	63.3	77	589	21.83	50	99.9
Dhar	63.4	79	658	28.9	36.5	35.7
Dindori	62.6	89	1088	22.4	77.1	17.6
Khandwa	57.7	79	846	24.8	56.7	42.8
Guna	53.5	89	814	29.8	30.7	36.3
Gwalior	65.3	118	1313	30.52	52.6	61.8
Harda	55.6	104	807	24.8	71	42.6
Hoshangabad	55.6	94	962	28.7	71	42.6
Indore	69.7	69	509	27.6	68.9	72
Jabalpur	57.5	102	973	25.7	50.9	44.4
Jhabua	55.8	73	793	36.23	17.4	22.4
Katni	57.5	84	638	27.3	50.9	44.4
Mandla	62.6	79	796	23.42	77.1	17.6
Mandsaur	58.5	78	660	26.92	40.4	46.4
Morena	57.4	91	977	28.53	18.6	33
Narsinghpur	56.9	88	770	23.6	68.7	27.8
Neemach	58.5	79	645	26.6	40.4	46.4
Panna	53	86	954	30.65	10.5	13.3
Raisen	55.3	129	1277	39.9	70.6	29.4
Rajgarh	54.2	86	846	28.29	28	34.2
Ratlam	58.1	91	737	28.02	48.8	60.4
Rewa	53.6	90	797	33.3	65	20.8
Sagar	54	91	903	31.47	32.4	43

(Contd.)

TABLE 2 *(Contd.)*

1	*2*	*3*	*4*	*5*	*6*	*7*
Satna	49.6	87	894	27.31	35.9	16.9
Sehore	54.5	103	747	29.1	26.8	38.5
Seoni	59.9	98	871	29.3	69	42.6
Shahdol	57.1	99	922	24.7	39.7	51.7
Shahjahpur	58.3	98	874	28.82	24.8	39.7
Sheopur	57.4	82	674	34.52	18.6	33
Shivpuri	47.3	80	737	29.85	63.2	47.3
Sidhi	58	75	729	23.9	40.8	10.4
Tikamgarh	52.8	91	903	29.1	17.3	29.5
Ujjain	59.8	73	561	27.67	57.6	68.5
Umaria	57.1	82	874	28.4	39.7	51.7
Vidisha	54.7	68	864	30.4	44	27.8
Khargone	59.6	76	622	27.4	31.8	34.5
Mean	57.41	88.27	833.89	28.23	46.89	38.74
S.D.	4.25	12.46	163.07	3.57	20.23	17.31
C.V.	7.40	14.12	19.56	12.64	43.15	44.67
Madhya Pradesh	54.40	82.00	834.00	28.23	46.88	38.74

(Contd.)

TABLE 2 (Contd.)

Health Indicators for Madhya Pradesh

Districts	Sex Ratio	Child Sex Ratio	Drinking water fully covered	% villages partially covered	allo. ins/ village	beds/ hosp.	% villages having Angan-wadi workers
1	8	9	10	11	12	13	14
Balaghat	1022	968	73	20.1	0.01	10.44	90.37
Barwani	971	970	63.1	22.6	0.01	12.87	85.12
Betul	965	969	69.6	21.4	0.02	8.93	94.64
Bhind	829	832	61.1	9	0.01	16.14	63.65
Bhopal	895	925	90.7	6	0.05	11.42	56.03
Chattarpur	869	917	67.8	24.1	0.03	7.04	76:97
Chindwara	952	958	90	3.1	0.02	9.24	95.18
Damoh	901	935	76.5	16.3	0.01	11.82	77.84
Datia	857	874	53.3	12.3	0.01	12.00	91.22
Dewas	930	930	43.8	40.3	0.02	13.83	97.07
Dhar	955	943	73.8	10.5	0.01	9.20	84.75
Dindori	991	990	73.4	12.5	0.01	1.00	85.98
Khandwa	936	941	71.9	21.5	0.02	11.95	89.45
Guna	885	931	88.1	6.4	0.01	16.24	80.49
Gwalior	848	853	83.7	8	0.03	7.19	89.01
Harda	919	925	98.3	1	0.02	13.40	86.34
Hoshangabad	896	927	89	3.3	0.02	21.00	73.3
Indore	912	908	40.4	57	0.05	10.47	98.82
Jabalpur	986	974	81.1	8	0.02	16.60	76.7
Jhabua	902	931	78.6	14	0.00	10.98	86.58
Katni	941	952	88.7	0.6	0.02	11.68	87.94
Mandla	996	981	65.8	10.7	0.01	11.03	76.8
Mandsaur	956	946	23.3	69.5	0.04	8.71	66.44
Morena	822	837	78.7	10.9	0.01	17.14	84.11
Narsinghpur	909	917	70.9	1.1	0.01	15.56	82.08
Neemach	950	931	49.6	27.1	0.02	10.68	78.27
Panna	901	932	60.1	24.6	0.01	13.50	71.09
Raisen	881	936	63.6	32.9	0.01	11.76	69.4
Rajgarh	932	938	45.5	51.7	0.02	11.55	58.47

(Contd.)

TABLE 2 *(Contd.)*

1	*8*	*9*	*10*	*11*	*12*	*13*	*14*
Ratlam	958	957	57.2	39.6	0.02	22.03	81.74
Rewa	941	926	79.5	10.4	0.01	7.14	84.58
Sagar	884	931	55.3	34.3	0.02	14.26	64.74
Satna	925	931	50.6	33.9	0.01	9.22	79.59
Sehore	909	927	66.9	19.7	0.02	15.68	76.44
Seoni	981	977	82.6	14.3	0.01	12.82	79.95
Shahdol	957	972	85.7	6.3	0.01	8.91	94.32
Shahjahpur	927	936	50.9	48.2	0.02	14.75	82.04
Sheopur	895	929	65.7	19.2	0.01	1.00	81.59
Shivpuri	858	906	89.1	6.9	0.01	19.30	84.35
Sidhi	932	954	59	38.2	0.01	8.37	93.75
Tikamgarh	886	916	49.3	29.8	0.01	12.84	81.23
Ujjain	938	938	53.3	33.3	0.02	22.32	99.26
Umaria	946	959	83	8.6	0.01	6.62	78.02
Vidisha	875	943	70.11	27.2	0.01	17.00	55.21
Khargone	949	962	63.8	16.3	0.02	7.97	85.68
Mean	921.56	934.11	68.34	20.73	0.02	12.08	81.26
S.D.	44.82	33.81	16.14	15.96	0.01	4.60	10.82
C.V.	4.86	3.62	23.61	77.02	60.22	38.09	13.32
Madhya Pradesh	919.00	932.00	70.50	18.50	0.01	11.86	85.27

TABLE 3

Health Indicators for Madhya Pradesh

District	*Comp. Index*	*Ranks*
1	*2*	*3*
Balaghat	12.43	9
Barwani	10.63	28
Betul	11.79	16
Bhind	10.67	26
Bhopal	16.64	3
Chattarpur	9.43	37
Chindwara	12.30	11
Damoh	9.30	40
Datia	10.97	25
Dewas	16.80	2
Dhar	11.46	21
Dindori	11.35	23
Khandwa	12.71	8
Guna	9.35	39
Gwalior	15.25	4
Harda	12.00	14
Hoshangabad	11.74	17
Indore	19.36	1
Jabalpur	11.63	18
Jhabua	8.19	44
Katni	11.92	15
Mandla	11.59	19
Mandsaur	14.17	6
Morena	9.82	35
Narsinghpur	11.35	22
Neemach	12.39	10
Panna	7.88	45
Raisen	10.12	32
Rajgarh	10.21	31
Ratlam	13.50	7
Rewa	9.21	41
Sagar	10.49	30
Satna	8.51	43
Sehore	10.67	27

(Contd.)

TABLE 3 *(Contd.)*

1	2	3
Seoni	12.17	12
Shahdol	11.30	24
Shahjahpur	12.14	13
Sheopur	9.42	38
Shivpuri	9.87	34
Sidhi	10.09	33
Tikamgarh	9.13	42
Ujjain	15.14	5
Umaria	10.55	29
Vidisha	9.53	36
Khargone	11.47	20
Composite Index of		
Mean	11.48	
S.D.	2.34	
C.V.	20.38	

TABLE 4

Total Variance Explained

Component	*Initial Eigenvalues*			*Rotation Sums of Squared Loadings*		
	Total	*% of Variance*	*Cumulative %*	*Total*	*% of Variance*	*Cumulative %*
1	3.23	24.86	24.86	2.25	17.33	17.33
2	2.40	18.45	43.31	2.20	16.94	34.28
3	1.88	14.49	57.80	2.15	16.50	50.78
4	1.40	10.75	68.54	2.13	16.42	67.19
5	1.07	8.22	76.76	1.24	9.57	76.76
6	0.93	7.14	83.90			
7	0.70	5.35	89.25			
8	0.47	3.61	92.86			
9	0.37	2.81	95.68			
10	0.23	1.74	97.41			
11	0.21	1.65	99.06			
12	0.07	0.51	99.57			
13	0.06	0.43	100.00			

Extraction Method: Principal Component Analysis.

TABLE 5

Rotated Component Matrix

Variable/Component	*1*	*2*	*3*	*4*	*5*
Life Expectancy	0.752	-0.004	-0.173	0.131	-0.352
IMR	0.040	0.244	0.800	-0.116	-0.033
MMR	-0.137	0.214	0.849	-0.097	-0.134
Birth Rate	-0.201	-0.149	0.495	-0.356	0.058
Children Immunised %	0.529	0.366	0.160	0.510	0.121
Safe Delivery %	0.778	-0.029	-0.285	-0.087	0.211
Sex Ratio	0.060	-0.026	-0.234	0.915	-0.186
Child Sex Ratio	-0.139	-0.059	-0.133	0.906	-0.069
Per cent Villages (FC) drinking water	-0.063	0.893	0.164	0.040	0.062
Per cent Villages (PC) drinking water	0.149	-0.933	-0.064	0.053	0.021
Allopathic institutions/ village	0.804	-0.388	0.061	-0.097	0.073
Beds/hospital	0.081	0.086	-0.108	-0.163	0.894
Per cent Villages with aganwadi workers	0.200	0.333	-0.531	0.028	-0.435

Rotation converged in 6 iterations

TABLE 6

Results of Multiple Regression

	T Lit	*WFP*	*PVWAW*	*B/H*	*H/V*	*PVWSDWS*	*Sex ratio*
	b7	*b6*	*b5*	*b4*	*b3*	*b2*	*b1*
Beta values	0.003	-0.035	0.066	0.069	191.358	-0.034	0.015
SE	0.028	0.029	0.016	0.042	22.139	0.024	0.005

R^2	0.809	SE y	1.114
F	22.438	d of	37.000
SS		SS	
regression	195.042	residual	45.945

Note: T Lit.: Total literacy
WPR: Workforce Participation Rate
PVWAW: Percentage of villages with anganwadi workers
B/H: number of beds per hospital.
H/V: number of hospitals per village.
PVWSDW: Per cent villages with safe drinking water

39

Regional Disparities in Education with Special Reference to Secondary Level: Issues and Challenges

VINAYAK KANT MISHRA AND PRAHLAD KUMAR

INTRODUCTION

There is a broad consensus on the overall improvement of the economy and quality of life during the last few years, there are significantly differing perceptions about the distributional impacts of these gains. Disparities in economic and social development across the regions and intra-regional disparities among different segments of the society have been the major planks for adopting planning process in India since independence. Apart from massive investments in backward regions, various public policies directed at encouraging private investments in such regions have been pursued during the decades of planned development. While efforts to reduce regional disparities were not lacking, achievements were not often commensurate with these efforts.

The ongoing economic reforms since 1991 with stabilization and deregulation policies as their central pieces seem to have further widened the regional disparities. The seriousness of the emerging acute regional imbalances has not yet received the public attention it deserves.

The scope of this study is restricted to a comparative analysis of the emerging trends in fifteen major states in respect of a few key parameters which have intrinsic bearing on social and economic development, especially regarding the educational attainment at secondary level of schooling. The fifteen states together account for 96 per cent of the population of India. The remaining 4 per cent is spread out in 10 smaller states and seven Union Territories including the National Capital Territory of Delhi. Leaving out these states and UTs from detailed study is mainly due to non-availability of all relevant data and also to keep the data sets analytically and logistically manageable.

The fifteen states taken up for the detailed study are: Andhra Pradesh, Assam, Bihar, Gujarat, Haryana, Karnataka, Kerala, Madhya Pradesh, Maharashtra, Orissa, Punjab, Rajasthan, Tamil Nadu, Uttar Pradesh and West Bengal.

Table 1 presents the growth of population during the period 1991 to 2001 in these states. It is quite evident that the states like, Rajasthan, Haryana and Bihar have showed a comparative high rate of population growth of 28.41 per cent, 27.88 per cent and 27.08 per cent, respectively. While the states, like Kerala, Tamil Nadu and Andhra Pradesh have showed a growth of 9.28 per cent, 11.09 per cent and 13.83 per cent, respectively. To make it more clear, Figure 1 is plotted so as give a more presentable picture of this fact.

Following the study of K.V. Ramaswamy, we conclude that there is a concentration of poverty and backwardness in a group of contiguous states accounting for about as much as 50 per cent of the total population of the major states of India. The gap between the highest and the lowest per-capita income (in 1993-94 prices) among the fifteen states increased from 2.55 times to 3.76 times (in absolute figures, from Rs. 5,735 to Rs. 14,967) in this period, indicating a stark widening of income disparity among the states. This difference was more in current prices (in 2004-05, the per-

TABLE I

Population in Millions

States	*1991 Census*	*2001 Census*	*Population Growth in%*
Andhra Pradesh	66.5	75.7	13.83
Assam	22.4	26.6	18.75
Bihar	86.4	82.9	27.08
Gujarat	41.3	50.6	22.52
Haryana	16.5	21.1	27.88
Karnataka	45.0	52.7	17.11
Kerala	29.1	31.8	9.28
Madhya Pradesh	66.2	60.4	22.66
Maharashtra	78.9	96.7	22.56
Orissa	31.7	36.7	15.77
Punjab	20.3	24.3	19.70
Rajasthan	44.0	56.5	28.41
Tamil Nadu	55.9	62.1	11.09
Uttar Pradesh	139.1	166.0	19.34
West Bengal	68.1	80.2	17.77

Note: Bihar and Madhya Pradesh contains the figures of Jharkhand and Chhattisgarh also for 2001.

Source: Office of the Registrar General and Census Commissioner, India (2006): "Census of India 2001", GOI.

FIGURE I

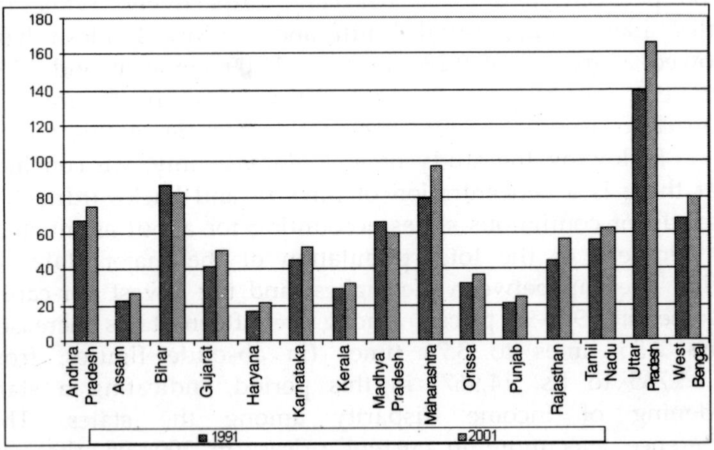

FIGURE 2

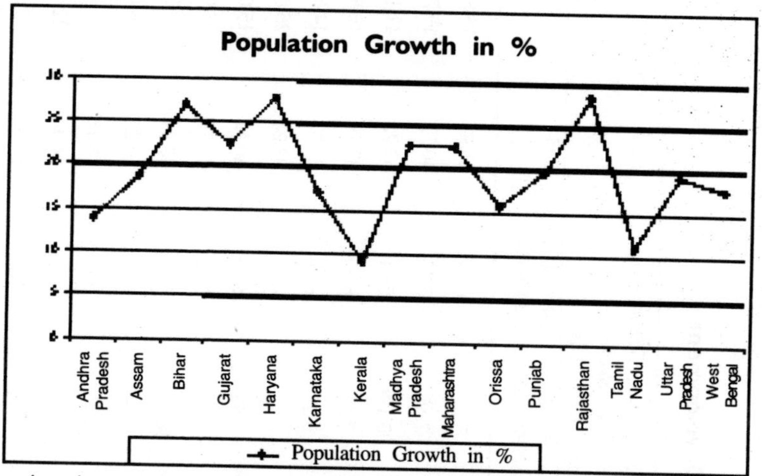

capita income of Maharashtra at Rs. 36,423 was 4.01 times larger than that of Bihar at Rs. 9,082). The gap between the average per-capita income (GSDP) of Bihar, Uttar Pradesh, Assam, Orissa, Madhya Pradesh and Rajasthan and Andhra Pradesh, Gujarat, Haryana, Kerala, Karnataka, Tamil Nadu, Maharashtra and Punjab (in 19993-94 prices) drastically increased from Rs. 1,862 in 1980-81 to Rs. 8,908 in 2004-05, both because the average GSDP of Bihar, Uttar Pradesh, Assam, Orissa, Madhya Pradesh and Rajasthan grew at a slower rate than that of Andhra Pradesh, Gujarat, Haryana, Kerala, Karnataka, Tamil Nadu, Maharashtra and Punjab and also because the average population of Andhra Pradesh, Gujarat, Haryana, Kerala, Karnataka, Tamil Nadu, Maharashtra and Punjab grew much faster (Figure 2).

The poverty ratio (2004-05) was 46.4 per cent in Orissa and 41.1 per cent in Bihar as against 8.4per cent in Punjab. The infant mortality rate (IMR) (2005) was 14 in Kerala but 76 in Madhya Pradesh. The male (female) life expectancy (2001-06) was only 59 yrs (58 yrs) in Madhya Pradesh as against 71.7 (75) in Kerala. Bihar had the lowest literacy rate (2001) of 47 per cent and female literacy rate of 33.1 per cent, while Kerala had the highest literacy rate of 90.9 per cent and female literacy of 87.7 per cent. The Human Development Index (2001) of Bihar was only 0.37 and of Kerala was 0.64. (Table 2).

TABLE 2

Syate-wise Indices of Economic Development

States	Per-capita GSDP (Rs.) in 1993-94 Prices			Average Annual GSDP (1993-94 Prices) Growth Rate (%)#			Poverty Ratio (%)#	
	1980-81	1995-96	2004-05	1981-82 to 1989-90	1990-91 to 1999-2000	2000-01 to 2004-05	1983	2004-05*
Andhra Pradesh	5142(10)	9015(8)	13805(8)	6.66	5.27	6.54	28.91	15.80
Assam	5117(11)	6530(12)	7807(13)	4.18	2.68	5.23	40.77	19.70
Bihar	3711(15)	4107(15)	5430(15)	4.42	3.19	5.01	62.22	41.13
Gujarat	7361(4)	14871(1)	19899(2)	6.37	7.02	6.85	32.79	16.80
Haryana	8636(2)	13186(4)	19323(3)	6.32	5.27	6.86	21.37	14.00
Karnataka	5476(8)	9429(7)	15431(6)	5.65	6.93	6.12	38.24	25.00
Kerala	6092(5)	9803(6)	15401(7)	3.34	5.92	6.88	40.42	15.00
Madhya Pradesh	5522(7)	7685(11)	9457(11)	4.30	5.75	3.32	49.78	38.96
Maharashtra	7963(3)	13556(3)	20397(1)	6.29	6.79	5.13	43.44	30.70
Orissa	4469(14)	6022(14)	8255(12)	5.36	3.09	6.01	65.28	46.40
Punjab	9446(1)	14664(2)	19002(4)	5.74	4.45	3.95	16.18	8.40
Rajasthan	4783(12)	8169(10)	10995(10)	7.23	6.69	5.39	34.46	22.10
Tamil Nadu	5861(6)	11361(5)	16035(5)	5.55	6.44	4.14	51.66	22.50

Uttar Pradesh	4615(13)	6120(13)	7380(14)	4.96	3.79	4.24	47.07	33.13
West Bengal	5410(9)	8254(9)	13403(9)	4.27	6.64	7.01	54.85	24.70

Notes:
1. Figures in parentheses indicate the relative rankings of states in terms of per-capita income.
2. # for each year, % change over previous year is computed and using them the average growth over the years is computed.
3. $ 2004-05 data based on URP consumption procedure.
4. * Bihar's (combined) data are the weighted average of Bihar and Jharkhand values, UP and MP are also the weighted averages

Source: CSO (website) and EPW Research Foundation for GSDP and GDP figures; Planning Commission (2003, 2007) for Poverty Ratios.

Thus, from the Table 3, we observe not only the widening disparity among states but also that the situations in most of the Group B states in terms of development indicators are really bad. About 38 per cent of poor people in India live in the two states of Bihar and Uttar Pradesh alone.

TABLE 3

Syate-wise Indices of Social Development

State	*IMR (2005)*	*% of Child Under-nourish-ment (2002-04)*	*Life Expectancy (2001-06) Male*	*Female*	*HDI (2001)*	*Literacy (2001) Person*	*Female*
Andhra Pradesh	57	42.3	62.8	65.0	0.416	60.5	50.4
Assam	68	32.2	59.0	61.0	0.386	63.3	54.6
Bihar	61	53.9	65.7	64.8	0.367	39.0	27.6
Gujarat	54	46	63.1	64.1	0.479	69.1	57.8
Haryana	60	35.6	64.6	69.3	0.509	67.9	55.7
Karnataka	50	44.8	62.4	66.4	0.478	66.6	56.9
Kerala	14	35.8	71.7	75.0	0.638	90.9	87.7
Madhya Pradesh	76	53.7	59.2	58.0	0.394	52.7	41.7
Maharashtra	36	47.7	66.8	69.8	0.523	76.9	67.0
Orissa	75	42.8	60.1	59.7	0.404	63.1	50.5
Punjab	44	40	69.8	72.0	0.537	69.7	63.4
Rajasthan	68	58.1	62.2	62.8	0.424	60.4	43.9
Tamil Nadu	37	38.3	67.0	69.8	0.531	73.5	64.4
Uttar Pradesh	73	55.1	63.5	64.1	0.388	46.3	34.9
West Bengal	38	44.9	66.1	69.3	0.472	68.6	59.6

Source: Planning Commission (2002) for HDI; 'Reproductive and Child Health Report' (2002-04); *Economic Survey*, (2006-07).

SECTION II

STUDIES ON REGIONAL DISPARITIES IN INDIA

A number of studies have looked at the trends in regional disparities among the states in India. Conventionally, scholars working on SDP data have restricted their analysis to only major Indian states in view of data limitations associated with smaller states and union territories in India. Breaking from this trend, Shetty (2003) calculates the regional disparity based on all states and union territories of India and finds that the disparity is much higher compared to that which is based on major states only.

Kumar, Prahlad and Ashutosh Shukla (1997) in their study concluded a direct relationship between the expenditure on education by states and their respective literacy rates. They had highlighted the fact that Kerala with the highest literacy rate spent more than one-fourth of its revenue expenditure on education. Further, they stated that expenditure on education since is primarily done by states; per-capita expenditure on education has wide inter-state disparity. The states with less educational attainment and progress are suffering from the lack of resources.

Ahluwalia (2000), used population-weighted Ginni Coefficient to show that inequality in real per-capita gross state domestic product (GSDP) has tended to rise particularly in the 19990s. The estimated Ginni coefficient from both Ahluwalia and Shetty show that during the 1980s, regional disparity remained stable till about 1986-87, and started increasing slowly thereafter, but not as fast as in the 1990s.

Bhattacharya and Sakthivel (2004) reveal that disparities in per-capita GSDP has accentuated in the 1990s as compared to 1980s. The coefficient of variation of per-capita GSDP was 0.22 per cent per annum in 1980s, doubled to 0.43 per cent per annum during the 19990s.

Das Gupta *et al.* (2000) have studied the period from 1970 to 1995 and concluded that it is primarily the agricultural sector, and to a certain extent the manufacturing sector that had important roles to play in the regional divergence over this period, while the tertiary sector had a stabilizing influence, with regional inequality decreasing in this sector.

Sabyasachi, Kar and Sakthivel (2007) in their study attempt to fill the lacuna of dearth of contributions that use the 'new economic geography' framework to analyze regional disparity in India, and study the impact of the pro-market reforms adopted in the early 1990s, on regional inequality during this period. Further, it tries to analyze the effect of reforms on the trend in regional inequality in India.

Ramaswamy, K.V. (2007) in his study investigated the growth and structure of employment in fourteen major states of India during 1983 and 2004-05. Ramaswamy estimated the Ginni coefficient for two years, 1993-94 and 2004-05, using per-capita GSDP data. It is found that to have risen from 0.28 in 1993-94 to 0.36 in 2004-05.

A deep insight on the above studies makes it clear that though education as a parameter of social development indices has found a place in these studies, yet there is no specific study on regional disparity in education in India. Thus, there is a dearth of contribution in the field of education; the present study therefore, is an attempt to fill this lacuna.

SECTION III

DISPARITIES IN EDUCATIONAL ATTAINMENT

At the time of Independence India inherited a system of education which was not only quantitatively small but also characterized by the persistence of large intra- and inter-regional as well as structural imbalances. Only 14 per cent of the population was literate and only one child out of three had been enrolled in primary school. The low levels of participation and literacy were aggravated by acute regional and gender disparities.

The reform and restructuring of educational system was recognized as an important area of State intervention. The need for a literate population and universal education for all children in the age group of 6-14 years was recognized as a crucial input for nation-building and was given due consideration in the constitution as well as in the successive five year plans. This has resulted in a manifold increase of spatial spread, infrastructural facilities, increased coverage of various social groups, but the goal of providing education to all continues to be elusive. The experience of the last five decades of planning has shown that the educational development in India is neither homogeneous in regional spread nor neutral to social formations. It has a strong bias in favour of economically developed areas with strong infrastructural support and against backward regions of the country. Inspite of planned efforts spread over decades, regional disparities continues to be glaring.

Further, the regional disparity in educational development has not attracted adequate attention of planners. The vast body of literature dealing with problems of disparities, largely focuses on group disparities and very little has been done in the context of regional framework. The country displays vast disparities in the domain of education. Starting from the Ernakulam district of Kerala where 100 per cent literacy has been attained, the country has areas with literacy rate of about 2 per cent. This contrast is more glaring when seen in the context of groups in a regional context. It is not very difficult to find areas where the rural female literacy for SC and ST is less than 1 per cent. (NIEPA). The implications are obvious. Education will have to come to terms with realities at the grass-root level as they unfold themselves over space.

According to a Report of the Central Advisory Board on Education (CABE) released recently, 15 states and union territories (out of 35) have reported an enrolment rate lower than the national average. The report has pointed to glaring regional disparities in enrolment." The enrolment ratio in higher education is as high as 29 per cent in Chandigarh—a union territory—but less than five per cent in states like Jammu & Kashmirand Nagaland," the report said. Among the States with low enrolment ratios are Orissa (8.71%), Uttar Pradesh (7.03%), Madhya Pradesh (7.77%) and West Bengal (8.21%).

A Report released by the National Council for Applied Economic Research (NCAER) confirms the regional disparities in both higher and primary education. It shows how southern states have outperformed northern and eastern regions in respect of economic growth and literacy. In order to remove disparities in higher education, the central government earlier identified 370 districts—as educationally backward—having enrolment ratios lower than the national average of 9 per cent.

SECTION IV

DISPARITIES IN EDUCATIONAL ATTAINMENT AT SECONDARY LEVEL

The recent NSS survey on education and training points out that in India, among the persons of the age of 15 years and above, only 2 per cent had technical degrees or diplomas or certificates. The constraint of skilled labour (human capital) is likely to be the binding constraint for growth and employment in many states in India. It is well argued that secondary education is crucial for economic growth. A workforce with secondary school attainment will turn out to be the best bet for a job in modern industries like telecommunication, which emphasizes training and skill acquisition on the job.

TABLE 4

Gross Enrolment Ratios, 2003-04

States	*Upper Primary (11-14 years)*	*Secondary (14-18 years)*
Andhra Pradesh	64.9	44.6
Assam		
Bihar	25.3	16.9
Gujarat	70.4	40.0
Haryana	65.5	45.5
Karnataka	76.2	41.7
Kerala	93.6	48.0
Madhya Pradesh	63.3	34.9
Maharashtra	87.6	53.9
Orissa	54.0	32.7
Punjab	60.1	39.0
Rajasthan	61.5	32.6
Tamil Nadu	100.4	56.9
Uttar Pradesh	48.6	37.9
West Bengal	64.3	32.6
All-India	62.4	38.9

Source: Selected Educational Statistics, 2003-04 and Rani (2007, Table A2).

Table 4 gives data on gross enrolment ratios for upper primary and secondary schooling in India for the selected states (except Assam) for the year 2003-04. The relatively better development of education in the states of Kerala, Tamil Nadu, Haryana and Andhra Pradesh, emerges clearly.

Ramaswamy, K.V. (2007) addressed to the question that do states with better initial gross enrolment ratios (GER) in secondary education have better labour productivity growth. Ramaswamy found a positive relationship observed and concluded that labour productivity is the key proximate determinant of output and employment. Incidentally, these are all relatively well endowed states with an educated workforce. Thus, it is quite clear that there is a widespread disparity with regard to educational attainment. States with better supply of secondary school educated workers are likely to attract more investment and jobs coming in their way.

FIGURE 3

Gross Enrolment Ratios for Upper Primary and Secondary Level, 2003-04

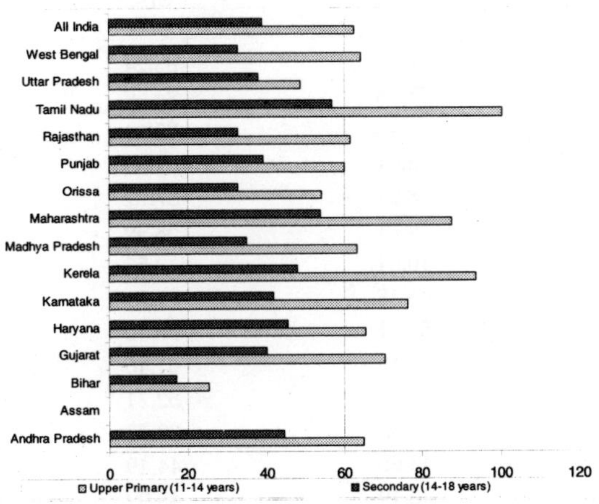

There is an urgent need that the states with low GER at secondary level must make sincere efforts to make it at par with the national average of 51.65 for classes IX-X (14-16 years) and 27.82 for classes XI-XII (16-18 years).

States with better supply of secondary school educated workers are likely to get more investment and jobs coming in their way. It is now well established that a major chunk of investment, domestic and foreign direct investment, has gone into states like, Maharashtra, Gujarat, Karnataka, Andhra Pradesh and Tamil Nadu (Bagchi and Kurian, 2005).

Table 5 clearly shows that the dropout rates of all categories of students is significantly less in Kerala, which has a role model dropout rates of 10.64 for boys and 3.52 for girls, aggregating to 7.15 in total, as against this the national average of dropout rates for boys is 60.41, for girls is 63.88 and a total of 61.92, while Bihar has the poorest performance with regard to dropout rates as it is 81.46 for boys, 85.64 for girls and averaging to 83.06 in total, it is followed by West Bengal and Rajasthan.

TABLE 5

Dropout Rates of All Categories of Students in Classes I-Xth

States	*Boys*	*Girls*	*Total*
Andhra Pradesh	62.30	65.24	63.69
Assam	75.18	74.69	74.96
Bihar	81.46	85.64	83.06
Gujarat	58.01	61.05	59.29
Haryana	28.01	37.72	32.48
Karnataka	59.71	58.99	59.38
Kerala	10.64	3.52	7.15
Madhya Pradesh	60.48	70.31	64.70
Maharashtra	52.11	56.40	54.16
Orissa	66.40	61.46	64.42
Punjab	57.27	52.71	55.19
Rajasthan	69.33	80.72	73.87
Tamil Nadu	43.68	44.49	44.06
Uttar Pradesh	40.49	48.99	43.77
West Bengal	75.92	80.34	78.03
All-India	60.41	63.88	61.92

Source: Selected Educational Statistics, 2004-05.

FIGURE 4

Dropout Rates of All Categories of Students in Classes I-Xth

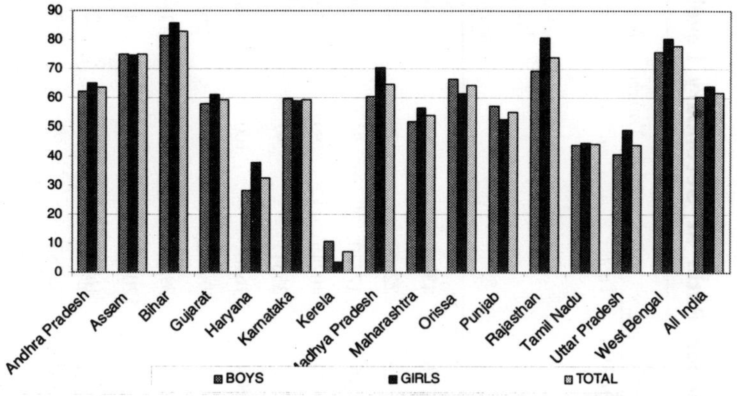

The Table 6 clearly shows that on one hand there are states like West Bengal which has a pupil-teacher ratio of 50 as against national average of 33, followed by Karnataka with 47, Uttar Pradesh with 45, Maharashtra with 42 and Gujarat with 35, while on the other hand there are states like Kerala

FIGURE 5

Pupil-Teacher Ratio at Secondary Level

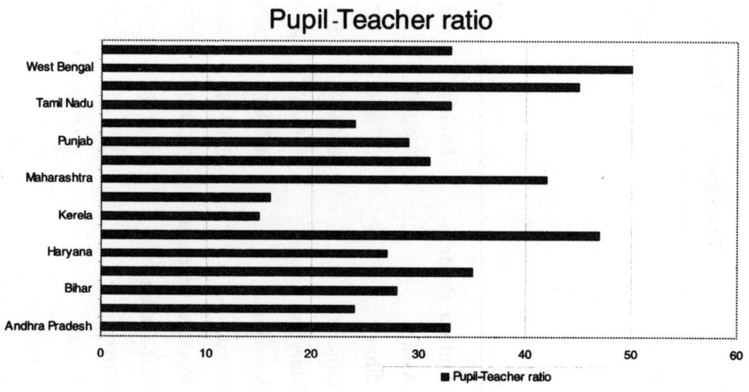

TABLE 6

Number of Teachers, Enrolment and Pupil-Teacher Ratio at Secondary Level

States	Enrolment			Number of Teachers			% of Trained Teachers	No. of female Teachers per 100 male teachers	Pupil-Teacher ratio
	Boys	Girls	Total	Male	Female	Total			
Andhra Pradesh	861154	604156	1465310	32224	11736	43960	95	36	33
Assam	358219	197716	556035	16384	6525	22909	29	40	24
Bihar	377072	127139	504211	15513	2207	17720	96	14	28
Gujarat	834107	576162	1410269	28821	11424	40245	99	40	35
Haryana	549687	419682	969329	19006	16535	35541	97	87	27
Karnataka	417062	365603	782665	12658	3824	16482	100	30	47
Kerala	290144	282657	572801	9728	28907	38635	99	297	15
Madhya Pradesh	612020	317297	929317	27435	32275	59510	79	118	16
Maharashtra	2774233	2258826	5033059	84935	35492	120427	99	42	42
Orissa	359140	159140	159340	12991	3710	16701	100	29	31
Punjab	625092	514440	1139532	16573	22209	38782	99	134	29
Rajasthan	943924	459433	1403357	39987	17714	57701	94	44	24
Tamil Nadu	2525087	2230728	4755815	56440	85922	142362	100	152	33

Uttar Pradesh	3612424	2744749	6357173	119176	20730	139906	97	17	45
West Bengal	1816372	1275061	3091433	43855	17940	61795	85	41	50
All-India	19048791	14322380	33371171	614269	385843	1000112	90	63	33

Source: Selected Educational Statistic,s 2004-05.

with a pupil-teacher ratio of 15, followed by Madhya Pradesh with 16, Rajasthan with 24 and Assam with 24.

Further, Orissa, Karnataka, Tamil Nadu have 100 per cent trained teachers and Kerala has 99 per cent of trained teachers, while Assam has only 29 per cent of trained teachers. In Kerala out of 38635 teachers, about 75 per cent are female, while in Uttar Pradesh out of 1339906 teachers only about 15 per cent are female, West Bengal 29 per cent, Orissa 22 per cent, while Bihar has only 12 per cent out of 17720 teachers as female.

The number of female teachers per 100 male teachers is 297 in Kerala, followed by Tamil Nadu with 152 and Punjab 134, while Bihar has only 14, followed by Uttar Pradesh which has 17 female teachers per 100 male teachers.

Literates with general education level secondary and above including diploma/certificate courses have been considered to be educated, as per the definition of NSS Report No. 517, p. 25. Following this definition, the numbers in table indicate large inter-state variation in educational attainment. Table 7 presents the inter-state differences in educational attainment of persons in different states in India in 2004-05.

Bihar, Orissa, Uttar Pradesh, Rajasthan and Madhya Pradesh suffer from a serious shortage of educated persons. In these states, only 17 per cent are found to be educated and more seriously only 12 per cent are found to have secondary education or higher secondary education as against the all-India average of 24 per cent and 16, respectively.

Expectedly, Karnataka, Tamil Nadu, Gujarat and Maharashtra emerge as educated states. The educational performance of Kerala is well known. In brief, high income states also have better potential supply of educated persons. This will prove to be a great source of comparative advantage for these states in the years to come.

Table 8 as well as Figure 6 presents the secondary and higher education attainment ratios for various states in India in 1999-2000. Inter-State variations and also rural-urban differences are quite marked, While states like Orissa, Bihar, Madhya Pradesh and West Bengal have less than 15 per cent of their population having secondary and above education,

TABLE 7

Educational Differences by States, 2004-05 per 1000 Persons

States	*Not Literate*	*Literate and upto Primary*	*Middle*	*Secondary*	*Higher Secondary*	*Diploma/ Certificate*	*Graduate and above*
Andhra Pradesh	491	193	109	99	45	13	48
Bihar	516	198	118	92	40	2	33
Gujarat	318	229	189	124	63	16	61
Haryana	351	218	117	150	78	15	71
Karnataka	382	200	171	124	58	11	55
Kerala	94	268	305	154	63	58	58
Madhya Pradesh	456	252	115	61	55	8	54
Maharashtra	271	199	226	132	69	29	71
Orissa	412	252	177	75	35	5	43
Punjab	315	213	126	175	87	19	65
Rajasthan	524	192	125	62	47	5	44
Tamil Nadu	293	278	160	117	68	18	66
Uttar Pradesh	478	178	144	82	61	4	52
West Bengal	325	321	162	82	49	3	58
All-India	382	228	160	102	58	12	57

Source: NSS 61st Round Report No. 517, Table 3.8.1 (p. 66) on per 1,000 Distributions of Persons of 15 years and above by General Educational Level.

Punjab and Kerala have more than 25 per cent of the adult population being educated up to secondary and above level. Rural-urban differences seem to extremely sharp in several states.

The Eleventh Plan rightly recognizes that in the context of rapidly changing technology and the growth of the knowledge economy, 'a mere eight years of elementary education would be grossly inadequate for our young children'. Accordingly, Scheme for Universal Access and Quality

At the Secondary Stage (SUCCESS) was launched as a centrally sponsored scheme, the main objective of the scheme is to make secondary education of good quality "available,

TABLE 8

Percentage of Population with Secondary and above Education for 1990-2000

States	*Rural*	*Urban*	*Total*
Andhra Pradesh	7.1	26	15.2
Assam	9	32.1	16.7
Bihar	6.7	24.9	13.3
Gujarat	9.4	28.2	20.1
Haryana	12.8	27.6	21.3
Karnataka	9.4	33.2	18
Kerala	19.7	27.7	25.6
Madhya Pradesh	5	23.8	13.3
Maharashtra	10.5	29.2	24.2
Orissa	6.1	22.4	11.9
Punjab	14.6	30.9	29
Rajasthan	4.9	23.5	12.8
Tamil Nadu	11.1	28	17.5
Uttar Pradesh	7.8	22	15.3
West Bengal	6.3	27.9	14.4

Source: NSSO (2001).

FIGURE 6

Percentage of Population with Secondary and above Education for 1990-2000

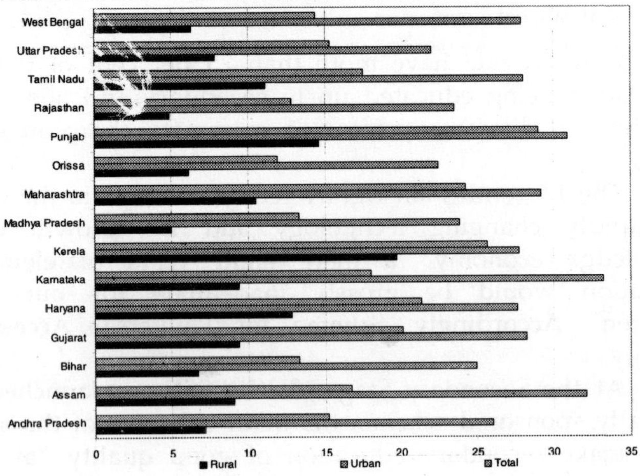

accessible and affordable" to all young students in the age group of 15-16 years, i.e., for classes IX-XIth, the scheme aims at universal access of secondary education to all students by 2015 and universal retention by 2020.

It also sets targets of a gross enrolment ratio of 65 per cent by 2011-12, and a reduction in gender disparity in all enrolment ratio by 5 per cent, improvement in pupil-teacher ratio to 25 : 1 and pass percentage rates in board exams at the end of grades X and XII to 75 per cent. (Annual Report, 2006-07, MHRD, GOI).

Besides, SUCCESS and other ongoing Programmes/ schemes, the current union budget has provided for a few important new programmes/schemes. They include establishment of 6,000 new high quality model schools- one in each block and new Jawahar Navodaya Vidyalayas in 20 districts that have large concentration of SCs/STs. The Programme of model schools by includes setting up of 3500 schools by the government (3000 as Kendriya Vidyalayas and 500 Navodaya Vidyalayas) and 2500 schools through public-private partnerships.

Thus, this is a welcome step and if special measures are adopted to check elitism and to promote equity and inclusive growth, it will reduce regional disparity in educational attainment to a considerable extent.

CONCLUSIONS AND SUGGESTIONS

A federal system involves explicit and explicit balancing of the interests of its constituents units can matter as well as the objective material gains from being part of the larger nation. India has faced these issues since independence, and central policies have always incorporated inter-regional to inter-state considerations. The evidence presented in this paper suggests that there are some indicators of increase in regional inequality, but they are not uniform.

The gap between the highest and the lowest per-capita income (in 1993-94 prices) among the fifteen states increased from 2.55 times to 3.76 times (in absolute figures, from Rs. 5,735 to Rs. 14,967) in this period, indicating a stark widening of income disparity among the states. As per the

NSSO, 2001 data Punjab has about 29.0 per cent population with secondary and above education, followed by Kerala with 25.6 per cent and Maharashtra with 24.2 per cent, on the other hand, Orissa had only 11.9 per cent population with secondary and above education, followed by Rajasthan with 12.8 per cent, Bihar and Madhya Pradesh with only 13.3 per cent population with secondary and above education. On one hand there are states like West Bengal which has a pupil-teacher ratio of 50 as against national average of 33, followed by Karnataka with 47, Uttar Pradesh with 45, Maharashtra with 42 and Gujarat with 35, while on the other hand there are states like Kerala with a pupil-teacher ratio of 15, followed by Madhya Pradesh with 16, Rajasthan with 24 and Assam with 24.

In Kerala out of 38635 teachers, about 75 per cent are female, while in Uttar Pradesh out of 1339906 teachers only about 15 per cent are female, West Bengal 29 per cent, Orissa 22 per cent, while Bihar has only 12 per cent out of 17720 teachers as female. The number of female teachers per 100 male teachers is 297 in Kerala, followed by Tamil Nadu with 152 and Punjab 134, while Bihar has only 14, followed by Uttar Pradesh which has 17 female teachers per 100 male teachers.

The dropout rates of all categories of students is significantly less in Kerala, which has a role model dropout rates of 10.64 for boys and 3.52 for girls, aggregating to 7.15 in total, as against this the national average of dropout rates for boys is 60.41, for girls is 63.88 and a total of 61.92, while Bihar has the poorest performance with regard to dropout rates as it is 81.46 for boys, 85.64 for girls and averaging to 83.06 in total, it is followed by West Bengal and Rajasthan.

Thus, a vast disparity lies in educational attainment among states. However, the policies of state government can make a difference, governments in states such as Bihar, Uttar Pradesh, Madhya Pradesh and Rajasthan can make major strides by improving educational attainments.

Though, educational attainments differs widely across states, yet the budget allocation to education sector in union budget 2008-09 marks, in nominal prices, a 35 per cent increase over the previous year's revised estimates of budgeted expenditure. The allocation of resources to create new model schools at the secondary level in selected districts of these states can bridge the gap of educational attainment in these states. Thus, despite of the fact that regional disparity in education exists, it is now clearly reflected that the sincere efforts of both central and state governments can reduce it to a greater extent along with an active participation of people. A holistic convergent framework for implementation of various schemes in secondary education is required to make quality secondary education available, accessible and affordable to all young students. We should be optimistic about achieving the target of universal access of secondary level education to all students by 2015 and universal retention by 2020 as stated in the Scheme for Universal Access and Quality at the Secondary Stage (SUCCESS).

REFERNCES

Aggarwal, Yash (1983), "Regional Aspects of Literacy among Scheduled Caste and Non-Scheduled Population in India: A District-wise Analysis", NIEPA, New Delhi.

Aggarwal, Yash (2000), "DPEP 2000: An Assessment of Trends in Access and Retention District-wise Analysis", NIEPA, New Delhi.

Ahluwalia, M. S. (2000): "Economic Performance of States in Post-Reforms Period", Economic and Political Weekly, May, Sameeksha Trust Publication.

Bagchi, Amresh and John Kurian (2005), "Regional Inequalities in India: Pre and Post-Reform Trends and Challenges for Policy", in John Mooji (Ed.), 'The Policies of Economic Reforms in India', Sage Publications, New Delhi.

Bhattacharya, B.B. and S. Sakthivel (2003), "Regional Disparities in Growth: A Comparison of Pre and Post-Reform Period", Discussion Paper No. 73/ 2003, Institute of Economic Growth, New Delhi.

Bhattacharya, B.B. and S. Sakthivel (2004), "Economic Reforms and Jobless Growth in India", Working Paper Series No. E/245, Institute of Economic Growth, New Delhi.

Bhattacharya, B.B. and S. Sakthivel (2004), "Regional Growth and Disparity in India: A Comparison of Pre- and Post-Reform Decades", *Economic and Political Weekly*, Vol. XXXIX, No. 10, March 6, pp. 1071-77, Sameeksha Trust Publication.

Carron, G. and Chau Ta Ngoc (Ed.) (1980), "Regional Disparities in Educational Development: A Controversial Issue", IIEP, Paris.

Carron, G. and Chau Ta Ngoc (Ed.) (1980), "Regional Disparities in Educational Development: Diagnosis and Policies for Reduction", IIEP, Paris.

Chanana, Karuna (2000),"Treading the Hallowed Hall: Women in Higher Education in India", *Economic and Political Weekly*, Vol. XXXV, No 12, March, 18-24, pp. 1012-22, Sameeksha Trust Publication.

Chelliah, Raja J. and K.R. Shanmugam (2007), "Strategy for Poverty Reduction and Narrowing Regional Disparities", *Economic and Political Weekly*, Vol. XLII No 34, August 25-31, pp. 3475-81, Sameeksha Trust Publication.

Das Gupta, D. *et al.* (2000), "Growth and Inter-State Disparities in India", *Economic and Political Weekly*, Vol. XXXV, No 27, pp. 2413-22, Sameeksha Trust Publication.

Dreze', J. and Amartya Sen (Eds.) (1996), "Indian Development: Selected Regional Perspectives", Claredon Press, Oxford.

http:/www.esocialsciences.com

Kar, Sabyasachi and S Sakthivel (2007), " Reforms and regional Inequality in India", *Economic and Political Weekly*, Vol. XLII, No. 47, November 24-30, pp. 1069-73, Sameeksha Trust Publication.

Kumar Prahlad and Nisha, (2007): "तकनीकी शिक्षा एवं विकास की चुनौतियां", परिप्रेक्ष्य, नीपा अंक, 14 अप्रैळ ।

Kumar, Prahlad and Ashutosh Shukla (1997), ''माधयमिक शिक्षा में वित्त की समस्या: विश्लेषण एवं सुझाव दसवीं पंचवर्षीय योजना के संदर्भ में'' परिप्रेक्ष्य, नीपा अंक 1-2, अप्रैल-अगस्त.

Lewin, K and F. Caillods (2001), "Financing Secondary Education in Developing Countries: Strategies for Sustainable Growth", UNESCO, IIEP, Paris.

National Sample Survey Organization (2006), "Employment and Unemployment Situation in India ", Jan.-June 2004, NSS 61st Round, Report No. 515, Parts I and II, GOI.

National Sample Survey Organization (2006), "Status of Education and Vocational Training in India, 2004-05, NSS 61st Round, Report No. 517, GOI.

Office of the Registrar General and Census Commissioner, India (2006), "Census of India 2001", GOI.

Planning Commission (2002), "National Human Development Report", GOI.

Ramaswamy, K.V. (2007), "Regional Dimension of Growth and Employment", *Economic and Political Weekly*, Vol. XLII, No. 49, December 8-14, pp. 47-56, Sameeksha Trust Publication.

Rani, Geetha (2007), "Secondary Education in India: Determinants of Development and Performance", Working Paper, NIEPA, New Delhi.

Rao, Hanumantha, C.H. (2006), "Growing Regional Disparities in Development in India: Post-Reform Experience and Challenges Ahead", The *Indian Economic Journal*, Vol. 54, No. 1, April-June, *Indian Economic Journal*, Academic Foundation, New Delhi.

Raza, Moonis and Yash Aggarwal (1983), "Inequalities in the Level of Literacy: The Regional Dimension", NIEPA Occasional Paper No 4, NIEPA, New Delhi.

Shetty, S.L (2003), "Growth of SDP and Structural Change in State Economics: Inter-State Comparisons", *Economic and Political Weekly*, Dec., Sameeksha Trust Publication.

Singh, Nirvikar, Laveesh Bhandari, Aoyu Chen and Aarti Khare(2003), "Regional Inequality in India: A Fresh Look", *Economic and Political*

Weekly, Vol. XXXVIII, No. 11, March 15-21, pp. 1069-73, Sameeksha Trust Publication.

Srivastava, Ravi (1994), "Planning and Regional Disparities in India", in Terence Byres (Ed), 'The State and Development Planning in India', Oxford University Press, New Delhi.

Tripathi, Mahendra Prahlad Kumar (2006): "उत्तर प्रदेण में प्राथमिक णिक्षा का सार्वभौमीकरणण परिप्रेक्ष्य, नीपा अंक 13, अगस्त

40

Inter-State Disparities in Technical Education in India: Challenges for 2030

NISHA AND PRAHLAD KUMAR

India has the potential to be a technology leader. The Indian economy has been growing at the rate of 9 per cent per year. The Indian industry has also become globally competitive in several sectors and can increase its global market share. A critical factor in this will be the success of the technical education system in India. (Muley, 2007) Technical Education is one of the most crucial components of human resource development having potential for adding value to products and services thereby improving the quality of life of people.

Since technical education determines the development and socio-economic condition of a nation, there is a greater need for high quality technical education to produce technically skilled manpower in India. Technical education is imparted at three different levels in India:

— Industrial Training Institute (ITI), which conduct trade courses for skilled workers.

- Polytechnic Institutes, which conduct diplomas to produce middle level technicians.
- Engineering colleges, which conduct undergraduate and post-graduate degree courses in engineering and technology.

There are engineering institutes and colleges that are supported by the state and central governments, and also a la rge number of private engineering colleges and institutes that provide technical education in India. Since the early eighties, due to rapid industrialization and economic growth, engineering and technical education in India have been developing faster, and India has the second largest number of engineering students in the world. (Palit, 1998)

GROWTH OF ENGINEERING INSTITUTIONS

As a consequence of continuous efforts, phenomenal growth has occurred in the field of Technical Education in the country since 1947. This has been possible through planning and setting the objectives, implementation and conducting reviews and corrections whenever and wherever needed. The formal educational opportunities have increased tremendously and this can be gauged from the fact that there has been a ten-fold increase in the number of engineering colleges and almost a twenty-fold increase in the diploma polytechnic institutions since independence. In 1947, there were 44 degree-level institutions with a student intake of 2, 500, this became 142 by 1975-76 showing about three-fold increase between 1947 to 1975-76, which increased to 547 institutions with a student intake of 130,947 in 1997.

Table 1 shows the rapid growth of engineering institutions in India. It is seen that there have been a phenomenal increase in the number of engineering institutions in the period 1955-56 to 1960-61. The percentage increase is very low during 1980s. Due to initiatives taken during successive plan periods and particularly because of large-scale private sector participation, in recent years, the number of All-India Council of Technical Education (AICTE) approved technical and management institutions have risen to 4,791 in 2001-02 with an annual intake of 6.7 million students. (Tenth Five Year Plan, 2002-07) At the end of 2006, there were 1,559 engineering colleges in the country. Table 2 shows ten fold increases during 26 years, from 1980-2006. If we look at figures from 1990, than number of institutes increased about five times. (Krishna, 2008). The intake capacity of the technical education system has increased manifolds over the years. As on 31st July 2007, the total intake capacity in AICTE approved institutions is to the tune of 6,27,082 students in the 1617 undergraduate degree engineering institutions.

The Indian technical education system during the post-Independence period is, therefore, characterized by a massive growth in the number of institutions and student enrolment, vast coverage of subject areas and specialization, establishment of institutions of national importance, establishment of regional-level institutions of excellence, emergence of unaided private institutions and the emergence of non-formal sector in technical education besides establishment of national and State-level distance learning programmes.

TABLE 1

Growth of Institutions in Engineering in Post-Independence Era (1950-73)

Year	*Numbers*	*Index No. (1950-51=100)*	*Percentage Increase*
1950-51	49	100	
1955-56	65	132.6	32.6
1960-61	102	208.1	56.9
1965-66	133	271.4	30.4
1970-71	138	281.6	3.7
1975-76	142	289.8	2.9

Source: Various Five Year Plans, Government of India.

TABLE 2

Growth of Institutions in Engineering in Post-Independence Era (1980-2004)

Year	*Numbers*	*Index No. (1950-51=100)*	*Percentage Increase*
1980	158	322.4	
1990	337	687.7	113.3
1995	375	765.3	11.3
1997	471	961.2	25.6
1998	558	1138.8	18.5
1999	662	1351.0	18.6
2000	776	1583.7	17.2
2001	838	1710.2	8.0
2002	1,057	2157.1	26.1
2003	1,208	2465.3	14.3
2004	1,346	2746.9	11.4
2005	1495		
2006	1559		

Source: (i) Technical Education in Independence India, 1947-97.
(ii) AICTE Annual Reports.

FIGURE I

Growth of Institutions in Engineering in Post-Independence Era (1947-2006)

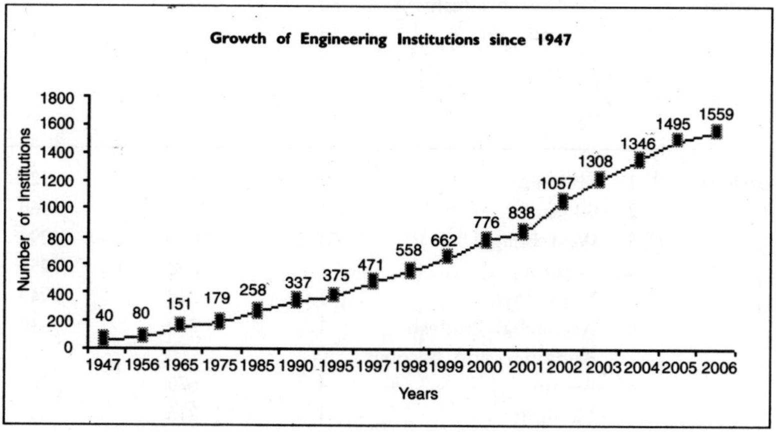

INTER-STATE DISTRIBUTION OF ENGINEERING INSTITUTIONS AND ENGINEERING MANPOWER

When we see the region-wise growth of technical education, some of the industrially developed states, such as Maharashtra, Karnataka, Tamil Nadu and Andhra Pradesh have experienced phenomenal growth both in number of students and engineering and technical institutions. In 2001-02, 69 new colleges in the Tamil Nadu, 26 in Karnataka, 58 in Andhra Pradesh and 13 in Maharashtra have come up (113th Report, 2001). If the number of institutions goes on increasing at this rate there numbers will reach approximately about 37 thousand by the year 2030

Table 3 shows the sanctioned intake break-up for 2006-07 as per AICTE. This does not include the IITs. If these are included the total number of sanctioned seats for UG engineering education in India is 5,54,000. (Muley, 2007)

TABLE 3

Number of Technical Institutions and Intake Approved for 2006-07 (As on Sept. 2006)

Region		*State/Union Territory*	*No. of Institutions*	*Sanctioned Intake*	*Average Intake per Institute*
Central	1.	Madhya Pradesh	84	30060	358
	2.	Chhattisgarh	15	5130	342
	3.	Gujarat	43	14086	328
		Total			
Eastern	1.	Mizoram	1	120	120
	2.	Sikkim	1	465	465
	3.	West Bengal	54	15671	290
	4.	Tripura	1	250	250
	5.	Meghalaya	1	240	240
	6.	Arunachal Pradesh	1	210	210
	7.	Andaman and Nicobar	0	0	0
	8.	Assam	4	670	168
	9.	Manipur	1	115	115

	10.	Nagaland	0	0	0
	11.	Orissa	48	15033	313
	12.	Jharkhand	9	3198	355
		Total			
North	1.	Bihar	6	1690	282
	2.	Uttar Pradesh	110	40418	367
	3.	Uttaranchal	13	3905	300
		Total			
North-West	1.	Chandigarh	5	788	158
	2.	Haryana	45	16325	363
	3.	Himachal Pradesh	6	1282	214
	4.	Jammu & Kashmir	6	1401	234
	5.	New Delhi	16	6359	397
	6.	Punjab	47	16961	361
	7.	Rajasthan	47	16051	342
		Total			
South	1.	Andhra Pradesh	280	107575	384
	2.	Pondicherry	5	2295	459
	3.	Tamil Nadu	268	105318	393
		Total			
South-West	1.	Karnataka	128	56542	442
	2.	Kerala	93	29165	314
		Total			
West	1.	Maharashtra	171	58989	345
	2.	Goa	3	794	265
	3.	Daman and D, Dadar, N.H.	0	0	0
		Total			
		Grand Total	1511	550986	365

Source: AICTE, Handbook for Approval Process.

Higher concentration of technical institutions in southern states viz. Andhra Pradesh, Tamil Nadu, Karnataka and Maharashtra giving rise to sub-standard technical institutions. On the other hand, it has led to lopsided development of technical education in the country. For proper growth of technical education, focus should be on proper planning and coordinated development. Concentration in certain pockets has already given rise to regional imbalance. Therefore, focus should be on the country as a whole. There has been phenomenal increase in the number of engineering colleges in southern states. AICTE should make all conceivable efforts for encouraging both Government and private initiatives in setting up technical institutions in N-E region.

Table 4 shows the sanctioned intake and the number of engineering institutions during 1996-2006. The maximum number of engineering institutions and the sanctioned intake is in the South. It is clear that there is a disproportionate growth in engineering colleges and output in a few states (Tamil Nadu, Karnataka).

Engineering is a preferred career choice for a large number of students at the 10 + 2 level in India. Many of the reputed engineering colleges (IITs and NITs) are highly selective in their admission process with the number of available seats being only 1-2 per cent of the number applying. A large number of private engineering colleges have been set-up. Upto 2003, there are 1,208 engineering colleges, of which 986 are in the private sector (U.R. Rao Committee Report, 2001).

In the state of Tamil Nadu, during the period 1997-98 to 2001-02, Government Engineering Colleges remained same (only 7), the number of Self-Financing institutions has gone up from 76 to 212. In Karnataka, during the same period, the number of Government Engineering Colleges remained only 13 and Self-Financing institutions went up from 50 to 90. In the state of Andhra Pradesh, during this period whereas there is no increase in the number of Government Engineering Colleges (i.e. 9), Self-Financing institutions went up from 48 to 153, and in Maharashtra, Government Engineering Colleges remained only 10 whereas Self-Financing institutions increased from 102 to 141. (113th Report, 2001)

TABLE 4

Region-wise Distribution of Sanctioned Intake and Number of Engineering Institutions

Region	1996		1998	2003		2004		2005		2006	
	NOI	Intake	Intake	NOI	Intake	NOI	Intake	NOI	Intake	NOI	Intake
Central	31	6565	8315	82	25914	112	37195	115	39434	147	49238
Eastern	24	4547	3862	99	24019	114	34016	110	33343	121	36437
North	37	5684	8597	99	26356	106	32298	107	34748	140	43613
North-West	45	7627	11294	119	32042	153	50645	155	51295	169	58304
South	112	28195	40884	471	145372	496	165757	502	178637	523	196013
South-West	68	23964	28869	184	58243	207	70788	206	72063	221	77972
West	99	24869	33074	154	47775	158	48990	160	49867	175	55441
Total	416	101451	134895	1208	359721	1346	439689	1355	459407	1496	517018

Source: AICTE Reports.

FIGURE 2

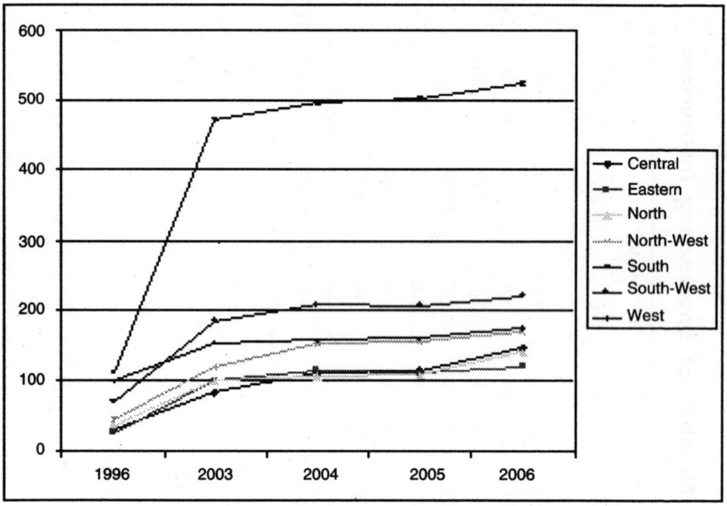

During the same period, in Uttar Pradesh the number of Government Engineering Colleges remained 12 and the number of Self-Financing institutions has gone up from 25 to 62. (Technical Education in Uttar Pradesh Handbook, 2001). In the year 2005, number of private institutions affiliated to UP Technical University is 210. (www.uptu.ac.in) With the advent of these self-financing colleges, availability of resources for improvement and development has become a more difficult proposition. Though there is a mechanism for accreditation (National Board of Accreditation) and an umbrella agency, the All-India Council of Technical Education (AICTE) set-up to monitor and control engineering education, the quality of engineering education in many institutions is suspect. (Banerjee and Muley, 2007)

UNEMPLOYMENT AMONG TECHNICAL MANPOWER

The National Technical Manpower Information System (NTMIS) provides information on the activity status of technical manpower through its graduate-follow-up surveys. A remarkable feature, which emerges from the data, is the decreasing unemployment among the technical degree and diploma-holders during the reform period across the states.

TABLE 5

Unemployment among Technical Degree Holders in Selected States

State	*1994 (%)*	*1998 (%)*
Gujarat	14.73	10.74
Karnataka	16.22	19.75
Kerala	20.80	12.13
Punjab	24.59	24.05
Assam	26.35	26.44
Tamil Nadu	32.00	24.58
West Bengal	5.56	4.91
Himachal Pradesh	18.75	11.45

Source: NTMIS, Annual Technical Manpower Reviews (Various Issues), I.A.M.R, New Delhi.

(NTMIS Bulletin, 1999) It decreased by about 8 percentage points in Kerala and Tamil Nadu but surprisingly it increased by about 3 percentage points in Karnataka during 1994-98.

In Punjab and Assam unemployment rate is almost at the same level during this period. It was found to be lowest in West Bengal but highest in Assam, followed by Tamil Nadu and Punjab. (Rajendra P. Mamgain, Vandana Parashar, 2000)

Realizing the potential of this vital sector of education, the National Policy of Education (NPE) 1986 and Programme of Action (POA) 1986 emphasized the need of reorganizing and revamping the technical education system to meet effectively the challenges posed by the changing socio-economic scenario. The All-India Council for Technical Education (AICTE) has been vested with Statutory powers through an Act of Parliament (Act 52 of 1987) with a view to plan for coordinated development of technical education system throughout the country, to promote qualitative improvement of such education in relation to planned quantitative growth and to regulate and maintain norms and standards in the technical education system and matters connected therewith.

For proper growth of technical education, focus should be on proper planning and coordinated development. Concentration in certain pockets has already given rise to regional imbalance. Therefore, focus should be on the country as a whole. There has been phenomenal increase in the number of engineering colleges in southern states AICTE should make all conceivable efforts for encouraging both Government and private initiatives in setting up technical institutions in N-E region.

We are a country with one of the largest trained and educated manpower with considerable scientific and technical capabilities. (India Development Report, 2008) Since the number of technical manpower is increasing year after year, it is imperative that their skill is fully utilized for the development of the country. Government is sincere in its efforts to produce efficient technical manpower that can be suitably utilized for the development of the country. (Kumar Prahlad and Nisha, 2005) Various Indian plans have emphasized the importance of removing/eliminating under-employment and unemployment in the country along with some other socio-economic objectives. As part of the strategy for development, efforts have been put for both quantitative and qualitative expansion of facilities for development of engineering and technical manpower in the country. (Kumar Prahlad and Nisha, 2007) According to planning commission the meaningful development consists in mobilizing the skills, strength and creative capabilities of the masses of the people and securing their active participation. (Kumar Prahlad, 1995)

In India engineering is one of the preferred choices for good students at the 10+2 level. The competition for the top institutions is intense with students spending a lot of time and money. This demand for engineering has resulted in a mushrooming of a large number of engineering colleges in the country. Despite this, the industry complains of an absence of trained quality engineers. According to Kumar, if the shortage of educated skilled persons or of highly technical and professional persons persists for long periods, it may hamper the productive activities, makes economies more dependent on other countries and may retard the process of economic growth. (Kumar, 1996) India has produced a large number of competent, qualified engineers who have contributed to the success of many Indian companies and industries. A large number of our engineering graduates have also made an impact in the corporate world internationally. Despite these positive outcomes, a critical analysis of trends is required before we can attempt to make any recommendations for the future. Universities and institutions should adopt more job and object-oriented engineering education curricula linked with industries and research organizations to meet the present and future challenges of rapid technological changes and industrial development in India. (Palit, 1998).

The thrust in technical education during the Eleven Plan period will be coped with challenges and dimensions. The plan that in order to ensure inclusiveness, much larger scholarships and a loaning mechanism without collateral will be offered is very encouraging. The acceptance of a Central University in each state and a good college in each district would be like a dream come true. The real challenge lies in improving the system. (Alagh, 2008) Besides sustaining and consolidating the infrastructure developed during the recent Five Year Plans, the emphasis will be towards enhancement in the quality of output, the introduction of certain new and innovative thrusts and an attempt to gradually usher in a new ethos and thinking in the system. Not only more equitable development of engineering institutions in various regions/states of the country is required but as part of the strategy for development, efforts should be made to make engineering education more qualitative and industries -based.

REFERENCES

Alagh, K. Yoginder (2008), "Education and Skills in the Eleventh Plan", in *The Indian Journal of Labour Economics*, Vol. 51, No. 1.

Banerjee, Rangan and Muley P. Vinayak, (2007), "Engineering Education in India", Observer Research Foundation, Energy Systems Engineering, IIT, Bombay, Powai, Mumbai

Government of India, Tenth Five Year Plan, Planning Commission, New Delhi.

Government of India, Department-Related Parliamentary Standing Committee On Human Resource Development Hundred -Thirteenth

Report On Technical Education (Presented To The Rajya Sabha On 13th December, 2001), Rajya Sabha Secretariat, New Delhi.

Government of India, (2001), "Technical Education in Uttar Pradesh Handbook", New Delhi.

Government of India, (2001), Report of Task Force on Employment Opportunities, Planning Commission, New Delhi.

Kumar Prahlad, (1995), "Craze for Liberalization in India and Its Impact on Manpower Utilization", in Singh, B.N.P (Ed.) "Economic Liberalization in India", Ashish Publishing House, New Delhi.

Kumar Prahlad, Nisha, Upadhyay Pratima (2003), "Some reflections on ICT Intervention in Higher Education", Paper presented in a national seminar on 'Information and Communication Technology in Higher Education with Special Reference to Teacher Education' Organized by Education Department, University of Allahabad.

Kumar, Prahlad and Nisha, (2007), "Whither Technical Manpower in India: Directions for the Future", Paper published in a book entitled "Socio-Economic Development and Population Dynamics in India", Edited by R.B.S. Verma, Manoj Kumar Agrawal and R.K. Singh published by New Royal Book Centre, Lucknow.

Kumar, Prahlad and Nisha (2005), "Development and Utilization of Engineering Manpower in India: A Study", in Business Perspective, Birla Institute of Management Technology, New Delhi, Vol. 7, No. 1, Jan.-June.

Kumar, Prahlad (1996), "Re-Structuring Educational Programmes in the Changing Liberalized Environment: Some Prescriptions for Growing Economies like Malaysia", *The Indian Journal of Economics*, Vol. LXXVI, No. 303.

Mamgain Rajendra P. and Vandana Parashar (2000), Enhancing Employability of Youth Through Education and Training, *The Indian Journal of Labour Economics*, Vol. 43, No. 4.

Nisha, (2007), "Development and Utilization of Graduate Engineering Manpower in India: With Special Reference to Allahabad", unpublished thesis, Department of Economics, University of Allahabad.

NTMIS Bulletin, Publication of National Technical Manpower Information System (NTMIS), Vol. IV, No. 4, Jan.-March, 1999.

Palit, Sajal K. (1998), "The Development of Engineering and Technical Education in India", *Global Journal of Engineering Education*, Vol. 2, No. 3, UICEE, Australia.

Parekh, P.P. and Sukhatme, S.P., "Women Engineers in India", *Economic and Political Weekly*, Vol. XXXIX, No. 2, Jan. 10-16, 2004.

Prakash, Shri (1977), "A Review and Pre-Review of Indian Education: Analysis of Supply-Demand Relation and their Repercussions", in "Educational System of India: An Econometric Study", Concept Publishing Company, New Delhi.

Prakash, Shri (1977), "Educational System of India: An Econometric Study", Concept Pulishing Company, New Delhi.

Prasad, Krishna (2008), "Quality Assurance of Technical Education in India".

Radhakrishna, R. (2008), India Development Report, 2008, Oxford University Press, New Delhi.

Ramachandran, "Warning Bells: U.R. Rao Committee Report", *Frontline* (2004), Vol. 21, Issue 6, 13-26 March, Department of Science and Technology, Government of India, Research and Development Statistics (1990-91), New Delhi.

Report on Educational Development in India (1981-83).

Sukhatme, S.P. and Parikh, P.P. (2006), "A Silent Revolution: Assessing Output of Women Graduates and Post-graduates from IIT Bombay", at http://www.ircc.iitb.ac.in/~webadm/update/Issue1

The Engineering Profile, 2006, website URL:http://www.asee.org/publications/profiles/upload/2006ProfileEng.pdf

URL: http://www.engineergirl.org

URL: http://www.eng.rpi.edu/soe/profile_womentech.cfm

41

Human Development in India: An Inter-State Analysis

MINATI MALLICK AND JAGANNATH LENKA

I. INTRODUCTION

Human Development (HD) in fact is at the heart of today's policy agenda of governments' world over. It is vindicated by the fact that in addition to several regional reports, more than 360 national and sub-national Human Development Reports have been prepared by 120 countries. These reports have injected the human development concept into national policy dialogues not only through human development indicators and policy recommendations but also through the country specific process of consultation, data collection and report preparation. Furthermore, there are more than one Human Development Index (HDI) such as Income inequality adjusted Human Development Index (IHDI), Gender-related Development Index (GDI), Gender Empowerment Measure (GEM), Capability Poverty Measure (CPM) and Human Poverty Index (HPI) constructed for different purposes. Indeed the Human Development Reports (HDRs) have helped to put forward forcefully the message that economic development has no meaning unless it expands human choices. Fundamental to enlarging these choices is building human capabilities—the range of things that people can do or be in life. The most basic capabilities for human development are to lead a long and healthy life, to be knowledgeable, to have access to the resources needed for a decent standard of living and to be able to participate in the life of the community. However, the practical usefulness and relevance of HDI may be seriously restricted if it is not used to facilitate disaggregated analysis and policy actions.

The overall index of a country conceals the fact that different regions within the country have very different levels of human development whereas disaggregated HDIs reveal a more detailed profile of human development. One important aspect of disaggregated analysis is that it becomes clear precisely what the deficiencies in human capabilities in different regions are and what specific aspect of human development should concern policy-makers in future regional plans. It is realized that in every component of HDI (Whether income, education and health) there are glaring interstate disparities in India. When coupled with rural dimensions this disparity seems to be more intensified. This is corroborated by the world's best known welfare economist (A. Sen) that the success achieved in urban and industrial development has not made the lives of three-fourths of more than .one billion Indians living in the villages any easy. The affluence in the urban centres has no assurance of development in the peripheries.

The aim of this paper is to reflect the underlying features of Human Development in major states of India. Materials and methods of the analysis are presented in Section-II. The salient features of Human Development across fifteen major states are discussed in Section-III. The findings and suggestions are presented in the concluding Section.

II. MATERIALS AND METHODS

The present study makes use of secondary data collected from different publications of the Directorate of Economics and Statistics of respective State Governments;

Ministry of Home affairs and Ministry of Human Resources Development, Government of India. Per-capita Income, Literacy rate, Gross Enrolment Ratio, Life Expectancy and Infant Mortality Rate are used to construct Income, Education and Health Indexes. The formula used for calculating the indices is as per the UNDP norms.

$$\text{i.e., } Z_i = \frac{\text{Actual } X_i \text{ value - Minimum } X_i \text{ value}}{\text{Maximum } X_i \text{ value - Minimum } X_i \text{ value}}$$

where X_i refers to the value of the variable of ith state and Z_i is the corresponding index of the ith state. It may be noted here that for the purpose of the present analysis, per-capita income is used to construct Income Index, literacy rate with two-thirds weight and gross enrolment ratio with one-third weight are used to construct Education Index and life expectancy with two-thirds weight and infant mortality rate (where the numerator in the formula is taken as the absolute value of Minimum X_i value - Actual X_i value) with one-third weight are used to construct Health Index. A composite index called Human Development Index is constructed which is the simple Arithmetic Mean of the Income Index, Education Index and Health Index. The value of these indices lies in between '0' and '1' for which the value of HDI also lies in the same range for individual state. HDI does not measure the absolute level of human development rather assess the relative position of the states and ranks them in relation to each other. This helps to know how far the states have come from the lowest levels and how far they will have to travel towards present highest level of development on each of the three indicators.

III. RESULTS AND DISCUSSION

The HDI value for each state indicates how far it has to go to attain certain goals of human development or the present level of highest human development. The most desirable value of HDI is given as unity. The closer this value of a state is to one, the smaller the distance to be traveled by that state. UNDP has categorized human development into high HDI as above 0.8, medium as between 0.5 to 0.8, low as between 0.4 and 0.5, lowest as below 0.4. None of the states considered in the study fall under the category of high HDI as mentioned by UNDP, i.e. above 0.8 both in 2001 and 2005. Therefore, present study has categorized human development into high HDI as above 0.6, medium as between 0.4 and 0.6 and low as below 0.4.

The income index, education index, health index and

TABLE I

Human Development Index for Major States, 2001

Sl. No.	Major States	Income Index	Education Index	Health Index	HDI	Rank	Rank as per PC NSDP
1.	Andhra Pradesh	0.57	0.33	0.47	0.46	9	8
2.	Assam	0.22	0.52	0.29	0.34	11.5	12
3.	Bihar	0.00	0.00	0.35	0.12	15	15
4.	Gujarat	0.64	0.65	0.46	0.58	6	6
5.	Haryana	0.94	0.38	0.55	0.62	5	2
6.	Karnataka	0.63	0.57	0.48	0.56	7	7
7.	Kerala	0.76	0.90	0.67	0.78	1	5
8.	Madhya Pradesh	0.20	0.47	0.30	0.32	13.5	13
9.	Maharashtra	0.87	0.75	0.51	0.71	2	3
10.	Orissa	0.13	0.44	0.40	0.32	13.5	14
11.	Punjab	1.00	0.42	0.62	0.68	3	1
12.	Rajasthan	0.32	0.47	0.43	0.41	10	10
13.	Tamil Nadu	0.78	0.65	0.48	0.64	4	4
14.	Uttar Pradesh	0.24	0.41	0.37	0.34	11.5	11
15.	West Bengal	0.53	0.50	0.43	0.49	8	9
	Average	0.52	0.50	0.45	0.49		
	CV	60.94	41.15	23.64	37.17		

Human Development Index reflecting the household's welfare characteristics of major states of India are shown in Table 1 and Table- 2 for 2001 and 2005 respectively .In addition to these indices the rank of the states based on the HDI and Rank of the states as per their Per-capita Net State Domestic Product (PCNSDP) are also shown in the table for a

TABLE I

Human Development Index for Major States, 2005

Sl. No.	*Major States*	*Income Index*	*Education Index*	*Health Index*	*HDI*	*Rank*	*Rank as per PC NSDP*
1.	Andhra Pradesh	0.50	0.36	0.50	0.45	9	8
2.	Assam	0.20	0.39	0.33	0.31	14	11
3.	Bihar	0.00	0.00	0.41	0.14	15	15
4.	Gujarat	0.82	0.56	0.47	0.62	5.5	4
5.	Haryana	1.00	0.41	0.57	0.66	3	1
6.	Karnataka	0.54	0.52	0.49	0.52	7	7
7.	Kerala	0.68	0.86	0.67	0.73	1.5	5
8.	Madhya Pradesh	0.17	0.67	0.33	0.39	11	12.5
9.	Maharashtra	0.93	0.78	0.49	0.73	1.5	2
10.	Orissa	0.15	0.55	0.39	0.36	13	14
11.	Punjab	0.85	0.38	0.64	0.62	5.5	3
12.	Rajasthan	0.17	0.53	0.46	0.39	11	12.5
13.	Tamil Nadu	0.65	0.76	0.47	0.63	4	6
14.	Uttar Pradesh	0.22	0.56	0.40	0.39	11	10
15.	West Bengal	0.46	0.52	0.41	0.47	8	9
	Average	0.49	0.52	0.47	0.49		
	CV	66.33	39.84	20.90	34.48		

Bihar, Madhya Pradesh and Uttar Pradesh include Jharkhand, Chhattishgarh and Uttarakhand respectively.

comparative analysis.

It is observed that in 2001 Punjab (1.00) tops the list followed by Haryana (0.94) so far as income index is concerned while Bihar lies at the bottom. However, in 2005 Haryana comes to the top most position. Maharashtra, that was having an income index of 0.87 in 2001, follows it with 0.93. Kerala and Tamil Nadu have the index little higher than 0.7, i.e. 0.76 and 0.78 respectively in 2001. But their per-capita income situation deteriorated by 2005 so as to put them in 0.4 to 0.6 ranges. States like Andhra Pradesh, Gujarat, Karnataka and West Bengal have this index between 0.4 and 0.6 in 2001.

By 2005 only Gujarat could manage to get its income index improved from 0.64 to 0.82 while the position of the other states remained unchanged. The rest of the states have it below 0.4 indicating their poor performance. A temporal analysis of the income index of all the states reveals that the per-capita income of more than 50 per cent of the states considered has deteriorated while that of only four states has improved. This indicates that poor states remain poor even when the country grows and they are not able to reap the benefit of liberalization and globalisation.

A cursory glance at education index reveals that the literacy is highest in Kerala followed by Maharashtra and Tamil Nadu. Bihar lies at the bottom with lowest literacy preceded by Andhra Pradesh in both the years. However, states like Madhya Pradesh, Haryana Orissa, Rajasthan, Tamil Nadu and Uttar Pradesh have shown tremendous improvement in their literacy level over the years. The mission of Total literacy is found to have made no headway in the states of Andhra Pradesh, Assam and Bihar. It may be pointed out that these states are home to a large percentage of disadvantaged people, mostly scheduled tribes. Though the other states have fared well but still they have to go miles compared to the national average.

So far as health index is concerned it is observed that Kerala is at the top followed by Punjab and Haryana in both 2001 and 2005. This may be attributed to the high literacy and missionary activities in Kerala and for Haryana and Punjab higher health index may be the contribution of better income position. Health care and health provision facilities are found to be better in the states of Andhra Pradesh, Gujarat, Maharashtra, Karnataka, Rajasthan and Tamil Nadu for which the health index seems to be almost satisfactory. Rest of the states fare badly and require immediate attention.

Looking to the level of HD (Table 3) it is seen that among top five states in terms of high HDI value are Kerala, Maharashtra, Punjab, Tamil Nadu and Haryana in 2001 while Gujarat joined the group in 2005 by taking a giant leap in terms of per-capita income even though its education and health index present a gloomy picture. These, except Punjab and Haryana are all coastal states with satisfactory values of

TABLE 3

Levels of Human Development Index for Major States

2001 States	2005 States	Levels of HD
Kerala, Maharashtra, Punjab, Tamil Nadu, Haryana	Kerala, Maharashtra, Tamil Nadu, Haryana, Gujarat, Punjab	High
Andhra Pradesh, Gujarat, Karnataka, Rajasthan, West Bengal	Andhra Pradesh, Karnataka, West Bengal	Medium
Assam, Bihar, Madhya Pradesh, Orissa, Uttar Pradesh	Bihar, Madhya Pradesh, Assam, Orissa, Uttar Pradesh, Rajasthan	Low

income, education and health indices. The lowest positions are occupied by states such as Assam, Bihar, Madhya Pradesh, Orissa and Uttar Pradesh with low HDI values less than 0.4. Due to drastic deterioration in income index, Rajasthan's rank in terms of human development has also come down in 2005. These states are the backward and some of them are with Naxalite problems. The rest of the states like Andhra Pradesh, Karnataka, and West Bengal are having medium level of human development. The temporal analysis reveals that while Rajastan's position has deteriorated that of Gujarat has improved in terms of HDI values. The level of Human development has remained the same for all other states.

It is evident from the table that the average HDI of the states stands at 0.49 in 2001 that remained unchanged in 2005, which reflects the poor human development of the states and their incapability in improving the same. This low average HDI during 2001 is due to low average health index while low average income and health indices of poorer states accounted for it. Though the average income index value is 0.52, which pushes up the average HDI, it is seen that the co-efficient of variation is maximum (61%) for this index in 2001. The co-efficient of variation for education and health indices stand in the order of 41 per cent and 23 per cent. Looking into the indices during 2005 it can be observed that the coefficient of variation for income index is even greater than that in 2001 while the value of average income index has not increased .It may be construed that poor performance in income generation is widespread among the poorer states. Education though seems to give some comforts is concentrated in non-backward states. Health consciousness and health services are found to be dismal throughout.

Finally it is worked out that the correlation co-efficient between the HDI for the states and the Per-capita Net State Domestic Product is high and stands in the order of 0.94 and 0.92 for 2001 and 2005 respectively. This conveys the idea that though economic growth is argued to be inadequate for human development, lower educational and health attainment are found to be the consequence of low income and impedes the real human development.

IV. CONCLUSION

The main findings that emerged from the present study are as follows:

- The value of HDI for states as a whole turns out to be 0.49 in both the years of study that is considered to be low by UNDP standard. But as per our classification there is medium level of human development. Of the three components of HDI, the education index is found to have maximum weight (0.52%) in 2005 while that of income index is highest (0.52%) in 2001. The health index has lowest weight in both the years.
- Though the education index is bettered of during the study period, the interstate variation (41% in 2001 and 40% in 2005) is still a matter of concern.
- The average income index is found to have decreased from 0.52 per cent in 2001 to 0.49 per cent in 2005. This is mainly due to the decrease in the average per-capita income during the study period. The coefficient of variation is also found to have increased which is reflective of the fact that

poor states have become poorer and the rich states have fared well over time.

- Though the average performance of the health sector is dismal it is found that the variation across the states is also low.
- The rank correlation co-efficient between income and human development indexes stands in the order of 0.94 and 0.91 in the years 2001 and 2005 respectively. This vindicates the fact that economic growth is the major determinant of human development.
- As expected the low-income category states like Assam, Bihar, Madhy Pradesh, Orissa, Rajasthan and Uttar Pradesh have low levels of human development. It is disheartening to note that the measures taken by the central and state governments have not helped much even after more than one and half decades of economic reforms.

This necessitates to rethink and reformulate our policy approaches so as to break the vicious cycle of underdevelopment that is widespread in the low-income category states.They need development of both physical and social infrastructure. The sector that needs immediate attention is health sector. In addition to the existing literarcy programmes, more health programmes are at the moment highly essential for human development. This may be possible by organizing more health awareness programmes so as to help people give up superstitious beliefs and accept health related schemes launched by government from time to time. To accelerate income on a sustainable basis, the employment programmes are to be designed in such a way that physical infrastructure is created particularly for agricultural development that holds the key to development of low-income states. These responsibilities are to be shared by the governments at all levels to see that the policy of inclusive growth is fruitfully implemented.

REFERENCES

Kamdar, S. and Basak, A. (2005), "Beyond the Human Development Index, Preliminary notes on Deprivation and Inequality", *EPW*, Vol. XL No. 34.

Human Development Report (2004), Government of India.

Economic Survey (2004-05), Government of India.

Human Development Report (2001), Oxford University Press, New York.

Meyer, P. (2001), Human Development and Civic Community in India, Making Democracy Perform, *Economic and Political Weekly*, Vol. XXXVI, No. 8, pp. 624-92.

42

A Review of Inter-State Disparities in Telecom Sector in India

ARCHANA RANI SRIVASTAVA AND JAGDISH NARAYAN

I

India is a country where unity exists in diversity. It has different cultures, languages, religions, regions, etc. With all these differences, our country is unite. Being all that there is disparity in India. The word 'disparity' may be defined as "the condition or fact of being unequal, as in age, rank or degree." Disparity may be synonymous to inequality, unlikeness, disproportion and difference. Regional disparity is a familiar phenomenon for a country. In India regional disparity is found both at the national and state levels. Every state or region of an economy does not develop identically or homogeneously due to historical, natural, economic, geographical climatic and even political factors.

The objectives of the study are—

1. to access the regional disparity among the states of India on the basis of NSDP,
2. to analyze the contribution of telecom sector, and

3. to analyze the inter-state disparities in telecom sector in India on the basis of teledensity and NSDP

In order to fulfil the above objectives, for the study we have collected secondary data from various published sources namely, data obtained from Directorate of Economics and Statistics of respective state governments and Central Statistical Organization, Annual Report, 2003-04 of the Department of communication, Ministry of communications and information technology.

The analyses of data is based on some specific statistical tools namely, tables and regression analyses. We have used t-statistics to test the significance of regression analyses.

In the process of planning regional disparity widened the gap between rich and poor regions. When India got freedom it was in the category of developing country with poor infrastructural resources. The administrator had to decide the path of development process for achieving the targeted goal of development. In Economic literature two approaches are stated for development: 1. Balanced growth, 2. Unbalanced growth. Ragner Nurkse, Rosenstein Rodan, Arthur Lewis are the economists who supported balanced growth approach, while professor Singer and Hirschman supported unbalanced growth approach: According to balanced growth approach economists, an economy must develop all the sectors simultaneously with demand sector and supply sector, while unbalanced growth approach advocates that an economy must develop those sectors which are important for the point of the priorities of the economy and the development of these sectors will be followed by the development of another less priority sectors.

India decided to follow the unbalanced growth approach. For fulfiling the objective of development India choose 'economic planning as a device of economic management. It is a centralized method, which is applied at macro level to attain the objectives of socio-economic and structural adjustment for development. In spite of all the precautions and hardships India adopted in the path of planning, there exists disparity in various regions or state of the country.

We may analyze disparity among the states of India on the basis of per-capita net state domestic product (PSDP), as we know that the most common indicator of the economic development of a society is the per-capita annual income generated by it. After adopting the path of planning in the country it is found that disparities and inequalities in different regions, sub-regions, stats have widened the gap. Disparities and inequalities have also increased during the planning period, which may be observed by the table given below.

TABLE I

Per-capita Net State Domestic Product at Current Prices

Sl. No.	*Name of States/Year*	*2001-02*	*2002-03*	*2003-04*	*2004-05*	*2005-06*
1.	Andhra Pradesh	18630	19568	22041	23729	26211
2.	Arunachal Pradesh	17893	17434	19707	22542	23788
3.	Assam	13153	14600	15687	16825	18598
4.	Bihar	6197	6928	6913	7467	7875
5.	Jharkhand	10972	11865	12941	17493	19066
6.	Goa	44110	48839	54577	66135	70112
7.	Gujarat	19823	22683	26922	29468	34157
8.	Haryana	26077	28295	31509	35044	38832
9.	Himachal Pradesh	24608	26627	28333	31140	33805
10.	Jammu & Kashmir	15031	164252	17528	18630	-
11.	Karnataka	17776	19041	20515	24199	27291
12.	Kerala	21047	23207	25645	27864	30668
13.	Madhya Pradesh	12697	12303	14306	14534	15647
14.	Chhattisgarh	12443	13145	16098	18068	20151
15.	Maharashtra	24450	26697	29770	32979	37081
16.	Manipur	12801	13250	14728	18386	20326
17.	Meghalaya	17936	18756	20729	2115	23420
18.	Mizoram	19430	20896	21963	22417	-
19.	Nagaland	18961	20407	20821	20998	na
20.	Orissa	11075	11788	14252	16306	17299
21.	Punjab	28949	29443	31192	32945	34929
22.	Rajasthan	14165	13126	16704	16800	17863
23.	Sikkim	17324	19428	21476	23791	26412
24.	Tamil Nadu	20924	21813	24106	27137	29958

25.	Tripura	18368	19059	21138	22836	24706
26.	Uttar Pradesh	9781	10435	11250	11941	13262
27.	Uttaranchal	16408	18819	20519	22093	24585
28.	West Bengal	17826	18746	20806	22522	25223
29.	Andaman and Nicobar Islands	27112	30050	33150	31004	34853
30.	Chandigarh	52385	58772	66512	75181	86629
31.	Delhi	43587	45483	49825	55215	61676
32.	Pondicherry	39138	44903	48547	44908	48477
	All-India	17800	18899	20936	22946	25716

Source: http://indiabudget.nic.in

The table sharply shows that PSDP is significantly differing state-by-state and year-by-year.

TABLE 2

Growth Rate in PSDP

Sl. No.	*Name of States/Year*	*2001-02*	*2002-03*	*2003-04*	*2004-05*	*2005-06*
1.	Andhra Pradesh	8.0	5.0	12.6	7.7	10.5
2.	Arunachal Pradesh	15.8	-2.6	13.0	14.4	5.5
3.	Assam	2.8	11.0	7.4	7.3	10.5
4.	Bihar	-3.1	11.8	-0.2	8.0	5.5
5.	Jharkhand	6.6	8.1	9.1	35.2	9.0
6.	Goa	0.9	10.7	11.7	21.2	6.0
7.	Gujarat	7.8	14.4	18.7	9.5	15.9
8.	Haryana	8.0	8.4	11.5	11.2	10.8
9.	Himachal Pradesh	8.0	8.2	6.4	9.9	8.6
10.	Jammu & Kashmir	5.1	9.5	6.5	6.3	0.0
11.	Karnataka	1.8	7.1	7.7	18.0	12.8
12.	Kerala	5.7	10.3	10.5	8.7	10.1
13.	Madhya Pradesh	7.0	-3.1	16.3	1.6	7.7
14.	Chhattisgarh	13.3	5.6	22.5	12.2	11.5
15.	Maharashtra	6.3	9.2	11.5	10.8	12.4
16.	Manipur	3.5	3.5	11.2	24.8	10.6
17.	Meghalaya	11.4	4.6	10.5	5.7	6.9
18.	Mizoram	9.0	7.5	5.1	2.1	0.0
19.	Nagaland	12.2	7.6	2.0	0.9	0.0

(Contd.)

TABLE 2 *(Contd.)*

20. Orissa	6.0	6.4	20.9	14.4	6.1
21. Punjab	3.9	1.7	5.9	5.6	6.0
22. Rajasthan	9.8	-7.3	27.3	0.6	6.3
23. Sikkim	7.8	12.1	10.5	10.8	11.0
24. Tamil Nadu	0.0	4.2	10.5	12.6	10.4
25. Tripura	14.9	3.8	10.9	8.0	8.2
26. Uttar Pradesh	2.5	6.7	7.8	6.1	11.1
27. Uttaranchal	6.0	14.7	9.0	7.7	11.3
28. West Bengal	7.9	5.2	11.0	8.2	12.0
29. Andaman and Nicobar Islands	7.7	10.8	10.3	-6.5	12.4
30. Chandigarh	12.3	12.2	13.2	13.0	15.2
31. Delhi	5.2	4.3	9.5	10.8	11.7
32. Pondicherry	8.1	14.7	8.1	-7.5	7.9
All-India	6.90	6.2	10.8	9.6	12.1

Compiled from the above table

We may draw some interesting figures from the table. In the year 2001-02 maximum growth rate of PSDP occurred in Arunachal Pradesh while Bihar had minimum growth rate even negative growth rate of -3.1.

Even Growth rate of PSDP in Tamil Nadu in the same year was zero. In the year 2002-03 PSDP of Arunanchal Pradesh showed surprisingly negative growth rate by -23.6, while it ranked first in the year 2001-02 with maximum growth rate of 15.8. Uttaranchal and Pondicherry showed highest growth rate in the same year by 14.7 and Gujarat followed these states with 14.4 growth rate. Three states—Arunachal Pradesh, Madhya Pradesh and Rajasthan Showed negative growth rate in PSDP, while Rajasthan showed minimum growth rate with -7.3 per cent.

In the year 2003-04, Rajasthan surprisingly ranked top with 27.03 per cent growth rate followed by Chhattisgarh with 22.5 per cent growth rate. Bihar again was at lowest rank with -0.2 per cent growth rates in the same year. No other state showed negative growth rate in this year.

Two states namely Andaman-Nikobar islands and Pondicherry showed negative growth respectively 6.5 and -7.5

per cent, in the year 2004-05. Jharkhand ranked first among the states with 35.2 per cent growth rate in PSDP. Pondechery was at lowest rank in this year. In the year 2005-06 Gujarat ranked top with 15.9 per cent growth rate followed by Chandigarh with 15.2 per cent growth, while Arunachal Pradesh and Bihar shared the last position with 5.5 per cent growth rate. Surprisingly none state got negative growth rate. We may analyze in another way. We compare PSDP of the states with the per-capita net domestic product of the whole India in the year 2001-02 and 2005-06.

TABLE 3

Name of the States having Average above India

(India's per-capita net domestic product Rs. 25716) 2001-02	*(India's per-capita net domestic product Rs. 17800) 2005-06*
1. West Bengal	1. Andhra Pradesh
2. Arunachal Pradesh	2. Sikkim
3. Meghalaya	3. Karnataka
4. Tripura	4. Tamil Nadu
5. Andhra Pradesh	5. Kerala
6. Nagaland	6. Himachal Pradesh
7. Mizoram	7. Gujarat
8. Gujarat	8. Andaman and Nicobar Islands
9. Tamil Nadu	9. Punjab
10. Kerala	10. Maharashtra
11. Maharashtra	11. Haryana
12. Himachal Pradesh	12. Pondicherry
13. Haryana	13. Delhi
14. Andaman-Nicobar Islands	14. Goa
15. Punjab	15. Chandigarh
16. Pondicherry	
17. Delhi	
18. Goa	
19. Chandigarh	

(Contd.)

TABLE 3 *(Contd.)*

2001-02	2005-06
1. Bihar	1. Bihar
2. Uttar Pradesh	2. Uttar Pradesh
3. Jharkhand	3. Madhya Pradesh
4. Orissa	4. Orissa
5. Chhattisgarh	5. Rajasthan
6. Madhya Pradesh	6. Assam
7. Manipur	7. Jharkhand
8. Assam	8. Chhattisgarh
9. Rajasthan	9. Manipur
10. Jammu & Kashmir	10. Meghalaya
11. Uttaranchal	11. Arunanchal Pradesh
12. Sikkim	12. Uttaranchal
13. Karnataka	13. Tripura
14. West Bengal	

Compiled from the above table.

From the compiled table given above we summarize the findings as following:

In the year 2001-02 maximum PSDP was in the state Chandigarh and after 5 years in the year 2005-06 Chandigarh maintained its PSDP. Lowest PSDP was in Karnataka in 2001-02, while it was lowest in West Bengal in 2005-06. The data for PSDP was not available for three states, Jammu-Kashmir, Mizoram and Nagaland in the year 2005-06 but we can draw a very interesting inference from the table. In the year 2001-02 there were nineteen states having PSDP above India, while in the year 2005-06 there were only fifteen stats above all-India per-capita domestic product. PSDP of the three states namely Meghalaya, tripura, and West Bengal were above PSDP of India in the year 2001-02, but they were below in the year 2005-06

II

TELECOMMUNICATIONS IN INDIA

(a) Historical Perspective

India is the world's largest democracy and it holds second highest population and seventh largest area of the world. In terms of purchasing power, India is the fourth largest economy. India's telephone network, including mobile phones, is one of the largest in the world and second largest among the emerging economies (after China).

Telegraph is a kind of telecom services. In India telecommunications were introduced through telegraph in 1851 near Calcutta by the British government. When India got freedom in 1947, it had 321 switching centres (telephone exchanges) in urban areas and a teledensity of 0.025, Telecommunications was controlled and managed by the government under monopoly till the mid-1980's and it was centered around the urban and metropolitan cities because of "the perception that phones were a luxury and rather than essential infrastructure for efficient administration of government and industry." Rajiv Gandhi has been the pioneer person for bringing revolution in telecommunications in the country in 1985. It is his longer run vision that we are having the facilities of ultra modern telecommunication techniques; TVs Internet communications and computer-based a number of telecommunication services. The new telecom policy allowed private firms to manufacture telephones while DOT (Department of Telecommunications) licensed switching technology from various foreign firms. In 1984 the government set-up the centre for Development of telematics (C-DOT) and separated the Department of Post and Telegraph in 1985 by setting up the Department of Posts and the Department of Telecommunications.

The second phase liberalization in telecom sector started with New Economic Policy, 1991. Telecom equipments manufacturing was delicensed and value added services were opened to the private sector. National Telecom Policy was announced in 1994 with the objectives of universal service and qualitative improvements in telecom services.

The third phase reforms are important landmark in telecom sector. The new telecom policy 1999 was launched with the new dimensions that telecommunications was a very important service for a common man which could be used as an important driver of economic growth.

Milestonnes in Telecom Reforms

1984	-	Manufacturing of subscriber terminal equipments to private sector.
1985	-	Telecom was constituted into a separate department with a separate board.
1986	-	MTNL and VSNL were created as corporations.
1989	-	Telecom commission formed
1991	-	Telecom equipment manufacturing opened to private sector.
1992	-	Value-added service sectors opened for private competition.
1993	-	Private Networks were allowed in industrial areas.
1994	-	1—Licenses for radio paging (for 27 cities) issued. 2—Licenses for cellular mobiles and basic services opened up.
1997	-	The telecom regulatory authority of India (TRAI) was established.
1998	-	Several VAS available through private operators. The first private basic service becomes operation.
1999	-	Migration to revenue share.
2000	-	Formation of Bharat Sanchar Nigam Limited (BSNL). NLD sector opened up.
2002	-	BSNL launched nation-wide cellular services, ILD sector opened up.
2004	-	Rationalization and further reduction of license fees, Broadband policy announced.
2005	-	Foreign Direct Investment (FDI) increased to 74%. ILD/NLD regime liberalized.
2006	-	One India plan introduced to allow calls at 'One Rupee' per minute across India.

We may summarize reforms in telecommunications sector as follows:

(b) Present Scanario of Telecom Sector in India

Presently India has the third largest subscriber Base in the world. It is subscriber base in the world in telecom sector. It is the fastest growing telecom market in the world, surpassing China. The India telecom sector has crossed US $ 100 billion (almost Rs. 4.5 lakh crore) in terms of valuation, which approximates to 13 per cent country's GDP.

India has becomes the second most attractive destination for FDI among manufacturing investors. As against a target of 250 million telephone connections by December 2007, 264 million telephone connections have already been installed by November 2007. The over-all teledensity is 23.21. For the purpose of popularizing broadband services in villages BSNL has named the year 2007 as the "Year of Broadband". As on October 2007, about 3 million broadband connections have been provided in more than 1100 towns. Under 'Bharat Nirman Programme', about 90 per cent villages and have already been provided with Village Public Telephones (VPTs). The target of the programme is to provide VPTs in 66822 uncovered villages by June 2008. Against this target the number of villages provided with VPTs till October 2007 is 51136. Apart from this, those villages are provided Rural Community Phone (RCP), which have no VPTs, and their population exceeds 2000. The number of RCPs in such villages upto October 2007 is 37911.

The mobile sector is also growing at exponential growth rate. There were 10 million mobile subscribers in 2002. Now the number of mobile subscribers is 150 million by early 2007, which is registering an average growth rate of over 90 per cent year over year. The two main reasons for expansion of mobile sector are low tariffs and falling handsets prices.

(c) Highlights and Opportunities of Telecom Sector

- India has the highest monthly minutes of usage (MOU) per subscribers in the Asia-Pacific region with usage of 500minutes a month.
- Every 11th person is an Indian who is using cell phone as a tool to access the Internet.
- Global consultancy firm, Earnest and young will invest up to US $ 25 billion over the next five years.
- According to the technology research conducted by firm Gartner, India will record the highest growth with handset production over 51 million units in 2007 in Asia-Pacific region.

- According to the estimation of TRAI, India will need about 350000 telecom towers by 2010, as against 125000 in 2007.
- The combined revenue of all operators from their mobile business would more than double to US $ 33.1 billion by 2010 from about US $ 12.8 billion in 2006.
- The total revenue will also be doubled to US $ 43.6 billion by 2010, from US $ 22.5 billion in 2006.
- The share of telecom in FDI rose from 3-4 per cent to 12-15 in the year 2006.
- The world's largest mobile player, Vodafone has announced to invest one fifth of its global expenditure in India in 2007, which is about US$ 2 billion.
- Virgin Mobile is entering the Indian market through a 50:50 joint venture with the Tata group.
- Nearly US $ 1.1 billion is invested in 2007 to roll out close to 18000 towers, collectively by Essar Telecom Tower and Infrastructure, GTL infrastructure and Sri Group's Quipo.
- Intec Telecom system has lined up a US $ 12 million expansion plan for its Bangalore office for operational support.
- Ericson Company plans to invest US $ 100 million every year in India for enhancing its services.
- Indian cellular operators have planned investments of about US $ 20 billion over the next two years to bring over 80 per cent of the population under mobile coverage.
- Highest growth rate in mobile connection with an investment of about US$ 650 million was achieved in 2007.
- Addition of about 8 million connections per month is highest in the world.
- Lower prices of handsets, even it touched to Rs. 1000.

III

STATE-WISE ANALYSIS OF TELEDENSITY IN INDIA—TOTAL AND RURAL-URBAN

TABLE 4

(a) International Comparisons of Teledensities

Country	*Population (Million)*	*GDP (US $, 2004)*	*Teledensity (Dec. 2005)*
USA	298.21	36273.0	122.7
UK	59.67	26369.0	158.5
Australia	20.16	25436.0	148.3
Brazil	186.41	3338.0	59.8
Mexico	107.03	6328.0	62.6
Srilanka	207.74	1031.0	22.2
Korea (Republic)	48.29	14136.0	128.6
Japan	128.08	31324.00	119.86
Indonesia	222.87	1156.00	26.79
China	1315.84	1268.00	56.53
Pakistan	153.96	614.00	11.72
India	1115.59	634.00	12.74
World	6728.08	5944.00	49.45

Source: International Telecom Union.

When we compare teledensity among some important countries of he world we find that there has been variations in the teledensity in the countries of the world. On comparing the distribution of teledensity among the countries it has been maximum, i.e. 158.51 in United Kingdom followed by 148.25 in Australia and 128.56 in Korea (Republic). While minimum value of teledensity is in Pakistan with 11.72 teledensity followed by India with 12.74 and Sri Lanka with 22.20. Comparing teledensity with the world and other countries we observe that four countries namely Pakistan, India, Sri Lanka and Indonesia have teledensity below the world average teledensity while China and other countries have teledensity above the world's average teledensity.

Teledensity has been defined as number of telephones per hundred people. The status of teledensity is not same in all the states. There are some states, which have higher teledensity than that of India, and some have lower teledensity. Comparing the teledensity in the year 2003 and 2004, for different states, it is observed that states, which are rich in economical terms, also have high teledensity. There have been some variations in teledensity between rural and urban sub-groups of population due to the considerable accentuation of the process of urbanization.

(a) Overall Teledensity

Following are the states, which have above all-India average teledensity, and then we have states, which have below all-India average teledensity in the years 2003, and 2004.

TABLE 5

Overall Teledensity above All-India Average in States

Sl. No.	*Circle/States*	*2003*	*2004*	*Growth rate*
1.	Andaman and Nicobar	10.15	11.56	13.89
2.	Andhra Pradesh	5.66	7.85	38.69
3.	Gujarat	7.77	10.14	30.50
4.	Haryana	6.21	8.38	34.94
5.	Himachal Pradesh	8.50	10.14	19.29
6.	Karnataka	6.67	9.46	41.83
7.	Kerala	11.33	14.87	31.24
8.	Maharashtra	6.03	8.00	31.58
9.	Punjab	11.76	17.33	47.36
10.	Tamil Nadu	6.22	8.54	37.30
11.	Kolkata	13.47	18.92	40.46
12.	Chennai	22.97	38.81	68.96
13.	Delhi	27.38	41.79	52.63
14.	Mumbai	24.22	36.08	48.97
	All-India	5.11	7.02	37.38

Annual Report, 2003-04, Department of Telecommunications.

When we compare average teledensity overall for two respective years 2003-04 for the country as a whole, we find that absolute level of average teledensity has increased in the year 2004. Its level has become up by 1.91 point of the country as a whole. On comparing the distribution of teledensity among the states of the country. It has been maximum, i.e. 27.38 in Delhi in the year 2003, followed by Mumbai with 24.22 and Chennai with 22.97 in the respective year. While minimum value of teledensity in the year 2003 has been in Bihar, i.e. 1.32 followed by Chhattisgarh with 1.47 and Jharkhand with 1.68 in the respective years.

TABLE 6

Overall Teledensity Below All-India Average in States

Sl. No.	*Circle/States*	*2003*	*2004*	*Growth rate*
1.	Assam	1.94	2.13	9.79
2.	Bihar	1.32	1.67	26.52
3.	Chhattisgarh	1.47	1.63	10.88
4.	Jammu & Kashmir	2.48	3.01	21.37
5.	Jharkhand	1.68	2.00	19.05
6.	Madhya Pradesh	3.02	3.99	32.12
7.	North-East I	3.00	3.35	11.67
8.	North-East II	2.35	2.71	15.32
9.	Orissa	2.29	2.95	28.82
10.	Rajasthan	3.47	4.50	29.68
11.	Uttaranchal	4.25	5.10	20.00
12.	Uttar Pradesh (E & W)	2.15	2.96	37.67
13.	West Bengal	1.85	2.18	17.84
	All-India	5.11	7.02	37.38

Annual Report, 2003-04, Department of Telecommunications.

Since the telecommunications process is providing upgrading infrastructure facilities and people are becoming more conscious and aware about the telephones and telecommunication services therefore, in spite of that increasing level of average level of teledensity the distribution pattern of teledensity among the states remains same in the two respective years 2003 and 2004.

On comparing the growth rates of teledensity among the different states we observe that growth percentage are also heteroscedastic in nature in the states having average above and below than all-India average.

(b) Urban Teledensity

When we compare urban average teledensity for the two respective years 2003 and 2004 for the country as a whole, we find that absolute level of urban average teledensity has increased in the year 2004 by 6.42. We observe that urban teledensity growth rate in India is higher than overall teledensity growth rate in the respective year.

On comparing the distribution of teledensity, it is maximum in Himachal Pradesh with 36.08 and minimum value of urban teledensity in the respective year 2003 has been in Uttar Pradesh (E & W), i.e. 2.15. In the year 2004, Himachal Pradesh again ranked first with highest teledensity of 51.12, while Chhattisgarh ranked lowest position in the respective year with 6.02 teledensity.

TABLE 7

Urban Tendensity above All-India Average in States

Sl. No.	*Circle/States*	*2003*	*2004*	*Growth rate*
1.	Andaman and Nicobar	14.82	-	18.08
2.	Andhra Pradesh	15.42	22.70	47.21
3.	Gujarat	16.44	22.46	36.62
4.	Haryana	15.30	22.01	43.86
5.	Himachal Pradesh	36.08	51.12	41.69
6.	Karnataka	14.78	22.58	52.77
7.	Kerala	21.28	32.82	54.23
8.	Maharashtra	14.96	-	33.62
9.	Punjab	23.99	38.25	59.44
10.	Chennai	22.97	38.81	68.96
11.	Delhi	29.24	44.48	52.12
12.	Mumbai	24.22	36.08	48.97
	All-India	14.32	20.74	44.83

Annual Report, 2003-04, Department of Telecommunications.

Following are the states, which have below all-India average of urban teledensity—

TABLE 8

Urban Teledensity Below All-India Average in States

Sl. No.	Circle/States	2003	2004	Growth rate
1.	Andaman and Nicobar	-	17.50	18.08
2.	Assam	11.54	12.47	11.54
3.	Bihar	8.46	11.64	8.46
4.	Chhattisgarh	5.55	6.02	5.55
5.	Jammu & Kashmir	8.34	10.12	8.34
6.	Jharkhand	6.11	7.34	6.11
7.	Madhya Pradesh	9.68	12.91	9.68
8.	Maharashtra	-	19.99	33.62
9.	North-East I	9.88	10.89	10.22
10.	North-East II	8.22	9.07	10.34
11.	Orissa	10.12	13.86	36.96
12.	Rajasthan	10.73	14.83	38.21
13.	Tamil Nadu	12.28	17.21	40.15
14.	Uttaranchal	12.57	15.17	20.68
15.	Uttar Pradesh (E & W)	8.12	12.12	50.74
16.	West Bengal	7.82	9.79	25.19
17.	Kolkata	13.47	18.92	40.46
	All-India	14.32	20.74	44.83

Annual Report, 2003-04, Department of Telecommunications.

When we compare the two tables of urban teledensity for above average and below all-India average for the respective years 2003 and 2004. We find that Andaman and Nicobar and Maharashtra states have above average teledensity in 2003 but they declined their position in the year 2004 and they joined the group of below average teledensity.

Comparing the growth rates of urban teledensity in the respective years we conclude that above average states have faster growth rates than the states of lower growth rates. Highest growth rate is shown in the state Chennai, while it was lowest in Jharkhand.

When we compare the table of overall teledensity and urban teledensity we find that there are fourteen states above overall all-India average teledensity, in the year 2003 and 2004. But when we observe the table of urban teledensity, we find that there are only twelve states above all-India average in 2003 and this number reduces to ten in the year 2004.

(c) Rural Teledensity

On comparing rural average teledensity for the respective two years 2003 and 2004 for the country as a whole, we find that absolute level of rural average teledensity has increased nominally only 0.08 points.

Comparing the distribution of rural teledensity among the states for the respective years 2003 and 2004, it is maximum in Kerala while it is minimum in Chhattisgarh and Jharkhand in 2003. Again Kerala toped among the states in the year 2004 and it is minimum in Jharkhand and slightly greater with 0.02 in Chhattisgarh.

Following are the states, which have above all-India average for rural teledensity.

TABLE 9

Rural Teledensity above All-India Average in States

Sl. No.	*Circle/States*	*2003*	*2004*	*Growth rate*
1.	Andaman and Nicobar	7.74	8.40	8.53
2.	Andhra Pradesh	2.03	2.33	14.78
3.	Gujarat	2.48	2.52	1.61
4.	Haryana	2.32	2.42	4.31
5.	Himachal Pradesh	5.43	5.51	1.47
6.	Karnataka	2.37	2.41	1.69
7.	Kerala	7.85	8.60	9.55
8.	Maharashtra	2.19	2.31	5.48
9.	Punjab	4.60	4.81	4.57
10.	Tamil Nadu	2.12	2.35	10.85
	All-India	1.49	1.57	5.37

Annual Report, 2003-04, Department of Telecommunications.

Following are the states, which have below all-India average for rural teledensity—

TABLE 10

Rural Teledensity Below All-India Average in States

Sl. No.	Circle/States	2003	2004	Growth rate
1.	Assam	0.50	0.56	12.00
2.	Bihar	0.48	0.50	4.17
3.	Chhattisgarh	0.40	0.47	17.50
4.	Jammu & Kashmir	0.52	0.61	17.31
5.	Jharkhand	0.40	0.45	12.50
6.	Madhya Pradesh	0.56	0.68	21.43
7.	North-East I	0.95	1.08	13.68
8.	North-East II	0.79	1.01	27.85
9.	Orissa	0.87	0.95	9.20
10.	Rajasthan	1.25	1.32	5.60
11.	Uttaranchal	1.30	1.48	13.85
12.	Uttar Pradesh (E & W)	0.56	0.47	-16.07
13.	West Bengal	0.89	0.95	6.74
14.	Kolkata	0.00	0.00	0.00
15.	Chennai	0.00	0.00	0.00
16.	Delhi	0.00	0.00	0.00
17.	Mumbai	0.00	0.00	0.00
	All-India	1.49	1.57	5.37

Annual Report, 2003-04, Department of Telecommunications.

Analysing the tables of above and below averages for rural teledensity we find that ten states are above the average and seventeen states/circles are having below average. Rural teledensity has increased in the year 2004 against he year 2003, except Uttar Pradesh that shows negative growth in teledensity.

By analysing all the tables for teledensity we observe that none state maintains its position in the next year respectively 2004.

TABLE 11

Name of states	Net state domestic product 2003 (Rs. Crore)	Net state domestic product 2004 (Rs. Crore)	Per-capita net state domestic product 2003 (Rs.)	Per-capita net state domestic product 2004 (Rs.)	No. of telephones 2003	No. of telephones 2004	Teledensity 2003	Teledensity 2004
Andaman Nicobar	1118	1276	30050	33150	37980	44293	10.15	11.56
Andhra Pradesh	152066	173274	19568	22041	4404179	6188869	5.66	7.85
Assam	39397	42914	14600	15687	536832	599491	1.94	2.13
Bihar	59278	60235	6928	6913	1150235	1489300	1.32	1.67
Chhattigarh	28131	35094	13145	16098	315446	357239	1.47	1.63
Gujarat	118130	142534	22683	26922	4131348	5501783	7.77	10.14
Haryana	61710	70181	28259	31509	1377696	1905951	6.21	8.38
Himachl Pradesh	16751	18127	26627	28333	534309	647381	8.5	10.14
Jammu & Kashmir	17400	18992	16452	17528	264077	328750	2.48	3.01
Jharkhand	32910	36501	11865	12941	473349	574696	1.68	2
Karnataka	102765	112123	19041	20515	3634888	5238457	6.67	9.46
Kerala	75090	83888	23207	25645	3681305	4875828	11.33	14.87
Madhya Pradesh	76661	90871	12303	14306	1907635	2577355	3.02	3.99
Maharashtra	265290	300576	26697	29770	5170868	6930891	6.08	8
Orissa	44208	54047	11788	14252	865881	1133495	2.29	2.95
Punjab	73832	79665	29443	31192	3078825	4619822	11.76	17.33
Rajasthan	76697	99606	13126	16704	2064943	2742619	3.47	4.5
Tamil Nadu	138145	153997	21813	24106	3599903	4988595	6.22	8.54

Uttaranchal	16408	18193	18819	20519	373439	456245	4.25	5.1
Uttar Pradesh	178990	196826	10435	11250	3746736	5273067	2.15	2.96
West Bengal	153580	172551	18746	20806	1290660	1545828	1.85	2.18
Delhi	65923	74439	45483	49825	4078904	6463003	27.38	41.79

Source: http://indiabudget.nic.in (first four columns)
Annual Report, 2003-04, Department ofTtelecommunications (last four columns).

Relationship between Net State Domestic Product and Number of Telephones.

We have data about net state domestic product (NSDP) of various states and number of telephones for the years 2003 and 2004. We have tried to test whether there is any relationship between NSDP and number of telephones.

We may draw a relationship that T=F (NSDP) for the year 2003 and 2004 and for this relationship we formulate a model that is

$$T= b_o+b_1N$$

where; T is number of telephones in the states and N is net state domestic product.

Relationship between NSDP and number of telephones for the year 2003.

By fitting the linear regression for the data in the year 2003 we find the estimates of b_o and b_1 Estimated regression function of number of telephone and NSDP is:

$$T = b_o + b_1N$$
$$T = 445102 + 20.58\ N$$
$$(362976.4)\ (3.523)$$

Values in the parenthesis are the standard error of the estimates. This relationship holds for the year 2003.. As well as $R^2 = 0.63$ which indicates that 63 per cent variations in dependent variable, i.e. number of telephones are explained by the explanatory variable, i.e. NSDP.

Now we will test whether the estimates are significant or not, for the estimated relationship. We will conduct the 't' test.

Null Hypothesis: $b_1 = 0$
Alternative Hypothesis: $b_1 \neq 0$

We find that tcal is 5.840. Since the theoretical (tabular) valued of t at 5 per cent level of significance for 20 d.f. is 2.086. That is tcal > t tab implying that H_o is rejected or H_1 may be accepted for b_1. Meaning thereby slope of the regression is not equal to zero. Our regression estimate is statistically significant. Now we will test the hypothesis—

$$H_o : b_o = 0$$
$$H_1 : b_o \neq 0$$

T_{cal} for b_o is coming out to be 1.226. Further t_{tab} at 5 per cent level of significance for 20 d.f. is 2.086, that is $t_{cal} < t_{tab}$, implying that H_o is accepted that is the regression line may pass through origin.

Positive sign of b_1 shows that slope is increasing one quantitatively, which is a good sign for number of telephones. In other words number of telephones depends on NSDP or large size of NSDP will correspond to larger number of telephones.

Relationship between NSDP and number of telephones for the year 2004.

By the same process of calculation we have drawn conclusions for the year 2004. We find the regression equation as follows:

$$T = \underset{(558313.5)}{624707.3} + \underset{(4.785)}{24.92N}$$

where T is estimated number of telephones in the various states for the year 2004 and N is NSDP for the year 2004. As well as $R^2 = 0.58$ which indicates that 58 per cent variation are explained through the explanatory variable. By comparing the values of R^2 for the respective years 2003 and 2004 we find that explanatory power of the variable has been reduced.

For testing the significance of the estimates we calculate t-values for the estimates b_0 and b_1, t_{cal} for b_1 is coming out to be 5.208 . Further ttab at 5 per cent level as significance for 20 d.f. is 2.086. Hence $t_{cal} > t_{tab}$ we reject our null hypothesis that is b_1 is not equal to zero and is statistically significance. Its positive sign also shows that the slope of the regression equation is increasing.

T_{cal} for b_o is 1.119 and t_{tab} at 5 per cent level of significance for 20 d.f. is 2.086. Since $t_{cal} < t_{tab}$ we accept our null hypothesis that is regression line may pass through its origin.

Curve Fitting for Number of Telephones and Net State Domestic Product for the Year 2003

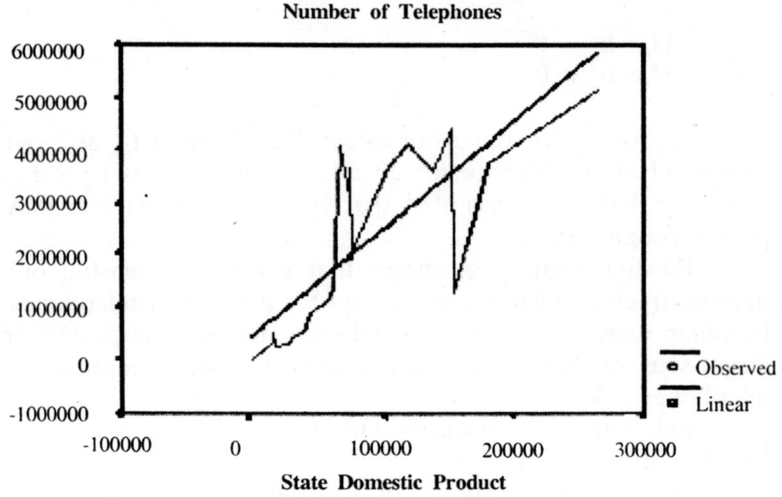

Curve Fitting for Number of Telephones and Net State Domestic Product for the Year 2004

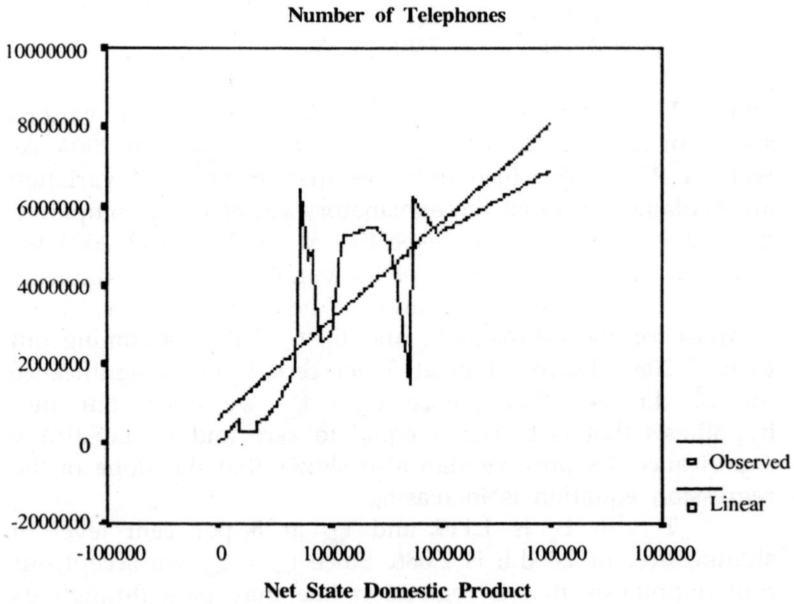

These relationships show that states, which have higher NSDP, number of telephones is also higher while states having lower NSDP have lower number of telephones. Thus NSDP may be conceived as a cause of telecom disparity among states in India.

Per-capital State Domestic Product (PSDP) and Teledensity

We will now formulate a model that is;

TD=f(P) where; TD=teledensity; P=PSDP

Meaning thereby teledensity is a function of PSDP, that is teledensity is dependant variable while PSDP is an explanatory variable now,

$$TD=b_0+b_1P$$

Relationship between Teledensity and PSDP for the Year 2003

We fit a regression line for the year 2003 and find the results as follows—

$$TD=-5.837 + 5.942\ P$$
$$(1.388) \quad (0.0)$$

The value of R^2 is 0.813, which indicates that 81 per cent variation in teledensity has been explained by PSDP.

Now we use t-test for testing estimates of b_0 and b_1.

t_{cal} for the b_0 is coming out to be -4.206 and t_{tab} at 5 per cent level of significance for 20 d.f. is -2.086 Since tcal<ttab we conclude that null hypothesis for b0 is equal to zero is accepted, that is, the regression line may pass through its origin.

Similarly, t_{cal} for b_i is coming out to be 9.334 and ttab at 5 per cent level of significance for 20 d.f. is 2.086 . Thus $t_{cal} > t_{tab}$ we reject our null hypothesis that is b_1=0 and accept alternative hypothesis. That is our estimate is significant.

Relationship between Teledensity and PSDP for the Year 2004

As formerly we have developed the model, here we

will consider the same model and fitting the regression we find the following relationship—

$$TD = -9.713 + 2.413P$$
$$(8.038) \quad (0.0)$$

The value of R^2 is 0.763, that is 76 per cent various in dependent variable, i.e. teldensity is explained by the explanatory variable, i.e. PSDP. One thing that is noted down to be here is explanatory power of model has been declined in the year 2004 against the year 2003. It was 81 per cent in the previous year while it was 76 per cent in the considering year.

We use t test for the significance of the values of b_0 and b_1. t_{cal} for b_0 is coming out to be 4.025 while t_{tab} at 5 per cent level of significance for 20 d.f. is –2.086.

Since $t_{cal} < t_{tab}$ we conclude that H_o is accepted that is the regression line may not have intercept and it will pass through its origin.

Curve Fitting for Teledensity and Per-capita Net State Domestic Product for the Year 2003

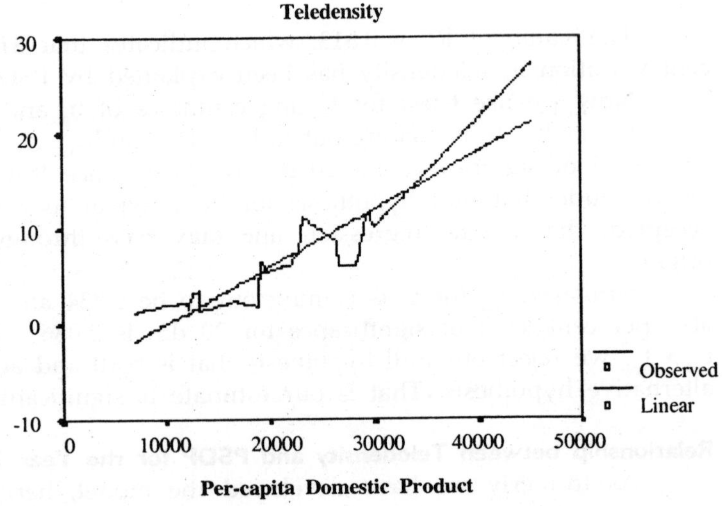

t_{cal} for b_1 is 8.034 and t_{tab} at per cent level of significance for 20 d.f. is 2.086 as $t_{cal} > t_{tab}$ we may draw the inference that is value of b_1 is statistically significant and its positive value shows that slope of the regression line is increasing.

Curve Fitting for Teledensity and Per-capita Net State Domestic Product for the Year 2004

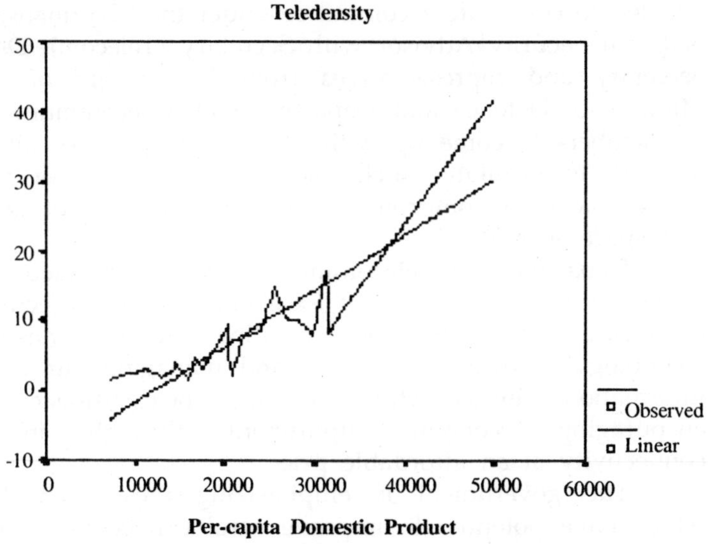

We may summarize as follows:

1. The number of telephones is significantly dependent on NSDP.
2. Teledensity is significantly dependent on PSDP.
3. In both the cases linear regression function is proportional in the year 2003 and 2004 for various states.

CONCLUSION

As we have discussed above it is clear that the Indian Telecom sector is currently witnessing a resurgent growth and has emerged as the fastest growing telecom market in the world with the addition of over 7 million subscribers per month. As well as we have discussed about disparity in telecom sector among states. It is very necessary that the government should adopt such policies, which make telecom services accessible to all the urban and rural areas providing equal opportunities. It is also an important objective of NTP 99 and the aim of this policy is to ensure rapid expansion of teledensity.

Keeping in the view the government of India has decided to constitute a committee under the Chairmanship of National Security Advisor with Secretary (Telecom), Defence Secretary and representatives from Department of Space, Ministry of Defence and Department of Telecommunications as members to come up with a workable plan for alternate network to facilitate quick release of spectrum for mobile services without compromising the requirements of Defence and space services.

Department of Telecommunications has decided to set-up seven Telecom centres of Excellence for the objectives of enhancing the talent pool, creating an environment of technology innovation, securing and managing our national information infrastructure during peace/disaster and encouraging economic upliftment through increased connectivity at an affordable price.

The government is emphasizing those technologies, which have potential to improve rural connectivity, so it is adopting modern technology including wireless Broadband, 3G, etc.

Mobile communication channels are giving strong competition to the basic telephones in the country. In order to stop cut-throat competition our telecom policy should be made eco-friendly as well as based on private-public partnership.

References

Annual Report, 2003-04 of the Department of Communication, Ministry of Communications and Information Technology.

Dhir, K.S., "A Challenges of Introducing Advanced Telecommunications in India."

Jain, R. and Chhokar, J. (1993), "Reorganization of the Telecom Sector: Past and Future", *Economic Times*, Feb. 3.

Jain, R., "Operationatizing a Regulatory Framework in India."

Jain, R. and Santry, T. (1997), "Rural Telecom Services in India", Paper presented at the Telecom Policy Research Workshop, Feb. 28-March.

Jussawaal, M., "Is the communication Link Still Missing?"

Littlechild, S.C., "Elements of Telecommunication Economics."

N.J. Kurion, "Regional Disparities in India."

N.J. Kurion, "Growing Inter-State Disparities."

Ravi, N. (1992), "Telecommunications in India: Post, Present and Future, *IEEE Communication Magazine*", March.

Saunders, Robert J., Warford Jeremy, Wellenious Bjorn, "Telecommunication and Economic Development."

Tyler, K.M. and Bednarizyk, S. (1993), "Regulatory Institutions and Process in Telecommunications: An International Study of Alternatives: Telecom Policy, Dec.

Vehara, T., "Privatization and Reorganization of Nippon Telegraph and Telephone", Restructuring and Managing the Telecommunication Sector.

Website—www.indiabudget.nic.in

43

Infrastructure Disparity and Role of MPLAD Scheme: A Case Study of Allahabad (UP)

GIRISH CHANDRA TRIPATHI, ABHISHEK KUMAR PANDEY AND SHILPI TIWARI

Most of the countries of the world either developed or underdeveloped are faced with the problems of regional imbalances and regional inequalities. Even the most advanced nations of the world are not able to solve these problems, and there are glaring disparities/inequalities at all levels of development between and within countries. Most of the developed countries as well regional imbalances/inequalities are present in substantial proportions.

Because of the glaring economic bankruptcy, regional disparities and inequalities in the India, a planning process initiated in 1951. It recognized the significance of regional imbalances/inequalities and advocated regional development of the economy. This was incorporated as an important objective of the planning in India. Consequently, "the constitution of free India resolved that, we the people of India, having solemnly resolved to constitute India into a sovereign, democratic, socialistic and secular republic and to secure to all its citizens...." The constitutional pledge to the people of India aimed an establishment of a "welfare state" which in its socuo-economic policies shall try to attain certain given objectives enshrined in the constitution of India.

The will of the people for a balanced regional economic development thus, draws force from Indian constitution itself. The directive principles, become the guiding principles, become the guiding principles of India's socio-economic policy and planning became the tool through which these aims were to be realized. The need and motivation for balanced regional economic development of all sections thus, while derives force from the directive principles of Indian constitution; the federal structure of Indian union lends credence to the demand for the balanced regional development.

Indian planners seem to be conscious of the desirability of balanced regional development in some sense too. Right from the very beginning as evident from the nature of the economic policy formulation the objective of balanced regional development was explicitly maintained during the five year plan (GOI, First Five Year Plan, 1951). The Second Five Year Plan observes that, "In comprehensive plan of development, it is axiomatic that the special areas receive due attention. The pattern of development must be so devised so as to lead balanced regional development..." (GOI, Second Five Year Plan, 1956). The Plan mentioned further, "as the development proceeds and large resources become available for investment, the stress of development programmes should be on extending the benefits of investments to underdeveloped regions." The Second Five Year Plan adopted the following programmes for the balanced regional development:

1. The programmes of agricultural, community development and local development works, etc. which spread over the entire area within the shortest possible time.
2. Facilities such as power, water supply, transport and communication, training institutions, etc. provided in backward regions that faced acute problems of unemployment.

3. Programmes of the expansion of village and small-scale industries.
4. Keep the claim of under-development regions in mind while deciding the location of new enterprises (GOI: Third Five Year Plan, 1963).

Here we emphasized on infrastructure development in terms of disparity. Infrastructure plays an important role in development at all the levels. Myrdal, Nurkse, Lewis, Rostow, Rodan and many others economist describes the importance of infrastructure in economic development. In fact development activities depend upon infrastructure facilities. It is the prerequisite of development. Therefore lack of adequate infrastructure facility is an obstacle in development. Without development of road, school, drinking water facility, sanitation, and health facility no country can develop. But unfortunately disparity can be seen at various levels in these facilities. A region is developed where all of these basic infrastructures are available on the other hand rest of the regions continuous goes worse-off. In our country decentralization adopted for development under this system various developmental plans, schemes and projects formulated and implemented through various authorities such as administrative authority, people representatives (MPs, MLA, Panchayat, Municipal Corporation, etc.) and district planning committee. Government of India introduced many of the schemes for infrastructure development since First Five Year Plan, in this paper we focused on Member of Parliament Local Area Development Scheme (MPLAD). This is a very ambitious scheme of infrastructure development. In these days this is one of the controversial scheme among of the hundreds developmental scheme. Electronic media, print media, various governmental reports expose misutilisation of the funds that is why a group of the majority continuously demanded to discontinue of the scheme on the other hand MPs wants to raise this fund so that they can developed their constituency smoothly present amount is not sufficient for development. Therefore, here a contradiction can be seen in these two approaches. In this paper an attempt has been made to know the efficacy of the scheme and how can we make it more effective? Should it continue or discontinue? Fund should be raised or not? These are an important to know, after data analysis we conclude findings and according to the problems an attempt to have given suggestion, which may be helpful to policy-makers and government.

This scheme was introduced in December 1993 to enable the members of Parliament (MPs) to identify and get implemented small works of capital nature based on locally felt needs with emphasis on creation of durable assets in their respective constituencies. Under this scheme each MP receives Rs. 2 crore annually. India is perhaps, the only country where such schemes are operating. The Ministry of Rural Development (since renamed as ministry of rural areas and employment) initially administered the scheme. Since October 1994, it has been transferred to the Ministry of Statistics and Programme implementation (henceforth, the Ministry). The Ministry prepared guidelines to be followed, covering various aspects of the scheme and amended this from time to time. The main objective of the scheme is to enable the members of parliament to recommend and get executed small works of capital nature in their constituencies. Those works can be taken up under the scheme as are development in nature and based on locally felt needs, with emphasis on creation of durable assets.

REGIONAL DISPARITY IN SELECTED CONSTITUENCIES

Three constituencies have been selected for the analysis, which are Allahabad, Phulpur and Chayal. There are wide disparity can be seen not only amongst the constituencies but also within a constituencies. Wide regional variation have found in three constituencies. Regarding infrastructure facility such as road availability, literacy rate, drinking water facility and electrification. A brief scenario of the disparity has been explained as follows:

Allahabad Constituency

The geographical area of Allahabad Constituency is 2934.76 sq. km. This is widest area among these Constituencies. There are 9 blocks in the Constituency e.g.

Chaka, Karchana, Jasara, Shankargarh, Meja, Manda, Koraon, Kaundhiyara and Uruva. Further urban area also included in the constituency, but in the study only rural area has been analysed, therefore disparity are explain only amongst the blocks. Table (A) shows the basic infrastructural disparity among the blocks. The table is based on Census 1991 inter-block disparity can be seen regarding various development indicators. According to the literacy rate Uruva (46.2%) is in highest position followed by Chaka (41.6%) and Karchana (40.6%), it is lowest in Kaundhiyara (29.6%), followed by Koraon (29.9%) and Shankargarh (34.7%). According to the pucca road availability per thousand km., it is highest for Jasara (711.3) followed by Chaka (481.8) and Koraon (467.5). On the other hand Manda (198.6) is at lowest position followed by Shankargarh (273.4) at Karchana (393.6). With 72.3 per cent electrification of the villages Karchana in the highest position followed by Uruva (62.5) and Chaka (67.0). On the other hand villages of Meja electrification only 47.3 per cent followed by Manda (48.2%) and Koraon (49.3%). dependencies on type sources of water are different amongst the blocks with the 159 number of villages Koraon take first place on the dependency of India Marka hand pump, followed by Shankargarh (149) and Manda (120). On the other hand, dependency on India Marka is lowest in Kaundhiyara (0) followed by Uruva (68) and Chaka (72). Further number of villages are also different among the blocks on the dependency of other sources.

It is highest for Kaundhiyara (83) followed by Meja (46) and Manda (46) on the other hand, it is lowest for Karchana (12) followed by Jasara (18) and Uruva (23).

Dependency on the other water sources includes wall, hand pump and tap in this context Manda (46) has highest number of villages which are depends on wall and only 9 villages of Karchana block depends on this source take lowest position. For the hand pump point of view Kaundhiyara (72), has highest number of villages depend upon this source and with zero number of villages each Manda and Uruva let lowest position.

Availability of number of schools per lakh population includes primary, middle and secondary also different among

Table (A)

Infrastructure Disparity in Allahabad Constituency

Block	*Literacy rate (%)*	*Road development (Per 1000 km.)*	*Electricity availability (Per cent)*	*India-marka villages*	*Rest of water source villages*
Chaka	41.6	481.8	67	72	25
Karchana	40.6	393.6	72.3	107	12
Jasara	38.2	711.3	67.9	91	18
Shankargarh	34.7	273.4	50.8	149	36
Meja	35.9	443.3	47.3	102	46
Manda	38.5	198.6	48.2	120	46
Koraon	29.9	624.3	49.3	159	44
Kaundhiyara	29.6	467.5	56.6	0	83
Uruva	46.2	420.8	62.6	68	23

Source: Statistical Diary (1991), Allahabad, Vikas Bhavan.

the blocks. Shankargarh (129.6) has highest number of primary schools and Chaka (72.3) has lowest number of primary schools. For the secondary schools of points Shankargarh (70.2) has highest number of schools and Jasara (29.4) has lowest number of schools with (25.9 number of middle school Chaka let highest position and Manda (6.8) has lowest number of schools.

Phulpur Constituency

The geographical area of the Phulpur constituencies is 2299.30 sq. km. and 11 blocks situated in this constituency. The name of the blocks has given in the following Table (B). According to the 1991 Census regional variation can be seen among the blocks. Mooratganj (27.2), for the pucca road availability at per thousand km. Chayal (487.6) ranked number one followed by Mooratganj (432.5) and Kaurihar (405.7). On the other hand, Sirathu (265.4) has lowest position following Nevada (265.8) and Sarsavan (349.9). Number of electrification of villages in highest in Chayal (83.74%) followed by Manjhanpur (79.82) and Sarsavan (79.49). On the other hand, Sirathu (66.44) ranked lowest position followed by Nevada (70.77) and Kada (73.05).

TABLE (B)

Infrastructure Disparity in Phulpur Constituency

Block	*Literacy rate (%)*	*Road develop-ment (Per 1000 km.)*	*Electricity availability (%)*	*India-marka villages*	*Rest of water source villages*
Phulpur	36.4	481.8	79.1	114	34
Pratappur	36.4	467.5	74.4	72	57
Handia	35.6	417.7	77	100	26
Bahadurpur	40.9	600.5	77.9	116	38
Dhanupur	34.5	357.6	81.6	172	18
Holagarh	36.5	357.6	65.6	90	0
Soraon	38.7	711.3	71.7	99	7
Mauaima	32.3	417.7	61.3	93	0
Baharia	38.4	273.4	84.4	178	21
Saidabad	37.7	365.6	78.8	98	58
Kaurihar	38	365.6	81	196	31

Source: Statistical Diary (1991), Allahabad, Vikas Bhavan.

The above table shows that literacy rate is highest in Bahadurpur (40.9%) followed by Soraon (38.7%) and Kaurihar (38.0%), on the other hand Mauaima (32.3%) let lowest position followed by Dhanupur (34.5%) and Handia (35.6%). In the pucca road at per thousand km., Soraon (711.3) let highest position followed by Bahadurpur (600.5) and Phulpur (481.8), on the other hand with 273.4 km. Baharia let lowest position followed by Dhanupur (357.6) and Holagarh (357.6). As far as electrification percentage, Baharia (84.6) shows highest position followed by Kaurihar (81.6) and Saidabad (78.8) against this Mauaima (61.3) is in lowest position followed by Holagarh (65.6) and Soraon (71.7). Finally, sources of water are also varies among the block Kaurihar (196) has highest number of villages also depends on India-Marka hand pump for water availability following Baharia

(178) and Baharia (172) on the other hand dependency is very low in Pratappur (72) followed by Holagarh (90) and Baharia (93). Further dependency on the other sources for water availability is highest in Saidabad (58), followed by Pratappur (57) and Bahadurpur (38), it is lowest in Holagarh (0) and Mauaima (0) followed by Soraon (7) and Dhanupur (18).

Other sources of water include wall, hand pump and tap. Pratappur (45) has highest number of villages depends on wall and with zero number of villages Holagarh, Soraon, Mauaima and Kaurihar let lowest position as far as hand pump concern Baharia (15) has highest number of villages which depends a hand pump and Dhanupur, Holagarh and Baharia have no number of villages depends on this source.

Availability of school as per lakh population is different among the block. Phulpur (89.4) has highest number of primary schools are Bahadurpur (56.7) has lowest number of primary schools with 37.5 number of secondary school Holagarh let highest position and Mauaima (15.2) let lowest position. In the number of middle school concern Saidabad (13.2) get highest position and Dhanupur (5.3) has lowest number of schools.

Chayal Constituency

The geographical area of the Chayal constituency is 2686.26 sq. km. and that constituency is a part of Kaushambi District. 8 blocks are situated under this constituency named Chayal, Nevada, Mooratganj, Kaurihar, Manjhanour, Sarsavan, Kada and Sirathu. The following table shows the development scenario of the constituency.

The table represents that with 30.7 per cent literacy rate Kada is a highest position followed by Chayal (30.4) and Sarsavan (27.9). On the other hand, Nevada (20.7) had lowest position in literacy rate followed by Manjhanpur (22.5) and Kada (27.2) and Mooratganj (27.2), for the pucca road availability at per thousand km. Chayal (487.6) ranked number one followed by Mooratganj (432.5) and Kaurihar (405.7). On the other hand, Sirathu (265.4) has lowest position following Nevada (265.8) and Sarsavan (349.9). Number of electrification of villages is highest in Chayal (83.74%) followed by Manjhanpur (79.82) and Sarsavan (79.49). On the other hand, Sirathu (66.44) ranked lowest position followed by Nevada (70.77) and Kada (73.05)

TABLE (C)

Infrastructure Disparity in Chayal Constituency

Block	*Literacy rate (%)*	*Road development (Per 1000 km.)*	*Electricity availability (%)*	*India-marka villages*	*Rest of water source villages*
Chayal	30.4	487.6	83.74	99	8
Nevada	20.7	265.8	70.37	118	1
Mooratganj	27.2	432.5	79.05	34	49
Kaushambi	27.6	406.7	79.28	70	21
Manjhanpur	22.5	492.0	79.82	99	0
Sarsavan	27.9	349.9	79.49	76	3
Kada	30.7	377.1	73.05	81	29
Sirathu	27.2	265.4	66.44	122	14

Source: Statistical Diary (1991), Allahabad, Vikas Bhavan.

Disparity can also seen about the different sources of water, Sirathu (122) is at highest position on the dependency of India-Marka hand pump followed by Nevada (118) and Manjhanpur (99) and Chayal (99). On the other hand, lowest dependency in this regard is in Mooratganj (34) followed by Sarsavan (76), and Kaushambi (70). Further dependency on other water sources are highest for Mooratganj (49) followed by Kada (29) and Kaushambi (21), on the other hand no number of villages depends on other sources in Manjanpur block. Nevada and Sarsavan have respectively 1 and 3 number of villages that depends on other sources. Other sources as includes wall, hand pump and tap. Dependency on wall is highest in Mooratganj (32) and lowest (0) in many of the blocks such as Chayal, Nevada, Manjhanpur and Sirathu, with 17 number of villages Mooratganj again at top position on the dependency of hand pump is lowest in Manjhanpur (0).

According to the number of schools per lakh population Kaushambi (69.4) has highest number of primary schools followed by Manjhanpur (63.1) and Sarsavan (61.9), Chayal has only 47.8 primary schools. For the secondary school point of view it is highest in Manjhanpur (19.1) and lowest in Kada (10.2). With 5.8 Kada get highest position to the number of middle school as it is lowest (2.2) in Sirathu.

RESEARCH METHODOLOGY

Uttar Pradesh is the state of highest Population, therefore parliamentary seats are also highest in the state both for Lok Sabha and Rajya Sabha, and it is 80 and 31 respectively. The study has tries to know feedback of MPLAD Scheme at gross root level, further where and what is the main problem in the execution of scheme. In this study only Lok Sabha constituencies has been selected for the analysis because these MPs are represent at a particular region or area, they can spend their fund in these Particular regions from where they elected while Rajya Sabha MPs are representatives of the state. They can spend their fund in any where within the state. Actually they do not elected by Public directly, so peoples' expectations and interaction are not to much with him. For the Lok Sabha MPs, peoples directly elect them and they can approach with them regarding any demand in developmental works if they have any requirements, Lok Sabha MPs accountable for this because they elected by Public and for Public. That is why only Lok Sabha constituencies have been selected in the studies.

From each constituency two blocks has been selected on the basis of highest and lowest expenditure under MPLAD scheme. From Allahabad constituency Koraon and Chaka, Bahadurpur and Holagarh from Phulpur Constituency and Kaushambi and Chyal from Chyal constituency have been selected. In this way six blocks have been finalized for the study. Most of the fund has spent on road and bridges, schools, drinking water and electricity. These are also basic needs of the people therefore study has covered only these four sectors enumerated below:

TABLE I

MPLADS Expenditure and Indicators of Infrastructure Development of Phulpur Constituency

Phulpur	30.01	36.4	87.66	481.8	2.95	79.1	0.17	114	34
Pratappur	24.56	36.4	119.71	467.5	00	74.4	38.11	72	57
Handia	43.08	35.6	113.45	417.7	1.6	77	0.16	100	26
Bahadurpur	36.74	40.9	114.15	600.5	2.18	77.9	42.44	116	38
Dhanupur	13.10	34.5	89.51	357.6	1.6	81.6	00	172	18
Holagarh	45.38	36.5	51.41	357.6	00	65.6	00	90	0
Soraon	25.12	38.7	98.74	711.3	1.15	71.7	2.2	99	7
Mauaima	11.25	32.3	90.85	417.7	00	61.3	4.95	93	0
Baharia	30.37	38.4	104.71	273.4	3.59	84.4	5.61	178	21
Saidabad	30.25	37.7	159.05	365.6	2.6	78.8	2.91	98	58
Kaurihar	20.29	38	72.46	365.6	1.00	81	20.01	196	31

Source: Compiled from MPLDS expenditure and Statistical Diary (1991).

- Road and Bridges
- Schools
- Drinking Water
- Electricity

The Reference Period

Although this scheme was introduced in December 1993, but in this study those work has been selected which have done between 1996 to 2006. The reason behind this is that secondary data regarding expenditure of the scheme are available from 1996 when computerization has been done in sample constituencies. Therefore 1996-2006, ten years time period has selected for the analysis.

The Sample Size

During the period of 1996 to 2006, 301 works has been done in sample blocks regarding four selected sectors. In these works 81 works (26.91%) has proportionally selected amongst the various four sectors, from road and bridges, school, drinking water and electricity.

We have selected four basic infrastructure development indicators, e.g. school development, road development, electricity and water availability for the year 1991. The reason behind the selection of this year is that the MPLADS starts from 1993 and work for infrastructure development in local area, there has to be some rationale for expenditure under this scheme. It has to need basis or those areas where infrastructure development indicators performing low demands more expenditure through this scheme.

Table 2 shows that the highest expenditure were made for school infrastructure development through this scheme is for Karchana where literacy rate is satisfactory as compare to other blocks in this constituency. Here lowest literacy rates occurs in Manda and Kaundhiyara blocks where demands more expenditure but data shows that only Rs. 3.5 lakh and Rs. 4.4 lakh respectively spent during 1996-2006 under this scheme, which shows that the MPLADS does not focus on the development of infrastructure to enhance the literacy and education facilities according to the demand basis. For the Road development the highest expenditure were made

TABLE 2

MPLADS Expenditure and Indicators of Infrastructure Development of Allahabad

Block	*Exp. on school (in Lakh)*	*Literacy rate (%)*	*Exp. on road (in Lakh)*	*Road development (Per 1000 km)*	*Exp. on electricity (in Lakh)*	*Electricity availability (%)*	*Exp. on water (in Lakh)*	*India-marka villages*	*Rest of water source villages*
Chaka	19.25	41.6	72.6	481.8	00	67	00	72	25
Karchana	59.11	40.6	81.28	393.6	00	72.3	0.34	107	12
Jasara	8.65	38.2	145.52	711.3	00	67.9	00	91	18
Shankargarh	29.5	34.7	71.23	273.4	3.58	50.8	52.95	149	36
Meja	47.24	35.9	185.24	443.3	00	47.3	1.17	102	46
Manda	3.5	38.5	163.94	198.6	00	48.2	5.00	120	46
Koraon	38.47	29.9	272.38	624.3	00	49.3	0.86	159	44
Kaundhiara	4.4	29.6	109.04	467.5	00	56.6	0.32	0	83
Uruva	30.84	46.2	115.52	420.8	00	62.6	9.45	68	23

through this scheme for Koraon block where already the second longest road developed in 1991. Here again Manda needs more expenditure through this scheme. For electricity availability there has no proper work made through this scheme except the Shankargarh block. This is not the one of lowest electrically developed block and not the highest one so the reason has to be found for this expenditure otherwise the fair analysis for this could not be possible. The water availability is shown on the basis of number of villages with different

According to the local need Mauaima had the lowest literacy rate while the expenditure of MPLADS is also low in this block, which has, be high to develop the literacy and education facility in this block. Apart from that in this constituency the expenditure on education were made according to the needs of other blocks, e.g. Handia, Holagarh. Therefore, the correlation coefficient value is good for this as compare to other indicators and MPLADS expenditure (see Table 4). For road development Phulpur performance is poor when we compare this to Allahabad where again discrepancy occurs in expenditure and development. Again the expenditure on road development is made in those blocks where already road exist in satisfactory manner. The expenditure on road development is made almost in every block with marginal difference it doesn't consider the development status of road in these blocks.

Here the expenditure on electricity is quite satisfactory as compare to other constituencies. But again the pattern of distribution of expenditure in these blocks is quite irrational. Those blocks where electricity availability is lowest e.g. Mauaima, Holagarh and Pratappur, the expenditure under this scheme is nil, or those blocks where electricity availability is satisfactory the expenditure of MPLADS is also high, therefore the value of correlation coefficient is high (see Table 4), which is quite disturbing. Water availability in this area is more or less depends on India-marka but the ratio behind the expenditure on water resources

Through MPLADS is not understandable. Here one more interesting thing is that the expenditure on water resources is very less as compare to expenditure on other items. The reason behind this is very political and interest making between center and state government.

Table 3 shows the situation of infrastructure development of Chayal constituency and related MPLADS expenditure. The situation of this constituency according to the expenditure of MPLADS on selected indicators is very poor. First of all we taken the school development then we find that Chayal pursue very low level of literacy overall, therefore it needs more expenditure on it, but contemporary there were very few amount spent on it and specially those blocks, which needs more fund to generate education facilities were lacking behind to avail expenditure of MPLADS e.g. Nevada, Mooratganj, Sarsavan, Kada and Sirathu. The large amount of expenditure is for Kaushambi under this head but the reason behind this is unexplainable.

The relationship between road development and MPLADS expenditure is also not satisfactory in this constituency.

Resulting this discrepancy we find the correlation coefficient value of MPLADS expenditure in this constituency with school development is negative (see Table 4).

Sarsavan and Kada did not avail single amount of expenditure through this scheme while there is possibility to develop Kada as a religious tourist place. Here again Kaushambi avail the large amount of expenditure on road development. The expenditure pattern is almost same for Nevada and Mooratganj while road development situation in both locks were very different. In Chayal constituency the MPLADS expenditure is not made for water and electricity facility, which is quite surprising. Therefore, for this area the last two indicators analysis could not be possible. The Table 4 shows the correlation coefficient values of selected indicators and MPLADS expenditure on it in selected constituencies for the study. MPLADS do not perform well on expenditure of any one of selected indicator except from electricity availability in Phulpur constituency.

In some sectors they were negatively correlated. Table 5 also shows that in Phulpur constituency MPLADS expenditure perform better in education facility (.452) as compare to correlation coefficient values of other selected

TABLE 3

MPLADS Expenditure and Indicators of Infrastructure Development of Chayal

Block	*Exp. on school (in Lakh)*	*Literacy rate (%)*	*Exp. on road (in Lakh)*	*Road development (Per 1000 km)*	*Exp. on electricity (in Lakh)*	*Electricity availability (%)*	*Exp. on water (in Lakh)*	*India-marka villages*	*Rest of water source villages*
Chayal	4.98	30.4	37.1	487.6	00	83.74	00	99	8
Nevada	6.42	20.7	8.00	265.8	00	70.37	00	118	1
Mooratganj	00	27.2	8.26	432.5	00	79.05	00	34	49
Kaushambi	34.10	27.6	63.61	406.7	00	79.28	00	70	21
Manjhanpur	4.00	22.5	12.49	492.0	00	79.82	00	99	0
Sarsavan	00	27.9	00	349.9	00	79.49	00	76	3
Kada	00	30.7	00	377.1	00	73.05	00	81	29
Sirathu	00	27.2	14.44	265.4	00	66.44	00	122	14

Source: MPLADS Expenditure and Sstatistical Diary (1991), Allahabd.

indicators e.g. road development (.104), water availability (.150). (Here we cannot leave the correlation value of electricity availability and expenditure of MPLADS, which is 762, but we were earlier said that it is not because of better results of MPLADS in this area but it is because of some basic statistical reason like the both series moving with same pattern).

Table 4 shows that in Chayal constituency MPLADS expenditure perform better in road development (.318) for literacy rate or development of education facilities the scheme performance is very poor and it is negatively correlated (-.035). The correlation coefficient values of rest of two indicators of Chayal constituency were not computed because there was no expenditure made in these items during 1996-2006, which is quite surprising. While the area demands more development in these indicators in Chayal as compare to other selected constituencies.

TABLE 4

Pearson (Linear)-Correlation between Selected Indicator of Infrastructure Development and MPLADS Expenditure during 1993-2006

(Significant at the 0.05 Level)

	Literacy rate	*Road development*	*Electricity availability*	*Water availability*
Allahabad Constituency				
Expenditure	.138 (.362)	.382 (.155)	-.280 (.233)	.393 (.148)
Phulpur Constituency				
Expenditure	.452 (.081)	.104 (.381)	.762 (.003)	.150 (.330)
Chayal Constituency				
Expenditure	-.035 (.467)	.318 (.221)	**	**

Calculated with the help of Tables 1, 2 and 3.
Note: *Means; cannot compute at least one of the variables is constant.

On the basis of above we find that linkages between the expenditure of MPLADS and indicators of infrastructure development were really very poor; there is such no rationale behind the funding of project and the local needs under this scheme. In Allahabad constituency on the basis of infrastructure development Manda is one of the poorest block, therefore, this need more focus but on the contemporary the expenditure for infrastructure development through MPLADS is almost negligible in this block. Meanwhile for the same constituency at Karchana blocks the indicators of infrastructure development is almost high as compare to other blocks in 1991 at the same time the expenditure under MPLADS is also very high for the same. In Phulpur constituency Mauaima, Holagarh and Pratappur is least developed block and in Chayal Sarsavan and Nevada is one of the least developed blocks and demands more expenditure through MPLADS but the scheme is lacking behind to generate fruitfulness of this scheme according to the demand of local people. The above analysis is tested through t-test and find correct.

FINDINGS

The findings of the study are following:

(1) Lack of adequate information available to MPs seems to be one of the contributing factors leading to such an undesirable situation. Many of the MPs do not have complete information even about the works they have recommended

(2) Unfortunately MPLAD scheme increases regional infrastructure disparity. They always sanctioning fund for those area where they can gets maximum vote and not concerned regional science.

(3) To know the needs of the People as well as area MPs do not have developed any mechanism. They do not try that how can they utilise these funds in developmental works. It is the reason; this scheme does not success to reduce regional disparity. Many of the blocks in constituencies of many MPs

have not given any fund for selected items during last 10 years. (See expenditure of chayal constituency)

(4) Most of the funds are allocates for roads and schools. Drinking water and electricity are avoidable sectors MPs are not seems too interested in these sectors, no or nominal funds have been spent in these sectors. In this regard MPs admitted that they have not sufficient fund, therefore, they cannot give similar consideration for all of the sectors. Further they slightly emphasised they are Political Persons and they cannot avoid political consideration in sanctioning projects. They have to tries satisfy all of them, this is the reason that share of small projects are high in overall works which have been done under MPLAD Scheme.

(5) There are wide mismatch between the works, which have preferred by the local people and the work, which have done by concerning MPs. Although people accept that the works, which have done, are useful for them but according to Priority based they are not satisfied with this. For example, most of the area in sample constituencies suffers with drinking water facility but maximum fund has been allocate for road and bridges by MPs. Therefore, MPs fail to recognize need-based Priority of the area.

(6) Most of the MPs while allocating funds to individual works seem to be thrifty, despite of the fact that there is large unspent balance of MPLADS. All the works in the sample constituencies when cross-tabulated by sectors and amount allocated depicts a distribution, which is skewed towards lower allocation irrespective of the sectors. At the aggregate level about 42.6 per cent an allocation less than Rs. 1 lakh, while works with allocation of Rs. 5 lakh or more constitute only 17 per cent of the works. Many of these small works are so small that one may classify these as petty works. A large number of

these come under roads and bridges. The roads thus constructed are often Kachcha and have short length and durability because of inadequate funds. Such roads often fail to connect effectively one village with another or the village with other important places. This perhaps is not in conformity with the objective of creating durable assets.

(7) Monitoring and supervision is perhaps the weakest part of the scheme. This seems to be largely due to inadequate infrastructure available to the collector vested with the responsibility. Despite suggestion in the guidelines, the number of visits to the sites by the head of the district was far short of the norm. Collectors largely depended on other development functionaries for monitoring. Collectors are administrative authority to the execution of the work. During discussion they accept that they have suffered with higher workload. Therefore, they cannot proper monitor the works.

(8) Maintenance of assets created is another area of weakness of the scheme. This seems to have received lesser attention than it deserves. Despite suggestion in the guidelines collectors could not ensure some Provisions of maintenance before sanctioning works. For many of the assets created there seems to be no arrangement, either physical or financial, for maintenance. In fact no body seems to know how and who is maintaining these assets. Therefore, it is urgently needed to taken some strict steps so that maintenance of assets may be secure.

(9) Lack of co-ordination among the MPs, MLAs and district planning committee is a serious problem. MPs and MLAs do not consulted to each other. In this situation it may be possible that fund for any particular items sanction by both representatives. Therefore overlapping possibilities are always remaining in sanctioning fund.

(10) One thing is very important to mention here that, MPs often depends on their representatives for recommendation of the work. They does not seems interested to know, what types of the work should have been sanctioned in any particular area. Every MP has their agents in different areas of their constituency. Works recommended for materialisation, are based on such agents and the agents representing only a section of people not the whole. On all occasion due to local politics these agents recommends the works only to satisfy their ego.

(11) If we look on the performance of MPLAD scheme, it is appeared that it is a pivotal cause of regional disparity within a constituency. It is revealed that the MPs are always interested to develop only those areas of their constituencies wherefrom they get maximum votes for their win. Means they use this scheme to satisfy their loyal only. In a broad view this scheme is now become an effective mean of satisfaction.

SUGGESTION

For improving the performance of the scheme and achieving optimum benefits out of it certain changes are inevitable. These are given as follows:

(1) Many of the MPs do not have full information even about the works they have recommended for effective monitoring and supervision of the works in progress. Adequate arrangements need to be made for making all relevant information available to the MPs. In addition, to it emphasis on co-ordination between MPs (both Lok Sabha and Rajya Sabha) and between MPs and nodal department is required for the selection of districts. Upper limit of number of projects and completion of the same as per specifications with appropriate fund need to be ensured in the guidelines.

(2) The state nodal departments will need to be strengthened in terms of staff and other infrastructure. At the ground level, the PRI may be involved in execution as well as monitoring to a larger extent. The collector may continue to receive fund from the ministry and recommendation of the works from MPs. he may also scrutinize the recommendations, according to administrative sanction and release fund for individual works. The execution, monitoring and supervision may be largely shared between the strengthened state nodal department and the PRI's. The PRI's may send monitoring reports to the state nodal department and the collector periodically. The collector on receipt of these reports can then make it available to the ministry and the concerned MP. Relevant information about other developmental activities in the district may also be made available to the MP equipped with these detailed informations the MPs are likely to be in a more comfortable position to recommendation of specific works.

(3) To help the MPs to determine priorities the felt needs of various groups of population, the PRI's may be asked to provide a list of works to be recommended to the MP annually. This list may also be displayed conspicuously for public information.

(4) To avoid inadequate allocation of fund for individual works, the assets intended to be created may be described in more details so that its cost implication is clear. The MP may consider allocation of fund only after the cost estimation is prepared and the detailed work plan and coordination mechanism are made available to him.

(5) For some of the assets there is a natural agency for maintenance, upkeep and use. For others it is necessary to locate an agency to maintain the assets. This should preferably be done before the

work is sanctioned. Availability of adequate fund for this purpose will also need to be insured either from Public fund or through user charges to be collected, wherever possible.

(6) Awareness among the people is prerequisite for successful implementation of any scheme. Displaying the details of the work at the site may be made mandatory. In addition, full details about all the ongoing works under MPLADS (and other such schemes) in the district may be displayed prominently at collector's office. Other methods of publicity through local newspapers and electronic media may be explored. In addition, explaining the scheme in a meeting of the Gram Sabha for the benefit of those who can not read and write is likely to be very effective.

(7) Finally morality is almost an essential requirement in the absence of honest no scheme can be successful. Corruption is the major problem in this scheme now it is necessary for the efficacy of the scheme that MP, administrative authority and other players who play an important role in this scheme must be honest.

(8) There is no need to raise the amount of the fund, it is fully illogical this amount of the fund is sufficient for development it will be definitely effective if implicate honestly.

44

Inter-State Pattern of Technology Achievement in India

ALPANA KATEJA

INTRODUCTION

India has emerged as a powerful global player in Information and Communication Technology (ICT) market. The phenomenal growth of ICT sector has also contributed in spectacular growth of Indian economy (Joseph and Abraham, 2005). The pace of growth of the IT sector in India has been rapid and continuous; the share of IT sector output in GDP has risen to 4.5 per cent in 2004-05 from a mere 0.44 per cent in 1990-91 (NASSCOM, 2006). This sector has not only grown in size but also in complexity (Joseph and Harilal, 2001). The IT export market alone brings about two third of its total revenue to the industry. Indian software industry accounts for roughly about two per cent of the four hundred billion US$ global software industry. However, the growth rate of Indian software industry has been substantially higher than the global software industry. In fact, India is the only country in the world to register a growth rate of around 50 per cent in the software industry (Kumar, N., 2001). NASSCOM (2006) indicates that the Indian IT-ITES (Information Technology Enabled Services) sector continues to chart double-digit growth. IT-ITES industry continues to grow five times as fast as the global IT services industry, clocking a compound annual growth rate of 28 per cent since 1999-2000. Out of this, software and services exports are estimated to grow by 32 per cent, to reach $23.4 billion in 2005-06 (NASSCOM, 2006). NASSCOM (2006) has forecast that a growth rate of over 25 per cent is expected to continue and would help Indian IT-ITES exports exceed US$ 60 billion by 2010.

Every state in India is making serious effort to participate in the digital economy. But the fact is that Indian states resemble little nations and there exists vast interstate inequalities in infrastructure, human resources and policies. So, it is essential to take stock of the preparedness of states. With this objective, ministry of information technology (MIT) brings out "e-Readiness Survey" which presents e-Readiness Index and accordingly ranks all states of India. At the state level, the value of e-Readiness Index—composed of large number of variables that fall into three broad categories; environment, readiness and usage—reflects the capacity of a state to participate in the networked economy in relation to the country at large.

The aim of this article is first, to prepare an alternative Technology Achievement Index (TAI) for states of India to gauge the preparedness and achievements of states and second, to compare this rather crude measure with sophisticated 'e-Readiness Index'.

The paper is organized in four sections. Section I summarizes components of TAI. Section II presents methodology and data, Section III discusses important results and compares TAI with e-Readiness Index, and finally, Section IV concludes.

I

ASSESSING CAPACITY: TECHNOLOGY ACHIEVEMENT INDEX

The technological transformations of the past decade and the emergence of the global marketplace in India have raised the stakes for all states of India to become technologically connected to be able to create, adapt and use global technological innovations. Yet the challenges of competing in the technology-based global marketplace and of harnessing technology as a tool for development are very different across states, which vary greatly in their technological capacity and needs. This section presents a measurement approach to assess the technological achievements of major states of India, as an aid to policy-makers in identifying policy priorities.

TAI, similar to e-readiness Index (MIT, 2005), attempts to measure "the ability of a state to provide business, the capacity to participate in the provincial level digital economy and further networking with the national level digital economy." True e-readiness is very difficult to measure. However, without measurement, governments and other policy and decision-makers would be "flying blind." TAI would reflect the level of technological progress and thus the capacity of a state to participate in the network age. It would help a state situate itself relative to others, especially those farther ahead. Many elements make up a state's technological achievement, but an overall assessment is more easily made based on a single composite measure than on dozens of different measures. TAI aims to capture technological achievements of a state in four dimensions: Infrastructure, Human Capital, Information Technology Achievements and Communication Technology Achievements. Thus, it is not a measure of technology development alone, but focuses on how well the state as a whole is participating in creating and using technology. The TAI focuses on four dimensions of technological capacity which are important to reap the benefits of the network age. These indicators relate to important technology policy objectives for all states, regardless of their level of development.

I. Infrastructure

Even though all states need not to be at the leading edge of global technological development, but the infrastructural capacity is relevant for all states and constitutes the highest level of technological capacity. All states need to have the infrastructural capacity to innovate because the ability to innovate in the use of technology cannot be fully developed without the capacity to create, especially to adapt products and processes to local conditions. In the absence of perfect indicators and data series, the TAI uses two indicators to capture the level of infrastructure in a society. The first is the urbanization rate, to reflect the current level of urbanization and modernization. The second is percentage of households electrified, as ICT usage is directly dependent on electricity.

2. Human Skill

A critical mass of skills is indispensable for technological dynamism. Both creators and users of new technology need skills. Today's technology requires adaptability-skills to master the constant flow of innovations. The foundations of such ability are basic education to develop cognitive skills. Cognitive skills are hard to define and measure. The first indicator used is the Gross Enrolment Ratio and the second indicator used to gauge human skills is the out turn of undergraduates from technical institutions. This measure gives an idea of the current effort in developing advanced skills in science, mathematics, engineering and technology. Every state needs this skill base to be able to innovate and adapt to new technologies. Although it would be desirable to include indicators of vocational training, the data are not available.

3. Information Technology Achievements

All states must adopt innovations to benefit from the opportunities of the network age. This is measured by diffusion of the Internet, indispensable to participation, and by exports of IT (high-technology and medium-technology) products. While the number of internet connected computers does not tell us how many users there are, it gives a fairly good indication and data are available for practically all states. By dramatically increasing the access to information while decreasing the cost, the Internet has vast potential to aid political participation, to increase people's incomes, and to improve healthcare. Second indicator used for measuring the diffusion of recent technology is software exports. It is used assuming that the higher the diffusion of new technology the higher the software exports. In India, currently exports are the major contributors in the total IT sector revenue.

4. Communication Technology Achievements

Participation in the network age requires diffusion of many old innovations. Although leapfrogging is sometimes possible, technological advancement is a cumulative process, and widespread diffusion of older innovations is necessary for adoption of later innovations. Two indicators used here, landline and mobile density are especially important because they are needed to use newer technologies and are also pervasive inputs to a multitude of human activities.

II

WEIGHTING AND AGGREGATION

The methodology used to calculate the TAI is similar to HDI (UNDP, 2001): a simple average of the dimensions of the index, which in turn is calculated based on the selected indicators. The TAI has eight indicators, two in each of the four dimensions; Infrastructure, measured by the urbanization rate and by percentage of households electrified; Human Skills measured by Gross Enrolment Ratio and Out turn of undergraduates from technical institutions; Information Technology achievements, measured by the number of Internet users per thousand population and total IT exports and Communication Technology achievements measured by telephones (mainline and cellular) per hundred population.. The values of the different indicators are normalized to a scale from 0 to 1 using goalposts, such that an indicator value that is equal to the upper goalpost will be normalized to 1 and a value equal to the lower goalpost will be normalized to 0, according to the formula:

$$\text{Indicator index} = \frac{\text{Actual value - Observed minimum value}}{\text{Observed maximum value - Observed minimum value}}$$

A second important issue is that of weighting of different indicators and dimensions. The index for each dimension is calculated as the simple average of the indicator indices in that dimension. The TAI, in turn, is the simple average of these four dimension indices. The indicators in each dimension are given equal weight, and the dimensions are given equal (one-quarter) weight in the final index. This means that diffusion of technology is, effectively, given more weight since two of the four dimensions deal with this.

III
RESULTS

While Karnataka is doing better than Maharashtra and Tamil Nadu in entering the high technology export market, with its world class hubs and pioneering policies, Maharashtra and Tamil Nadu do well in the index, ranking top out of seventeen major states. Their high score is due, first and foremost, to outturn from undergraduate technical institutions. In both these states number of internet users per thousand people is also at the highest levels in the country. It shows that top ranker states Maharashtra, Tamil Nadu and Karnataka have responded very positively to the niche opportunities that are being created in the global market.

Punjab occupies high rank only due to better performance in infrastructure and communication technology achievement. Yet other indicators show that Punjab has long way to go in developing its technological capacity and translating that for the purpose of promotion of business and exports.

Gujarat, Kerala and Himachal Pradesh rank high in TAI. It reflects their considerable capacity in the way of modern society equipped with essential capabilities to reap the benefits of e-readiness. Yet the technological advances are not widespread. In contrast, Andhra Pradesh, though ranked moderate in TAI, reflects its technological success in using advanced technology and the ability to compete successfully in the technology based global market place. The state's consistent performance in all components places it on the top in e-readiness Index. In Andhra Pradesh, initiatives like Rajiv

Internet Village (RAJIV), launched in 2004, seeks to provide a host of services to the rural populace through its 22, 000 kiosks. The State Government has also taken proactive steps like attractive investment promotion policies. Due to these measures it is estimated that Andhra Pradesh would capture 33 per cent of the national IT and IT enabled services market by 2009 (MIT, 2005).

Haryana follows the list. In last few years the state has registered commendable improvement in ICT performance. Gurgaon in Haryana has been the IT destination in the North. Almost all big names in the IT section have registered their presence in this town. The state Government has been proactive in having an IT policy, web policy, a number of incentives to software firms and an e-Governance policy to provide effective governance to business and people.

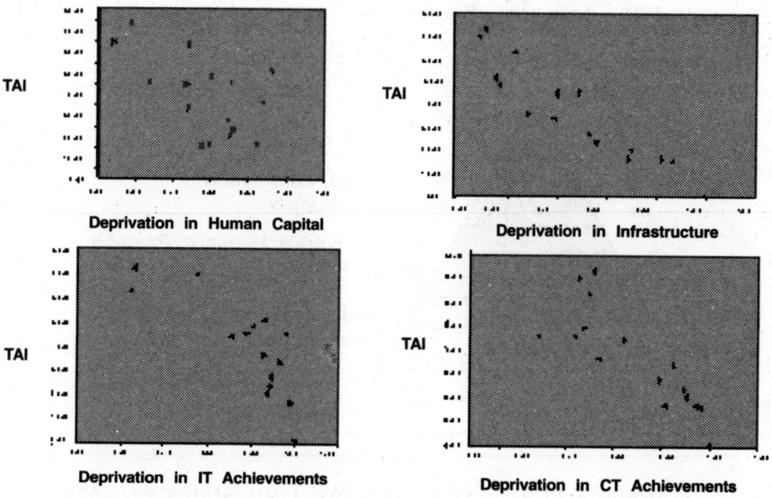

Economically backward states sometimes referred to as BIMARU states lag behind in the index, holding the low positions. TAI has significant high correlation (0.798) with per-capita NSDP. This suggests that economic well-being of a state is directly related to ICT growth. There is significantly high positive rank correlation between TAI and e-Readiness Index (0.8137).

The results show great disparities among states with TAI values ranging from 0 for Bihar to 0.74 for Maharashtra. On the basis of TAI values all states can be classified among four categories viz. leaders, aspiring leaders, followers and least achievers.

Leaders (TAI > 0.50): This category is at the cutting edge of technological innovations. Four states, Maharashtra, Tamil Nadu, Karnataka and Punjab fall in this category. These states have high achievements in all components except that Punjab which is on the margin of this category does not perform well in human capital and diffusion of new technology.

Aspiring leaders (TAI = 0.35 to 0.49): This group characterizes excellent infrastructure and diffusion old innovations but rather lags behind in developing human skills and also in diffusion of new innovations. Gujarat, Kerala, Himachal Pradesh, Andhra Pradesh and Haryana fall in this category.

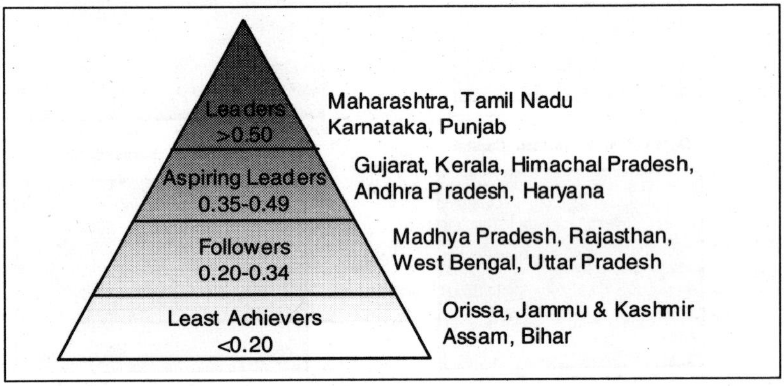

Followers (TAI = 0.20 to 0.34): Four states viz. Madhya Pradesh, Rajasthan, West Bengal and Uttar Pradesh falling into this category do neither have developed infrastructure nor have vital human skills. These states have a very long way to travel. Even diffusion of old technology is not satisfactory. So, development of human skills accompanied with essential infrastructure especially electricity and teledensity is the policy prescription for these densely populated states.

Least Achievers (TAI < 0.20): Four major states namely Orissa, Jammu & Kashmir Assam and Bihar are just like dark black spots on the shining India. Very poor performance of these states is clearly evident in all spheres. In fact, on the basis of e-readiness value these four major states are far behind small state like Goa and union territories like Chandigarh and Pondicherry (MIT, 2005).

IV

CONCLUSION

It is true that TAI does not capture all dimensions of ICT achievements. However, to the extent that it focuses on significant components of ICT achievements, there is merit in using it to measure states' performance. India being a large country with huge heterogeneity among the states in socio-economic indicators, regional ICT indicators are also expected to vary widely across regions. Therefore, analysis of state-wise performance is even more important in ICT sector. TAI values and state rankings based on it indicate great disparities among seventeen major states of India. In general, southern states have performed well while technological advances are not widespread among the states in the central belt. The study of different components of TAI reveals that lack of development of human skill and deficient diffusion of recent technology are the chief causes for the states to trail behind. Follower states and least achiever states should concentrate on quick formulation and efficient implementation of appropriate policies to put them in the mainstream. At the same time in view of ever increasing global market, there is substantial scope for leaders too, to attain new heights.

REFERENCES

Joseph, K.J. and Abraham, Vinoj (2005): "Moving up or Lagging Behind? An Index of Technological Competence in India's ICT Sector" in Saith and Vijayabaskar, ICT's and Indian Economic Development (Ed), Sage Publications, New Delhi.

Joseph, K.J. and K.N. Harilal (2001): "Structure and Growth of India's IT Exports: Implications of an Export-Oriented Growth Strategy", *Economic and Political Weekly*, 36(34).

Kumar, N (2001): "Indian Software Industry Development: National and International Perspectives", *Economic and Political Weekly*, 36(44).

MIT (2005): "E-Readiness Survey", Report by Ministry of Information Technology, Government of India.

NASSCOM (National Association of Software and Service Companies) (2006): "Indian IT Software and Services Directory", New Delhi, NASSCOM.

UNDP (2001): Human Development Report, Oxford University Press.

TABLE I

State-level Achievements in ICT

State	Infrastructure		Human Capital		IT Achievement		CT Achievement	
	Urbanisation Rate (2001)	Electrified Households	Gross Enrolment Ratio (2005)	Outturn from Undergraduate Technical Institutions (2003)	IT Exports (2006)	Internet Users/ 1000 Popn. (2003)	Tele-Density (2004-05)	Mobile Density (2007)
1	2	3	4	5	6	7	8	9
Andhra Pradesh	27.08	67.17	86.99	20099	12620.32	2.89	9.48	17
Assam	12.72	24.9	91.92	n.a.	0	0.54	2.79	9
Bihar	10.47	10.25	65.16	n.a.	4.22	0.23	2.36	7.6
Gujarat	37.35	80.41	101.7	6944	443.12	3.86	12.73	21.5
Haryana	29	82.9	80.01	1950	8410.25	1.05	10.83	20.6
Himachal Pradesh	9.79	94.82	108.74	n.a.	12.5	1.02	13.12	22.7
Jammu & Kashmir	24.88	24.3	74.45	n.a.	1	0.53	5.09	13.7
Karnataka	33.98	78.55	98.76	14550	41429.94	4.91	12.19	21.2
Kerala	25.97	70.24	95.35	3944	852.89	4.29	18.77	23.6

(Contd.)

TABLE I

1	2	3	4	5	6	7	8	9
Madhya Pradesh	26.67	69.98	124.95	3439	201.98	1.48	5.21	11.7
Maharashtra	42.4	77.49	105.7	27157	19644.79	9.8	9.96	22.9
Orissa	14.97	26.91	108.47	4316	466	0.61	3.96	8.3
Punjab	33.95	91.91	72.57	2944	265.28	2.88	21.94	34.2
Rajasthan	23.38	54.69	102.67	1976	459.17	2.15	6.12	13.8
Tamil Nadu	43.86	78.18	113.96	28107	14573.96	5.31	11.21	24.7
Uttar Pradesh	20.78	31.9	87.04	8083	8455.3	0.75	4.06	10.4
West Bengal	28.03	37.45	94.67	3834	2721.84	1.78	2.98	12.7

TABLE 2

Technology Achievement Index (TAI)

S. No.	*State*	*Index of*				*Composite Index of TAI*	*Rank (TAI)*	*Rank E-Readiness*
		Infra-structure	*Human Capital*	*IT Achievement*	*CT Achievement*			
1.	Andhra Pradesh	0.59	0.56	0.29	0.36	0.45	8	1
2.	Assam	0.13	0.45	0.02	0.04	0.16	16	15
3.	Bihar	0.01	0.00	0.00	0.00	0.00	17	16
4.	Gujarat	0.82	0.43	0.20	0.53	0.49	5	8
5.	Haryana	0.71	0.16	0.14	0.46	0.37	9	7
6.	Himachal Pradesh	0.50	0.73	0.04	0.56	0.46	7	12
7.	Jammu and Kashmir	0.30	0.16	0.02	0.18	0.16	15	17
8.	Karnataka	0.76	0.56	0.74	0.51	0.64	3	3
9.	Kerala	0.59	0.32	0.22	0.72	0.46	6	4
10.	Madhya Pradesh	0.60	0.56	0.07	0.15	0.35	10	14
11.	Maharashtra	0.88	0.85	0.74	0.48	0.74	1	5
12.	Orissa	0.17	0.44	0.03	0.05	0.17	14	13
13.	Punjab	0.84	0.11	0.14	1.00	0.52	4	6
14.	Rajasthan	0.46	0.35	0.11	0.21	0.28	11	10
15.	Tamil Nadu	0.90	0.94	0.44	0.55	0.71	2	2
16.	Uttar Pradesh	0.29	0.33	0.13	0.10	0.21	13	9
17.	West Bengal	0.43	0.32	0.11	0.11	0.24	12	11

45

Inter-State Disparities in Banking Operations in India: A Study of UP and Uttarakhand

Nisar Ahmad Khan

Banks act as the mobiliser of savings and allocator of credit for production and investment. Banks boost economic growth by identifying the entrepreneurs with the best chances of successfully initiating new goods and production processes (King and Levine, 1993) and facilitates long-run investments in high return projects (Bencivenga and Smith, 1991, p. 196). Schumpeter (1934, p. 74) assigned an important role to banks in economic development. According to him:

The banker, therefore, is not so much primarily a middleman in the commodity "purchasing power" as a producer—and stands between those who wish to form new combinations and the possessors of productive means. He is essentially a phenomenon of development though only when no central authority directs the social process. He makes possible the carrying out of new combinations, authorizes people, in the name of society as it were, to form them. He is the ephor of exchange economy.

An aspect of banking development, which seems to reflect the general pattern of economic development, is the acute and growing form of regional as well as sectoral concentration. In India the social control over banking and the policies associated with bank nationalisation had infused a centrifugal tendency to the spread of banking so as to prevent its concentration in urban and well-developed regions. With the financial sector reforms initiated in the mid-1990s and with the freedom given to scheduled commercial banks to operate in a liberalised environment, a centripetal tendency has been in vogue whereby banks' operations have been increasingly attracted by those sectors and regions which are relatively well-endowed and rich. This tendency has obviously resulted in jettisoning the widely-known supply-leading approach to financial development embedded in the philosophy behind bank nationalisation. In such an approach, banking services would make an advance presence so to that they provide positive externalities for underdeveloped regions and poorer sectors. Bank credit has a dynamic role to play in such regions and sectors, for the millions of self-employed production units, small farmers and small-scale enterprises alike, depend on external finance for survival and growth. Such institutional credit can effectively substitute non-institutional sources of funds and thus help to bring about a modicum of egalitarianism in the pattern of development. In this respect, amongst the segments of banking, cooperative institutions and non-banking financial companies (NBFCs) have limited resources and thus a limited role to play in the totality of financing activities. On the other hand, a pivotal role has to be played by scheduled commercial banks, the deposits of which constitute near 90 per cent of the total bank deposits including those of cooperatives.

In the 1980s, the growth of bank deposits and credit in the backward states was impressive; it was even better than that of the forward states. Contrariwise, in the 1990s, forward states generally sustained their earlier performance in deposit growth and to an extent even in credit growth, but backward states suffered the steepest fall in bank credit growth. It is true that to an extent, credit absorptive capacity of backward regions may have suffered, but at the same time it also appears true that the supply of credit is found to have fallen behind demand for it.

The bulk of the territorial spread of branch network, particularly in rural areas and underdeveloped regions, took place prior to the 1990s. Between 1969 and 1990, the bank branch offices increased by 51,000 with about 80 per cent of them having been opened in rural and semi-urban areas. The regional distribution also shifted away from Maharashtra, Gujarat, and South India, which accounted for close to 60 per cent of the total branch offices in the late 1960s, to the rest of the country. The share of South India, Maharashtra and Gujarat came down to about 40 per cent by the late 1980s and the share of Uttar Pradesh, Bihar, Madhya Pradesh and Rajasthan increased from less than 25 per cent to close to 35 per cent during this period. The credit-deposit ratio also began showing less variation across the states of India during this period. Though the reform process of the 1990s did not prevent the banks from expanding rural branch network - and in fact, the Narasimham Committee did specifically emphasize the importance of rural institutions and branch banking, in reality quite the contrary has happened. There was a branch expansion programme monitored by the RBI, which was disbanded after it expired on March 31, 1995. Combined with focus on the bottomline and the prudential requirements, the scheduled commercial banks halted the spread of rural branches and branches in underdeveloped regions (EPWRF, 2006).

The present study will focus on banking development in Uttar Pradesh (UP) and Uttarakhand. UP is the most populous province in India and occupies 7.3 per cent of the country's area. In 2001 in response to the long-term movement of the hilly region for the creation of a separate hill state, UP was bifurcated and a new state, Uttaranchal, comprising thirteen districts of the hilly region, was created. In January 2007, the name of the state was officially changed from Uttaranchal to Uttarakhand according to the wishes of a large section of its population. Since Uttarakhand was part of UP before the year 2001, comparison of UP and Uttarakhand in terms of banking development would be very interesting.

The comparison would help us to know as to whether Uttarakhand as a separate state has done well in terms of banking development. Our study would also highlight the inter-district banking variation. in UP and Uttarakhand. The paper is organized as follows. Section II reviews the inter-state literature on disparities. Section III compares the banking development in UP and Uttarakhand. The last section concludes the study.

SURVEY OF LITERATURE ON INTER-STATE DISPARITIES

Inter-State disparities in India have been studied in a number of contexts. Studies exist on inter-state and intra-state inequality in the distribution of income and also the inequality in rural-urban areas within the states (Mishra and Parikh, 1997). Pant (2004) attempted to find out the factors responsible for widening intra-state disparities in per-capita income. Kathuria and Shankar (2005) examined inter-state disparities in the performance of public health system in rural areas of the major states. Inter-State disparities have been related to caste too (Deshpande, 2001, 2003). Poverty and inequality across the states have been extensively examined by many studies. Dholakia (2003) examined the regional disparities using per-capita income and human development indicators and has also examined the causality between the two.

A critique of the economic reforms in India has been an 'increase in spatial inequalities in the development process' (as expressed by Williamson, 1965). A number of studies examined the regional disparities in the economic performance of states in the pre-reform and post-reform period (Ahluwalia, 2000, 2002; Bhattacharya and Sakthivel, 2004; Kurian, 2000; Nagaraj, Varoudakis, and Veganzones, 1998; M.G. Rao, Shand, and Kalirajan, 1999; Sachs, Bajpai, and Ramiah, 2002; Shand and Bhide, 2000) have observed that the regional disparity in India has widened, especially during the nineties. Per-capita SDP growth is positively related to their initial levels States with better infrastructure and human resources have had an edge over the others in attracting investment in the post-reform era. These studies have emphasized the need for reducing inequalities across the states and raise the per-capita income of less developed states. Bhide, Chadha *et al* (2005) examined the spill-over effect of the growth rate among the states. Their results suggested that the spill-over effects have been limited which could be due to inter-state barriers in trade and other regulations. On a similar note Chelliah (2003) pointed out the need to develop the less developed states on the grounds that these would create large potential markets for the more developed states. He also urged for the removal of inter-state trade regulations. Some studies have examined whether convergence in incomes has occurred across the states. Prominent among these are (Cashin and Sahay, 1996; D. Dasgupta, Maiti, Mukherjee, Sarkar, and Chakrabarti, 2000; Nagaraj *et al*., 1998; Purfield, 2006; M.G. Rao *et al*., 1999; also see Subrahmanyam, 1999). While Cashin and Sahay (1996) found that convergence across the states did take place between the period 1961-91, Nagraj *et al*. (1998) for the period 1970-94 find evidence of conditional convergence. Rao, Shand *et al*. (1999) find divergence in the growth of per-capita incomes of the states. Among the recent studies Purfield (2006) found that the gap in per-capita income between rich and poor states has widened and that state policies matter in influencing pattern of economic growth. Using different reference periods all these studies have arrived at different results on convergence/divergence. Overall these studies examine regional disparities in various dimensions.

Though a lot has been said and discussed on the disparities across the states, there is a grey area as to whether the underprivileged areas have been affected adversely by the lack of credit and low investment, which are already caught in a vicious circle of lower investment, low growth and increasing poverty. The concern on poor credit flow and the emerging regional and sectoral inequalities in the deployment of commercial credit was highlighted by Narayana (2000) and Shete (2002). Reddy (2004) expressed concern over the decline in credit and raised issues relating to credit delivery and the role of credit in liberalized banking system. EPW Research Foundation (2004, 2006) in its analysis of the banks, noted low levels of credit to the agriculture, less developed regions and small-scale sector. The macro approach of these studies however, ignores the micro aspects including differences between states in trends in credit within and across the states. Burgess and Venables (2003) and Stern (2001) highlighted the importance of studying micro-level heterogeneity and diversity.

In spite of our best effort, we have not been able to find any study pertaining to banking development in UP and Uttarakhand.

BANKING DEVELOPMENT IN UP AND UTTARAKHAND

The total scheduled commercial banks (SCBs) in India are 178 of which 28 are public sector banks, 25 private sector banks, 28 foreign banks and 96 regional rural banks. The total number of branches of SCBs in India at the end of March 2007 was 73199 of which 41.5 per cent branches were in rural areas. The average population covered per bank branch in the country was 15000 in 2007. This was a significant improvement from the population coverage of 64000 per branch in 1969 at the time of nationalization of banks. In UP the total number of bank branches were 747 in 1969, much higher than in most of the states. The average population per bank branch was 114000, way higher than the all-India average. In 2007 the total number of bank branches in the state increased to 9063 and the population covered came down to 17748 per bank branch.

Looking at the banking development in UP in the initial period of economic reforms in the country, we find that UP has not done very well. The share of UP in the total credit of SCBs in the country declined from 7.86 per cent in 1990-91 to 5.55 per cent in 1999-00. The share of the state in total number of branches and total deposits of SCBs in the country also declined during the said period. But the decline was more in case of credit as compared to deposits, as a result the credit-deposit ratio of the state dropped from 47.58 in 1990-91 to 30.87 in 1999-00. The fall in the share of the state in total credit of SCBs in the country was primarily because of the failure of the state to create necessary environment and infrastructure required to boost up the bank

TABLE I

Share of UP in the Total Credit and Deposits of SCBs

	1990-91	*1999-00*
Share in total no. of offices (%)	13.92	13.51
Share in total credit (%)	7.86	5.55
Share in total credit to agriculture (%)	11.85	11.00
Share in total deposits (%)	10.23	10.06
Share in total no. of rural offices (%)	16.4	16.54
Share in total rural deposits (%)	18.34	18.58
C/D ratio (%)	47.58	30.87
C/D ratio (all-India) (%)	60.40	53.32

Source: Money and Banking, 1999 and 2004, CMIE.

credit to various sectors of the state. In fact the economic reforms in the state were introduced only in 1998-99 due to political instability and the preoccupation of the government with the rise of communalism and castiesm (Hasan, 2005). However, the state has done marginally well in case of rural branches and rural deposits. Its share in the total number of rural branches of SCBs in the country increased from 16.4 per cent in 1990-91 to 16.54 per cent in 1999-00. Similarly, its share in the total rural deposits of SCBs in the country increased from 18.34 per cent in 1990-91 to 18.58 per cent in 1999-00. But it does not mean that the number of rural branches of SCBs has increased in the state during the said period. In fact the number of rural branches of SCBs declined in UP as well as in the country during the period 1990-91-1999-00. But the decline was relatively less in UP, as a result its share in the total number of rural branches of SCBs in the country increased during the period.

A comparision of banking development in UP and Uttarakhand reveals that Uttarakhand is far ahead of UP in all spheres of banking activity. Table 2 gives some basic indicators of banking development in UP and Uttarakhand during the period. The table shows that the share of UP in total number of branches of SCBs in the country came down from 12.22 per cent in 2000-01 to 12.02 in 2006-07. Whereas the share of Uttarakhand in total number of branches of SCBs

TABLE 2

Progress of Banking in UP and Uttarakhand

	2000-01		*2005-06*		*2006-07*	
	UP	*Uttara-khand*	*UP*	*Uttara-khand*	*UP*	*Uttara-khand*
Credit per-capita (Rs.)	1638	2634	3893	7858	4426	8442
Deposit per-capita (Rs.)	5137	11020	8403	25415	9808	31593
SDP per-capita (Rs.)	11028	17449	15382	28140	15095	32113
Share in total no. of offices (%)	12.22	1.25	12.1	1.3	12.02	1.3
Share in total no. of rural offices (%)	14.94	1.62	15.04	1.73	15.16	1.73
Share in total credit (%)	5.05	0.41	4.61	0.48	4.21	0.40
Share in total deposits (%)	8.99	0.99	7.30	1.13	7.00	1.13
Share in total rural deposits (%)	16.60	1.98	15.75	2.29	15.76	2.33
C/D ratio (%)	31.85	23.87	46.33	30.92	45.13	26.72
Credit/SDP ratio (%)	15.52	17.47	32.30	28.27	34.76	26.29
Credit per-capita (Rs.) (India)	5194	13614	17192			
Deposit per-capita (Rs.) (India)	9707	19052	23247			
C/D ratio (India) (%)	53.51	71.46	73.95			
Credit/GDP (India) (%)	27.49	46.36	51.53			

Source: 1. Money and Banking, 2007, CMIE.
2. Basic Statistical Returns of SCBs in India, 2007, RBI.
3. SDP, National Accounts Division, CSO, 2008

in the country increased from 1.25 per cent in 2000-01 to 1.3 per cent in 2006-07. The per-capita credit to UP was 62.20 per cent of the same to Uttarakhand in 2000-01. It declined to 52.43 per cent in 2006-07 owing to rapid growth of credit to Uttarakhand during the period 2000-01—2006-07 (Table 3). In fact the annual average rate of growth of per-capita credit to Uttarakhand was same as the all-India annual average rate of per-capita credit. The high rate of growth of credit to Uttarakhand has been among others, an important factor responsible for the relatively high rate of growth of state

TABLE 3

Compound Growth Rate (CGR) 2000-01—2006-07

	UP		*Uttarakhand*		*All-India*	
	CGR (%)	R^2	*CGR (%)*	R^2	*CGR (%)*	R^2
Per-capita Credit	18.1	0.99	22.23	0.99	22.52	0.98
Per-capita Deposit	10.73	0.99	17.99	0.98	15.43	0.99
Total Credit	20.27	0.99	24.25	0.99	24.50	0.99
Total Deposits	12.76	0.99	19.93	0.99	17.25	0.99
Credit to Agriculture	25.39	0.99	27.35	0.98	28.20	0.99
Credit to Industry	14.14	0.97	23.20	0.96	20.69	0.98
Bank Offices	0.96	0.93	1.88	0.97	1.3	0.94
State Domestic Product	4.70	0.98	8.52	0.99		
Per-capita SDP	2.67	0.93	6.75	0.99		
Agriculture	1.30	0.79	2.42	0.74		
Industry	7.75	0.95	14.7	0.99		
Services	5.37	0.99	8.07	0.99		

Source: Author's calculations using data from the sources mentioned in Table 2.

domestic product (SDP). The per-capita SDP of UP at current prices was 63.20 per cent of Uttarakhand's per-capita SDP in 2000-01. It declined to 47.00 per cent in 2006-07 due to relatively high growth of Uttarakhand's SDP. Table 2 shows that credit SDP ratio of UP and Uttarakhand have been quite low as compared to the credit GDP ratio of the country during the period 2000-01—2006-07. The higher credit SDP ratio of UP as compared to that of Uttarakhand in recent years as shown by the Table 2 has not been because of the relatively rapid credit growth rather it has been because of the relatively slow growth of SDP of the state (Table 3). Thus, there is not only the need to enhance the amount of bank credit to these states but also to ensure that there is better utilization of the credit.

Table 3 gives the rate of growth of per-capita real SDP, agriculture, industry and service sector of UP and Uttarakhand during the period 2000-01—2006-07. A look at the table reveals that Uttarakhand has done remarkably well as compared to UP. The annual average rate of growth of per-capita real SDP of Uttarakhand was almost three times of

TABLE 4

Share of Different Sectors in Total Credit

(In %)

Years	UP			Uttarakhand		
	Agriculture	Industry	Others	Agriculture	Industry	Others
2000-01	21.72	34.53	43.75	16.03	31.88	52.09
2001-02	20.50	31.15	48.35	13.79	31.76	54.45
2002-03	22.50	33.07	44.43	15.20	26.84	57.96
2003-04	22.70	26.88	50.42	14.85	25.92	59.23
2004-05	24.28	26.12	49.60	13.31	32.48	54.21
2005-06	25.77	24.04	50.19	17.77	26.40	55.83
2006-07	25.57	25.52	48.91	14.89	29.14	55.97

Source: 1. Money and Banking, 2007, CMIE.
2. Basic Statistical Returns of SCBs in India, 2007, RBI.

that of UP. Though the share of agriculture in total credit has been lower in Uttarakhand as compared to UP (Table 4), yet the rate of growth of agriculture has significantly been higher in Uttarakhand as compared to UP. The low share of agriculture in total credit to Uttarakhand has been because of its low agricultural base as compared to UP. But the growth of credit to agriculture has been higher in Uttarakhand as compared to UP. Similarly, the share of industry in total credit has almost been same in UP and Uttarakhand (Table 4), but industrial growth has significantly been higher in Uttarakhand as compared to UP due to very high rate of growth of industrial credit in the state.

Uttarakhand has also done well in case of bank deposits as compared to UP during the period from 2000-01 to 2006-07. The per-capita deposit of UP was 46.61 per cent of that of Uttarakhand in 2000-01. It declined to 31.04 per cent in 2006-07 due to rapid growth of deposits of Uttarakhand during the period. Table 3 shows that the annual average rate of growth of per-capita deposit of Uttarakhand has been higher than the all-India annual average rate of growth of the per-capita deposit. Consequently, the share of Uttarakhand in total bank deposits of the country increased from 0.99 per cent in 2000-01 to 1.13 per cent in 2006-07. Contrary to that, the share of UP in total bank deposits of the country declined from 8.99 per cent in 2000-01 to 7.00 per cent in 2006-07.

Though the per-capita deposit of Uttarakhand has been very high and its rate of growth has also been very high, only a small fraction of that is utilized by the state as credit. The credit-deposit ratio of the state in 2006-07 was almost one third of the all-India credit deposit ratio. Credit deposit ratio of UP has also been significantly higher than that of Uttarakhand during the period 2000-01 to 2006-07. However, in spite of low credit-deposit ratio of UP and Uttarakhand, these states have higher credit deposit ratio as per utilization than sanction, meaning thereby that there has been net inflow of credit to these states (Table 5).

There have been a lot of variations in banking activities within the state. In order to measure the inter-district variations in banking activities within the state, we have calculated coefficient of variation of bank branches, per-capita deposit and per-capita credit. The results are given in Table-6. The table shows that inter-district variations in per-capita credit and per-capita deposit have been higher in UP as compared to Uttarakhand. It is not surprising keeping in mind the large size of UP. But the same has not true in case of number of bank offices. The Table 6 shows that inter-district variations of bank offices has been higher in Uttarakhand as compared to UP. It means that banks have been more careful in opening branches in Uttarakhand as compared to UP. The banks have opened branches in Uttarakhand according to the demand for banking services as a result in spite of relatively large variation in bank branches in Uttarakhand the variations in per-capita credit and per-capita deposit are significantly lower in the state as compared to UP. The Table 6 shows that inter-district variation in bank branches has not only been higher in Uttarakhand as compared to UP but it has also increased more in Uttarakhand as compared to UP over the period from 2000-01 to 2006-07. In order to have a more clear view, we analysed the trends of bank branches in the districts of Uttarakhand and UP during the period from 2000-01 to 2006-

TABLE 5

Outstanding Credit of SCBs According to Place of Sanction and Utilisation, March 2007

(Amount in Rupees Lakh)

Region/States	*Total Credit Sanctioned in the State*	*Credit Utilised in the State of Sanction*	*Credit Sanctioned in the State but Utilised in Other States*	*Credit Utilised in the State but Sanctioned in other States*	*Total Credit Utilised in the State*	*Credt-Deposit Ratio (%)*	
						As Per Sanction	*As Per Utilisation*
Northern Region	417196,30	398532,94	18663,36	28018,89	426551,83	69.6	71.2
Eastern Region	155908,60	151507,46	4401,14	23154,86	174662,33	54.1	60.6
Western Region	715045,28	597656,97	117388,31	15848,57	613505,54	90.1	77.3
Southern Region	500074,15	484573,42	15500,72	70753,87	555327,29	87.0	96.6
Central Region	142582,15	137698,59	4883,56	19870,30	157568,89	47.4	52.3
Uttar Pradesh	82023,62	77734,14	4289,48	13804,15	91538,30	45.1	50.4
Uttarakhand	7855,69	7769,71	85,98	1658,20	9427,91	26.7	32.1
All-India	1947099,62				1947099,62	75.0	75.0

Source: Basic Statistical Returns of Scheduled Commercial Banks in India, March 2007.

TABLE 6

Inter-District Variations in Banking Operations in UP and Uttarakhand

State/Region	*Coefficient of Variation*					
	2000-01			*2006-07*		
	No. of Offices	*Per Capita Deposit*	*Per Capita Credit*	*No. of Offices*	*Per Capita Deposit*	*Per Capita Credit*
Uttarakhand	64.12	69.5	87.46	74.75	133.18	89.55
UP	53.6	117.49	133.87	59.84	169.82	141.45
Eastern UP	48.4	51.56	71.72	52.71	55.42	60.04
Western UP	46.7	84.01	68.27	49.98	189.53	129.85

Source: 1. Basic Statistical Returns of SCBs in India, 2007, RBI.
2. www.India.gov.in/knowindia

07. We found that bank branches declined in only 11 out of the 70 districts of UP from 2000-01 to 2006-07. Whereas in Uttarakhand bank branches declined in 5 out of the 13 districts during the same period. This explains as to why inter-district variation in bank branches has increased more in Uttarakhand. It is noteworthy that the districts in which bank branches have declined are backward districts irrespective of fact as to whether theses districts belong to UP or Uttarakhand. It support the hypothesis that during the post-reforms period banks have carried out banking activities keeping in mind profitability and have ignored the backward areas. So there has been increasing concentration of banking operations during the post-reforms period.

Table 6 also gives the inter-district variation in banking activities in eastern and western UP during the period from 2000-01 to 2006-07. A look at the table reveals that inter-district variation in per-capita credit has gone down in eastern UP, but it has increased significantly in western UP during the said period. The fall in the inter-district variation in per-capita credit to eastern UP has not been because of the increased bank credit to backward districts, rather it has been because of the slow growth of credit to relatively advanced districts due to lack of necessary infrastructure and industrial

TABLE 7

Development of Cumulative Number of Self Help Groups Financed

State	*Development of cumulative No. of SHGs financed*						
	March 2001	*March 2002*	*March 2003*	*March 2004*	*March 2005*	*March 2006*	*%age change 2002 to 2006*
UP	23,152	33,114	53,696	79,210	119,648	163,439	
Uttarakhand		3,323	5,853	10,908	14,043	16,060	
All-India	263,825	461,478	717,360	1,079,091	1,618,456	2,238,565	

Source: Report of the Committee on Financial Inclusion, January 2008.

environment. The inter-district variation in per-capita credit to western UP has gone up mainly because of the rapid industrial growth in some of the districts due to their proximity to New Delhi.

In the current development literature, credit and development are often associated with microfinance, i.e. credit in small quantities given to the poor to help them emerge out of poverty. In India too, the microfinance is used as a tool for poverty alleviation. In India three models of microfinance are being followed. Under Model-I, banks' form and nurture the groups themselves, open their saving accounts and provide with bank loans. Up to March 2006, 20 per cent of the total Self Help Groups (SHGs) financed belonged to this category. Under Model-II, SHGs are formed by NGOs and formal agencies but are directly financed by banks. This model has a major share, with 74 per cent of the SHGs financed up to March 2006, falling under this category. Under Model-III, SHGs are financed by banks using NGOs and other agencies as financial intermediaries. Up to March 2006, only 6 per cent of the total SHGs financed belong to this category. Women are often the targeted groups of these programmes. As against the southern states, where SHGs are mostly comprised of women, in UP mixed groups of men and women or men only with a few women groups only are found (P. Basu and Srivastava, 2005). The role of SHGs in

TABLE 8

SHG Credit Linkage by RRBs: March 2006

State	*% SHGs credit linked (RRBs)*
Uttar Pradesh	56%
Uttarakhand	15%
Central Region	48%
All-India	33%

Source: Report of the Committee on Financial Inclusion, January 2008

capital accumulation and poverty reduction is limited in UP and Uttarakhand due to its inadequate outreach. Table 8 gives the cumulative number of SHGs in UP and Uttarakhand. UP accounted for 7.71 per cent of SHGs in the country in March 2002 which increased to 7.30 per cent in March 2006. Uttarakhand had 0.72 per cent of SHGs in the country in March 2002. It remained same in March 2006. Table 8 shows that RRBs have been more active in promoting SHGs in UP as compared to Uttarakhand. Though the share of UP and Uttarakhand in total number of SHGs in the country is small but there has been rapid growth of SHGs in these states.

CONCLUSION

Uttarakhand has been far ahead of UP in all spheres of banking activity. The credit deposit ratio of Uttarakhand has been lower than that of UP. But the credit deposit ratio of both the states have significantly been lower as compared to all-India credit deposit ratio. Thus, there is a need to enhance the amount of credit in both the states. The banks have opened branches in Uttarakhand according to the demand for banking services as a result in spite of relatively large inter-district variation in bank branches in Uttarakhand the inter-district variations in per-capita credit and per-capita deposit are significantly lower in the state as compared to UP. The inter-district variation in bank branches has not only been higher in Uttarakhand as compared to UP but it has also increased more in Uttarakhand as compared to UP. It is because bank branches declined in only 11 out of the 70 districts of UP from 2000-01 to 2006-07. Whereas in Uttarakhand bank branches declined in 5 out of the 13 districts during the same period. It is noteworthy that the districts in which bank branches have declined are backward districts irrespective of fact as to whether these districts belong to UP or Uttarakhand. It support the hypothesis that during the post-reforms period banks have carried out banking activities keeping in mind profitability and have ignored the backward areas. So there has been increasing concentration of banking operations during the post-reforms period.

References

Ahluwalia, M.S. (2000). Economic Performance of States in Post-Reforms Period. *Economic and Political Weekly*, 1637-48.

Ahluwalia, M.S. (2002). State Level Performance Under Economic Reforms in India. In A.O. Krueger (Ed.), Economic Policy Reforms in the Indian Economy (pp. 91-125). New Delhi: Oxford University Press.

Basu, P., and Srivastava, P. (2005). Exploring Possibilities, Microfinance and Rural Credit: Access for Poor in India. *Economic and Political Weekly*, 1747-55.

Bencivenga, V.R., and Smith, B.D. (1991). Financial intermediation and economic growth. *Review of Economic Studies*, 58(194), 195-209.

Bhattacharya, B.B., and Sakthivel, S. (2004). Regional Growth and Disparity in India: Comparison of Pre- and Post-Reform Decades. *Economic and Political Weekly*, 1071-77.

Bhide, S., Chadha, R., and Kalirajan, K.P. (2005). Growth Interdependence among Indian States: An Exploration. *Asia-Pacific Development Journal*, 12(2), 59-80.

Burgess, R., and Venables, A.J. (2003). Towards a Microeconomics of Growth. Paper presented at the Annual Bank Conference on Development Economics, Bangalore, India.

Cashin, P., and Sahay, R. (1996). Regional Economic Growth and Convergence in India. Finance and Development (March), 49-52.

Chelliah, R.J. (2003). Reducing Poverty through State-level Reforms. In S. Howes, A.K. Lahiri and N. Stern (Eds.), State level Reforms in India: Towards More Effective Government (pp. 35-42). New Delhi: Macmillan.

Dasgupta, D., Maiti, P., Mukherjee, R., Sarkar, S., and Chakrabarti, S. (2000). Growth and Inter-State Disparities in India. *Economic and Political Weekly* (July 1), 2413-22.

Deshpande, A. (2001). Caste at Birth? Redefining Disparity in India. *Review of Development Economics*, 5(1), 130-44.

Deshpande, A. (2003). Recasting Economic Inequality. In W. Darity, Jr. and A. Deshpande (Eds.), Boundaries of Clan and Color: Transnational comparisons of inter-group disparity (pp. 112-29). London: Routledge.

Dholakia, R.H. (2003). Regional Disparity in Economic and Human Development in India. *Economic and Political Weekly* (September 27), 4166-72.

EPW Research Foundation. (2004). Critical Neglect of Social Banking. *Economic and Political Weekly*, 39(31), 2072-78.

EPW Research Foundation. (2006). Special Statistics Issue, *Economic and Political Weekly*, 41(11), March 18-24.

Hasan, Z. (2005). Communal Mobilization and Changing Majority in Uttar Pradesh. In D. Ludden (Ed.), Making India Hindu: Religion, Community and the Politics of Democracy in India (Second ed., pp. 81-97). New Delhi: Oxford University Press.

Kathuria, V., and Sankar, D. (2005). Inter-State Disparities in Health Outcomes in Rural India: An Analysis Using a Stochastic Production Frontier Approach. *Development Policy Review*, 23(2), 145-63.

King, R.G., and Levine, R. (1993). Finance and Growth: Schumpeter might be right. *Quarterly Journal of Economics*, 108(3), 717-38.

Kurian, N.J. (2000). Widening Regional Disparities in India: Some Indicators. *Economic and Political Weekly* (February 12), 538-550.

Mishra, P., and Parikh, A. (1997). Distributional Inequality in *Indian States. Journal of Income Distribution*, 7(1), 89-108.

Nagaraj, R., Varoudakis, A., and Veganzones, M.A. (1998). Long-Run Growth Trends and Convergence Across Indian States (OECD Technical Papers No. 131): Organisation for Economic Cooperation and Development (OECD).

Narayana, D. (2000). Banking Sector Reforms and the Emerging Patterns in Commercial Credit Deployment in India. *Review of Development and Change*, 5(2), 248-67.

Pant, N. (2004). Trends in Groundwater Irrigation in Eastern and Western UP. *Economic and Political Weekly*, 3463-68.

Purfield, C. (2006). Mind the Gap—Is Economic Growth in India Leaving Some States Behind? Washington, D.C.: Asia and Pacific Department, International Monetary Fund (IMF).

R.B.I. Report on Trend and Progress of Banking in India, Mumbai, India, (Various Issues).

Rao, M.G., Shand, R.T., and Kalirajan, K. P. (1999). Convergence of Incomes Across Indian States—A Divergent View. *Economic and Political Weekly*(March 27), 769-78.

Reddy, Y. V. (2004). Credit Policy, Systems and Culture. *Reserve Bank of India Bulletin*, 58(3), 303-11.

Sachs, J., Bajpai, N., and Ramiah, A. (2002). Why some Indian States have Grown Faster than the Others? Retrieved. February 21, 2006

Schumpeter, J.A. (1934). The Theory of Economic Development: An Inquiry into Profits, Capital, Credit, Interest and the Business Cycle (Translated from the German by Redvers Opie, Trans.). Cambridge, Massachusetts: Harvard University Press.

Shand, R., and Bhide, S. (2000). Sources of Economic Growth—Regional Dimensions of Reforms. *Economic and Political Weekly*, 3747-3757.

Shete, N.B. (2002). Priority Sector Advances of Banks During the Post-Reform Period,. *Prajnan*, 31(1), 21-37.

Stern, N. (2001). A Strategy for Development. Paper presented at the Annual World Bank Conference on Development Economics.

Subrahmanyam, S. (1999). Convergence of income across Indian States. *Economic and Political Weekly* (November 20), 3327-28.

Williamson, J.G. (1965). Regional Inequality and the Process of Economic Development: A Description of the Patterns. *Economic Development and Cultural Change*, 13(4), 3-45.

46

Regional Imbalances in India—An Analysis of Industrial Disparity in UP, MP, Rajasthan and Maharashtra

SHAKSHI CHAUDHARY

INTRODUCTION

The most common indicator of the economic development of a society is the per-capita annual income generated by it. The level of poverty or the share of population which do not have minimum income to meet its basic requirements is an indicator of the level of economic development as well as the inequality in the income distribution. India is a vast country possessing diverse demographic trends on population density, employment opportunities, social sector investments and overall economic development, etc. across different states. One of the major objectives of the development planning initiated immediately after Independence has been, among other things, reduction of regional disparities in social and economic development.

Direct investment by the Central Government and Centrally directed investment of the private sector have been two powerful instruments to achieve this objective.

During the first four decades of development planning, most of the large units in basic and heavy industries were set-up in the public sector in a regionally well-balanced manner. Indeed, their location, other things being equal, was biased towards backward regions as natural endowments such as mineral deposits were concentrated in those regions. Massive public investments have been made to provide economic and social infrastructure in the backward regions to accelerate their overall development. The natural tendency of the private sector is to set-up industries and other related activities in developed regions. To counter-balance this tendency, various incentive and disincentive schemes have been introduced as public policies to direct private investments to backward regions. Fright equalization scheme was just one of them.

The efforts of the first four decades of planned development to reduce various imbalances across the regions have been only partially successful. At best they have ensured that regional disparities in terms of various indicators of development are not aggravating. Of course, even this is no mean achievement.

Economic reforms initiated in 1991 implied among, other things, that the private sector would be the principal engine of economic growth. Most of the restrictions on private investment have been removed. Mounting debt burden of the government has imposed a cap on public investment. As a result, while there was significant increase in the quantum of private investment, there was a sharp fall in the public investment over the last decade. The flow of private investment, both domestic and foreign, has been extremely biased in favour of the more developed regions of the country. This has enabled the developed regions to achieve accelerated economic growth during the 1990s. On the other hand, backward regions of the country, which were unable to attract any significant private investment flows, experienced decelerated economic growth during this period.

The net result of this divergent growth performance of

the developed and backward regions has been a widening of the regional disparities in the country in terms of per-capita income and other indicators of well-being of the people.

OBJECTIVES OF THE STUDY

The overall objective of the present study is to capture the disparity in industrial development across the states in India and recommending fruitful suggestions to encounter the industrial disparity. This has been supported by the following sub-objectives,

1. to unfurl the growth pattern of number of factories in UP, MP, Rajasthan and Maharashtra,
2. to peep into the pattern of Invested Capital in factories in UP, MP, Rajasthan and Maharashtra,
3. to analyse the employment opportunities available in factories in UP, MP, Rajasthan and Maharashtra, and
4. to enquire into the output of the factories in UP, MP, Rajasthan and Maharashtra,

RESEARCH METHODOLOGY

In the light of abovementioned objectives, relevant literatures, journals and research papers, etc. have been reviewed and adhered to. The present study made use of secondary data from two important sources, viz. Annual Survey of Industries and Economic Survey of India. Various websites like www.econostates.com, www. indiastates.com, etc. have also been used for collection of data and information. For preparation of present study various journals and magazines like Indian Journal of Commerce, Vikalpa, *Economic and Political Weekly*, etc. have also been used. The study covers the period from 1998-99 to 2004-05. However, the period varies according to the availability of data and information. The period has been chosen on the ground of consistency of available data and information. The states covered under the study are UP, MP, Rajasthan, which are less developed, and Maharashtra which is comparatively highly developed. The study has been initiated with relevant percentages, statistical averages and trend analysis, etc.

FINDINGS OF THE STUDY

The industrial development and disparity in India *vis-a-vis* UP< MP, Rajasthan and Maharashtra has been analysed in Tables 1, 2, 3, and 4 covering the period from 1998-99 to 2004-05. The major findings of the study are outlined below:

1. Table 1 reveals that the number of factories in UP, MP, and Rajasthan are very much lower as compared to Maharashtra. Maharashtra alone, on an average, accounts for 14.04 per cent of total factories in India whereas the proportion of UP, MP, Rajasthan are 7.35 per cent, 2.37 per cent and 4.02 per cent respectively. The situation calls for establishing more factories in UP, MP, and Rajasthan.

TABLE I

Number of Factories

Year	*All-India*	*UP*	*MP*	*Rajasthan*	*Maharashtra*
1998-99	131706	10508(7.98)	3216(2.44)	4778(3.63)	19390(14.72)
1999-00	131558	10303(7.83)	3269(2.48)	5063(3.85)	19009(14.45)
2000-01	131268	9635(7.34)	3221(2.45)	5112(3.89)	18528(14.11)
2001-02	128549	9157(7.12)	3019(2.35)	5279(4.11)	17853(13.89)
2002-03	127957	8980(7.02)	2995(2.34)	5409(4.23)	17570(13.73)
2003-04	129074	9237(7.06)	2982(2.31)	5452(4.22)	17474(13.54)
2004-05	136353	9582(7.03)	3028(2.22)	5740(4.21)	18912(13.87)
Average		7.35	2.37	4.02	14.04

Note: Figure in brackets are percentages of all-India.
Source: Annual Survey of Industries, Government of India, Various Issues

2. The invested capital of the factories have been analysed in Table 2. The table depicts that the invested capital of the factories in Maharashtra on an average accounts for 17.98 per cent which is very much more than that of other states covered under the study. The invested capital in the factories in UP, MP, and Rajasthan must be increased in order to encounter the regional disparity.

Table 2

Invested Capital

Year	*All-India*	*UP*	*MP*	*Rajasthan*	*Maharashtra*
1998-99	53706813	6457333(12.02)	2230263(4.05)	1583978(2.95)	8618508(16.05)
1999-00	56663430	5085709(8.98)	2369511(4.08)	2467886(4.36)	10469124(18.48)
2000-01	57179940	4901000(8.57)	1973342(3.45)	1855306(3.24)	10363120(18.12)
2001-02	60591285	4423859(7.30)	1881102(3.10)	1498125(2.46)	10508270(17.34)
2002-03	63747308	4399806(6.90)	1947125(3.05)	1839425(2.93)	11891264(18.65)
2003-04	67959786	4761440(7.01)	2044016(3.01)	1954894(2.88)	12401930(18.25)
2004-05	75869399	5160774(6.80)	2445337(3.22)	2119235(2.79)	14368443(18.94)
Average		8.23	3.45	3.09	17.98

Note: Figure in brackets are percentages of all-India.
Source: Annual Survey of Industries, Government of India, Various Issues.

3. Maharashtra accounted for 14.78 per cent of total employment provided by industrial sector in India during the period of analysis (Table 3). The

Table 3

Employees

Year	*All-India*	*UP*	*MP*	*Rajasthan*	*Maharashtra*
1998-99	8588581	621155 (7.23)	301438 (3.51)	237521 (2.77)	1393688 (16.23)
1999-00	8172836	571719 (7.0)	267685 (3.28)	234651 (2.87)	1217260 (14.89)
2000-01	7987743	539737 (6.76)	253444 (3.17)	232177 (2.91)	1172782 (14.68)
2001-02	7750366	513190 (6.62)	209035 2.70)	348668 (4.50)	1162542 (15.00)
2002-03	7935948	542160 (6.83)	208874 (2.63)	244265 (3.08)	1170461 (14.75)
2003-04	7870081	569603 (7.24)	214140 (2.72)	245274 (3.12)	1114070 (14.16)
2004-05	8453628	587702 (6.95)	216563 (2.56)	268437 (3.18)	1162346 (13.75)
Average		6.95	2.94	3.20	14.78

Note: Figure in brackets are percentages of all-India.
Source: Annual Survey of Industries, Government of India, Various Issues.

proportion of UP, MP, and Rajasthan captured only 6.95 per cent, 2.94 per cent and 3.20 per cent respectively during the said period. The availability of equal employment opportunities is a must for balanced development of a nation. The employment opportunities in the concerned states should be accelerated by involving public as well as private investments.

4. The average share of UP, MP, and Rajasthan in the output of factories is very much lower than that of Maharashtra. The average output of the factories in Maharashtra has registered 19.82 per cent of all-India whereas the relative share of UP, MP, and Rajasthan remained only 7.0 per cent, 3.71 per cent, and 3.07 per cent respectively during the period covered under the study (Table 4).

TABLE.4

Output

Year	*All-India*	*UP*	*MP*	*Rajasthan*	*Maharashtra*
1998-99	78377081	5811990	2858558	2382042	16115975
		(7.42)	(3.65)	(3.04)	(20.56)
1999-00	89793835	6104692	4408900	2995996	18133252
		(6.80)	(4.91)	(3.34)	(20.19)
2000-01	92690185	6485418	3671234	3078418	18497146
		(7.0)	(3.96)	(3.32)	(19.96)
2001-02	96245663	6703704	3822625	3122742	18122281
		(6.97)	(3.97)	(3.24)	(18.83)
2002-03	113056111	8052063	3805750	3311696	21759551
		(7.12)	(3.37)	(2.93)	(19.25)
2003-04	128740055	9340116	4274433	3763555	23832495
		(7.26)	(3.32)	(2.92)	(18.51)
2004-05	167256142	10913874	4696851	4488205	35887957
		(6.53)	(2.81)	(2.68)	(21.46)
Average		7.0	3.71	3.07	19.82

Note: Figure in brackets are percentages of all-India.
Source: Annual Survey of Industries, Government of India, Various Issues.

CONCLUSION

The ability of the governments at the Centre and in the States to counter trend of disparity by effecting countervailing public investment has been reduced considerably. In the context of macro-economic stabilization policies initiated in 1991, the ability of the Centre to finance public investment by borrowings has been severely constrained. Revenues of the Centre also experienced reduced buoyancy in the wake of tax reforms especially due to reduction in customs tariff to levels comparable to those of our trading partners.

The factors which attracted more and more private investments to developed regions have been their better developed economic and social infrastructure as well as more efficient and investor friendly State governments. The backward regions, to be attractive to the private investors, have to improve their infrastructure facilities, both economic and social, considerably. This needs substantial public investment.

Almost all the State governments in the backward regions find that their entire revenues are not sufficient to meet even the committed revenue expenditure like interest liability, salaries and pensions. A sizable share of their borrowings is diverted to fill the gap between the revenue receipts and revenue expenditure. There are several States where borrowings have been steadily increasing, but investments have been decreasing secularly.

The adverse impacts of the deteriorating State finances are much more severe for the backward States as compared to the developed States, where investments of the past have created adequate social and economic infrastructure to attract private investments. The backward States are facing multiple dilemmas. They are not able to attract investments due to lack of infrastructure. They are not in a position to provide these facilities on their own due to lack of investible funds. Unlike in the past, Centre is not in a position to help them either as the Centre itself has a serious fiscal constraint.

Along with social and economic infrastructure, efficiency of administration and the quality of governance including law and order situation are important factors in attracting private investment. Studies conducted by NCAER and some of the apex associations of industries have indicated that prospective investors give higher weightage to these factors than various incentives, including fiscal incentives offered by the State governments. Indeed, there are enough evidences to the effect that the investors don't mind paying speed money to get things done fast. In other words, a corrupt but efficient regime is preferred to an honest but inefficient regime in the context of investment decisions. Other aspects of governance like the law and order situation, trade union activism, etc., are also important factors affecting the flow of private investments.

To sum up, it will be appropriate to state that there are hardly any signs of reversing the recent trend of accentuating regional disparities in the country in the coming decades. Indeed, almost all the relevant forces are such that the disparities are likely to widen deriving the next quarter century. It will require Herculean tasks on the part of the Centre and the leadership in the concerned regions to ensure that the gap does not widen further.

47

Regional Disparities in Growth and Employment in India

SAMIK SHOME

INTRODUCTION

One of the major areas of concern for India is the regional disparity. It is true that in a large economy like India, different regions with different resource bases and endowments would have a dissimilar growth path over time. One of the reasons why centralized planning was advocated in India earlier was that it could restrain the regional disparity. However, in spite of planning, the regional disparity remained a serious problem in India. A new controversy in this respect is whether growth rates and standard of living in different regions will eventually converge or not. The convergence theorem (Barro, 1991) postulates that when the growth rate of an economy accelerates, initially some regions with better resources would grow faster than others. But eventually after sometime, when the law of diminishing marginal returns set in, first growth rates would converge, due to differential marginal productivity of capital[1] and this in turn would bridge the gaps in the levels of income across regions. The empirical evidence on this is however very controversial. It has also been observed that when an economy is liberated, especially after controls on investment are lifted, then regions with better infrastructure would attract more investment, especially foreign capital, through market mechanism, and this in turn would lead to regional inequity.

The reforms[2] in 1991 led to a lot of structural changes in the Indian economy. The post-reform period also witnessed a sharp decline in public investment due to fiscal constraint. At the aggregate level, the average share of public investment in total investment has declined from 45 per cent in the early 1980s to about one-third in early 2000s. The RBI data on capital flows show that only four to five developed states[3] have cornered the major chunk of foreign direct investment (FDI) in India. The poorer states with inadequate infrastructure are not able to attract foreign investment which leads to disparities among states.

Under this background, the present paper will try to look at and analyze the growth and disparity among the major states in India. Over the years, a number of studies (for instance, Bhattacharya and Sakthivel, 2004; Ahluwalia, 2000 and 2002; Kurian, 2002; Shand and Bhide, 2000; Rao, Shand and Kalirajan, 1999; Nagaraj, Varoudakis and Veganzous, 1998; Datta Roy Choudhury, 1993), among others, have observed that the regional disparity in India has widened, especially during the 1990s. These studies on India have focused not only on the bright side of reform and open door policy, as seen in the country's remarkable economic growth, but also on the dark side as shown by serious inter-regional disparities. Two crucial points have to be investigated to address these issues. First, why then, despite of this remarkable growth, are inter-regional disparities widening? Second, whatever the causes, can solutions or remedies be found for them in the coming years? Answers to these questions would be quite meaningful in helping to deepen the understanding of problems faced by India.

The paper uses several types of data relating to demographic, economic and social characteristics and also employment. The data related to India and its states are collected from various census reports, RBI bulletins and other publications of Government of India. This analysis includes 15 major states of India. Jammu & Kashmir is excluded because some data is not available due to political disturbance during 1990s. Delhi, Goa and the states of North-East are excluded because they are too small to reflect general economic behaviour of states in India. Three newly created states, namely, Chhattishgarh, Jharkhand and Uttaranchal are also excluded because there are no time-series data on these states. Bihar, MP and Uttar Pradesh therefore refer to as undivided states.

The study is divided into five sections. Section I of the paper highlight questions relating to the inter-state disparities in terms of social and demographic characteristics. Section II highlights the disparities among the states of India with reference to growth comparison. Disparity in per-capita growth is highlighted in Section III. Section IV deals with the disparity in employment growth and the last section contain concluding remarks.

REGIONAL DISPARITIES IN INDIA

Along with faster economic growth and reduction in poverty, there has been accelerated improvement in various indicators of human development in India since the early eighties whether it is in the case of demographic characteristics or social development indicators. During the last two decades, the country has also made major strides in health and education sectors. The economy got diversified significantly and the share of the manufacturing and service sector in employment and incomes improved considerably. While there is a broad consensus on the overall improvement of the economy and quality of life during the period under consideration, but there are significantly differing perceptions about the distributional impacts of these gains.

SECTION I

DEMOGRAPHIC AND SOCIAL CHARACTERISTICS

Disparities in demographic and social development

across the regions and intra-regional disparities among different segments of the society have been the major planks for adopting planning process in India since independence. Apart from massive investments in backward regions, various public policies directed at encouraging private investments in such regions have been pursued during the first three decades of planned development. While efforts to reduce regional disparities were not lacking, achievements were not often commensurate with these efforts. The reforms since 1991 with stabilization and deregulation policies as their central pieces seem to have further widened the regional disparities.

A few major demographic and social characteristics of the 15 States under consideration are presented in Table 1 along with corresponding all-India figures. The state-wise population is given in column (2).

The state-wise sex ratio given in column (3) is, perhaps, the most revealing index of gender disparities among the States of the Indian Union. The all-India sex ratio of 933 females per 1000 males itself is a reflection of the neglect of women's' health due to relatively lower economic and social value assigned to women, in general, in India. Among the 15 States considered in the study, seven states have sex ratio above the national average and eight have below national average. Economic theories reveal that as a society develops economically, the sex ratio turns more favourable towards women. Within India, however, this does not appear to hold good. The highest sex ratio is that of Kerala. Indeed, Kerala is the only State in the country which has a sex ratio favourable to women (1058). It is interesting to note that, the two developed states, viz. Haryana and Punjab, has the lowest sex ratio within the country.

The average annual rate of growth of population for the decade (1991-2001) based on the two censuses for the different states is presented in column (4). There are six states with growth rate higher than the all-India figure of 1.92. The highest growth rate is shared by Rajasthan and Haryana at 2.84. While migration may be important for a smaller state, it is the natural growth which contributes mainly to the population growth in larger states. A higher population

TABLE I

Some Demographic and Social Characteristics

States	*Population (in millions)*	*Number of females per 1000 males (2004)*	*Growth of population (1991-2001)*	*Literacy Rate (2001)*	*Number of females per 100 males (Till class X) 2004*	*People below poverty line (2000) (in per cent)*
(1)	(2)	(3)	(4)	(5)	(6)	(7)
Andhra Pradesh	76.2	978	1.46	60.5	85	15.77
Bihar	82.9	919	-0.39	47.0	44	42.60
Gujarat	50.6	920	2.27	70.0	67	14.07
Haryana	21.1	861	2.84	67.9	72	8.74
Himachal Pradesh	6.0	968	1.75	76.5	85	7.63
Karnataka	52.8	965	1.75	66.6	88	20.04
Kerala	31.8	1058	0.94	90.9	99	12.72
Madhya Pradesh	60.3	919	-0.88	63.7	56	37.43
Maharashtra	96.8	922	2.27	76.9	84	25.02
Orissa	36.8	972	1.63	63.1	80	47.15
Punjab	24.3	876	2.01	69.7	88	6.16
Rajasthan	56.5	921	2.84	60.4	42	15.28
Tamil Nadu	62.4	987	1.17	73.5	90	21.12
Uttar Pradesh	166.1	898	1.95	56.3	53	31.15
West Bengal	80.1	934	1.78	68.6	76	27.02
All-India	999.6	933	1.92	64.9	71	26.10

Source: Col (2) – Census of India, 2001; Col. (3) and (5) – Women and Men in India, 2006, CSO; Col. (5) – Selected Educational Statistics, 2004-05, Ministry of HRD, GOI; Col. (7) – www.indiastat.com

growth in the Indian context is a reflection of a state in early stage of demographic transition where death rate has come down but birth rate has not yet followed suit.

The level of literacy is, perhaps, one of the most important indexes of development of a society. The literacy rate is given in column (5). State-wise number of females per 100 males attended till class X is given in column (6). Invariably, male literacy is higher than female literacy in any society. Often there may be significant gender gap in literacy. The true index of development of a society is the level of female literacy which can be considered as the bottom line as far as literacy is concerned. Ten states have female attending class X level above the national average of 71. The distinction of highest female attending class X level goes to Kerala with 99 out of every 100 males. The gap between Kerala and the rest of the country is, indeed, phenomenal. Rajasthan (42) has the least number of females attending class X level followed by Bihar (44) and Madhya Pradesh (56).

There is a steep fall in the share of poor in the country during the nineties. Column (7) reflects the state-wise percentage of people below poverty line in 2000. It can be noted that the developed states have the percentage of people below poverty line much less than that of the national average of 26.1. No doubt, this establishes the close positive relationship between poverty reduction and economic growth.[3]

SECTION II

INTER-STATE GROWTH COMPARISON

State Domestic Product (SDP) growth rates have also shown a fair degree of variation among the states. While some states have witnessed rapid and phenomenal growth, the rest lagged behind the all-India growth rate. The comparative average growth rates of SDP for 15 major states at 1993-94 prices for the decades 1980s (1980-81 to 1989-90) and 1990s (1990-91 to 1999-2000) as well for the overall period (1980-81 to 1999-2000) are given in Table 2. It may be seen that except two states, Andhra Pradesh and Kerala, all the other major states had recorded over five per cent growth during the 1980s, against the all-India growth rate of 5.6 per cent per annum. Rajasthan, Haryana, Tamil Nadu, Himachal Pradesh and Karnataka have progressed rapidly during the 1980s with over six per cent per annum growth, with Rajasthan recording the highest (7.1). In general, there was a comparatively balanced regional growth during the 1980s, even though the disparity widened across the states. However, the 1990s belongs to the relatively industrialized states. Highly industrialized states like, Gujarat (8.2), Karnataka (7.0) and Maharashtra (6.8) grew at a very high rate. It is interesting to note that West Bengal (7.2%) has grown not only faster than the all-India average, but also more than many developed states, such as, Andhra Pradesh (5.1%) and Punjab (4.6%) during the reform era. The poor performance of both Punjab and Andhra Pradesh during the reform era came as a surprise. Punjab's slow growth may be attributed to stagnation in agriculture and fiscal mismanagement. The reason for slow growth in Andhra Pradesh needs a careful scrutiny. Among other states, Rajasthan, Kerala, Haryana, Himachal Pradesh and Tamil Nadu have recorded above average growth rate during the reform era.

TABLE 2

Growth Rate of SDP at Constant Prices

(per cent per annum)

States	*1980-81 to 1989-90*	*1990-91 to 1999-2000*	*1980-81 to 1999-2000*
Andhra Pradesh	4.8	5.1	5.1
Bihar	5.2	3.4	3.8
Gujarat	5.7	8.2	6.8
Haryana	6.7	6.7	7.8
Himachal Pradesh	6.1	6.9	6.2
Karnataka	6.1	7.0	6.5
Kerala	4.5	6.0	5.9
Madhya Pradesh	5.2	5.4	5.8
Maharashtra	5.9	6.8	6.3
Orissa	5.8	3.6	3.9
Punjab	5.1	4.6	4.7
Rajasthan	7.1	6.4	6.9
Tamil Nadu	6.3	6.6	6.5
Uttar Pradesh	5.9	4.3	5.1
West Bengal	5.2	7.2	6.1
All-India	5.6	6.0	5.6
CV	0.14	0.29	0.22

Source: Various reports of Central Statistical Organisation.

Some of the high growth states during reform era, notably, Gujarat, Maharashtra, Karnataka and Tamil Nadu got major shares in foreign investment in the 1990s. On the other hand, poor states like, Bihar, Orissa and Uttar Pradesh have attracted less foreign and domestic capital and performed badly with SDP growth below 4 per cent per annum. Apart from lack of investment, poor infrastructure combined with poor governance might have also restrained growth in these states.

The coefficient of variation[4] of average growth rates among states has jumped from 0.14 in the 1980s to 0.29 in the 1990s. And this has happened despite a very modest rise in average growth rate at the all-India level from 5.6 per cent in 1980s to 6.0 in 1990s. This reflects an uneven regional development in the post-reform era.

Section III

DISPARITY IN PER-CAPITA SDP GROWTH

The study of the growth of per-capita SDP gives a broader and better picture of regional disparities. The growth of per-capita SDP for 15 major states along with all-India average is presented in Table 3. It may be seen that the regional disparities in standard of living, as measured by per-capita SDP at constant prices, have accentuated in the 1990s. In the 1980s, Andhra Pradesh recorded the lowest per-capita SDP growth at 2.5 per cent per annum and Tamil Nadu the highest at 4.8 per cent. As against these, the all-India growth rate was 3.4 per cent. In the 1990s, the disparity range has widened from 1.8 for Bihar to as high as 6.4 for Gujarat and 5.4 for Tamil Nadu and West Bengal. In comparison, the all-India rate has improved only marginally to 4.1 per cent in the 1990s. Maharashtra, Tamil Nadu, Karnataka and Himachal Pradesh have also improved the standard of living by over 5 per cent per annum during the post-reform period. Gujarat's performance is particularly noteworthy, as the growth rate has jumped from a moderate 3.6 in the 1980s to 6.4 per cent in the 1990s. West Bengal has also managed to push up its per-capita income growth tremendously, from a mere 2.9 per cent in the 1980s to 5.4 per cent in the 1990s. In case of Maharashtra and Karnataka also per-capita income growth rate jumped significantly in the 1990s.

TABLE 3

Growth Rate of Per-capita SDP

(per cent per annum)

States	*1980-81 to 1989-90*	*1990-91 to 1999-2000*	*1980-81 to 1999-2000*
Andhra Pradesh	2.5	3.6	3.1
Bihar	2.9	1.8	1.9
Gujarat	3.6	6.4	4.8
Haryana	4.1	4.4	5.3
Himachal Pradesh	4.3	5.1	4.2
Karnataka	4.0	5.2	4.6
Kerala	3.0	4.7	4.6
Madhya Pradesh	2.7	3.2	3.0
Maharashtra	3.6	5.0	4.8
Orissa	3.9	2.1	2.1
Punjab	3.1	2.7	2.7
Rajasthan	4.4	4.0	4.2
Tamil Nadu	4.8	5.4	5.1
Uttar Pradesh	3.4	1.9	2.9
West Bengal	2.9	5.4	3.9
All-India	3.4	4.1	3.5
CV	0.22	0.43	0.34

Source: Various Reports of Central Statistical Organisation.

While the standard of living improved faster in 1990s in comparison to 1980s in most states, the opposite picture can be viewed in case of Bihar, Orissa, Punjab, Rajasthan and Uttar Pradesh. One of the probable reasons for this could be the comparatively higher growth of population in these states. In Rajasthan, the per-capita growth rate declined in spite of a fairly high SDP growth in 1990s. Punjab, which was the richest state in India in the 1980s with its strong agriculture base, performed relatively worse in terms of per-capita income growth in the 1990s. In case of per-capita growth also, the coefficient of variation of per-capita growth rates among states has jumped from 0.22 in the 1980s to 0.43 in the 1990s, which is almost double. This also clearly highlights the unequal development among the states in the 1990s.

It can be observed that, in general, the Southern states of India have performed better than the Eastern and the Central states. West Bengal is a major exception in this regard. The standard of living in the Southern states increased faster in the 1990s due to a combination of slackening of population growth and acceleration of SDP growth. Even in Andhra Pradesh, despite a below national average SDP growth, per-capita SDP growth accelerated in the 1990s over 1980s due to a significant fall in population growth rate. In the Western states, however, per-capita SDP growth accelerated mainly due to higher SDP growth rate.

Section IV

DISPARITY IN EMPLOYMENT GROWTH

One of the major weaknesses of India, especially in case of rural India, is the huge volume of surplus labour in the form of disguised as well as open unemployment. The growth of population in India has been rapid, intensifying the pressure on land. The population pressure has not only led to a tremendous fall in the land-man ratio but also to the fall in the productivity of labour in agriculture. So expanding productive employment is central for sustained poverty reduction as labour is the main asset for majority of the poor. Over time it has also been recognized that high growth does not necessarily create employment. Labour absorption depends more on the pattern of growth (i.e., labour-intensive or capital-intensive).

Now, agriculture is the backbone of the economy and it will remain as the mainstay of the country, in spite of the fact that it is moving towards industrialization. Now, since the early 1990s, with the introduction of economic reforms, many changes have taken place also in the agriculture and allied sector in India. It has been argued that liberalization measures relating to regional and international trade had a positive impact on the growth of commercial and other service activities in rural India, ushering in a process of sectoral diversification. The growth of employment for the decades 1990s (1993-94 to 1999-2000) and 2000s (1999-2000 to

2004-05) as well for the overall period (1993-94 to 2004-05) separately for rural and urban and also the overall are given in Table 4.

The compound annual growth rate of employment shows a fair degree of variation not only among the states but also within the rural and urban areas of the states. There are only five states with growth rate higher than that the all-India figure of 0.71 in 1990s in rural areas. In 2000s, the all-India average went up to 2.45 in the rural areas with only six states above the national average. Haryana showed a tremendous growth in the rural areas in this period. The main reason for this is the rapid growth of rural non-farm sector. Though the rural employment growth rate has increased in 2000s, but the disparity range among the states has widened. Andhra Pradesh had a growth of only 1.24 whereas for Haryana it was as high as 5.68. This indicates that probably by trying to concentrate on the industrialization of Andhra Pradesh, the rural development has been ignored, which can be a probable reason for farmer suicide. In case of urban areas, the all-India average went up to 4.14 from 1990s to 2.36 in 2000s in the urban areas. It can be noted that, in Gujarat the employment growth rate of urban areas (7.17) in 1990s is much more than that of the rural areas (2.02), which reflects a disparity among the rural and urban areas within the state and it leads to a rural-urban migration with the hope of better opportunities in the urban sector. In case of total employment growth, considering rural and urban together, the all-India average is only 1.89 between 1993-94 and 2004-05 and Gujarat has the highest employment growth rate with 3.09 followed by Haryana 3.01, which is an effect of rapid industrialization in these states in the post-reform period.

It can be concluded that, in case of employment growth Western states have performed better than other parts of the country. One of the main reasons can be the huge flow of foreign direct investments in these states which made them industrialized states and showed them the ways of better employment opportunities.

TABLE 4

State-wise Growth of Employment in India

States	*Rural*			*Urban*			*Total*		
	1993-94 to 1999-00	*1999-00 to 2004-05*	*1993-94 to 2004-05*	*1993-94 to 1999-00*	*1999-00 to 2004-05*	*1993-94 to 2004-05*	*1993-94 to 1999-00*	*1999-00 to 2004-05*	*1993-94 to 2004-05*
Andhra Pradesh	0.29	1.24	0.72	0.27	3.82	1.87	0.29	1.76	0.95
Bihar	1.87	2.06	1.96	-0.56	3.79	1.39	1.59	2.26	1.89
Gujarat	2.02	1.85	1.94	7.17	4.40	5.90	3.34	2.61	3.01
Haryana	0.76	5.68	2.97	1.94	5.33	3.47	1.06	5.59	3.09
Himachal Pradesh	-0.12	2.26	0.96	1.59	9.94	5.30	-0.01	2.82	1.27
Karnataka	0.13	3.06	1.45	3.31	3.39	3.35	0.94	3.15	1.94
Kerala	1.27	1.62	1.43	1.20	0.62	0.93	1.25	1.37	1.31
Madhya Pradesh	0.68	2.15	1.35	2.87	4.57	3.64	1.06	2.62	1.76
Maharashtra	0.39	2.54	1.36	2.05	4.78	3.28	0.93	3.32	2.01
Orissa	0.59	2.37	1.39	-0.20	3.44	1.44	0.49	2.49	1.40
Punjab	1.96	2.22	2.08	5.13	3.54	4.40	2.85	2.62	2.74
Rajasthan	0.50	2.64	1.46	1.11	3.94	2.38	0.61	2.88	1.63
Tamil Nadu	-1.36	0.35	-0.90	6.84	4.58	5.81	1.12	1.56	1.32
Uttar Pradesh	0.61	3.64	1.98	0.65	4.40	2.34	0.62	3.79	2.05
West Bengal	0.37	2.96	1.54	0.53	3.43	1.84	0.42	3.10	1.63
India	0.71	2.45	1.50	2.36	4.14	3.16	1.09	2.86	1.89

Source: Calculated from NSSO Report No. 516

SECTION V

CONCLUDING REMARKS

The analysis so far clearly establishes that there are considerable disparities in development across the Indian States. Efforts through the planning process had only partially succeeded in reducing regional disparities. The reforms since 1991 with stabilisation and deregulation policies as their prime instruments and a very significant role for the private sector seem to have further aggravated the inter-state disparities.

An analysis of the growth in domestic product of Indian states in the last two decades reveals that the development process has been uneven across states. The regional disparity in the growth rates becomes sharper in terms of per-capita income. The poorer states have not only performed poorly but their failure to control population growth has left them in even worse position. These states with higher population growth are not able to attract investment, both public and private, due to a variety of reasons, like poor income and infrastructure and probably also poor governance. The immediate requirement of these states is more investment in their social and infrastructural sectors. To improve the level of social services massive investment in primary education and primary health services are required[5].

The population pressure has not only led to a tremendous fall in the land-man ratio but also to the fall in the productivity of labour in agriculture which is reflected in the growth pattern of rural employment. As a result majority of Indian farmers now requires off-farm income for sustained rural livelihood. It has been observed recently that in rural India, most of the households pursue a multiple of activities as part of their survival strategy. So they are not only depending on agriculture for their livelihood but also depend on a diverse portfolio of activities and income sources. There is an urgent requirement of the growth of non-farm employment across the country and it can be a good avenue for other sources of income within the village. This can lead to a reduction in both the inter-state and intra-state disparities.

Another way of improvement in the basic infrastructural facilities in the less developed states is the introduction of public-private-partnership (PPP). PPP is a mode of implementing government programs or schemes in partnership with the private sector. It involves a long-term relationship between the public sector and the private sector. PPP brings in greater professionalism to bear through introducing meaningful concepts. This can also lead to a reduction in the inter-state disparities.

In conclusion one can say that, if the existing trends in differential rate of development continue regional disparities in India are bound to accentuate. Therefore, it is imperative that the present trends are arrested and preferably reversed. This will require serious efforts on the part of both the concerned State governments and the Centre.

Notes and References

1. Higher in poorer regions and lower in richer regions.
2. For example, deregulation of investment, liberalization of trade, exchange rate, interest rate, capital flows and prices.
3. Andhra Pradesh, Gujarat, Karnataka, Haryana and Maharashtra.
4. The most widely used measure of inter-regional inequality is the coefficient of variation, first popularized in this field by Williamson (1965). The coefficient is simply a weighted dispersion measure, standardized by the mean.
5. The Improvement in literacy and health indicators like infant mortality and expectation of life at birth will bring down the rate of growth of population.

References

Ahluwalia, Montek S. (2002), "State Level Performance Under Economic Reforms in India", in *Economic Policy Reforms and the Indian Economy*, ed. by Anne O. Krueger, Oxford University Press, New Delhi, pp 91-125.

Ahluwalia, Montek S. (2000), "Economic Performance of States in Post-Reforms Period", *Economic and Political Weekly*, May 6, pp. 1637-48.

Barro, Robert J. (1991), "Economic Growth in a Cross Section of Countries", *Quarterly Journal of Economics*, 106, 2 (May), pp, 407-43.

Bhattacharya, B.B. and S. Sakthivel (2004), "Regional Growth and Disparity in India: A Comparison of Pre and Post-Reform Decades", *Economic and Political Weekly*, Vol. 39, No. 10, pp. 1071-77.

Central Statistical Organisation: Various Issues of the National Accounts Statistics.

Datta Roy Choudhury, Uma (1993): "Inter-State and Intra-State Variations in Economic Development and Standard of Living", New Delhi: National Institute of Public Finance and Policy.

Kurain, N.J., "Widening Regional Disparities in India", Planning Commission Paper.

www.planningcommission.nic.in/reports/articles/ncsxna/art_wide.pdf

Nagaraj, R., Aristomene Varoudakis and Marie-Ange Veganzones (1998), "Long-Run Growth Trends and Convergence Across Indian States", OECD Technical Papers, No. 131, January, pp. 1-58.

Reserve Bank of India: Finances of State Governments, various issues.

Rao, M. Govinda, R.T. Shand and K.P. Kalirajan (1999), "Convergence of Incomes Across Indian States—A Divergent View", *Economic and Political Weekly*, March 27,

Shand, Ric and S. Bhide (2000), "Sources of Economic Growth – Regional Dimensions of Reforms", *Economic and Political Weekly*, October 14, pp. 3747-57.

Williamson, J.G. (1965), "Regional Inequality and the Process of National Development: A Description of Patterns", *Economic Development and Cultural Change*, 13, pp. 3-45.

48

Regional Disparities and Level of Employment in India

MOHAMMAD ASIF AND JYOTI OBIA

I. INTRODUCTION

The existence of large disparities in the economic indicators is widely believed to be an important cause of prevailing social, political and economic unrest. Many economist hold the view that inequalities are growing and that this trend, if unchecked would aggravate tensions and endangers economic stability. The regional disparity thus, a matter of serious concern. In our large economy with substantial regional differences in physical endowment, climatic conditions and difference in the initial level of development, growth rates are bound to vary among regions. It is the task of the state policy to implement compensatory measures. to push forward the lagged regions and spread growth and development more equally. However, during almost the entire periods of National planning, a steady widening of Regional disparities has taken place. These disparities are also shown in the levels of employment. Thus, in India, different regions with different resources base and endowment would have dissimilar growth pattern over time. It is generally recognized that inter-regional disparities increases in the early stages of National Economic development. As a result, government everywhere used to initiate deliberate policy measures to reduce these disparities. But in this liberalized scenario, the faith in the market mechanism created a tendency to withdraw such measures under the implicit assumptions that the invisible hand will deliver the goods in this regard.

In the recent years considerable attempts have been made by many economists including Ratan Kumar, Angus Deaton and Jean Dreze, Abhiji Sen and Himanshu, Jayati Ghosh, Gaurav Nayyar and many more to understanding the regional dimensions of economic growth in India. Understanding the causes and nature of differences in the levels and growth of economic indices across the regions is very important because even small differences in the growth rates, if cumulated over a period of time, may have substantial adverse impact on the economy. Further, in equalities in any respect gives rise to unequivocal negative effect on subsequent growth and development and worsens, economic, social and political tensions among regions leading to misallocation of resources.

This paper attempts to estimate the levels and trends in the regional disparities for the major states and the impact of liberalization leading to openness of the economy on regional disparities is studied. This paper is divided into five parts. Section 1 deals with introduction, section 2 discusses the growth of employment and its trend. Section 3 presents the Regional Disparities in the incidence of employment. Section 4 shows the employment prospects and government efforts in this direction. Last section throws some light on the conclusion and Policy Recommendations. The objective is to analyze the growth and disparity among major states in the pre and post-reform period. In the recent period a number of studies have been observed that regional disparity in Indian has widened especially during Nineties.

The period of study is 1980-81 to 1990-91, i.e. a period of pre-reform period and 1991-92 to 2006-07 being the post-reform period. The unemployment is taken as the major indicator for the analysis. The secondary data as available in standard publications have been used.

2. EMPLOYMENT: GROWTH AND ITS TREND

The most significant link between growth and poverty reduction is employment generation, which is why pattern of economic employment growth are usually critical in determining both changes in income distribution and the incidence of poverty. One of the daunting challenges facing India is to provide employment not only for the additions to the labour force but also to reduce the backlog of unemployment accumulated from the past. This should be seen in the context of acceleration in the growth rate of the labour force as well as a secular downward pressure on the employment intensity of the growth process. Economic growth and employment opportunities in themselves may not be sufficient to improve the living conditions of the poor. It is therefore, necessary to shift the force of employment strategies towards creating conditions whereby employment opportunities leads to significantly better living and working conditions of the people and to uphold the dignity of labour

Here we deals with two major questions:

(1) What has been the trend rate of growth of employment?
(2) How has this trend varied between the pre and post-reform period?

During the period of 1972-2003, eighteen NSSO employment surveys have been conducted, out of which six survey (1972-73, 1977-78, 1983, 1987-88, 1993-94 and 1999-2000) were based on large samples.

The Table 1 shows that during the period how employment has changed with the increasing population, there is a steady increase in the number of labour force. But unemployment level has also increased in the pre reform period, i.e. upto 1991. The year 1992 is the year having the highest rate of unemployment, i.e. 5.2 per cent but since then there is decrease in that rate of growth. Thus, here we can

TABLE I

Employment, Unemployment and Growth Rates

(millions unless otherwise indicated)

Survey Round	*Year*	*Labour force*	*Unemployment*	*Rate (%)*	*Employment*
27*	1972	231	10	4.3	221
32*	1977	245	11	4.5	234
38*	1983	275	12	4.5	263
43*	1987	296	14	4.8	282
45	1989	317	11	3.5	306
46	1990	328	13	4.0	315
47	1991	338	15	4.4	323
48	1992	349	18	5.2	331
50*	1993	359	13	3.6	346
51	1994	352	7	2.0	345
52	1995	355	8	2.3	347
53	1997	363	9	2.5	354
54	1998	358	13	3.6	345
55*	1999	385	17	4.4	368
56	2000	377	10	2.7	367
57	2001	396	13	3.3	383
58	2002	394	13	3.3	381
59	2003	405	12	3.0	393

(* based on large samples).

Source: NSSO Reports on Employment and Unemployment available at (mospi. Mic. In/stat_act_t14. htm).

say that reforms have contributed in covering down the level of unemployment.

Employment in the Organized Sector

The employment growth in the organized sector, public and private can be shown in Table 2.

In 1981, the total number of persons employed in the public sector was 162.5 lakhs, which rose to 190.6 lakhs in 1991. In this way, in 1981-91, the rate of growth of public sector employment was 2.1 per cent per annum. But in the post-reforms period (1991-98), public sector employment,

TABLE 2

Employment in the Public and Private Sector

(in millions)

Year	*Public Sector (end March)*	*Private Sector (end-March)*
1970-71	11.1	6.73
1971-72	11.69	6.96
1972-73	12.4	6.72
1973-74	12.73	6.75
1974-75	13.13	6.79
1975-76	13.63	6.79
1976-77	14.18	6.95
1977-78	14.73	7.11
1978-79	15.58	7.23
1979-80	15.12	7.24
1980-81	15.48	7.4
1981-82	16.28	7.53
1982-83	16.75	7.39
1983-84	17.22	7.36
1984-85	17.58	7.43
1985-86	17.68	7.37
1986-87	18.24	7.39
1987-88	18.32	7.39
1988-89	18.51	7.45
1989-90	18.77	7.58
1990-91	19.06	7.68
1991-92	19.21	7.85
1992-93	19.33	7.85
1993-94	19.45	7.93
1994-95	19.47	8.06
1995-96	19.43	8.51
1996-97	19.56	8.69
1997-98	19.42	8.75
1998-99	19.41	8.7
1999-00	19.31	8.65
2000-01	19.14	8.65
2001-02	18.77	8.43
2002-03	18.58	8.42
2003-04	18.2	8.25
2004-05	18.01	8.45

Source: Directorate General of Employment and Training.

which was 190.6 lakhs in 1991, slowly increased to 194.1 lakh in 1998. Thus, in the eight year period (1991-98) the rate of growth of public sector employment slowed to merely 0.2 per cent per annum—a highly pessimistic scenario and then employment raised 180.1 lakhs in the year 2004-05.

The share of Central Government employment was 20.6 per cent in 1981, it fell to 17.9 per cent in 1991 and further to 16.8 per cent in 1998. The growth rate of Central Government employment was 0.7 per cent in 1981-91, but in the post-reform period it became negative 0.6 per cent. As far as the state Government are concerned, employment growth in this sector was 2.3 per cent in 1981-91, but post-reform, it fell to a mere 0.69 per cent. The share of state Government's employment, which was 26.7 per cent in 1981, increased marginally to 38.4 per cent in the post-reform era.

Data reveals that organized private sector employment in 1981 was 74 lakhs, which increased to 76.8 lakhs in 1991, accounting for an annual average, growth rate of 0.4 per cent but post-reform private sector rose to 87.5 lakh in 1998, signifying an annual average growth rate of 1.7 per cent. The highest contribution to the growth of employment was provided by the manufacturing sector and, to some extent, by finance, insurance, real estate and service sectors. But if this growth of employment is reviewed in the light of the increase in the overall labour force, it becomes obvious that the organized public sector is unable to provide employment to the growing labour force.

But a review of the increase in employment, both in public and private sectors, shows that the Public sector employment growth rate was just 0.2 per cent per annum and private sector employment growth was 1.7 per cent in the post-reform period. But unfortunately the period of reforms reveals that the overall growth of employment was only one per cent. It may also be noted that since the reform process is limited to the organized sector, rate of growth of employment in the organized sector also decelerated to 0.6 per cent in the post-reform period as against 1.7 per cent witnessed in the seven year pre reform period of private sector.

All these trend make us to think about the utility of an exclusive policy in resolving poverty and unemployment.

Thus, a new strategy of growth must be adopted which may focus on promoting growth with equity and social justice.

The employment growth in the organized sector, public and private combined has declined during the period between 1994-2005. The trend of employment in both public and private sector can be graphically shown in Chart 1 and Chart 2 as:

CHART 1

Employment in Public Sector

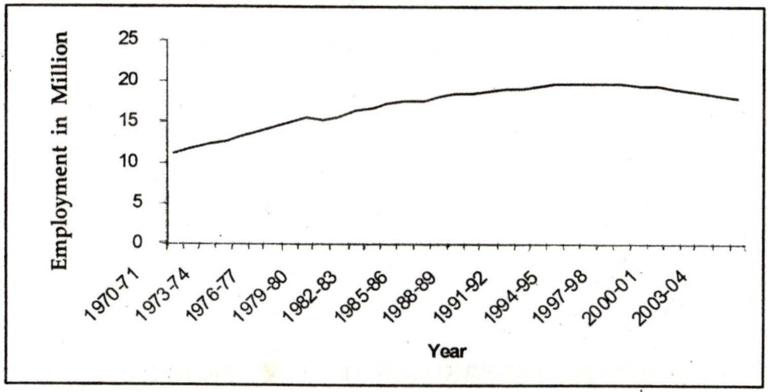

Trend Value is -2.56035.

CHART 2

Employment in Private Sector

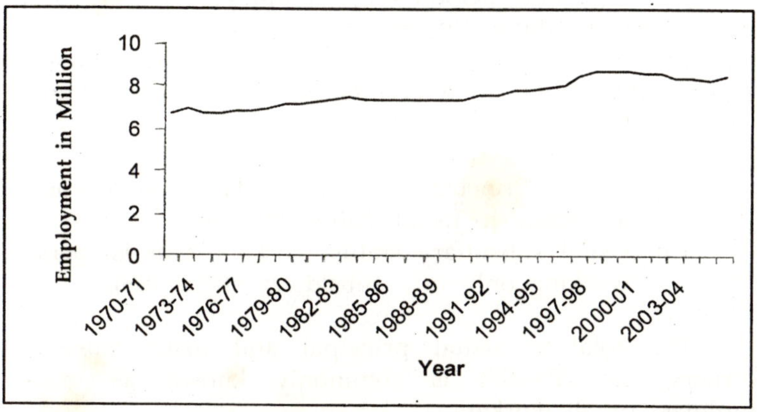

Trend Value is 4.223093.

This has primarily happen due to decline of employment in establishments covered by employment market information system of the ministry of labour grew at 1.20 per cent per annum during 1983-94 but decelerated to -0.31 per cent per annum during 1994-2004.

However, the latter decline was mainly due to a decrease in employment in public sector establishments, whereas the private had shown acceleration in the pace of growth in employment from 0.44 per cent to 0.58 per cent per annum (Table 3)

TABLE 3

Rate of Growth of Employment in Organized Sector

(per cent per annum)

	1983-84	*1994-2005*
Public sector	1.53	-0.70
Private sector	0.44'	0.58
Total organized	1.20	-0.31

Source: Eleventh Plan documents.

3. REGIONAL DISPARITIES IN THE INCIDENCE OF EMPLOYMENT

Worker Population Ratio (WPR) is defined as the number of persons/person days employed per thousand persons/person days (in the population). This ratio is employed in the discussion on the incidence of employment. Worker population ration (WPRs) for usual status workers viz.,

(a) Usual Principal status workers, i.e. workers according to usual status (PS), and
(b) Usual subsidiary status workers, that is, persons working only in a subsidiary status (SS).

The total of usual principal and usual subsidiary workers, i.e. (PS+SS) is commonly known as usually employed or all workers.

Tables 4 and 5 depicts workers population ratio for states and union territories separately for males and females.

TABLE 4

Number of Employed per 1000 Persons according to Usual Status taking Both Principal and Subsidiary Status (PS+SS)

State/UT's	Males					
	2004-05		*1999-00*		*1987-88*	
	R	*U*	*R*	*U*	*R*	*U*
Andhra Pradesh	605	560	605	511	595	503
Arunachal Pradesh	500	461	422	399	524	535
Assam	551	551	529	522	514	572
Bihar	477	452	492	432	500	448
Chhattisgarh	565	529	-	-	-	-
Delhi	516	535	520	528	426	510
Goa	524	534	539	498	521	474
Gujarat	593	578	584	536	559	510
Haryana	522	511	475	506	475	553
Himachal Pradesh	555	619	536	499	539	466
J & K	552	526	548	478	535	431
Jharkhand	535	472	-	-	-	-
Karnataka	623	576	595	545	568	494
Kerala	559	547	553	558	506	530
Madhya Pradesh	544	525	536	488	546	480
Maharashtra	566	560	531	532	546	496
Manipur	524	456	495	445	437	375
Meghalaya	572	454	557	393	583	517
Mizoram	594	484	555	471	591	509
Nagaland	549	457	518	393	(No survey)	585
Orissa	586	504	551	575	566	493
Punjab	549	572	530	549	560	540
Rajasthan	510	508	500	486	512	471
Sikkim	554	545	502	519	487	487
Tamil Nadu	547	593	494	563	587	558
Tripura	549	504	504	494	519	463
Uttaranchal	523	519	-	-	-	-
Uttar Pradesh	446	524	481	490	518	489
West Bengal	574	595	534	567	550	539

A & N Islands	632	578	547	632	536	547
Chandigarh	602	512	784	547	616	497
D & N Haveli	547	689	582.	656566 (No ...)		-
Daman and Diu	591	652	655	549	-	-
Lakshadweep	611	436	497	432	437	363
Pondicherry	569	536	560	555	518	495
All-India	656	549	531	518	539	506

Source: NSSO Survey—61st Round and earlier Surveys.

Among the major states, in 2004-05, the rural male WPR was the highest in Karnataka at 62.3 per cent and among Union territories Andaman and Nicobar Island had the highest WPR ratio at 63.2 per cent in 2004-05. This was followed by Andhra Pradesh (61%), Tamil Nadu (60%), Gujarat (59%) and Orissa (59%), West Bengal and Maharashtra also have a WPR of 57 per cent each, that is, well above the all-India level of 55 per cent. All other states have WPR's higher than the average WPR for all-India.

As against the above, on the other side Bihar with 48 per cent, UP with 50 per cent and Rajasthan with 51 per cent is the lowest three employed states. These states were showing a decline in the WPR's ratio since 1987-88.

Among the urban males, the WPR was above all-India level of 55 per cent in 9 states with 62 per cent in Himachal Pradesh followed by West Bengal and Tamil Nadu with 60 and 59 per cent of WPR respectively. In the lower spectrum, Bihar along with north-eastern states like Manipur, Meghalaya, Nagaland and Mizoram form lower than 50per cent WPR states.

Among rural females, Himachal Pradesh, Andhra Pradesh, Maharashtra, Tamil Nadu, Karnataka and Chhattisgarh reported higher WPRs. than all-India WPR's of 33 per cent. Assam, Bihar, Goa, Haryana, Jammu & Kashmir, Jharkhand, Kerala, Orissa, Punjab, Sikkim, Uttar Pradesh and West Bengal reported lower WPR than all-India.

Among Urban females a few major states namely, Tamil Nadu, Himachal Pradesh, Andhra Pradesh and Kerala reported higher than all-India average WPRs.

TABLE 5

Number of Employed per 1000 Persons according to Usual Status taking Both Principal and Subsidiary Status

	Females					
State/UT's	*2004-05*		*1999-00*		*1987-88*	
Andhra Pradesh	483	224	478	178	470	215
Arunachal Pradesh	410	148	310	100	305	142
Assam	209	109	151	112	162	84
Bihar	138	65	173	75	193	79
Chhattisgarh	454	181	-	-	-	-
Delhi	47	88	29	105	51	90
Goa	188	188	181	106	239	145
Gujarat	427	151	413	135	381	112
Haryana	317	132	202	98	297	123
HP	506	241	471	130	480	156
J & K	267	112	327	62	347	145
Jharkhand	313	134	-	-	-	-
Karnataka	459	101	380	178	377	196
Kerala	256	200	238	203	286	198
Madhya Pradesh	366	154	362	134	410	144
Maharashtra	474	190	434	137	462	159
Manipur	351	221	253	211	191	123
Meghalaya	478	303	418	197	512	352
Mizoram	441	281	440	259	409	358
Nagaland	504	257	441	199	(No survey)	65
Orissa	322	148	299	145	276	125
Punjab	322	133	280	125	317	123
Rajasthan	407	182	388	138	450	191
Sikkim	318	168	241	200	298	117
Tamil Nadu	461	241	430	215	461	227
Tripura	85	100	73	75	136	91
Uttaranchal	427	127	-	-	-	-
Uttar Pradesh	240	117	201	94	219	94
West Bengal	178	155	160	117	196	125
A & N Islands	243	155	180	206	177	112
Chandigarh	54	142	128	136	122	192
D & N Haveli	478	194	354	112	490	No urban
Daman and Diu	168	225	300	186	Included in Goa	-
Lakshadweep	50	108	115	179	110	154
Pondicherry	361	154	287	169	340	186
All-India	327	166	299	139	323	152

Source: NSSO Survey—61st Rounds and earlier survey.

4. EMPLOYMENT PROSPECTS AND GOVERNMENT'S EFFORTS TO EMPLOYMENT GENERATION

The increasing rate of economic growth, is unable to generate high employment growth. Infact it is accompanied by a slow down in employment growth in recent years, that has led many economist to portray the experience of 'Jobless Growth'. The author's basic contention is the number of new jobs created each year, since the reforms may be low, and that does not translate into a high unemployment rate because the increase in labour force has itself been low.

A brief account of the performance of employment growth shows that in organized sector, growth of employment in the public sector has decelerate, but there is rapid increase in the rate of growth in private sector. It has also been shown that since 1972 there is a steady increase in the level of employment. Since 1991, Indian economy became more integrated with the Global Economy, we can make some inferences about the effect of globalization on the level of employment:

Firstly, the globalization era has reduced the rate of growth of employment in the public sector but there is expansion in the private sector which seems the globalizations effect on labour productivity and capital Intensity.

Secondly, in the post-reform era, there has been a divergence in employment growth rates. This makes it increasingly important for policy-makers to ensure that workers are equipped with the skills to move from low growth to high growth of employment in various sectors.

In most parts of India, the level of unemployment and under employment remains high. The vicious circle of falling employment rising poverty and increasing social tension is most dark in all states of India. Planning in India focused at realizing a high rate of growth of output in the long-term. A basic assumption was that shortage of capital goods in relation to employable persons conducted a fundamental constraint on growth of the economy. Therefore, the planning process made no attempt to define an independent employment strategy; the focus on economic growth was viewed as essential for improving the employment situation.

Thus, in the Five Year Plans, the generation of employment was viewed as part of the process of development and not as a goal in conflict with or to be pursued independently of economic development.

The approaches to tackling the task of unemployment have varied from time to time. In the initial years of planning reliance was placed primarily on the expectations of a rapid Industrial development and control of population. These expectations did not materialized and it was observed that the rate of growth of employment was generally much than the GDP growth rate of an economy. Successive plans, strategies, policies and programmes were, therefore, re-designed to bring about a special focus on employment generation as a specific objectives. Various schemes were initiated by the government to achieve this objectives. These includes; NREP, RLEGP to provide wage employment through public work programmes and schemes to promote self employment and entrepreneurship through provision of assets, skills and other support to the unemployed and the poor. Pradhan Mantri Gram Sadak Yojana (PMGSY), India Awaas Yojana (IAY), Swarnjayanti Gram Swarozgar Yojana (SGSY), Sampoorna Grameen Rozgar Yojana (SGRY), Swarna Jayanti Shahri Rozgar Yojana (SJSRY) were also planned.

The objectives of the employment generation policies:

- To develop a vision and strategy for employment generation and to prepare a time bound action plan for implementation of the same.
- To suggest measures to desire synergy of the plans and programmes of various departments working directly or indirectly for employment generation.
- To advice on institutional and organizational mechanism for effective implication of the action plan for employment generation.
- To regularly monitor and oversee employment generation action plans in the economy and advice on the future steps to be taken.
- To initiate public debate on important policy issues related to employment generation and build consensus for policy reforms related to it.

- To facilitate manpower planning in key sectors of the economy.
- To identify and advise on the regulatory aspects of training.

Strategies

To realize these objectives, World Development Report (WDR) has a recommended following strategies:

- Timely Investment in skill development and training at enhanced level.
- Enhancement of education and skill level of workers.
- Responsive training system.

Following areas can be concentrated for convergence:

1. Convergence of programmes aimed at employment Generation Mission.
2. Convergence of actuaries within the sectors (self-help groups leading to self-help employment leading to entrepreneurship).
3. Convergence among sectoral growth of agriculture and Industries leading to the growth of service sector further contributing to the growth/ diversification of Agriculture and Industrial sectors.

Focused Areas

Employment Generation Mission focus on certain areas for increasing employment potential as—

1. Establishing more technical and enhancing the capacity of existing institutions.
2. Sharpening training and development institutes by following duster development approach.
3. Focus on certain emerging growth engines like information technology, health care, etc.
4. Harnessing the potential of various self-help youth groups, etc.

5. POLICY RECOMMENDATIONS AND CONCLUSION

Planning Commission set-up a Task Force under the Chairmanship of Dr. M.S. Ahluwalia to go into the details of employment generation taking place in the economy and suggest measures for creation of 100 millions jobs in a period of 10 years.

The task force has recommended intervention in five major areas as under:

- Accelerating the rate of growth of GDP, with a particular emphasis on sectors likely to ensure the spread of income to the lower income segments of the labour force.
- Pursuing appropriate sectoral policies in Indian dual sectors, which are particularly important for employment generation.
- Implementing focused special programmes for creating additional employment of enhancing income generation from existing activities aimed at promoting economic growth.
- Pursuing suitable policies for education and skill development, which would upgrade the quality of the labour force and make it capable of supporting a growth process which generates high quality jobs.
- Ensuring that the policies and legal environment governing the labour market encourages labour absorption, especially in the organized sector.

A special group in the Planning Commission was constituted under the chairmanship of Dr. S.P. Gupta, Member, Planning Commission to suggest strategies and programmes in the Tenth Plan for creating gainful employment opportunities for one crore people per year. The special group suggested restructuring in the following sectors:

(a) Agriculture and allied sector.
(b) Greening the country through Agro Forestry.
(c) Energy Plantation for Biomass Power Generation.

(d) Rural sector and small and medium enterprises (SMEs).
(e) Education and Literacy.
(g) Health, Family and Child Welfare.

This paper has attempted a somewhat preliminary account of the pattern and growth of employment inequalities in India during pre- and post-reform period. It has been found that growth of employment in the public and private sector was characterized by instability. It would be instructive to extend the analysis to sectoral growth rates and identifying the sector contribution to instability.

Inter-State disparities in the employment levels and growth rates has increased over time in the post-reform era. However, the relative positions of many states remained unchanged.

This paper has also made an attempt to throw light on some of the government's efforts in narrowing this inequality gap, in the form of various policies, strategies and schemes. Thus, it is imperative that reform processes be such that which promotes growth with equity. For this, the policies of employment expansion will have to be adopted rather than employment contraction.

References

Ahluwalia, Montek (2000): "Economic Performance of States in the Post-Reforms Period", *Economic and Political Weekly* (May 6): 1637-48.

Ahluwalia, Montek (2002): "Report of the Task Force on Employment Opportunities." In Planning Commission Report on Labour and Employment, edited by R. Kapila, and U. Kapila, New Academic Foundation.

Bardham, P. (2001): 'Social Justice in the Global Economy', *Economical and Political Weekly*, 36(5/6), pp. 467-80.

Bell, M. (2001): 'Bhagwati Counters Critics of Globalization, Stresses its Social and Economic Benefits, IMF Survey, 2 April, pp. 114-16.

Bhattacharya, B.B. and S. Sakhivel (2004). "Regional Growth and Disparities in India, Compression of Pre- and Post-reform Decades", *Economic and Political Weekly*, Vol. 29(10), March 6, pp. 1071-77.

CSO (2001): National Accounts Statistics, Back series, 1950-51 to 1992-93, Department of Statistics, Ministry of Planning, New Delhi.

Dholakia, R.H. (1985): Regional Disparities in Economic Growth in India, Himalaya Publishing House, Bombay.

Dollar, D. (2001): Globalization, Inequality and Poverty since 1980, World Bank, mimeo.

Government of India (2004): *Economic Survey,* 2003-04, New Delhi, Ministry of Finance.

Government of India (2008), *Economic Survey,* 2007-08, New Delhi, Ministry of Finance.

Kurian, N.J. (2000): 'Widening Regional Inequalities in India: Some Indicators'. *Economic and Political Weekly,* 35(7), pp. 538-50.

Kurian, N.J. and A. Bagchi (2002): 'Regional Inequalities in India—Pre and Post-Regorms Trends and Challenges for Policy, Planning Commission, GOI, mimeo.

Mahbubul Haq (2002): Human Development in South Asia, 2001: Globalization and Human Development, Oxford University Press, New York.

Marjet, S. and A. Mitra (1996): "Convergence in Regional Growth Rates: Indian Research Agenda", *Economic and Political Weekly,* Vol. 31(33), August 17.

Ric, Shand and S. Bhede (2000): "Sources of Economic Growth: Regional Dimension of Reforms", *Economic and Political Weekly,* Vol. 35(42), October 14, pp. 3747-57.

49

Regional Development and Occupational Shift in Madhya Pradesh: An Inter-temporal Analysis

ROOPALI SHEVALKAR

INTRODUCTION

The contemporary production relations determine the division of labour and thereby the employment and occupational composition in the economy. It is argued that economic development is accompanied by employment generation and in developed regions there has been steady increase in employment. In contrast to the above it is observed that backward economies fail to generate employment. Therefore, the regional development and employment has been characterised by four factors and reflects strong relationship between the two. These are an increase in employment is followed by the increasing labour force, productivity of labour which enhance the per-capita income, the increasing wage earner labour force results into fall in the self employment, and finally there is employment a shift occupational structure from primary to non-primary with advancement of the economy. Therefore, a direct relationship may be observed between the levels of development and employment/occupational structure. Theoretically the above statements are seen in the light of the aggregate economies at macro level, but when one comes to the regional level where there is strong diversification of resource base and the levels of development, the theoretical premises do not stand to be correct. The initial stage of development supports a large number of persons in labour force and finds employment in the primary production. The rate of shift is extremely slow.

Many studies have been conducted on employment, occupational pattern, sectoral shift and development, regional development, but little work has been done on the determinants of most of studies confined to macro trends and structure of employment. It has been observed that unemployment rate has increased in 1990's along with decline in the share of agricultural sector in urban areas (Amitabh Kundu). On the contrary it has been observed that after liberalisation unemployment has declined (Parthsarthy, 1995). Although India had to opt for Globalisation forcefully, but still situation has not worsened. Employment growth picked up after liberalisation in spite of rigidities. (S. Mahendra Dev 2000). Economic and demographic factors have always been influential on employment structure (V.N. Kothari, 1966). With the development process there is sectoral shift in, occupational pattern as share of agricultural sector declines and share of secondary sector and tertiary sector increases. (Colin Clark). Similarly shift in employment, from agricultural to non-agricultural sector. Educated unemployment is growing in terms of job opportunities (A. Vaidyanathan, 1994). Therefore, self-employment is increasing as educated youth is creating job opportunities for himself. (Amitabh Kundu, 1997). Various other aspects of employment and unemployment such as disguised unemployment self employment, under-employment, visible unemployment have been studied by different scholars like K.K. Mohanti and Sakti Padhi, N.A. Majumdar. Sectoral employment specifically agricultural sector and modern sector have also been a key area for scholars. (K.R. Patel, Sumati Kulkarni, Dr. Radha Devi, 1994).

Gender related studies on employment have also conducted by scholars such as Rachel Kumar, Nitya rao, Rana. In spite of many studies on employment and various other aspects of employment and unemployment and development, very little has been done to relate employment and development specifically for Madhya Pradesh. Madhya Pradesh, even though a resourceful state, had always been at the periphery of development during colonial era which continued even in the post-independence era too. The economy is basically agrarian and the state is considered backward by any measure of indicators. In such situation change in occupational pattern requires two things; the pace of regional development has to be increased and deliberate measures to increase employment potential is pertinent for regional development.

In the light of above statement, the present paper is focused to analyse shift in the occupational pattern and levels of regional development and their relationship in Madhya Pradesh at district-level.

Sector theory examines the process of economic development that is accompanied by a shift in the employment pattern first from primary to secondary latter to tertiary sector. Stage theory visualized economic development as a process of transfer through successive stages of development from agricultural to industrial economy. This process is due to relative difference in the income elasticities of the products of different sectors and relative earnings per worker in different sectors. It will be interesting and worthwhile to observe the process in case of MP and also to understand how far development has accompanied shift in occupational pattern. In the light of above statements the Objective of the Paper are:

1. To study the shifts in the occupational/ employment pattern of MP during 1981 and 2001.
2. To study the shifts in the levels of development throughout the period of study.
3. To analyse the relationship between Regional Development and Occupational structure.
4. Data Base and Methodology.

The present study is based on secondary data which has been colleted from different statistical publications of Madhya Pradesh government ,census of India, Directorate of Economics and statistics department of Madhya Pradesh

For the purpose of structural analysis of occupational pattern ,data has been transformed into comparative units by using percentages, ratio, etc. For further study, statistical measures such as central tendency, dispersion, coeffient of variation are used. Factor analysis method has been used to construct composite index of development.

The study is carried out for two point of time, i.e. 1981 and 2001. The following indicators are used for construction of composite index.

INDICATORS

Percentage of net sowed area to the Geographical area, Irrigation Extent, Irrigation Intensity, Cropping Intensity, Number of registered factories per thousand population, Number of employees in registered factories per thousand populations, Output capital ratio, Output-input ratio, Net value added per thousand populations. Capital labour ratio, Per-capita deposit, Per-capita credit, Credit deposit ratio, Literacy rate, Total road length per 100 sq. km. Consumption of fertilizers kg/hec, Number of primary students enrolled per lakh population, Number of secondary students enrolled per lakh population, Per-capita power consumption, Percentage of villages electrified.

SECTION I

SHIFT IN OCCUPATIONAL PATTERN 1981-2001

Table 1 reveals that the percentage of cultivators to total main workers has declined during the two decades. In 1981, in category A, Jhabua ranked highest with 83 per cent of cultivators. In 2001, the per cent has declined to 73.3 per cent, i.e. almost 10 per cent Also it is visible that number of districts have been reduced from 20 in category A in 1981 to 15 in the same category in 2001. Another alarming fact is that in category B number of districts has increased from 15 in

TABLE I

Percentage of Cultivators to Total Main Workers

Category	*1981*	*2001*
High 50% and above	Ujjain, Jhabua, Morena, Datia, Tikamgarh, Shivpuri, Mandla, Morena, Dhar, Guna, Mandsaur, Sidhi, Rajgarh, Panna, Balaghat, Betul, Khandwa, Seoni, Shahdol, Shajapur	Jhabua, Shivpuri, Tikamarh Barwani, Dindori, Datia, Chhatarpur, Bhind, Rajgarh, Mandsaur, Dhar, Sidhi, Neemuch, Guna
Medium 25% to 50%	Sehore, Dewas, Chhindwara, Reewa, Raisen, Satna, Khargon Narsinhpur, Damoh, Gwalior, Sagar, Chhatarpur, Jabalpur Hoshangabad	Shajapur, Panna, Khargon, Ratlam, Sehore, Mandla, Reewa, Sheopur, Ujjain,Betul, Dewas, Seoni, Umaria, Harda, Shahdol, Chhindwara, Vidisha, Kandwa, Satna, Raisen, Narsinhpur, Damoh, Sagar
Low Below 25%	Bhopal, Indore, Vidisha	Gwalior, Bhopal, Jabalpur, Balaghat

1981 to 24 in 2001. This indicates that per cent of cultivators has reduced in some of the districts.

The same is supported from Table 2 which indicates an increase in per cent of agricultural labourers in both the categories, i.e. A (above 40%) and B (20% to 40%) the number of districts have gone up by 3 and 5 respectively in 1981 and 2001. Increase in per cent of agricultural labourers reflects speedy casualisation of labour in rural areas due to increase in population that decreases land man ratio which results into subdivision and fragmentation of holdings.

Table 3 reveals that the percentage of workers in household industry is excessively low except for Chattarpur, Sagar and Damoh in 1981, although Chattarpur has shifted to C category in 2001. The status of household industry is quite low which could otherwise provide employment

TABLE 2

Percentage of Agricultural Labourers to Total Main Workers

Category	*1981*	*2001*
High above 40%	—	Seoni, Narsinhpur, Malwa
Medium 20% to 40%	Sehore, Dewas, Chhindwara, Reewa, Raisen, Satna, Khargon Narsinhpur, Damoh, Seoni Jabalpur, Vidisha, Khandwa, Hoshangabad, Shajapur, Betul, Shahdol, Sidhi, Panna, Dhar, Balaghat, Ujjain, Mandla, Rajgarh.	Shajapur, Panna, Khargon, Ratlam, Sehore, Balaghat, Reewa, Sheopur, Barwani, Betul, Dewas, Hoshangabad, Umaria, Chhaterpur, Katni, Chhindwara, Vidisha, Dhar, Khandwa, Satna, Raisen, Damoh, Sidhi, Rajgarh, Guna, Dindori, Mandsaur, Ujjain, Jabalpur, Neemuch, Shahdol,
Low Below 20%	Bhopal, Indore, Guna, Sagar, Ratlam, Mandsaur, Jhabua, Tikamgarh, Datia, Bhind, Gwalior, Chhatarpur, Morena	Gwalior, Bhopal, Morena, Jhabua, Indore, Datia, Bhind, Shivpuri, Tikamgarh

opportunities to those who are working as agricultural labourers and marginal workers.

Table 4 of the section represents the percentage of workers for 1981 and 2001. For both the periods percentage of workers being higher than 50 per cent, i.e. in category A are found to be developed districts of Madhya Pradesh. These districts are Bhopal, Indore, Gwalior and Jabalpur .Most of districts are in category B and C in both the decades which proves that work participation in agricultural sector is high and low in other sectors of the economy.

TABLE 3

Percentages of Workers in Household Industry to Total Main Workers

Category	*1981*	*2001*
High above 20%	Chhatarpur, Sagar	Sagar, Damoh
Medium 10% to 20%	Damoh	—
Low Below 10%	Raisen, Shajapur, Sehore, Mandsaur, Jhabua, Bhopal, Tikamgarh, Bhind, Morena, Narsinhpur, Rajgarh, Panna, Balaghat, Shivpuri, Reewa, Khandwa, Seoni, Dhar, Sidhi, Mandla, Ujjain, Guna, Dewas, Hoshangabad, Gwalior, Betul, Ratlam, Datia, Vidisha, Indore, Shahdol, Chindwara, Khargone.	Narsinhpur, Guna, Raisen, Shivpuri, Tikamgarh, Betul, Harda, Panna, Balaghat, Dhar, Shajapur, Sehore, Khargone, Reewa, Rajgarh, Dindori, Sidhi, Seoni, Mandla, Dewas, Chhatarpur, Indore, Vidisha, Umaria, Gwalior, Shahdol, Hoshangabad, Ujjain, Bhind, Bhopal, Morena, Khandwa, Ratlam, Chhindwara, Dewas, Neemuch, Shivpuri.

SECTION II

REGIONAL DISPARITIES AND DEVELOPMENT: A COMPARATIVE ANALYSIS

The present section deals with the comparative analysis of regional disparities and composite index of development for 1981 and 2001. Factor analysis method has been used for the above purpose.

It is evident from Table 5 that regional disparities has gone down from 1981 to 2001 as coefficient of variation has decreased from 97.4 in 1981 to 66.49 in 2001. This is due to industrial dispersal with in the state as growth centre strategy has been adopted during 80's by Madhya Pradesh

TABLE 4

Percentage of Workers in other Services To Total Main Workers

Category	*1981*	*2001*
High above 40%	Bhopal, Indore, Gwalior, Jabalpur	Bhopal, Indore, Gwalior, Jabalpur
Medium 20% to 40%	Dewas, Chhindwara, Sagar, Satna, Khargon, Datia, Chhatarpur, Ratlam, Vidisha, Hoshangabad, Shahdol, Balaghat, Ujjain, Mandla, Rajgarh.	Ujjain, Neemuch, Shahdol, Ratlam, Morena, Bhind, Reewa, Sheopur, Sagar, Dewas, Hoshangabad, Umaria, Chhaterpur, Katni, Chhindwara, Vidisha, Khandwa, Satna, Raisen.
Low Below 20%	Raisen, Shajapur, Sehore, Mandsaur, Jhabua, Damoh, Tikamgarh, Bhind, Morena, Narsinhpur, Rajghat, Panna, Balaghat, Shivpuri, Reewa, Khandwa, Seoni, Dhar, Sidhi, Mandla, Ujjain.	Narsinhpur, Damoh, Guna, Jhabua, Badwani, Mandsaur, Shivpuri, Tikamgarh, Betul, Harda, Panna, Balaghat, Dhar, Shajapur, Sehore, Khargone, Reewa, Rajgarh, Dindori, Sidhi, Seoni, Mandla.

TABLE 5

Regional Disparities in Madhya Pradesh

	1981	*2001*
Mean	6.31	10.02
Standard deviation	6.14	6.66
Coefficient of variation	97.4	66.49

government. 23 growth centers have been established in Madhya Pradesh among which flourishing are Pithampur, Malanpur, Mandideep, Maneri, Ghinori, etc.

TABLE 6

Coefficient of Variation of Selected Indicators—1981

	Indicators	*C.V.*
1.	Percentage of net sowed area to the Geographical area	27.51
2.	Irrigation Extent	85.30
3.	Irrigation Intensity	5.66
4.	Cropping Intensity	7.31
5.	Number of registered factories per thousand population	125.3
6.	Number of employees in registered factories per thousand population	180.57
7.	Output-capital ratio	258.30
8.	Output-input ratio	88.15
9.	Net value added per thousand populations	248.76
10.	Capital-labour ratio	154.23
11.	Per-capita deposit	136.47
12.	Per-capita credit	132.21
13.	Credit-deposit ratio	42.21
14.	Literacy rate	29.98
15.	Total road length per 100 sq. km.	31.38
16.	Per cent of villages electrified	45.02
17.	Per-capita power consumption	96.1

Tables 6, 7 deals with the coefficient of variations of individual indicators for 1981 and 2001. It was found that most of indicators of industrial sector has high coefficient of variation in 1981 which declined marginally in 2001. In 1981 coefficient of variation output per-capital ratio and Net value added per thousand population is above 200 per cent. In 2001 coefficient of variation for infrastructural and agricultural sector indicators is high.

Factor Analysis

Factor Analysis is a method of data reduction of a large set of N number of variables to a smaller set of n number of factors which are orthogonal in nature.

Tables 8 and 9 indicates, factors extracted and variance explained for 1981 and 2001. Factor analysis, which was carried out for 17 indicators of regional development in 1981, brought out six factors, which together explained 79.2 per

TABLE 7

Co-efficient of Variation of Selected Indicators—2001

Indicators	*C.V.*
1. Percentage of net sowed area to the Geographical area	26.24
2. Percentage of double cropped area to the Geographical area	57.17
3. Irrigation Extent	54.17
4. Irrigation Intensity	16.36
5. Cropping Intensity	10.04
6. Consumption of fertilizers kg/hec	51.99
7. Number of registered factories per thousand population	118.5
8. Number of employees in registered factories per thousand population	181.34
9. Output-capital ratio	624.05
10. Output-labour ratio	30.76
11. Net value added per thousand population	196.98
12. Capital labour ratio	110.3
13. Per-capita deposit	69.78
14. Per-capita credit	110.09
15. Credit-deposit ratio	149.14
16. Literacy rate	15.32
17. No. of primary students enrolled per lakh population	15.41
18. No. of secondary students enrolled per lakh population	15.41
19. Total road length per 100 sq. km.	36.52
20. Per cent of villages electrified	3.48
21. Per-capita power consumption	51.25

TABLE 8

Factor Analysis Extracted and Variance Explained—1981

Variable	*Factor extracted*	*Eigen Value*	*Percentage of Variance explained*	*Cumulative Percentage*
N_1	1	5.42	31.91	31.91
N_2	2	2.49	14.7	46.61
N_3	3	1.88	9.9	56.55
N_4	4	1.51	8.9	65.48
N_5	5	1.25	7.3	72.84

TABLE 9

Factor Analysis Extracted and Variance Explained—2001

Variable	*Factor extracted*	*Eigen Value*	*Percentage of Variance explained*	*Cumulative Percentage*
N_1	1	5.28	22.00	22.00
N_2	2	14.33	36.34	36.34
N_3	3	2.77	11.57	47.91
N_4	4	1.99	8.31	56.23
N_5	5	1.69	7.04	63.28
N_6	6	1.41	5.91	69.19

cent of variance. The Ist factor, which explains maximum variance, is highly correlated with number of registered factories per 1000 population, number of employees in registered factories per 1000 population, per-capita deposits, per-capita credit. In 2001 factor I is highly correlated with infrastuctural and agricultural indicators. It not factor I but factor II which explains 14 per cent of the total variance is highly correlated with the above indicators of industrial development (1981). This analysis strongly supports the fact that industrial development disparities have gone down and infrastructural, agricultural disparities have increased from 1981 to 2001.

In 1981 Madhya Pradesh economy was totally dependent on agriculture sector that generated very little income in the hands of people, which further reduced demand for processed commodities leaving industry at its infancy stage. Later on it was realized that industrialization should be promoted in back ward districts of MP for which growth centre strategy based on growth pole concept has been adopted. Which resulted in reduction in industrial development disparities. Growth poles are the centers in economic space from which growth trickles down to the peripheral areas through centrifugal forces and also it attracts economic activities and people to concentrate at such centers need to have leading industry or propulsive firms for polarization (perroux). This further requires strong infrastructure to generate spread effects, which further

TABLE 10

Comparative Analysis of Levels of Development in Madhya Pradesh

Rankings and Categories of Districts Based on Composite Index for 1981 and 2001

Category	1981		2001	
	Rank	District	Rank	District
A	1	Jabalpur	1	Jabalpur
	2	Bhopal	2	Katani
	3	Indore	3	Indore
	4	Ujjain	4	Bhopal
	5	Gwalior	5	Dewas
	6	Dewas	6	Dhar
	7	Khandwa	7	Bhind
	8	Mandsaur	8	Gwalior
	9	Satna	9	Khargone
	10	Ratlam	10	Ujjain
	11	Hoshangabad	11	Raisen
			12	Ratlam
			13	Badwani
			14	Mandsaur
			15	Khandwa
			16	Neemuch
B	12	Shahdol	17	Hoshangabad
	13	Rajgarh	18	Seoni
	14	Sehore	19	Sagar
	15	Chhidwara	20	Morena
	16	Sagar	21	Datia
	17	Morena	22	Damoh
	18	Dhar	23	Harda
	19	Vidisha	24	Sehore
	20	Raisen	25	Reewa
			26	Sheopur
			27	Chhindwara
			28	Tikamgarh
			29	Rajgarh
			30	Narsinhpur
			31	Shajapur
			32	Vidisha
			33	Balaghat
			34	Betul

C	21	Shajapur	35	Chhatarpur
	22	Reewa	36	Umaria
	23	Khargone	37	Sidhi
	24	Damoh	38	Shivpuri
	25	Seoni	39	Jhabua
	26	Datia	40	Dindori
	27	Narsinhpur	41	Shahdol
	28	Balaghat	42	Mandla
	29	Jhabua	43	Satna
	30	Bhind	44	Panna
	31	Chhatarpur	45	Guna
	32	Guna		
	33	Betul		
	34	Tikamgarh		
	35	Shivpuri		
	36	Sidhi		
	37	Panna		
	38	Mandla		

facilitates to break vicious circle of under development. (Gunnar Myrdal). This also attracts private and MNC'S in industrial sector. Unfortunately growth centers were missing leading industries and due to wrong location in Madhya Pradesh, the strategy was not of much success. Later on government realized the importance of private participation and role of infrastructure in industrial development and as a result industry promotion policy 2004 and action plan to develop MP as industry state. The policy envisages on creating an industry friendly administration, maximizing employment opportunities and encouraging private sector participation. (Sunil Rajeshwar) by investment promotion assistance, setting up of SEZ. A power policy has also been developed to facilitate industrialization.

The above table reveals different categories of districts based on composite index of development. There are some interesting observations which comes out after analyzing the table. First there is wide gap in terms of composite scores between category A districts and category C districts and there is no gap between underdeveloped districtS as indicated by their composite scores which varies only marginally. Secondaly, number of districts in category C of CID has reduced during the period of study. Major upward shift is observed only for Dhar, Bhind and Khargone which are ranked high in 2001 as compared to 1981. Lastly districts which have gone down remarkably in ranking from 1981 to 2001 are Ujjain, Khandwa, Ratlam, Sehore, Chindwara, Vidisha, Shajapur. For some of the districts, this downward shift may be attributed to decrease in per cent of cultivators and increase in per cent of agricultural workers during the period of study.

Section III

RELATIONSHIP BETWEEN INDEX OF REGIONAL DEVELOPMENT AND OCCUPATIONAL PATTERN 1981

Last section deals with the direction of shift in occupational pattern and regional development between two decades for this purpose two tables have been prepared for 1981 and 2001 respectively. From both the tables it is observed that higher order districts have highest percentage of worker in other services such as Bhopal, Jabalpur, Indore and Gwalior. No major shift is observed in occupational pattern of higher order districts between 1981 and 2001 except for Ujjain which is ranked higher in 1981 and has higher percentage of cultivators, but in 2001 has gone down in ranking and has observed occupational shift from cultivators to other services marginally.

Middle order districts have maximum people engaged in primary sector as is evident from the fact that most of the districts falls in C category of other workers and A or B category of cultivators and agricultural labourers.

During 1981 lower order districts have major occupation as cultivators and agricultural labourers, and minor occupation in household industry and other services. There is no major change in the situation in 2001, except for Damoh which has shifted from lower to higher order districts from 1981 to 2001, where percentage of workers in household industry has increased (from 19% to 23.08%).

It is not that agricultural development cannot lead to regional development but a miserable aspect of MP economy is that it has less developed agriculture because of traditional

Relationship between Index of Regional Development and Occupational Pattern, 1981

S. No.	District	per cent of Cultivators to T.M.W.	per cent of Agricultural Labourers to T.M.W.	per cent of workers in Household Industry T.M.W.	per cent of Other Workers to T.M.W.
1.	Jabalpur	C	B	C	A
2.	Katni	C	B	C	B
3.	Indore	C	C	C	A
4.	Bhopal	C	C	C	A
5.	Dewas	B	B	C	B
6.	Dhar	A	B	C	B
7.	Bhind	A	C	C	B
8.	Gwalior	C	B	C	A
9.	Khargone	B	B	C	B
10.	Ujjain	B	B	C	B
11.	Raisen	B	B	C	B
12.	Ratlam	B	B	C	B
13.	Barwani	A	B	C	C
14.	Mandsaur	A	B	C	B
15.	Neemach	A	B	C	B
16.	Hyderabad	B	B.	C	B
17.	Seoni	B	A	C	C
18.	Sagar	B	B	A	B
19.	Morena	A	C	C	B
20.	Dalia	A	C	C	C
21.	Damoh	A	B	A	C
22.	Harda	B	B	C	C
23.	Sehore	B	B	C	C
24.	Rewa	B	B	C	C
25.	Shivpuri	B	B	C	B
26.	Sheopur	B	B	C	C
27.	Chindwara	B	B	C	C
28.	Tikamgarh	B	C	C	C
29.	Rajgarh	A	B	C	C
30.	Narsinghpur	B	A	C	C
31.	Shajapur	B	B	C	C
32.	Vidisha	B	B	C	B
33.	Balaghat	C	B	C	C
34.	Betul	B	B	C	C
35.	Chhattarpur	A	B	C	B

36.	Umariya	B	B	C	B
37.	Sidhi	A	B	C	C
38	Shivpuri	A	C	C	C
39.	Jhabua	A	C	C	C
40.	Dindori	A	B	C	C
41.	Shahdol	B	B	C	B
42.	Mandla	B	A	C	C
43.	Satna		B	C	B
44.	Guna	A	B	C	C
45.	Panna	C	B	C	C

Relationship between Index of Regional Development and Occupational Pattern, 2001

S. No.	*District*	*per cent of Cultivators to T.M.W.*	*per cent of Agricultural Labourers to T.M.W.*	*per cent of workers in Household Industry T.M.W.*	*per cent of Other Workers to T.M.W.*
1.	Jabalpur	B	B	C	A
2.	Bhopal	C	C	C	A
3.	Indore	C	C	C	A
4.	Ujjain	A	B	C	C
5.	Gwalior	B	C	C	A
6.	Dewas	B	B	C	B
7.	Khandwa	A	B	C	C
8.	Mandsaur	A	C	C	C
9.	Satna	B	B	C	B
10.	Ratlam	A	C	C	B
11.	Hoshangabad	B	B	C	B
12.	Shahdol	A	B	C	B
13.	Rajgarh	A	B	C	C
14.	Sehore	B	B	C	B
15.	Chindwara	B	B	C	B
16.	Sagar	B	C	A	B
17.	Murena	A	C	C	C
18.	Dhar	A	B	C	C
19.	Vidisha	C	B	C	B
20.	Raisen	B	B	C	C
21.	Sajapur	A	B	C	C

22.	Rewa	B	B	C	C
23.	Khargone	B	B	C	B
24.	Damoh	B	B	C	C
25.	Seoni	A	B	C	C
26.	Datia	A	C	C	B
27.	Narsinghpur	B	A	C	C
28.	Balaghat	A	B	C	C
29.	Jhabua	A	C	C	C
30.	Bhind	B	C	C	C
31.	Chhattarpur	B	C	A	B
32.	Guna	A	C	C	B
33.	Betul	A	B	C	C
34.	Tikamgarh	A	C	C	C
35.	Shivpuri	A	C	C	C
36.	Sidhi	A	B	C	B
37.	Panna	A	B	C	C
38.	Mandla	A	B	C	C

methods of agriculture, less use of proper fertilizers, lack of proper marketing and storage facilities, small and fragmented land holdings, power cuts and low productivity. Therefore in spite of dominance of agriculture sector in occupational pattern most of the districts have low percentage of cultivators and are less developed.

CONCLUSION

From over all study it can be concluded that there has been reduction in regional disparities during the two decades however there is no major shift in occupational pattern during the same period. Also there is no major change in the rankings of districts during the study except for two or three. Regional development can be enhanced by focusing on development of resource base of the regional economy.Punjab is example where agricultural sector is contributing in development.Therefore strategy for regional development should be to develope resource base of the districts. Agricultural sector being the resource base for most of the districts should be developed along with house hold industry to generate employment opportunities.

REFERENCES

Kundu, Amitabh (1997): "Trends and Structure of Employment in the 1990's—Implication for Urban Growth", *Economic and Political Weekly*, Vol. 28, 7, pp. 1399-1404.

Nagraj (1994): "Employment and Wages in Manufacturing", Growth and Reforms in India: *Economic and Political Weekly*, Vol. 29, No. 4, pp. 177-86.

Prof. Rao, V.K.R.V.: Employment in a Developing Economy with Reference to India", Unemployment Problem in India, pp. 13-23.

Kulkarni, Sumati (1994): "Dependence on Agricultural Employment", *Economic and Political Weekly*, pp. 3260.

Vaidyanathan, A. (1994): "Employment Situation: Some Emerging Perspectives, *Economic and Political Weekly*, pp. 3147-56.

Devi, Radha (1994): "Anomaly in Employment in Some Modern Sector Occupations, *Economic and Political Weekly*, pp. 3255-59.

Parashsarthy, G. (1995): "Employment and Unemployment in Andhra Pradesh—Trends and Dimensions", *Economic and Political Weekly*, pp. 811-21.

Dev, Mahendra S. (2000): "Economic Liberalisation and Employment in South Asia-I, *Economic and Political Weekly*, pp. 40-51.

Dev, Mahendra S. (2000): "Economic Liberlisation and Employment in South Asia-II, *Economic and Political Weekly*, pp. 135-46.

Kumar, Rachel (1994): Development and Women's Work in Kerala Interactions and Paradoxes, *Economics and Political Weekly*, pp. 3249-62.

Mathew, E.T. (1995): "Unemployed and Self-employed—Job Preferences and Employment Perspectives", *Economics and Political Weekly*, pp. 2815-26.

Mandal, S.K. (1987), "Regional Disparities and Imbalances in India's Planned Economic Development", Deep & Deep Publications Pvt. Ltd.

Rao, Hemlata (1984) "Regional Disparities and Sevelopment in India", Ashish Publishing House.

Tewari, R.T., "Interregional Disparities in the Levels of Development", Ashish Publishing House.

50

Need of an Integrated Price Policy in an Inter-Regional and Inter-Sectoral Frame of the Indian Economy

BINOY N. VERMA AND ABHAS SAURABH

The typical federal structure of the Indian economy has unique contrast of modern, affluent, predominantly agricultural economy of Punjab, Haryana on the one hand and on the other hand stagnating, Bihar economy having strong base of agriculture with alluvial Gangetic soil and effective reservoir of abundant water base. The prices of agricultural output and input along with prices of industrial sectoral commodities play an important role. Therefore, the need of development and planning is a successful orientation towards functioning of the economy on the basis of an integrated price policy of both the sectors.

The critical evaluation of agricultural price policy in this section clearly shows the absence of a well-defined, clear-cut and perfect agricultural, price policy. Un-co-ordinated schemes and inconsistent policies have been predominantly responsible for the undesirable price-behaviour. Our past experiences suggest that *ad-hoc* price control measures hardly provide any permanent solution and generally fail in timely redress of the situation. In fact, a sound price policy meant to further agricultural development has to be a combination of a number of measures taking into consideration the complex character of the inter-relationship of prices with other aspects of the economic system. A price policy for agriculture does not merely mean a price policy for agricultural products, whether it be in the sense of price restraint or a price support, it would no doubt constitute a basic element of an integrated price policy.[1]

Thus, what we really need is a comprehensive well-knit, long-term integrated price policy. As pointed out earlier a price policy is not separate from the rest of the economic activity and it cannot be viewed in isolation as a thing in itself. It is to be viewed as an integral part of the general economic policy. The integration of price policy must be with the current dynamic variables which determine the prospect of the economy. According to Mr. M.L. Dantwala, "When we are advocating a price policy we are not thinking of integrating the prices with some historical situation, some relationship in the past. In a period of planning the integration has to take place with a developing and dynamic economy.[2]

Introducing and implementing an integrated price policy, a proper relationship should be insured between the policy of agricultural commodities and manufactured articles so that the terms of trade do not turn too sharply against one or the other. At the same time such a policy should ensure an appropriate relationship between the prices of competing crops, especially, subsistence and commercial crops so that undue preference and hence bias will not be imparted to one or the other as related to a crop plan.[3]

The integration of prices over space, i.e. "regional price integration" is another important aspect of the integrated price policy. The necessity of regional price integration stems from the fact that with progressive integration of the national economy and the objective of doing away with unnecessary regulation requires that as a long-term aim we must move towards a uniformity of producer's prices and that the differences in these prices from region to region should not be higher than warranted by reasonable calculation of transport and other costs.

Broadly, an integrated price policy in agriculture should take into account the following factors:

First, as mentioned above there should be a proper relationship between the agriculture prices and the prices of other commodities which the agriculturists purchase so that the terms of trade should not turn violently against the agriculturists. Secondly, there should not be violent fluctuations in agricultural prices otherwise the agricultural income will not be projected. Thirdly, the seasonal fluctuations in agricultural prices must be reduced to a minimum. Fourthly, such a strategy of agricultural prices should be made which arrest the cost of agricultural development. Fifthly, which may ensure a proper crop pattern in the economy. Sixthly, which may safeguard the interests of all the consumers or some particular vulnerable section of society. Seventhly, which may reduce the price to a reasonable level. Eighthly, which insures that the regional variations in prices is not more than the transport and other genuine costs. Ninthly, which may accelerate technical progress in agriculture.[4]

Besides, an unimportant aspect of an integrated price policy is to maintain the proper monetary and fiscal balance because if wages bills rise more rapidly than the real production it accentuates the inflationary pressure in the economy. A perfectly integrated price policy aims at allocating such a "wage-price behaviour" that the rate of increase in incomes (and particularly the wages and salaries) should not exceed the rate of increase in real production. So, there should be a perfect co-ordination between the price policy and the income policy in the economy.

Further, integrated price policy should be framed in a manner that it maintains a proper distribution of income in the economy. Various studies on the implications of rising prices (especially in the context of "green revolution") have established that the big and medium farmers have gained much more than other farmers. The tax policy and credit policy should be formulated and implemented mainly with a view to reduce income inequality by taking out extra income from the pockets of the big farmers which may be used for the development of the small farmers.

The credit policy should be more liberal for the small and marginal farmers and attempts should be made to make their units viable. This implies that a co-ordinated approach should be made in formulating the agricultural price policy keeping in view the general objective to achieve growth with "Social Justice."[5]

References

1. Jain, S.C., Priniciples of Agricultural Marketing and Prices.
2. Dantwala, M.L., *Indian Journal of Agricultural Economics,* April to June 1956, p. 175.
3. Mathur, P.N. and Hanna, Ezekiel, Marketable Surplus of Food Grains and Price Fluctuations in a Developing Economy, 1966.
4. Agricultural Price Policy in India, Ministry of Food and Agriculture, Food and Supply Dept. Government of India.
5. Verma, B.N., Inter-Regional Trend Analysis of Agricultural Price in India, Since 1939, Atma Ram and Sons, Delhi, Lucknow, 1980.

51

Inter-Regional Disparity of Foreign Direct Investment in India after Economic Reforms

Brajesh Srivastava

The existence of substantial regional disparity in a large country, such as India, in physical endowments, climate conditions, social traditions and differences in the initial levels of development, growth rates are bound, to vary among regions. All the five year plans stressed the importance of balanced regional development and Policies were designed to direct more investment to the relatively backward areas. Nevertheless, regional disparity continue to remain a serious problem. In the post-reforms period, due to deregulation, the degree of control of the central government declined in many sectors. State government can now take more initiatives for economic development than ever before. After adoption of economic reforms, in the changing scenario, it is the task of state policy to implement compensatory measures to push forward the lagged regions and spread growth and development more evenly. However, during almost the entire period of national planning, as is well known, a steady widening of regional disparities has taken place. This disparity is in growth rates, poverty and also in attracting FDI.

In India, globalization has produced paradoxical results in the sense that the states have been engaged in fierce competition among themselves for Foreign Direct Investment, giving rise to a new division among the states such as developed and backward states. Many states have entered the FDI race which they now see to be inherent to development strategy. They hold 'location tournaments' and compete for FDI through tax benefits, concessions and incentives like land or loan allocation priorities. Even then just a few get the lion's share of FDI and skewed inflows account for much of the difference between states. Extremely skewed inter-state distribution of Foreign Direct Investment (FDI) has also contributed to increased inter-regional disparity in India. State-wise data on (aggregate) FDI approvals between 1991 and 2002 show that only a handful of states have managed to attract a very high share of FDI (Figure 1). From the figures, it can be seen that the top 10 Indian states attracted more than 63 per cent of total foreign direct investment in India. In contrast, the bottom 10 states together received less than 1 per cent of total FDI. There is also a strong regional disparity in the pattern of FDI flows, with the southern and western states faring much better than the other parts of the country. Three southern states (Andhra Pradesh, Karnataka and Tamil Nadu) received more than 20 per cent of total FDI, while Maharashtra and Gujarat (both in western India) received 17.35 per cent and 7.7 per cent of FDI respectively. In contrast, the seven North-Eastern states together received only 0.03 per cent of total FDI during the same period. This unequal distribution of FDI across states in India is not unexpected, as FDI inflows tend towards states with better infrastructure and development. The concentration of FDI in a few pockets in India therefore did not help to reduce inequality during the reform period.

Apart from its very skewed regional distribution, FDI flows in India also exhibit a strong sectoral bias. In India, a very high proportion of FDI has gone into high-end consumer goods and financial services like banks, insurance companies

FIGURE 1

States of India with FDI Share of more than 1 per cent

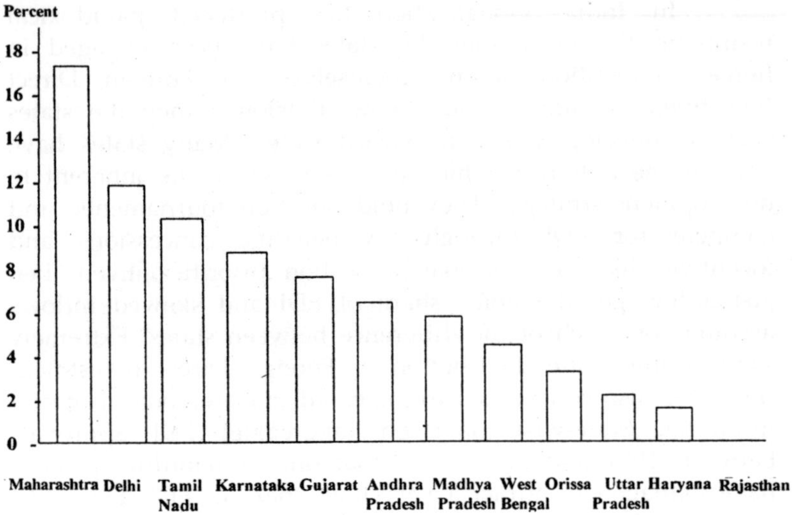

Source: Reserve Bank of India, Handbook of Statistics on Indian Economy (various issues).

and consultancy services. It has also flowed into information technology areas where India's human resources and research and development (R&D) base have pockets of international competitiveness. A large part of the inflow also went into the non-tradable infrastructural sector, attracted by special concessions, including guaranteed returns, offered by the government for such investments. However, benefits accruing from FDI in terms of fixed investments, exports and technological upgrading have been less than expected. This happened because since the 1990's a significant part of FDI came in the form of mergers and acquisitions (M & As). As opposed to green-field FDI investment, M & As do not create productive capacity and hence do not benefit the host country as much. In fact, there are some negative consequences if M & As lead to the formation of monopoly powers in an industry. Also typically with such mergers, employment stagnates or falls. This often counterbalances or even negates the increase in employment of multi-national corporation (MNC) affiliates, so that employment increases tend to be the least buoyant of all the major variables associated with MNC production.

Secondly, though FDI worth around and 30 billion has come into India since 1991, it has not contributed to an increase in expoıts. Most analysts suggest that a high proportion of FDI came into India during the early 1990s to jump the 'tariff wall' and service the Indian markets, rather than to use the country as an export hub. There were also apprehension that the initial inflow of direct investment would be followed by large and persistent outflows on account of imports, royalties, technical fees and dividends, with adverse balance of payments consequences. There have also been a few instances of anti-competitive practices by some large foreign companies in India. The most famous cases include the tussle between the government of Maharashtra and the entry giant Enron and the buyout of a rival Indian cold drink company Parle Exports by Coca Cola.

Pattern of FDI inflow in India suggest that the inflows are highly concentrated in a few states and in some sectors where India can offer either a big domestic market or cheap and skilled labour. The concentration of FDI in relatively small areas has created some illusion of prosperity, but has hardly done anything to reduce overall levels of poverty or inequality in India. On the other hand, in a bid to attract FDI to their states, many state governments have completely overlooked the rural sector and concentrated their development expenditure in the urban areas. This has resulted increased rural-urban inequality and has give rise to political tension in these states.

There are 'haves' and 'have-nots' amongst states and before a foreign investor commits investments in a 'green-field' venture in a region, he reviews the state's infrastructure position and whether it has an enabling government. The five high FDI inflow States have better infrastructure. Their rail and road networks, airports and seaports, dependable power supplies, communication networks, skilled manpower and competitive labour markets make them more attractive. Plus, states have a Major role to play in project implementation, which explains why an investor-friendly, transparent official decision-making process is so important. Single window authorities like Tamil-Nadu's Guidance Bureau, or Andhra Pradesh's centralized Documentation and clearances centre reduce ground level hassles and coordinate the multiple requirements of a new investment in a time bound way.

But even if the above factors influence FDI, they also affect investments in general. Hence, high FDI-receiving states also get lots of domestic corporate investment as part of a sort of 'crowding-in' effect. Internal investment and FDI tend to choose the same states/regions for 'co-location' benefits. A foreign investor's presence alongside a domestic one's benefits both from external economics. Domestic firms also want to be located near foreign ones for the spillover benefits of technology and better management practices. That is why Bangalore and Hyderabad are sought-after destinations for IT-related FDI of late, Maharashtra too has shown its capacity for receiving FDI in the Knowledge sector. Foreign investors also want to capitalize on the scientific manpower outputted by technical institutes like the IISc and IITs, and want to use the R&D that emerges from central labouratories. They also want to benefit from the location of technology-intensive PSUs (like BHEL and BEL) and India's IT firms.

FDI, thus, does not occur in a vacuum. Forward and backward linkages demand the presence of other foreign and domestic firms in the same regions. For instance, FDI in Tamil Nadu's automobile sector has seen Ford, Hyundai and Mitsubishi setting up shop in Chennai. A strong manufacturing and engineering industry, supported by a well-developed component-supplier base determine these investments. The Murugappa and Rane groups, and companies under the TVs umbrella have large, diversified, product portfolio related to the auto-industry.

Mumbai, Chennai, Bangalore, Mysore, Pune and Hyderabad also emerged as clear winners in the recent Business. Today-Gallup survey ranking cities by quality of work-life, social life and the suitability of doing business. These cities has a large number of overseas investors. In other words, FDI is attracted by better infrastructure, high levels of development, prominent centres of Industry and a relatively more urbanized populace. So FDI, instead of driving growth, is really gravitating to those states which are already have high levels of FDI receive more. We must bridge the investment-gap, and the resultant development-gap. But how?

Heads of various state governments are used to going abroad and wooing foreign investors by promising all types of sops. But the taxation benefits and special concessions they offer are only short-term measures, whereas foreign investors seek advantages going beyond just financial package. So, states must do much more in a sustainable manner to achieve substantial investment inflows. In that context, the unchanged composition of the top five states in FDI points to the direction in which the other states too must reform to make themselves aggressively and catch up with the leaders.

Thus the massage is clear: improve basic infrastructure, build up human capital, quicken official dealing and make them more transparent and up hold the rule of law. Develop and promote the state into a hub for a particular industry, as have Tamil Nadu, Andhra Pradesh and Karnataka. Also, spread investment growth into new regions to increase the total size of the incoming FDI cake. States like Himachal Pradesh and Uttarakhand, for example, have vast expanses of virgin territory and can become important FDI locations if they improve basic physical infrastructure—especially telecom—and arrange for skill-based training to enrich their literate manpower. The ultimate aim must not only be to bring in more FDI but also to achieve a high volume of investment in general and spread it to new destinations in particular.

References

Parthapratim Pal and Jayanti Ghosh (2007), *"Inequality in India: A Survey of Recent Trends", Economic and Social Affairs,* DESA Working Paper No. 45, July.

Professor Dr. Harihar, Bhattacharyya (2007), "Globalization and Indian Federalism: Current Trends", An In-house Seminar presentation at the institute of federalism, Fribourg (Switzerland), 16 May.

Raja J. Chelliah and K.R. Shanmugam (2007), "Strategy for Poverty Reduction and Narrowing Regional Disparities", *Economic and Political Weekly*, August 25.

S. Mahendra Dev (2008), "Post-reform Regional Variations", 7 January.

The Economic Times (2006), "Regional Disparity Widens, Rich States Corner Benefits of Reforms", 23 May.

The Economic Times, "Niceties of FDI inflows into States", 13 March, 2004.

52

Inter-State Income Disparities and the Transfer of Resources from the Union to the States

R.K. Bansal and J.R. Gupta

Marked inter-state income disparities is the striking feature of the Indian federation. In spite of the favourable treatment meted out to the poorer States by the federal agencies like Finance Commission and Planning Commission, these disparities have grown over the period. The situation has particularly worsened during the post-reform period. It is a matter of serious concern that growth rates of NSDP in the poorer States have decelerated in the nineties while these have accelerated in the richer states.

OBJECTIVES AND MYTHOLOGY

In the present paper an attempt has been made to examine the relationship between transfer of resources from the Centre, particularly through the Finance Commission and the Planning Commission and the per-capita income of the

States. An attempt has also been made to examine the extent of inter-state variations in the per-capita NSDP (net state domestic product).

The paper is based on the secondary data collected from various government publications, viz. Reserve Bank of India Bulletins, Finance Commission Reports, Plan Documents, and Reports on Currency and Finance, etc.

RESULTS AND DISCUSSION

Table I examines the per-capita NSDP of different States during the period of different Finance Commissions. The table observes that except for Punjab, the ranks of richer States have either improved or remained almost static, whereas the poorer States could not improve their ranks. States like UP had rather moved from 11th position occupied during the period of Seventh Finance Commission (1980-81 to 1984-85) to 13th during the period of Twelfth Finance Commission. The only State which has consistently improved its rank over the period is Kerala. Insofar as the inter-state NSDP co-efficient of variation is concerned, it has been consistently on the rise from 31.54 per cent during the Seventh Finance Commission period to 48.55 per cent during the Eleventh, though during the Twelfth Finance Commission it declined to 36.52 per cent.

In order to examine the relationship between per-capita NSDP and per-capita total transfers by the Finance Commissions, the coefficients of rank correlation between these two variables were worked out for the various Finance Commission's period. These coefficients were negative and were generally increasing over the period implying that per-capita transfers by the successive Finance Commissions were more and more progressive, i.e., poorer States were getting more and more. Yet no dent was made on the inter-state income disparities. The above observation also implies that the better-off States were depending mainly on their own resources. Therefore, in order to study the fiscal self-reliance of different States, ratios of own revenue to revenue expenditure (per cent) were also examined and these are given in Table 3. It was observed that these ratios were generally higher for better-off States. For poorer States not only these ratios were lower but over the period these ratios have declined. For example, for poorer States like Bihar, Orissa, Rajasthan and Uttar Pradesh these ratios were 34.21 per cent, 37.56 per cent, 52.03 per cent and 42.55 per cent respectively during 1993-94 through 1995-96, whereas the respective ratios were 24.78 per cent, 34.32 per cent, 45.81 per cent and 41.48 per cent during 2000-01 through 2002-03.

Another significant source of transferring resources from the centre to the States is the Planning Commission. Ever since the advent of planning plan assistance, in the form of loans and grants, is given to different states to finance their plan expenditure. During the Eighth Plan Period the per-capita plan outlay of different States was inversely related with per-capita income. But during the Ninth and Tenth Plan periods, though this relationship turned out to be positive, yet was not significant. Similarly, per-capita plan assistance from the Centre to the States did not have any significant relation with the economic status of the State. However, insofar as the mobilisation of own resources for financing the plan was concerned, the better-off States appeared to be at an advantageous position because the coefficients of correlation between the ranks of per-capita NSDP and those of own resources were 0.61 for the Ninth Plan and 0.75 for the Tenth Plan and both were significant.

CONCLUSION

Therefore, it may be concluded that self-dependence of the better-off states is more responsible for keeping them ahead of others than the distribution of sources from the centre. The dependence of the poorer States on the Centre has become counter-productive. Until and unless the poorer States themselves learn to tighten their own belt in the matter of financing their expenditure, the Centre cannot do much insofar as the growing inter-state income disparities are concerned.

TABLE I

Per-capita NSDP (Rs.) and Ranking of States during the Period of Different Finance Commissions

States	*Seventh*		*Eighth*		*Ninth*		*Tenth*		*Eleventh*		*Twelfth*	
	NSDP	*Rank*	*NSDP*	*Rank*	*NSDP*	*Rank*	*NSDP*	*Rank*	*NSDP*	*Rank*	*NSDP*	*Rank*
Andhra Pradesh	1785.00	8	2914.67	8	6430.00	8	12373.00	8	18554.25	8	26211.00	8
Bihar	1156.60	14	1903.33	14	3006.00	14	4069.00	14	5406.75	14	7875.00	14
Gujarat	2630.80	4	3983.67	4	8553.80	4	16847.00	4	21840.50	5	34157.00	4
Haryana	2891.80	3	4677.33	3	9855.60	3	17759.80	3	23745.50	3	38832.00	1
Karnataka	2035.40	5	3180.67	7	6728.80	6	13292.00	7	19393.25	7	27291.00	7
Kerala	1784.80	9	2829.33	9	6544.60	7	14783.20	6	21915.50	4	30668.00	5
Madhya Pradesh	1463.40	13	2415.33	12	5306.60	11	9702.00	11	12099.00	11	15647.00	12
Maharashtra	2906.80	2	4777.67	2	10251.40	2	19226.00	1	25358.25	2	37081.00	2
Orissa	1495.60	12	2472.67	10	4357.80	13	7951.60	12	10443.50	12	17299.00	11
Punjab	3408.60	1	5719.33	1	11221.20	1	19105.40	2	25922.75	1	34929.00	3
Rajasthan	15630	10	2431.00	11	5554.80	9	10938.20	10	13591.50	10	17863.00	10
Tamil Nadu	1883.20	7	3308.67	5	7380.20	5	15239.20	5	21442.50	6	29958.00	6
Uttar Pradesh	1516.80	11	2415.00	13	4565.40	12	7814.60	13	9792.25	13	13262.00	13
West Bengal	1973.80	6	3195.33	6	5541.00	10	11807.60	9	18272.50	9	25223	9
Co-efficient of Variation	31.54		32.13		38.72		46.25		48.55		36.52	

TABLE I

Per-capita NSDP (Rs.) and Ranking of States during the Period of Different Finance Commissions

States	*Seventh*		*Eighth*		*Ninth*		*Tenth*		*Eleventh*		*Twelfth*	
	NSDP	*Rank*	*NSDP*	*Rank*	*NSDP*	*Rank*	*NSDP*	*Rank*	*NSDP*	*Rank*	*NSDP*	*Rank*
Andhra Pradesh	1785.00	8	2914.67	8	6430.00	8	12373.00	8	18554.25	8	26211.00	8
Bihar	1156.60	14	1903.33	14	3006.00	14	4069.00	14	5406.75	14	7875.00	14
Gujarat	2630.80	4	3983.67	4	8553.80	4	16847.00	4	21840.50	5	34157.00	4
Haryana	2891.80	3	4677.33	3	9855.60	3	17759.80	3	23745.50	3	38832.00	1
Karnataka	2035.40	5	3180.67	7	6728.80	6	13292.00	7	19393.25	7	27291.00	7
Kerala	1784.80	9	2829.33	9	6544.60	7	14783.20	6	21915.50	4	30668.00	5
Madhya Pradesh	1463.40	13	2415.33	12	5306.60	11	9702.00	11	12099.00	11	15647.00	12
Maharashtra	2906.80	2	4777.67	2	10251.40	2	19226.00	1	25358.25	2	37081.00	2
Orissa	1495.60	12	2472.67	10	4357.80	13	7951.60	12	10443.50	12	17299.00	11
Punjab	3408.60	1	5719.33	1	11221.20	1	19105.40	2	25922.75	1	34929.00	3
Rajasthan	15630	10	2431.00	11	5554.80	9	10938.20	10	13591.50	10	17863.00	10
Tamil Nadu	1883.20	7	3308.67	5	7380.20	5	15239.20	5	21442.50	6	29958.00	6
Uttar Pradesh	1516.80	11	2415.00	13	4565.40	12	7814.60	13	9792.25	13	13262.00	13
West Bengal	1973.80	6	3195.33	6	5541.00	10	11807.60	9	18272.50	9	25223	9
Co-efficient of Variation	31.54		32.13		38.72		46.25		48.55		36.52	

TABLE 2

Ranking of States on the Basis of Per-Capita Total Transfers Recommended by the Different Finance Commisions

(Rs.)

States	(1956-57 to 1984-85)		Eighth		Ninth		Tenth		Eleventh		Twelfth	
	Total Transfers	Rank	Total Transfers	Rank	Total Transfers	Rank	Total Transfers	Rank	Total Transfers	Rank	Total Transfers	Rank
Andhra Pradesh	504	5	514	6	1386	6	2558	3	4664	7.5	6608	6
Bihar	426	12	573	2	1579	2	2737	2	6574	1	9044	2
Gujarat	466	6	416	12	1120	10	1940	11	2906	11	5061	12
Haryana	389	14	331	14	981	13	1552	14	2564	13	3812	13
Karnataka	465	7	461	9	1218	9	2231	9	4664	7.5	5950	9
Kerala	611	2	495	8	1306	7	2480	5	4386	9	6166	8
Madhya Pradesh	428	11	534	4.5	1426	4	2308	7	5295	5	7965	4
Maharashtra	461	8	417	11	1099	11	1629	12	2457	14	3739	14
Orissa	708	1	635	1	2032	1	2892	1	6568	2	10039	1
Punjab	405	13	364	13	1012	12	1558	13	2687	12	5302	11
Rajasthan	553	3	452	10	668	14	2338	6	5361	4	6914	5
Tamil Nadu	446	9.5	505	7	1414	5	2260	8	3871	10	5880	10
Uttar Pradesh	446	9.5	534	4.5	1468	3	2481	4	5432	3	8348	3
West Bengal	524	4	560	3	1303	8	2072	10	5179	6	6352	7

Rank correlation	-0.225ns (t=0.796)	-0.729* (t=3.685)	-0.754* (t=3.975)	-0.824* t=8.890)	-0.962* (t=12.206)	-0.947* (t=10.219)

Ns Stands for not significant; * Stands for five per cent level of significance.

Sources: 1. Figures from 1956-57 to 1948-85 (i.e. upto Seventh Finance Commission) have been taken from Gupta, J.R. and Manjit Kalra, Federal Transfers and Inter-State Disparities in India, 2005.

2. For rest of the Finance Commissions the figures have been taken from Singh, Ajit Kumar (Ed.) Twelfth Finance Commission Recommendations and Their Implications for the State Finances, 2008.

TABLE 3

Index of Fiscal Self-reliance in Different States

States	Ratio of Own Revenue to Revenue Expenditure (Per cent) Average 1993-94 to 1995-96	Average 2000-01 to 2002-03
Andhra Pradesh	59.22	59.46
Bihar	34.21	24.78
Gujarat	79.57	58.81
Haryana	75.48	77.62
Karnataka	73.62	61.52
Kerala	63.69	54.24
Madhya Pradesh	56.68	48.83
Maharashtra	80.09	67.50
Orissa	37.56	34.32
Punjab	69.59	57.71
Rajasthan	52.03	45.81
Tamil Nadu	68.36	64.60
Uttar Pradesh	42.55	41.48
West Benngal	50.77	32.20

Source: Report of the Twelfth Finance Commission, Annexure 7.10, p. 418.

TABLE 4

Ranking of the States on the Basis of Per-capita State Plan Outlays, and Per-capita Plan Assistance and Per-capita Own Resources during the different Plan Periods

(Rs.)

States	Eighth Plan						Ninth Plan					
	State Plan Outlays	Rank	Plan Assistance	Rank	Own Resources	Rank	State Plan Outlays	Rank	Plan Assistance	Rank	Own Resources	Rank
Andhra Pradesh	1491.47	11	1007.10	5	484.37	13	3366.80	11	2311.64	3	1055.16	12
Bihar	1408.45	13	666.42	12	742.03	9	1761.35	14	1106.08	13	655.27	13
Gujarat	2619.59	4	587.47	13	2032.12	2	5833.34	1	2359.42	2	3473.92	2
Haryana	3220.34	1	1091.65	4	2128.69	1	4702.01	4	1962.09	4	2739.92	7
Karnataka	2589.47	5	809.00	8	1780.47	4	4543.69	5	1666.49	8	2877.20	5
Kerala	1796.05	8	956 54	6	839.51	8	5047.02	2	1312.13	11	3734.89	1
Madhya Pradesh	1563.38	10	534.39	14	1028.99	7	2694.63	12	1251.59	12	1443.04	11
Maharashtra	2199.52	7	739.13	10	1460.39	6	4024.12	9	1045.21	14	2978.91	4
Orissa	2976.19	3	1094.36	3	1881.83	3	4201.68	6	2585.85	1	1615.83	9
Punjab	3070.09	2	2889.06	1	181.03	14	4914.53	3	1790.06	6	3124.47	3
Rajasthan	2426.16	6	778.90	9	1647.26	5	4135.34	7	1355.41	10	2779.93	6
Tamil Nadu	1761.65	9	1153.13	2	608.52	11	4078.31	8	1381.02	9	2697.29	8
Uttar Pradesh	1413.18	12	869.16	7	544.02	12	3412.37	10	1914.33	5	1498.04	10
West Bengal	1351.79	14	692.16	11	659.63	10	2161.13	13	1701.22	7	459.91	14
Rank Correlation	-0.63* (t=2.95)		-0.44 Ns (t=1.76)		0.22 Ns (t=0.83)		0.44 Ns (t=1.76)		-0.09 Ns (t=0.32)		-0.61* (t=2.78)	

(Contd.)

TABLE 4 (Contd.)

States	Per-capita		Per-capita		Per-capita	
	State Plan Outlays	Rank	Plan Assistance	Rank	Own Resources	Rank
Andhra Pradesh	5290.58	6	2524.62	4	2765.96	8
Bihar	1881.71	14	1050.30	13	831.41	14
Gujarat	6792.35	4	2233.67	5	4558.68	2
Haryana	4530.84	9	1400.88	9	3129.96	7
Karnataka	7296.14	1	3013.87	3	4282.27	4
Kerala	7207.21	2	3254.82	2	3952.39	5
Madhya Pradesh	3577.73	11	1389.09	11	2188.64	10
Maharashtra	5161.27	7	756.81	14	4404.46	3
Orissa	4773.87	8	3670.28	1	1103.59	12
Punjab	7203.47	3	1536.29	7	5667.18	1
Rajasthan	3941.99	10	1391.13	10	2550.86	9
Tamil Nadu	5822.41	5	2184.29	6	3638.12	6
Uttar Pradesh	2083.31	13	1235.52	12	847.79	13
West Bengal	2928.53	12	1466.82	8	1461.71	11
Rank Correlation	0.45 Ns (t=0.48)		-0.04 Ns (t=1.83)		0.75* (t=4.09)	

Note: Rank correlations have been calculated between per-capita NSDP and the respective variable.
Ns Stands for not significant; * Stands for five per cent level of significance

References

Government of India (1980), Report of the Seventh Finance Commission for 1980-85, Akalank Publications, New Delhi.

Government of India (1985), Report of the Eighth Finance Commission for 1985-90, Akalank Publications, New Delhi.

Government of India (1990), Report of the Ninth Finance Commission for 1990-95, Akalank Publications, New Delhi.

Government of India (1995), Report of the Tenth Finance Commission for 1995-2000, Akalank Publications, New Delhi.

Government of India (2000), Report of the Eleventh Finance Commission for 2000-05, Akalank Publications, New Delhi.

Government of India (2005), Report of the Twelfth Finance Commission for 2005-10, Akalank Publications, New Delhi.

Government of India, Eighth Five Year Plan, 1992-97, Planning Commission, New Delhi.

Government of India, Ninth Five Year Plan, 1997-2002, Planning Commission, New Delhi.

Government of India, Tenth Five Year Plan, 2002-07, Planning Commission, New Delhi.

Gupta, J.R. and Manjit Kalra (2005), Federal Transfers and Inter-State Disparities in India, Atlantic Publishers, New Delhi.

Singh, Ajit Kumar (2008), Twelfth Finance Commission Recommendations and their Implications for the State Finances, APH Publishing Corporation, New Delhi.

Index